A Textbook of Economics

A Textbook of Economics

MURRAY WOLFSON

Methuen & Co Ltd

First published 1978 by Methuen & Co. Ltd.
11 New Fetter Lane, London EC4P 4EE
© 1978 Murray Wolfson
Printed in Great Britain by
J. W. Arrowsmith Ltd., Bristol BS3 2NT

ISBN 0416 77080 0 (*hardback*)
ISBN 0416 77090 8 (*paperback*)

Contents

viii   Contents

Acknowledgements

The author and publishers wish to thank the following for permission to reprint figures and tables:

The Bank of England Economic Intelligence Department for extracts from *Bank of England Quarterly Bulletin* (March 1974); Professor Abram Bergson for table from 'Toward a new growth model', *Problems of Communism* (April–March 1973), p. 3; The Brookings Institution for tables from E. F. Denison, assisted by J.-P. Poullier, *Why Growth Rates Differ: Postwar Experience in Nine Western Countries* (© 1967 by The Brookings Institution, Washington, DC); Department of Applied Economics, Cambridge University, for extracts from *The British Economy Key Statistics 1900–1970*, Table E, p. 8; Field Newspaper Syndicate for Andy Capp cartoon from the *Daily Mirror* (8 February 1973); The Controller, Her Majesty's Stationery Office, for extracts from *Annual Abstract of Statistics 1971*, Table 339, pp. 320–1, *National Income and Expenditure 1971*, pp. 2, 3 and 5, *Abstract of Regional Statistics 1971*, pp. 30 and 97, *Economic Trends* (June 1973), and table from the *106th Report of the Commissioners of Inland Revenue* (1962–3), Cmnd. 2283; Imperial Chemical Industries Ltd for balance sheet and profit and loss statement from *Annual Report to Stockholders* (1970); Macmillan Publishing Company Inc. for figure from G. Ackley, *Macroeconomic Theory* (1961), p. 225; North-Holland Publishing Company for figure from E. Malinvaud, *Statistical Methods of Econometrics* (Chicago, Rand McNally, 1966), p. 117; Dr George Stigler for figure from Testimony before Senate Subcommittee on Anti-Trust and Monopoly (1965), p. 1552; *Three Banks Review* for tables from A. P. Jacquemin, 'Size, structure and performance of the largest European firms' (June 1974), pp. 62–3; United Nations Department of Economic Affairs for tables from *Economic Survey for Asia and the Far East 1964*, pp. 30–3; John Wiley & Sons Inc. for table from J. S. Bain, *Industrial Organization* (1968), p. 84; Yale University Press for extracts from J. S. Bain, *International Differences in Industrial Structure* (1966), p. 78.

Preface to the student

Purpose

This book has a purpose. It is to present economics in an up-to-date and straightforward way. We do this by introducing a simplified but useful picture of the economy called input-output analysis. Then, by investigating practical problems, we press on with the limitations of the simple model, and move on to the more sophisticated considerations.

The text is not directed toward the student with advanced mathematical training. On the contrary. The input-output system was designed by Nobel Prize winner Wassily Leontief as a sufficiently simple model of the economy to actually measure the structure of interaction between industries.

Our study is first approached from the point of view of organization for production – the *supply* of goods and services. How are the production inputs directed in coordinated stages of manufacture from one industry to another until they become available for final use? Then we enquire into the structure of *demand* for those goods and services. Who will buy the goods produced for final use? Consumers? Businessmen investing in additional equipment? Government? Britain's export customers?

Nowadays every country attaches great importance to using the economic structure in planning. Planning inevitably requires a choice between alternative courses of action. Therefore we need to understand how to choose among plans so as to make the best use of resources. Choice is exercised at the individual level as well as the national one. The mythology of capitalist society suggests that all the economic decisions are made individually by businessmen and private citizens. Yet every existing capitalist society is actually a mixture of private decisions and government plans for the public interest. Official communist doctrine, on the other hand, pretends that decision making is in the hands of the central planning boards and political authorities. Nonetheless, individual decisions remain in deciding what goods to buy, or where to seek a job. Private plots tilled by Soviet peasants account for much of Russia's agricultural produce. Most nations live under mixed economies where the issue of the extent of individual choice versus delegation of decisions to collective authorities is a burning issue. We shall study how effective consistent decisions can be made by firms, individuals and by governmental planners in achieving the goals they set.

The reader should understand the refusal of most economists to make judgements about what the social goals ought to be. As individuals, economists have their vote. However, their feelings have nothing to do with analysis of the economic processes at work. Value judgements about what ought to be are called *normative* statements. Scientific statements about matters of fact or cause and effect are *positive* statements. This book's focus on positive science is simply designed to avoid wishful thinking, which confuses what we think ought to be with what is actually the case. Science is not a ploy to avoid social issues. On the contrary, it provides the means to help to cope with them in an effective way. Life without normative judgements is impossible. Yet, if the point is to change the world, we must know how it actually works.

Exercise: Often positive or normative judgements are confused. How would you classify the following passage from the American Declaration of Independence?

> We hold these truths to be self-evident: that all men are created equal; that they are endowed by their Creator with certain inalienable rights; that among these rights are Life, Liberty and the Pursuit of Happiness.

Maths for economists: linear equations

To master this book the reader need have only two mathematical skills. He must (1) solve a pair of simultaneous linear equations, and (2) compute the sum of a geometric series.

The solution of simultaneous linear equations

Effective planning of production demands that each industry plan its outputs consistent with the needs of the others. We shall write equations expressing these industry outputs. We are interested in *systems* of equations each representing an industry, since such a system will be a mathematical model of the economy. Solving these equations will be the way in which we can determine proper, consistent outputs for industries. In order to solve any one of these equations, we have to solve all the others at the same time – simultaneously. This mathematical face mirrors the interdependence of industries.

Let us review the simple algebra required. Consider the following system of equations:

$$6x + 3y = 7$$

$$2x - 3y = 1.$$

Each of these equations represents a *set* of values of x and y that satisfies the condition it sets forth. Thus, the first equation really limits the infinity of numbers to a set, such that six times the first number, x, plus three times the second number, y, sums to seven. Likewise, the second equation refers to all number pairs, such that twice the first minus three times the second is equal to 1.

Now, in the first equation, if $x = 1$, then $6x + 3y = 7$ becomes $6 + 3y = 7$, and it is easy to see by solving that $y = \frac{1}{3}$. But, if $x = 2$, then $12 + 3y = 7$ shows that $y = -\frac{5}{3}$. Since we are free to choose any value for x in the first equation, we can find the corresponding value of y by simple algebra. Evidently, since there are an infinite number of x-values we will produce an infinite set of corresponding values for y.

Obligatory exercise: For each of the two equations in the text, complete the following table of y-values corresponding to the given x-values. Then plot these points on graph paper, measuring the x-values horizontally and the corresponding y-values vertically. Verify that each equation has a straight line as its graph.

First equation

x	-2	-1	$-\frac{1}{6}$	0	1	2	$3\frac{1}{2}$
y							

Second equation

x	-2	-1	$-\frac{1}{6}$	0	1	2	$3\frac{1}{2}$
y							

Now we can ask the key question. Of the collection of pairs of numbers satisfying the first equation, and the different collection corresponding to the second equation, what pair of numbers is able to satisfy both equations simultaneously? The answer can be found by graphing the equations. Graphs are pictures of the sets of numbers that satisfy each equation. We will look for the numbers that are in both sets. That is to say, we seek the point where the graphs cross.

Graphing of equations of straight lines is most readily accomplished by putting them into *slope-intercept form*. Take the first equation, $6x + 3y = 7$, and subtract $6x$ from both sides; then divide by 3. Now y appears alone on the left hand side. The equation has become:

$$y = -2x + \tfrac{7}{3}.$$

The reader should apply the same procedure to the second equation and obtain:

$$y = \tfrac{2}{3}x - \tfrac{1}{3}.$$

In the first equation, when $x = 0$, substitution in the equation tells us that $y = \tfrac{7}{3}$, since y is two times zero plus $\tfrac{7}{3}$. $\tfrac{7}{3}$ is a constant term appearing alone on the right hand side of the equation. It is known as the *y-intercept* because when $x = 0$ the graph of the equation will cross the y-axis at a value where $y = \tfrac{7}{3}$. The other constant, -2, can be seen to be the *slope* of the line. Each time we increase x, the y-value will be changed by -2 times as much, because x is multiplied by -2. The slope tells us the *vertical change* in y per unit *horizontal change* in x.

Graphing the equations is done most easily by first finding the y-intercept. Set the x-value equal to zero and solve for y ($x = 0$, $y = \tfrac{7}{3}$). Graph that point. Now increase x by 1 and change y by the slope, -2. A second point is $x = 1$, $y = \tfrac{1}{3}$. Two points are enough to determine a straight line. We know we are dealing with a straight line because the slope of the equation is constant. Indeed, it is the constancy of slope which makes a straight line straight! Connect the two points. We may extend the line indefinitely in both directions to take in any points that satisfy the first equation (Figure P.1).

Do the same thing for the second equation, showing all the points that satisfy its conditions. By superimposing one graph on the other (Figure P.2) we see the one common point which satisfies both equations simultaneously. It is where $x = 1$ and $y = \tfrac{1}{3}$, the point of intersection which lies on both lines.

We may find the common point by algebraic means. This method is more powerful than graphics because it leads to the solving of larger systems of many equations which would be impossible to do graphically. (Why?) We can add or subtract the equations from one another without violating the equality: Equals added to equals are equal. Also, we are free to multiply all the terms in an equation by a number, since equals multiplied by equals are equal. Using these operations, our strategy is to first convert the pair of

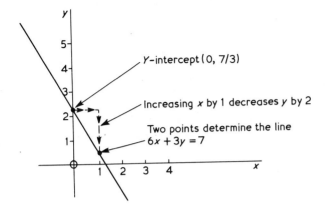

Figure P.1

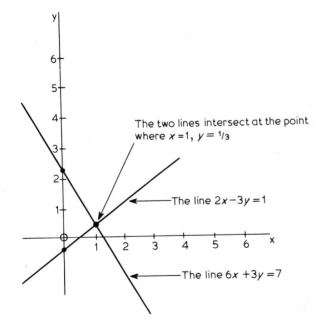

Figure P.2

xvi Preface to the student

equations involving two unknowns into a single equation involving only one unknown which we can easily solve. Starting with the original pair of equations,

$$6x + 3y = 7$$
$$2x - 3y = 1$$

we eliminate the terms involving x in two steps. First, we perform a suitable multiplication of the second equation making its coefficient of x equal to that of the first equation. Then we subtract the second equation from the first. The x terms will cancel leaving only one equation in x. For example, multiply the second equation by 3:

$$6x + 3y = 7$$
$$6x - 9y = 3.$$

Subtract the second equation from the first so that

$$12y = 4$$

and

$$y = \tfrac{1}{3}.$$

To find x, we repeat the procedure. Happily, in this case, the coefficient of y is 3 in the first equation and -3 in the second. Simply add the original equations:

$$8x = 8,$$

so that

$$x = 1.$$

Exercise: Verify that the point $x = 1$ and $y = \tfrac{1}{3}$ satisfies the second equation as well as the first.

This method can be applied to systems of equations involving three unknowns in three equations. Indeed the method applies to any number of equations in the same number of unknowns, for it is always possible to take a pair of equations and eliminate one of the variables between them. Doing this repeatedly, one arrives at two equations in two unknowns and then one equation in one unknown.[1]

---

[1] There are queer cases where solutions do not exist because the lines are parallel and do not intersect. Then there are no solutions. In some cases the lines may coincide, in which case there are infinitely many common points. The algebra of these situations can safely be postponed to a more advanced course.

Clearly this elimination method can get very tedious. There are more efficient, computer driven methods which really do not concern us. That is a problem for mathematicians who devise quick solutions for large systems of equations. Yet it is crucial for us to appreciate that, in principle, seventy equations in seventy unknowns present no new challenges. If you have seen two, you have seen them all!

Exercise:
(1) Solve the following systems of linear equations.

(a) $3x - 2y = 6$
    $2x - 7 = 7$

(Ans. $x = 8$, $y = 9$)

(b) $3x + 3y + 2z = 6$
    $x + y + z = 0$
    $x = 1$

(Ans. $x = 1$, $y = 5$, $z = -6$)

(c) $3x_1 + 2x_2 = 4$
    $x_1 + \frac{1}{2}x_2 = -1$

(Ans. $x_1 = -8$, $x_2 = 14$)

(d) $3x - 2y = a$
    $2x - y = b$

(Ans. $x = -a + 2b$, $y = -2a + 3b$)

(e) $ax + by = c$
    $dx + ey = f$

$$\left(\text{Ans. } x = \frac{ce - fb}{ae - bd}, \ y = \frac{af - cd}{ae - bd}\right)$$

(f) $0 \cdot 21x + 0 \cdot 03y = 1 \cdot 70$
    $3 \cdot 21x - 0 \cdot 70y = 3 \cdot 56$

(Ans. $x = 5 \cdot 33$, $y = 19 \cdot 36$)

(2) What are the slopes and y-intercepts of the equations in examples (a), (c) and (d) in the preceding set of problems?
(3) Why is $y = x^2$ not a linear equation? Illustrate graphically.

In the real world of planning, we must solve equations representing a large number of industries. To write them out as we have been doing is too cumbersome. It is more convenient to simply make a table of the coefficients, taking care to include the minus signs when they are present. The variables can also be listed in tabular form as a column just to the right of the table of coefficients. Thus the table of coefficients and the column of variables is equivalent to the left hand side of the system of equations. The right hand side can also be shown as a column of numbers. Thus we convert our original equations:

$$6x + 3y = 7$$
$$2x - 3y = 1$$

into:

$$\begin{bmatrix} 6 & 3 \\ 2 & -3 \end{bmatrix} \begin{bmatrix} x \\ y \end{bmatrix} = \begin{bmatrix} 7 \\ 1 \end{bmatrix}.$$

A rectangular table or array of numbers may be called a matrix. Instead of speaking of a table of coefficients, we could say that $\begin{bmatrix} 6 & 3 \\ 2 & -3 \end{bmatrix}$ is a *matrix* of coefficients. This matrix is *square* because it has as many rows as it has columns. The columns $\begin{bmatrix} x \\ y \end{bmatrix}$ and $\begin{bmatrix} 7 \\ 1 \end{bmatrix}$ are also matrices, but not square. A matrix consisting of a single column, or a single row, is called a *vector*.

Exercise: From the newspaper clip several matrices such as share prices, Premium Bond winners, weather reports. Indicate the number of *rows* and number of *columns* (in that order). These are the *dimensions* of the matrix. Indicate whether your matrices are *square or rectangular matrices, row vectors or column vectors.*

For the purpose of explanation, we usually will deal in two-equation examples; but the reader should bear in mind that the power of the matrix device stems from its ability to deal with large systems of equations in a simple form.

Exercise: (1) Express the following systems of equations in matrix form:

        (a) $5x + 2y = 6$
             $x - 2y = -5$

        (b) $3x - 2y + z = 10$
             $x - z = -5$
             $x - 0 \cdot 1y + 3z = 0$

(2) Express the following matrix equations as a pair of ordinary equations:

(a) $\begin{bmatrix} 6 & 3 \\ 2 & 1 \end{bmatrix} \begin{bmatrix} x \\ y \end{bmatrix} = \begin{bmatrix} 5 \\ 1 \end{bmatrix}$

(b) $\begin{bmatrix} 5 & -1 \\ 2 & 0 \end{bmatrix} \begin{bmatrix} x \\ y \end{bmatrix} = \begin{bmatrix} a \\ b \end{bmatrix}.$

Once having written the system of equations in matrix notation, we get an additional insight. The matrix equation is a *function* as the term is used in mathematics. The familiar expression $y = 3x$ is a function because it is a clear unambiguous rule which tells us how to take a set of x-values and for each one of them find a single corresponding y-value. For any x, we have all learnt to compute the corresponding y. Sometimes it is said that the set of all x-values is *mapped into* the set of y-values, or that the x-set is *transformed into* the y-set. Likewise, the matrix equation provides us with a clear set of directions to take the vector of variables, multiply them by the elements of the coefficient matrix, and add them up to get the vector of values on the right hand side. In other words, we may very conveniently think of the matrix equation as a *function* which transforms, maps or converts the variables $\begin{bmatrix} x \\ y \end{bmatrix}$ into the values $\begin{bmatrix} 7 \\ 1 \end{bmatrix}$. In order to understand the process better, we ought to express the constants on the right hand side in a more general way. Instead of the constants $\begin{bmatrix} 7 \\ 1 \end{bmatrix}$, let us use the vector $\begin{bmatrix} a \\ b \end{bmatrix}$. Then,

$$\begin{bmatrix} 6 & 3 \\ 2 & -3 \end{bmatrix}\begin{bmatrix} x \\ y \end{bmatrix} = \begin{bmatrix} a \\ b \end{bmatrix}$$

is a function that converts the vector $\begin{bmatrix} x \\ y \end{bmatrix}$ into $\begin{bmatrix} a \\ b \end{bmatrix}$.

The imaginative reader might well ask: If we can map from one set of values to another, can we not go back again to the original values? Often we can. The process involves finding an *inverse* function to transform back again. Thus, $y = 3x$ is a rule which tells us to take the x-value and multiply it by three to get the y-value. For example, if x is 6, then by multiplying by 3 we get y equal to 18. How should we convert back to 6? Easy, multiply by $\frac{1}{3}$. Multiplication by 3 is the original operation; the inverse is multiplication by $\frac{1}{3}$. It is important to notice that we can discover the inverse by solving the original equation for x and observing the coefficient of y. Thus $y = 3x$ can be solved to get $x = \frac{1}{3}y$. Literally $\frac{1}{3}$ is 3 inverted!

Query: Find the inverse of $y = 6x$.

Now we want to suggest that when we solve the *set* of simultaneous equations the same inversion process is involved. Thus the original matrix mapped $\begin{bmatrix} x \\ y \end{bmatrix}$ into $\begin{bmatrix} a \\ b \end{bmatrix}$. What inverse matrix will map $\begin{bmatrix} a \\ b \end{bmatrix}$ into $\begin{bmatrix} x \\ y \end{bmatrix}$?

Find it by solving:

$$6x + 3y = a$$
$$2x - 3y = b.$$

Add the second equation to the first to eliminate y: $8x = a + b$, so that $x = \frac{1}{8}a + \frac{1}{8}b$. To find y we multiply the second equation by 3. Then:

$$6x + 3y = a$$
$$6x - 9y = 3b.$$

Subtracting the second equation from the first: $12y = a + 3b$ and $y = \frac{1}{12}a = \frac{1}{4}b$. Summarizing our results we have:

$$\frac{1}{8}a + \frac{1}{8}b = x$$
$$\frac{1}{12}a + \frac{1}{4}b = y.$$

In matrix form we can write:

$$\begin{bmatrix} \frac{1}{8} & \frac{1}{8} \\ \frac{1}{12} & \frac{1}{4} \end{bmatrix} \begin{bmatrix} a \\ b \end{bmatrix} = \begin{bmatrix} x \\ y \end{bmatrix}$$

We have it! This matrix $\begin{bmatrix} \frac{1}{8} & \frac{1}{8} \\ \frac{1}{12} & \frac{1}{4} \end{bmatrix}$ is the inverse matrix to $\begin{bmatrix} 6 & 3 \\ 2 & -3 \end{bmatrix}$. It transforms whatever the $\begin{bmatrix} a \\ b \end{bmatrix}$ values might be, back into $\begin{bmatrix} x \\ y \end{bmatrix}$.

Exercise:

Test this out by substituting $\begin{bmatrix} 7 \\ 1 \end{bmatrix}$ for $\begin{bmatrix} a \\ b \end{bmatrix}$ in the universe function to arrive at the solution for $\begin{bmatrix} x \\ y \end{bmatrix}$ achieved on p. xvi. Now substitute $\begin{bmatrix} 1 \\ \frac{1}{3} \end{bmatrix}$ for $\begin{bmatrix} x \\ y \end{bmatrix}$ in the original function and transform back to $\begin{bmatrix} 7 \\ 1 \end{bmatrix}$.

We found this inverse matrix by solving the equations. That is all there is to it! Students have been inverting matrices since before they were 15 years old taking O-level maths. It reminds one of Molière's play, *Le Bourgeois Gentilhomme*, in which the foolish hero was flattered to discover that he had been speaking prose since infancy!

Exercise:

(1) Any matrix equation can be written as ordinary equations by putting the variables back in place. Thus,

$$\begin{bmatrix} 6 & 5 \\ 7 & -1 \end{bmatrix} \begin{bmatrix} F \\ R \end{bmatrix} = \begin{bmatrix} H \\ J \end{bmatrix} \text{ is the same as } \begin{array}{l} 6F + 5R = H \\ F - R = J. \end{array}$$

Now apply this idea to the inverse equation just derived and write out:

$$\begin{bmatrix} \frac{1}{8} & \frac{1}{8} \\ \frac{1}{12} & \frac{1}{4} \end{bmatrix} \begin{bmatrix} a \\ b \end{bmatrix} = \begin{bmatrix} x \\ y \end{bmatrix}$$

for the case where $a = 16$ and $b = 24$. Find x and y.

(2) Explain why the inverse of $\begin{bmatrix} 6 & 3 \\ 2 & -3 \end{bmatrix}$ is *not* $\begin{bmatrix} \frac{1}{6} & \frac{1}{3} \\ \frac{1}{2} & -\frac{1}{3} \end{bmatrix}$.

Geometric series

In economics we frequently find ourselves using the mathematical notion of a *sequence* to describe a set of events that occur one after the other according to some rule. HM Office of Population Census has observed the population of the UK starting in 1960 to be (in thousands): 52,559, 52,932, 53,431, 53,755, 54,156, 54,520, 54,806, 55,112, 55,391, 55,643, and finally in 1970 the population was 55,812. Based on these figures, they made a mathematical calculation which permitted them to forecast that the population of the UK in 2001 would be 66,488.

Another situation with which we may all be familiar is a decision to save money by deposits in a bank. Thus we may start in 1973 and deposit £10 each year. The sequence would be 10, 10, 10, . . . for as long as we carry out our savings programme. Alternatively, we may start in 1973 depositing £10, and each year plan to save one more pound than the year previous. Then our sequence would be £10, £11, £12, ... If we allow D to stand for deposits each year, and L the amount by which we increase our annual deposit the sequence would be: $D, D+L, D+2L, D+3L, \ldots$ and so on. A sequence in which the terms are generated by adding a specified amount is called an *arithmetic sequence*.

Of course there are any number of rules which might be adopted to define the sequence. Thus we might decide to start a savings programme in which the deposits each year were a multiple of the year previous. Thus if a young person were to embark on a programme of increased savings as he increased his earnings, he might start with £10 a year at school leaving, and each year *multiply* that amount by 10 per cent. Then the sequence would be £10, £11, £12·1, £13·32, . . . and so on. Another savings plan, which would be appropriate to a person presently earning his maximum income and planning to save less as the years go on, would be to multiply by 50 per cent. Then if the first term of the sequence were £100, the next term would be £50, then £25, £12·50, £6·25, . . . and so on. In general, if the first term of the sequence were D, and a the multiplying factor, the sequence would be $D, aD, a^2D, a^3D, \ldots$. A sequence defined by successive multiplication is called a *geometric sequence*. We shall be concerned mostly with geometric sequences.

Obviously a very important question is: How long is the sequence to continue? This is clearly related to the exponent of the last term. Thus if the last term were a^3D, the sequence has four terms, D, aD, a^2D, and a^3D. We can generalize this idea and write the sequence according to the general rule

$a^n D$. In this case $n = 3$. Notice that the sequence will have $n + 1$ terms in it, since n is the number of years after the first. Sometimes we will wish n to be infinitely long. Clearly if n is indefinitely large, so is $n + 1$!

Query: Give examples of sequences that consist of terms that are stated in terms of *space* rather than *time*. Can sequences be defined in terms of economic variables such as income, employment, prices?

Any sensible person engaged in a programme of savings is concerned with his *total* bank balance as well as his annual deposits. That is to say, he is concerned with the *sum* of the sequence. The sum of a sequence is called a *series*, and is usually designated by S. Thus, in the case of the man depositing £100 at first, and then half as much in each succeeding year, the series for four years would be:

$$S = D + (0 \cdot 5)^1 100 + (0 \cdot 5)^2 100 + (0 \cdot 5)^3 100.$$

In general, for any n:

$$S = D + aD + a^2 D + a^3 D + \ldots + a^n D.$$

What happens when n gets to be very large? Does the sum of the terms in the series get to be indefinitely large or does it converge to some finite number? The answer turns out to depend on a. We will now show that if a is less than 1 (or 100 per cent), the series converges. Otherwise it gets indefinitely large.

Suppose we had a geometric series for three years, so that $n = 2$.

$$S = D + aD + a^2 D.$$

Multiply both sides of this equation by a to get another series:

$$aS = aD + a^2 D + a^3 D.$$

Subtract the second equation from the first. The right hand side would be the first term of the original series minus the last term of the second series, $D - a^3 D$. All the intervening terms common to both would cancel. That is to say, $S - aS = D - a^3 D$. Factoring S on the left side and dividing by $(1 - a)$,

$$S = \frac{1}{1-a} D - \frac{a^3}{1-a} D.$$

Now generalize this to n years:

$$S = D + aD + a^2 D + a^3 D + \ldots + a^{n-1} D + a^n D$$

and

$$aS = aD + a^2 D + a^3 D + a^4 D + \ldots + a^{n-1} D + a^n D + a^{n+1} D.$$

After subtracting, only the first and last terms remain:

$$S - aS = D - a^{n+1}D$$

or:

$$S(1-a) = D - a^{n+1}D$$

and finally:

$$S = \frac{1}{1-a}D - \frac{a^{n+1}}{1-a}D.$$

Exercise: Suppose the original deposit in a cheque account were £100. Each year an amount was deposited equal to 50 per cent of the deposit made in the preceding year. What would be the balance after three deposits according to the formula for S?

The formula for the sum consists of two parts. The first part, $(1/1-a)D$, does not depend on how many terms there are in the series since n does *not* appear. In the second part, $(-a^{n+1}/1-a)D$, n matters. But if a is less than 1, as n gets bigger and bigger, the size of this second part will get smaller and smaller as a is raised to higher powers. If $a = \frac{1}{2}$, then $a^1 = \frac{1}{2}$, $a^2 = \frac{1}{4}$, $a^3 = \frac{1}{8}$, and so on. As n gets larger and larger, approaching infinity, a^{n+1} approaches zero. The second part of the formula becomes very small, effectively leaving $S = (1/1-a)D$ as the sum of the series.

Provided that a is less than 1, we conclude that the geometric series *converges* closer and closer to a finite value. This is so even though each of the terms adds a little more on to the preceding term! The point is that each additional term adds so little that the total never gets beyond the limit specified in the formula. For a equal to or greater than 1, S gets indefinitely large.

We can now calculate how much money would be deposited in the bank if the deposits were carried on forever. In the first year we deposited £100, so $D = 100$. Each year thereafter, we deposit half of the previous year's deposit, so $a = 0{\cdot}5$. Then if this process continued indefinitely we would have a bank account that approached

$$S = \frac{1}{1-0{\cdot}5}(100) = \frac{100}{0{\cdot}5} = £200.$$

Isn't it interesting the bank balance does not get indefinitely big even though the deposits go on forever!

Exercise:

(1) Suppose a person deposited £500 in his bank. Each year thereafter further deposits were made at the rate of 25 per cent of the previous year's deposit.

   (*a*) What would be the balance if this process were carried on forever?

   (*b*) What would the balance be in three years? In five years?

   (*c*) What would the balance be if 125 per cent of the previous deposit were added each year for three more years? Forever?

   (*d*) What if the same £500 deposit were made forever?

(2) What is the formula for the sum of the series if $a = 1$? Explain.

(3) Suppose a gardener plants a rose cutting that grows 1 foot in the first year. Then he allows it to grow $\frac{3}{4}$ of the previous year's growth, pruning off the rest. How big will his rose be if he were to do this for a very long time?

These mathematical tools are sufficient for a first course. With their help, the complex economic world will be seen to contain elements of regularity that we can understand and often utilize in the interest of society. A word of advice. Learning is an *active* process. You must do as many of the exercises as you possibly can. This book is written so that the reader is shown how to reach conclusions for himself rather than receiving them spoon-fed.

One word more. Economics developed as a science using ordinary words in a technical, precise sense. When such terms appear for the first time, they will be printed in italics to alert the reader to be sure he understands their meaning.

Preface to teachers
of economics

The purpose of this book, I have told the student reader, is 'to present economics in an up-to-date and straightforward way'. Certainly there is no shortage of 'principles' textbooks on the market written by outstanding economists and embodying some of the fruit of recent research. Yet I am impelled to write still another because, despite the growing restiveness of teachers and students, the basic concept of the first year course has remained unchanged for thirty years. Students come to economics expecting to grapple with the urgent problems of our times, yet they find that as a prerequisite they must confront an abstruse theoretical structure – the maximization of an unlikely entity, utility, by an abstract 'consumer'. If, in the interest of motivation, the course starts with 'macro', the focus of attention is on those problems thrown up by aggregate demand, an apparent looking-glass world in which output is limited by what people are willing to buy rather than by what they can produce. Is it any wonder that students complain of the distance between economics and common sense, and that teachers test the boundaries of their conscience in watering down the course so as to make it more 'relevant'?

Students are right to be restless. The world of partial equilibrium, of four cost curves, of elasticity of demand, no longer occupies the centre of attention of economics, precisely because it is not adequate to deal with consistent and efficient coordination of industries, planned production activities, pollution control, and the interdependence of national economies. Aggregate demand no longer is a matter only of the Keynesian cross diagram, but is part of larger models that show the interaction of demand upon all the other sectors of the economy. Of course the traditional doctrine retains its value, but the thrust of modern economics has been toward general equilibrium concepts of interdependence for reasons that are explicitly understood by economists, and I believe, intuited by the dissatisfied students. Is there not a way to transmit the core notion of interdependence to students as the basic integrative idea, and then particularize into microeconomics or aggregate into the familiar macroeconomics?

Why not start the study of economics with Leontief's simplified input-output system? Why not use the mathematical simplification for pedagogical purpose? The student then can start from the palpable world of production, with meaningful data and immediate application ready to hand. Our generation learned input-output as an advanced topic only because we already knew too much to simply accept its simplifications. Yet the precognitions of young people coming to economics for the first time are different. We can start them with a simple system – outputs proportional to inputs – and then introduce all the complications one step at a time.

Put the matter differently. No matter how we try to sugar the pill, the traditional economics curriculum involves the application of difficult calculus (marginal) concepts to the process of optimization. Once having committed students to this approach, it is impossible in a first course to retrace the steps and deal with structure and interdependence. Having lost innocence, general equilibrium becomes so difficult as to make it inaccessible. If, however, we start from structural interdependence, the underlying algebra can be illustrated with two linear equations which students have been solving since the age of fourteen. It is not necessary to hide such simple mathematics! Then optimization, first in production and later in consumption, can be expounded in a graphical exposition of linear programming. The concept of interdependence of activities is retained. All the traditional material of price theory is made available. Shadow price – opportunity cost – becomes a palpable, computable datum which the student must use at every turn rather than a metaphysical nicety.

Once having accustomed the student reader to think in terms of linear systems of equations, the structure of aggregate demand becomes a natural parallel to that of production. A miniature system of national income determination is built and later expanded to include international implications as well.

In writing this book, I have been guided by the notion that economics is an applied science. The unity of theory which the presentation permits has as its purpose the constant and immediate application to matters of social concern. From early on, the student is led to feel that he has an adequate grasp of sufficient theory to come to an informed judgement on the issues presented. Theory, problems and institutional descriptive material are complementary inputs into the learning process if a sufficiently wide ranging conceptual framework is prepared at the outset.

In writing this book I have been encouraged and guided by many people. Mr Alastair MacLean of Shaw-MacLean in London has been a constant source of wisdom. I was heartened by the American Joint Council on Economic Education which awarded the First Prize for Excellence in College Teaching of Economics (1970) for the curriculum embodied in this text. The greatest support, however, came from students in America, Britain and Nigeria, who grappled with the concepts of this book, and who rewarded me with that electric moment of suddenly 'catching on'. They have my heartfelt thanks. I am grateful also to Professor A. D. Brownlie (University of Canterbury), the late Charles B. Friday and Richard E. Towey (Oregon State University), G. H. Peters (University of Liverpool) and Ranjit S. Bhambri (Ahmadu Bello University, Nigeria) for advice and comments at various stages. I especially wish to thank my family, my wife Betty, and Paul, Susan and Deborah, for their love and their help.

Murray Wolfson
Department of Economics
Oregon State University
March 1976

1 Principles of economics

Science, social science and economics

It is a commonplace of the scientific method that the advance of knowledge proceeds in three steps:

1 Observation of the facts.
2 Generalization of observations into logically consistent theories.
3 Testing theory against further observation.

The tried and true method still serves, but it has one serious drawback: it does not tell us what facts to observe. Usually this is not considered much of a problem. Apprentice physicists merrily roll balls down an inclined plane, confining their attentions to facts of distance, mass and time. If a laboratory partner has bad breath that has nothing to do with the law of gravity. Or does it? How does the physicist really know what influences may safely be neglected? Should he consider the imperfect roundness of the ball? The wobble in the rotation of the earth? Perhaps the bad breath of the lab partner is important after all? He cannot record all of these facts? He cannot observe everything!

In physics it is usually fairly easy to specify what to observe. In advance of entering the laboratory, we have a fair idea of the degree to which certain causes are likely to affect the outcome. Most of the time we can decide what to neglect. But we are never really sure! Even in physics, there may be an ugly surprise in store showing that we have omitted some important factor. Ideas held in advance may turn out to be wrong, and we must try again.

Nonetheless the relative ease with which the key elements can be identified permitted the early translation of physics into precise mathematical terms. One should not be so overawed by its long chains of mathematical reasoning to forget that only the ease with which physical observations can be isolated from 'outside' influences makes this elegant treatment possible. Yet by omitting these influences the physicist never deals with the whole reality. In his formulae and experiments, he makes a simplified *theoretical model* of reality leaving a great deal out. By experimental test he hopes to show that his theory has some important relation to the infinitely complex universe. Ultimately this becomes a practical question of the *degree of accuracy* required. The model survives its test if its predictions come close enough for the theory to fit the facts well enough for us to *use*. In an uneasy sense we are always more or less wrong!

We often have several theories to account for the same experience. The theory we choose often depends on the sort of practical problem we intend to solve. Thus, if we are to be asked, 'Why does water boil?', one answer might be: 'It is in a hot pot!' To cook a pot of porridge is a perfectly adequate explanation. If we are interested in designing a steam engine we should talk about the number of calories required to convert liquid water to steam. Which is the true explanation—hot pot or heat flow? Neither represents the ultimate truth, as advanced courses in physics show. The 'hot pot' explanation is more useful when cooking breakfast, and the 'calories to create steam' is appropriate to driving a locomotive.

In a study of human affairs such as economics we also make appropriate models of social behaviour. Economics will never get 'the truth' any more than physics, but it can solve a wide variety of problems.

A particularly nasty complication in economics is the problem of *time*. How do we know that the reality we study will not change even while we study it? Human affairs are subject to continuous variation so that we can rely less on the constancy of nature than physical scientists. This difficulty can be overestimated. There are very important elements of uniformity in economic life. The resources available for production change slowly compared with such economic events as purchase and sale. Productive capability embodied in the 'state of the technical arts' certainly changes, but this does not happen all at once. Most important, human beings are creatures of habit. If they were not, we could hardly expect to survive for long since each one of us relies on the 'normal conduct' of others. We expect business acquaintances to be concerned for their own self-interest. At the same time we do not anticipate such grossly antisocial behaviour as a merchant biting off a great chunk of the bank manager's ear if he is refused an overdraft. It is from humdrum regularities of behaviour that economic analysis has built a surprisingly powerful science.

Economics can be studied through three different models labelled micro-economics, macroeconomics, and interindustry analysis. Each approach focuses on the facts relating to different aspects of the economy.

(1) *Microeconomics* is concerned with the behaviour of individual consumers and producing firms. It studies how the outputs of firm contribute to the *supply* of goods offered by industry. Microeconomics is also concerned with the decisions by consumers to use their incomes to buy or not to buy particular products. The sum of individual decisions to buy is the *demand* for the products of the industry in question. In most practical applications microeconomics is *partial* analysis. Attention is limited to one industry at a time. All other aspects of the economy – the activities of other industries, the level of general business activity, the tastes of the consumers and the technical possibilities available to producers – are taken as constant facts of life. Supply and demand adapt to these conditions which are taken as given. In the economist's phrase, *ceteris paribus*, we assume all other things remaining the same.

This method permits us to understand a great deal about the way in which a type of goods is produced and sold, but it does not explain how one industry and its constituent firms are related to the general level of business or the conditions of other industries. Microeconomics cannot give such answers precisely because it has decided to take these things as remaining the same.

(2) *Macroeconomics* deals with the aggregate, overall, workings of the economic system. The total value of all the goods and services produced by a country in a year is called its *gross national product* (GNP). On one hand the GNP represents the ability of the country to produce (supply) goods and services; on the other it also depends on the willingness of the country to buy (demand) these products.

Macroeconomic models seek to determine if there is sufficient total demand for goods and services to match society's capacity to supply. If so, there will be a condition of full employment; otherwise depressed business conditions will cause unemployment. Perhaps the demand for the GNP is greater than can be supplied. Then firms and individuals will be bidding against one another for goods that cannot be supplied and prices will rise.

The macroeconomic model is only part of the whole truth. It cannot discuss prices, output or employment in a particular industry precisely because it has added them all up. Nevertheless it can tell us a great deal about how to cope with unemployment or inflation (the nub of our present predicament is that we do not know how to cope with both of these problems at once).

(3) *Interindustry analysis* (*input-output*) occupies an intermediate position. Whilst microeconomics studies the consumers and firms within an

industry, and macroeconomics investigates the total supply and demand of all the industries, interindustry analysis analyses how the various industries *fit together*. *Input-output analysis* is a particularly simple form of inter-industry study in which many of the complications are put aside in the interest of easy measurement and understanding.

Interindustry analysis is called upon to show how the demand for a particular type of goods would affect other industries – for example, how a programme of building motorways in the UK alters the whole economy. Clearly there must be an increase in production of road building equipment and materials. But these industries are supplied by others, which are in turn supplied by still others. How much must each industry ultimately produce to supply the others and still satisfy public demand for its own product? How much labour, capital and natural resources must be employed? Will these be available? Is it possible to build the motorways on the projected scale without directly or indirectly drawing resources away too much from other worthwhile projects such as ship building?

Input-output is useful for learning economics because of its intermediate position between micro- and macroeconomics. Once we understand the working of interindustry relations, we can more easily make sense out of the microeconomic position of separate industries. We can sum the outputs and demands for all industries and relate the totals to macroeconomics. Before concentrating on input-output we need to examine the three models in more detail.

Query: What industries are likely to be discouraged by motorways?
How would you go about deciding whether the motorway pro-gramme is good or bad?

Microeconomics

Information about business – or individuals – is reflected in two financial statements: *The balance sheet* and *profit and loss statements*.

(1) *The balance sheet* shows the *stock of wealth* in the hands of the firm at any instant in time. Positive items of wealth are called *assets*. Negative wealth, debts, are *liabilities*. The difference is *net worth*. Frequently accountants call net worth *capital and reserves*, even though economists wince since they prefer to use capital to mean physical productive assets such as equipment, buildings, and stocks of goods.

(2) *The profit and loss* statement shows the flow of wealth over a period of time. It records the *inflow* of income or revenue from sales of merchandise or services. It also makes a record of the *outflow* of expenses of production or other operations. The difference is *profit*.

Stocks of wealth – the balance sheet

Consider the balance sheet for Imperial Chemical Industries Ltd (ICI), published in their *Annual Report to Shareholders* for 1970. We ask the reader to read through this balance sheet rather carefully and total all the assets as they appear at various places in the statement, subtract all the liabilities, and verify for himself that net worth (capital) is equal to assets minus liabilities.

ICI Group Balance Sheet (£ million)
at 31 December 1970

Assets employed:

Fixed assets:			
Land and buildings	349.3		
Less depreciation	118.0		
Net book value	231·3		
Plant and equipment	1512·1		
Less depreciation	666·9		
Net book value	845·2		
Total net book value of fixed assets			1076·5
Goodwill			38·7
Interest in subsidiaries			62·0
Interest in associate companies			112·3
Net current assets:			
Current assets:			
Stocks of finished goods	184·5		
Raw materials and stores	136·8		
Total stocks		321·3	
Debtors to ICI		351·0	
Quoted investments	10·8		
Short term deposits	90·2		
Cash	19·4		
Total liquid resources		120·4	
Total current assets			792·7
Current liabilities:			
Trade and other creditors	217·5		
Gross dividends	35·4		
Current taxation	77·1		
Total creditors		330·0	
Bank overdrafts	76·4		
Other short term borrowing	17·9		
Total short term borrowings		94·3	
Total current liabilities			424·3

ICI Group Balance Sheet (£ million) at 31 December 1970 (continued)

Assets employed (*continued*):

Net current assets (current assets minus current liabilities)			368·4
Total assets employed			1657·9

Financed by:

Capital and reserves:

5% cumulative preference stock	8·6		
Ordinary stock	468·7		
Total issued capital	477·3		
Reserves employed in business	464·0		
Total capital and reserves		941·3	
Investment grants		80·5	

Deferred taxation:

UK corporation tax payable 1 Jan. 1972	38·4		
Deferments due to accelerated capital allowances	38·9		
Total deferred taxation		77·3	

Loans (fixed interest stock):

Repayable within 5 years	70·0		
Not repayable within 5 years	372·0		
Total loans		442·0	
Total finance			1657·9

We said that the balance sheet was a statement of condition at a moment of time. This is reflected in the dating of the ICI statement at the close of business on New Year's Eve. This is a single date and not an interval of time. The balance sheet is an instantaneous photograph of positive and negative *stocks of wealth* which may have been accumulated over many years.

The form of the balance sheet is an *identity*. The assets of the company are always equal to the liabilities and net worth because net worth is defined as the difference between assets and liabilities. To see this, let A stand for assets, L for liabilities, and W for net worth. The balance sheet has the equation: $A = L + W$. The net worth is defined as $W = A - L$. Substitute $W = A - L$ in the first equation. We get: $A = L + (A - L)$, or $A = A$. Ultimately the balance sheet can only tell us that assets are equal to assets are equal to assets...a rose is a rose is a rose. Trite but certainly true!

Very frequently in economics we will have to deal with accounting identities of various kinds. This is a source of confusion if one is not careful, because an *identity* is different from an *equation*. An equation is a question, a search for values, that will satisfy certain prescribed conditions. Thus

$x + 5 = 7$ is an equation. It asks for the particular value of x that will make the statement true. On the other hand, $A + 2A = 3A$ is an identity, because it is true for any value of A that one can possibly think of. The identity does not tell us anything special about A. But the equation permits us to find that x which equals 2.

As an identity, the fact that a balance sheet balances only proves that the accountant can add, and tells us nothing about the condition of the firm. Nonetheless, the balance sheet is a convenient way of displaying the assets, liabilities and net worth of the company.

Query: (1) Would a balance sheet still balance if the firm were so deeply in debt that it had a negative net worth?

   (2) What information would you look for in the ICI balance sheet to decide whether to buy shares in the company? What other information would you like to have before deciding?

   (3) Is $x^2 = 4$ an identity or equation? What of $x \times x = x^2$?

A particularly nasty problem facing accountants is assessing the value of partially worn out *fixed assets* such as machinery and equipment. Their historical purchase price is interesting but irrelevant: an obsolete machine is worthless. A precious painting picked up for a song at a rummage sale may be worth a fortune. Economists have a ready but sometimes impractical answer to what an asset is worth: 'Sell it and find out!' This wholesome advice usually falls on deaf ears. The chief accountant is not about to urge that ICI sell off all its equipment to help him draw up the balance sheet more easily.

Accountants list the historical purchase price of the fixed assets and then subtract some estimate for the depreciation or wear and tear. This can be tricky. How is one to know if the value of a machine declines at a constant percentage each year? How can anyone know in advance how long the machine will actually last?

The matter is complicated by the fact that the depreciation apportioned each year enters as a *cost* into the profit and loss statement (see p. 11). More rapid depreciation lowers the profit shown and hence reduces income tax. As a result, the depreciated value of the fixed assets assigned by accountants often has very little to do with the amount that wear and tear have reduced their actual market valuation. Generally, in the UK, 15 per cent is the standard annual rate at which depreciation is accepted by tax authorities for industrial machinery, although it may go as high as 25 per cent for some types. Buildings are depreciated much more slowly at 4 per cent and some business assets may not claim a depreciation allowance against tax at all. This sort of regulation becomes a guideline for accountants.

Depreciation regulations are also a means to stimulate business since accelerated depreciation has the effect of lowering taxes. Investment in new machinery is encouraged as firms tend to replace fully depreciated assets.

Query: (1) How long does the Inland Revenue seem to think machinery lasts? Longer or shorter than buildings?

(2) What are the pros and cons of influencing investment by tax allowances such as accelerated depreciation? Are direct investment grants better? Do you think investment ought to be aided at all?

There is another method of valuing assets called *capitalization*. The theory is that the value of a productive asset to its owner ultimately depends on the income which the asset generates over its lifetime. Suppose, after deducting repair and maintenance costs, that a machine increased the output of a firm by £100 each year over and above what could be earned without it. The value of the machine could be compared to some other use of funds of comparable risk such as lending money out at interest. Let us say that the interest rate was 10 per cent. The question is now: how much money would have to be loaned out in order to earn the same £100 each year? The machine should have a value equal in amount. Let the amount that has to be loaned be A. Then 10 per cent of A equals £100, or $0 \cdot 1A = £100$. Therefore $A = £100/0 \cdot 1$ or £1000. The machine would be worth £1000 if it could be maintained indefinitely to produce £100 each year, and if the interest rate was 10 per cent.

In general, $rA = i$, where i is the additional income that the asset generates, and r is the interest rate for loans of similar risk. Then the capitalized value of the asset is given by the formula: $A = i/r$. This calculation has been made on the simplified assumption that the asset can be made to last indefinitely: a machine that is kept constantly in repair, or a sum of money that is always kept loaned out by relending. The calculation for more short-lived assets is set out in the appendix to this chapter (pp 34–6).

Exercise:

(1) What would a rational farmer be willing to pay for a harvester that increased his annual income by £1000 net of repair costs to keep it indefinitely as good as new? Assume that he had to borrow money from the bank at 5 per cent. What would he be willing to pay if he used his own money?

(2) Suppose it costs £500 for a university lecturer to move from one position to another. Suppose that the rate of interest were 10 per cent per annum. By how much would the salaries paid at the new institution have to exceed the old for him to be willing to pack up? Does your answer help explain why some teachers call themselves migratory workers?

(3) How would you decide what damages to pay to the surviving family of a mother of five, killed in an automobile accident? What is a human life worth? If you object to the capitalized value method, propose another system. Can we put a value on human life?

(4) What is the value of a university education? Suppose you had to vote for one of three public projects: a university, a technical school for under-privileged youth, a medical centre in the suburbs of a metropolitan city. How would you choose?

Liabilities are grouped according to the time within which the obligations are payable. One way or another, they are contracts to repay a specified amount of money in the future, plus an interest charge. For the long-term loan, fixed interest stock, and bank overdrafts, the *interest* charge is cus-tomarily added to the original *principal*. In the case of some short-term commercial debt, firms are offered a *discount* if they pay within the specified thirty or ninety days. Clearly the discount is simply another form of interest charge that must be paid by making remittance later rather than sooner. Firms can borrow cash for short periods in a similar way by simply selling their promise to pay at a discount.

The nature of debt liability is often misunderstood. As individuals we usually want to pay debts off as soon as we can, simply because the interest charges are a constant drain on our pocketbook. 'Buy now and pay later' means that we have to pay more later. To be sure, we can decide to remain permanently in debt by *refinancing* again each time an old loan comes due. But there is the danger that unforeseen circumstances might later temporar-ily reduce our income. Lenders could not be sure we could always pay the interest charges, and refinance may be impossible. Excessive fixed interest charges often cause serious trouble as a result of this uncertain aspect of economic life.

Businesses face the same problem of uncertainty but its significance is different for productive business enterprises. Interest charges continue to represent fixed expenses that have to be met out of revenues; refinancing of loans can be difficult if the prospects are uncertain. Yet there is one very important difference: Unlike a consumer, the firm does not simply use up the loan in consumption, but spends it to earn more money. It borrows to meet a payroll, to buy machinery and materials. As long as the income that the loan generates exceeds the interest cost, there is no reason at all why the firm should not borrow indefinitely. The expenditure that the businessman makes with the money he gets for a sound loan provides him with the means of paying the interest charge. It is using the savings of people who do not have immediate use for them, and putting them to a profitable purpose.

Of course, business uncertainty is a problem. A firm that has earmarked most of its revenue to pay interest may find that even the smallest drop in sales will make the fixed interest burden of debt overwhelming. Prudence in this matter is important, but sensible debt management is normal good business.

Net worth of the firm is the difference between assets and liabilities and reflects its form of organization. The firm is a *sole proprietorship* if the net worth is wholly owned by one person. A *partnership* can be described as a *multiple proprietorship*. Each partner owns the firm and can bind it to contract. At the same time each is fully liable for *all* of the debts.

These two forms are only suitable for small enterprises. Partnership provides for pooling individual savings but is a hazardous form of business organization, since each partner can fully bind the others even to foolish decisions. A partnership is much like a marriage. The prevalence of both monogamy and divorce suggests that the number of partners ought to be limited. Indeed, it is often more difficult to extricate oneself from a partnership than a marriage, since the remaining partner must be induced to take all of the business obligations on himself. That can be sticky and expensive.

The *corporation* is the form of most larger firms. A corporation is an artificial person created by a government. It can buy and sell, borrow and lend, sue and be sued, make profits or go into bankruptcy. In other words, the corporation can do the same sorts of economic activities as flesh and blood individuals, subject to the purposes specified in its charter.

The advantages to the corporate form follow from its nature as an artificial entity. If the business fails it is the corporation that fails not the individuals who own it. Individual liability is *limited*. Ownership in a corporation is in the form of *shares*. If a corporation fails, they may become worthless, but no further legal liability is involved to the shareholder. In the balance sheet shares are shown at the 'par' value printed on them – usually £100 – but may be traded at more or less than that amount.

Since the actual value of the assets of a firm accumulate over time, the net worth of a firm may exceed the total of the par value of the shares. The difference is shown in the balance sheet as reserves. Individuals can buy shares in a firm and withdraw from it without the consent of the other shareholders. As a result, the element of risk is further reduced. Funds can be tapped from individuals who otherwise would not be willing to form a business.

Obviously the corporation is an immensely useful invention. It is a device for mobilization of savings by reducing the risk each owner must bear to manageable proportion. At the same time it may become so large that it represents a monopolistic danger to competition. There may also be drawbacks in the separation of the ownership of the corporation by shareholders and its *de facto* control by the managers and officers they employ. We return to this problem in Chapter 9.

The flow of income and expenses: the profit and loss statement

The profit and loss statement is a record of *flows* of revenues and expenditures over a period of time, usually a year. The profit and loss statement for ICI is 'for the year ending 31 December 1970'.

ICI Group Profit and Loss Statement
(£ million for year ending 31 December 1970)

Sales and other income:			
Sales to United Kingdom	693		
Sales overseas	769		
Royalties	13		
Other trading income	5		
Investment income	18		
Total sales and other income	1498		
Disposition of income:			
Raw materials and purchased services	868		
Wages and salaries	318		
Pensions and pension fund contributions	21		
Depreciation	114		
Interest payable	35		
Employees' profit-sharing bonus	8		
Taxation less investment grants	35	} Profits	⎱ Profits
Distributed as dividends	71⎰ Profits	} before	⎰ before
Retained in the business	28⎰ after taxes	taxes	bonus
Total disposition of income	1498		

To find profits for the year, we take sales and other income (S), subtract expenses (E) leaving profits (P). Profits are defined by the *identity* $P = S - E$. The ICI statement tends to lump profits and expenses together into the category of 'disposition of income'. In effect, it prefers the identity to be written as $S = E + P$. To determine ICI's profits we must draw the line somewhere between E and P. This is not always easy. Should we include profit-sharing bonus in profits? How about taxes? We are in the same quandary as the virgin in the arms of her seducer: we are certain that we ought to draw the line somewhere but are not sure where. In any case, ICI profits after bonus and taxes were £99 million. Some of the profit is distributed to the shareholders as *dividends*. Undistributed *retained* profits are added to the stock of net worth, recorded in the balance sheet as *reserves*. Retained profit flow is the rate of change over time of the net worth of the firm.

Query: What is the ratio of ICI's depreciation expense to total value of plant and equipment? How does it compare with the 15 per cent figure mentioned on p. 7?

The profit and loss statement shows the *flow of inputs* into production represented by the *expenses* of the firm. Economists call these inputs *factors of production* and recatalogue the accounting classifications into *labour, land, capital, entrepreneurial effort.*

(1) *Labour* is understood by all and avoided by most. That is why wages have to be paid. But what of the person who enjoys his work? Why is he paid? The impoverished lecturer who turns in his gown at prestigious Scroogeville University for a job at grimy Hopeful Polytechnic is always rebuked, 'Shame on you for thinking of money! Are you not dedicated to teaching?' To which the proper reply is, 'I *am* dedicated. The only *relevant* question is *where* I should be dedicated!' Whether or not it is painful or sheer ecstasy, wages are paid by the employer because labour is scarce. Workers must be bid away from other employers as well as induced to give up *leisure* time.

(2) *Land* is a traditional term for all the scarce *natural resources* that enter into production: water, soil, mineral, pure air and the like. As in other endeavours, persons who look for land in the virgin state are apt to be disappointed. Over the centuries man has applied labour and capital and transformed his environment for better or worse.

Nonetheless it is useful to employ the notion of a factor of production that more reasonably may be considered to be the product of natural rather than human efforts. Again the key to its value is scarcity. Even if it is a 'free gift of nature', land is limited in supply. Everyone cannot use the land at the same time. Rent is the payment that has to be made to induce one owner of the resource to apply it to a different use. The use of land will go to the highest bidder, who must therefore also have the most productive use to which it can be put. One may think of rent as the payment making it worthwhile to sacrifice the next best alternative use of the resource.

(3) *Capital* to economists means the *products of past production to be used in the present and future* (it differs from the accountant's use of the term in the balance sheet). Capital is accumulated buildings, machinery and stocks of goods. Capital does not mean money. To be sure, buildings, machinery and inventories are bought and sold for money. Nonetheless, money is only the measure of the capital, just as it is of labour and land.

The expenses using capital are more than wear and tear, *depreciation* or *capital consumption*. Since it is the product of an earlier date to be used now or in the future, capital always involves an element of waiting, for which its provider must be paid interest. Consider a businessman who is faced with a choice whether to use more or less equipment in production: Would it be sensible for him to use more capital rather than less if he were only able to recover the cost of capital depreciation? Only later would he get back the investment he advanced. His wealth would not be available for him to use now. Consequently, he must also receive *interest* to induce him to wait.

The interest received by owners of capital operates as an incentive to others to save part of their income. Interest as an inducement to save and a necessary cost to investment applies to every economic system, even one based on barter or central planning. In an economy such as ours, financial intermediaries such as banks pay interest to individual savers and lend the money at higher interest to businessmen anxious to accumulate more capital. Capital accumulation is called *investment*. Investment is the purchase of additional buildings, machinery and stocks of goods. The interest earned by the industrial investors of capital must at least equal the interest charged by banks for investment to take place. In a monetary economy interest is also a payment to induce lenders to hold their assets in a less negotiable form than cash, such as bonds or rates receivable. Some authors tend to give this preference for liquidity a more prominent place than the incentive to save; this issue will be explored more thoroughly in Chapter 12.

(4) *Entrepreneurship*. Imagine that the revenues of ICI were just enough to pay for the factors of production considered thus far. ICI would not stay in business very long. Why not? A successful business involves more than hiring land, labour and capital. Ultimately someone must take responsibility for decisions that cannot be made in a routine way. What is to be produced? How? Not the least of shareholder decisions in a large corporation is who to hire as manager.

Decisions are made in an uncertain world, involving the entrepreneur in responsibility for failure. Why should a person take on such responsibility unless he had a better than even chance to benefit? The entrepreneur must make a profit on the average of the good years and the bad, otherwise he will leave his occupation and go to work for somebody else. True, profit appears as a *residual*, money left over from sales after deducting expenses; certainly profit is not a *contractual*, prearranged, sort of income; yet profit is one of the necessary costs of the business operation, for without it business ceases as surely as if wages are not paid. Indeed, the scarce entrepreneurial ability it buys is frequently the crucial 'bottleneck' factor in large business enterprises.

Exercise:
(1) Review the profit and loss statement and show that all the income is resolved into payments to factors of production (before taxes), depreciation and payments to other firms.

(2) Who is the entrepreneur in ICI? The shareholders? The officers? The workmen? All of them? Who gets the profits?
(3) Do you think there are entrepreneurs in the USSR? If so, who are they?
(4) Why could one not obtain an insurance policy for all business uncertainties, thus eliminating the cost of entrepreneurship?

Planning for profit

We are now in a position to look for stable relationships which will permit a firm to plan its future. Planning begins by calculating the ratio of expenses to sales, the amount spent to manufacture and sell £1 worth of merchandise. Call this ratio the *technical coefficient of production* and symbolize it by a. Let us take it that a turns out to be fairly consistent from one year to the next. Then $a = E/S$, and consequently $E = aS$.

Query: Compute a for ICI.

We shall continue this result with the profit and loss identity, $S - E = P$. We call this the *balancing equation*. It also might be written as $E + P = S$, showing that the sales of the firm just equal the disposition of funds, i.e. the cost of inputs including the profit.
Substituting aS for E in $S - E = P$, we get:

$$S - aS = P.$$

Factoring out S we have:

$$(1 - a)S = P_1$$

and dividing by $(1 - a)$ (multiplying by $1/(1 - a)$), we finally have: $S = (1/1 - a)P$. Now we have it! The sales required to achieve *any* specified profit can be found by multiplying that profit by $1/(1 - a)$; the *multiplier* $1/(1 - a)$ can be written $(1 - a)^{-1}$ and read 'one minus a inverted'.
To illustrate, suppose that Fictitious Foundations Ltd, makers of mountains from molehills, applies for a loan from a bank, on the expectation that it will be able to earn £3,000,000 in profit next year. Using our method the bank manager can calculate the sales required to earn that much profit. Suppose prior years showed expenses were £8,000,000 and sales were £10,000,000; then the *technical coefficient*, a, is 0·8, and the *multiplier* is $1/(1 - 0·8) = 5$. If £3,000,000 profit is to be earned, then £15,000,000 worth of Fictitious Foundations must be sold. 'Is the sales expectation unrealistic?' the banker asks. Do the sales prospects reflect inflated figures? If not, the loan is good business for both borrower and lender.

Exercise:
(1) Compute S if the firm wished to make £4,000,000 profit. Suppose the technical coefficient were to change from 0·8 to 0·9. Would the needed sales increase or decrease? How would an increase in efficiency change the multiplier?
(2) Suppose ICI planned to earn £200 million profit before taxes. How much must it plan to sell (treat profit-sharing bonus as a wage expense)?

There is another way to look at multipliers that will carry over from this problem to many others. The firm's ultimate goal is profits, but some of the revenue 'leaks out' of the company revenue in the form of expenses. Multipliers are used to compute the sales needed to compensate for the leakage.

Suppose a firm foolishly tried to make an amount of profit, P, by making and selling only the same amount of goods. That is, suppose it set $S = P$. It would soon discover to its sorrow that, in order to produce, expenses must be incurred. To pay the expenses, $S = P + aP$ must be produced and sold, where aP is the direct expense requirement. But now the greater production of the extra aP incurs additional indirect expenses! How much? a times as much as aP, or a^2P. The firm must now make $S = P + aP + a^2P$. Alas, the manufacture of the additional a^2P requires that new indirect expenses must also be met; these are a^3P. So it goes, on and on indefinitely. Now how much must really be sold to earn P and still meet direct and indirect expense? Clearly S is the sum of the infinite geometric series:

$$S = P + aP + a^2P + a^3P + \ldots + a^nP.$$

If a is less than 1, the sum of this series is:

$$S = \frac{1}{1-a}P.$$

Behold! Our multiplier formula again in which S equals P is multiplied by $1/(1-a)$! As long as a is less than 1, the series converges to $(1-a)^{-1}$.

Exercise:
(1) Suppose the ratio of expenses to sales is 0·8 and the firm is trying to earn £4,000,000. Compute the sales in the case in which the firm only makes three additions of indirect sales necessary to meet expenses. By how much will their sales fall short of the actual amount needed to make the desired profit?
(2) Why must a be less than 1 for a viable enterprise?

The meaning of the market: supply and demand

The private sector of the economy is a vast market for goods and services. Participants react to *prices* in such a system: consumers buy more when the price is low, and less when high; firms produce more when offered greater prices and supply less when the price is low. To understand the market is to understand the mechanism of price formation.

In a market economy, price is determined by *demand* and *supply*. Demand is a reflection of the willingness of individual consumers to spend their money on products offered to them by business firms. Supply is the corresponding willingness of business firms to produce and sell amounts of the various products in response to the prices that consumers offer. The balance of demand and supply on the market means that the price of products depends on the interaction of the individual decisions of consumers and producers.

Not every economy is coordinated by supply and demand. In a *command society*, such as the USSR, the exchange of goods and services for factors of production takes place through the directives of the government authorities rather than through the inducement of offers of money. Traditional village societies in pre-industrial societies allocate human effort and the distribution of product on the basis of tribal or family 'right', their traditional concepts of justice and morality.

No matter how the arrangements are made, there must be some system for allocating goods and services and the factors of production to create them. Since they are scarce, factors of production are not available to satisfy every desire. Choosing the optimum allocation of scarce resources among alternative ends is the basic economic issue facing every social system.

Exercise:

In the following table we designate the three ways of allocating scarce resources by:

   T = Traditional economy
   C = Command economy
   M = Market economy

We symbolize the possibilities of planning by:

   P = Planned
   U = Unplanned

We show ownership of productive property as:

   O = Private ownership
   N = No private ownership

	P		U	
	O	N	O	N
T				
C				
M				

(1) Tick those boxes which you believe represent possible combinations of social systems.
(2) Give examples of societies that correspond to the boxes. Where they actually exist in the world?
(3) Designate the boxes you have checked either with a D for democratic or an L for non-democratic society.
(4) Is it possible for a single country to combine several types of economy? Give examples.

We have said that the market economy operates through buying and selling goods and services at money prices. We shall see how the market operates to find the price at which the willingness of consumers to buy a certain amount of goods matches the willingness of producers to provide them. That is to say, prices adjust until the quantity of goods demanded equals the quantity supplied.

The demand for a good is a *schedule* which relates the amounts that consumers will buy at alternative prices. It is certainly reasonable to suppose under ordinary circumstances that if a product is offered at a cheaper price more of it will be bought. For example, consider the following hypothetical schedule of demand for hats; corresponding to each price alternative it

DEMAND SCHEDULE

Price of hats (£)	Number of hats (in millions)
10	5
9	6
8	7
7	8
6	9
5	9·5
4	10
3	10·5
2	10·5
1	11
0	14

shows the number of hats consumers would buy. We can make a graph of the schedule by measuring prices on the vertical axis, and showing quantities bought horizontally. The graph is called the *demand curve* (Figure 1.1). The

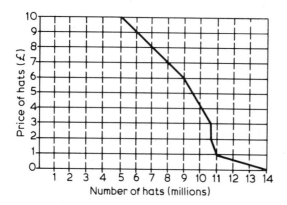

Figure 1.1   Demand curve

demand curve slopes downward reflecting the fact that price and quantity purchased vary inversely. Higher prices mean lower quantities, and lower prices imply greater quantities bought by consumers.

Exercise:
(1) Do you think it more likely that 14 million hats would be bought if the price were zero or do you think that people would take an unlimited number of hats if they were free? Does medical care have similar demand? How about fresh fish?
(2) Why might the demand curve for alcoholic beverages be nearly vertical?

The production of hats is summarized by a *supply schedule*; its graph is the *supply curve* (Figure 1.2). It is certainly reasonable to suppose that if a hat company were offered a higher price it would be able to find a way to make more hats. Suppliers react in the opposite way to consumers: a high price for hats means more hats, and a low price means fewer hats supplied. Price and quantity vary directly, so the supply curve slopes upward.

Superimposing the curves upon each other, supply and demand are seen to cross at the point where the price of hats is £6, and 9 million hats are sold (Figure 1.3). It is easy to see that a competitive market would tend toward this price and quantity. Suppose the price was above the £6 per hat, say £8. The schedule of supply shows that the amount offered for sale would be 11

SUPPLY SCHEDULE

Price of hats (£)	Number of hats (in millions)
10	13
9	12
8	11
7	10
6	9
5	8
4	7
3	6
2	5
1	4
0	0

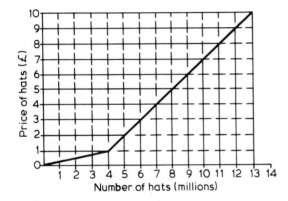

Figure 1.2   Supply curve

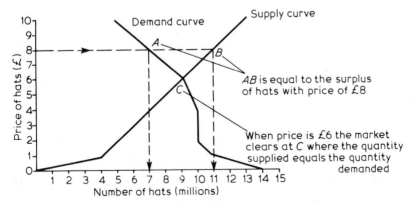

Figure 1.3   Supply and demand combined

million hats (read over from £8 on the vertical price axis to the supply curve, and down to the horizontal quantity axis at 11). But at a price of £8 the demand schedule indicates that only 7 million hats would be purchased (read over from £8 to the demand curve and down to the quantity axis). Therefore at a price of £8 there would be a surplus of unsold hats. Unless there were monopolistic firms that can protect the high price, competition will force sellers to sell at lower prices. If one seller does not, another will.

Query: How big is the surplus?

As the price of hats falls, the surplus of hats tends to disappear. At £7, only 10 million hats will be supplied, but 8 million hats will be demanded. Finally, at the £6 equilibrium price, the market clears at 9 million hats. There is neither surplus nor shortage, and therefore no tendency for the price to change further.

Reasoning in exactly the same way, we can see that if the price of hats were lower than the equilibrium price there would be a shortage of hats. More would be demanded than supplied. Consumers would bid for the scarce hats and the price would rise. But as the price rose, fewer hats would be demanded and more would be supplied until equilibrium were once more restored.

Exercise:
(1) How much would the surplus or shortage of hats be if the price were £4?
(2) Suppose somebody thought it only 'fair' that hats should be sold for £4. What difficulties would result? What solutions could you offer? Is the price system a fair rationing device?
(3) What might be meant by stable and unstable equilibrium in the physical world? Are prices in stable or unstable equilibrium? Explain.

Supply and demand is a useful model. It enables us to forecast prices and outputs as they are influenced by the choices made by producers and consumers. If the pattern of choice changes, then the price and quantity resulting from the intersection of supply and demand also changes. For instance, if it becomes the fashion to wear hats to bed, then the quantity of hats demanded will be greater at each price in the schedule. The demand curve shifts to the right. Intersection with the upward sloping supply curve will indicate a higher price reflecting the increased desire for headwear. Now examine a situation of supply shift. Technical progress such as a more inexpensive blockhead would cause the quantity producible by suppliers of hats to rise for each price alternative. The supply curve shifts to the right. The intersection of the new supply curve with demand causes the price of hats to fall and more of them to be manufactured.

Exercise:
(1) Draw graphs illustrating the *shifts* of supply and demand curves described in the text. Show the prices and quantity changes.
(2) What would be the likely effect of an increase of *income* to consumers of hats?

Macroeconomics

Before the Depression in the 1930s supply and demand was thought to be sufficient to explain important economic events. Yet how could the Depression have come about? Did we not show that at the equilibrium price the market cleared? How could there possibly have been unsold goods for an extended period of time? The supply and demand models can be applied to the labour market. Wages as the price of labour should have adjusted to market conditions making mass unemployment impossible! Yet in 1932 the stubborn fact was that 22 per cent of the UK labour force was unemployed! Moreover, for the twenty years 1921–39, unemployment was always over 9 per cent and most frequently close to 15 per cent. Apparently it was possible for the economy to be in equilibrium under conditions of less than full employment. Evidently something more was involved than the supply and demand of goods like hats and tomatoes. But what?

In what was probably one of the most important and controversial books of the century, *The General Theory of Employment, Interest and Money* (1936), John Maynard Keynes argued that there was a fundamental difference between the market for individual commodities and the demand for goods and services taken as a whole. Keynes freely conceded that a competitive market clears for one good at a time, just as the 'classical' microeconomic analysis suggested. The reason that the market clearing tendency is effective, Keynes argued, is that the market for a particular good is dominated by the possibility of substitution of other goods. Because of the substitution effect, if the price of peas is too high, consumers do not demand as many peas. They buy carrots. If the price of peas is low, farmers who formerly supplied peas grow some other crop. They produce the carrots.

Of course, it never really was lost on thoughtful people (and even one or two professors of economics) that the income of buyers has a great deal to do with demand. For most goods, the income effect works so that the more or less a person has to spend, the more or less he will buy. Keynes went further: when the economy as a whole was considered, the tendency of the substitution effect to strike a balance at full employment might be outweighed by the income effect which could lead to unemployment when people bought less.

The Keynesian argument as elaborated by others[1] is that a change in the price of goods affects incomes as well as prompting substitution. If the price of hats falls, the potential buyer of hats has a higher real income since his money goes further; at the same time, the seller of hats may suffer a fall in income if he does not sell a good many more hats. In turn these changes in income affect the demand for hats.

Usually the income effect arising from a price change is so small as to be safely ignored. Hats are only one small item in a consumer's budget. Income effects may not be ignored when we take a price which is a large element in incomes, such as wages; nor when we consider large, macroeconomic, aggregate categories of expenditure, such as total national consumption.

Take, for example, the effect of a change in the price of labour. If the wage rate falls, the possibility of quickly substituting great amounts of cheap labour for relatively dear machinery is limited. Hence the immediate effect of lower wages usually is lower labour incomes. Since demand by workers is so important in the total demand for consumer goods, one would expect aggregate demand to weaken. The result might be a further reduction of demand for labour and still lower wages. Whether the process stabilizes or continues into the abyss of depression depends on whether cheaper wages are quickly reflected in cheaper goods prices. It may be that lower prices will cause more goods to be sold restoring the demand for labour. But the timing of the price and wage changes is critical and the result is uncertain.

What is not problematical, Keynes showed, is that, when we take the whole economy in the macroeconomic sense, the income effect becomes very important. Aggregate consumption expenditures depend critically on personal incomes. To be sure, if interest rates offered by banks and building societies were very much lower, people might be tempted to save less and consume more. They might substitute consumption for savings out of their present income. Keynes insisted that the income effect dominates. Since the demand by consumers is such a large part of total demand, a change in incomes which changes demand by consumers, will also change the demand for the goods produced by labour and other factors of production. Keynes hoped to understand and ultimately control the level of national income so as to maintain a satisfactory level of employment.

National income accounts

Keynes's new ideas demanded new facts – macroeconomic information about aggregate production of goods and services as well as the sources of demand for this output. In the UK these are published quarterly in *Economic Trends*, and summarized annually in the invaluable 'Blue Book',

---

[1] Notably John R. Hicks (Oxford) in *Value and Capital* (1939) and Paul A. Samuelson (MIT) in *Foundations of Economic Analysis* (1947).

National Income and Expenditure. The search for appropriate facts starts with gross national product (GNP), new value added by production in a year. In compiling GNP the Central Statistical Office might have been tempted to simply add the sales of all firms as reported in profit and loss statements. Yet this would involve a degree of double counting since it would record materials purchased from other firms passed on, perhaps several times, in altered form. Rather than record these *intermediate goods*, the CSO reports total *final sales*. The value of intermediate goods is included in final sales to the public, to be sure, but only once.

In practice, how are final sales to be distinguished from intermediate ones? Aggregate final sales are most easily identified by examining the purpose for which goods are sold. This is the *expenditure method* which adds sales of consumer goods, investment in additional capital, sales to government, and net exports. The sum is the GNP (Table 1.1). We shall briefly review these components.

Table 1.1   Expenditure of UK gross national product and national income 1970

	£ million	Conventional symbols
Consumers' expenditure	31,238	C
Public authorities' current expenditure on goods and services	9,055	G
Gross domestic fixed capital formation	8,886 ⎫	⎫
Value of physical increase in stocks and work in progress	454 ⎭	⎬ I_g
Exports and property income from abroad	13,775 ⎫	X ⎫Net exports:
Less Imports and property income paid abroad	−12,979 ⎭	M ⎭ $E = X - M$
Less Taxes on expenditure*	−8,458	
Plus subsidies†	848	
Gross national product	42,819	GNP
Less Capital consumption	−4,132	
National income	38,687	Y

* 'Indirect' taxes are included in *both* the expenditures of government and the price of other items such as consumption and investment goods. They must be subtracted once from total expenditure to avoid double counting.
† These subsidies are intended to reduce the price of goods below their cost. They must therefore be added on to other expenditures to get back to the value of goods and services produced.
Source: *National Income and Expenditure 1971* (Blue Book), p. 3.

Little must be said about *consumption*, the largest component of GNP. Symbolized by C, it includes durable and perishable goods, as well as services. *Public expenditure* by national and local authorities, *G*, is largely the result of defence, National Health and education expenditures. It is important to notice that *G* refers to the purchase of goods and services, and not to such items as superannuation payments to pensioners or subsidies to firms. Such items are called *transfer payments* because they represent changes in ownership of wealth rather than reflecting current production (private transfer payments, such as the sale of previously produced property, shares of stock, or inheritance, are also excluded from GNP because they do not represent goods produced this year).

Exercise: Sometimes it is hard to decide whether an expenditure is a transfer or not. Are interest payments transfers? Government investment in the Upper Clyde shipyards? Is bribing a policeman in Chicago a transfer? How about taxes?

Gross investment, I_g, is carried on in roughly equal proportions by the private and public sector. It consists of *gross domestic fixed capital forma-tion* – additional durable items of capital as buildings and machinery – as well as the increase of *stocks of goods and work in progress*.

The reader may well object. GNP was to exclude 'purchases from other firms'; is not investment such a purchase? Are we not double counting? Not really, because we need to exclude only those intermediate purchases from other firms that are processed and passed on to this year's product. The accumulation of extra capital simply represents the final destination this year of the new product of the capital equipment industry. Suppose Birmingham Turning Machinery Ltd sells a lathe to Manchester Screw and Bolt Ltd. The value of the lathe is a final sale of the Birmingham firm and does not enter into the value of the product of their Manchester customers this year.

Foreigners buy *exported goods and services, X*. Since they are manufac-tured in the UK they are part of its GNP. By the same token, imported goods, *M*, are not part of the UK GNP. Since the figures for consumption, investment and government all include imported goods, the import compo-nent of these expenditures must be subtracted out again. In practice, instead of subtracting the import component of the other categories, we subtract total imports from exports. That is, we simply include *net* exports, *E*, in GNP along with the other elements of consumption, investment, and so on. This will do the trick since net exports are defined as exports minus imports, $E = X - M$, readily available as the *balance of trade* figures produced by the CSO.[2]

---

[2] Part of the GNP of the UK comes from property and other income earned abroad. To measure only the income generated on these islands, we subtract the *net property income from abroad*. Then we have *gross domestic product*, GDP.

Gross national product, then, is concisely expressed by the formula:

$$GNP = C + I_g + G + E.$$

One difficulty remains with gross investment, I_g. Think back to the example of the lathe sold by Birmingham Turning Machinery Ltd to Manchester Screw and Bolt Ltd. The lathe certainly was a final sale, but as the lathe is used and wears out its depreciation expense will have to be recovered by Manchester Screw and Bolt in order to replace it, and so enters into the price of the screws. GNP is more than new value added in a year because it counts investment, once as a final sale of capital equipment, and partly again as depreciation. This could be avoided if we were to include as investment only *new* additions to capital excluding replacement of old, depreciated machinery. This would constitute *net* investment, I, contrasted with *gross* investment, I_g, which contains both replacement of depreciation and new capital. Accountants being what they are, it is very difficult to obtain a precise estimate of depreciation, and so the CSO measures gross investment. The 'gross' in I_g makes GNP 'gross' as well. If we were to include only net investment, we would have *net* national product. As we shall see, net national product is the same as national income, symbolized by Y. Hence $Y = C + I + G + E.$

Strictly speaking, instead of the word depreciation, we should use the wider term *capital consumption*, which comprises reductions of stocks of merchandise as well as wear and tear of machinery and buildings. Gross national product is the value of goods and services produced in a year *including* replacement of capital consumption; national income is the value added *excluding* capital consumption.

Exercise:
(1) Consult *The British Economy, Key Statistics 1900–1970,* published for the London and Cambridge Economic Service by Times Newpapers Ltd. Make a graph of gross national product of the United Kingdom from 1900 to the present time. Locate the depressions and prosperity.
(2) Consult the *United Nations National Accounts Yearbook* and find the GNP of the United States, USSR, Nigeria and Mexico. Express them as percentages of the GNP of the United Kingdom (be sure that the currencies are converted to dollars). Find out the *per capita* GNP of these countries and compare with the United Kingdom.
(3) Make a table of the components of UK GNP, in percentage terms, for the following important years:

	1929	1932	1950	1970
1 Gross national product				
2 Personal consumption				
3 Gross domestic investment				
4 Net exports				
5 Government other items				
	100%	100%	100%	100%

There is another important method for estimating GNP. Again our point of departure is the profit and loss statement of individual firms. Recall that we eliminated transfer payments and 'purchases from other firms' from reported sales. Now, instead of looking at what was *excluded*, look at the categories that were *included*: payments to *factors of production* and *capital consumption*. Therefore, a second estimate of GNP can be made by adding the payments to factors of production, taking care to include profits in the form of *gross* profits computed before capital consumption costs are subtracted. From the estimate of GNP subtract capital consumption to arrive at national income (Table 1.2).

Table 1.2   UK gross national product at factor cost 1971

	£ million
Income from employment	30,487
Income from self-employment	3,345
Gross trading profit of companies	5,028
Gross trading surplus of public corporations	1,379
Gross trading surplus of other public enterprises	112
Rent	2,988
Less Stock appreciation*	−976
Less Residual error	−56
Gross domestic product at factor cost	42,307
Plus Net property income from abroad	512
Gross national product	42,819
Less Capital consumption	−4,132
National income	38,687

* This is an adjustment for increases in the price of stocks of goods in the course of the year.

Source: *National Income and Expenditure 1970* (Blue Book), p. 2.

National income is now seen to have a twofold character. On one hand it represents the *net* new value added by production. On the other, it equals the sum of payments to factors of production. In fact this should have been obvious all along. After all, new value is added by production through the efforts of people and incorporated firms, their work and the use of their property. These efforts are measured by the money they fetch on the market. National income is the payment of wages, rents, interest, and profits.

As a further refinement, we sometimes estimate the income of individual persons – *personal income*. To do this we subtract the *undistributed profits* of corporations, and add transfer payments to individuals such as National Insurance payments. Further subtraction of personal taxes and transfers abroad brings the account to *disposable personal income*, which individuals decide either to *consume* or to *save* (Table 1.3).[3]

Table 1.3   Disposition of personal income 1971

	£ *million*
Personal income	42,833
Less: Tax and National Insurance payments	8,807
Equals: Disposable personal income	34,026
Less: Personal consumption	31,238
Equals: Personal savings	2,788

Source: *National Income and Expenditure 1970* (Blue Book), p. 5

Exercise: Using the data you collect from *The British Economy* make a table of the percentage components of GNP by factor payments.

	1929	*1932*	*1950*	*1970*
1 Employment				
2 Self–employment				
3 Gross profits and surplus of private companies and public enterprises				
4 Rent				
5 Other items				

Controlling income and employment

The twofold character of national income as *new value added by production* and *use of factors of production* permits us to study and plan employment. That is to say, the expenditures on consumption, investment, government,

[3] Of course, individuals are not the only ones who save. Businesses also save by retaining earnings instead of distributing them as dividends.

and exports are also the demand for labour, capital, land, and entrepreneur-ial skill. The maintenance of full employment involves the demand for planning C, I, G and E. To study the quantitative relations involved, we shall confine ourselves for the moment to the *private, domestic* sectors of demand, neglecting government and exports. Thus, for simplicity, we suppose that $Y = C + I$.

In the long run – say fifty years or so – it appears that aggregate consump-tion is roughly proportional to national income.[4] People spend a fairly constant amount of their income on consumer goods and save the rest. This proportionality permits us to calculate the national income which will result from a given amount of investment demand in a way which is strikingly similar to the way in which the firm calculated sales for a given level of profits.

First we calculate the long-run ratio of consumption to income, called the *average propensity to consume*, a_c; $a_c = C/Y$. We can express C in terms of Y by using the average propensity to consume, $C = a_c Y$. Since $Y = C + I$, we see that $Y = a_c Y + I$, and $(1 - a_c)Y = I$. The inverse is:

$$Y = \frac{1}{1 - a_c} I.$$

Another multiplier! The *income-investment* multiplier. To illustrate, sup-pose the average propensity to consume is 0·8. 80 per cent of national income is spent on consumer goods. Then the multiplier is:

$$\frac{1}{1 - a_c} = \frac{1}{1 - 0·8} = 5.$$

If businessmen invest £9000 million then income will be:

$$Y = \left(\frac{1}{1 - a_c}\right) I = 5 \times 9000 \text{ million} = £45,000 \text{ million}.$$

The multiplier really expresses the result of a geometric series of induced expenditures. A decision to invest by firms increases income, since $Y = C + I$. The increase in income increases consumption, which increases income – increasing consumption further – and again increasing income. The process continues indefinitely. The ultimate income is the direct investment demand plus the sum of all indirect consumption demand that it induces!

---

[4] It is not so clear that this is still the case for shorter periods of time, such as the length of a trade cycle of prosperity and depression. The matter is not unimportant, as we shall see in Chapter 13. Keynes himself argued that only the *change* in consumption is proportional to the *change* in income.

Obviously it is the initiating decisions of businessmen to invest that are crucial. Consumers can be expected to behave themselves in a reasonably stable way. The unstable element is the willingness of businessmen to take a chance on the future. It is clear that those things that motivate investment – technical progress, expectations of increased profits, general optimism – are powerful forces toward increasing employment. As a self-fulfilling prophesy, depressed expectations by businessmen about the future lead to depression. If firms expect business to be bad, they will invest little, and business will be bad. After the event, they congratulate themselves for being able to outguess the market; but their very attitudes brought the market conditions about.

The art of macroeconomic planning consists of estimating the level of private investment and comparing it with the amount needed to maintain enough demand to provide full employment, but not excessive demand so as to induce inflation. The practising planner must find the means to make up the difference – the 'gap' – between forecast and desired investment. Sometimes this can be done by influencing private decisions of firms, and sometimes by government making up the difference by its own power to spend or tax. Therefore even though the multiplier relationship is straightforward, its application often is a hazardous exercise in gazing into the uncertain future. We shall reexamine this black art in more detail in Chapter 13.

Exercise:
(1) Go back to the exercise 3 on p. 25 of this chapter in which you computed the average propensity to consume as the percentage of consumption to GNP (not quite the same as consumption divided by national income, but never mind).
   (*a*) Compute the multiplier for the four years under review.
   (*b*) What would the gross national product have been in 1932 if businessmen could have been persuaded to invest £100 million more in fixed capital formation? By what means do you think this could have been done?
   (*c*) Suppose businessmen could not be persuaded to invest the £100 million. Could government have spent the money?
(2) Prove that the investment–income multiplier can be derived as the sum of an infinite geometric series. What would happen if people spent more on consumer goods than they earned? Is it possible?
(3) What do you think is meant by the *average propensity to save*? How is it related to the average propensity to consume?
(4) Compare what you have learned about microeconomics with what you have learned about macroeconomics in the light of the statement: 'The whole is equal to the sum of its parts.'

Interindustry economics

The history of the last fifty years has been associated with the rise of *planning* as an essential aspect of economic life. Until the Great Depression planning in industrialized nations was restricted to the sales and output plan of the business firm. Yet, as we saw, maintaining full employment turned out to be a problem that could not be solved by the automatic working of supply and demand. There must be a *macroeconomic plan* to maintain full employment. In the United Kingdom this necessity was recognized in the 1944 White Paper on Employment Policy (Cmnd. 6527). Following on from a forecast by the Treasury staff, the Chancellor of the Exchequer prepares his budget to meet the goal of full employment. His plan requires the support of the Bank of England and other agencies.

Other countries are even more deeply committed to planning. Certainly communist countries are committed to total planning as a matter of principle. Enterprises are not only publicly planned, but publicly owned. Underdeveloped countries emerging from colonial or semicolonial status almost universally have a plan for industrialization and growth. Clearly countries such as these simply must know that the plans that are made for each industry fit together. It is not possible for the planning authorities simply to order people to produce so many tons of copper, pounds of meat and yards of cloth. Material, equipment and labour must be available in sufficient quantity.

The problem is that these materials must come from other industries which must, in turn, be supplied. Consumer final demand for copper teakettles, for instance, creates a demand for electric power to purify the ore. Matters do not end here, for this *direct* requirement must be met by further indirect requirements; inputs such as coal are needed to generate the electric power. Some of these indirect demands come from the copper itself; the production of electric power requires large amounts of copper as well as coal. Copper is needed for turbines, wires, and dynamos. Copper kettle production involves many industries; all of their demands for materials either must be satisfied simultaneously, or the teakettle plan cannot be carried out.

Western countries are more thoroughly committed to macroeconomic planning to maintain full employment than to the direction of particular firms or industries. To a larger degree free market forces are supposed to govern the coordination of activities and the allocation of resources. Nonetheless, national policies have been specifically directed toward changing the industrial, regional or employment structure. Even when that is not the purpose, it has proven impossible to prevent macroeconomic plans from influencing industry outputs.

In practice, macroeconomic policies cannot be limited to controlling the *total demand* for goods and services without stimulating or holding back some industries, either directly or indirectly. After all the government of the United Kingdom cannot spend in excess of £9000 million on current purchases, and another £4000 million on capital, out of a national income of £38,687 million without spending it for something! It is simply a vital necessity to know the ultimate effects of these expenditures. It might turn out that when the indirect as well as the direct effects are added up, a result occurs that was not at all intended.

For example, at the time of writing (1971), the UK government is committed to high levels of demand so as to maintain high levels of employment. In order to do this without excessive inflation, the government is also attempting to hold down the general level of wage claims. At the same time, since the last war, the government has committed itself to the support of employment in certain industries. In particular, it is committed to maintaining the coal mining industry through nationalization, keying electric power production to coal fuel, and investing capital to modernize as many pits at it can. The question that has come to a crisis is whether the structural decision to closely link the economy to the coal industry was compatible with the macroeconomic goals.

In 1972 the miners declared their wage level intolerably low. The National Coal Board replied that at the prevailing level of productivity, it could not afford more without closing more mines, increasing the price of coal, and thus adding to inflation. The government asserted that it could not permit another round of wage and price increases. Yet as a result of a strike the government ultimately did declare the coal mines a 'special case' and conceded the justice of the miners' claim.

As if to underline the importance of structural analysis, the miners' strike showed just how interdependent a modern economy is. The reduction in coal stocks brought the whole economy to a virtual standstill. As the rota cuts in electric power took hold, industry after industry came to a halt when the direct and indirect linkages to coal snapped.

In hindsight, should the decision have been made to rescue coal mining? Perhaps linking the energy source to oil would have been worse? Nonetheless, it is clear that the pattern of postwar employment-generating expenditures created structural problems for Britain which have made the present employment and inflation problems difficult to manage.

Query: What structural changes in British industry have brought on the distress in coal mining? Who should bear the burden of any low productivity 'lame duck' industry?

The very success of macroeconomic planning for full employment has served to bring problems of structure into sharper focus. Consider the *regional* aspect. Table 1.4. shows the unemployment rate (for both men and women) and average hourly earnings of men in manufacturing as a percentage of the UK average.

Table 1.4.   Hourly earnings and unemployment by region 1970

Region	Unemployment rate (per cent)	Hourly earnings of male manual workers (per cent of UK)
United Kingdom	2·7	100
North	4·8	97·3
Yorkshire	2·9	93·8
East Midlands	2·3	95·7
East Anglia	2·1	90·9
South East	1·7	102·4
South West	2·8	93·6
West Midlands	2·3	107·7
North West	2·8	99·4
Wales	4·0	101·1
Scotland	4·3	97·0
N. Ireland	7·0	86·6

Source: *Abstract of Regional Statistics 1971*, pp. 30, 97.

Some regions face a declining demand for their products. Wages and employment sag below the general level. This situation is different from the depression years when insufficient demand resulted in mass unemployment for all. It was easier to know what to do in the past: increase investment by business and by government, and trust the multiplier to increase aggregate demand for factors of production. But the same medicine will not work as effectively now. To increase overall demand for factors of production would probably succeed in markedly bidding up prices rather than employing many more shipyard workers in the Upper Clyde, or improving the lot of the Catholic minority in Belfast. The overall guarantee of full employment to both labour and business has tended to keep labour dear. To reduce labour costs industry has become more and more automated. Labourers need more skill and training. Those who are from deprived backgrounds do not generally obtain an adequate education and are trapped in poverty. They cannot find work in modern industry, and at the same time their poverty prevents them from getting – or even seeking – the education they need to escape.

Exercise:
(1) Consult the *Annual Abstract of Statistics* (1971). Find life expectancy at birth by region. Relate your findings to the table of earnings and unemployment.
(2) Consult the *Statistical Abstract of the United States* and find the wage and unemployment figures by race, sex and region. Are the problems similar to those of the UK?

Environmental protection problems are another area in which neither the overall macro nor the piecemeal micro approach is satisfactory. While some writers do approach the problem through opposition to growth in the aggregate national income, most of these problems involve the way in which the operations of individual firms or industries affect others. What makes problems of pollution so difficult is precisely the fact that its costs are not borne by the polluter. They fall into the category of what economists call *external* effects. If we are concerned to deal with such problems, we must first understand how each industry is related to the others. Then we will be able to trace out how pollution 'bads' are produced along with the goods and services normally sold on the market.

We have only mentioned a few of the structural problems which make it necessary for planners to try to fit the economic system together like a gigantic jigsaw puzzle. Indirect effects must be anticipated unless planners are prepared for ugly surprises. To be sure, even the best of programmes are subject to jolts and to error, but clearly planners must do their best to deal with the interaction of the various sectors of the economy.

Until very recently, this was thought to be a practical impossibility. Conceptually, the inputs and outputs of each industry could be written into equations; conceivably all these equations could be solved simultaneously. Such theorizing tended to be impractical. The equations might take on all the hideous complexities that mathematicians delight in inflicting upon their students. Furthermore, there are bound to be a great many of these equations; then there is the practical question of generating all the detailed statistical information to put into all the myriad equations. It seemed hopeless. *General equilibrium* was a theorist's plaything.

A way out of the situation was proposed by Wassily Leontief, a Russian-born Harvard economist. His Nobel Prize winning plan was both simple and bold. Leontief suggested an interindustry accounting system recording the flows of inputs from each industry to the others. He supposed that the necessary input to an industry from each of the others was simply proportional to its output. The dependence of one industry on the production of others was expressed as a simple linear equation relating the output of that industry to the contribution of others to it. No squared terms, logarithms or other complicated relations were employed. Since every industry requires inputs from others, the whole productive structure can be expressed as a system of simultaneous linear equations. Devising a consistent plan reduces to the solution of a system of linear equations essentially by methods that were discussed in the Preface.

One might object. Inputs are not always proportional to outputs! Production equations are not always linear! Leontief agreed. But the really important question is: How wrong will we be if we assume that they are linear? If the error is not great, then we will be able to cope with vital problems that once were beyond our grasp. It turns out that for reasonable periods of time, and for a coarse sort of grouping of firms into eighty or so industries, the error is surprisingly small. To be sure we will not know the ultimate truth about the economy. After all, nobody ever knows the ultimate truth about anything. The best we can do is make an approximate model which gives us results accurate within the practical limits we can tolerate for our purposes.

In this book we first will go as far as we can within the limits imposed by the Leontief simplifications. Then as we tackle additional problems, we shall be forced to develop more sophisticated models to cope with them. With each bit of realism we introduce, we will gain insights into particular problems, such as the behaviour of money, of the consumers, of choices in productive techniques and the like. That is to say, ultimately we will come to the traditional content of macro- and microeconomics as they relate to the overall picture of an interrelated economy.

Exercise:
(1) When the Automobile Association provides us with a paper map of the road from London to Manchester, are they saying that the world is flat?
(2) Express the recipe: 4 cups of sugar
                           1 pound of flour
                           3 teaspoons of water
                           ―――――――――――――――――
                           Yield: 5 water biscuits
    as a linear equation? What is the recipe for 10 biscuits?
(3) Are the following equations linear? What is their graph?
    (a) $3x + 5y = 10$
    (b) $3x + 5y + 3z = 5$
    (c) $x = 2$
    (d) $3x^2 + 2y = 10$
    (e) $3x + 2y = 0$.

Appendix: The capitalized value of assets

We said that the value of an asset A that would yield a fixed amount of i pounds forever is $A = i/r$, where r is the annual market rate of interest, and i

is the income derived from the asset each year. This seems peculiar. One would assume that such income adds up to an infinite amount of money. The explanation stems from the fact that I would not pay £10 today for the right to get £10 a year from today. Why not? Really the answer is obvious. There are other opportunities to lend or invest money at interest which I would give up.

£10 tomorrow is worth less than £10 today. How much is it worth? What is its *present value*? Call the present value of income received one year from now P_1; then the present value plus the interest it could earn in a year is equal to the future value, £10. Algebraically, $P_1 + rP_1 = £10$, so $(1+r)P_1 = £10$. Therefore the present value of £10 is $P_1 = £10/(1+r)$. In general, if the money to be received next year is i, then the present value of that income is $P_1 = i/(1+r)$. The value of i is said to be *discounted* by multiplying by $1/(1+r)$.

Query: Suppose the market rate of interest is 10 per cent per year. What is the present value of £10 which will be paid a year hence?

Suppose I have to wait two years to get i. Call its present value P_2. One year from now I still have to wait an additional year to get i amount of money. If P_1 is the value of i a year from now, P_2 is P_1 discounted once more. That is to say, $P_2 = P_1/(1+r)$. But $P_1 = i/(1+r)$, so $P_2 = 1/(1+r)^2$. Extending this idea, $P_3 = i/(1+r)^3$, $P_4 = i/(1+r)^4$, and for any year n, $P_n = i/(1+r)^n$.

Now suppose that by acquiring a long-lived àsset I am going to get i forever, starting a year from the date of purchase. The worth of the asset to me is the sum of the series of present values. That is to say, for an indefinitely large n, $A = P_1 + P_2 + P_3 + \ldots + P_n$, or

$$A + \frac{i}{1+r} + \frac{i}{(1+r)^2} + \frac{i}{(1+r)^3} + \ldots + \frac{i}{(1+r)^n}.$$

To make our algebra easier, let us set $1/(1+r) = R$. Then the series becomes:

$$A = iR + iR^2 + iR^3 + \ldots + iR^n.$$

This is similar to the infinite geometric series, $S = i + iR + iR^2 + iR^3 + \ldots + iR^n$. Only the first term, i, is missing from the series A. Consequently, we can say that $A = S - i$.

Now notice that R is positive and less than one. (Why?) From our knowledge of the sum of a geometric series, $S = i/(1-R)$. Hence:

$$A = \frac{i}{1-R} - i.$$

The rest is only a bit of algebra, messy but not profound. Replacing R by $1/(1+r)$ and simplifying gives $A = i/r$ as required.

Questions:
(1) What would be the value of £10 received annually forever if the interest rate were 20 per cent? What if *r* were higher?
(2) This analysis has been stated in terms of simple interest. If the compound interest formula is:

$$A = P(1+\frac{r}{n})^{nx}$$

where *n* is the number of times interest is compounded each year, and *x* is the number of years, compute the present value of £10 two years from now compounded quarterly at 5 per cent interest. Compare results with simple interest by computing the present value of £10 two years from now at simple interest (it is a lot of arithmetic – but do it anyway).
(3) It is common to express the price of a bond in terms of its *yield*. The yield is the rate of interest computed by dividing the *stated interest income* (e.g. 6 per cent of £1000) by the market price. If yields rise what can be said about the price of bonds? Having borrowed at 6 per cent can the firm pay less than £60 if the market rate of interest falls to 5 per cent? What might it do to save interest charges?
(4) Economists are forever preaching that the real cost of any factor of production is not money spent, but alternatives foregone. How does this be applied to the present case?
(5) Carry out the substitution suggested in the last sentence to prove that $A = i/r$.

Part 1 Interindustry economics

2 The input-output system

The reader should have before him:

(1) The Input-Output Transactions Matrix, 1968, for the UK reproduced in part on pp. 42–3, and in full at the end of the book.[1]

(2) The 'dollar flow' table presented for the American economy in *Scientific American*, April 1965[2]. This is the transactions matrix for the United States arranged in an interesting way which will bring out some important points about the structure of economic systems in general.

The transactions matrix

The transactions matrix (sometimes called the interindustry flow matrix) is a record of all the sales of goods and services produced in a single year. This large table is nothing but a national bookkeeping record of the flow of products through the economy. As such it reveals the sales and expenses of the various industries, as well as the net final use they ultimately make available to the public. If we think of final use as the net gain to society from production, the transactions matrix will be seen to be analogous to a national profit and loss statement. By keeping this analogy in mind, we shall appreciate the utter simplicity of the Leontief system, despite the imposing

---

[1] *National Income and Expenditure 1971* (Blue Book). A much more detailed table is given in *Input-Output Tables for the United Kingdom 1963*.

[2] Leontif, W. W. 'The structure of the US economy', *Scientific American*, Vol. 212, No. 4, April 1965. Pp. 26–32 of this issue presents the transactions matrix and related tables which will be discussed in this and later chapters. A wall chart illustrating these tables is available from the same company.

size of the tables it uses. Classifying the transactions of firms into interindustry flows permits us to study structural patterns of production.

In this chapter we measure the flow of products in money terms. The records show the *value* of goods transacted. Chapter 3 will discuss input-output in physical terms. As a practical matter, it is much easier to record the value of sales from one industry to another, rather than attempt to count the actual number of nuts and bolts, screws, and bales of cotton.

It will be recalled that the profit and loss statement was a means of expressing the relationship: Profits = Total sales − Expenses, or $P = S - E$. We can rearrange these terms to say: Expenses + Profits = Sales, or $E + P = S$. In bold outline − there are some finicky accounting problems to worry about − the input-output transactions matrix is nothing but such a re-arranged statement.

The total *sales* of each industry of goods and services to the rest of the economy is shown as the last column of the transactions matrix as *Total output*. *Expenses*, products used up in further manufacture, appear as the shipments from each industry to all the other industries. These are called *interindustry transactions*. Lastly, for each industry the difference between total output and interindustry transactions is *final use* (or *final demand*). It is the new value added by production, the net gain analogous to the 'profit' of society. The final use is available for private consumption; it may also be ploughed back as investment in accumulated capital, such as machinery, new buildings, or additional stocks; it may be used by governments for public use; or it may be exported to foreign countries. Final use is therefore seen to be the contribution of each industry to the gross national product.

Reading across the transactions matrix, we see that it is divided into three main blocks. They are: Interindustry use + Final use = Total output, corresponding to Expenses + Profits = Sales. Notice that the total interindustry use is called the 'total intermediate output' in the input-output table in order to stress the fact that the goods shipped from one industry to another are in the process of being worked up into the elements of final output.

Interindustry use

The distinctive characteristic of the input-output system is the *disaggregation* or breaking down of the blocks in an interesting and important way. Each *row* running across the table records the destination of the products of an industry. The industry named in the rows ships its goods to destinations shown in the *columns*. Some row product goes to interindustry expenses in columns and some to final uses.

For instance, industry 1 in the Blue Book table is Agriculture. The total output of that industry is £1892 million. Of this, approximately half (£972·8

The transactions matrix   41

million) is used by other industries (shown in the columns) in the further fabrication of different goods. Thus half of the agricultural output represents an intermediate stage in the productive process, and is recorded in the interindustry use portion of the table. The remainder (£919·3 million) is available for final use. Reading across the first row, we are not surprised to see that the largest industrial user of the products of agriculture is column 5, the Food industry. Nor are we surprised to see Consumption as the largest final use of Industry 1.

Query: How much is shipped from coal mining to coke ovens? From coke to coal.

A further insight is obtained if we read *down* one of the columns. These are the shipments *to* the column industry *from* all the rows. For instance, the most important industry supplying goods to the Communications industry (No. 32) is the Transport industry (No. 31), providing £42·2 million. This only slightly exceeds the contribution of the Electrical Engineering industry (No. 14) which provides £41·7 million to Communications.

Query: What are the third and fourth most important supplying industries to Communications?

Value added

The inputs read from the columns consist of shipments of inputs produced by industries during the current year. But there are other inputs. These are the *primary inputs* – land, labour, capital, and entrepreneurship. They are either not produced by the other industries at all, as in the case of land, labour and entrepreneurship; or they represent the payment for the use of the *capital stock* of wealth produced in earlier years. Primary inputs are nothing but the *factors of production.* When factor inputs are added to the intermediate inputs shown in each column, we get the value of *all* the inputs. Since the sum of the value of the inputs equals the value of the outputs, the value of the output of each industry is to be found at the foot of every column as well as the total of every row.

Thus the sum of payments to households and businesses supplying the factors of production – wages, rents, interest, and profit – have a twofold nature. On one hand they are expenses to each industry; on the other hand they are the *increase in value* as a result of human effort and the use of private property in production. Very frequently, we will loosely refer to this primary input as 'labour', since that is the largest element in the value added. We must be careful to note that we are using the word labour in a broad sense to indicate *all* human participation in production including providing property in the form of land and capital as well as physical or mental labour.

Table 2.1 UK transactions matrix 1968

Sales by \ Purchases by	Agriculture (1)	Forestry and fishing (2)	Coal mining (3)	Other mining and quarrying (4)	Food (5)	Drink and tobacco (6)	Mineral oil refining (7)	Coke ovens (8)	Chemicals, etc. (9)	Iron and steel (10)	Non-ferrous metals (11)	Mechanical engineering (12)	Instrument engineering (13)	Electrical engineering (14)	Shipbuilding, etc. (15)	Motor vehicles, etc. (16)
1 Agriculture	—	—	—	—	881·7	41·5	0·3	—	4·0	—	—	—	—	—	—	
2 Forestry and fishing	—	—	—	—	28·0	—	—	—	0·4	—	—	—	—	—	—	
3 Coal mining	1·6	—	—	0·8	5·4	2·5	0·5	138·1	16·6	5·7	1·1	2·1	0·2	1·5	0·2	2
4 Other mining and quarrying	7·6	—	0·1	—	2·1	—	0·7	—	22·6	15·6	21·5	0·7	—	—	—	
5 Food	413·3	0·5	—	2·6	—	32·8	1·7	—	87·6	0·1	—	—	—	6·7	—	
6 Drink and tobacco	3·9	—	—	—	7·7	—	—	—	4·9	—	—	—	—	—	—	
7 Mineral oil refining	26·1	5·3	2·6	11·7	16·1	6·3	—	0·6	60·2	30·2	5·2	12·5	0·9	6·0	1·4	10
8 Coke ovens	0·9	—	0·1	0·3	1·4	0·4	0·3	—	28·1	102·2	2·3	2·5	0·1	0·8	0·3	0
9 Chemicals, etc.	119·1	0·1	4·5	14·7	41·6	19·3	38·4	7·9	—	40·1	13·6	31·5	14·9	75·0	5·2	2
10 Iron and steel	0·6	—	32·6	0·9	6·2	0·6	1·6	1·6	4·7	—	7·7	363·5	4·6	77·1	39·3	22
11 Non-ferrous metals	1·3	—	0·3	0·1	11·1	8·8	0·3	0·1	42·2	63·6	—	112·0	8·8	119·6	12·3	68
12 Mechanical engineering	7·6	0·6	38·5	14·7	14·7	15·2	12·4	3·9	28·5	74·3	16·4	—	5·0	106·7	19·0	5
13 Instrument engineering	0·3	—	0·6	0·4	0·4	0·4	0·3	—	11·7	1·6	1·8	19·0		68		
14 Electrical engineering	1·4	—	12·0	3·6	6·1	5·1	0·8	1·2	20·0	21·2	33·7	81·3				
15 Shipbuilding, etc.	—	6·7	0·4	0·2	0·3	0·2	0·1	—	0·3	2·2	0·8					
16 Motor vehicles, etc.	5·1	0·4	1·6	2·2	3·0	1·6	0·5	0·3	5·7	19·4	5·3					
17 Aerospace equipment	—	—	0·2	0·2	0·3	0·2	0·1	—	0·7	1·4	2·0	2·9				
18 Other vehicles	—	—	1·2	0·1	0·6	0·4	—	0·1	0·6	6·5	2·4	3·0	—	1·2	0·1	2
19 Other metal goods	20·0	0·5	7·6	5·3	63·4	31·7	10·7	1·1	68·4	31·0	36·6	181·9	6·9	113·0	64·9	16
20 Textiles	5·0	5·6	8·6	0·9	8·1	0·5	0·1	—	27·6	1·3	—	6·5	3·4	12·9	1·8	2
21 Leather, etc.	—	—	—	—	—	—	—	—	1·8	0·1	—	2·0	—	—	—	2
22 Clothing and footwear	0·3	—	3·1	—	—	0·3	—	—	0·4	0·1	0·2	0·1	—	—	—	
23 Bricks, etc.	18·6	—	6·2	2·6	11·9	27·1	—	0·2	24·8	33·0	1·4	18·5	2·2	33·9	2·6	14
24 Timber and furniture	3·9	0·4	9·8	0·9	4·1	15·5	0·7	—	8·5	4·0	1·0	17·3	4·9	35·0	8·2	5
25 Paper and printing	4·2	0·2	1·8	6·0	118·9	72·4	3·0	0·4	82·9	6·4	8·3	26·9	11·7			
26 Other manufacturing	9·0	—	5·5	2·6	14·2	5·5	0·8	0·2	43·6	13·0	2·9	59·7	6·3			
27 Construction	41·1	2·2	19·4	5·6	4·2	14·6	0·4	0·3	24·9	5·9	1·5	10·8	0·5	6·2	2·7	5
28 Gas	0·6	—	0·1	0·1	6·0	0·4	0·2	7·7	4·6	39·4	6·6	10·2	1·0	5·8	1·0	5
29 Electricity	23·6	0·5	31·8	7·2	26·5	6·5	8·8	2·5	68·6	63·9	14·4	29·7	3·3	18·4	5·3	2
30 Water	7·0	0·2	2·7	0·4	3·3	1·7	1·3	0·3	8·0	0·4	0·8	2·5	0·1	1·3	0·2	
31 Transport	22·2	6·6	16·6	55·7	133·9	27·5	182·8	14·6	87·9	73·4	25·7	43·8	12·7	24·9	3·6	3
32 Communication	6·4	0·5	1·3	1·5	9·3	4·5	0·3	0·2	13·8	4·0	2·1	21·9	2·7	11·4	1·2	
33 Distributive trades	146·8	2·9	11·5	6·9	77·1	19·9	5·3	0·9	50·8	50·6	33·4	83·1	5·3	49·7	13·0	5
34 Miscellaneous services	44·3	7·4	1·4	28·5	144·1	100·3	36·5	1·0	220·6	17·1	25·8	129·7	11·5	130·5	23·0	
35 Public administration, etc.(1)	—															
36 Imports of goods and services	108·0	1·4	6·6	4·6	722·0	155·6	492·5	0·6	377·6	143·4	399·9	134·9	19·5	231·2	20·7	11
37 Sales by final buyers(2)	1·5	—	—	0·7	−1·6	2·3	0·5	0·2	6·4	48·9	51·8	10·8	1·3	7·3	1·6	
38 Total goods and services (1 to 37)	1051·3	42·0	228·7	182·2	2372·3	621·7	802·0	184·0	1460·0	920·0	726·3	1457·3	161·2	1249·1	249·2	121
39 Taxes on expenditure *less* subsidies	−198·2	−4·6	−0·5	13·1	55·6	21·6	6·7	2·1	47·2	26·6	7·5	23·7				
40 Income from employment	329·0	40·0	511·0	66·0	596·9	203·2	38·2	22·7	545·4	509·3	157·1	1176·9				
41 Gross profits and other trading income(3)	710·0	46·0	74·0	45·0	322·6	263·7	45·2	22·1	410·8	179·5	70·9	358·7				
42 Total input(4) (38 to 41)	1892	123	813	306	3347	1110	892	231	2463	1635	962	3017	404	2302	481	206

(overlaid labels: "Quadrant — Interindustry", "Exports", "Quadrant — Primary")

(1) Public administration and defence, public health and educational services, ownership of dwellings, domestic services to households and services to pr[ivate] non-profit-making bodies serving persons.
(2) The sales by final buyers consist of scrap materials and fees and charges for government services. These inputs are not the output of any industry in 196[8] and are therefore treated as primary inputs.

Sum of Final Use equals Gross Domestic Product. (Imports must be subtracted from this figure to include only <u>net</u> exports in GDP (£51 861 m. − £9181 m. = £42 680 m.)

Handwritten annotations on this page: **Quadrant I — Output / Final Use** (18·9, 19·7); **+ 'Profit' = 'Sales'**; **Quadrant IV — Totals**; **M** (arrow to 9181); **Sum of Primary Input Equal to Gross Domestic Product (£42 680 m.)**; **Gross Social Product**.

[25]	26 Other manufacturing	27 Construction	28 Gas	29 Electricity	30 Water	31 Transport	32 Communication	33 Distributive trades	34 Miscellaneous services	35 Public administration, etc.[1]	36 Total intermediate output (1-35)	37 Consumers (C)	38 Public authorities (G)	39 Fixed (Ig)	40 Stocks	41 Exports (X)	42 Total final output (37-41)	43 Total output[4] (36+42)	
·4	—	—	—	—	—	3·8	—	—	16·5	—	972·8	791·1	42·6	18·1	−5·9	73·4	919·3	1892	1
—	—	—	—	0·4	—	—	—	—	—	—	42·1	42·0	1·6	—	31·9	5·8	81·3	123	2
·6	2·8	1·6	57·2	313·5	0·6	0·8	0·4	1·0	0·9	—	595·3	177·4	34·1	10·0	−15·7	12·1	217·9	813	3
·7	0·2	106·7	13·9	—	0·6	0·1	1·1	—	—	—	250·7	7·7	10·3	2·7	1·9	33·0	55·6	306	4
—	8·2	—	—	—	—	10·9	—	—	15·6	—	590·5	2475·6	87·4	—	47·3	146·6	2756·9	3347	5
—	—	—	—	—	—	—	—	—	15·5	—	32·0	811·6	4·9	—	15·4	246·3	1078·2	1110	6
·3	5·0	31·6	60·0	42·1	1·1	98·1	2·0	33·1	30·6	—	570·0	100·9	38·6	—	7·5	175·1	322·1	892	7
·5	0·7	0·5	2·1	0·6	0·2	—	—	0·5	2·2	—	155·1	57·7	12·9	0·2	−1·8	6·8	75·8	231	8
·1	161·2	67·0	1·9	3·2	2·0	19·8	0·3	14·3	111·8	—	1186·7	364·5	206·3	19·6	41·1	645·2	1276·7	2463	9
·8	7·6	162·5	22·3	1·3	7·9	13·2	0·1	1·2	2·5	—	1344·7	11·6	5·1	8·9	11·5	253·6	290·7	1635	10
·2	5·4	61·1	1·4	0·1	1·0	0·5	—	0·6	12·7	—	747·9	10·0	2·4	2·3	11·7	187·5	213·9	962	11
·4	10·3	100·4	12·8	15·6	4·0	11·0	0·2	15·4	8·6	—	732·3	41·4	92·9	1237·5	−10·7	923·2	2284·3	3017	12
0·9	2·4	0·4	0·5	0·2		3·8	0·4	4·5	5·7		154·6	22·4	53·3				18·9		13
4·9	127·4	2·8	60·1	1·1		30·1	41·7	17·6	119·7		851·8	245·4	202·1				19·7		14
	0·9	0·2	0·4	—		49·5	—	0·2	0·2		81·2	0·3							15
	11·6	1·1	1·7	0·3		32·7	0·9	7·5	55·0		220·0	350·3							16
	0·3	1·4	—	0·2	—	28·2	0·2	0·2	0·8		47·8	0·9							17
·8	0·4	1·5	0·9	1·4	0·3	64·2	—	—	0·8	—	92·7	9·0	2·4	25·7	−2·6	38·7	73·2	166	18
·3	26·9	128·8	5·0	5·1	0·8	14·5	0·5	41·3	79·9	—	1265·7	170·1	17·0	69·2	11·2	293·9	561·4	1827	19
·7	61·6	12·7	—	—	1·5	0·2	—	92·8	13·8	—	633·6	667·7	20·8	0·6	7·3	432·0	1128·4	1762	20
·5	2·5	0·1	—	—	—	—	—	—	1·8	—	80·6	43·1	0·3	—	2·6	50·4	96·4	177	21
·6	0·4	0·3	0·2	—	0·4	6·1	3·0	8·0	9·6	—	35·8	787·2	30·2	0·1	13·8	120·1	951·4	987	22
·2	1·6	573·9	6·1	4·7	1·0	2·7	—	0·3	4·8	—	813·3	54·1	8·3	16·6	6·4	99·1	184·5	998	23
·9	10·8	329·3	0·2	4·1	—	4·0	—	18·3	0·7	—	558·6	266·4	33·6	40·1	15·2	19·6	374·9	934	24
	9·0	7·3	2·6	0·3	31·3	11·8	125·6	480·0			1231·?	343·5	11			179·9	56·0	1000	25
	90·0	0·9	1·1	1·0	36·1	1·9	36·7	50·7			671	158·5	4			181·4			26
·8	1·7	—	20·5	3·3	0·6	21·5	4·7	54·1	34·3	—	310·3	594·9	399·0	3753·6	10·8	37·7	4796·0	5106	27
·5	1·7	1·6	—	0·9	0·2	—	—	9·2	34·8	—	166·8	339·5	19·4	31·6	−3·8	4·7	391·4	558	28
·0	17·9	12·0	6·9	—	9·9	30·0	9·9	113·8	90·2	—	755·2	620·0	98·4	124·9	0·6	2·2	846·1	1601	29
·7	0·7	0·5	1·6	—	—	2·0	0·1	4·4	8·2	—	56·7	74·7	10·2	30·2	—	0·3	115·4	172	30
·2	28·4	56·3	18·8	57·0	0·1	—	42·2	378·8	30·6	—	1685·0	807·9	100·0	34·6	1·0	1273·2	2216·7	3902	31
·6	5·3	18·5	3·5	5·2	1·2	9·6	—	172·5	206·4	—	574·5	261·0	84·0	48·0	—	38·5	431·5	1006	32
·6	18·8	76·9	10·0	9·9	1·6	37·3	4·2	—	28·2	—	1067·5	4026·3	149·2	288·9	—	426·0	4890·4	5958	33
·9	66·8	176·2	18·5	44·1	0·5	63·4	8·6	363·9	—	—	2170·9	3675·7	928·4	241·9	—	633·5	5479·5	7650	34
—	—	—	—	—	—	—	—	—	—	—	—	2308·0	4084·0	—	—	M	6392·0	6392	35
·4	91·1	177·8	36·7	17·6	0·5	889·7	39·9	40·4	77·6	—	5594·8	2012·7	445·5	583·3	79·0	465·7	3586·2	9181	36
·8	2·6	17·9	—	—	—	—	—	34·7	38·0	—	276·9	529·0	−597·3	−335·5	—	126·9	−276·9	—	37
·0	588·4	2358·4	313·2	596·7	39·0	1515·0	174·1	1591·0	1588·7	—	26617·2	23260·1	7400·5	7713·3	211·0	8827·4	47412·3	74029	38
	17·4	216·9	15·0	64·6	16·1	99·7	28·9	464·9	468·7	—	1597·3	3975·9					4448·7	6046	39
	349·5	1873·0	149·0	310·0	54·0	1578·0	575·0	2487·0	4054·0	4584·0	25305·0	—					—	25305	40
	658·0	81·0	630·0	63·0	709·0	228·0	1415·0	1539·0[5]	1808·0		11329·0	—					—	11329	41
	1085	5106	558	1601	172	3902	1006	5958	7650	6392	64848	27236	7739	7884	211	8791	51861	116709	42

[3] Before providing for depreciation, but after deducting stock appreciation.
[4] Measured free from duplication.
[5] Including the Residual error.

We must put up with some unavoidable accounting detail to make the column totals exactly equal to the row totals. First of all we must define 'Gross profits and other trading income' (row 41) to include capital consumption as well as the payment for capital, entrepreneurship and land. This is similar to the GNP calculation.

Secondly, we must add taxes (less subsidies) to the other primary inputs since they also enter into the market value of the goods of each industry. In the case of Agriculture, we see that subsidies are greater than taxes, so row 39 is a negative number – the market value of all the agricultural produce is *less than* the total recorded inputs.

Thirdly, we have to do something about imports. These are inputs into, say, agriculture originating from abroad. Row 36 shows them to be £108 million. By definition imports are not one of the UK industries. Therefore there is no *column* representing imports – only a row.

Fourthly, 'sales by final buyers' (row 37) consists of scrap materials and fees for government services as explained by a footnote in the Blue Book. The footnote goes on to say: 'These inputs are not the output of any industry . . . and are therefore treated as primary inputs.'

Now that is over with, the important thing to see is that the total expenses of production are the primary inputs and the intermediate interindustry inputs. Production consists of the transformation of intermediate goods into final use by human beings through their efforts and their stock of productive property.

Exercise:
(1) What is the value of shipments from the Mechanical Engineering industry to the Shipbuilding industry? What is the shipment from Shipbuilding to Mechanical Engineering?
(2) From what industry does the Paper and Printing industry get most of its materials?
(3) Which industry produces the biggest amount of total product? The biggest final use?
(4) Find two industries that ship to many other industries, and two that ship to very few other industries. Why do they show this pattern?
(5) What industries seem to make the greatest use of primary inputs? Which least?

Final use

Final use is the output available for consumption, investment, public use and export after interindustry expenses are met. Clearly for people to be able to consume and accumulate additional capital, a surplus must be forthcoming from production over and above the material inputs used up. An economy that did not provide for such net product would soon die.

A transatlantic controversy

The economy's expenses are of two types:

(1) *Intra*-industry sales occur within an industry. Various stages of semifinished products are sold from firm to firm before they are made available to other industries or final use at the end of the production pipeline. For example, seed is sold from some agricultural firms to others.

(2) *Inter*industry sales show intermediate goods sold from one industry to another. Thus the cell consisting of the first row and second column shows £881·7 million of goods shipped from Agriculture to the Food industry.

The cell in the first row and first column shows shipments from Agriculture to itself; *intra*-industry flows of feed, seeds, fertilizers, cattle and so on are used up in the production of agricultural goods. British practice is not to show such intra-industry flows. Consequently all the cells corresponding to the same row as column are empty in the Blue Book table.[3] This procedure is recommended by the United Nations. In contrast, American practice is to include such flows. There are advantages and disadvantages to each procedure.

The British procedure is based on the idea that intra-industry transactions only show up in the statistics when goods are bought and sold on the market. The US procedure misleads the reader into thinking that the entries shown represent the total of goods shipped within an industry. After all, in a large integrated factory, a semifinished part is moved around from one machine or department to another; it represents an intra-industry transaction that does not appear in the sales statistics. Yet if the same manufacturing process were performed by a group of smaller jobbing firms which sell the semifinished goods to one another for further fabrication, the intra-industry transaction would appear. The British procedure avoids this dilemma and does not report intra-industry sales at all. We will follow UK procedure in this chapter.

The American procedure has its advantages too in that it links up more closely with the idea that the shipments we are discussing represent the expenses of industry. Intra-industry shipments are expenses as much as interindustry shipments. We shall need this idea when we discuss the theory of input-output in Chapter 3. Consequently, even though it is a bit awkward, we shall use the American idea when theoretical considerations are involved. It is easy to see which method is in use simply by looking at the cells with the same row as column number. These lie on the so-called *principal* (or *leading*) *diagonal* running from the 'north-west' corner of the table to the 'south-east'.

---

[3] In the older 1963 table these elements are shown in brackets, but are not included in the totals.

46   The input-output system

The transactions matrix as a whole

We are now in a position to bring together all the parts of the transactions matrix (Table 2.1). In broad outline, the matrix is divided into four *quadrants*:

Quadrant I   *Final use*: Consumption, Investment, Government, Export of goods and services produced by the industries named in the rows.

Quadrant II   *Interindustry use*: Flow of intermediate products from the industry shown in each row to the industries listed in the columns.

Quadrant III   *Primary input* or *value added*: Flow of payments for factors of production used by the industries named in the columns.

Quadrant IV   *Totals.*

Row equalities

Each cell in the interindustry quadrant II shows how much output is shipped from its row to the corresponding column. Each cell in the final use quadrant I shows the value of the goods sent from the industry in the row to the final use to which it is destined. Consequently the total output for each industry is the sum of all the entries in its row in quadrant I plus quadrant II. Adding up the total output of all the rows gives the entry (£450 in Table 2.2) shown in the lower right hand cell of quadrant IV. It is *total* of all the *row totals*, and may be called *gross social product*.

Query: How big is gross social product in Table 2.1?

Column equalities

Each cell in the interindustry quadrant II also shows what is received by the industry indicated by the column in which it lies. These *inputs* are received from the corresponding row industries. Reading down a column we see the list of inputs into that industry. Included in the inputs are the primary inputs – value added or 'labour' – shown as the row constituting quadrant III. Each entry in quadrant III shows the amount of inputs from individuals' work or property that goes to each of the column industries. Consequently, the total money value of all the inputs into each industry column is found by adding up the interindustry inputs from quadrant II and the human inputs in quadrant III. Adding up the column totals we get the sum of all the inputs; this sum is the total of all the entries in quadrant II and quadrant III. The

Table 2.2   The relations of quadrants in a transactions matrix

	Industries				Final Use				Total Final Use	Total Output
	1	2	3	4	C	I	G	E		
1	–	15	50	20	10	10	20	5	45	130
2	5	–	100	20	5	10	5	5	25	150
3	50	100	–	5	10	20	10	20	60	215
4	50	5	50	–	5	10	20	15	50	155
Value Added	25	30	15	110	I = III = 180					
Total Input	130	150	215	155	I+II II+III 450					

The total of all the industry outputs equals the sum of all the entries in Quadrants I and II

The sum of Quadrants I+II equals that of II+III. Hence the sum of the elements in Quadrant I equals that of III. Quadrants I and III are two different expressions for Gross National Product

The total of all the industry inputs equals the sum of all the entries in Quadrants II and III

total of all the column entries also is shown in the lower right hand cell of quadrant IV as gross social product.

Balancing equalities and GNP

The *value of the outputs* of each industry is equal to its total sales to other firms and to final use. This is shown as the row total. The *value of the inputs* into each industry consists of purchases from other firms and primary inputs of factors of production. These are column totals. Hence, including profit the sum of all the inputs is equal to the sum of the outputs of each industry. Any possible difference between them must appear as a profit (or loss) and is included as one of the human primary inputs. Adding up rows and columns, quadrants $I+II = II+III$ in the lower right hand box of quadrant IV, illustrates two ways of arriving at the gross social product. But, by subtracting the intermediate use in II from both sides of the equality we see that $I = III$. That is to say, quadrant I and quadrant III are the two different ways of expressing gross national product (GNP): the money measure of the *value added by production* on one hand, and the *payment to factors of production* on the other.

Now we can see the meaning of gross national product more clearly. The *total sales* of goods and services is gross social product. But gross social product is not the new value added by production because it contains all of the transactions of intermediate goods in quadrant II which are used up in the course of production. The goods and services made available for the nation are the final use, quadrant I; excluding intermediate interindustry use from gross social product yields GNP in the sense of new value added by national production. We have just seen that this new value equals the payments to factors of production that produced it, the elements of quadrant III.

Some accounting refinements

There are minor problems of definition and accounting procedure that we have swept under the rug in identifying the sum of final use to the UK with GNP (the USA table fully coordinates final use with GNP, the UK table requires a few adjustments).

International transactions

There are two problems here. First, strictly speaking, final use should be called gross domestic product (GDP) rather than GNP, because it represents goods produced by factors of production located in the UK. To record GNP accurately, income from UK factors of production operating abroad should be added; income of foreigners located in the UK should be subtracted.

A second problem is accounting for *imported goods*. This is done by treating imports as if it were just another industry (row 36) providing intermediate goods and final use. Final use in the table is greater than new value added by British factors of production. To make the reconciliation, we must subtract imports from final use.

Taxes on goods

Net taxes on expenditure (taxes minus subsidies) add to the market value of the output of each industry and are included as a primary input (row 39). Taxes on final use add a further problem. They are included in quadrant IV even though they do not really correspond to the GNP in the factor-use sense of the word; consequently, we must subtract them out again.

Capital consumption

This irritating problem came up before in macroeconomic national income accounting. Recall that by capital consumption is meant using up the stock of capital in the course of production – wear and tear on buildings, machinery and running down of stocks of inventory. Since it is a practical impossibility to assign how much of the depreciation was involved in the shipments to each of the receiving industry of any row, we simply record gross domestic capital formation (*gross* investment) as part of final use. For each row industry, gross investment includes both the replacement of depreciated fixed capital and the net investment in new capital accumulation. To ensure that the value added quadrant II equals the total value of final use shown in quadrant I, we must also include capital consumption in *gross* profits and in other trading income (row 41), rather than *net* profits.

The structure of production in differing economies

Now, to more interesting matters, and a look at forests as well as trees! Suppose we step back from the details and look for overall patterns. Almost all of the cells in the interindustry use quadrant record at least a small shipment from row to column. The pattern of shipments is made clearer if we distinguish the significantly large cells from the small.

Leontief has done this in a hypothetical example, shading in those cells that represent more than their proportional share of each industry's total output.[4] That is to say, if there are fifteen industries, he shaded those cells

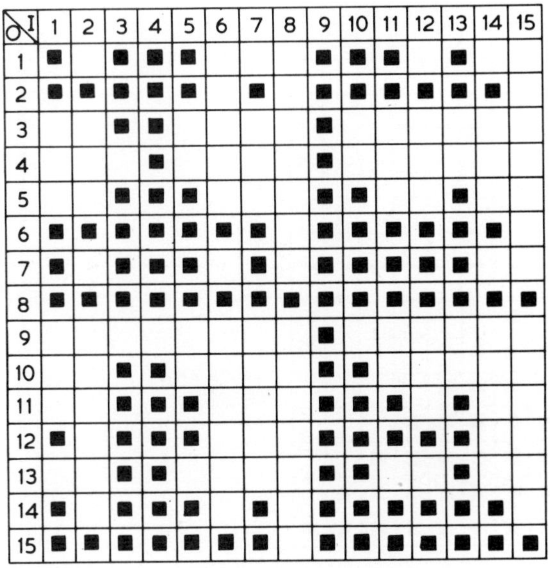

I/O	1	2	3	4	5	6	7	8	9	10	11	12	13	14	15
1	■		■	■	■				■	■	■		■		
2	■	■	■	■	■		■		■	■	■	■	■	■	
3			■	■					■						
4				■					■						
5			■	■	■				■	■			■		
6	■	■	■	■	■	■	■		■	■	■	■	■	■	
7	■		■	■	■		■		■	■	■	■	■		
8	■	■	■	■	■	■	■	■	■	■	■	■	■	■	■
9									■						
10			■	■					■	■					
11			■	■	■				■	■	■		■		
12	■		■	■	■				■	■	■	■	■		
13			■	■					■	■			■		
14	■		■	■	■		■		■	■	■	■	■	■	
15	■	■	■	■	■	■	■		■	■	■	■	■	■	■

Figure 2.1   (W. Leontief, 'The structure of development', *Scientific American*, September 1963)

[4] W. Leontief, *Input-Output Economics* (1966).

that account for more than $\frac{1}{15}$ of each industry's total shipments to others. This is surely an arbitrary criterion, but we have to draw the line somewhere between 'small' and 'large'.

Now we have a picture of the structure of an economy. At first we get something like the illustration in Figure 2.1. There seems to be no pattern at all. Perhaps if we renumber the rows and columns, we might make more sense out of it. After all there is no reason why Agriculture must be industry 1 in the Blue Book rather than industry 9. Suppose we interchange industry 9 with industry 1. Then industry 9 would occupy the first row and the first column. The change would have the effect of making the first column consist entirely of shaded cells. But only the first cell of the first row would be shaded; all the others would be blank.

Continuing to rearrange rows and columns, we can place the old fourth industry in the place of industry 2. Then all but the first cell in column 2 is shaded, and the first two cells of row 2 are shaded. It might be possible to rearrange our matrix in triangular form. Figure 2.2 shows an ideal case where complete triangulation is possible.

O\I	9	4	3	10	13	5	11	1	12	7	14	2	6	15	8
9	■														
4	■	■													
3	■	■	■												
10	■	■	■	■											
13	■	■	■	■	■										
5	■	■	■	■	■	■									
11	■	■	■	■	■	■	■								
1	■	■	■	■	■	■	■	■							
12	■	■	■	■	■	■	■	■	■						
7	■	■	■	■	■	■	■	■	■	■					
14	■	■	■	■	■	■	■	■	■	■	■				
2	■	■	■	■	■	■	■	■	■	■	■	■			
6	■	■	■	■	■	■	■	■	■	■	■	■	■		
15	■	■	■	■	■	■	■	■	■	■	■	■	■	■	
8	■	■	■	■	■	■	■	■	■	■	■	■	■	■	■

Figure 2.2　(W. Leontief, 'The structure of development', *Scientific American*, September 1963)

In fact, the table for many of the advanced industrial countries can be put roughly in this triangular form. Despite their differences, the numbering scheme which triangulates one country also does fairly well for the others. This suggests that developed countries seem to have strikingly similar interindustry structure. Seemingly the pattern is the result of technical linkages between industries. Steel production requires coke, iron ore, limestone, coal or electric energy and labour in roughly the same proportions wherever steel is made in the world. Either steel is made this way or not made at all.

This may not seem surprising until one reflects on the many different ways in which steel could be produced. For a long time, economists preached that the way in which goods were produced depended on the different supplies of resources available in different countries. Production technology was supposed to adapt to local circumstances. Of course, adaptation occurs and we will study the mechanism that brings it about. But, it appears that this adaptation takes time. Over the short run it may be less important than was thought.

Especially if one is in a hurry to get on with production, there are only a few reasonable ways of producing most things. While less developed countries might be motivated to use special methods adapted to their cheaper labour force, they often find it so costly to develop new production methods as to make it cheaper to imitate the way things are done in the United States, the Soviet Union or Japan. In fact, Russian and Japanese industrialization proceeded very rapidly, partly because they started late and simply took over the technology developed elsewhere.

The structure of a developed economy

Scientific American magazine has prepared a triangulated table for the USA economy. Industries in this economy can be arranged in a hierarchy. The industries at the top of the triangle fall into the category of Final Non-Metal goods: footwear and leather products, furniture and fixtures, tobacco manufactures, apparel and textiles, drugs and toiletries and food. These industries ship relatively little of their products to other industries. The rows exhibit small interindustry entries; most of their output goes directly to final use for consumption.

Query: Industries 2 and 3 in the *Scientific American* table do not supply consumption as much as the others. Why are they still at the top of the triangle?

While Final Non-Metal industries do not supply many other industries with intermediate goods, they receive inputs from many other industries. Read down the columns corresponding to these industries, and observe that the industries with the nearly empty rows are the very ones with the nearly full columns. Industries such as these are at the end of the long chain of production processes by which goods are increasingly fabricated by being passed from industry to industry until they reach final form.

Contrast the industries at the top of the triangle with those at the bottom. The latter have almost complete rows indicating that they ship goods to many other industries. Their columns are almost empty. These industries receive little from other industries, but ship much to them. They provide the basic services and materials of manufacture. As we read up to the top of the triangle, we move from more basic industries supplying primary labour and raw materials to those producing goods mostly for consumption and other final uses. Proceeding from the bottom to the top, the categories are: Services, Energy, Basic Non-Metal, Basic Metal, Final Metal, and Final Non-Metal.

The most extreme case of an input that contributes to every industry is not really an industry at all, but the 'labour' included in quadrant III. None of the labour directly provides final use – it is all channeled through one or another industry. Primary input is used indirectly in serving the public by working for all the other industries of the economy. One might object and point out that such efforts as teaching, the work of domestic servants, the army, all provide labour services which enter into final use, but which do not involve providing input to other industries. These labour efforts are included in the category of Service industries.

Service industries are at the base of the interindustry triangle and are almost entirely produced by labour with few inputs from other industries. Some service industries such as medical and educational services, amusements, automotive repair, hotels and the like provide final use in the form of consumption, and very little to other industries. Other service industries such as research and development cater to industry needs and supply little to final use.

Questions:
(1) Which service industry has the largest interindustry use? The largest final use?
(2) Is government an industry?
(3) What is a non-profit-making industry? How do you think it decides on the outputs it produces and the prices it charges?
(4) How does the table show that the service industries receive few inputs from other industries?
(5) How large a portion of GNP in the USA is made by service industries? Which industries make the greatest use of the products of service industries? Which least?

Energy is the next industry group. As one might expect, these industries provide for many others, but receive inputs from relatively few. Nevertheless, their situation is not as extreme as the Service industries.

Query: (1) Which industries are most likely to be harmed by the 'energy crisis'?

(2) In the United Kingdom what energy source produces the largest value of output? Describe the input and output relationship between energy and service industries.

The Basic Non-Metal and Basic Metal industries lie above Energy. They extract and refine the material used in further production. The fact that these industries lie in the middle of the table means that they use the products of many other industries as well as supply them with raw materials. The raw materials industries themselves must be supplied by others. There is an important element of interdependent linkage here. Before the raw materials can be forthcoming, the equipment needed to extract them must be available. At the same time the equipment itself is produced with raw materials extracted. In developed countries this 'chicken and egg' problem of balance has been solved in the course of their history. Unfortunately the supply links are not as well established in less developed countries.

Final Metal industries are the next stage in the production hierarchy. These industries provide goods for further fabrication to a fairly restricted set of other industries. Examination of the group of cells formed by the rows and columns of these industries shows how tightly they are dependent upon each other. Little is shipped from Final Metal to Final Non-Metal or to other groups except services. Whilst fitting into the larger triangulation pattern, the Final Metal industries form a triangle of their own. They produce highly fabricated metal products which they use themselves, and which they ship to final use.

Query: (1) Do the Final Metal industries receive important inputs from other industries?

(2) Describe the pattern of final use of the Final Metal industries.

The production triangle ends at last in the Final Non-Metal group. These are the industries that are dependent upon many of the others, but which supply little to other intermediate use in the interindustry quadrant. Their product is mostly designed for final use, converting what they receive from the industries further down in the table into final consumption, investment, government and export.

Exercise: Notice that in the hierarchy, the metal industries occupy an intermediate position between the Basic Non-Metals and the Final Non-Metals. Explain how this arrangement justifies the description of our technology as the 'steel age'. What was the Bronze Age? The Stone Age? Could there be a Plastic Age?

The interdependence of the industries in the developed economy is the outstanding conclusion that can be drawn from the triangular array. Industries at the apex of the triangle largely supply final use, but they receive inputs from others. Those at the base of the triangle contribute to the end product of social production only indirectly by supplying other industries. Most industries supply both final use as well as each other.

This interdependence works in a distinctive way, passing demand down the triangle. Suppose final demand for the first industry were to increase. In the *Scientific American* table, this is the Footwear and Leather Products industry. Obviously the output of the footwear industry could increase only if further inputs into that industry were made available. Consequently shipments in all the cells in the first column would have to increase. But for each of these industries to enlarge their supply, their inputs must increase in turn. The *Scientific American* table shows that an increase in footwear demand means the Apparel industry (5) must be stimulated; if apparel is stimulated, so will its suppliers, and so on down the matrix.

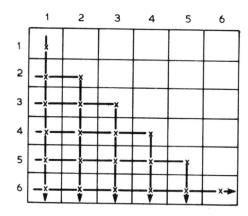

Figure 2.3

In Figure 2.3 we sketch a triangulated interindustry transactions matrix by inserting an *x* for 'large' values, leaving the zero or small cells blank. Then increased demand for industry 1 increases the demand for industries 2–6.

But the increased demand for 2 increases 3–6, and so on. Demand 'cascades down the diagonal', to use Leontief's striking phase.

If the table were strictly triangulated, so that there were zeros above the principal diagonal, the direction of causation only will work down the triangle. The stimulation of demand for an industry will spread to others which supply it. These supplying sectors lie lower down in the production hierarchy. This is called *forward linkage*. Industries above the expanding one would not be affected. In practice, since the upper cells are not completely empty we can expect that the increase in demand will require an increase in output by those industries higher in the triangle. Thus there is always some *backward linkage*. For instance, an increase in the output of the Printing and Publishing industry (No. 42) will require an increase in output by the Wholesale and Retail Trade industry (No. 72). But, an increase in industry 72 requires a substantial increase in industries lying above both of them, such as drugs, cleaning and toilet preparations (No. 7) and food and kindred products (No. 8). These increased indirect demands will then 'cascade down' and triangle once again. The main linkages, nonetheless, are seen to be forward in the developed economy.

For the complete, developed country, there are no gaps in the chain of interdependence. Even if all the columns are not quite full the chain is not broken. There are enough remaining linkages to transmit the demand from one industry to the next. This is not the case in underdeveloped countries. As a result, progress is more difficult as demand in one sector induces further expansion only slowly and with blockages.

Exercise:
(1) In Figure 2.3, suppose the second industry were stimulated. Show the effect on the others. Suppose the entries in the third row second column were blank. Would your chain be broken? Illustrate. What is the largest number of blanks that can exist for the chain not to break? Sketch the matrix that illustrates your conclusion.
(2) Judging from the transactions matrix shown in *Scientific American*, which industries are likeliest to be most affected by changes in demand? Which least? What industries are likeliest to be most stable and steady in their output? Which least?
(3) In the following transactions matrix, Figure 2.4, draw arrows to show how an increase in the final demand for the fifth industry will stimulate all the others. Where would the off-diagonal x have to be for only the industries 2–6 to be stimulated?
(4) Trace out the consequences of an increase in output of the Lumber and Wood Products industry through several trips down the *Scientific American* triangle.

	1	2	3	4	5	6
1	x					x
2	x	x				
3	x	x	x			
4	x	x	x	x		
5	x	x	x	x	x	
6	x	x	x	x	x	x

Figure 2.4

The structure of incomplete economies

The triangular pattern of complete industrialized economies provides a powerful insight into planning the development of incomplete economies. It shows what linkages are *missing* in its interindustry structure.

Open incomplete economies – less developed nations   A national economy heavily dependent upon other nations is said to be open. Clearly the UK and Japan are open since much of their final use is destined for export, and much of the raw produce is imported. These industrialized nations may be open, but they hardly can be called incomplete because their interindustry structures can be triangularized. Within their boundaries the linkages exist to process raw materials in stages until final use is produced.

Less developed 'third world' countries are open for a different reason. Their interindustry quadrants show gaps in the linkages between industries. Goods are not fabricated internally, but exported in raw materials or crudely processed form such as cotton, crude petroleum, and the like. Even when manufacture takes place internally, it is based on an intermediate process completed elsewhere, such as automobile assembly plants in Brazil or Nigeria using components produced by Fiat or Ford.

The interindustry quadrant of such nations cannot be triangulated by a rearrangement of rows and columns. Development economists analyse the breaks in linkage by numbering the industries according to the pattern established in the complete developed economies, and observing the gaps. These are then candidates for more concentrated development programmes.

The decomposed economy – regions, races and nations   An interindustry structure might also be split up, *decomposed*, into groups of industries that are largely unrelated to one another. The grouping into sectors might, in the UK, reflect regional structures. In the extreme, such groups would be independent; that is to say, they would not have a single row or column in common (Figure 2.5). Industries in one group would neither provide nor require the outputs of the other. For this to be the case, quadrant II would have to be *block diagonal*, as shown in the figure.

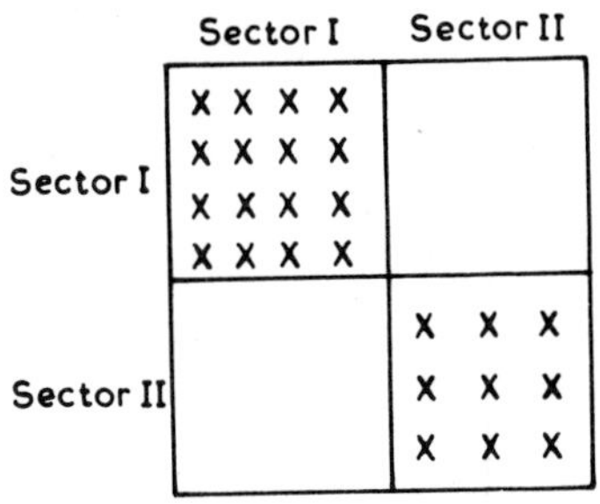

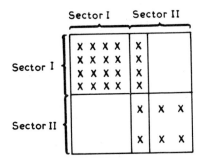

Figure 2.5   Block-diagonal decomposed interindustry matrix

Block diagonal decomposition need not entail absolute separation. One or two columns with non-zero entries might remain common to both sectors. For instance, in Figure 2.6, the industries in sector I share a column with

Sector I   Sector II

Sector I

Sector II

Figure 2.6

sector II. The industries classified in sector II do not supply any of their products to sector I because they do not have a row in common. But sector I does supply some of the inputs to sector II through the linking fifth industry. The first four industries making up the first sector provide inputs into the fifth industry, which in turn provides inputs into both sectors. Consequently, an increase in demand for the products of the four industries in sector I will have no effect on the output of sector II. There is no forward linkage between sectors. But there is backward linkage; an increase of any of the outputs of sector II will require more of the intermediate goods furnished by the linking industry, which in turn, will necessitate increased output by the industries in sector I.

Exercise:
(1) What would Figure 2.5 look like if it consisted of six blocks of one industry each?
(2) What would be the pattern of interdependence in Figure 2.6 if the industries had only a row in common? Would the location of the row make a difference?
(3) What would be the pattern of interdependence if the sectors only had one column in common but if sector I occupied the upper right hand side of the quadrant, and sector II was located in the lower left? What sort of economic situation would that indicate?

The analysis of industry sectors and their linkages has numerous applications. In the UK the obvious use is in the solution of regional problems. The government is committed to support the 'development regions' which are suffering from unemployment and depressed levels of income. If a proper study is made of the inter-regional linkages, it may be possible to study the way in which these regions may be advanced as a result of increased demand elsewhere in the UK. A unified approach to development in the whole nation would include the study of the linking industries – the sinews that bind the nation's economy together. The study of regional interdependence is in its infancy in the UK, with only a few attempts to make regional input-output tables, but the issue will doubtlessly be pressed further in the future.

Exercise:
(1) What changes in the pattern of regional development are likely to occur as a result of Britain's entry in the Common Market? Review the parliamentary debate on the question and advocate a programme for development regions.
(2) No nation is completely independent of linkages to others. Nevertheless, a national economy is likely to be much more closely linked with domestic industries than with foreign. Use the analysis presented in the text to evaluate the following statements or to show what sort of data would be needed to do so.
   (*a*) In economic terms Britain is a part of Europe rather than a member of the Commonwealth or a trans-Atlantic trading community.
   (*b*) Ulster is a part of Ireland and not part of the United Kingdom.
   (*c*) The blacks in the United States really represent a nation within a nation.

(d) African nations are the accidental result of the way Europeans drew the boundaries of the colonies in the struggle for empire. Hence a country like Nigeria is made up of at least three major tribal groups and is not a nation at all.

3 The theory of input-output

Three steps to the inverse

The transactions matrix is to the economy what the profit and loss statement is to the firm. Just as we used the profit and loss statement to compute the *sales* required to earn a desired *profit* for a firm, we shall use the input-output accounting system to compute the *output* of each industry required to meet a specified bill of *final use*. Suppose the government or the market decides that the nation ought to have so much coal, textiles, food and so on for its final uses of consumption, investment, government and export. How much must each industry produce so that the national expenses in the form of interindustry use are met, and still the desired final use is made available by each industry's contribution?

Unlike the typical firm, the national economy produces the goods in its various industries that serve as the inputs into the others. It does not buy these intermediate goods from others, but manufactures them itself. Government planners who expect that the final use they desire will actually be forthcoming must be sure that each of the industries will also be able to supply the needs of other industries. That means that each industry must produce the right amounts of the right kinds of goods for the plan to be anything but a fiasco.

Different nations and social systems use different methods to determine the desired final use and enforce the required industry outputs. Leaving these aside, let us examine the overall principles of the proper output consistent with final use and interindustry needs. The analysis proceeds in three steps analogous to the profit and loss calculation:

Step 1

Start with the record of transactions in a previous year. For the firm, the profit and loss statement showed expenses plus profits equal to sales: $E + P = S$. For the economy, the transactions matrix shows that interindustry inputs plus final use equals the total output of the various industries.

Step 2

For the firm, we assumed that the ratio of expenses to sales would be the same in future years as it was in the year for which the information was gathered. Even though E and S were subject to changes, the technical coefficient of production was the same: $a = E/S$. If $E = £80$ and $S = £100$, then $a = 0.80$; then if $S = £200$, E must be £160.

For the economy, we consider the expenses of each industry to be the whole column of inputs into it. The technical coefficient of any industry, then, is the column of ratios of the various inputs into it divided by the total output of the industry whose name (number) is shown at the head of the column. The collection of such columns for all the industries is called the *technology matrix*.

Step 3

(*a*) In order to compute the sales required to meet the profit target for the firm, we first substituted $E = aS$ in the basic profit and loss equation. Factoring, we arrived at the relationship: $P = (1 - a)S$. For the economy we will have to find a tabular expression corresponding to $(1 - a)$ to be called the *Leontief matrix*.
(*b*) We then found the multiplier which gave us the required sales when applied to the firm's profit target. This was obtained by inverting the previous relationship. Thus S was found by the formula:

$$S = \frac{1}{1-a}P \text{ or } S = (1-a)^{-1}P.$$

In order to invert the Leontief matrix we will have a bit more difficulty. The inverse of an ordinary number like $(1 - a)$ is simply $1/(1 - a)$. The same is not true of a matrix of numbers. The inverse of a matrix will be explained in detail in this chapter, but even now, we can see what the outcome ought to be. The *inverse Leontief matrix* when applied in the proper way to final use should tell us how much total output is required. That is to say, the inverse matrix must turn out to be a table of multipliers which will reflect the direct and indirect requirements of all the industries.

Finding the inverse: The three steps in detail

Step 1: The transactions matrix

In Chapter 2 we permitted ourselves the convenience of recording inputs and outputs in money terms. At the same time we suggested that the determining factors of these flows were technical and physical relationships. The interindustry flows to steel makers depended, we said upon the physical amounts of coke, limestone and iron required. These are not the same. After all, £1000 worth of goods depends on both the physical units and their prices. The value of the shipments might change due to price changes, and yet the physical relationships could be unaltered.

Statistically, there is not much choice but to use money values. Like it or not, the multitude of physical transfers is almost impossible to record. In order to understand the *workings* of our economy, however, we use a theoretical model, and are freed from the problems of data gathering. So we imagine that we have been able to measure and record production in physical units – tons of steel, bushels of wheat, hours of labour, feet of newsprint, and so forth. Much can be learned from studying the input-output system in physical units. We can then return and use the theoretical ideas in application to the statistical material we do have.

One consequence of dealing in diverse physical units is that they cannot be added together. Everyone recalls the admonition of his maths teacher: 'You cannot add apples and pears!' Yet the sum of five apples and six pears is eleven pieces of fruit! Summation is possible provided we have a common unit. The trouble is that we have just decided to relinquish our only common unit – money. We cannot add up the columns of inputs because the inputs come from various industries consisting of diverse things. But all is not lost. We can still add up across each row, showing the distribution of the output of each industry. Row entries are in the same units.

To simplify matters, let us illustrate only two industries in the transactions matrix shown below. We express the relationship in general algebraic symbols in the left hand panel; a parallel numerical example is given on the right.

In manipulating this table it is probably a good idea for the reader to accustom himself to think of industries as simply industry 1 and industry 2, instead of agriculture and manufacturing, although temporarily, for concreteness, we shall continue to name the industries in the examples. This will involve us in some tortuous expressions when we try to illustrate the physical interindustry flow because these are very large and clumsy categories. The reader should really have in mind the manipulation of a large detailed table. Furthermore, for simplicity, let us identify all primary inputs with 'labour' without committing ourselves to the Marxian idea that it is the sole social

Transactions matrix

General theory					Example				
	Inputs					*Inputs*			
	1	2	*Final use*	*Total*		*Ag*	*Mfg*	*Final use*	*Totals*
Outputs					Outputs				
1	x_{11}	x_{12}	y_1	X_1	Ag	50	75	75	200
2	x_{21}	x_{22}	y_2	X_2	Mfg	100	200	100	400
Labour	b_1	b_2	0	B	Labour	40	60	0	100

cost. Finally, for each industry, let us lump together all the final uses into a single final use for each industry.[1]

Now study the table starting with quadrant II. It shows the shipment of product from the industry shown by the row to the industry in the column. A lower case x such as x_{12} designates the amount of the shipment. The *originating row* industry is indicated by the first subscript and the *receiving column* industry by the second subscript. Thus x_{12} is the physical amount of product shipped from industry 1 to industry 2. Caution! x_{12} is not the same as x_{21}; x_{21} is the amount shipped from the second industry to the first. In our example, x_{12} is the amount of agricultural produce shipped to manufacturing. It might consist of raw materials like cotton, grains, or vegetable oils. On the other hand, x_{21} is the amount of manufactured products shipped to agriculture, such as chemical fertilizer, or fuel for tractors. If we torture ourselves into saying that all agricultural products come in bushels, then the numerical illustration shows that 75 bushels of produce go from agriculture to manufacturing: $x_{12} = 75$. Contrariwise, to quote Tweedledee, if manufactured products are measured as truckloads of chemical fertilizer, $x_{21} = 100$ means that 100 truckloads of chemical fertilizer are shipped from manufacturing to agriculture. In both cases the shipments are of intermediate goods which will be further processed toward final use.

From a formal point of view, the x indicates the amount of goods shipped; the first subscript indicates the row, or source of the shipments; the second subscript indicates the column, or destination of the goods. This permits us to express the whole of the second quadrant of the transactions matrix in terms of its typical element, x_{ij}. The i stands for the rows, and in our little example takes on the values 1 and 2 in turn. Likewise, j stands for the

---

[1] Each industry will be taken to produce a single product rather than a whole line of goods as is frequently the case. Joint products will be taken up in Chapter 5. Combinations of several factors of production will be treated in Chapter 6.

column numbers running from 1 to 2. The x is the size of the shipment and the i and j are subscripts identifying the row and the column respectively.

We can go further and write the general interindustry quadrant for any number of rows or columns as x_{ij}, where $i = 1, 2, 3, \ldots n$ and $j = 1, 2, 3, \ldots n$. Customarily we speak of the ith row or jth column when we want to discuss a typical situation and still do not want to specify a particular row or column. These subscripts can get a bit confusing, but there is no more convenient way of keeping track.

Exercise:
(1) Consult the large CSO Transactions Table for 1963 and write down the values for the following: $x_{2,4}$; $x_{70,32}$; $x_{32,70}$. What units are used?
(2) What sort of products might fit into cell entries x_{11} and x_{22}?
(3) Where would one find all the cells of x_{ij} for which $i = j$? Where is i greater than j? Where is i less than j? Describe a triangulated matrix in terms of x_{ij}.

In quadrant I we have condensed all the categories of final use into a single column. The elements of this vector are y_1 and y_2. In general y_i is the symbol for the final use provided by the ith industry.

Questions: (1) How much agricultural product goes to final use in the example on p. 63?
(2) Why is the typical element y_i and not y_j?

An upper case X is the total amount of an industry's product. Thus X_i is the total output of the ith industry. When writing by hand, it is advisable to write a bar over the X, to make sure that there is no doubt that an upper case symbol is intended. Read $\bar{X}$ as 'X bar'. Since the total output of the first industry is distributed between the interindustry use and the final use, the first row equality is: $x_{11} + x_{12} + y_1 = X_1$. For the second row: $x_{21} + x_{22} + y_2 = X_2$.

In quadrant III, b represents the amount of labour which is used in each of the industries. In general, b_j is the amount of labour employed in industry j. The total labour employed is designated by B. The sum of the labour employed in all the industries is $B = b_1 + b_2$.

Query: Why is there no b entry in the final use vector? Why do we write b_j not b_i? Do the b_j form a row or column vector?

Step 2: The technology matrix

How much of each input is directly required to produce a unit of the product? Following the pattern of a single firm, it is the ratio of interindustry expense to total output. Since x_{ij} represents the goods shipped from industry i to industry j, the ratio a_{ij} is found by dividing x_{ij} by X_j the output of the receiving industry: $a_{ij} = x_{ij}/X_j$.

For example, since the goods shipped from industry 1 to industry 2 is x_{12}, $a_{12} = x_{12}/X_2$. According to our example, x_{12} is 75 bushels of farm goods shipped from agriculture to manufacturing. The output of industry 2 is X_2, 400 truckloads of manufactured goods. Hence:

$$a_{12} = a_{ag,mfg} = \frac{x_{ag,mfg}}{X_{mfg}} = \frac{75\,\text{bushels}}{400\,\text{truckloads}} = 0 \cdot 18 \text{ bushels per truckload.}$$

It takes $0 \cdot 18$ bushels of agricultural products to turn out one truckload unit of manufactured goods. Notice that the units in which a_{12} (or $a_{ag,mfg}$) is stated are two different physical units. In computing a_{ij} always check the units to be sure that the receiving industry in the denominator X_j is the same as the second subscript in the numerator x_{ij}.

Query:
(1) Why would it be wrong to say that $a_{12} = x_{12}/X_1$? In what units would the ratio be stated?
(2) Can an a_{ij} value be larger than 1? Could a_{11} or a_{22} exceed 1? If the matrix were drawn up in money value of shipments rather than physical units would you change your answer?
(3) Why can we construct the ratio between bushels of farm goods and truckloads of manufacture even though we cannot add bushels and trucks?

In order to find the technical coefficients that show how much labour is required per unit output we follow a similar procedure. The labour shipped to the jth industry, b_j, is divided by the output of that industry, X_j. The ratio is $l_j = b_j/X_j$. For instance, the labour required to produce a single truckload of manufactured goods is l_2 (or l_{mfg}).

$$l_2 = l_{mfg} = \frac{b_{mfg}}{X_{mfg}} = \frac{60}{400} = 0 \cdot 15 \text{ hours per truckload.}$$

It takes $0 \cdot 15$ hours of labour per truckload of manufactured goods.

Query: Why is there only one subscript in the labour technical coefficient and two in the interindustry coefficients?
What are the *units* in which l_j is stated?

The technology matrix is a table composed of all the technical coefficients of production. The matrix of all the a_{ij} is analogous to the firm's single ratio of expenses to sales, a. Since there are two industries receiving inputs from two industries we have two-times-two kinds of interindustry expenses. The collection of a_{ij} values is called the A matrix. Attached to the interindustry A matrix is a row of l_j values representing the labour technical coefficients of production. The technology matrix is often referred to as the matrix of *direct requirements per unit of gross output*. Reading down each column we see how much each row industry contributes per unit output of the column industry. Continuing the earlier example we have:

Technology matrix

Industry	1	2		Industry	Ag	Mfg
1	a_{11}	a_{12}		Ag	0·25	0·18
2	a_{21}	a_{22}		Mfg	0·50	0·50
Labour	l_1	l_2		Labour	0·20	0·15

Questions:
(1) Which quadrants in the transactions matrix have no counterpart in the technology matrix?
(2) By what quantities are each of the outputs from manufacturing divided to compute the technical coefficients of production? What of the inputs into manufacturing?
(3) Explain the technical coefficient of production in words. Explain how the coefficients exhibit the importance relation of one industry to others.
(4) Invent a hypothetical transactions matrix. Be sure it balances. Derive the appropriate technology matrix.

Step 3: The Leontief matrix and its inverse

The Leontief matrix Still following the analogy with the profit computation, our next step is to express the interindustry expenses, x_{ij}, in terms of the total output, X_j. That is not hard to do. The technical coefficients of production, a_{ij}, are equal to the amount of product shipped from the ith industry to the jth, per unit output of the jth industry. Therefore the amount actually shipped is equal to a_{ij} multiplied by X_j, the number of units produced by the jth industry. That is to say, since $a_{ij} = x_{ij}/X_j$, it follows that $x_{ij} = a_{ij}X_j$. Thus $x_{11} = a_{11}X_1$, $x_{12} = a_{12}X_2$, and so on. Concretely, suppose it took 100 tons of coke to make 500 tons of steel. The technical coefficient of production would be: $a_{coke,steel} = 100 \ coke/500 \ steel = 0·2$ tons of coke per ton of steel. Hence, to produce X amount of steel the amount of coke shipped to steel firms must be: $x_{coke,steel} = 0 \cdot 2 X_{steel}$. To produce 1000 tons of steel, $x_{coke,steel} = (0 \cdot 2)(1000) = 200$ tons of coke.

What could be simpler than Leontief's basic idea that inputs are proportional to outputs? Yet, as we shall now see, it turns out to be a very fruitful insight. Instead of writing the row equations as:

$$x_{11} + x_{12} + y_1 = X_1$$
$$x_{21} + x_{22} + y_2 = X_2$$

we can write the interindustry terms using the a_{ij} and X_j values:

General theory	Example
$a_{11}X_1 + a_{12}X_2 + y_1 = X_1$	$0 \cdot 25 X_1 + 0.18 X_2 + y_1 = X_1$
$a_{21}X_1 + a_{22}X_2 + y_2 = X_2$	$0 \cdot 50 X_1 + 0 \cdot 50 X_2 + y_2 = X_2$

Our ultimate goal is to compute the appropriate output of each industry (X_1 and X_2) which is consistent with final uses which, presumably, will be told to us. To do so we first use the foregoing equations to isolate y_1 and y_2 on the right hand side.

$(1 - a_{11})X_1 - a_{12}X_2 = y_1$	$0 \cdot 75 X_1 - 0 \cdot 18 X_2 = y_1$
$-a_{21}X_1 + (1 - a_{22})X_2 = y_2$	$-0 \cdot 50 X_1 + 0 \cdot 50 X_2 = y_2$

This step corresponds to the calculation of profit as dependent on sales in the firm's calculation. There, since $E = aS$, we could write $E + P = S$ as $aS + P = S$ and then $(1 - a)S = P$. Let us take the time to spell out the analogous process for the economy in some detail. Here the interindustry expense has four parts – two for each industry:

$x_{11} + x_{12}$ –interindustry expense for industry 1

$x_{21} + x_{22}$ –interindustry expense for industry 2

We have shown that we can write these expenses as:

$$a_{11}X_1 + a_{12}X_2$$
$$a_{21}X_1 + a_{22}X_2.$$

Suppose we now detach the coefficients and label these various a_{ij} values as the technology matrix, A:

$$A = \begin{bmatrix} a_{11} & a_{12} \\ a_{21} & a_{22} \end{bmatrix}.$$

We can also make a vector list of the outputs of the two industries, called X:

$$X = \begin{bmatrix} X_1 \\ X_2 \end{bmatrix}.$$

Then the interindustry expenses in matrix terms can be written as a matrix function:

$$\begin{bmatrix} a_{11} & a_{12} \\ a_{21} & a_{22} \end{bmatrix} \begin{bmatrix} X_1 \\ X_2 \end{bmatrix},$$

or even more compactly as AX. Interindustry expenses are seen to be the matrix of technology coefficients operating on outputs; in the case of the firm, expenses were the single technical coefficient multiplied by total sales.

We can now move on to express the complete set of equations in matrix terms. The original pair of equations:

$$a_{11}X_1 + a_{12}X_2 + y_1 = X_1$$
$$a_{21}X_1 + a_{22}X_2 + y_2 = X_2$$

may be restated in matrix terms as:

$$\begin{bmatrix} a_{11} & a_{12} \\ a_{21} & a_{22} \end{bmatrix} \begin{bmatrix} X_1 \\ X_2 \end{bmatrix} + \begin{bmatrix} y_1 \\ y_2 \end{bmatrix} = \begin{bmatrix} X_1 \\ X_2 \end{bmatrix} \quad \text{where} \quad Y = \begin{bmatrix} y_1 \\ y_2 \end{bmatrix}.$$

More compactly this equation is $AX + Y = X$, where $Y = \begin{bmatrix} y_1 \\ y_2 \end{bmatrix}$.

Clearly this is the analog of the firm's equation $aS + P = S$.

Now to express the dependence of final use on total output, we proceed as before to isolate y_1 and y_2 on the right hand side.

$$(1 - a_{11})X_1 - a_{12}X_2 = y_1$$
$$-a_{21}X_1 + (1 - a_{22})X_2 = y_2.$$

Detaching coefficients these equations may be expressed in matrix terms:

$$\begin{bmatrix} (1 - a_{11}) & -a_{12} \\ -a_{21} & (1 - a_{22}) \end{bmatrix} \begin{bmatrix} X_1 \\ X_2 \end{bmatrix} = \begin{bmatrix} y_1 \\ y_2 \end{bmatrix}.$$

The matrix operating on the vector of total outputs is called the Leontief matrix. We can understand its significance more clearly by first defining the *identity matrix*, I, as one with unity down the principal diagonal and noughts everywhere else:

$$I = \begin{bmatrix} 1 & 0 \\ 0 & 1 \end{bmatrix}.$$

Since matrix subtraction is the difference between the corresponding elements of two matrices, the Leontief matrix is seen to be the identity matrix minus the technology matrix. Thus $I - A$ is:

$$\begin{bmatrix} 1 & 0 \\ 0 & 1 \end{bmatrix} - \begin{bmatrix} a_{11} & a_{12} \\ a_{21} & a_{22} \end{bmatrix} = \begin{bmatrix} (1 - a_{11}) & -a_{12} \\ -a_{21} & (1 - a_{22}) \end{bmatrix}.$$

The progression of equations can now be fully expressed in matrix terms. Start from the balancing equations $AX + Y = X$. Then isolating Y, $Y = X - AX$ and therefore $Y = (I - A)X$. The analogy between input-output and the profit and loss calculation is unmistakable:

Profit and loss	*Input-output*
$aS + P = S$	$AX + Y = X$
$P = S - aS$	$Y = X - AX$
$P = (1 - a)S$	$Y = (I - A)X$

One more step. So far we have been able to compute Y from the X –final use from the total outputs. Planners need to do just the opposite – compute the required outputs to release the desired final use – just as the firm must compute sales to earn desired profits. We must somehow complete the process by inversion to get:

For the firm	*For the economy*
$S = \dfrac{1}{1-a}P$	$(I - A)^{-1}Y = X$

or

$$S = (1-a)^{-1}P$$

The inverse Leontief matrix   An inverse function or operation is the undoing of the change wrought by another. If the first operation is 'I pound a nail into this piece of wood', the inverse is 'I pull it out again'. Solving an equation involves an inverse function. Thus $6x = 3$ may be solved by undoing the multiplication of x by 6 by dividing both sides of the equation by 6. Equivalently, the inverse of multiplying by 6 is to multiply by 'six inverted', i.e. $\frac{1}{6}$ or 6^{-1}. This gives us x alone on the left hand side, and $\frac{1}{2}$ on the right: $x = \frac{1}{2}$.

Previously we inverted $(1-a)S = P$ to get $S = [1/(1-a)]P$ for the firm. We must do the same for the economy. The system of simultaneous equations

$$(1 - a_{11})X_1 - a_{12}X_2 = y_1$$
$$-a_{21}X_1 + (1 - a_{22})X_2 = y_2$$

can be thought of as the application of the Leontief matrix to X to get Y: $(I - A)X = Y$. If we can invert the operation $(I - A)$ on X we will have X alone on the left hand side and $(I - A)^{-1}$ operating on Y. This would be an extremely important result because it would give us the X_1 and X_2 which represent the output of each industry directly and indirectly needed to produce the final use y_1 and y_2.

How to invert the function? Simply solve the two equations simultaneously for X_1 and X_2. That will give us the X-values alone on one side of the pair of equations. The other side will consist of the y_i-values tied up with the a_{ij}-values by various operations of addition and multiplication. That is to say, we will have computed the total output of each industry in terms of the goal of final use and the technical coefficients of production.

We compute the inverse in general and continue on with the working of the numerical example. The reader should bear in mind that while the resulting computations look imposing, they merely consist of solving two linear equations in two unknowns. One must not be intimidated by the untidy appearance of the problem resulting from the subscript notation.

We already have the Leontief equations:

General theory

$$(1-a_{11})X_1 - a_{12}X_2 = y_1$$
$$a_{21}X_1 + (1-a_{22})X_2 = y_2$$

Example

$$0\cdot75X_1 - 0\cdot18X_2 = y_1$$
$$-0\cdot50X_1 + 0\cdot50X_2 = y_2$$

Solving[2] these equations for X_1 and X_2 yields:

$$X_1 = \left[\frac{(1-a_{22})}{(1-a_{11})(1-a_{22}) - a_{12}a_{21}}\right]y_1 + \left[\frac{a_{12}}{(1-a_{11})(1-a_{22}) - a_{12}a_{21}}\right]y_2$$

$$X_1 = 1\cdot72y_1 + 0\cdot62y_2$$

$$X_2 = \left[\frac{a_{21}}{(1-a_{11})(1-a_{22}) - a_{12}a_{21}}\right]y_1 + \left[\frac{(1-a_{11})}{(1-a_{11})(1-a_{22}) - a_{12}a_{21}}\right]y_2$$

$$X_2 = 1\cdot72y_1 + 2\cdot59y_2$$

Obligatory exercise: Verify the result of X_1 and X_2 both in general and numerical illustration. Do not proceed any further with this book until you do! Your numerical result may differ slightly from the text depending on how you round off.

---

[2] The actual computation for X_1 is as follows. We eliminate the terms involving X_2. Multiply the first equation by the coefficient of X_2 which appears in the second equation. Likewise, multiply the second equation by the coefficient of X_2 in the first equation. The result is:

$$(1-a_{11})(1-a_{22})X_1 - a_{12}(1-a_{22})X_2 = (1-a_{22})y_1 \quad \text{in general. The}$$

numerical example is $(0\cdot75)(0\cdot50)X_1 - (0\cdot18)(0\cdot50)X_2 = 0\cdot50y_1$.

Then, $a_{12}a_{21}X_1 - a_{12}(1-a_{22})X_2 = -a_{12}y_2$ in general. The

example becomes $(0\cdot18)(0\cdot50)X_1 - (0\cdot18)(0\cdot50)X_2 = -0\cdot18y_2$.

Subtracting the second equation from the first eliminates the X_2 terms:

$$[(1-a_{11})(1-a_{22}) - a_{12}a_{21}]X_1 = (1-a_{22})y_1 + a_{12}y_2 \quad \text{in general}$$

and numerically $[(0\cdot75)(0\cdot50) - (0\cdot18)(0\cdot50)]X_1 = 0\cdot50y_1 + 0\cdot18y_2$.

After dividing by the parenthesis on the left hand side we have solved for X_1 in terms of y_1 and y_2. The solution for X_2 is similar.

Look at the new pair of equations derived by inverting the Leontief relationship. Just as anticipated, the y_i values of final use are multiplied by a messy looking collection of a_{ij} values hitched together by various operations such as addition, multiplication and so on. We have collected the multipliers of y_1 and y_2 together in brackets. These ugly looking quantities are the elements of the inverse Leontief matrix. Detaching them into a matrix table they constitute the function which, when applied to Y, carries over into X. That is to say, when the inverse matrix is applied to a bill of final use, it tells us how much each industry should produce to directly and indirectly make that final use available.

In order to make the relationship clearer, and to show a little bravado in the face of such algebraic dragons, let us designate these coefficients as J_{ij}, J standing for junk. Once again i stands for rows, j for columns. The inverse matrix, $(I-A)^{-1}$, is the collection of J_{ij} values:

$$(I-A)^{-1} = \begin{bmatrix} J_{11} & J_{12} \\ J_{21} & J_{22} \end{bmatrix}$$

In equation form, $X = (I-A)^{-1}Y$, is:

$$X_1 = J_{11}y_1 + J_{12}y_2$$

$$X_2 + J_{21}y_1 + J_{22}y_2.$$

We understand, by comparison with the solution just completed, that

$$J_{11} = \frac{1-a_{22}}{(1-a_{11})(1-a_{22})-a_{12}a_{21}}; \quad J_{12} = \frac{a_{12}}{(1-a_{11})(1-a_{22})-a_{12}a_{21}}$$

$$J_{11} = 1 \cdot 72; \quad J_{12} = 0 \cdot 62$$

$$J_{21} = \frac{a_{21}}{(1-a_{11})(1-a_{22})-a_{12}a_{21}}; \quad J_{22} = \frac{1-a_{11}}{(1-a_{11})(1-a_{22})-a_{12}a_{21}}$$

$$J_{21} = 1 \cdot 72; \quad J_{22} = 2 \cdot 59$$

There is something remarkable about the collections of junk that constitute the inverse matrix. Each of the J_{ij} is a constant because it is a combination of constant a_{ij} values. Hence, once computed, the inverse matrix can be applied to any bill of final use to compute the X vector of industry outputs. Even though the goals that society builds into its desired final use may undergo change, so long as the technology embedded in the a_{ij} values does not, we can carry on with the same inverse to plan for each industry. Obviously, Leontief fashioned a very powerful tool out of a very simple idea. Still another view of the inverse is contained in a brief appendix to this chapter.

Exercise:

(1) Suppose $y_1 = 50$ and $y_2 = 25$. Using the numerical example in the text find required outputs of industry X_1 and X_2.

(2) If one doubles both y_1 and y_2, what is the effect on X_1 and X_2? What is the effect on the various a_{ij}?

(3) If y_1 and y_2 are as exercise (1), compute the four interindustry flows, x_{11}, x_{12}, x_{21}, x_{22}.

Interpreting the three input-output matrices

(1) The transactions matrix is a record of the flow of output between industries and to final use. In the previous chapter we showed the actual flows in terms of the money value of goods shipped. In this chapter we discussed the properties of a theoretical transactions record measured in physical units.

(2) The technology matrix is the collection of technical coefficients of production based on the assumption that the proportions between inputs and outputs would be roughly the same from one year to the next. The coefficients were derived from the transactions matrix by dividing the flow of goods from one industry to another.

Exercise: Using the Blue Book Transactions Matrix compute the five largest technology coefficients for the Paper and Printing industry.

(3) The inverse Leontief matrix, usually called the inverse, tells us how much each industry must produce in order to turn out the bill of final use. A cell in the table is a coefficient (a multiplier) which tells how much the row industry must produce per unit of final use of the column. Stated in money terms, each cell of the inverse matrix shows the value of output required from the industry shown in its row per pound's worth of final use associated with the industry shown in its column. The total output from the row industry is the sum of the products of the final use times the corresponding inverse coefficient.

The difference between the technology and inverse matrices is vital. The technology matrix is the ratio of inputs shipped from rows to columns. The inverse matrix relates total production of the row industry to the final use of industries shown in the column headings. Look at this matter in concrete terms. The CSO (1963) inverse table in money units is called the 'Total requirements, direct and indirect, per £1 of final industrial output'. Read across row 10 representing the Iron and Steel industry to column 17 representing Aerospace Equipment. The entry in this cell formed by the nineteenth row and the seventeenth column is 0·0586. This entry in the inverse table tells us that for every £1 worth of aerospace equipment delivered to final use, Iron and Steel must, directly and indirectly, supply £0·0586 worth of iron and steel. Be sure to understand that the iron and steel are not only sent to aerospace producers. The Aerospace industry requires inputs from other industries which, in turn, require iron and steel inputs. These latter industries require inputs from still other industries, which also require iron and steel. Thus to increase the final product from the Aerospace industry by £1, it is necessary that the Iron and Steel industry increase its output by £0·0586 in order to meet direct and indirect needs. National planners who ignore even small indirect effects are in for big trouble.

Exercise:
(1) Go back to the transactions matrix and trace out the indirect ways in which Aerospace is supplied by Iron and Steel.
(2) Find ten cases in which 'large' cells in the inverse correspond to 'small' cells in the transactions table. In what sort of industries is the difference most marked?
(3) If the final demand for construction increased by 10 per cent what would be the effect on the rest of the economy? Illustrate by computing the output required for the twenty most affected industries. What kind of industries are they?
(4) Suppose the United Kingdom were to cut its military expenditures by 20 per cent. List ten industries whose final use would be most likely to contract. What would the indirect effects be?
(5) Why are the principal diagonals of the transactions matrix empty, but not those of the inverse matrix? What does that tell you about the meaning of output computed by the UK–UN method compared with the US method?
(6) Do people chop down trees with soap? Answer by reference to the appropriate entries in the UK technology and inverse matrices.
(7) Given the following transactions matrix:

Input

Output	*Agriculture*	*Manufacturing*	*Final demand*	*Total output*
Agriculture	25	20	55	100
Manufacturing	14	6	30	50
Household inputs (labour)	80	180		

(*a*) Find the technology matrix.

(b) Find the Leontief or $I - A$ matrix.

(c) Compute how much *ag* and *mfg* would have to produce for y_1 amount of farm products and y_2 amount of manufactured products for final use.

(d) Write down the inverse matrix, $(I - A)^{-1}$.

(e) Compute how much would have to be produced for agriculture to deliver 110 units of final demand, and manufacturing to deliver 60.

(8) Prepare a model report to the government in which you use the inverse input-output table for the UK to explain methods for dealing with the shortage of oil.

(a) Consult the row entitled Mineral Oil Refining. Explain the relationship of total output of this industry to the final uses shown in the column including petrol as a final use of the Mineral Oil Refining industry.

(b) Explain to the government that there are many ways to cope with a 10 per cent reduction in the value of output of this industry. Show that it could be done by reducing the availability of petrol for final use. Show how this could be done by reducing the final use of other products as well. Identify other final uses that might be the most likely candidates for reduction in final use to supplement the petrol reduction program.

(c) Study the final uses of the Mineral Oil industry in the transactions matrix and recommend which components ought to be cut back most. Do the same for the other industries that you thought should be reduced.

Appendix: inverse matrices

Further insight into the nature of the inverse matrix is available if we reconsider the solution of the ordinary equation $y = 3x$ first suggested in the Preface (p. xix). Solving for x, we said, consisted in disengaging the x from the 3 with which it was associated by multiplication. Once having made x stand alone, the solution of x would be whatever was on the other side of the equals sign. Thus we divided – un-multiplied – by 3 to learn that $x = \frac{1}{3}y$ or x equals y times 3 inverted. It was at this point that we suggested that finding the inverse to a matrix consisted in the solution of a system of equations.

Now look back to $y = 3x$. Releasing x from the grips of its coefficient 3 may be understood as multiplying $3x$ by the inverse, $\frac{1}{3}$. Since we must multiply both sides by $\frac{1}{3}$ to preserve the equality we are saying that $\frac{1}{3}y = \frac{1}{3}3x$. All of us were brought up to use the word 'cancel' as the reason for eliminating $\frac{1}{3}$ and 3 from the right hand side; but cancelling only means crossing things out. The point is that $\frac{1}{3}$ times 3 equals the number 1, and 1 times x is x. Thus the solution can be seen as multiplying both sides by the inverse of 3, leading to 1 times x on one side and the solution on the other. 1 is an *identity* number under ordinary multiplication – 1 times anything is the number itself.

The identity element in matrices is the *identity matrix*,[3]

$$I = \begin{bmatrix} 1 & 0 \\ 0 & 1 \end{bmatrix}.$$

The identity matrix applied to another matrix is that matrix itself. To see this we need to know how one matrix is applied to another. This is merely an extension of the way in which a matrix is applied to a column vector, since a matrix can be seen as a collection of column vectors. Thus if we wish to apply the matrix L to the identity matrix I, where L is $\begin{bmatrix} 5 & 3 \\ 2 & 4 \end{bmatrix}$, we write the problem: $LI = \begin{bmatrix} 5 & 3 \\ 2 & 4 \end{bmatrix}\begin{bmatrix} 1 & 0 \\ 0 & 1 \end{bmatrix}$. First we apply L to $\begin{bmatrix} 1 \\ 0 \end{bmatrix}$ to get a first column $\begin{bmatrix} 5 \\ 2 \end{bmatrix}$. Then applying to the second column of I we get $\begin{bmatrix} 3 \\ 4 \end{bmatrix}$. Putting the columns together we again get $LI = \begin{bmatrix} 5 & 3 \\ 2 & 4 \end{bmatrix}$, which is the same as L in this case. Customarily this application of matrices to each other is called *matrix multiplication*, even though it is an amalgam of operations involving multiplication and addition of terms.

Now, multiplication of a matrix by its inverse gives us the identity matrix, just as multiplying an ordinary number by its inverse is unity. This is proven in general in courses in mathematics, but illustration will suffice here. Consider the example on p. xiii of the Preface:

$$\begin{array}{l} 6x + 3y = a \\ 2x - 3y = b \end{array} \quad \text{which can be rewritten} \quad \begin{bmatrix} 6 & 3 \\ 2 & -3 \end{bmatrix}\begin{bmatrix} x \\ y \end{bmatrix} = \begin{bmatrix} a \\ b \end{bmatrix},$$

or, even more compactly, $MX = C$. M is the matrix of coefficients, X is the vector of variables and C is the vector of constants on the right hand side. If we knew M^{-1} then we could apply it to both sides of the equation[4] to get $M^{-1}MX = M^{-1}C$. Since $M^{-1}M = I$, then $IX = M^{-1}C$ or $X = M^{-1}C$. This is a sterile exercise as a means of solving systems of only two equations in two

---

[3] We only show the 2×2 identity matrix, although the size can be made as large as necessary as long as it consists of unity down the principal diagonal and zero everywhere else.

[4] In this sort of multiplication it is important to preserve the order of multiplication by multiplying both sides on the left or both on the right. Unlike ordinary multiplication, the order makes a difference in the result, so that the matrix multiplication of AC is not the same as CA.

unknowns since good old O-level methods will suffice. For large systems rapid computational methods make it possible to find the inverse directly so that one can solve more efficiently. Thus if we knew that the inverse of $\begin{bmatrix} 6 & 3 \\ 2 & -3 \end{bmatrix}$ was $\begin{bmatrix} \frac{1}{8} & \frac{1}{8} \\ \frac{1}{12} & \frac{1}{4} \end{bmatrix}$ we could immediately write down the solution to the previous problem by multiplying both sides of the matrix equation by the inverse:

$$\begin{bmatrix} \frac{1}{8} & \frac{1}{8} \\ \frac{1}{12} & \frac{1}{4} \end{bmatrix} \begin{bmatrix} 6 & 3 \\ 2 & -3 \end{bmatrix} \begin{bmatrix} x \\ y \end{bmatrix} = \begin{bmatrix} \frac{1}{8} & \frac{1}{8} \\ \frac{1}{12} & \frac{1}{4} \end{bmatrix} \begin{bmatrix} a \\ b \end{bmatrix}$$

amounting to:

$$\begin{bmatrix} x \\ y \end{bmatrix} = \begin{bmatrix} \frac{1}{8} & \frac{1}{8} \\ \frac{1}{12} & \frac{1}{4} \end{bmatrix} \begin{bmatrix} a \\ b \end{bmatrix} \quad \text{or} \quad \begin{aligned} x &= \tfrac{1}{8}a + \tfrac{1}{8}b \\ y &= \tfrac{1}{12}a + \tfrac{1}{4}b. \end{aligned}$$

The original problem was a mapping from x and y to a and b. Application of the inverse resulted in the desired mapping from a and b to x and y. Put differently, x and y are solved in terms of a and b. If a and b were given to us as numbers, the numerical value of x and y could be written down at once.

Exercise: Verify that the product of the two matrices on the left equals I.

Now apply this notion to the input-output problem. Originally we had a mapping from total outputs, X, to final uses, Y, $(I-A)Y = X$. We sought to find the inverse relationship from Y to X so that we should know the required outputs. Therefore we multiplied both sides by the inverse of the $I-A$ matrix, namely $(I-A)^{-1}$:

$$(I-A)^{-1}(I-A)X = (I-A)^{-1}Y$$

which became:

$$X = (I-A)^{-1}Y.$$

How did we find the elements of the $(I-A)^{-1}$ matrix? By O-level methods of direct solution of $(I-A)Y = X$ for X. The elements of this matrix were what we so cavalierly labelled as junk, J_{ij}. With many equations, one must resort to more powerful methods, computing the inverse directly from $(I-A)$, but here the economist may feel free to call in the consulting mathematician or computer programmer.

Exercise for the unconvinced:
Carry out the matrix multiplication for the $(I-A)$ matrix in the example with the $(I-A)^{-1}$ found in the text for the two industry example. Verify that the results are the identity matrix subject to error due to rounding.

4 Prices and plans in communist, capitalist and mixed economies

In this chapter we shall study how communist, capitalist and mixed economies go about coordinating their efforts to achieve their society's desired final use. We shall discover that the methods of coordination differ, as do the means for deciding upon the final use. Nonetheless we shall find a greater core of common problems in achieving the goals of final use than political ideology would suggest. By expounding each system in turn, and then subjecting it to criticism, we shall learn something of their strengths and weaknesses.

The planned economy: the Soviet Union

Working through the stages of input-output analysis, we have actually been grappling with the problem of how to coordinate the activities of the teeming number of firms, industries and consumers that make up a national economy. We have seen how each industry affects all the others, and is itself affected by them. Yet, whatever means society employs to coordinate the industries, the solution must be the one prescribed by the inverse matrix.

How is this to be done as a practical matter? Unclouded by ideological issues, common sense might well suggest the communist solution of total planning: let government economists and engineers give direct instructions to the firms and industries. With computers, slide rules and sharp pencils, they might construct an input-output table and issue directives accordingly. Such complete central planning in physical terms would be an extreme form of the method of coordination practised in countries such as the Soviet Union.

The opposite of central planning is a market system in which goods are bought and sold according to prices determined by supply and demand. For the market method to work, the prices would have to amount to a system of signals and incentives that directed individuals and businesses toward the inverse solution. Although there is some experimentation with the market mechanism in communist countries, by and large the market system is associated with capitalism in which the factors of production are privately owned. Individuals have to be induced to use their own resources in a certain way rather than ordered to do so.

In the early years of the Soviet Union intense debates raged about the nature and direction of planning in the new economy. Karl Marx has said little on the subject even while condemning the 'anarchy of production' which he asserted characterized capitalism. Marx was convinced that public ownership and central planning were better than allowing the capitalist market to choose the final use and regulate the interindustry distribution of products.

The years after the Bolshevik revolution in 1917 were characterized by continuous warfare. Civil war broke out immediately. Inevitably under the circumstances, coordination of the flow of goods and services to military and civilian uses was carried out by direct command of the authorities. The priorities of society and their implementation were dominated by military considerations. This period became known as the era of *war communism*.

At the close of hostilities in 1920, the economy of the USSR was in a state of collapse. In addition to the physical destruction, the disruption of mechanisms for coordinating production and distribution interfered with the use of such resources as were available. To meet the situation, Lenin proposed the New Economic Policy under which small-scale production, farming, trade and commerce were returned to private enterprise. To be sure, Lenin argued, the economic 'commanding heights' were to remain solidly in government hands; large factories, banks and international trade remained public monopolies. Under the existing conditions, Lenin contended, the market system and money incentives constituted the only practical coordinating device available.

It is a matter of some debate whether Lenin meant the NEP to be a permanent feature of the Soviet economy or only a passing phase until central planning could be instituted. In the event, Lenin was succeeded by Stalin who instituted the directly planned economy with the first five-year plan in 1928. Industry and commerce returned completely to government hands. Goods were produced according to directive and sold to firms and to the public at established prices. Only agriculture retained a trace of institutions of private property. By a combination of incentives, propaganda and coercion, peasants' holdings of land were amalgamated into large *collective farms*. In addition, the Soviets operate large farms owned and directed by the government.

Stalin's critics in the Soviet Union argued that a plan originating from Moscow could not succeed. Their life expectancy was short. Western economists such as F. A. Hayek[1] maintained that in order to plan an economy from a single centre, it would be necessary to do an impossible statistical job. All the supply and demand curves for all the goods and services would have to be statistically estimated, and then solved simultaneously. Otherwise the plan would be internally inconsistent. An inconsistent plan would mean shortages of some goods and useless surpluses of others. They held that starvation and waste would be the natural result of any arrangement other than the market mechanism.

Economists more sympathetic to the Soviet experiment, such as the late Oskar Lange, proposed schemes whereby prices and outputs of factories would be regulated by rules which in effect simulated the capitalist market solution to the coordination problem.[2] At the same time, they insisted, industrial property could be held in public hands so that the growth decisions could be made by public authority rather than private persons. Lange was promptly damned by his conservative colleagues as a communist, and excoriated by the communists for advocating unplanned capitalist 'anaemic socialism' and 'anarchy of production'.

Although marred by some glaring examples of waste and inefficiency, the five-year plans of the USSR held together surprisingly well in spite of the maledictions of Hayek and the ignored friendly advice of Lange. How did the Russians manage to solve the coordination problem?

The five-year plans in the USSR are constructed by the *method of material balances*. This is neither a market nor an input-output technique. The Soviet central planning authorities first suggest a set of production goals. These are essentially estimates based on desired final use for the future years tempered by past experience with the amount of total output required to produce them. Tentative production targets then are passed down to the district and local industry administrations, and on to factories and their managers. These lower echelons of industry reply by 'criticizing' the plan. In effect their comments help to specify the inputs they would need to fulfil the plan. The plan is revised in light of the criticism and local needs and sent down the chain of authority again. The procedure is repeated several times until the authorities are convinced that the plan is workable.

---

[1] F. A. Hayek, *Collectivist Economic Planning* (1935).
[2] O. R. Lange and F. M. Taylor, *On the Economic Theory of Socialism* (1938).

Undoubtedly the reader can now see why all the predictions of chaos were wrong. Each time the plan is submitted for revision, the firms and industries reply with their inputs, expenses they would need to cover. On a vast scale, the USSR is operating like the individual firm which gropes toward the sales needed to meet its profit target by adding a geometric series of corrections to meet the expenses it incurs. Of course, the Soviet problem is more complicated since they have to plan the corrections for each industry in light of interindustry use expenses. In effect, they are successively applying the A matrix of technical coefficients to proposed final use, just as the firm repeatedly multiplied profits by the a coefficient and summed. Starting with the first proposal for final use, the A matrix is being applied again and again. The method of material balances amounts to what is called an *iterated* solution to the inversion of the $I - A$ matrix. That is, each circulation of the proposed plan brings it closer and closer to convergence to the consistent inverse set of outputs. A discussion of the mathematics of iterated methods of inversion is given as an appendix to this chapter.

In practice, the Soviet Union uses the material balances procedure to grope toward the solution of the inverse Leontief matrix.[3] In principle, there can be no objection to this procedure. One practical disadvantage is that there are only a limited number of corrective rounds possible in the available time. Inevitably, there will be a discrepancy between the plan and the correct inverse. Nevertheless, since a great deal of the error disappears after the first few corrections the inconsistency may not always be unbearably large. Inevitably there are situations in which 'crash programmes' have to be instituted to make up for an inconsistent plan. Suddenly there is not enough capacity in the chemical industry to make the fertilizers to make the expanded agricultural production needed to supply raw material to manufacturing industries. Stalin put this in positive terms by saying that the bottleneck industry was the 'link in the chain' that had to be seized in order to move the whole chain along. Critics of such heroic efforts have been less charitable of inconsistencies.

Another problem with the centralized method of material balances is that the actual requirements of each firm and industry are not identical with what the factory managers say they are. For one thing, the managers cannot know exactly what inputs they will need to fulfil the plan. Furthermore, industrial executives have a chronic and human tendency to overstate the inputs they need and minimize the output they promise to produce. If they exceed the promised output or use less of the inputs allotted, the manager is praised as a hero and awarded accordingly. He has 'overfulfilled the plan'. Of course, one must not overdo this sort of thing lest the plan targets are raised next

[3] J. M. Montias, 'Planning with material balances in Soviet type economies', *American Economic Review* (December 1959).

year. In order to be able to continue to be a hero year in and year out one must not be too much of a hero this year. The repeated corrections take on something of a bargaining character. Managers seek the maximum leeway in taking on plan obligations while the authorities try to whittle down on inputs and boost output targets.

Now that Stalin is dead, why have not the Soviets simply planned directly by inverting the Leontief matrix on a computer and be done with the clumsy old method. As a matter of fact, Soviet planners have been impressed with input-output and have started to use it. They have not adopted it as their main planning tool. This is partly because old ideas die slowly. Much more important is that the Hayek objection to central planning does have some validity. Even the best matrix cannot possibly take into account local and changing conditions, even if it were a marvellously complex document. The reader certainly must feel that the United Kingdom table is complex enough, yet it has grouped all the industries of the country into thirty-five or so coarse categories, when actually each industry is composed of many firms producing many different products. Finer tuning requires decentralized decision making.

The fundamental theorem of economics

No matter how much Soviet planners distrust market prices and money transactions, they have not tried to run their country completely without them since the desperate days of war communism. For even the best and most finely detailed material plan must add up quantities of things which are physically different: even nuts and bolts come in a bewildering array of sizes, shapes, materials and screw threads; the same objects are produced at different places and times, satisfy different wants. All of these detailed dimensions of material production simply cannot be included in the plan. Planners simply must find a common unit.

Could the unit be weight in tons? The tale is told of a quota in tons established for a Soviet nail factory. The ingenious manager promptly overfulfilled his plan with a single enormous nail. The story is certainly a myth, but the principle is important. Could the common unit be labour employed? If so, then the wasteful factory which uses up the most work time will be rated the best. That will not do either. Prices related to the real cost of production are needed in order to accomplish the 'accounting and control' with which Soviet planners are always rightly concerned. Money revenues from sales have to be examined, and money budgets have to be allocated to the firms as well as supplies of certain specific inputs.

Meaningful control of budgets requires the meaningful calculation of the costs of production. In turn cost control requires that the prices of the inputs into industries be rationally calculated. There is a chicken and egg aspect to a cost of production method of pricing. What is the cost of production? The costs of the goods going into production! Correct pricing must start somewhere. But where?

The Soviet consumer also uses prices. He must decide what to buy and what to forgo. He can't have everyting, so prices will determine what he buys. If these prices do not reflect the true costs of production, people will be buying too much of goods which are really costly to manufacture and which should have a high price. At the same time, they will be deterred from taking goods which ought to be attractively priced.

On one hand Soviet planners are anxious to produce proposed final use, working toward the inverse of the $I - A$ matrix in their method of balances. On the other hand they find themselves groping toward a set of prices that are consistent with the expenses of production. Can these both be accomplished at the same time? The vital point which we shall now explore is that the same technical considerations leading to the consistent planning of production implies a set of prices that consistently match the costs of production. Conversely, if the planners adopted the proper prices and sold their goods on the open market to other firms and consumers, the result would be the same as if they directly allocated production according to the inverse Leontief matrix. For every society the way in which the scarce primary inputs are used in the industries determines a set of relative values for the final goods turned out. There is no avoiding of prices even in a command economy directly planning production. In later chapters we shall spell out the converse: the prices arrived at by a capitalist market economy cannot avoid amounting to a means of direction of output and consumption.

We have come to the fundamental theorem of economics: *The allocation of scarce primary inputs to alternative final goals implies a system of relative prices.* In view of the fact that there is a limited amount of primary input available for productive use, no society can have as much as it could want of every possible final use. Therefore, a choice must be made among alternative bills of final goods which it is feasible to produce. But the amount of one good that must be given up in order to get another means the relative price of the two goods. So many tomatoes are worth one chicken, because in order to grow more tomatoes on a farm, less labour and other factors of production are available for chickens. It is that simple. The amount of one good given up measures the price of another good obtained.

Of course the prices involved are relative prices: one chicken is worth so many tomatoes, not so many pence. In Chapter 12 we shall translate relative prices into familiar money prices, but the main point will not be affected. The underlying idea is simply that there is no Father Christmas who has unlimited toys to give good little girls and boys. Alas, to get more of a good produced with scarce inputs it is necessary to give up others which might have been manufactured. The ratio at which the choice is made is the relative price of the goods.

Society as well as chicken farmers has to choose among alternative final uses which are feasible to produce. The distinction between a feasible and infeasible bill of final use is whether sufficient primary input is available to provide both the intermediate and final use it requires. For simplicity, let us continue to assume that labour is the only primary input (in Chapter 5 we will deal with the more complicated cases where there are many scarce primary inputs such as land and capital). A bill of final use can be produced if it does not call for any more labour for direct or indirect purposes than is available.

This condition can be expressed by continuing our earlier analysis of planning production. Recall that the inverse equations for determining outputs from final use were:

$$X = (I - A)^{-1} Y \qquad \qquad X_1 = 1 \cdot 72 y_1 + 0 \cdot 62 y_2$$

or

$$X_1 = J_{11} y_1 + J_{12} y_2 \qquad X_2 = 1 \cdot 72 y_1 + 2 \cdot 59 y_2$$
$$X_2 = J_{21} y_1 + J_{22} y_2$$

How much labour is required to produce X_1 and X_2? The labour used in each industry is its output times labour required per unit output. Thus we must multiply each X_j by the appropriate labour coefficient, l_j, to get b_j, the amount of labour for each industry ($b_j = l_j X_j$).

$$b_1 = l_2 X_1 \qquad b_1 = 0 \cdot 20 X_1$$
$$b_2 = l_2 X_2 \qquad b_2 = 0 \cdot 15 X_2$$

To express the labour absorbed in each industry in terms of the two final uses, we need only multiply the rows in the inverse equation by the proper labour coefficient. The left hand side of each equation becomes the labour used up to produce the total outputs of that industry. The right hand side is also the labour consumed, but expressed in terms of the final uses.

$$b_1 = l_1 X_1 = l_1 J_{11} y_1 + l_1 J_{12} y_2 \qquad b_1 = (0 \cdot 20)(1 \cdot 72) y_1 + (0 \cdot 20)(0 \cdot 62) y_2$$
$$b_2 = l_2 X_2 = l_2 J_{21} y_1 + l_2 J_{22} y_2 \qquad b_2 = (0 \cdot 15)(1 \cdot 72) y_1 + (0 \cdot 15)(2 \cdot 59) y_2$$

Carrying out the arithmetic indicated:

$$b_1 = 0 \cdot 34 y_1 + 0 \cdot 12 y_2$$
$$b_2 = 0 \cdot 26 y_1 + 0 \cdot 39 y_2$$

We now have the amount of labour directly and indirectly required by each industry to produce final uses y_1 and y_2.

Obligatory exercise: Suppose $y_1 = 150$ and $y_2 = 300$. How much labour will be needed by industry 1? By industry 2? Why must the labour employed in industry 1 depend on the final use of both industries?

To find out how much labour is needed by the whole system, all we need do is to sum the labour at work in each industry. The total labour that must be employed to meet the bill of final use is $b_1 + b_2 = B$. Adding up each side in the previous pair of equations and collecting the coefficients of y_1 and y_2 in parentheses we have:

$$B = b_1 + b_2 \quad \mid \quad B = (0{\cdot}34 + 0{\cdot}26)y_1 + (0{\cdot}12 + 0{\cdot}39)y_2$$

$$B = (l_1 J_{11} + l_2 J_{21})y_1 + (l_1 J_{12} + l_2 J_{22})y_2 \quad \mid \quad B = 0{\cdot}60y_1 + 0{\cdot}51y_2$$

This is a very important relationship because it presents us squarely with the limits to feasible programmes of final use; it is called the *production possibility frontier*. Let the planning authorities specify the final use they wish to accomplish, y_1 and y_2. Then we, as economists, calculate how much labour is required to accomplish the goals. We are therefore able to determine whether the goals of final use are feasible or impossible. If there is not enough primary input, then the goal is not feasible. Full stop! All the shouting and storming, all the political power in the world, all the ideological exhortation and great leaps forward cannot make an infeasible plan possible.

Once having accepted this reality, we define the options actually open to planners. They can have more of y_1 by producing less of y_2. They can substitute more of one final use for less of another, but only those combinations of final uses are feasible that do not need more labour than is available. One must choose.

Now let us avoid writing the equation of the production possibility frontier in such an awkward many-jointed way. Instead, call all the messy stuff in the two parentheses T_1 and T_2 respectively. The production possibility frontier simply becomes a linear equation:

$$B = T_1 y_1 + T_2 y_2 \quad \mid \quad B = 0{\cdot}60y_1 + 0{\cdot}51y_2$$

T_1 represents the labour directly and indirectly required in both industries for one unit of final use 1; T_2 is the labour directly and indirectly needed for a unit of final use 2.

A graph of the production possibility frontier will show us how much of y_1 we can produce for any specified y_2. In the following numerical example let B, the amount of labour, be 50 man-hours. To graph, put the equation in slope-intercept form with, say, y_1 as the dependent variable:

$$B = T_1 y_1 + T_2 y_2 \qquad\qquad B = 50$$

$$T_1 y_1 = -T_2 y_2 + B \qquad\qquad 50 = 0 \cdot 60 y_1 + 0 \cdot 51 y_2$$

$$y_1 = -\frac{T_2}{T_1} y_2 + \frac{B}{T_1} \qquad\qquad 0 \cdot 60 y_1 = -0 \cdot 51 y_2 + 50$$

$$y_1 = -\frac{0 \cdot 51}{0 \cdot 60} y_2 + \frac{50}{0 \cdot 60}$$

$$y_1 = -0 \cdot 85 y_2 + 83 \cdot 33.$$

The result is the straight line frontier pictured in Figure 4.1. If the final use of y_2 were zero, the line would intercept the vertical y_1 axis at the point B/T_1. The vertical intercept in our numerical example is 83.33. Its significance is easy to see if we recall that T_1 is the amount of labour directly and indirectly required for a unit of final use 1. If all the labour is going to be directed at producing only y_1, the amount of it released to final use will be the total labour force divided by T_1, the amount of labour needed directly and indirectly for one unit of final use 1. If no y_2 is to be left over for final use, we can use 50 units of labour to make 83.33 units of y_1.

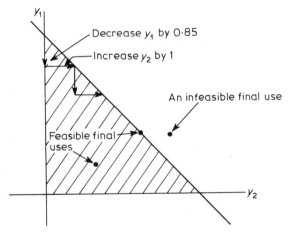

Figure 4.1   Production possibility frontier

The slope of the line is $-T_2/T_1$. In the example, it is $-0 \cdot 85$. The slope is negative, because if y_2 is increased by 1 unit, then y_2 must be decreased by $0 \cdot 85$. There is only so much labour available; if more of it is to be devoted to y_2, less is available for y_1.

Exercise:
(1) What is the final output of y_1 in the numerical illustration if y_2 is increased from zero to 1? What would it be if y_2 were increased one unit further? Suppose y_2 were 10 units?
(2) What is the maximum number of units of y_2 that could be produced? Express your answer numerically, in general algebraic terms, and on the graph.
(3) Why must T_1, T_2 and B all be positive numbers? Why is this consideration essential for our belief that the frontier has a negative slope and a positive intercept?
(4) If final use $y_2 = 0$, does it follow that $X_2 = 0$?
(5) Express the frontier with y_2 as the dependent variable.

The production possibility frontier divides the space that represents all the conceivable final uses into the feasible and the impossible. Any point on or within the shaded triangle bounding the frontier is a feasible final use. A point located beyond the frontier requires more labour than exists. The points on the line are combinations of final uses for which all the labour is employed. Attempts to produce beyond the frontier can result only in an excessive demand for labour. Within the frontier there is an excess supply of unemployed labour which could be used to provide further final product. The only efficient points from the point of view of the planners are those that lie on the frontier, where society gets the most that is possible. On earth we live with scarcity as well as sin, and one must choose in order to make the best of the situation.

The frontier tells us more. It is possible, as we have said, to move to different points along the negatively sloped boundary. The slope of the line tells the planners how much of y_1 they must sacrifice in order to be able to manufacture another unit of y_2. The ratio between the increase in one and the decrease in the other is the rate at which planners are mentally trading y_2 for y_1. To be sure, there is no market in sight, but this ratio is a price nonetheless.

In our example, one additional unit of y_2 requires that $0 \cdot 85$ units of y_1 be foregone anywhere along the frontier. That means that y_2 costs society only 85 per cent as much as y_1. The price of commodity 2 is $0 \cdot 85$ times the price of commodity 1. If we designate the prices by p_1 and p_2, then $p_2/p_1 = 0 \cdot 85$. The relative price of p_2 is also the slope of the production possibility frontier. In general, $p_2/p_1 = T_2/T_1$. The ratio of prices holds regardless of the money units which might be involved in particular economic systems. If commodity 1 is worth £1, then commodity 2 is worth 85p; alternatively, if good 1 sold for £2, then good 2 would go for £1·70.

Exercise: 1 apple = 2 bananas. What is the price of apples compared to bananas? What is the price of bananas compared to apples?

This is the fundamental theorem of economics at work. The slope of the production possibility frontier is the relative price of commodity 2, in terms of commodity 1. The scarcity of labour makes it necessary to choose between the two commodities, and the technical conditions of production combined, as we have discussed, determine the ratio at which the choice is to be made. Economists call such prices *shadow prices* to indicate that they are coercive realities operative behind the scenes in every situation involving choice, regardless of social arrangement. Surprising as it may seem at first, *real costs* involve the ratio of goods – how much of one final use one good is given up for another. Prices stated as amounts of money are more superficial: they are convenient ways of expressing the underlying ratio in many (not all) societies (see Chapter 12 for a discussion of money).

Soviet growth and efficiency

It now should be evident to the reader that planners have a lot less control over their situation than even unlimited political power suggests. Certainly the Soviet authorities have the power to decree official prices. Yet if these are different from the shadow prices, they will not work. Prices are the basis for decision making, for accounting and control, and evaluation of performance by firms, farms and households. They are the signals to which individuals and enterprises respond. If they are the wrong signals – if they do not reflect real costs – they will elicit the wrong response. The result is wasted effort: shortages of some goods and surplus of others. Consumers buy those goods with artificially low prices; firms operate at a loss, and nobody knows whether they are more or less efficient than those showing a profit; engineers are unable to choose between alternative techniques of production since the low cost operation at official prices might be the high cost method at the proper shadow prices; and the international foreign trade programme becomes national, since it is impossible to determine which items ought to be produced internally and which imported from abroad.

The theory we have developed has shown us the shadow prices the Soviet authorities ought to make official. Their practical problem is discovering them from existing input-output tables, which is not so easy. First of all the tables deal with coarsely defined industries, so they are plagued by the same sort of problem in pricing that they are in direct planning of output.

Secondly, most input-output tables are in money terms rather than the physical units. To use the theoretical model developed in this chapter with money data, they would have to presume that the official prices are correct shadow prices. Put somewhat differently, the very power of the Soviet authorities to make arbitrary price decrees serves to make their decrees arbitrary. The prime example is agriculture, where low prices for collective farm produce resulted in disastrously low agricultural outputs, under-estimation of the need for such inputs as chemical fertilizers, and the like. The result has been that agriculture has been a bottleneck in the whole development programme of the country.

The power of Soviet planning has not come from superior coordination of activities, but the control that the central authorities have over final use. In particular, they have control over how much will be allocated to consumption and how much to investment in additional capital. Soviet investment accounted for only 8 per cent of GNP in 1928, but increased to 21 per cent in the 1930s and since the 1950s has been at a phenomenal rate of 31 per cent.

Query: Find comparable figures for the United Kingdom, United States, Japan and Nigeria.

The result was extremely limited supplies of consumer goods, such as are produced in the Final Non-Metal industries. Much effort was devoted to producing equipment for the supporting Final Metal, Basic Metal and Energy industries. The bias of Soviet planning was toward the earlier stages in the production pipeline. Communist leaders insisted on producing heavy machinery, such as are found in the basic lower rows of the Final Metal sector. They put off the manufacture of equipment for light industry which is closer to the production of consumer goods.

In the backward state of Soviet technology at the start, the shadow price of investment goods compared to consumption final uses was very high indeed. Stalin's decision to invest massively in capital implied privation for many and starvation for some, especially at the early stages. It is questionable whether the individual Soviet citizen would have been willing to make the same decision. But it was not up to him. Stalin made the choice, for better or worse. Great strides were made in Soviet output. Over the thirty-eight year period between 1928 and 1966, Western economists such as Raymond Powell estimate the growth in Soviet GNP to be between 5·4 and 6·7 per cent.[4] This is smaller than the Soviet claim of 9·2 per cent, but still impressive; over the same period the United States economy growth has averaged 3·3 per cent per year.

[4] R. P. Powell, 'Economic growth in the USSR', *Scientific American* (December 1968), p. 22.

In addition to massive accumulation of capital, Soviet economic growth was achieved by more and better labour, and by increased use of natural resources. During the period up to 1966 the Soviet labour force grew at twice the growth in population. Labour was moved from rural areas to industrial labour in the city factories. Furthermore, the Soviet government instituted very intensive programmes of education at all levels. The Russian worker laboured harder and more skilfully. Powell estimates that very roughly this contributed 2·8 per cent per year. The opening up of a new farm and timber land, and exploitation of natural mineral, and other resources resulted in about a 1·6 per cent increase in output per year.

Including the increase in all three factors of production – capital, labour and natural resources – Powell estimates that the increase in inputs accounted for between 3·5 and 4·3 per cent of the average annual growth in Soviet output. He concludes that 'the growth of resources would appear to account for somewhere between one-half and four-fifths of the GNP growth.' The balance of the Soviet growth was made as a result of increased productivity.

In the language of the current Soviet five-year plan, the past growth was achieved by 'extensive' rather than 'intensive' efforts. While there certainly were impressive gains in the productivity of each factor of production as modern technology was adopted, 'catching up' with the already industrialized nations, the main source of the growth was simply more primary input. The considerations of efficiency and consistency of plan which are emphasized in this chapter were given second place, and overridden by sheer effort and sacrifice.

Now the Soviets face a new era in which the opportunities for extensive growth are sharply limited, and the issues we have raised apply with new force as the growth rate slows down dramatically. Table 4.1 tells the story.

While there is disagreement as to the magnitude of the growth of national income, it is clearly declining. The reasons are plain:

(1) The pace of accumulation of new capital is slowing, partly as a result of the slowing in the growth of national income from which investment comes. Partly investment is declining because the Soviet citizens are insisting on higher levels of consumption. The new five-year plan places new emphasis on consumer goods, at least in part because it is realized that workers need a 'material incentive', and that after fifty years ideological commitment and centralized power is not sufficient to engender the desired effort on the part of individuals.

(2) The increase in the labour force is declining. It is already down to 1·7 per cent, and the forecast is for a rate of 1·2 per cent growth in employment in the 1970s. The movement from rural to urban society is largely completed, so that those farm family members formerly not included in the

Table 4.1   Selected economic indicators for the USSR 1950–75
(average annual rates of growth, in per cent)

	1950–8	1958–67	1967–70	1970–5 (planned)
National income, Soviet official data	10·9	7·2	7·3	6·7
GNP, Cohn calculations	6·4	5·3	3·4	n.a.
Capital investment, Soviet official data	12.9	7.6	7.5	6.7
Gross investment, fixed capital, Moorsteen-Powell calculations	11.4	6.9	n.a.	n.a.
Gross investment, Moorsteen-Powell calculations	12.2	6.1	n.a.	n.a.
Fixed capital stock including livestock, Soviet official data	8·3	8·3	7·5	n.a.
Net fixed capital stock, Moorsteen-Powell calculations	10·0	9·4	n.a.	n.a.
Net capital stock, Moorsteen-Powell calculations	9·0	9·0	n.a.	n.a.
Employment, Feshbach calculations	1·8	1·7	1·7	n.a.
Total input of capital and labour	4·6	4·6	n.a.	n.a.
Factor productivity (GNP per unit of labour and capital)	1·7	0·7	n.a.	n.a.

Source: Abram Bergson, 'Toward a new growth model', *Problems of Communism* (March–April 1973), p. 3.

labour force have now been moved into it. Female workers have already been integrated into the work force. Like all other nations, as its GNP grows, the Soviet Union has experienced a decline in the growth of population. This process has been accelerated by the high female labour force participation.

(3) Although the possibilities remain for exploitation of natural resources, it is important to see that these require substantial amounts of capital and labour. It is one thing to say that 70 per cent of the Soviet coal reserves lie untapped in Siberia, and it is another to supply the capital and skilled labour to dig it out from beneath the tundra. The energetic efforts made by Soviet officials to involve other nations – Japan, Germany and the United States – in supplying capital for this purpose are testimony to the seriousness of the problem.

The only remaining source of growth is increased 'factor productivity' – intensive growth. This has been declining, as the cumbersome planning mechanism, irrational pricing and inadequate material incentive to labour take their toll. Factor productivity has declined from 1·7 per cent in the period 1950–8 to 0·7 per cent in 1958–67.

Stalin's emphasis on capital as the main source of productivity gains may have been misguided. The triangular transactions matrices of developed industrial countries gives us an important insight into the problem. The emphasis was, as we have said, on developing the Basic Metal and Final Metal industries, since these were thought to be the industries that supported all the others. The table shows that these industries that have taken up so much of Soviet capital and manpower are actually supported by the Basic Non-Metal industries. A glance at the list of industries in this category shows up the sector which gave the Russians so much difficulty: agriculture, livestock, forestry, chemicals and chemical fertilizers. The Soviets were preoccupied excessively with iron hardware. Insufficient attention was also paid to the Final Non-Metal industries making consumer goods because they both were 'light industry' and did not appear to be the kind of capital using sectors that Marx associated with increased productivity. The transactions matrix triangle shows us that the distinction between light and heavy industry is misleading. What is important is not the degree to which an industry uses capital in imposing quantities, but its stage in the production triangle.

The difficulty faced by a centrally planned economy is in planning its outputs in a consistent way, in evaluating its alternatives at meaningful prices, and providing adequate incentives to its work force. It remains to be seen whether the Soviets will find a way out of their dilemma. Certainly strenuous efforts are now being made to introduce more detailed input-output studies, including attempts to record physical rather than money flows. Still at a very abstract level, Soviet mathematicians and economists are discussing improved methods of planning with wider use of computers and mathematical techniques. Sporadically, attempts are made to 'reform' prices and decentralize planning procedures so as to leave greater flexibility at the enterprise level. This tendency has been more marked in the other communist countries but is also at work in the USSR. Foreign trade is becoming more important and more attuned to the world market economy. It remains to be seen how effective this combination of efforts will be in rationalizing the present Soviet difficulties within the structure of their social system.

Exercise:
(1) In the example in the text suppose there is a different set of labour coefficients: $l_1 = 0.50$, $l_2 = 0.10$.
  (a) Recalculate the amount of labour required directly and indirectly to fulfil bill of final use in a production possibility frontier. Let the amount of labour available be called B. Suppose B equals 50 man-hours. Graph the production possibility frontier. Now, let B equal 70 and graph. What can be said about these two graphs and the shadow prices they reveal?

(b) Suppose y_1 were final use of capital goods and y_2 were consumer goods. Interpret the meaning of the relative prices in terms of strategies for growth.

(2) State the fundamental theorem of economics in your own words as you might to someone who has not studied economics. Can you describe an economic situation in which this theorem might not apply?

(3) What do you think the Soviet Union and the rest of the world would be like if Lenin's New Economic Policy were the permanent model for the economy of the USSR? Was Stalin necessary?

Review the Industrial Revolution in Great Britain and show in what ways it was similar to and different from the Soviet pattern of industrialization.

(4) Consider Table 4.2 below of the sources of economic growth in the United Kingdom. Compare growth in the UK and USSR at the present time.

Table 4.2   Sources of growth of national income in the United Kingdom 1950–62

Source national income			National income per person employed	
Contribution to rate of growth		Per cent of total growth	Contribution to rate of growth	Per cent of total growth
Adjusted national income*	2·38	100	1·72	100
Total factor input:	1·11	47	0·45	26
Labour	0·60	25	0·10	·6
Capital	0·51	21	0·37	22
Land	0·00	0	−0·02	−1
Adjusted output per unit of input:*	1·27	53	1·27	74
Advance of knowledge	0·76	32	0·75	44
Change in lag in application of knowledge	0·03	1	0·04	2
Improved allocation of resources	0·12	5	0·12	7
Economies of large scale	0·36	15	0·36	21

* Excludes effects of irregularities in pressure of demand on output per unit of input.
Source: Adapted from E. F. Denison, assisted by Jean-Poullier, *Why Growth Rates Differ, Postwar Experience in Nine Western Countries*, pp. 314–15 (© 1967 Brookings Institution, Washington, DC).

Optional exercise:

Consider the production possibility frontier for three final uses $B = T_1y_1 + T_2y_2 + T_3y_3$. Suppose $T_1 = 2$, $T_2 = 3$, $T_3 = 6$. Derive the shadow prices between y_1 and y_2, and y_2 and y_3, and for y_1 and y_3. (*Hint:* this can be done by transposing the final use not involved on the LHS along with B). Draw the frontier as a plane on three dimensions. Explain how any number of goods can be involved by this calculation of shadow prices.

The rise of the unplanned economy

The Soviet Union is not the world's first planned economy. Before the Renaissance it was unthinkable that any human activity could operate without conscious direction. The nobility directed the lives of the peasants and also appropriated much of the peasant production in the form of taxes, rents and church tithes. It seemed that this was as it ought to be in a society built on the legal obligations of the social classes.

The growth of trade exerted a corrosive effect on the traditional economy. Everything had a price. Merchants had to be paid. All the battle axes, inquisitions and torture racks could not manufacture the goods brought by traders. Yet even the mercantilist mind still was affected with the need for planning and control. Trading companies were certain that their profits depended on monopoly privileges to sell in a restricted, captive market at high prices. The mercantilist view boiled down to two basic beliefs: first the gains of one business or nation must be at the expense of others; second, governments must direct and protect the economy in order to insure that the gains did not go elsewhere.

In 1776 these views were challenged in a remarkable book by an eccentric Scottish professor of moral philosophy, Adam Smith. In *The Wealth of Nations*, he applied the radical notions of the Enlightenment that the world ran by itself according to natural law. Smith denied that economic affairs needed constant regulation. Governmental planning and control hindered the automatic, self-directing tendency toward maximum economic growth. Monopolistic privileges served only special interests and did not increase the total national wealth. They lowered the standard of living, slowed the accumulation of capital, and weakened the strength of countries that adopted such policies. Smith's work was the economic counterpart of the political thinkers who argued that freedom was the 'natural state' of man. Governments were designed solely to protect this freedom. The fact that the *Declaration of Independence* and *The Wealth of Nations* both appeared in 1776 is far from coincidence.

What is to insure order in a society of people free to pursue their own self-interest? Smith answered in one word: *competition*. Should a firm become inefficient or charge higher prices than necessary, it faces the ultimate penalty – economic death! Standing ready in the wings were new businessmen, ready to take the place of those who faltered, or who attempted to exploit the public. It was competition that led to efficiency and ultimately to the benefit of all. Greater harmony was achieved than if society were directed by a benevolent monarch. In a famous passage, Smith decried the hypocrisy of those who 'feign to trade for the public good'. The businessman who is frankly out for the biggest profit in a competitive society serves the public best. In a famous phrase, the self-seeking individual was said to act as if led by an 'invisible hand' to achieve a result 'that was no part of his intention'.

Smith saw that an increase in productivity was the result of *division of labour*. As he concentrated on a limited set of operations each worker became more skilled at his job. Capital equipment evolved into specialized machinery and, like labour, was directed toward occupations for which it was best suited. Moreover, the division of labour in the factory was a miniature of the division of labour in society where each man, parcel of land or piece of equipment is used to produce a specialized product.

Greater division of labour will mean greater productivity. Yet if people specialized where would they get the goods and services they need but do not produce themselves? The *market mechanism* permits the exchange of products. Each specialized person works to the best of his ability, directed by competition. He exchanges with others who are similarly specialized. The market is the coordinating device and replaces the planner.

No wonder Smith denounced the mercantilists for obstructing economic growth. Growth occurs as a result of the division of labour and, Smith insisted, the division of labour is limited only by the extent of the market. By interfering with the working of the competitive market, government direction only served to reduce the real wealth of nations. Government policy, Smith concluded, should restrict itself to such obviously public functions as enforcing the law and providing for defence, and should otherwise leave the economy alone. *Laissez-faire, laissez-passer.* We shall take a hard look at Smith's view after we have analysed prices under such a regime.

Exercise:
(1) Explain how the triangular transactions matrix reflects the division of labour in industrialized countries. Describe the degree of division of labour in underdeveloped countries.
(2) Compare the argument for free political institutions with Smith's argument for *laissez-faire*. Is there a political equivalent of a hidden hand of competition?

(3) Are there drawbacks as well as advantages to unlimited competition? Explain. Offer alternatives to competition and weigh their costs and benefits. Evaluate Britain's entry into the Common Market in terms of the greater division of labour and competition it might provide.

Prices and competitive capitalism

Adam Smith claimed that his unplanned capitalist society worked perfectly through perfect competition. But when we try to define perfect competition in a precise way, we are led to conditions so exacting that it is questionable whether any society has ever achieved it. Nevertheless, we shall first examine the properties of this ideal. Then, just as we did in the case of a planned communist society, we shall examine the degree to which actual capitalist societies fall short of the ideal.

The conditions for perfect competition are:

(1) Each industry consists of a very large number of firms, none of which is large enough to plan its profitability in terms of altering the market price of its product. Unlike a monopoly a minor firm cannot measurably raise the price of its product by restricting the amount of goods it offers to sell. Firms in perfect competition are *price takers*, not price makers. They must accept the market prices as beyond their control, given by forces of supply and demand.

(2) Buyers and sellers have perfect knowledge of the nature of goods and factors of production. In particular, everybody knows the prices of these goods, so that identical goods sell at the *same price* everywhere, except for transportation costs. At any point in space and time each good sells at only one price.

(3) There are no barriers to firms entering or leaving an industry in search of profit. Neither monopolistic power nor government regulation interferes with this self-seeking process. Hence there is an equal rate of return in all industries when adjusted for degrees of riskiness. Workers and owners of other resources are free to switch their employment, so that the return to each factor is equalized.

(4) The product of each firm in an industry is identical with that of its competitors; we exclude degrees of monopoly which a firm might achieve by making its product slightly different from others.

In Part 2 we shall see how these conditions serve to determine what and how each firm will produce. We will study the equilibrium of the firm as it fits into the larger equilibrating process of supply and demand. At this point we are not so much concerned with the process of attaining equilibrium as with the features of consistency which competitive industries must achieve as a result of the balance of market forces.

Whilst each firm is out for the maximum profits, and hence always tries to get the highest prices for its goods at equilibrium enforced by competition, it is compelled to settle for prices that just cover its costs of production and no more. Any other situation would not be one of equilibrium: firms earning additional revenue would attract competitors; firms that fail to cover costs must sooner or later go out of business reducing output. Hence the ultimate prices at which the supply and demand mechanism settles in a competitive economy must exactly equal the cost of production. Hence a competitive market economy can be viewed as searching for a consistent set of prices for all its industries that will just cover their production cost. Consistent pricing is a critical feature of equilibrium because the cost of the inputs to one industry depends on the prices charged by other industries. Equilibrium entails a simultaneous explanation of all of prices.

It turns out that the consistent prices of a perfectly competitive capitalist society are precisely the same as the shadow prices for a perfectly planned communist society! To see this, turn back to the technology matrix, and consider the inputs into an industry. Reading down a column we will find technology coefficients which tell us how much physical input is needed from each of the rows per unit output of the column industries. Thus, reading down the first column of the illustrated two-industry technology matrix used in Chapter 3, we have:

Theory	Example
a_{11}	0·25
a_{21}	0·50
l_1	0·20

Notice that the second subscripts are all 1, showing that the coefficients are inputs into industry 1. Thus a_{11} is the input of industry 1 into itself per unit output of the first industry; a_{21} is the input of industry 2 into industry 1 per unit output of industry 1; and l_1 is the amount of labour per unit output of industry 1 (remember that we are using labour in the loose sense to include all the necessary human efforts, including entrepreneurship, capital, land, and so on). In effect, each column is a cookbook recipe for the various inputs required for one unit of product.

Now we are looking for consistent prices of these inputs and outputs. Call the price of the goods produced by the first industry p_1. Goods produced by the second industry are p_2. The price of 'labour' is the wage rate, w. The value of the input of industry 1 to itself per unit of output is the price of 1 multiplied by the amount of it used for a of product, $p_1 a_{11}$. The cost of the inputs from industry 2 per unit output of the first is $p_2 a_{21}$. Finally, the labour cost is the amount of labour per unit product times the wage rate, $w l_1$.

Under competition, the sum of the unit costs to industry 1 just equals its price, p_1. Multiply each a_{ij} coefficient by the price of the row industry, p_i, and add down the columns; the total must equal p_j.

$$
\begin{array}{cc|cc}
p_1a_{11} & p_1a_{12} & p_1\,(0{\cdot}25) & p_1\,(0{\cdot}18) \\
+p_2a_{21} & +p_2a_{22} & +p_2\,(0{\cdot}50) & +p_2\,(0{\cdot}50) \\
+wl_1 & +wl_2 & +w\;(0{\cdot}20) & +w\;(0{\cdot}15) \\
\hline
p_1 & p_2 & p_1 & p_2
\end{array}
$$

These sums may be rewritten as equations:

$$
\begin{array}{l|l}
p_1a_{11}+p_2a_{21}+wl_1 = p_1 & 0{\cdot}25p_1+0{\cdot}50p_2+0{\cdot}20w = p_1 \\
p_1a_{12}+p_2a_{22}+wl_2 = p_2 & 0{\cdot}18p_1+0{\cdot}50p_2+0{\cdot}15w = p_2
\end{array}
$$

Notice that by writing the columns as rows of equations we have transposed the natural order of the technical coefficients. Thus the coefficients of the first column are now in the first row, and so on for all the columns.

The equations can be written in matrix form. A matrix such as A with rows transposed into columns is written A'. We now have the transposed matrix, A', operating on a column vector of prices which we designate by P, standing for p_1 and p_2. Added to this are the labour costs. These are the wage rate times the vector of direct labour coefficients l_1 and l_2, designated by L. The sum is equal to P, the column of prices.

$$
A'P+wL = P \quad\Bigg|\quad \begin{bmatrix} 0{\cdot}25 & 0{\cdot}50 \\ 0{\cdot}18 & 0{\cdot}50 \end{bmatrix}\begin{bmatrix} p_1 \\ p_2 \end{bmatrix}+w\begin{bmatrix} 0{\cdot}20 \\ 0{\cdot}15 \end{bmatrix}=\begin{bmatrix} p_1 \\ p_2 \end{bmatrix}
$$

This looks familiar. Before solving, however, observe that we have *two* equations in three unknowns, p_1, p_2 and w. We cannot hope to solve for all three of these with only two equations. Rather we shall have to content ourselves to solve these two equations for the prices in terms of the wage rate. First collect all the terms involving prices on the left hand side and the labour cost term on the right. Then group like terms by factoring:

$$
\begin{array}{l|l}
P-A'P = wL & 0{\cdot}75p_1-0{\cdot}50p_2 = 0{\cdot}20w \\
(I-A')P = wL & -0.18p_1+0.50p_2 = 0{\cdot}15w
\end{array}
$$

or

$$
\begin{array}{|l}
(1-a_{11})p_1 - a_{21}P_2 = wl_1 \\
-a_{12}p_1+(1-a_{22})p_2 = wl_2
\end{array}
$$

It is toil but no real trouble to solve these equations simultaneously for p_1 and p_2. The result is, in matrix terms, $P = w(-I - A')^{-1}L$, or:

$$p_1 = \frac{wl_1(1 - a_{22}) + wl_2a_{21}}{(1 - a_{11})(1 - a_{22}) - a_{12}a_{21}} \qquad p_1 = \frac{w(0{\cdot}20)(0{\cdot}50) + w(0{\cdot}15)(0{\cdot}50)}{(0{\cdot}75)(0{\cdot}50) - (0{\cdot}18)(0{\cdot}50)}$$

$$p_2 = \frac{wl_1a_{12} + wl_2(1 - a_{11})}{(1 - a_{11})(1 - a_{22}) - a_{12}a_{21}} \qquad p_2 = \frac{w(0{\cdot}20)(0{\cdot}25) + w(0{\cdot}15)(0{\cdot}75)}{(0{\cdot}75)(0{\cdot}50) - (0{\cdot}18)(0{\cdot}50)}$$

Factoring w in the numerator,

$$p_1 = w\left\{\frac{l_1(1 - a_{22}) + l_2a_{21}}{(1 - a_{11})(1 - a_{22}) - a_{12}a_{21}}\right\} \qquad p_1 = w\frac{0{\cdot}18}{0{\cdot}29}$$

$$p_2 = w\left\{\frac{(l_1a_{12} + l_2(1 - a_{11})}{(1 - a_{11})(1 - a_{22}) - a_{12}a_{21}}\right\} \qquad p_2 = w\frac{0{\cdot}16}{0{\cdot}29}$$

We have discovered the price of products 1 and 2 in terms of the wage rate, w. If we knew how much money was paid per unit of labour we could compute the money prices of the two goods. We do not know w, but it is relative or shadow prices that concern us at the moment. In fact, the expressions in the braces are nothing but T_1 and T_2 so that the price of each commodity is the value of the 'labour' directly or indirectly used in producing a unit of its final use.

How much of product 1 has to be given up in order to get a unit of product 2? What is the ratio of the prices of the two goods, p_1/p_2?

$$\frac{p_1}{p_2} = \frac{l_1(1 - a_{22}) + a_{21}l_2}{l_1a_{12} + (1 - a_{11})l_2} \quad\bigg|\quad \frac{p_1}{p_2} = \frac{0{\cdot}18}{0{\cdot}16} = 1{\cdot}12$$

In the division w cancels and so do the denominators $[(1 - a_{11})(1 - a_{22}) - a_{12}a_{21}]$.

Except for the slight discrepancy due to the rounding of numbers, the relative prices that we computed for the perfectly competitive unplanned economy are exactly the same as those under the perfectly planned economy $p_1/p_2 = T_1/T_2$! The allocation of scarce resources in any economy – socialist, communist, or capitalist – implies a set of relative prices. This is the fundamental theorem of economics showing itself again. A difference in relative prices in these two social systems could arise only because they have different technology matrices or from improper planning or pricing.

Furthermore, when a capitalist society is guided by competitive prices, every firm attempting to make the most money, it arrives at the same production possibility frontier as the planned communist society. Recall that our definition of gross national product was the money measure of all the final use produced by society. As such it is the price of each commodity times the amount of it that goes into final use: $GNP = p_1y_1 + p_2y_2$. Capitalist society attempts to maximize GNP, the total revenues of its firms.

Gross national product has another meaning, the money value of all the payments to primary factors of production which we are calling 'labour'. GNP is equal to the wage rate times the amount of labour used: $GNP = wB$. Taking both meanings of GNP together we get: $wB = p_1y_1 + p_2y_2$. We also know that prices are:

$$p_1 = wT_1 \qquad p_1 = \frac{0\cdot18}{0\cdot29}w = 0\cdot62w$$

$$p_2 = wT_2 \qquad p_2 = \frac{0\cdot16}{0\cdot29}w = 53w$$

So we now have the maximum GNP:

$$wB = wT_1y_1 + wT_2y_2 \qquad 50w = \frac{0\cdot18w}{0\cdot29}y_1 + \frac{0\cdot16w}{0\cdot29}y_2$$

$$= 0\cdot62wy_1 + 0\cdot532wy_2$$

Dividing out the wage rate w from both terms we get back into physical units:

$$B = T_1y_1T_2y_2 \quad | \quad 50 = 0\cdot62y_1 + 0\cdot53y_2$$

Compare this with the physical production possibility frontier for the communist country. Except for the rounding discrepancy, the results are exactly the same! Let perfect competition work itself out safe from government's good intentions or monopoly's evil ones, Smith said. Then each firm will come to competitive consistent prices or die. The system regulates itself as if it were perfectly planned.

The emergence of the mixed economy

During the Victorian era, England presented itself to the world as the model of economic liberalism. Government followed a *laissez-faire* policy towards business internally, and in external relations as well. Today's reader might not recognize this as liberalism. Yet to great minds of the last century, such as John Stuart Mill, economic freedom was the counterpart of political freedom as well as the source of the wealth of nations.

All this changed abruptly in 1914 for Britain and most of the industrialized world. New concerns since that time redefined the meaning of economic liberalism, which had to cope with: (*a*) unemployment, (*b*) monopoly, (*c*) inequity in the distribution of the wealth of nations, (*d*) external effects, growth of collectively consumed public goods and social costs. Let us look at these in turn.

Unemployment

Adam Smith's point was that the decentralized market economy was more flexible in meeting social needs than even the most benign government could be. Each man was the best judge of his own self-interest, which, when subject to competition, maximized the wealth of nations. It is possible for a market economy to be too flexible? Yes and no. Consider the possibility frontier once more. We have seen how a market economy translates the production possibility equation into money terms so that GNP equals $wB = p_1 y_1 + p_2 y_2$ and $p_1 = wT_1$ and $p_2 = wT_2$ (Figure 4.2). Now, suppose prices and wages are flexible, but adjust at different speeds. This can cause trouble in a market economy in which the decision to buy final use is an individual matter up to consumers or businessmen. Suppose that people decide to spend less of their money on buying the elements of final use, and prefer to hold it in the form of cash. The money value of GNP on the right hand side of the equation goes down, so it must do so on the left. Either the money wage rate or total employment must fall.

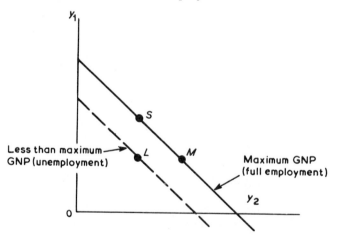

Figure 4.2

Of course, if there were instant flexibility in the money wage, w would fall as soon as anybody was in danger of being unemployed and B would be unaffected. But the money wage rate is sticky. People identify their standard of living with their money wages in the short run even though it may be only real wages that actually count. John Maynard Keynes called this 'money illusion'.[5] Money wages are written into union contracts. Many countries

[5] J. M. Keynes, *The General Theory of Employment, Interest and Money* (1936).

have wage regulations such as minimum or statutory wages (the same may be said for other factors of production). The result is that less of the labour force is employed and the decline is in B rather than w. Instead of choosing between points on the production possibility frontier of maximum, full employment GNP, such as S or M, production might be at a point within the frontier such as L, located on a less than maximum GNP line such as the dashed line in Figure 4.2. Labour and other inputs will be idle.

To be sure wages will tend to fall as people get over their 'money illusion' and accept smaller pay packets. But now it may well be that people receiving lower wages can spend even less for final use than before. Incomes tend to fall. Firms invest less in additional capital equipment. To achieve equilibrium wages would have to fall still faster and further. Maybe wages will never catch up before GNP has fallen considerably below the full employment level.

One must be careful not so say too much, since it is not at all certain that wage reduction will touch off the series of events described. After all, the prices of goods on the right hand side of the equation are also affected by the wage rate. As wages fall so do $p_1 = wT_1$ and $p_2 = wT_2$. The production costs of firms decline, and prices fall. As prices fall, people who have any money at all buy more rather than less. The danger is that there may be lags in the reduction of prices to the new appropriate level. There is a race between incomes, wages and prices. The result is uncertain. But the danger inherent in the lagged flexibility of prices is a cumulative decline in employment.

In the final analysis there is a lower limit to this process. People and firms do have money balances that they do not get out of current income. As prices fall very low these cash balances come to be worth a great deal in the real terms of what they can buy. The cumulative process of inadequate demand comes to a stop. This is called the *Pigou effect* after the Cambridge economist A. C. Pigou. When the Pigou effect finally takes over, the world economy may be in the midst of a disastrous depression. In the depths of the Great Depression almost one quarter of the labour force of the United Kingdom was out of work. In regions like Scotland the unemployment rates reached 27·7 per cent.

Depression may not quite be a bottomless pit, but it may be a very deep ditch. The flexibility of the market economy makes for efficiency. If the rate of adjustment of prices and wages were instantaneous there would be no problem. But if there are lags in adjustment, cumulative processes of declining demand can turn the very flexibility of the system against itself and in a downward spiralling disaster which only stops at an incredibly low level of employment and output.

What is to be done? In the Depression years Marxists suggested direct planning. J. M. Keynes offered an alternative. He suggested that we should

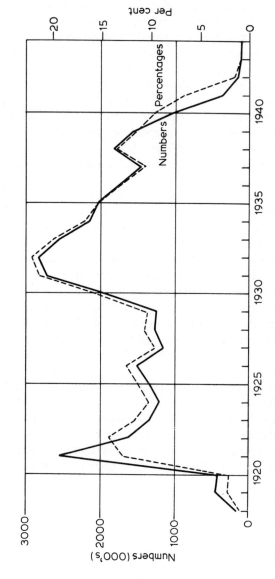

Figure 4.3 Unemployment during the pre-war years.
Source: Data from *The British Economy Key Statistics 1900–1970* (London, Times Newspapers Ltd.)

study the sources of demand for goods and services. Under conditions that prevailed in 1936, Keynes in effect asked us not to worry so much about efficient use of the market to determine shadow prices. We should be concerned to find sufficient final demand to employ the labour force. He was more concerned with getting to the production possibility frontier than with the problem of picking the most satisfactory point on it. The notion of a purely self-adjusting unplanned economy fell into disuse. Planning of aggregate demand has become a fixture of national policy. Rather than call this economy purely planned or unplanned, socialist or capitalist, it is probably most realistic to call it a mixed economy.

Monopoly

Modern capitalist economy differs from the perfectly competitive model. M. A. Utton drew on Inland Revenue reports to show that a large portion of the total income of firms in the United Kingdom is received by a very small number of firms. This point is made most strikingly in the last of his tables, in which he finds that two hundredths of 1 per cent of all the firms collect almost 30 per cent of all the earnings! These giant firms earn over £1,000,000 annually.[6]

It is not likely that such large firms are so subject to the rule 'compete or die'. Recent studies have discovered that these large organizations do not seem to set out to maximize their profits. Rather, there seems to be a minimum profit which has to be earned to satisfy the shareholders' dividend expectations. Over and above that, the goals of the modern corporation are unclear. First of all, there may be only the vaguest idea as to what the maximum profit might be. The flow of expenses from one department of a

[6] Statistics showing the concentrated ownership of assets are even more marked. These are a bit awkward to assemble for the UK, but evidence shows that the picture is not terribly different from the United States figures:

United States corporate structure in percentages 1962

Size of the individual corporation's total assets (in dollars)	Percentage of number	Percentage of total assets
Under 100,000	59·9	1·9
100,000–1 million	34·3	9·1
1 million–10 million	4·9	12·7
10 million–100 million	0·8	19·8
100 million–250 million	0·06	10·0
Over 250 million	0·05	46·5

Source: J. S. Bain, *Industrial Organization* (1968), p. 84.

Table 4.3 Size distribution of all concerns in the UK 1961–2, by net true income

Size (net true income)	Number (thousands)	Total amount (£ mill.)	Per cent of number	Per cent of net true income
Under 1000	1620·3	598·6	79·1	13·2
1000–9999	396·4	890·8	19·4	19·6
10,000–24,999	17·4	259·0	0·8	5·7
25,000–49,999	5·9	208·7	0·3	4·6
50,000–99,999	3·6	250·9	0·2	5·5
100,000–999,999	3·6	1005·7	0·2	22·1
1,000,000 and over	0·4	1336·9	0·02	29·4
Total	2047·6	4550·6	100·0	100·0

Source: Commissioners of Inland Revenue, *106th Report 1962–3*, Cmnd. 2283 (London, HMSO).

firm to another is not dissimilar to the transactions of a planned national economy; indeed the sales volume of some firms is larger than many nations. Prices assessed by the cost accounting department may be quite different from the shadow prices that are really relevant.

Secondly, a professional executive is not identical with the owners of corporate firms. He may build his career by showing what he can do rather than by maximizing profit. Thus a marketing manager may maximize sales at the cost of incurring greater expenses and lower profits. The gamesmanship of managerial success may dictate restricted profits in one year in order to be able to show continued progress in the next. The successful managing director may point to the overall growth or share of the market that he won for the firm. These various goals are often not the most efficient profit-maximizing ones that Smith relied upon for the 'hidden hand' to do its work. Indeed, the managerial goal may simply be 'do not rock the boat'.

It is ironic that the symptoms which we have described are similar to the rigidities of Soviet enterprises or other bureaucratic situations. Perhaps these stickinesses ultimately tend to be resolved in due course by competitive pressures. Competition works more slowly, efficiency is lost, and the hazard of economic spirals is increased. We shall look at these matters in greater detail in Chapter 9.

Concern over the equity (the fairness) of the economy

As the Victorian era applied Smith's ideas, it became increasingly difficult to identify equity with efficiency. Some people were very poor and others rich.

Social stratification contradicted the picture of an economy of equally circumstanced people who voted in the market place for the goods they preferred. Some people were more equal than others. In the present era the question of equity took another turn. Is it fair, people asked, for some people to bear the uncertainties of an unstable world? Should not everyone be protected from both unemployment and inflation, the expenses of illness, and from sudden shifts in demand for their services?

The trouble with the concept of fairness is that it is important and yet at the same time non-scientific. There is no way, for example, that one can prove to another house renter that it is fair to raise his rents in the same way that we have demonstrated that the efficient use of scarce resources implies a set of shadow prices. Loaded words evoking sympathy for the renter meet equally loaded words like 'sitting tenant' in rebuttal. Logic only can demonstrate that particular policies are inconsistent with stated value judgements, not that the value judgements are wrong. One man's justice is another's outrage.

Exercise:
(1) Is it equitable that 10 per cent of male and 86·2 per cent of female manual UK workers earned less than £15 per week in 1968? Can you convince women that this is just? Can you convince the men that this is unjust?
(2) Play devil's advocate and show that Scrooge was unfairly persecuted by irresponsible Christmas spirits bent on undermining the social fabric and respect for private property.

The public expects the economic system to work in a way that is equitable as well as efficient. That is easier said than done. Shadow prices have nothing at all to do with justice. They represent the slope of the production possibility frontier showing how much of one good has to be given up to produce another. There are only two possibilities. If prices embodying social justice are the same as efficient shadow prices, there is no need to talk about justice. If they are different, there is an irreconcilable conflict between equity and efficiency.

Thus, if the 'just price' of houses is controlled at less than their shadow price, some firms are asked to build or rent houses at below cost. Either government will tax some persons to subsidize housing for others, or the houses will not be built. Worse than this, only some housing may be controlled in price, and uncontrolled house prices and rents will skyrocket further in the situations where controls do not apply or are evaded.

Exercise: Illustrate the last paragraph with the aid of supply and demand diagrams.

The possibility of equity is not completely hopeless. After all, the reason people react to prices by calling them 'just' or 'unjust' is that incomes are altered by price changes. Perhaps it is possible to adjust incomes by taxes and grants and still allow prices to be determined by the market under competition. This is very difficult because most taxes affect prices one way or another. Even if they did not, individuals react to these measures by working or investing differently as a result of changed incentives. A truly perfect scheme would require that no one could plan his efforts in light of government contributions or taxes. Perfection would require a single lump sum tax or benefit which none of the affected persons could foresee! The fantasy nature of perfection in income transfers does not, of course, prevent efforts at adjusting distributive equity with tools that influence efficiency in a negative way. The judgement is made that the equity gain is worth the efficiency loss.

The commitment to equity also gives rise to the public provision of services to individuals outside the market. Health, schooling and the like are felt to be so important that they are distributed to individuals whether they can or wish to pay for them. Actually matters go deeper. Capital grants are made to specific industries and regions, such as agriculture, mining and aircraft. Depressed regions are encouraged. Industries such as steel, ship building and coal are nationalized, partly to ensure a 'fair' return to workers and the public.

In all these activities, equity plays a very important role often overriding efficiency considerations. Even when efficiency is deemed paramount, it is very difficult in a democratic society to actually enforce resolutions to maintain shadow prices and the most efficient methods. Once government makes changes in the impersonal workings of the market, there is somebody to blame. It is the very nature of equity considerations to cause problems. This is because it is impossible to say what is equitable, only what people think is equitable.

Exercise:
(1) Review the controversy over 'lame duck' industries in the UK. Choose a specific industry and show how equity and efficiency conflict.
(2) (*a*) Use the inverse tables to study the effect of a 10 per cent switch of final use from coal to gas. Study only the largest five supplying industries and tell by how much they would change their outputs.
     (*b*) Compute the labour coefficients for each of these industries from the transactions matrix. Compute the employment change which would result.
     (*c*) Decide whether you think the switch ought to be made. Don't fudge – answer yes or no. Somebody has to!

(*d*) Locate the coefficients showing both the direct and indirect flow of coal to electricity. Repeat for gas. Write a short description showing what would happen if electricity generation were redesigned in favour of gas so that the gas coefficient were 10 per cent less and the coal coefficient were 10 per cent more. Do not attempt a complete calculation, but explain the considerations involved.

(3) Do you think it equitable for the coal mines to have been nationalized by offering fixed interest stocks to the previous owners? Justify your view. Do you think the successful 'work in' at Upper Clyde Shipyards to prevent redundancies was equitable? Justify your view.

(4) Review the Hansard debates over the Value Added Tax and evaluate them in light of this section.

External effects, growth of collectively consumed public goods and social costs

The radical ideas of Adam Smith, as well as the Victorian liberalism of people like John Stuart Mill, were firmly rooted in individualism. This was the basis of their political credo as well as their economic policy proposals. An individual's welfare – his happiness – depended on the goods and services he received for his labours.

Yet some public goods obviously cannot be individually consumed. National defence is the classic example. The Royal Navy cannot protect only those who pay for the service! Hence no individual can be induced to pay for it. 'Let others pay, and I will get the service free', he reasons. He must be taxed. Defence, even in an era of contracting British military posture, amounted to £2·455 million in 1970 out of a total public expenditure of £21·5 million. Parks, libraries, prisons, education, child care, and environmental protection are also public goods.

The very fact that these goods are public means that they have little to do with the invisible hand of competition. Even when the goods are sold to the government by competing private contractors, the force of competition only works on the supply side of the relationship. Producers know what they must spend to make the goods, but the government has only the faintest idea of the worth of the goods they buy. How much good does an intercontinental ballistic missile do? What is the value of a green belt area about London? Crude estimates are made of the value of these goods to a mixed economy society by methods called cost-benefit or cost-effectiveness analysis. Fundamentally these techniques rely on comparing a proposed public project with one which is privately priced.

The importance of non-market considerations has also grown very rapidly for two other reasons. First of all, it becomes increasingly difficult to identify social benefits with individual decisions. We live too close together. Goods like land and open space, pure air, educated and peaceful associates, and safe and pleasant transportation are all things we must provide collectively for anyone to enjoy them. Also, we are too powerful in our technology for individual decisions to avoid injuring others. There are external social costs in driving a car, by producing exhaust over and above the cost of petrol internal to the calculation of individual motorists. Estimates can be made of these social costs by comparison with what people would pay to avoid them. The fact is that unless the public authority enters into the picture, these social costs are not paid. As a result the wrong signals are transmitted to private decision makers, and excessive social costs are incurred. This, in a nutshell, is the source of problems of pollution and neglect of environmental and often human resources.

Secondly, as productivity increases, it has become possible to become more concerned with public services. John K. Galbraith has emphasized this development.[7] Under conditions of extreme scarcity, Galbraith concedes, private concerns with subsistence predominate. As production increases, these recede in importance in favour of public parks, hospitals and other public facilities. The issue between Galbraith and his critics is their importance and price – both of which are devilishly difficult to estimate.

The dilemma of the mixed economy

The trouble with mixed economies is that they are mixed. The picture we have drawn of the modern bargained economy is one that contains a number of powerful groups, public and private, which, in the short run at least, seem not to respond rapidly to competitive pressure. They negotiate agreements with each other depending on their bargaining strength. Certainly the ultimate determinant of the bargaining power may be the underlying forces of competition which Adam Smith described, but they may work slowly behind the scene giving rise to the lags in adjustment that concern us so much.

On one hand, Western countries are unwilling to adopt the communist command economy. Thus far direct central planning has proven to be an awkward and inefficient way at arriving at the ideal inverse solution to the coordination problem. Moreover, most Western countries do not choose to allow the decisions on final use to be made by central political authorities to the exclusion of individual choice. Nor are they willing to accept the compulsion that must be employed when the central plan conflicts with individuals.

On the other hand, allowing the market to work itself out undisturbed by governmental intervention is not regarded as satisfactory for the four

<hr>

[7] J. K. Galbraith, *The Affluent Society* (1958).

reasons we sketched. Planning is inevitable. Inevitably it is painful. The more thoroughly planning becomes involved in setting prices, outputs and employment, the further will be the drift from the shadow prices which, in principle, are the guides to an efficiently run economy. It becomes more and more difficult to know if a public or private enterprise is being run efficiently, when costs do not reflect true scarcity. When prices are arbitrary, they cease to measure social as well as private benefits and costs.

Make no mistake, this is a dangerous situation in a democratic society. Governments are involved in directing the economy, and yet unable to find the courage to say that this 'lame duck industry' ought to founder, or that a public service or a wage increase is unjustified. A case always can be made by each group in its own interest with only little regard or knowledge of the total economy. In a mixed economy interest groups are safe, on one hand, from the rigours of communist 'criticism and self-criticism', and from the impersonal correction of competition on the other.

Inevitably, mixed economies are in the planning business. However they set their goals of final use, they must plan with an eye to direct and indirect effects so as to hold as close to shadow prices as possible. To be successful a country like Britain must use calculations similar to input-output to forecast what the private sector is likely to do as a result of public and private changes in final demand, and then to deliberately manipulate the public sector to meet the public goals. Clearly the analysis must be carried on in both output terms and price terms, precisely because the economy is mixed. Mixed economies have set themselves a formidable planning exercise, and an even more difficult political task in carrying out the plan.

Exercise:
(1) In the Blue Book find the Analysis of Public Expenditure and Gross Domestic Fixed Capital Formation. Compare the year 1960 with 1970 by expressing the main categories as percentages of total. Relate your figures to GNP. Adopt some graphic device to illustrate your conclusions. Write an interpretation of your results in the light of the analysis in this chapter.
(2) Look at the *Scientific American* triangulated table (see reference on p. 39). Suppose wages are sticky in the industries at the lowest levels of the triangle government services in nationalized industries. What can be said about the flexibility of prices in the rest of the economy? What would be the case if the price rigidity were characteristic of the apex of the triangle? Which is more likely to be the case?
(3) Evaluate the 'convergence thesis' that there is less difference between communist and capitalist societies than is ordinarily supposed, and that the two systems are in practice converging. Consider economic and non-economic dimensions.

Appendix: The inverse matrix as a series of adjustments to final use

The calculation of the direct as well as indirect output needed to produce a bill of final use can be thought of as a series of adjustments. In addition to final use, industries have to produce to meet interindustry needs. But this production requires inputs that have to be produced. These require further production, and so on. What guarantee is there that these adjustments will lead to the inverse?

Imagine that a first attempt at producing final use, Y, was simply to have industry 1 produce an amount equal to y_1, and industry 2 produce y_2. That is, suppose the total outputs X_1 and X_2 were set equal to the hoped for final use, y_1 and y_2. The goals could not be achieved because production involves an interindustry expense equal to the application of the technology matrix to the proposed output; AY would be used up in production and the first output would fall short of its goal by this amount. In order to make this up, it might be decided to produce an additional amount of product, equal to AY. A good idea. Produce $Y+AY$. But unfortunately, producing AY more product involves the additional expense of A applied to the extra produce, i.e. AAY or A^2Y. To meet this needed expense, an extra amount, A^3Y, must be turned out, and so on indefinitely.

The vector of total output, X, would have to be the target of final use Y plus an infinite series of corrections. The result is the matrix series:

$$X = Y + AY + A^2Y + A^3Y + \ldots + A^nY.$$

The sum of all these adjustments can be shown to be the inverse $Y = (I-A)^{-1}Y$.

We will not attempt a proof in matrix terms in this book, but it parallels the discussion of the sum of the infinite geometric series given in the Preface. The key idea is that for the infinite series to converge, each term in the series must be smaller than the preceding one. If that is the case, each additional correction gets smaller and smaller until it is of no importance. A similar process is at work in the matrix equation. If we keep up our correcting process long enough, the limiting sum of all the corrections will be approached. The whole system works toward the inverse Leontief matrix, $(I-A)^{-1}$, just as the firm adjusts successively until the inverse multiplier $(1-a)^{-1}$ is reached.

Let us now see if we can come to this result by direct computation. It is only fair to warn the reader that this is a lot of tedious arithmetic. Elegant mathematicians may turn up their noses at this working out of examples, but we mere humans must wade through the arithmetic to convince ourselves that our conclusion is correct.

Start from the Leontief $Y = (I - A)X$ equations:

$$y_1 = (1 - a_{11})X_1 - a_{12}X_2$$
$$y_2 = -a_{21}X_1 + (1 - a_{22})\bar{X}_2.$$

Suppose planners sought to have as final uses $y_1 = 100$ and $y_2 = 60$ and at first produced only those amounts. That is to say, suppose $X_1 = y_1 = 100$ and $X_2 = y_2 = 60$. Would the goals be achieved? To find out, substitute the proposed X-values. Let us call y_1^* and y_2^* the actual final use achieved compared to the hoped for y_1 and y_2. Substituting,

$$y_1^* = 0 \cdot 75 \ (100) - 0 \cdot 18 \ (60)$$
$$y_2^* = -0 \cdot 50 \ (100) + 0 \cdot 50 \ (60).$$

That means that:

$$y_1^* = 75 \cdot 0 - 10 \cdot 8 = 64 \cdot 2$$
$$y_2^* = -50 \cdot 0 + 30 \cdot 0 = -20 \cdot 0$$

That was a horrible plan! Not only have planners failed to achieve the goals of final use, 100 and 60, but they have used up so much of product 1 in satisfying the needs of industry 2 that they have a negative amount left over for final use. That will never do. They would have had to draw down on previously produced stocks of commodity 2 just to keep industry 1 going! And even then, industry 1 would still not meet its goal.

Suppose they try to correct their error. As a second approximation, add the shortage to the original production target. The new plans for X_1 and X_2 consist of the previous output plan plus the short fall in final use. The short fall of industry 1 was $100 - 64 \cdot 2 = 35 \cdot 8$. So the new trial output is $X_1 = 100 + 35 \cdot 8 = 135 \cdot 8$. For industry 2 the shortage was $60 - (-20) = 80$. The new $X_2 = 60 + 80 = 140$.

Substitute once more in the $(I - A)X = Y$ equations:

$$y_1^* = 0 \cdot 75 \ (135 \cdot 8) - 0 \cdot 18 \ (140) = 76 \cdot 7$$
$$y_2^* = -0 \cdot 50 \ (135 \cdot 8) + 0 \cdot 50 \ (140) = 2 \cdot 1.$$

That is a bit better. At least we no longer see the disconcerting negative value of y_2^*. But both industries fail to meet their goal.

Try once more: y_1^* is still short 23.3, so that the new $X_1 = 135 \cdot 8 + 23 \cdot 3 = 159 \cdot 1$; since y_2^* is deficient by 57.1, try $X_2 = 140 + 57.1 = 197.1$. Then:

$$y_1^* = 0 \cdot 75 \ (159 \cdot 1) - 0 \cdot 18 \ (197 \cdot 1) = 84 \cdot 3$$
$$y_2^* = -0 \cdot 50 \ (159 \cdot 1) + 0 \cdot 50 \ (197 \cdot 1) = 9 \cdot 0.$$

Better, but industry 2 is still sick. One more adjustment. Since y_1^* is deficient by 15·7, the next $X_1 = 159·1 + 15·7 = 174·8$; y_1^* is short by 51·0, therefore $X_2 = 197·1 + 51·0 = 248·1$. Here we go again:

$$y_1^* = 0·75\,(174·8) - 0·18\,(248·1) = 86·5$$

$$y_2^* = -0·50\,(174·8) + 0·50\,(248·1) = 37·3.$$

Each revision gets closer and closer to solving the Leontief equations for the inverse, the appropriate X_1 and X_2 values that will yield the final uses. A method of solution by repeated corrections is called an iterated solution.

Exercise: Correct twice more. Use the inverse Leontief matrix to determine the ultimate total outputs needed. How far away are you? What is the percentage error?

We portray this iterated solution graphically, showing X_1 on the vertical axis and X_2 horizontally (Figure 4.4). The intersection of the graphs of the Leontief equations will, of course, be their solution – the inverse applied to y_1 and y_2. To carry out this graphic inversion process, we first put the Leontief equations in slope-intercept form:

Equations

1: $(y_1 = (1 - a_{11})X_1 - a_{12}X_2)$ becomes

$$\left(X_1 = \frac{a_{12}}{(1 - a_{11})}X_2 + \frac{y_1}{(1 - a_{11})}\right)$$

2: $(y_2 = -a_{21}X_1 + (1 - a_{22})X_2)$ becomes

$$\left(X_1 = \frac{(1 - a_{22})}{a_{21}}X_2 - \frac{y_2}{a_{21}}\right)$$

Common sense tells a great deal about the nature of the graphs. They slope upward since the coefficients of the independent variable, X_2, is positive (the output of industry 1 has to increase if the output of industry 2 does). The first equation has a positive vertical intercept which is equal to $y_1/(1 - a_{22})$. That makes good sense! If X_2 were nil, and therefore did not place any demands on the output of the first industry, industry 1 would have to make an output equal to $[1/(1 - a_{11})]y_1$ to meet its own final use. The second equation crosses the horizontal axis for the same reason, and hence crosses the vertical axis below the origin.

The iterated solution can now be visualized. Start producing only final y_1 and y_2. This corresponds to point M^1 on the figure that does not satisfy the interindustry expenses for either industry. M^1 lies below the graph of the first equation indicating that too little X_1 is produced; it is also to the left of

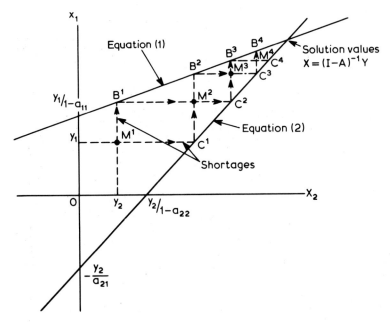

Figure 4.4   The iterated solution of the inverse

equation 2, showing that there is a shortage of X_2 as well. What to do? Increase output by the shortage. That is, increase X_1 by the distance $M^1 B^1$ and X_2 by $M^1 C^1$. That brings us to our second approximation, M^2. Once again we are short, since the increase in output from M^1 to M^2 involved us in further expenses. Correct again by the amount of shortage to M^3, then M^4, and so on.

Each time we correct the correction needed gets smaller, and we approach the inverse solution of the two equations where the lines cross and the requirements of both industries are met. When this happens the final use and the outputs of both industries are consistent with their interindustry expenses. We have arrived at the same result as if we were to solve the two equations simultaneously.

Part 2 Microeconomics: adaptation to scarce resources

5 Adaptation to scarcity by choice of product: the law of diminishing returns

Consistency, adaptation and substitution

Thus far we have laid great stress on the need for an economic system to act in a consistent way. We have shown that consistency in outputs and prices may be achieved by a competitive market economy – one in which goods are sold at uniform prices, and under which no excess profits are earned. But we have left a great deal unsaid. First, how are these prices enforced? By what mechanism do individual firms react to the prices in deciding what to produce? Second, we have assumed a given matrix of technology coefficients. What determines these? Why are some combinations of inputs chosen over others? Third, how do consumers interact with producers to satisfy their wants?

In Part 2 we shall show how competition works to solve these problems. Then we shall criticize actual market economies in the light of the distortions of monopoly. After making the case for competition, we shall enquire whether it is capable of dealing with problems of pollution and the preservation of the environment. We shall see whether it can be fair in its distribution of income.

The issues we have suggested arise once we consider alternatives in the use of factors of production and consumption. Alternatives open the door to choice. Our method will be to study the decision making process by analysing the best choices that could be made. Of course individuals and firms do not always make the optimum decision among the alternatives available to them, but most often they do. Moreover, in a thoroughly competitive economy there is no excess profit margin for error; those that do not make the optimum choice earn an insufficient return and are doomed to economic demise. Like biological organisms economic agents must adapt or die.

In previous chapters we have learnt that scarcity is the economic reality that must be faced. We constructed a production possibility frontier fixed by the limited supply of labour. Now we must enquire into the manner in which more flexible choice is possible when more than one factor is considered. The biological analogy of adaptation as the means to survival is worth pursuing. Natural history illustrates the amazing adaptations that living creatures make in structure and habits to meet nature's demands. Adaptation follows what in economics is called the *principle of substitution* – the use of one limited, scarce input in place of another. In living creatures, bodily organs are adapted to meet particular problems, necessarily at the expense of weakening the ability to meet with others. For example, the albatross has a very wide wing span which permits it to soar on wind currents over great areas of ocean in search of food. Its evolution has substituted this capacity for rapid take-off from the ground. The albatross, which is the marvel of grace once airborne, is the comical gooney bird struggling to work up enough speed to get off the ground. Substitution has adapted it to the environment of safe island shores and scarce ocean food. The bird is endangered if the environment should change to include carnivores – snakes and cats. Biological substitution in evolution can adapt life only by death for some species and replacement by others.

Man also faces the limitation of factors of production: labour, supply of capital, available natural resources and his own entrepreneurial ability. Individually he is more flexible than other creatures, he has the capacity to adapt by conscious, purposeful, planning. But what of an unplanned market economy? As a social system it has no conscious plan or purpose. How does it adapt?

To answer, we must drop the simplifying assumptions of the earlier chapters, one by one. They were designed to postpone the more complicated problem of substitution by assuming that there was only one way of 'doing things'. Choice among alternatives was irrelevant. Now we take a last look at these convenient simplifications before we give them up.

(1) *We assumed that there was only one scarce primary input, 'labour'.* There are in fact a very large number of primary inputs. They are roughly classified as land, labour, capital and entrepreneurship, but each of these categories is in reality composed of a myriad of subcategories of different kinds.

(2) *We assumed that each of the columns of the input-output matrix represented one industry and that each industry produced only one product.* By

assuming a one-to-one correspondence between product, production method and industry, we wished away two problems. First, we did not have to worry about *joint products*, situations where one firm makes several different products. The production choices of a company like General Motors which makes several kinds of cars as well as refrigerators and diesel engines were not allowed to trouble us. Second, we did not consider alternative *methods* of producing any one product. The method of production was specified by the column in the technology matrix; to produce one ton of steel there had to be just so much coke, electricity, iron ore, timber, railroad transportation, and so on. There was no allowance for the substitution of one of these inputs for another. Yet certainly there are many processes for producing steel. They start from a blacksmith pounding on a molten 'bloom' of wrought iron to include blast furnaces, oxygen reduction furnaces, and electric and coke operated open hearth processes. Moreover, these are methods that are in commercial use. Who knows what can be done in the laboratory? What is even now being considered on the drawing boards of the metallurgical engineers?

By these simplifications, we also managed to neatly sidestep the influence of consumer choice on technology. Of course, consumer choice in final use determined the outputs of the various industries. Indeed that is the whole thrust of input-output analysis. But we avoided the impact of the choice by consumers in response to the price of goods in the sense of which way goods were to be produced. The reason is too obvious. There was only one technology considered, and hence prices were technically fixed by the constant slope of the production possibility frontier.

In this chapter we drop the assumption of labour as the single primary input. Consider natural resources as a second limiting primary input. Now we face a land frontier as well. What we discover about the two frontier case can easily be generalized to a situation of any number of primary inputs and correspondingly many frontiers.

The land production possibility frontier is derived in exactly the same way as the labour frontier. The labour frontier, it will be recalled, was found by multiplying the total outputs of each industry, X_1 and X_2, by their labour requirements per unit output, l_1 and l_2. Since the Leontief inverse expressed X_1 and X_2 in terms of the final use y_1 and y_2, we could relate the labour supply, B, to the desired final uses. Thus in the frontier equation $B = T_1y_1 + T_2y_2$, T_1 and T_2 represented the *labour* directly and indirectly needed to produce a unit of each type of final use.

To compute the *land* frontier, we multiply the total outputs by the amount of land required per unit output. The frontier for land is $N = Q_1y_1 + Q_2y_2$, where N is the total amount of land, and Q_1 and Q_2 are the amounts of land required directly and indirectly to produce one unit of each final use.

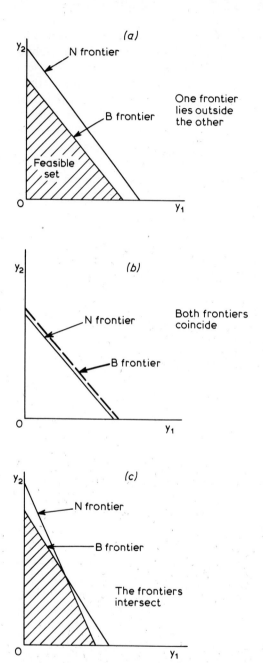

Figure 5.1   Land and labour production
possibility frontiers

By graphing the frontiers together (Figure 5.1), three possible combinations are exhibited, of which case (c) is the most important. In case (a) one frontier lies outside the other for all positive values of y_1 and y_2. Then only the inner frontier matters. If labour were the inner frontier, the limited amount of natural resources would be irrelevant; an economy would have run out of its scarce labour long before it had to worry about the scarcity of resources. A scarce labour situation existed in North America early in the last century. In Britain at about the same time the positions of the frontiers were reversed. British intellectuals were worried about overpopulation – recall Malthus and his theory – whilst Americans were busy trying to figure out how to chop down trees and populate the wilderness. When a resource is in surplus supply it is not an economic good. Economic goods are always scarce. Since more usually we have to worry about several scarce inputs, it is not likely that only one frontier will be relevant to all final uses.

Query: (1) Is not everything in limited supply? Therefore is every good an economic good?
(2) Is it possible for a resource not to be scarce now and become one in the future? Is it an economic good?

In case (b) where the two frontiers coincide, it makes just as good sense to consider one limitation as another. Because the frontiers coincide, we run out of both resources simultaneously. This is most unlikely; if these frontiers are to coincide throughout their entire length as in (b) they must also be parallel – have the same slopes. See what that would require. For the *labour* resource frontier we have: $B = T_1y_1 + T_2y_2$, or, in slope intercept form:

$$y_2 = \frac{B}{T_2} - \frac{T_1}{T_2}y_1.$$

For *natural resources* we have: $N = Q_1y_1 + Q_2y_2$, so:

$$y_2 = \frac{N}{Q_2} - \frac{Q_1}{Q_2}y_1.$$

If the slopes are equal, $T_1/T_2 = Q_1/Q_2$. This means that the ratio of *labour* directly and indirectly used in the production of the two final uses is the same as the ratio of the *land* used in the production of those net products. That is bizarre even though it is a logical possibility. It would require that every factor is just as useful in the production of every particular final product as any other. That is to say, it would mean that resources are not at all specialized toward the production of different products.

To see how absurd this is, take a concrete case in which we think of a particular natural resource, ocean water, and a particular kind of labour, pounding with a sledgehammer. Let the two final uses be fish and iron bars. The slopes of the respective frontiers mean that for the resource frontier:

$$\frac{Q_1}{Q_2} = \frac{\text{The amount of sea water directly and indirectly needed per fish caught}}{\text{The amount of sea water directly and indirectly needed per pound of iron}};$$

and for the labour frontier:

$$\frac{T_1}{T_2} = \frac{\text{The amount of pounding with a sledgehammer needed directly and indirectly per fish caught}}{\text{The amount of pounding with a sledgehammer needed directly and indirectly per pound of iron}}.$$

Only the wildest of coincidences would make these ratios identical. And yet that is precisely what would have to be asserted of all goods and factors for the frontiers to be parallel.

The third case, (c), is the only one that makes sense. Resources are specialized toward certain products in different ways. As the sea water and sledgehammer case illustrates, the more detailed our classifications of primary inputs, the more apparent it becomes that this must be so. In this case, the set of feasible combinations of y_1 and y_2 must satisfy both constraints. Long ago we said that for one constraint the feasible set of final uses constituted a triangle under that frontier. When we add a second constraint, the points in the feasible set must lie under both triangles. The feasible area is seen to be a convex polygon, bounded by the axes and the inner parts of each of the frontiers. The convex shape is given to the polygon by the fact that the innermost frontier is the one that is effective. This simple observation will be seen to have far-reaching consequences.

Exercise:
(1) Consider this transactions matrix with three primary inputs:

		Interindustry use		Final use	Totals
		1	2		
Interindustry inputs					
	1	25	175	50	250
	2	40	20	60	120

Primary inputs	Labour	10	40		50
	Land	100	20		120
	Capital	15	35		50

(a) Compute all three production possibility frontiers.

(b) Take the production possibility frontiers and graph them two at a time. Examine them to see if they follow the pattern (a), (b) or (c).

(c) Graph all three on the same chart. Are any of these frontiers ineffective?

(d) If a constraint is ineffective, what does that tell us about whether the primary input in question is fully employed?

(e) Construct a hypothetical numerical example in which you retain the interindustry and final use sectors of the transactions matrix above, but in which you reinterpret primary input in terms of skilled and unskilled labour rather than land, labour and capital.

(f) In what ways might a frontier that is not immediately constraining begin to be so even though technology does not change. Illustrate.

With two limiting inputs the production possibility frontier that matters is a composite one and it looks like a kinked line, convex outward from the origin (Figure 5.2). What are shadow prices now? Consider point A located on the portion of the compound frontier coming from the natural resources limitation. To add a bit more of y_2 one must give up an amount of y_1 equal to

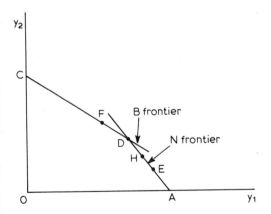

Figure 5.2. Shadow prices in a compound production possibility frontier

the slope of the natural resources frontier, Q_1/Q_2. As we have said so many times, the slope represents the shadow price of y_2 in terms of y_2.

Now suppose that consumers (or planners) decide to have more and more of y_2 and less of y_1. They will go to points like E or H assuming they are willing to pay the price. Until point D is reached, the shadow price will not change. If they choose still more of y_2 they must proceed to points on the portion of the frontier made up of the labour constraint. F is such a point. To go from D to F they must give up an amount of y_1 which is dictated by the slope of the labour frontier. The amount of y_1 given up for a unit of y_2 is T_1/T_2. This new shadow price will continue to rule for any further substitution of y_2 for y_1. The shadow price of the two commodities is not constant after all. The price of more y_2 depends on how much of y_1 and y_2 we already have. Between A and D, the cost of y_2 in terms of y_1 given up is Q_1/Q_2, but between D and C the shadow price is T_1/T_2.

Exercise:
(1) What is y_2 at point A? How does it differ from total output x_2?
(2) Explain why we are only considering points *on* the production possibility frontier and not *within* it. Are such interior points feasible? Can points be feasible and yet not be optimal?
(3) In the preceding set of exercises, suppose y_1 is 10. What is the shadow price of y_2? In order to solve this problem, first decide which is the effective frontier, and then determine its slopes. Would the price be the same if y_1 were 170? What can be said about prices if y_1 were 294·1?

The convex shape of the production possibility frontier shows the direction in which the shadow prices change as one continues to substitute y_2 for y_1. If more and more of y_2 is made its price rises sharply at point D where we switch from the B frontier to the N constraint. Figure 5.3 shows this to be so. Start from position A, producing only final use y_1, and none of y_2. Now, substitute some y_2 for y_1 and go to point E. The amount of y that has to be given up is shown as a movement to the left, Δy_1. The amount of y_2 gained is the vertical change, Δy_2.

Each additional unit of Δy_2 requires the same sacrifice Δy, up to point D. But once D is reached, the Δy_1 that must be given up for a unit of Δy_2 gets bigger. This is because the production frontier gets more nearly horizontal, and it takes a greater movement horizontally – a bigger reduction in y_1 – in order to get the same increase in y_2.

Geometry is telling us something important about the real world. The increase in shadow price or opportunity cost of y_2 is evidently a direct result of the shape of the production possibility frontier which gets flatter and flatter as we move to the left. The economic cause of this shape is a consequence of the specialization of inputs into production, causing the

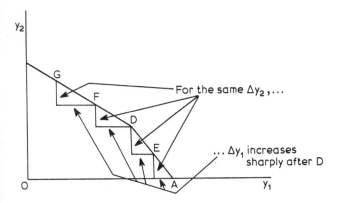

Figure 5.3.   Increasing shadow price for more of one
good and less of the other

frontiers to cross. Even allowing for unexpected effects, sea water is undoubtedly more conducive to the production of fish than of iron products!

As long as the production is carried out with more than one scarce primary
input, and as long as these primary inputs are differently specialized toward
the products, the shadow price of a good will increase as more of it is
produced. More of other goods will have to be given up to get another unit.
This is *the law of diminishing returns* in one of its several forms.

We started out with just one primary input, labour, and now we have
considered natural resources. Capital is still a third factor. These are very
crude categories of the multitudinous things that go into production. Actually there are an infinite variety of types of labour, each of which is in limited
supply at any one time. Likewise, capital consists of everything from ketchup
bottles to the great boring mills used in engineering works. Land comes in
various types, shapes, fertilities and climates. When we start to break down
the large categories of inputs – disaggregate them – we can go all the way and
realize that far from the economy being subject to one production constraint, it is limited by an infinite number of them.

What will be the shape of the composite production possibility frontier
then? It will consist of a smooth shape, which is the common inner envelope
of all constraints. If there are very many constraints, each of them will
contribute only one point at which it is just touching the frontier (Figure 5.4).
In this case, the composite frontier is a smooth curve whose slope changes at
every point on the curve. Nonetheless, the same principle applies as in the
polygon cases. More and more of commodity 2 is produced for final use,
the amount of commodity 1 that has to be given up for another unit of 2
gets bigger and bigger. The law of diminishing returns holds whether the

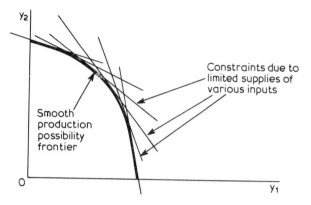

Figure 5.4   Composite production possibility frontier
with very many inputs

production frontier is smooth or made up of points of tangency with a set of
straight line segments.

This fundamental notion in economics is often stated in terms of *marginal
cost*. Marginal cost (*MC*) is the change in the total cost of producing a certain
good which results from producing another unit of it. We measure the cost of
y_2 in terms of y_1 foregone. Therefore:

$$\text{Marginal cost of } y_2 = \frac{\text{Decrease in } y_1 \text{ which can be produced}}{\text{Increase in } y_2 \text{ which can be produced}} = \frac{\Delta y_1}{\Delta y_2}.$$

Marginal cost of y_2 is nothing but the reciprocal of, or one dividend by, the
slope of the production possibility frontier:[1]

$$\text{Marginal cost of } y_2 = \frac{\Delta y_1}{\Delta y_2} = \frac{1}{\Delta y_2/\Delta y_1}.$$

With increased production of y_2 its marginal cost increases. Restating the
law of diminishing returns:

> Given the state of technical knowledge about methods of production
> and fixed supplies of several differently specialized primary inputs, the
> marginal cost of a product increases when the output of the product
> increases.

Further explanation is in order about the concept of marginal cost. The
reader may be disturbed by our frequent insistence that an additional
(marginal) unit of y_1 foregone is the cost of a unit of y_2 gained. We are

---

[1] Of course if we computed the marginal cost of y_1 in terms of y_2 we would have $\Delta y_1/y_2$ which
would be slope of the frontier itself.

accustomed to think of costs in terms of money expenditures. Even though we know that economic costs are not identical with money flows there is an element of truth to our feeling. For if a market economy is working properly under conditions of perfect competition, then the money cost of manufacturing another unit of a product should reflect its shadow price; if the system is doing its job, the expenditure of money prices should equal shadow prices. In a functioning competitive market, the marginal cost of product 2 in terms of 1 equals the ratio of their prices – p_2 divided by p_1. That is to say, the price of 2 is the amount of money spent on a unit of 2 measured in terms of the money price of a unit of 1. Symbolically:

$$\frac{\Delta y_1}{\Delta y_2} = \text{Marginal cost of product 2 measured in terms of product 1} = \frac{p_2}{p_1}$$

If commodity 1 is money itself, we are saying that the price of money is unity, $p_1 = 1$. Then we can conclude that under perfect competition the marginal cost of a product is equal to its money price.

Query: Why does Δy_1 appear in the numerator of the left hand side and p_1 in the denominator of the right hand side?

An application of the law of diminishing return: linear programming and the product mix problem

We now apply the law of diminishing returns to understand how a capitalistic market economy adjusts its combination of products so as to economize factors in most scarce supply. We examine the case of a firm which produces two products with given amounts of the several scarce inputs which it has at its disposal. How much of each of its joint products does it produce?

Consider the example of a lumber mill that produces plywood and structural timber. It has to decide how much of each of these final products to turn out. We can study how a firm makes the most profitable *product mix decision* under circumstances of limited inputs through a very important technique called *linear programming*. We shall see that the firm maximizes its profits by choosing that combination of outputs that makes the best use of its limited inputs. The law of diminishing returns will emerge as central to this calculation. The problem is: out of its possible outputs of final use, how many sheets of plywood, y_1, and how many timbers, y_2, should the firm produce to make the most money?[2]

[2] The reader will bear in mind that the distinction between final uses, y_1, and total outputs, X_i, arises because in the national economy some of the output is used up in the production of output. We are supposing the same situation in this firm in which some of the output of timber and plywood is used by the lumber mill itself in its operations. The money made through sale arises only from its final use to be sold. Frequently firms do not use their own products; then the distinction between output and final sales disappears.

We also need to specify the constraints on final use. These frontiers depend on the limited supply of factors that the firm owns or has hired. Take it that the woodworking firm is limited by the number of logs it can store in its millpond, c_1, the number of man-hours of labour at its disposal, c_2, the number of railway carriages available to haul the product to market, c_3, and finally the hours of saw and other machine time available, c_4. Final output and primary input symbols are summarized as follows:

Final outputs	Primary inputs
y_1 = sheets of plywood finally available for sale	c_1 = number of logs that can be stored in pond
y_2 = number of timbers finally available for sale	c_2 = number of man-hours of labour
	c_3 = number of railway carriages
	c_4 = number of hours of saw and other machinery

We also need to relate the final use to the constraining primary inputs. To do so we need to know the amount of each of these inputs directly and indirectly required for a unit of the final outputs. Instead of special symbols such as T_1 and T_2 for labour, and Q_1 and Q_2 for natural resources, we use the symbols M_{ij}, where the i designates the primary input, and j indicates the

Table 5.1 Coefficients of primary input directly and indirectly required per unit of final use of plywood and logs and the corresponding quantity of the primary inputs available

	Coefficients (M_{ij})		Primary input available (c_i)
	Plywood	Timber	
Log storage	M_{11}	M_{12}	c_1
Labour	M_{21}	M_{22}	c_2
Railway carriages	M_{31}	M_{32}	c_3
Saw and machine time	M_{41}	M_{42}	c_4

	Coefficients		Primary input available
	Plywood	Timber	
Log storage	0·5	0·4	100
Labour	0·4	0·2	80
Railway carriages	0·01	0·001	3
Saw and machine time	0·2	0·4	80

final output. For example, M_{11} is the log storage directly and indirectly required per sheet of plywood, and M_{12} is the log storage needed directly and indirectly for each timber. Then if all the available storage is utilized, $c_1 = M_{11}y_1 + M_{12}y_2$ is the log storage production possibility frontier. Table 5.1. consists of M_{ij} values and c_i values. Following our custom the information is presented in general algebraic form on the left and in illustrative hypothetical numbers on the right.

Since it is unlikely that all of the constraints will be effective at once, generally there will be some *slack* (unemployed or unused) inputs available. Consequently we must say that no more than the limited amount of the inputs can be used. In linear programming problems, therefore, the constraints imposed by the available inputs are written in the form of *inequalities*. For instance, the carriages used for carrying plywood and timbers must be less than or equal to the total number of carriages available; that is, the feasible mixture of final outputs is on or within the production possibility frontier represented by the railway carriage constraint.

The system of *structural constraints* can be written:

Theory	Example
$M_{11}y_1 + M_{12}y_2 \leqq c_1$	$0{\cdot}5y_1 + 0{\cdot}4y_2 \leqq 106$ (logs)
$M_{21}y_1 + M_{22}y_2 \leqq c_2$	$0{\cdot}4y_1 + 0{\cdot}2y_2 \leqq 80$ (labour)
$M_{31}y_1 + M_{32}y_2 \leqq c_3$	$0{\cdot}0y_1 + 0{\cdot}0y_2 \leqq 3$ (carriages)
$M_{41}y_1 + M_{42}y_2 \leqq c_4$	$0{\cdot}2y_1 + 0{\cdot}4y_2 \leqq 80$ (saw and machine time)

Since we cannot permit negative final use, it is also specified that the final outputs must be greater than or equal to zero, $y_1 \geqq 0$, and $y_2 \geqq 0$. Graphically these *non-negativity* constraints mean we confine ourselves to the first quadrant on our search for optimal output combinations. The feasible set is bounded by the positive axes as well as the frontiers comprising the *structural constraints* (Figure 5.5). Obviously the feasible set is convex. A combination of final outputs is feasible if it lies on or within all of the constraining frontiers. If it should lie outside any one of them, there would either not be enough of some input, or we would be contemplating negative final use. The production programme would be infeasible. Since a feasible point is not likely to be on the boundary of all of the constraints, it follows that some inputs will have slack, excess capacity.

Query: Interpret the expression 'production bottleneck' in terms of the diagram.

The problem of the lumber firm is to decide how much of each product to produce in order to make the most revenue. The making of the most money is the objective of the firm, so we identify revenue as the *objective function*. The revenue of the firm is the sum of the price of its products times the

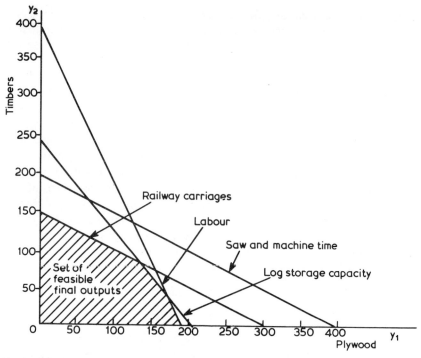

Figure 5.5 Constraints and feasible outputs of a lumber mill

quantity of them produced. Writing R for revenue, the objective function is the linear expression: $R = p_1y_1 + p_2y_2$. Linear programming is a method of maximizing a linear objective function, subject to the linear constraints which define the feasible set. The programme of final outputs chosen by the firm must be feasible – it must satisfy all the resource constraints. Of these feasible points, the best point is to be chosen; it is the optimal point that maximizes the objective function (it is also possible to use linear programming to minimize an objective function, but we will pursue this idea in the next chapter when we discuss minimizing cost).

There are a number of computational techniques for solving the linear programming problem. The principle behind all of them is illustrated in the simple illustration we shall give. The fact that a computer is used for efficient time-saving solutions to sizable linear programming problems should encourage, rather than disturb, the reader who is not a mathematician. If one understands the nature of the linear programming problem and how to interpret its results, there is no reason at all to go through the labour of computing the outcome. That is what the computer is for. The problem for practicing economists is, more often, to interpret the economic situation in linear programming form so it can be cast into the 'canned programme'. Thus the revenue objective function is written in linear form, prices being the constants, whilst the outputs are the variables to be chosen by the production decisions of the firm. This is really a statement that the industry of which the firm is a part is perfectly competitive. By holding back on output, a small firm is not going to be able to raise prices appreciably. All it will do is lose trade to competitors. The going price of the products is simply a fact – a take-it-or-leave-it proposition. If prices are not going to be affected by the amounts the firm produces, then revenue can be altered by program-ming the outputs. To maximize revenue the firm will therefore produce up to the point where it is held back by the constraints. That is to say, it will operate somewhere on the combined production possibility frontier formed by the various constraints.

But where on the frontier? To find out, let the price of a sheet of plywood be £4, and that of timber be £6. Then $R = 4y_1 + 6y_2$. The toal revenue is £4 times the amount of plywood sold, plus £6 times the number of timbers. For any particular revenue the objective function is a straight line which represents the set of all the various ways the firm has to make R amount of money. This is clearly seen to be the case if we cast the objective function in slope-intercept form: $y_2 = (-2/3)y_1 + R/4$. The negative slope of the line is the ratio of the prices, $-£4/£6 = -2/3$. Since these prices are taken as beyond the control of the competitive firm, the only way the firm can increase R is to move the line parallel to itself in a 'northeasterly' direction. Each time the revenue line moves this way, it describes a new set of plywood and timber combinations that will earn the increased revenue. The outward shifting of the revenue line is shown in Figure 5.6 superimposed on the set of feasible outputs originally shown in Figure 5.5.

What stops the firm from increasing its revenue indefinitely by producing more and more? A bottleneck eventually appears in the form of log storage, labour, carriages, or machine time. Eventually something must run out. We can represent this situation graphically by moving the objective function out, increasing revenue all the while, until it reaches the furthest extremes of the feasible set given by the constraints. Typically such an extreme point will be one of the corners of the convex polygon (conceivably the furthest value of the objective function might be on one of the line segments if the slope of the revenue line happens to be exactly the same as the effective constraint). The extreme points are called *basic solutions* and are candidates for the optimal output. Even if it should turn out that the objective function has the same slope of one of the constraints, then, as the reader can see for himself, there still is no better, higher revenue position than the two extreme points that lie on the line of the constraint.

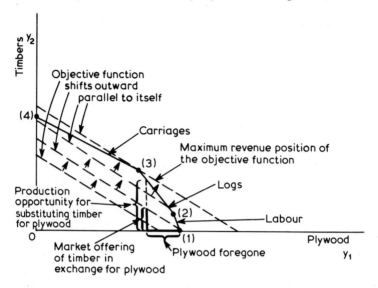

Figure 5.6   Linear programming maximizing the objective
function subject to constraints (point (3) is the optimal output of
plywood and timbers)

Linear programming is nothing but a systematic method of examining the extreme points and determining at which of them the objective function is greatest. Computer solutions first identify the extreme points as basic solutions by considering the points of intersection of the frontiers. If these points lie within all the other frontiers, then they are basic feasible solutions. Each of these basic feasible solutions represents an amount of plywood and timbers. Choosing the optimal solution consists of substituting the amounts of timbers and plywood into the objective function and computing R. The basic feasible solution which yields the maximum revenue is the optimum. It is that simple!

Whilst the principle is simple, computation time can get out of control if all the intersections of all the frontiers have to be considered. This is especially true if there are more than two products to be considered as well as many constraints. Even for a computer that can take too long, so methods have been devised with which to shorten the work. Starting from any basic feasible solution, the procedure calls for the programme only to go on to consider a better basic feasible solution. Should a given solution cause the objective function to decline, the analyst and his faithful computer know they have passed the optimum and should go back to the previous basic feasible solution.

Linear programming will be shown to be nothing but a fancy computational form using the law of diminishing returns. Let us work out the example to see this important result. The first step is to identify the basic feasible solutions. This can be done graphically. By inspecting the diagram, we can see that there are four basic feasible solutions numbered for reference. They are the intersections of pairs of frontiers that also lie on the boundary of the feasible set (intersections outside the set are infeasible and need not concern us). Table 5.2 summarizes these candidates for the optimum.

Table 5.2

Basic feasible solution in Figure 5.6	Relevant effective constraints	Equations	Coordinates of basic extreme point found by solving the pairs ·of equations
(1)	Labour frontier Horizontal axis	$0{\cdot}4y_1 + 0{\cdot}2y_2 = 80$ $y_2 = 0$	$y_1 = 200,\ y_2 = 0$
(2)	Labour frontier Log frontier	$0{\cdot}4y_1 + 0{\cdot}2y_2 = 80$ $0{\cdot}5y_1 + 0{\cdot}4y_2 = 106$	$y_1 = 180,\ y_2 = 40$
(3)	Log frontier Railway carriage frontier	$0{\cdot}5y_1 + 0{\cdot}4y_2 = 106$ $0{\cdot}01y_1 + 0{\cdot}02y_2 = 3$	$y_1 = 153{\cdot}3,\ y_2 = 73{\cdot}3$
(4)	Railway carriage frontier Vertical axis	$0{\cdot}01y_1 + 0{\cdot}02y = 3$ $y_1 = 0$	$y_1 = 0,\ y_2 = 150$

Take solution (1) where the labour frontier and horizontal axis intersect ($y_1 = 200$, $y_2 = 0$). There the objective function $R = 4y_1 + 6y_2$ is $R = 4(200) + 6(0) = 806$. If the lumber mill makes no timbers, but concentrates solely on making 200 units of plywood it will make £800, but no more because it would not have enough labour.

Is there a way to make more money? Consider extreme point (2) where the labour frontier is joined by the log frontier. At point (2) less plywood, ($y_1 = 180$) and more timbers ($y_2 = 40$) are produced. The revenue is $R = 4(180) + 6(40) = 960$. Point (2) is better than point (1) by £160. At point (1) the firm only used its labour to capacity, but had an excess supply of logs as well as the other inputs. By changing its product mix to include timbers the firm in effect has substituted logs for the scarce labour and increased its income. But now is has been stopped by the shortage of logs.

Let us see if the firm can make still more money. Consider point (3). Here $R = 4(153 \cdot 3) + 6(73 \cdot 3) = 1053 \cdot 33$. This product mix is still better by £93·33. Having run out of logs and labour at (2) the product mix is changed again to save still more labour by producing more timbers and less plywood. In fact there is excess labour at point (3), and output is limited by logs and railway carriages.

Thus far revenue has been increased at each successive point. But the increase in revenue has declined. Revenue increased by £160 from point (1) to point (2). But the increase in revenue from (2) to (3) is only £93·33. Up to (3) income from plywood has been sacrificed for greater income from timbers. All the while the production of timbers has become more difficult as it is necessary to make more and more awkward factor substitutions. The increase in the number of timbers for each sacrifice of plywood becomes smaller. This is the law of diminishing returns at work through the convex shape of the frontier. As a result the additional revenue earned by the substitution declines.

Would the revenues of the firm increase if a further substitution were made by going to point (4) producing only timbers ($R = 4(0) + 6(150) = 900$)? Revenue would be less then at (3). The firm would not choose this product mix, even though it is feasible. Substitution would stop at (3), where the firm makes the most money with the scarce resources at its disposal. In so far as the product prices also reflect the desires of the public for timbers and plywood, the firm has produced amounts of these two products that most satisfy the public with the limited resources of inputs at its disposal.

The process can be made more clear by comparing the shadow price of production alternatives to the firm with the market alternatives. The revenue line shows the market possibilities open to the firm, since its slope is the relative market price of timber compared to plywood. The market offers opportunities to exchange timber for plywood at the going price while the production possibility frontier shows the opportunity to manufacture more timber and less plywood at various shadow prices.

Self-interested revenue maximizing behaviour is the mechanism that brings shadow prices into line with the market price signals. For the fact that less timber is offered by the market in exchange for plywood means that the market price of timber is higher than its production shadow price. Obviously the firm should manufacture the timber itself at the *lower shadow price* and sell it on the market to take advantage of the *higher market price*. The process comes to an end at (3) where the slope of the production possibility frontier has caught up with that of the revenue line. The law of diminishing returns has operated to reduce the additional timber available in return for another unit of plywood not produced. This crucial result can be restated in terms of marginal cost. The marginal cost of plywood is $\Delta y_2 / \Delta y_1$, the amount of timber given up in return for an increase in plywood. Casting the revenue line in slope-intercept form, $y_2 = (-p_1/p_2)y_1 + R/p_2$, we see that the revenue maximization process amounts to making the marginal cost of plywood as close as possible to its price compared to timber, since the slope of the revenue line at the optimum is just in between the slopes of the two adjoining segments of the production possibility frontier.

Exercise:
(1) Suppose the prices of plywood and timbers were reversed, what would be the optimal production of these two products? What if the prices of plywood and timbers were doubled?
(2) How does the production possibility frontier show how alternate prices are offered to the public for timbers and plywood?

In economic literature the product mix problem is often discussed by assuming that the production possibility frontier is not only convex, but smooth. With a large number of constraints every point on the frontier would be a basic feasible solution. The maximum revenue would then be reached when the objective revenue function just touches one of these points. The product mix problem will be solved by the point of tangency between the smooth production possibility frontier and the revenue line (Figure 5.7).

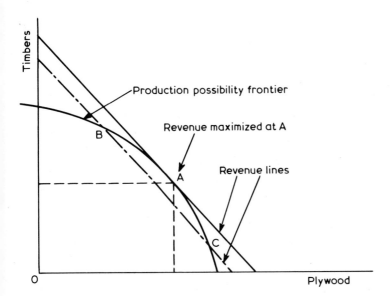

Figure 5.7   Tangency solution to product mix problem with smooth production possibility frontier

The smooth curve offers an infinite gradation of slopes, and so offers the possibility of a perfect match between shadow price and market price. Then marginal cost would exactly equal price. This is a case of complete adjustment which is only approximated in the polygon frontier. Finding the optimal solution to the product mix problem requires the application of calculus methods to the equation of the frontier rather than linear programming. As a practical matter, it is not always possible to obtain the necessary equation from engineering or other technical sources. More frequently the available information fits more readily into the linear form. Of course, the smooth function is still very useful and we shall have to be familiar with both.

The crucial function of prices as a means of harmonizing production and product mix demand can now be appreciated. For this to occur market prices must reflect shadow prices as well as consumer desires. It is now evident that failure to achieve this sort of harmonization will mean that the goods will be produced in the wrong quantities. Whatever the source of this disjointedness – monopoly disregard of competitive prices or government regulations – the result inevitably is a loss to the public.

Exercise:
(1) Show the working of the law of diminishing returns in the case of the smooth production possibility frontier.
(2) Do Soviet national planners face the product mix problem? How can they go about solving it?
(3) Consider a university that produces honours graduates in both English literature and economics. Designate the number of literature graduates by y_1 and the number of economists by y_2. To do so the university requires library space and computer facilities. Suppose the institution has at its disposal 50 square feet of library space and 40 hours of computer time to use for these two purposes. A literature honours student takes up 4 square feet of library space and the economist requires 10 square feet. The literature student requires 5 hours of computer time and so does the economics student.

Judging by the salaries they are paid in the market for graduates, economists are more valuable than literature students. Say that an economics graduate with a first class degree can earn £5000 a year after some years of experience and the literature graduate with the same class degree can expect £4000.

(a) Set up the equations and inequalities for the linear programming problem which would enable the university authorities to decide among three possibilities: (i) train only economists; (ii) train only literature honours graduates; or (iii) train some of each.

(*b*) Graph the equations and use your graphs to answer the problem facing the university authorities.
(*c*) Explain how the law of diminishing returns is operative in this setting. To what extent do you feel that the method used is useful to discuss the various products of the university such as: teaching, research and community service; arousing intellectual curiosity; providing exercise rooms, public spectacles, and museums of Egyptology; training skilled workers; providing a forum for political debate and an area for political action; providing an avenue for upward social mobility of deprived groups.

6 The costs of production to the firm

Production by alternative methods

In the previous chapter we considered the problem of adjustment to the limited supply of specialized primary inputs through changes in the products produced for final use. Yet a business firm does not only find itself concerned with what products to produce, but also with how to go about producing them. This area of choice was swept under the rug in input-output analysis, where it was assumed that each industry could produce its product in only one way.

An example will make the point. Petrol is produced by a process called 'cracking' of crude petroleum. The main inputs are crude petroleum and electric energy (we will ignore the other inputs to keep matters simple). Three goods are involved: (1) electrical energy, (2) petrol, (3) crude petroleum. Two technical coefficients are required to express the inputs required per gallon of petrol: $a_{12} = x_{12}/X_2$, which is the electricity per gallon of petrol; and $a_{32} = x_{32}/X_2$, which is the crude petroleum per gallon of petrol. The combination of inputs which defines the method of production may be expressed as the ratio of electricity to petroleum used. This is nothing but the ratio of the technical coefficients, for, on dividing one by the other, the X_2 in the denominators cancel leaving $a_{12}/a_{32} = x_{12}/x_{32}$. This brings to light one more hidden assumption in input-output analysis: since the coefficients are taken to be constants, so must be their ratio, which turns out to be equal to the ratio of inputs. We have been assuming that the ratio of inputs is the same regardless of the amount of output produced.

Exercise: Using the assumptions of input-output, suppose the labour coefficient for the plywood industry is 5 hours of labour per 1000 board feet of finished plywood. Suppose the natural resources input is 2500 board feet of uncut timber in the forest per 1000 board feet of finished plywood. Compute the amount of labour per board foot of timber in the forest used in the plywood industry. Do you think the same ratio will hold for 10,000 board feet of finished plywood?

Surely there is more than one way to produce a gallon of petrol. A small amount of petroleum can be very highly refined with a great expenditure of many kilowatts of electricity to 'crack' it into petrol; alternatively, a lot of crude petroleum can be processed with only a small amount of electrical energy. Crude petroleum and electricity are substitutes for each other in petrol production. Certainly, they are not perfect substitutes; one can't make much petrol with only electricity and no petroleum, but there are feasible alternative processes combining the two inputs. The opportunity for substitution amounts to saying that for each product there are several sets of technical coefficients, each of which corresponds to a different production process.

Each production process may be represented graphically, measuring electrical input vertically and crude petroleum horizontally (Figure 6.1). Suppose that a_{12} equals 3 kilowatt hours for each gallon of petrol, and a_{32} is 5 gallons of crude petroleum for each gallon of final product. Then the ratio of electrical energy to crude is 3 kWh/5 gallons of crude. Since the ratio is constant for any output using this process, we can double the output

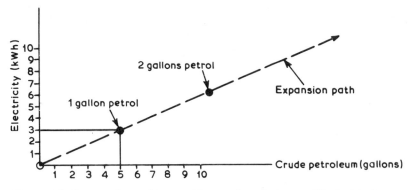

Figure 6.1 Output of petrol by cracking crude petroleum with electrical energy

of petrol by doubling the input of electricity and crude petroleum. Accordingly, we label the point (5, 3) as 1 gallon of petrol. To produce 2 gallons of petrol we must use 10 gallons of crude petroleum and 3 kWh of power. Label (10, 6) as 2 gallons of petrol. Connecting all such points we produce a line through the origin, which is called the *expansion path*. For every level of final output the expansion path tells us the amount of crude petroleum and energy that is used. The fact that the expansion path is a straight line through the origin tells us that the proportion of the two inputs never changes no matter how much is produced by the given process. This is because the slope of the path is the ratio of X_{12} to X_{32}, electricity to petroleum.

Exercise:
(1) Draw the expansion path for the plywood industry in the previous chapter.
(2) Does the fact that the expansion path is a straight line through the origin always require that if one doubles both inputs one doubles both outputs for this process? Give counter-examples where doubling all the inputs more than doubles output and less than doubles output. Does your conclusion conflict with constant proportions between the inputs?

Now we may introduce alternative processes, each of which has its own expansion path (Figure 6.2). The previous technical coefficients led to the expansion path labelled A. For different processes we will have different paths. If $a'_{12} = 8$ and $a'_{32} = 3$ we get expansion path A' with a slope of $\frac{8}{3}$. Still

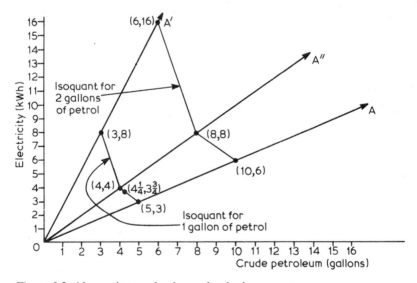

Figure 6.2 Alternative production technologies

another is $a''_{12} = 4$ and $a''_{32} = 4$, which gives expansion path A'' with a slope of 1. Each expansion path represents another way to make petrol from petroleum and electricity.

A firm could use any of these methods. It can also use any combination of methods in various proportions. Suppose, for instance, that it decides to produce one fourth of a gallon of petrol by method A and three fourths by method A''. Then it would need one fourth of the inputs for a gallon of petrol cracked by method A – namely, 1·25 gallons of crude petroleum and 0·75 kWh of electricity; it would also need three fourths of the inputs required for 1 gallon of petrol by production method A'', 3 gallons of petroleum and 3 kilowatt hours. One gallon of petrol produced by combining the two methods in the given proportion takes 4·25 gallons of petroleum and 3·75 kWh of electricity.

As the reader can verify for himself, this is a point which lies on the straight line joining (5, 3) and (4, 4). Such an intermediate point is only the weighted average of the two production methods for 1 gallon of petrol. Indeed the whole line segment between the two points represents different weighted averages for different proportions of each process used. Thus with two fundamental production methods, there are actually an infinite number of ways to produce a gallon of petrol. The firm might also use different proportions of A'' and another adjoining method, A'. It is now plain that the kinked line joining all three points is the set of combinations of electricity and petroleum that gives us the same quantity of petrol. Such a locus of equal output is called an *equal product curve*, or, in more pretentious jargon, an *isoquant*. Since we can construct an isoquant for 1 gallon of petrol, we can equally well construct one for 2 gallons, or for any desired output of petrol. Taken together they constitute an isoquant map of production technologies.

Exercise:
(1) If it takes 5 gallons of petroleum and 3 kWh to produce a gallon of petrol by method A and it takes 4 gallons of petroleum and 4 kWh by method A'', how much petroleum and electricity is required if half a gallon is produced by process A and half by process A''?
(2) Persons with interest in mathematics might want to prove that mixed processes always fall on the isoquant as drawn between the two points in Figure 6.2.

Efficiency and waste

The reader may have noticed that isoquants do not show all the possible ways of producing a given amount of final output. Would it be possible to produce 1 gallon of petrol with 4 kWh of power and 5 gallons of crude petroleum, instead of 4 gallons of crude? All one need do in production process A'' is to simply pour 1 gallon of crude petroleum down the drain! Certainly that is absurd, yet it makes the point that isoquants are made up of ways of producing with a minimum amount of inputs. Isoquants illustrate the set of alternative efficient methods.

By studying waste we shall learn more about efficiency. There are more interesting ways of being wasteful than the fanciful method just suggested. A wasteful process is one that uses more of some inputs without reducing the amount required of others. Consider process A''', illustrated in Figure 6.3, which requires 4·5 gallons of crude petroleum and 4 kWh. The firm can do better by using a combination of three fourths of a gallon of petrol produced by process A'', and one fourth by A. It would then require only 4·25 gallons of crude and 3·75 kWh to make the gallon of petrol. A''' is inefficient and does not contribute to the isoquant construction, since it is as wasteful as throwing petroleum and electricity away. Graphically the point on A''' corresponding to 1 gallon of petrol lies beyond the isoquant that could be built up out of the three other processes.

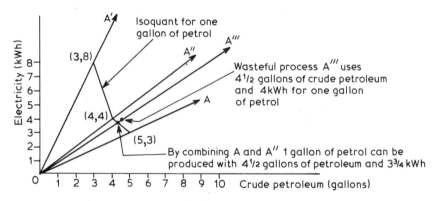

Figure 6.3   An inefficient production process, A'''

Exercise:
Consider production process A''' for which the technical coefficients of production are $a_{12} = 5$ and $a_{32} = 4$.
(1) Draw an expansion path A''' on Figure 6.3.
(2) Show that it is an inefficient process.
(3) From the graph, estimate what the technical coefficients would have to be for a process along expansion path A''' to be efficient.

One other form of waste is not as obvious, and yet is very important. A combined process of A and A' is also inefficient (Figure 6.4). It would

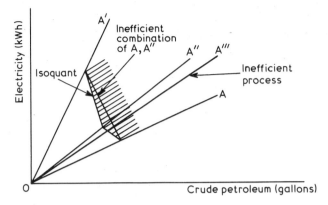

Figure 6.4   Efficient and inefficient combinations of
production processes (any point in the shaded region is
inefficient since it takes more inputs than necessary to
make 1 gallon of petrol)

consist of points on a line between the 1-gallon-of-petrol points on *A* and
A', but all of those points also lie beyond the isoquant. They use up more
crude petroleum and electricity than combinations of two adjacent efficient
methods. Only adjacent methods can go into building up isoquants. Hence,
as the diagram shows, the isoquant includes only points that form an inward
bending broken line, convex toward the origin. Input combinations within
the bends of the isoquant are inefficient, since one way or another it is
possible to make 1 gallon of petrol with less. Only the points on the isoquant
will be considered by a rational firm seeking to avoid waste.

Query: How is it possible for two production processes to be efficient, and
for combinations of those processes to be inefficient?

The law of variable proportions

The fact that isoquants slope downward and bend in toward the origin
means, in economic terms, that by switching from one efficient production
method to another a firm is in effect substituting one input for another. This
can be seen from Table 6.1, which summarizes the alternative efficient
methods for making 1 gallon of petrol.

   If the managers of the cracking plant were to change over from process *A*
to process *A''* they would use 1 gallon less petroleum and use 1 kWh more of
electricity in turning out 1 gallon of petrol. Now, suppose they were to switch
from process *A''* to process *A'*. Again they would use 1 less gallon of crude
petroleum input, but now they would refine it much more completely and

Table 6.1   Methods for producing 1 gallon of petrol

	Method		
	A	A″	A′
Inputs			
Crude petroleum (gallons)	5	4	3
Electricity (kWh)	3	4	8

would have to use 4 more kWh of electrical power. The increase in one input which must be substituted for the decrease in the other whilst staying on the same isoquant is called the *marginal rate of technical substitution*. Clearly the rate of technical substitution is the slope of the isoquant.

In the first instance the firm substituted 1 gallon of petroleum for 1 kWh. In the second changeover the rate of technical substitution was 1 gallon of petroleum for 4 kWh. The rate of technical substitution increases because electricity is only an imperfect substitute for crude petroleum in making petrol. When we used a lot of crude petroleum and only a little electricity, in process *A*, it was possible to substitute 1 kWh for 1 gallon of crude petroleum by going to process *A″*. But, once having made that change, it took 4 kWh to substitute for another gallon of crude petroleum when going from *A″* to *A′*. Because the isoquant is convex toward the origin, the slope increases as the amount of crude petroleum decreases, reflecting the imperfect substitution of inputs.

Query: What would be the behaviour of the rate of technical substitution if the isoquants were straight lines? How would this reflect the perfectness of substitution of electricity for petroleum? Could petrol be made without petroleum? Without electricity?

This insight into the nature of efficient production is called the *law of variable proportions*. The amount of an input into production which can be efficiently substituted for another input to get the same output depends on the amount of each input already in use. If only a little bit of one of the inputs is presently in use it will be very hard to substitute for it; a lot of the substitute factor is required. If a great deal is in use the substitution will be easier. The reason for the increasing difficulty of substitution is specialization. Production methods are biased or specialized towards the use of one or the other of the inputs, just as in Chapter 5 factors of production were seen to be biased towards various products. Thus method *A* uses a great deal of petroleum and little electricity, while the reverse is the case for method *A′*; more petroleum is used in *A* and electricity is more adapted to *A′*. The specialization appears as the different slopes of the two expansion paths that show the respective proportions of petroleum and electricity used.

Now consider that there may be a very large number of efficient processes. Actually the example of cracking petroleum is close to this situation since it is possible to vary the input mix by a bit more electricity, corresponding to a bit less crude petroleum. If the number of alternatives is large enough we may then consider that the isoquant is a smooth curve. The law of variable proportion tells us that the curve is convex towards the origin. Each of the infinite number of points on the curve represents a way to make petroleum and electricity efficiently into petrol. The constantly changing slope of the isoquant is the rate of technical substitution (Figure 6.5).

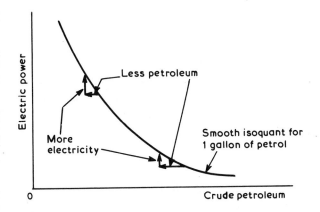

Figure 6.5   Isoquant of production with a large number of efficient processes

Query: Why would it be unlikely for an isoquant to double back on itself as in Figure 6.6? (Draw linear expansion paths for processes cutting the isoquant twice.) But can you think of a circumstance in which such a situation might exist?

The law of variable proportions, then, amounts to saying that all isoquants are convex toward the origin. If we drew isoquants for various levels of output, we would have graphed a set of nested isoquants spaced in some convenient way. Others could always be drawn for intermediate outputs. Isoquants are much like the elevation contours on a topographical map. They show equal outputs just as the contours show equal altitude. Figure 6.7 is a three-dimensional sketch of two mountains and the corresponding contour map. Continuing the analogy, the elevations correspond to outputs

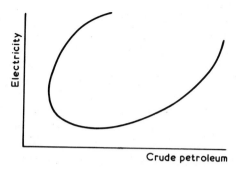

Figure 6.6   Backward bending isoquant

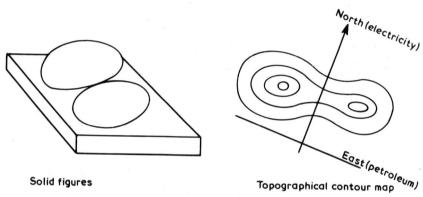

Solid figures   Topographical contour map

Figure 6.7   Solid three-dimensional figures and contours

of petrol, while the north-south distance indicates electricity input and the east-west dimension shows the input of crude petroleum. The elevation contours on the map correspond to the isoquants in our production analysis.

Isoquants can easily be shown never to cross each other. If they did, we would be saying that the same input yielded different outputs for two methods and yet that both methods were efficient. That is simply inconsistent with the idea that the isoquant is the locus of efficient points that gets the most production from the inputs of factors. It would be like saying that the altitude lines on a map showed a mountain which had two different heights at the same location.

Of course, an isoquant map does not consist of a set of closed contours like the map showing the elevation of the two mountains. As one moves across the map, the elevation increases and then gets lower. The contours go around the hill to form a closed loop. Production is different. The three-dimensional figure to which the isoquant contours correspond is the graph of a production function. The production function shows on the vertical axis the maximum amount of output that can be produced with a given combination of inputs shown on the two horizontal axes (Figure 6.8). Since each of the inputs adds something to output if more of it is used, our production function is likely to be a surface opening indefinitely out from the origin. The isoquants are created by passing an imaginary plane parallel to the horizontal input plane through the surface and observing that such planes cut the surface at points of equal output. We can then project the equal output contours on a common plane as an isoquant map. Isoquants do not come around to form a closed loop because output is not like a mountain – it does not decline again as we move across the surface increasing the inputs.

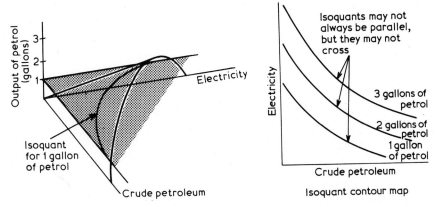

Figure 6.8   Three-dimensional production function and isoquant contour map

Choice of technique

Now we are in a position to deal with the question that motivated this chapter. How does a firm choose a production method among the many efficient ones available? How does the firm choose which combination of factors to use in order to get a desired amount of output? Should it choose a method which uses a great deal of petroleum and little electricity? Or should it choose a different production technology which uses more electric power and less crude petroleum? How does the firm solve the factor mix problem? The answer will depend on the price of factors of production.

Suppose the firm expects to spend a given amount of money, yet wants to get the maximum output for that expenditure on production costs. It will want to get to the highest possible isoquant subject to the limitation of the costs that it is going to undertake. The costs of production are nothing but the sum of the price of the various inputs times the amount of them used. Continuing with the petrol cracking plant example, we designate the price of one kilowatt hour p_k; the price of crude petroleum is p_c. Then if the amounts of these two inputs are symbolized by X_k and X_c respectively, total costs $C = p_k X_k + p_c X_c$. The line represents various combinations of X_k and X_c that can be purchased with the same cost expenditure. Cast in slope-intercept form, $X_k = (-p_c/p_k)X_c + C/p_k$, the line is seen to have a negative slope which is equal to the relative prices of the input factors of production.

Given the money that the businessman plans to spend, the cost line represents the set of feasible combinations of inputs. Any point beyond it costs too much. Any point within or on the boundary of the cost line is feasible. Of course, the firm wants the greatest output for its money, so – reasoning exactly as we did in the linear programming solution to the product mix problem – we see that the highest isoquant subject to the cost limitation is achieved at an extreme point involving one of the production methods. Any other point in the feasible set involves less output.

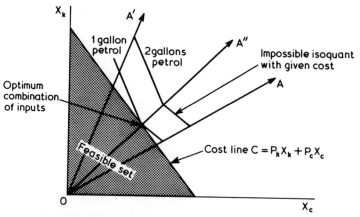

Figure 6.9   Solving the factor mix problem

Exercise: Demonstrate the same result as the text achieves by writing the factor mix problem as a minimization linear programming problem. Show the firm as attempting to minimize costs subject to the limitation that it will produce 1 gallon of petrol.

Once again, we can extend this analysis to the situation in which the isoquants are smooth convex curves (Figure 6.10). The inputs chosen to maximize output subject to a given cost of production will be where the cost line just touches or is tangent to a smooth isoquant. This tangency solution *B*

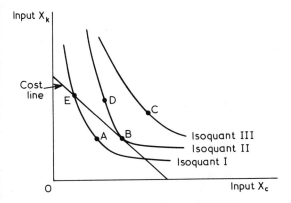

Figure 6.10   Tangency solution to factor mix
problem

is the highest output that can be obtained with the money that is to be spent. Points D and C clearly cost more than the firm plans to spend, whilst E and A are not too costly but do not represent the maximum output that can be produced. B is both feasible and optimal. The factor mix problem is solved.

Exercise: In the case of the petroleum cracking plant draw the cost line if £5 is to be spent and if the price of electricity is a fantastic 5p per kWh and crude petroleum sells for 5p per gallon. Find out by graphic means which of the three production methods would be used. Compute the amount of petrol turned out. Now suppose electricity were 5p per kWh and crude petroleum were 10p. What has happened to factor mix and output?

The return of diminishing returns

The solution to the factor mix problem in terms of the law of variable proportions took us a long way towards understanding the adjustment process of a competitive market economy. It is not the whole story. By applying a cost limitation to the law of variable proportion, we were able to determine how much of each factor would be used for a given outlay on factors of production. The fact remains that the amount a firm can spend is not constant. Unlike an individual consumer a firm does not really have a fixed budget because it can always borrow against future earnings. So long as the increase in revenues resulting from the enlarged production exceeds the increase in cost of production (including the cost of borrowing), it will be worthwhile for the firm to expand both costs and output.

Query: Cannot consumers borrow as well as firms? Explain the difference.

It is necessary to solve the problem of how much of the product the firm will produce, and hence the cost involved. Once we can identify the isoquant on which the firm is working, the law of variable proportions will then give us the factors to be employed. As the reader has no doubt anticipated, we are going to have to revisit the law of diminishing returns in a new guise in order to determine how much product will be produced by a profit maximizing firm under competitive conditions.

Explaining the law of diminishing returns in terms of the amount of output of a product compared to the input of several factors of production inevitably leads us back to the idea of a production function – the equation that relates the maximum output producible with various combinations of input. There are all sorts of equations that will do for a production function. I remember one very vividly. In the long and strenuous career that the author has had as a teacher, there was one particularly trying episode. One summer I taught a remedial class in mathematics to the American equivalent of second form. I recall trying to convince one girl that if she wanted to make two batches of cookies she should simple double the recipe for one batch. We both failed dismally. Let me try again. Twice as much sugar, flour, butter, water and chocolate chips makes twice as many cookies. Translated into our isoquant diagram, I was really assuming two rather special things about the nature of cookie baking.

First, I believed it possible to hold the proportions of factors of production the same whilst doubling the recipe. That is to say, I expected the production function to be such that I was able to expand output along an *expansion path* which was a straight line out from the origin (Figure 6.11). The expansion path would be generated by cookie bakers deciding to spend more and more

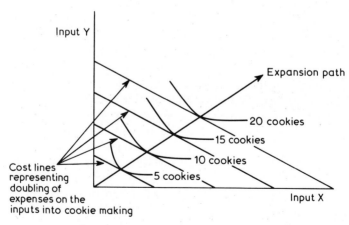

Figure 6.11   Expanding output

money. The path is the set of tangency points generated by moving the cost line outward. If the prices of factors of production are unchanged, the cost line will move parallel to itself as more money is spent on inputs. If the factor mix is in the same proportion regardless of output, the isoquants are also parallel to one another, as we have been drawing them all along. This amounts to assuming that if the prices of the ingredients do not change, cooks will not change the recipe no matter how many cookies they bake.

Query: What would the expansion path be if there were only one way to make cookies? What would the isoquants be like? How are they different from the present example?

Secondly, I was saying that the isoquants were equally spaced. That meant that if she doubled the inputs along an expansion path, she moved to an isoquant representing twice as much output. Using the same recipe, doubling the ingredients resulted in twice as many cookies, not three times as many or one and a half times as many.

Query: What would the three-dimensional production function look like if cookie output were measured vertically and the ingredients (say there were two) were measured on the horizontal axes?

The reader is doubtlessly a bit annoyed! Surely there are cases where neither of these two assumptions hold. Must it be the case that isoquants are always parallel? Increasing outputs with constant prices of factors often does result in different factor combinations. The expansion path may wiggle and change slope with increased output. Secondly, it certainly is easy to produce examples where doubling all the inputs will not double the output. These objections are well founded. The author's reason for discussing this simplified situation is to show the working of the robust law of diminishing returns below. It works even under conditions where doubling inputs actually does double outputs.

Exercise:
(1) Discuss the circumstances under which these simplifying assumptions might not hold. Give examples and draw graphs showing isoquants, cost lines and expansion paths.
(2) Criticize the accuracy of the two assumptions made in the text in the following conditions.
  (*a*) Increase the amount of freight carried in a freight car by increasing the size of the car. The two inputs to be considered are axles and wheels, and metal for freight car bodies. Compare with ocean-going oil tankers.
  (*b*) Production of cattle in some places in Australia or the western USA where the land is free, and the only cost is the barbed wire. The

inputs are square feet of land, and the barbed wire fence around the perimeter of the grazing land.

So, we take it that twice the recipe means twice the number of cookies. Or does it? Suppose one of the inputs were fixed in supply so that it were impossible to increase the amount of it in use. Normally, there is only one kitchen stove in a home. What happens when we are already using it twenty-four hours a day? How could we make more cookies? The answer is really obvious – change the recipe to bake faster. That is to say, we must alter the production method and proceed to a different expansion path. We could turn up the heat, use more labour to roll out the cookies thinner, or use more dry ingredients to get them to bake faster. We illustrate the law of diminishing returns to show how such successive recipe changes would become less and less fruitful as a substitute for the scarce kitchen stove input. While cookie output can be increased, the increase in output would become smaller as more and more cookie-rolling, heat and dry ingredients were added. That is to say, in the presence of a fixed factor of production – the stove – the increase in output resulting from increased use of the other factors will decline.

Look at the problem with one factor of production fixed. In Figure 6.12, we represent kitchen stoves, the fixed factor, on the vertical axis as input Y. Horizontally we show the variable factors lumped together as variable X. Isoquants are drawn for each level of output: one batch of cookies, two batches, three batches, etc. They are parallel and equally spaced to

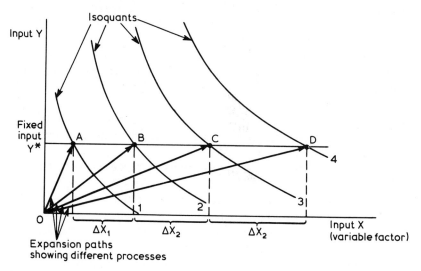

Figure 6.12   Expansion of output with one input fixed and the other variable

emphasize that if we could double all the inputs, including kitchen stoves, we would indeed double all the outputs. If input Y is fixed at some amount, say Y^*, then one can get from lower to higher isoquants only by increasing the variable factor X. Say Y^* is always used to capacity, so production will be carried on along a line parallel to the x-axis at the height of Y^*. More and more X is used with Y^*. Each time another dose of X is added, production moves on to the next isoquant, from point A to B, to C and so on. But observe that the production method is being changed since the factor proportions of X to Y is being altered each time! The expansion path changes from OA to OB, to OC and so on.

It is clear from the diagram that, in the presence of a fixed factor of production, the variable factor must increase by increasing amounts to increase the product by the same amount. As we move along the line parallel to the horizontal axis where the fixed input is unchanging, we move from isoquant to isoquant increasing output by the same amount – one additional batch of cookies. But the increase in X, indicated by the successive ΔX_1, ΔX_2, ΔX_3, ..., is getting bigger and bigger. Therefore, the extra amount of variable input required for an additional unit of output is increasing. These are the *marginal costs* of an increase in cookie output. Other goods which could have been produced with these additional variable inputs are now foregone.

Measuring variable costs in physical units of X, and output in physical units designated by Q, we write marginal costs as $MC = \Delta X/\Delta Q$. Customarily, however, we state inputs in money terms, by multiplying the variable factors by their price.

$$\text{Marginal cost} = \frac{\text{Increase in cost in money terms}}{\text{Increase in physical output}} = \frac{\Delta C}{\Delta Q}.$$

The law of diminishing returns can now be restated: Given the state of technical knowledge, in the presence of specialized fixed inputs into production, marginal cost eventually rises with output.

What makes the law of diminishing returns work? Two things. (1) The inputs into production must be specialized in favour of a particular process or a particular product. That is to say, the factors of production are less than perfect substitutes for one another. It is this that gives isoquants their characteristic convex shape associated with the law of variable proportions. (2) Some inputs must be fixed. As a result the only way to increase output is by adding a more readily available input for one that has been fully utilized.

We can be fairly sure that the law will apply to almost any business. Certainly the inputs are bound to be differently specialized. The fixity of inputs is less certain since they can frequently be purchased. But redesigning

factory plant to use them takes time. Thus in the very long run a firm
conceivably might multiply the number of assembly lines or even the
number of factories indefinitely. Yet at any moment there is a lag of time
between the moment of decision to expand and the time when expansion is
accomplished. During this time interval the factory capacities of the firm
must be regarded as fixed. Indeed, even if it were physically possible to
increase the basic plant and equipment in a short time, firms do not do so
unless they are fairly sure that such an investment would be profitable over
the long run. Consequently in practice some inputs are almost always fixed,
and diminishing returns is almost universally involved in the decision
making process of any business enterprise. Later we will look at this issue
again to see if there are fixed factors in even the very long run.

Exercise:
(1) Drop either of the two assumptions and show that the law of diminishing
    returns does not hold. (*a*) Let the inputs not be specialized; show that
    the isoquants are not convex but straight lines sloping downward. If
    these lines are equally spaced, show that marginal cost is constant. (*b*)
    Let the isoquants be convex and equally spaced, but allow both input X
    and input Y to be increased as long as the firm wants to buy them. Show
    that marginal cost is constant.
(2) When Leontief originated the input-output system with one scarce
    input, 'labour', he was criticized for suspending the law of diminishing
    returns. Why?

Diminishing returns and the supply of the product

The objective of a capitalist business enterprise is to make the most profit,
which in turn is equal to total sales revenues minus the cost expenses. To
discover how much of a product a firm will produce we relate these two
categories to the quantity of goods sold and compute the profit maximizing
output.

For each additional unit of product sold, the addition to revenue is simply
the price the item fetches on the market. Since we are discussing a firm
operating in competitive conditions, we take it that the market price is
beyond the control of the firm. That is to say, the firm is too small a portion of
the industry to hope to raise the price through restriction of output as a
monopolist might. Thus, treating price as a constant, the total revenue of the
firm is simply the price times the quantity it chooses to produce. In Figure
6.13 quantities produced are measured on the horizontal axis and prices
vertically. Each of the bars represents a unit of output horizontally, and the
price vertically. Market price is shown as a horizontal line at P^* to show that

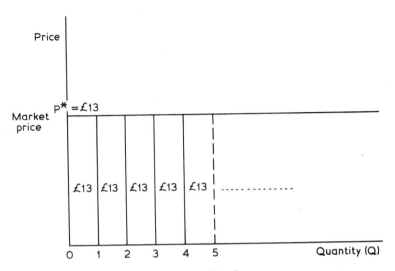

Figure 6.13   Revenues of the competitive firm

it is the same regardless of output. The area of each bar is one times P^* and represents the revenue from one unit of production sold. For any given quantity of output sold, Q, the revenue is the sum of these areas; the total revenue accruing to a firm is the area of the rectangle formed by the price, P^*, times quantity sold: $R = P^* \times Q$. Total revenue increases with quantity sold as the expanding area under the price line. Thus if the product sells for £13 and five units of it are sold, the revenue will be £65; if six units of it were sold revenue would be £78, and so on.

Calculations of costs can also be made in terms of output. We know from the previous section that marginal costs will rise with output. An illustrative table of these increasing increases in cost as the firm moves from one isoquant to another is given in Table 6.2.

The total cost of the variable inputs is clearly the running total of the marginal costs. Thus, if the first unit of output costs £10, and the second £9 more, the variable cost of two units is £19. Three units will cost £29 since the third unit adds £10, and so on (for the moment we put aside the problem of the cost of the fixed inputs, and promise to take it up in Chapter 8). Again representing units of output horizontally the height of the bars shows the marginal costs (Figure 6.14). For convenience we connect the midpoints of these marginal costs. Clearly the variable cost of the first unit is the area of the first bar, £10. The total variable cost of two units is'the area of the first bar plus the marginal cost area of the second and so on. Total variable costs as the sum of the marginal costs are thus seen to be the area of as many bars

Table 6.2

Quantity	Marginal cost*	Total variable cost
1	10	10
2	9	19
3	10	29
4	11	40
5	12	52
6	13	65
7	15	80
8	16	96

* The reader will note that for realism we have permitted marginal costs to decline for a bit until the barrier of the fixed factor of production is encountered.

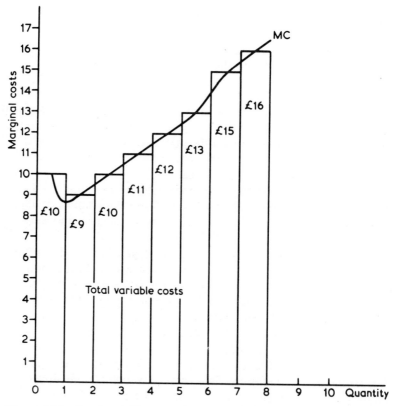

Figure 6.14   Total variable costs and marginal costs

as the firm produces units of output. Since the curve labeled *MC* (marginal cost) in the figure connects the midpoints of the bars, the total variable costs are seen to be the area under the marginal cost curve.

We are now in a position to make the profit maximizing calculation. The first unit of output brings £13 of revenue and costs £10, fetching a profit of £3. The second also fetches £13 but costs increase by £9, bringing £4 profit. Should a third unit be produced? Certainly, since *MC* is £10 and price £13, more profit is earned. Total profit is £3+4+3 = £10. More profit can be earned if four units are produced, since the *MC* of £11 is less than price. Indeed, any output programme for which marginal cost is less than price is operating on too small a scale, since further profits can be earned by increasing output. By the same token, if output is large enough to cause marginal cost to exceed price, a loss will be incurred on those last units. Thus if the firm were to produce seven units of output, marginal costs would be £15, while price would be £13. A loss of £2 would be incurred on the seventh item, which would have to be deducted from the profits earned on prior outputs. We conclude that the profit maximizing output for the competitive firm is that for which price equals marginal cost.

In our example the profit maximizing output is six units, where both price and marginal cost equal £13. Strictly, the profit is zero on the sixth unit, but if it were able to divide output more finely, profit would be earned up to five and a half units. The profit maximizing rule can be seen in Figure 6.15. The area under the marginal cost curve represents total variable costs, and the area under the price level represents total revenues. The difference between

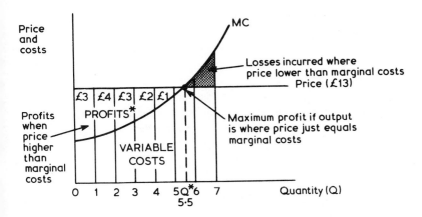

Figure 6.15   Price, marginal costs and profit maximization by a competitive firm

* Profits calculated before fixed costs

158 The costs of production to the firm

the two is the area labelled profits (before fixed costs are considered) which is maximized by obeying the rule $P = MC$.

The law of diminishing returns tells us that every time the firm produces another unit of product, the cost of that marginal unit rises. As long as the price is greater than the marginal cost the firm would be well advised to enlarge its output and sales. Inevitably, a point is reached where marginal costs catch up with price. Under competition it is not the difficulty of making sales that limits the firm's output, but the law of diminishing returns.

Exercise:
(1) Complete the following table for a firm in perfect competition.

Output of product (Q)	Costs of variable inputs (£)	Increase in costs MC (£ per additional unit)	Price of products (£)
0	0	0	15
1	2	2	
2	5	3	
3	7		
4	14		
5	20		
6	30		
7	42		
8	57		
9	74		
10	94		

(2) How much will the firm produce to make the most profit? Illustrate graphically.
(3) Draw a graph showing output horizontally and on the vertical axis show both total sales revenues and total variable costs. Find the profit maximizing output. Reconcile your result with (2). At what output would the firm 'break even' rather than maximize profit?
(4) Do these exercises again suspending the law of diminishing returns. Explain why the law of diminishing returns is necessary to explain levels of output under competitive conditions.

Since under competition a firm will produce where marginal cost equals price, we can determine how much the firm will produce at alternative prices simply by consulting the *MC* schedule. In the example in the previous section of the text, if the good sold for £15, seven units would be made. If it sold for £12, output would be reduced to five units. Graphically (Figure 6.16), for any price on the vertical axis, read over to the *MC* curve and down to find the corresponding quantity produced. If the market price of the

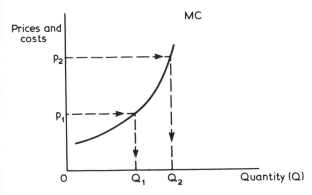

Figure 6.16   The marginal cost curve as the
supply curve of a single firm

product is p_1, firms will produce up to the point where MC equals that price, which is output Q_1. However, if the price were p_2, then the quantity produced would be Q_2. The marginal cost curve is therefore the supply curve of the firm, since it relates output to market price.

Since we know how much will be produced by each firm at each price we may add the output of the firms at various prices to get us to the supply curve for the industry. It will tell how much will be produced by all the firms in the industry at every price. Even though all the MC curves may not be identical for all the firms – they may be using different techniques of production – they all will slope upward due to the law of diminishing returns. As a result the supply curve for the product by the industry also will slope upward.

The demand curve for the product tells how much consumers are willing to buy at different prices. The equilibrium of supply and demand then is the balancing of the production possibilities against consumers' desires. In a market economy the balance is achieved by arriving at the equilibrium price at which the same quantity will be purchased as firms are willing to produce. This automatic process is remarkable. Not only does the market clear, but it also directs each firm to the production method and product mix that fulfils the desires of consumers who are able and willing to pay.

Exercise:
At the end of the previous chapter the reader was asked to do an exercise in which the product mix problem of a university was to be cast in linear programming terms. Now the reader should attempt to discuss the factor mix problem and the output problem as it faces the university.
(1) Discuss the problems involved in alternative methods of producing the university's products by teaching technique: lecture, television, libraries, informal education among students.

(2) Discuss the problems of the scale of operations of the university. What is the marginal cost of an additional student?

(3) Discuss the proper scale of operations of the university and how its product should be distributed to the public. Should education be auctioned off to the highest bidder? Should support of higher education be through a system of cash scholarships for students who would then enroll at universities run as profit making institutions? Contrast this last proposal with the present system.

(4) Distinguish between the university and a profit maximizing firm. Which principles of efficient management carry over and which do not?

7 The theory of demand

The efficient consumer

While there are important differences between the behaviour of consumers and that of business firms, there is one overriding similarity: they both want the most for their money! Firms want the most output and profits, but what do the consumers want? It is naive to think that consumers simply want the most things, because certainly they want fewer pollutants – less garbage rather than more. Evidently consumers want the most satisfactions that goods and services bring. We therefore define goods and services as those objects and activities that contribute to making the consumer feel better off. Pollutants are not goods, but the disposal activity which removes them is.

How much satisfaction does a consumer get? One cannot measure the increment in happiness a consumer receives with more goods in the same terms as a firm's increase in product with more inputs. In the production situation, if the owners of a competitive firm got twice as much product with twice as many inputs, they would count themselves twice as well off. At least they would have twice as much profit! Yet it is hard to believe that if a person achieves a certain level of satisfaction – economists use the word *utility* – from two sandwiches and one pint of beer he will be twice as happy if he downs four sandwiches and two pints.

Some might argue that the glutton is not really better off by overindulging himself. Perhaps that view makes sense from the point of view of the physician crusading against obesity, or the moralist who views it as a sin, but from the scientific point of view, describing consumer behaviour, asking if the consumer is really better off is nonsense. No one is forcing the glutton to eat and drink too much. Unwanted food can be thrown away. So if he does consume it all, he must feel that he gains satisfaction. In human behaviour, after all, it is the feeling of the individual that governs his decisions, not the feeling of other people who are passing judgement on him.

So whilst we are sure goods consumers purchase raise their level of utility, we still cannot say how much better off they become. Neither a consumer nor the economist watching him can count happiness in the same way as they can count gallons of petrol or pounds of profit. Nevertheless a person can rank the satisfactions he can get from various combinations of goods in some order which indicates whether one collection of goods makes him happier than another. To choose by ranking he need not say how much happier he is, only that he prefers one collection of goods to another. Indeed this is what we ordinarily do in the shops when selecting one basket of goods to take home rather than another which we can afford. We buy peas and pies instead of carrots and fish, thus revealing our preference ordering.

If it were a question of more of everything or less of everything, ranking would be easy. More of all of the items in a market basket will be ranked higher than less of each of the items. The beer-sandwich gourmand might rank his preferences as:

Input of food	Level of satisfaction
2 sandwiches & 1 beer	Good
4 sandwiches & 2 beers	Better
6 sandwiches & 3 beers	Better yet

Such an ordered ranking is called an *ordinal series* of classification. Compare it to the production situation for which we were able to assign quantitative values to the results:

Inputs of factors	Quantity of output
5 gallons of petroleum & 3 kWh	1 gallon of petrol
10 gallons of petroleum & 6 kWh	2 gallons of petrol
20 gallons of petroleum & 12 kWh	4 gallons of petrol

This latter series of outputs is called a *cardinal series*, which deals in amounts of output.

Query: Are all cardinal series ordinal? Are all ordinal series cardinal? Give examples.

A sensible consumer will choose the highest ranked utility level of satisfaction which his income permits. If he could only afford a 'good' outcome from the purchase of two sandwiches and one pint of beer he would have to be content with his lot. But if he could afford four sandwiches and two pints of beer he would buy that much which would make him 'better off'. A graph of such levels of satisfaction (Figure 7.1) is called an *income consumption curve* and looks very much like the expansion path we discovered in the theory of production. The only difference is that instead of the final product being gallons of petrol it is the states of satisfaction we have called 'good', 'better' and 'better yet'. We may number the levels of utility 1, 2, 3, provided we are very careful to remember that only a ranking is intended (we are not saying something ridiculous like: 'good' + 'better' = 'better yet', even though for cardinal numbers 1 + 2 does equal 3!).

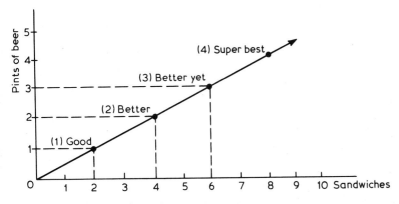

Figure 7.1   The happy consumer and his income consumption curve

Our reasoning now follows along the same route as the analysis of production. Many different activities involving combinations of sandwiches and beer can bring the consumer to the same level of satisfaction. The happiness level 'good' might be reached through a meal taken at home consisting of two sandwiches and one pint of beer. One might feel just as 'good' at the pub consuming two pints of beer and one sandwich. The first combination would be happiness producing process *A*, and the second, process *A'*. Just as in production theory, it would be possible to combine these processes in various proportions to give the 'good' level of utility. Thus some meals could be eaten at home, and others at the pub. Such mixed combinations would be a straight line joining the 'good' level for the different happiness processes. Further processes build up lines of equal satisfaction which have the somewhat unfortunate name of *indifference curves*. The reader is not meant to be indifferent to these curves; they show combinations for which a consumer is equally happy – indifferent.

For precisely the same reasons of efficiency that we studied in production, these indifference curves must be downward sloping and convex toward the origin. Furthermore, since people prefer more to less, an indifference curve lying 'northeast' of another signifies a higher level of satisfaction. This is so even though we do not pretend to know how much more happiness the goods that the consumer buys actually give him. All we know is that a curve lying beyond a given one represents more of everything, and that is 'better'. Since 'better' is different from 'good' combinations of sandwiches and beer, consistency requires that the indifference curves do not cross. If there are a large number of alternative activities the indifference curves become smooth just as in the case of the isoquants.

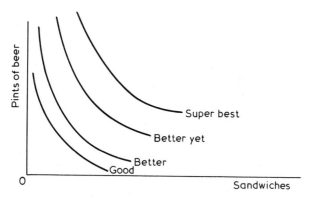

Figure 7.2   Indifference curves for sandwiches and beer

An individual may remain on the same indifference curve by substitution – by giving up sandwiches in order to get more beer. But the convexity of the indifference curve shows that substitution becomes more difficult as he gets more and more of one good. The more beer he already has (hence the fewer sandwiches he has), the greater will be the number of additional pints of beer an individual must substitute to relinquish sandwiches and still remain as well off. This compensating increase in pints per sandwich is called the *marginal rate of substitution* and is nothing but the slope of the indifference curve (Figure 7.3). The marginal rate of substitution is not constant, but increases as the amount of sandwiches declines, and declines as the number of sandwiches increases. All this really boils down to saying that the satisfaction a person gets from another unit of a good depends on how much of it he already has in hand.

Discussions about the theory of consumer behaviour frequently sound abstract and sometimes a bit silly. This is because careful analysis of everyday experience cannot avoid seeming like common sense made

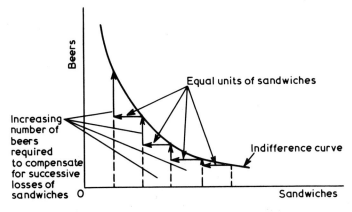

Figure 7.3   Marginal rate of substitution between sandwiches and beer

difficult. The marginal rate of substitution is only a measure of the relative importance of an additional unit of a product to an individual. The more sandwiches one has, the less important they are compared to beer, and conversely. How can we know that? Simple. Try it. It takes only a small amount of beer (perhaps a sip) to get a person to give up one sandwich if he has many sandwiches. But if the person has very few sandwiches, it will take a lot of beer to get him to give up what might be his only bite of solid food. The convexity of the indifference curve and the variation in the marginal rate of substitution is exactly analogous to the law of variable proportions in production theory. They represent processes whereby efficiently run consumption activities can be carried out.

Exercise:
(1) How would you represent the indifference map of an alcoholic? A teetotaller? A glutton?
(2) Describe another set of consumer activities involving alternative commodity inputs into happiness production.
(3) Imagine yourself a supplier of metals of various types such as steel, zinc, chrome, copper, to industries such as household appliances, structural parts for skyscrapers and plumbing ware. How might the decisions of the consumers in terms of happiness producing activities affect your sales planning?
(4) Can a person be too happy?
(5) Do you think happiness depends only on the goods a person consumes himself or on the consumption of others as well?

Demand curves

The amount of money that an individual can spend on himself is limited by his wealth. Even if he chooses to borrow money for consumption purposes, he cannot indefinitely live beyond his means. This is not true of the firm. If it sees profitable opportunities it can usually borrow to meet production expense. The firm produces new income which it can use to pay the costs of borrowing, while a consumer uses up his income by the very nature of the consuming process. The consumer cannot buy an unlimited amount of goods precisely because he does not have the money to do so.

Let us symbolize the consumer's budget limitation by Y. Let p_x stand for the price of one commodity and X stand for the physical amount of it purchased. Let M stand for the amount of everything else he might buy, and p_m the price of this composite commodity. A given budget is then spent on X or M, so that Y equals the price of X times the amount of it, plus the price of M times its amount: $Y = p_x X + p_m M$. The *linear budget equation* is shown graphically in Figure 7.4 where the physical amount of X is measured horizontally and M vertically. In slope-intercept form, the budget line becomes:

$$M = -\frac{p_x}{p_M}X + \frac{Y}{p_m}.$$

The slope $-p_x/p_m$ is the market price of X in terms of M. It tells us how much M must be given up to buy another unit of X on the market. Since the market price is not affected by how much any one individual buys in a

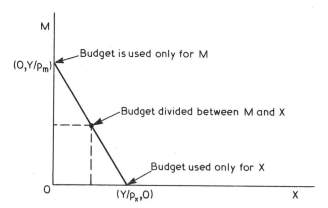

Figure 7.4   Budget line showing the combinations of commodities that can be purchased with a given income

perfectly competitive situation, the slope is constant. That is to say, the budget equation is a negatively sloped straight line.

The budget equation tells us how much of each commodity a consumer can buy with Y amount of money. He might choose to buy none of commodity X and instead keep his income in the form of 'everything else'. He then would be at the vertical intercept, where $X = 0$ and $M = Y/p_m$. Alternatively, he might compulsively spend all his income on X; if $M = 0$, $X = Y/p_x$. Usually the consumer chooses a point on the budget level somewhere in between these extremes.

Exercise:
(1) Suppose a person spends all his budget on X. How much will he buy if his income is £100 and the price of X is £2.
(2) What will happen if he changes his mind 'and spends $\frac{3}{4}$ of his income on X?
(3) Interpret the budget line if M stands for money-cash balances held in the bank or under a floorboard. Assume $p_m = 1$. What is meant by a miser and a spendthrift? Why is it unlikely that a complete miser will be observed in practice? What will happen if the price of money changes from 1 to 2? Would that be a case of inflation or deflation?

Continuing the analogy with production, the budget is a constraint on the consumption that an individual might carry on. Combinations of M and X on (or within) the constraint are feasible to the consumer, given the prices of the goods and the income he has to spend. If a consumer wants to be happy as possible – get to the highest indifference curve – he must go to the boundary of his budget constraint and search out the highest level of satisfaction obtainable. For exactly the same reasons that we studied in production theory, the consumer will either be best off at an extreme point of an indifference curve that is drawn as a polygon, or at tangency solution where a smooth indifference curve just touches the budget line (Figure 7.5). The shaded area under the budget line is feasible. Whilst indifference curve (3) would be very pleasant, the consumer cannot afford it. Portions of indifference curve (1) are feasible where it lies within the shaded region, but it is not the best consumption decision. Why not? Because with the same income it is possible to get to a point F which represents highest levels of utility. F is the *optimal feasible solution* to the consumer's problem and is a point of tangency equalizing the rate which consumers are willing to substitute (marginal rate of substitution) with market prices.

Query: Why is the convexity of the indifference curves so important? Imagine that they were straight lines or concave towards the origin and try to repeat the analysis in the text.

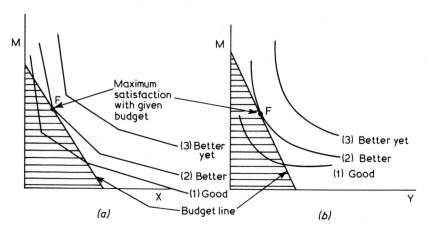

Figure 7.5 Consumer maximizing his satisfaction subject to a limiting budget constraint.

Suppose, now, that the market price of *X* falls. What happens to the budget line if P_m remains the same? The budget line has a less steep slope; with the same amount of money it is possible to buy more of *X* and the same of *M* (Figure 7.6).

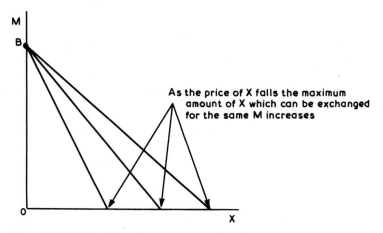

Figure 7.6 Budget lines change slope as the price of *X* falls

How much will the consumer buy at different prices? We can find this out by superimposing the various budget lines onto the indifference map (Figure 7.7). At any price slope of the budget line there is a tangency point that tells what a rational consumer will buy. These tangency points trace out a curve on the indifference map called the *price consumption curve*. We have labelled

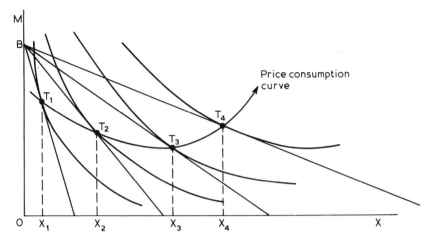

Figure 7.7   Purchases of X at different prices

the tangency points T_1, T_2, T_3, . . . , etc. Reading down from the M to the horizontal X-axis, we find the amount of X that would be held at each price. We label the amounts of X as X_1, X_2, . . . , etc. As one would expect, we observe that as the price of X goes down, more of it is purchased.

Query for the curious: Clearly the price of M in terms of X rises when the price of X falls. Now if we were to draw lines horizontally from T_1, T_2, etc., to the M-axis, we would find out how much M would be taken at each price. Observe that, as the price of M rises, at first less of it is taken but then more of it is taken. Isn't that curious? Can you explain why? Even more interesting in Figure 7.7, when price changes so that tangency switches from T_3 to T_4, the amounts of both X and M increase. How can both increase? What is going on here?

Although we are obviously very close, the price consumption curve is not yet the demand curve for which we are searching. The price consumption curve relates the amount of X to the amount of M which a person will hold at different prices. The demand curve we seek relates the amount of X to different prices of X. The price of X is the slope of the budget line as it swings around. The amount of X is given by reading off the values X_1, X_2, X_3, and so on from the horizontal axis at the points directly below tangency solutions. Consequently we can graph a demand curve by recording the slopes of the budget line on a vertical against the X-values to which they correspond on the horizontal.

The transition from the price consumption curve on the indifference map diagram to the familiar demand curve is illustrated in Figure 7.8. Panel (*a*) is an indifference map, and panel (*b*) shows prices and quantities of X. In the

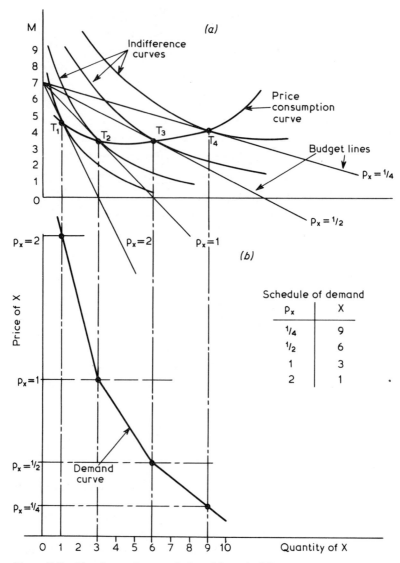

Figure 7.8   The demand curve deduced from indifference map

upper panel (*a*) of the diagram, we can see that, if $p_x = 2$, then the budget line would be tangent to the lowest indifference curve at T_1. The quantity of X corresponding to T_1 is 1 unit, as can be seen by reading down to the X axis. Now carry this quantity of X down to the horizontal axis of panel (*b*), but on its vertical axis chart the price of X. Consequently, panel (*b*) shows a point on the demand curve for X. That is to say, corresponding to a price of 2, the quantity this consumer will be willing to take is $X = 1$. Returning to panel (a), if the price of X were lowered to 1, then the point of tangency would be T_2 and the corresponding quantity would be 3. Carried down to panel (b) this is a second point on the demand curve. The process is repeated again for $p_x = \frac{1}{2}$, $p_x = \frac{1}{4}$, and so on. Thus, point by point the demand curve is constructed.

Connecting the points gives us the demand curve which is the graph of the schedule of demand of an individual consumer. The demand curve is a schedule which relates alternative price of a good to the amount of it that a person would buy at each of the prices. As common sense would suggest, the schedule slopes downward, since in the normal course of events a person will buy less of a product if the price is higher and vice versa. Of course we suspected this all along, but we now have the insight of relating this normal behaviour to the underlying calculations of a rational, efficient person. The demand curve for the market is nothing but the sum of rational individual decisions. Thus at each price, market demand for a good is the sum of the amounts all of the individuals would be willing to buy.

Query: (1) How might an irrational person behave?
(2) What would be the demand curve for the curious case in the preceding query?

We have now seen how the consumer adapts himself to market prices to maximize his utility. Although there are differences which we have noted, he, like the firm, is maximizing the outcome of his activities. In both cases the rational agent chooses a tangency (or extreme point) solution to a set of efficient alternatives shown by indifference curves or isoquants. This adaptation is more than passive response. The totality of consumers and producers interact on the market to create the very price to which they react. Supply and demand reflect willingness and capacity to produce on one hand and preferences for goods and income limitations on the other.

The balance of supply and demand reflects the balancing of marginal increments of effort against desire. The market clearing price is the device by which consumers and producers communicate. Tacitly they agree to produce this much and no more. At this point the gain in satisfaction is not worth the effort of further production when measured in money terms.

The argument in favour of an unrestricted market as a maximizer of satisfactions is not conclusive, for several reasons which we shall list here and enlarge upon in the remainder of this book:

(1) Consumers and producers are different people, so the costs and satisfactions are not directly comparable. Even though prices are agreed

upon, the significance of the money that changes hands is different to different individuals. In jargon, this is the difficulty of *interpersonal comparisons of utility*. Market supply and demand are aggregates of individual attitudes and are not necessarily those of each person taken separately.

(2) Since consumers express their preferences subject to their limited budget of wealth, market demand curves reflect the differences in wealth as well as human desires. This is the problem of the fairness or *equity of the distribution of wealth.*

(3) Consumption and production activities are not entirely personal affairs. The consumption of automobiles by some people affects some others: some must endure the negative utility (disutility) of the resulting smog and noise; others gain the positive utility of contact among persons living greater distances apart. A similar argument can be made for positive and negative spillover effects in production. Economists refer to such issues as *external effects.*

(4) Perfect competition is an ideal. Monopolistic industrial and labour organizations force a departure from the model of competitive supply and demand. Government operations are of such a magnitude as to dwarf market forces in some situations.

(5) The persistence of unemployment as well as the problem of inflation suggest that there are issues of stability of the market mechanism which remain to be solved.

On the basis of these five points it would be possible to reject the competitive market solution. Yet one suspects that the argument still retains some force. In specific circumstances the market solution often suggests at least a guideline to price and output decisions. One must make a judgement in these matters, and the weight and significance afforded to the market solution and its weaknesses is the source of continuing controversy.

Elasticity: a measure of demand

It is likely that the demand curves of individuals will be as irregular and full of kinks as people themselves. However, if we add up all of the amounts which all individuals will buy at each of the various prices, the irregularities smooth out and we are entitled to draw a smooth demand curve for the market without concern about individual eccentricities.

Robust common sense, as well as the refined theory of consumer demand, suggests that these curves normally slope downward. Due to the substitution effect price and quantity vary inversely as efficient, rational people will buy more of a good when its price falls. They decide to substitute more of it for other things. The ease of substitution will be reflected in the slope of the demand curve. If a small change in price of a good will bring about a large

change in the quantity of it purchased then the demand curve will have a
small slope and be close to horizontal (Figure 7.9 (*a*)). But if it takes a large
change in price to bring on a small change in quantity then the demand curve
will be very steeply sloped (Figure 7.9 (*b*)).

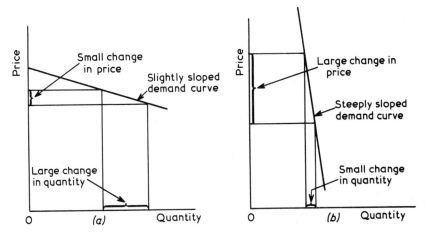

Figure 7.9   Demand curves

Exercise: Consider the following individual demand curves for hat

	Jones		Smith		Morgan
p	*q*	*p*	*q*	*p*	*q*
£0	10	£0	13	£0	Infinitely many
1	10	1	12	1	25
2	9	2	12	2	15
3	8	3	10	3	10
4	6	4	9	4	9
5	5	5	9	5	9
6	4	6	8	6	4
7	3	7	4	7	2
8	0	8	1	8	1
9	0	9	1	9	1
10	0	10	1	10	0

Compute the market demand curves. Graph market and
individual demand curves. Which of the three individuals is more
sensitive to price changes? Can you say which of these people
prefers hats most? Distinguish between the demand curve (or

schedule of demand) and the quantity demanded. Show that the demand curve may be constant but the quantity demanded changes. Can hats be made free? Could hats be free if Morgan were not involved? What goods are substitutes for hats?

Clearly the responsiveness of consumers to changes in the price of a product is a matter of first-rate practical importance to firms and planners. But it turns out that measuring consumer reaction in terms of the slope of the demand curve for a product is not usually convenient, because the slope relates price to the physical units of the commodity in question. Thus the demand curve for hats has a slope which is so many pounds per hat. How is that comparable to the slope for hamburgers stated as pence per pound of meat? Which of these commodities is more sensitive to changes in price? Suppose, for instance, the slope of the demand curve for hats were such that an increase in price by £1 causes a change in purchases by 5 hats. Then the slope is $\frac{1}{5}$. Now suppose that the change in price of mince by £1 causes a change in purchases by 4 pounds. Since the slope of the minced meat demand is $\frac{1}{4}$, one might conclude that the hat market is more sensitive to price. But suppose meat were sold in half-pound patties. Then a change in price by 50 pence will cause a change in quantity of 4 and the slope will be $\frac{1}{8}$! Precisely the opposite conclusion would be drawn!

Nothing profound is going on here. It is just that the units in which the minced meat is stated have been changed, and the slope is stated in those new units. The problem can be avoided if one expresses the changes in price and quantity in percentage terms. The percentage change in quantity demanded which is the result of a percentage change in price is called the *elasticity of demand*. Symbolize it by the Greek letter, η (eta).

$$\eta = \text{Elasticity of demand} = \frac{\text{Percentage change in quantity demanded}}{\text{Percentage change in the price}}.$$

Actually η is always a negative number since an increase in price means a decrease in quantity, but when the context is clear we usually omit the minus sign.

For example, suppose we have the following demand schedule for some commodity.

Price (£)	Quantity
1	10
2	9
3	8
4	5
5	5

Then the elasticity of demand for a price change from £1 to £2 – quantity changing from 10 to 9 – can be readily computed. The percentage change is the amount of the change divided by the original amount. Thus:

$$\text{Percentage change in quantity} = \frac{\text{Change in quantity}}{\text{Original quantity}}$$

$$= \frac{\Delta Q}{Q} = \frac{1}{10} = 10\%.$$

The percentage change in price is:

$$\text{Percentage change in price} = \frac{\text{Change in price}}{\text{Original price}} = \frac{\Delta P}{P} = \frac{1}{1} = 100\%.$$

Consequently the elasticity of demand is:

$$\eta = \frac{\Delta Q/Q}{\Delta P/P} = \frac{1/10}{1/1} = \frac{10\%}{100\%} = \frac{1}{10}.$$

This is a very inelastic demand since the per cent change in quantity is only one tenth of the per cent change in price. If firms in the industry were to reduce their price by 20 per cent they will only sell 2 per cent more product. The products of this industry are likely to have very poor substitutes. The classic example of inelastic demand is light bulbs. People do not install new electric lights or replace worn out bulbs with much regard to the price. Conceivably, if the price of electric bulbs were to go down, some people would convert from kerosene lanterns to electricity. Cheaper bulbs might mean fewer burnt out bulbs left in place. Yet the far-fetched nature of these substitutions suggests that the demand for bulbs is inelastic. Habit forming goods like alcohol, cigarettes and narcotics also have an inelastic demand. To the user, a certain amount of these goods must be consumed regardless of price.

In contrast, consumers are highly responsive to price changes in goods in elastic demand. Generally these goods have good substitutes. Thus the elasticity of demand for butter is high because margarine is a good substitute. A small percentage change in the price of butter will bring about a large change in the amount of it bought. If the price increases only a little, many people will switch over to buying margarine; if the price were somewhat lower, margarine would be replaced by butter.

Different brands of the same product often have high elasticities. Advertising notwithstanding, many people do not see much difference in the different brands of petrol. Thus if the local ICI petrol pump charges $\frac{1}{10}$ penny more per gallon for three star petrol, buyers will patronize the Shell establishment across the street. A small per cent change in price brings on a large relative change in purchases. Notice, though, that the elasticity for petrol in general may not be very great. Even though the price of petrol rises a bit for all brands, it is not likely that people will drastically reduce the amount of fuel they consume.

The elasticity of demand for goods in a perfect substitute situation is infinitely large. Farmer Brown who produced standard grade wheat sells exactly the same product as Jones. If Brown increases price by even the smallest fraction of per cent his sales will be zero, no matter how much he had been selling previously.

Exercise:
(1) Refer back to the demand schedule on p. 174 and compute the elasticity of demand if the price changes from £2 to £3.
(2) Explain why the elasticity of demand might be different at various points on a demand curve.
(3) Suppose the demand curve is a straight line such as $P = 6 - 2q$. By choosing various values for p and q show that the elasticity changes. Explain why.
(4) Compute the elasticity for a price *decrease* from £2 to £1 on p. 174. What explains the different result from a price increase from £1 to £2? (Hint: Remember the children's riddle: 'I am ten years old. When I am 15 years old my age will be increased by 50 per cent. What if some magician reduced my age by 50 per cent? Would I be 10 years old again?') Can you think of ways of redefining the elasticity of demand to get around this inconsistency?

At one extreme of elasticity the response of the consumer may involve percentage change in quantity equal to zero. Zero elasticity is the extreme case of an inelastic demand. In contrast, if the response of the consumer is such that an almost zero percentage change in price brings on an indefinitely large reaction in amount of the product purchased, the demand is infinitely elastic.

A reference for judging elasticities is the case where the per cent change in quantity is the same as the per cent change in price. The elasticity of demand would then be unity. Unit elastic demand curves serve as a convenient basis for comparison because every price-quantity combination on such a demand curve involves the consumers' expenditure of the same amount of money. This is so because every per cent increase in the price of the good is matched by an equal per cent decrease in the number of the goods sold. For all the prices and quantities involved the money expenditure of each price times the corresponding quantity remains the same. For this reason unit elastic demand curves are often called *constant outlay curves*. An example of a constant outlay behaviour might be exhibited by a housewife who budgets a certain amount of money to be spent on groceries for her weekly shopping expedition to the supermarket. If prices are 25 per cent lower than last week she will buy 25 per cent more tins and boxes of groceries. If prices are higher, she will buy that same percentage less. As long as she stays precisely within her budget, always spending it all, her demand for groceries is unit elastic.

Now if the expenditure is constant for any price (p) and any quantity (q) we can write the equation of this constant outlay demand curve as $pq = K$, where K is the constant amount of money that is going to be spent. Such a demand curve is called a *rectangular hyperbola* when it is plotted (Figure 7.10). It is convex towards the origin, and as p and q gets bigger the curve approaches closer and closer to each of the axes but it never touches them.

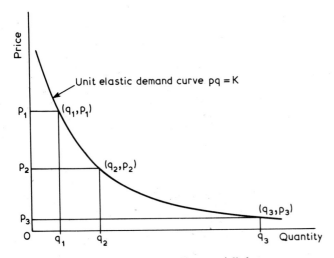

Figure 7.10   Unit elastic demand curve (all these rectangles have the same area, K; $p_1q_1 = p_2q_2 = p_3q_3 = K$)

This is so because pq is the area of a rectangle formed by dropping perpendiculars from any point on the curve to the axes. Since pq is a constant, it must be that for a very small q, p must be very large, to keep their product the same. If q were zero, however, there could be no p large enough to make pq equal K, so the curve never reaches the axes. The same argument applies for small values of p and large values of q. Hence, the demand curve approaches but does not touch the axes. Such an approach without actually touching used to be called unrequited love by romantic poets, but is called an *asymptote* by mathematicians.

Exercise:

(1) Graph the demand curve $pq = 10$ by computing and plotting points for $p = \frac{1}{4}, \frac{1}{2}, 1, 5, 10, 20, 40$. Compute the elasticity of demand between three of these points. Why do you not always get $\eta = -1$?

(2) Would the point $p = -5$, $q = -2$ satisfy the equation for the hyperbola? Why do we not show such points? Does the point $p = 5$, $q = -2$ satisfy?

(3) Name three other commodities for which it is reasonable to expect a unit elasticity of demand.

(4) (For calculus students only)

Since $\eta = \dfrac{dq/q}{dp/p} = -1$, prove that $pq = K$.

(5) Explain why some demand curves intersect the axes rather than approach them asymptotically.

There is certainly no reason to believe that the expenditures on every good will remain the same with a fall in price. Expenditures might increase or decrease. Indeed, it is not very likely that any demand curve will have the same elasticity throughout its length; the very responsiveness to price change may well depend on the original prices and quantities involved. Nevertheless, we can use the unit elastic curve as a reference to compare with other elasticities.

Suppose we want to describe the elasticity of demand curve D' in the region between the points F and J (Figure 7.11). We compare it with the unit elastic demand curve D, also drawn through point F. Demand curve D' can

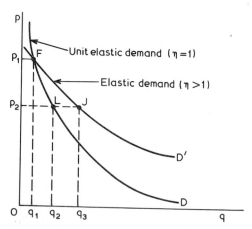

Figure 7.11   Elastic and unit elastic demands

be seen to be more elastic at F since a small percentage price change results in a larger per cent quantity reaction. Thus if price falls and quantity rises by a larger relative amount, the total expenditure increases.

Geometrically, the rectangle under an elastic demand curve increases in area as price falls. At the original price, p_1, both demand curves show that q_1 amount of goods will be taken at point F where the total expenditure is the area p_1q_1. Now let the price fall to p_2. Along unit elastic demand curve D the quantity would change to q_2 corresponding to point L. Expenditure would be p_2q_2. Since the curve is unit elastic the total expenditures would be the same, $p_1q_1 = p_2q_2$. But if the demand curve were elastic, such as D', then the corresponding quantity would be the greater amount, q_3. The result of the price fall in the case of elastic demand would be a change from point F to point J. As can be seen from the diagram, the area representing total expenditure would be p_2q_3; p_2q_3 is greater than p_2q_2, since the quantity is increased by a greater percentage than the fall in price. People would flock to buy the bargain goods in the case of elastic demand, more than making up for the fact that the goods were sold at a cheaper price. For elastic demands a fall in price means an increase in expenditures and a rise in price decreases expenditures.

A graphic test for elasticity, then, is to compare the demand curve with the unit elastic hyperbola through the same point. If the curve is flatter, the demand is elastic.

The limiting case of extremely elastic demand is *infinite elasticity*. Infinite elasticity of demand is illustrated by the horizontal demand curve in Figure 7.12. The demand curve is horizontal because price does not depend at all on quantity. In this case there is only one market price. The best illustration is the demand curve for the product of a single firm in a perfectly competitive

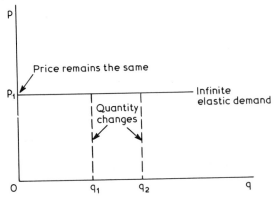

Figure 7.12   Infinite elasticity demand curve

industry. The product of such a firm is exactly the same as every other small firm. It also must charge the same price. If one firm were to sell at a lower price than others, it would simply throw money away, since it already can sell all it cares to produce at the market price. If it tries to sell at a higher price, it would lose all its customers who flock to the competition.

Query: (1) Give some examples of highly elastic industry demand curves. Can you think of any that are infinitely elastic?

(2) Why might the elasticity demand for a durable consumer good be greater than for a perishable one?

(3) How is total expenditure related to changes in quantity when $\eta = \infty$?

An inelastic demand is one that is more steeply sloped than the unit elastic hyperbola (Figure 7.13). If price falls from p_1 to p_2, then the rectangle representing total revenue for sellers of the product will decline. On the unit elastic curve the rectangle with area p_1q_1 equals the area p_2q_2. But if demand is inelastic, then the total expenditures fall to p_2q_3. Revenues at L are less than revenues at F or J. Conversely, if price rises, so will revenue. Consequently price and total expenditures move in the same direction if demand is inelastic.

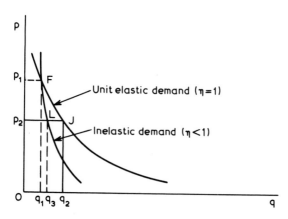

Figure 7.13   Inelastic and unit elastic demand curves

The limiting case of inelastic demand is where there is no change in quantity as a result of a change in price (Figure 7.14). Then, since the numerator of the elasticity of demand formula is zero, so is the elasticity of demand. Demand is completely inelastic. When the quantity has nothing at all to do with price the demand curve is a vertical line.

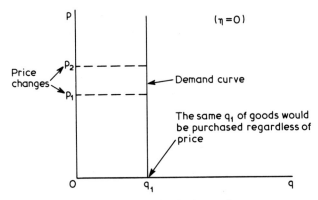

Figure 7.14   Completely inelastic demand

It is very hard to think of commodities which have completely inelastic demand curves for all imaginable prices. That would mean that no matter what the price – even if it were higher than the incomes of all the potential customers – the same amount would be purchased. Nonetheless there are goods which have inelastic demands for certain price ranges.

Questions:
(1) What do you think the elasticity of demand is for: (1) food, (2) rental housing, (3) chewing gum, (4) fur coats?
(2) As some of the students who read this book will find out, the teaching profession involves considerable migration, at least at first. In the course of one such move, I decided to auction off most of my household goods rather than try to move them. I had to have all of the contents of my house disposed of, and I was particularly worried about a sack of concrete that had been exposed to rain and had hardened. This made it somewhat less useful. When I confided my concern to the auctioneer he put his hand on my shoulder and reassured me: 'Don't worry, you can sell anything if the price is low enough.' As a matter of fact, he did sell it, by asking people to bid for it along with some garden tools and a still usable, rusty pickaxe. The package sold for £2. Sketch the demand curve you think he had in mind. Was the price that was paid for the concrete positive or negative? Was the auctioneer right?
(3) Why is the unit elastic demand a hyperbola and not a straight line?

A tale of booze, carrots and taxes

There are people in this world who are opposed to the use of alcoholic beverages. They make the point that booze is both expensive and habit forming. As a result, they say, too many men spend a good portion of their pay packet in the neighbourhood pub, and little is left over for wife and children. What to do? Illegalize drinking? The prohibition era in the United States showed that the result is both gangsters and bad booze. There must be a better way. How about a tax on drink? Would not a sufficiently high levy encourage people to stop drinking? In fact, the answer depends on the elasticity of demand. The demand for alcoholic beverages, it turns out, is very inelastic. Like so many other habit forming products, it has no really good substitute in the groggy mind of the booze user. Almost a constant amount of alcohol is consumed regardless of price.

Figure 7.15 shows what would happen as a result of a booze tax. Take a simple specific tax, in which the producer of drink pays over to the government so many pence for each bottle sold. The tax enters into his marginal cost of production. Whatever the output, the cost of producing another unit has increased by the amount of the tax. This amounts to shifting the supply curve upward a fixed distance equal to the tax from S to S'.

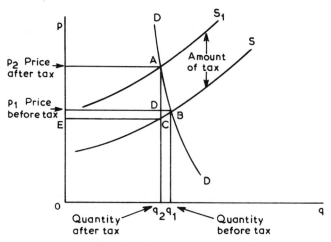

Figure 7.15 The demand for booze and the effect of a tax

How well does tax enforced virtue work? Since the demand for booze is inelastic, people will buy almost the same volume of drink after the tax, but will pay more for it. In the end the drinker spends more money on booze, not less. Thus in Figure 7.15, when price rises from p_1 to p_2, the rectangle formed at B representing expenditures before tax increases compares to the one formed by perpendiculars from A after tax, since price and revenue move in the *same* direction. In the case of inelastic demand wives and children get less, not more of the pay packet as a result of the tax!

There is one advantage to taxing alcohol. The government makes a great deal of tax money. Since people do not avoid drinking because of the higher price, consumers accept the tax in the price of the goods. After the tax has been imposed, the marginal cost including the tax is point A on supply curve S'. Excluding the tax, the cost of producing the same quantity of goods is point C on supply curve S. The tax take per unit product is the distance AC. And the total tax take is the area of the rectangle $ECAP_2$. Of this total the rectangle P_1DAP_2 represents the payments by consumers in the form of higher prices which they pay in order to get the booze. The balance of tax revenues is the small rectangle $ECDP_1$ reflecting lower marginal costs when output is slightly cut back as a result of the tax. Sometimes such a situation is described as shifting the burden of the tax forward to the consumer. The ultimate burden of a tax is called the *incidence of taxation*, and the division of the tax effect into higher prices to consumers and lower prices received by producers is called the *shifting* of incidence of taxation. Clearly the way in which this works out depends on the elasticity of demand and supply.

Exercise:
(1) We have interpreted the effect of the tax as a shifting upward of the supply curve. Interpret it in words as a shift to the left of the supply curve. Why does the cost of production after the tax become less than before the tax? If the effect of the tax is to raise the price of alcoholic beverages and the consumer is willing to pay the increased price, why have not the producers of the product been charging that amount all along?
(2) Repeat the analysis for the following two types of taxes.
   (A) *Ad valorem* tax. An *ad valorem* tax is proportional to the price of the product. For instance, if the original price of a bottle of whisky is £4.00, a 10 per cent *ad valorem* tax would be 40p.
   (B) *Lump sum tax*. This tax is a fixed amount and is not at all related to either output or price. An example might be a liquor licence fee.
   Who pays these taxes? Which type of tax is best? Why?
(3) We have been assuming that the booze consumer may be drunk but still rational in maximizing his satisfactions. Does this make sense?

Now suppose the government were to impose a tax on carrots, a product with many substitutes. If the price of carrots rises, people will switch to peas or beans. Consequently the demand for carrots is elastic (Figure 7.16). The effect of the tax is to shift the equilibrium from B to A.

People refuse to buy carrots at higher prices; output falls to q_2. The end result is that the new price of carrots including the tax, p_2, is not much higher than before at p_1. As a result of the elasticity even the small increase in carrot prices from p_1 to p_2 has caused a marked reduction in purchase. The tax take

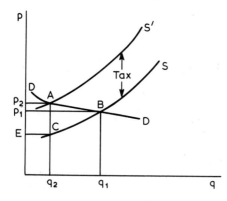

Figure 7.16   Effect of a tax on carrots

($ECAP_2$) is much smaller than in the booze tax. Most of the incidence of the tax is shifted backward on to the supplier of carrots, who must accept lower net prices after he turns the tax money into the revenue officers.

Exercise:
(1) If the government wanted to discourage the use of carrots would it be well advised to tax them? If it wanted to collect a tax revenue, should it tax carrots or whisky?
(2) If the government taxed wine, but not beer or whisky, how would the analysis be affected?

A tutorial fairy tale

Once upon a time there were two elves, Jones and Smith. These magical creatures were able to do more than ordinary people. You and I only rank our goods in preference, but these little fellows could tell exactly how much happiness they got from them.

Every morning and every night they looked at their precious possessions. Jones had 10 toadstools and Smith 10 magic wands. Jones often thought about magic wands. He knew how much happiness he would get if he could only obtain one. Smith too, cast covetous eyes on the toadstools of his little mate. They were sad because they wished they were happier.

One day a blue fairy came. She suggested that they ought to make a table of happiness. So they did.

When they made the table they found that it obeyed a law. It was a psychological law made especially for little men who are able to count happiness. The law was called the *law of diminishing marginal utility* and said that the more of any one thing a person has, the less additional satisfaction he gets from having another unit of it. Thus the first toadstool

Table of happiness

| Number of units | Jones | | Smith | |
	Toadstools	Magic wands	Toadstools	Magic wands
1	15	13	12	14
2	14	12	11	13
3	13	11	10	12
4	12	10	9	11
5	11	9	8	10
6	10	8	7	9
7	9	7	6	8
8	8	6	5	7
9	7	5	4	6
10	6	4	3	5

made Jones very happy. Indeed he was 15 happy. His second toadstool also increased his happiness, but by a bit less. As the table shows, his *marginal utility* from toadstools went down to 14. Together the two toadstools made him 29 happy.

Now, dearly beloved, calculate how happy Jones was with his ten toadstools and Smith was with his 10 magic wands. Put the number in little jeweled boxes called Totals:

Totals: Jones happiness_____   Smith happiness_____

Who was happier? Jones said he was happier because he had a bigger number in his box. But Smith said he was a much more sensitive person so that his happiness counted more than the other elf's. They quarrelled and almost came to blows. The blue fairy appeared just in time. She said: 'There is no way for you, Jones, to know how Smith really feels. Nor, Smith, can you know what emotions lie in the breast of your friend. When counting happiness, each little man is an island unto himself.' Jones and Smith thought and thought about what the blue fairy said. They could think of no way to make *interpersonal comparisons of utility*. If you can, explain how in this little space I have left for you. If not, tell us why not.

LITTLE SPACE FOR YOU TO USE ALL YOUR VERY OWN:

Then the blue fairy said to Jones and Smith: 'Do not worry if you cannot compare utilities. It will not make any difference.' The elves were astonished at this but they held their tongues. The fairy told them to call Jones's utility 'happies' and Smith's utility 'glads'. They were not to worry if many happies were equal to one glad!

'Since you are such good little elves', the fairy said, 'I will put you in a magic playroom called a *perfect market*. There you may trade toadstools for magic wands. But, remember, in a perfect market there can be only one price at a time regardless of the amount each individual person buys. So in this particular market, the price of a toadstool will equal the price of a wand. If you wish you may barter them in a one to one ratio.'

(1) Which toadstool did Jones trade off first? Which magic wand did Smith trade off first? Why? (The answer is so simple that it is often missed.)

(2) How many trades were carried out? Who was the first to refuse to trade? Why? Why did it make no difference that Jones could not compare his happiness with Smith's?

(3) How many happies did Jones have after the trading stopped? How many glads did Smith have after trading? Who gained more? Can you tell? Why was everybody happier? Where did the extra happiness come from? What improvement could a government wizard make upon the decisions of the elves themselves?

(4) Suppose Jones were a monopolist and could offer an 'all or none' bargain to Smith who was a good elf and sold his goods in a competitive way. How many toadstools could Jones get Smith to give up and still have both better off? What might the government wizard say then?

(5) What would happen if the elves did not obey the 'psychological law' and marginal utility increased? Is the psychological law really a law of psychology? Would the two elves still gain from trade if Jones started off with 10 toadstools and 5 wands and Smith had only 5 toadstools? What rational argument could you make for one initial distribution of wealth being better than another? If you can, use it to convince Jones to give up his 5 wands to Smith.

(6) If each elf traded until the marginal happiness he gives up equals the happiness he gets, we could say that, for each elf:

Marginal utility of toadstools = Marginal utility of wands.

Suppose the prices were different. Then each elf would trade up to the point where the additional happiness for each penny spent on toadstools equalled the additional happiness for a penny spent on magic wands:

$$\frac{\text{Increase in happiness}}{\substack{\text{Increase in price times quantity} \\ \text{of toadstools}}} = \frac{\text{Increase in happiness}}{\substack{\text{Increase in price times quantity} \\ \text{of magic wands}}}.$$

If U stands for happiness (utility) this can be written:

$$\frac{\Delta U}{\Delta(p_t Q_t)} = \frac{\Delta U}{\Delta(p_w Q_w)}.$$

Since prices are constant, we can say the change in spending on the two goods is just the changes in quantity ΔT or ΔW. That is to say:

$$\frac{1}{P_t}\left(\frac{\Delta U}{\Delta Q_t}\right) = \frac{1}{P_w}\left(\frac{\Delta U}{\Delta Q_w}\right).$$

Hence the marginal utility of toadstools per penny spent just equalled the marginal utility of wands per penny spent on one.

$$\frac{\text{Marginal utility of toadstools}}{\text{Price of toadstools}} = \frac{\text{Marginal utility of wands}}{\text{Price of wands}}$$

or,

$$\frac{\text{Marginal utility of toadstools}}{\text{Marginal utility of wands}} = \frac{\text{Price of toadstools}}{\text{Price of wands}}.$$

Now suppose the price of toadstools rises, but the price of wands remains the same. What will happen to maintain equality of the left hand side of the equation? How does this square with our previous analysis of demand curves?

Why will the utility measure cancel out on the left hand side so that it is the marginal rate of substitution? Is it necessary to count happies and glads or is a ranking of preferences enough?

What qualifications must you put on the elves' faith that the magic market playroom is the best place imaginable?

Does fairyland exist?

8 The firm and the market

The production decision revisited

In Chapter 6 we discovered the basic principle which determined how much a firm would produce under competitive conditions: it would choose that level of output at which marginal costs (MC) equal the market price of the good. This would be the profit maximizing level of output. Producing less would mean that profit making opportunities, where MC was less than price, were allowed to slip by; producing more would imply that the marginal cost on the extra items would exceed price and a loss would be incurred on them. The law of diminishing returns was the force that limited the output of a competitive firm. It was not the difficulty of making sales at the going price – the market clears at that price – but the fact that rising marginal costs overtook that price and caused the profit maximizing firm to produce so much and no more.

Put differently, the running total of MC was total variable cost (TVC). Graphically (Figure 6.14) TVC was the area under the MC curve. Total revenues (TR) was the area under the price line, or an infinitely elastic demand curve facing the competitive firm. Profit maximization amounted to making the area between these curves as large as it could be.

The MC curve, then, amounted to the supply curve for the firm, since it told us how much would be produced by that firm at alternative prices. In this chapter we plan to examine the firm and its relation to the supply of goods in greater detail, taking fixed costs into account and dealing with the problem of the time it takes for firms to adapt to market conditions.

Fixed costs and variable costs; marginal costs and average costs

Since the law of diminishing returns is central to the analysis, we should be clear about the distinction between the cost of fixed inputs that make it operative, and the variable inputs which are the increased costs of greater production. *Fixed costs*, sometimes called *overhead costs*, remain the same regardless of output. Examples are: rent of buildings, interest on long-term capital, salaries of supervisory personnel, and much of the heating and lighting expense. *Variable costs* are expenditures that increase as output increases, such as most labour, raw materials and the like. In the long run this distinction tends to break down because firms planning very far into the future adjust their buildings, capital and supervisory personnel to their output perspectives. But for the substantial period of time in which these costs are not altered, we may take it that some costs are fixed. The law of diminishing returns is therefore operative. In a flash of originality, economists have dubbed this shorter period of time the *short run*.

Before proceeding, it is necessary to clarify the distinction between marginal costs and average variable costs (AVC). Clearly variable costs are the only elements that enter into marginal costs, since fixed costs do not increase with output. MC is the ratio of the *increase* in total variable cost to the *increase* in output, $MC = \Delta TVC / \Delta Q$; conversely, the TVC is the cumulative running total of marginal costs. *Average variable cost*, on the other hand, is total variable costs divided by output, $AVC = TVC / Q$; and conversely, AVC multiplied by output gives TVC. Average and marginal costs do not mean the same thing. Marginal costs represent the increase in cost involved in producing another unit of product. MC is the additional cost of an additional unit of output. MC changes with levels of output due to the law of diminishing returns. Average cost also varies with output but it reflects more than the current increment in cost. Average cost, like every average, involves all the costs incurred by all the prior outputs divided by the quantity produced.

The distinction can best be seen by example (Table 8.1). For concreteness imagine we are analysing a wheat farm for which we know how TVC (column 2) corresponds to output (column 1). To find AVC, we divide the quantity of wheat into total variable cost. To find marginal cost we take the successive differences in TVC as quantity increases.

Observe that the schedule of MC is not the same as that of AVC. Division is not the same as subtraction! Observe that the AVC of 7 units of wheat, for instance, is £1·18 per bushel, while the MC is £1·70. MC is greater than AVC because, due to rising marginal costs, the average of the 7 bushels cost less to produce than the seventh bushel. To be sure, like the MC, the AVC curve is U-shaped – it declines and then rises. The important difference is

Table 8.1

(1) Quantity of wheat (bushels) Q	(2) Total variable cost TVC	(3) Marginal cost MC	(4) Average variable cost AVC
0	0	0	0
1	1·20	1·20	1·20
2	2·10	0·90	1·05
3	2·80	0·70	0·93
4	3·80	1·00	0·95
5	5.10	1·30	1·02
6	6·60	1·50	1·10
7	8·30	1·70	1·18
8	10·30	2·00	1·29
9	12·40	2·10	1·37
10	15·00	2·60	1·50

that the AVC lags behind the MC, which declines faster and starts to rise faster too. MC falls from £1·20 to 70p and then goes up to £2·60 by the time the tenth unit of product is manufactured. AVC falls from £1·20 to only 93p and only gets up to £1·50 on the tenth bushel of wheat. The reason for this lag is that the MC only reflects the additional costs of further output, and the AVC reflects *everything* that has gone on before.

Students often face a similar distinction between marginal and average quantities in examination grades. Suppose the first three test grades were 60, 50, 40. The average grade is 50. Each time an additional exam is taken the average changes because another, marginal, exam is given. Totalling up all the marginal exams gives the running total of points, which is divided by the number of exams taken up to that time to get the average grade. Students know how hard it is to raise an average grade after several tests. The past record weighs very heavily despite current (marginal) performance. If one wanted to raise the average grade, by taking a fourth exam, the next or marginal grade would have to exceed the average. It would have to be over 50. On the other hand, if the grade on the fourth exam were below the average, then the average would fall. And if the marginal and average grade were the same, then the average would be unchanged.

Query: There is a running debate between British and US educators on whether students should be continuously assessed, as in the US, or graded on their final examination performance as in the Commonwealth. Explain the justification for the British procedure on the grounds that the marginal performance reflects the actual achievement level rather than the history of early fumbling with subject matter. What is your opinion?

We may translate what was said about test results to cost curves. When marginal costs are below average costs, average costs are falling. True, marginal costs may themselves be increasing, but as long as they are less than *AVC* the latter continues to fall. When *MC* is greater than *AVC*, average values are rising. When *MC = AVC*, average costs can be neither rising nor falling. The average is then at the critical turning point in its U-shape, its minimum. This description can be visualized in Figure 8.1. The marginal curve slopes down, turns upward, due to the law of diminishing returns. As long as *MC* lies below *AVC*, the latter continues to fall. When the *MC* curve

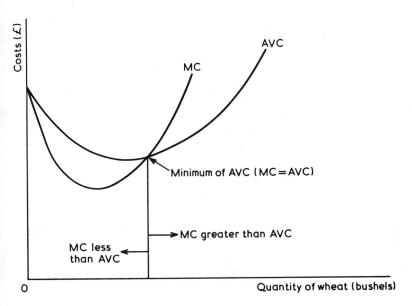

Figure 8.1   *MC* and *AVC* curves

crosses the *AVC* at its minimum they both proceed upward with *MC* always higher.

The profit maximizing firm and its industry

Now we are in a better position to understand the interaction of the firm and its industry. The key to this relationship is the firm's search for maximum profits. We have been working on the assumption that the firm attempts to maximize the difference between its total revenues (*TR*) and total variable costs (*TVC*). This is certainly correct, but it should be pointed out that this difference is not quite equal to profits because there are fixed costs to consider. The excess of revenues over variable costs goes by the somewhat outlandish name of *quasi-rent* (the origin of this bit of jargon will appear in Chapter 10 and need not trouble us here). Since fixed costs cannot be altered or avoided by the firm unless it quits business altogether, the search for profits is, in the first instance, a quest for the maximum quasi-rent. This maximum is achieved when the firm produces up to the point where *MC* equals the price at which the good sells on the market.

There is one problem with the rule $MC = P$ that requires amendment. Quasi-rent would turn out to be negative if at every level of production AVC is less than price. Since quasi-rent is the difference between *TR* and *TVC*, the quasi-rent per unit output is the difference between product price and average variable cost. If price were so low that there were no output at which the firm can avoid losing money, it might as well stop producing. Hence, the minimum of the *AVC* curve is also the *shut-down price*. Below the shut-down price, even though $P = MC$, it will be sensible to simply close the factory doors. Above the shut-down price the rule $P = MC$ still holds since there is some output that maximizes quasi-rent. Then fixed costs are deducted to arrive at maximum profit. Even if the quasi-rent should be more than eaten up by high overheads, it is still worthwhile to follow the rule $P = MC$ so as to use the quasi-rent to pay off as much of the overhead fixed costs. For all prices higher than the shut-down price, we can read off the amount that each firm will produce from its *MC* curve. This is shown in panel (*a*) of Figure 8.2. The firm will supply the quantity that makes *MC* equal to price. If we add all the outputs that all the firms in an industry produce, at each price we get a *market supply curve* from these *MC* curves. The market supply interacts with downward sloping market demand to determine an equilibrium price (panel (*b*)).

Exercise:
(1) Sketch a situation for farms in the wheat industry in which demand would shift due to a shift in tastes of consumers away from wheat. How far would the shift have to be for the firm illustrated on the left to cease production?
(2) What would happen to supply if a new firm entered this industry? Draw a sketch, and indicate prices and quasi-rent.
(3) Engineers speak of efficiency in terms of the ratio of the minimum of input to output. Show that this is the minimum of the *AVC* curve. Does the profit maximizing businessman aim for efficiency? What is quasi-rent at the most efficient point in your diagram?

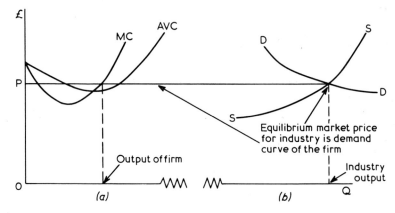

Figure 8.2   Firms and industry, output and price
(*a*) Costs and revenues for a typical firm
(*b*) Market for wheat industry

(4) Referring back to Table 8.1, suppose *MC* were constant at £2. What
would *AVC* be? Why is constant *MC* inconsistent with our description
of the firm under perfect competition?

A convenient way to display total variable costs relies on the fact that
average variable costs equal total variable costs divided by quantity:
AVC = *TVC*/*Q*. It follows that total variable costs are equal to ayerage
variable costs times quantity: *TVC* = *AVC* × *Q*. Therefore *TVC* for any
output, say *L*, is the area of a rectangle drawn from a point on the *AVC*
curve to the axes (Figure 8.3). *TVC* is equal to the area of rectangle *OLMT*,
as well as the area under the *MC* curve, *OFRL*.
Portrayal of *TVC* in these terms is useful to derive the profit or loss
situation of the firm because quasi-rent is shown as *TMRP*, the difference
between the rectangle of total revenues *OLMP* and the rectangle of total
variable cost *OLMT* (Figure 8.4).
Notice the order in which the analysis proceeds. First the profit maximizing quantity is determined where the *MC* curve intersects the price line.
Then the *TR* and *TC* areas are computed. The difference is quasi-rent.
Quantity is determined first because the competitive firm must adjust
quantity to meet market conditions. Price is beyond its control.

Exercise:
(1) Is it possible for a firm to have positive quasi-rent and yet have zero or a
negative profit?
(2) What is the relation between *TVC* and *TR* if the price were at the
minimum of the *AVC* curve? What is quasi-rent? Relate quasi-rent to

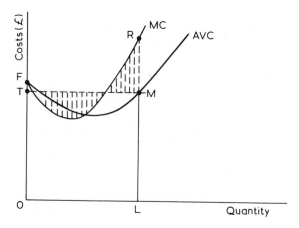

Figure 8.3   *TVC* equals *AVC* times quantity as well
as the area under *MC*

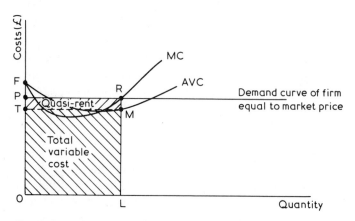

Figure 8.4   Quasi-rent

the shutting down of production in a business in order to avoid negative
quasi-rent. Is this still maximizing quasi-rent?

(3) Show that the price of the product can be expressed as average revenue,
since total revenue is equal to price times quantity. Express quasi-rent
per unit output as the difference between average revenue and average
cost. Relate this to the rectangle *TMRP*.

(4) What would happen to quasi-rent if the firm produced up to the point
where *AVC* equals price? Draw a diagram to illustrate.

(5) What would happen if the firm produced up to the point where the law of diminishing returns first was observed?

More on fixed (overhead) costs

A practical businessman reading this chapter might be forgiven for feeling that professors of economics are certainly impractical, and probably a bit mad. Who but a learned fool imagines that a firm attempts to minimize an entity as improbable as quasi-rent? Everyone knows that a businessman is simply out to make the most profit! Yet the truth of the matter is that, in order to maximize profit, the capitalist adjusts output so that he maximizes the return after variable costs are paid, which we have dubbed quasi-rent. To be sure, fixed costs must be included in the computation of profit by accountants and economists alike. But these unavoidable costs must be borne regardless of output. In order to maximize profit – or minimize loss – the firm will in fact maximize quasi-rent and simply accept the fact of overhead as something that cannot be changed in the short run. The capitalist maximizes quasi-rent whether he has heard of the word or not! Decisions leading to profit maximization do not depend on the level of fixed costs even though these help determine the amount of profit the firm earns. The important thing about fixed costs is that they are fixed; therefore they do not enter into MC!

Average fixed costs (AFC), fixed costs per unit produced, are equal to total fixed costs (TFC) divided by quantity of output (Q): $AFC = TFC/Q$. As a result, if Q were to increase, average fixed costs would decline. From the definition of AFC, $Q \times AFC = TFC$. But TFC is fixed. Therefore, the product of the horizontal measure and the vertical measure is a constant. The AFC curve is of the form $xy = c$, a rectangular hyperbola, which approaches both axes asymptotically (Figure 8.5). As output increases, the total amount of overhead costs is spread more and more thinly over the product. AFC gets closer and closer to zero, but it never gets there. The total overhead never gets any smaller, even though the fixed expenditure per unit produced gets less and less.

Query: Which demand curve was also a rectangular hyperbola?

Total variable costs and total fixed costs added together make up total costs: $TVC + TFC = TC$. Average total costs (ATC) are therefore composed of average variable costs plus average fixed costs: $ATC = AVC + AFC$. To find ATC for each output we add these average elements of cost together. Graphically, this amounts to adding the vertical distance of AFC to that of AVC for each point on the horizontal axis (Figure 8.6). As

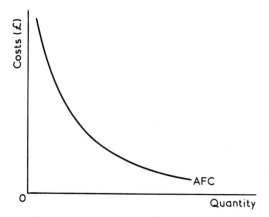

Figure 8.5   Average fixed costs

one would expect with increasing output the *ATC* curve approaches the *AVC* curve since the fixed cost per unit product becomes less and less significant.

The consequence of fixed costs being fixed is that there are no marginal fixed costs; the increase in total costs is through the increase in variable costs

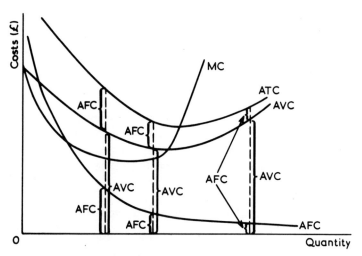

Figure 8.6   Average total costs

alone. Consequently the marginal cost curve is unaffected by the addition of fixed costs into calculation. The increase in total cost of production is the same marginal cost as before. Therefore the general relation between marginal and average quantities applies to average total costs as well as average variable costs. Another way of saying that is that the *MC* curve is marginal to both the *AVC* curve and the *ATC* curve. It crosses them each at their own respective minimum points. Even though *ATC* and *AVC* have different minima, *MC* crosses them where each one 'bottoms out'.

Exercise: To the illustration of costs of production to the wheat farmer add £10 total fixed costs. Compute *AFC* for each output. Then add total fixed cost to total variable cost (dare we call this 'total total cost'? – that is too much even for total totallers; let us continue to call it total cost). Compute *ATC*. Verify that the marginal values computed with respect to *TC* are the same as the marginal values to *TVC*.

Fixed costs are, of course, unavoidable by definition. Even shutting down production will not avoid them unless the firm goes out of business altogether. Consequently, it is entirely possible for a firm to find an output at which it can earn more than its variable costs – quasi-rent might be positive – even though it cannot cover its overhead expenses. Such a firm might run a loss, and yet it would pay the firm to produce up to the point at which price equals marginal cost. The resulting quasi-rent goes towards paying part of the fixed cost even though it cannot all be paid. The resulting loss is thereby minimized. The shutdown price, is, as we already said, at the lowest point of the *AVC* curve. Below that price, even variable costs could not be covered, and it is sensible to avoid further loss by shutting down. Fixed costs remain inescapable.

So long as variable costs are covered, our rule that firms produce up to the point where marginal costs equal price remains in force, and economic decisions are made at the margin of cost and price. Profits are maximized or losses are minimized. Figure 8.7 illustrates a firm that is earning a profit. Profit is maximized at output q^* where $MC = P$. At that quantity, total costs equal the area of the rectangle with q^* as the base and the corresponding *ATC* point on the curve as the height. Total revenues are seen to exceed costs. Their difference is profit. Quasi-rent is maximized at q^* also. Part of the quasi-rent goes to pay fixed overhead costs and the balance is the net profit.

Exercise:
(1) Illustrate a price at which the firm in Figure 8.7 would run a loss and yet not shut down. Show quasi-rent and loss.

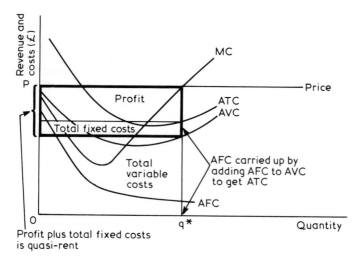

Figure 8.7   A profitable firm

(2) Graphically illustrate a price at which the firm would shut down. Show the loss that would be incurred. Show the loss it would suffer if it did not shut down but insisted on following the rule of producing up to the point where $P = MC$ even when quasi-rent was negative.
(3) Show that it would be foolhardy for a firm to produce 'as much as it can sell' to lower the burden of overheads even though overheads per unit product decline with output.

Of time, costs and efficiency

The only way to avoid overhead costs is to go out of business. That possibility should not be neglected. Nevertheless, should a firm fail to make a profit in some single year, it will not usually quit business. They will hope for better luck next year. But suppose the long-run prospects for eventual profit fade. In the face of long-run losses a firm will leave.

How does the departure of the firm from an industry affect market supply? At each price, fewer goods will be forthcoming because one less firm is producing. One less MC curve is added into the market supply schedule. The removal of one firm shifts the supply curve a bit to the left. The result is a rise in market price. The surviving firms, who presumably were in similar difficulties, are now able to pay their costs. They stay in business because they can earn normal profit which is included within costs. This process is illustrated in Figure 8.8. Before the firm left the industry, the diagram shows price at P. Typical firms suffered a loss. After a firm left, the supply curve

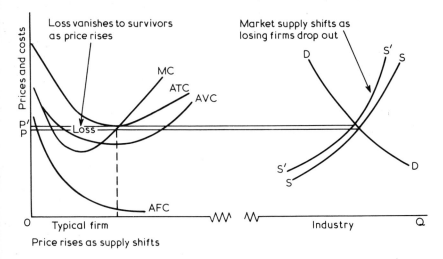

Figure 8.8.   Long-term adjustment of the industry to a loss by a firm

shifted to *S'*, and price rose to *P'*. The loss was eliminated. The typical firm covered its average total costs, which include the normal profits.

Think of the significance of all this in terms of Adam Smith's hidden hand of competition. Each individual capitalist seeks his own self-interest, to be sure. Yet he ends by serving the public good despite his egotistical goals. Why was the typical firm not able to earn a profit? The market demand curve was such that its intersection with supply gave rise to a price that did not cover costs. In effect this was the consumer's command to some firms to get out of that business. Take your factors of production, and get thee hence! Find some other way to satisfy our desires! It is a powerful command, that operates impersonally through the self-interest of the producers.

Just as losses drive firms out of an industry, opportunities to make a profit serve to attract firms into the industry. If the market price is higher than *ATC*, then the firms which obey the profit maximizing rule will earn more than enough to keep them in business. Other entrepreneurs will see their chance, and new firms will enter into the industry. The result will be increased output of goods that the consumer desires. At the same time, the addition of new firms shifts the supply curve to the right. Prices fall because firms are attracted to the industry until the excess profits disappear. Firms and factors of production are rearranged by this carrot and club method to produce products and to use methods that satisfy the wishes of those who have money to spend. No commands or central planning commissions are necessary. All they can do is to get in the way of the automatic adjustment process. 'I am not in business for my health', protests the businessman who finds himself losing money. 'No', replies the consumer, 'You are in business for my health.' 'I want two cars in my garage and an electric toothbrush that works', insists the affluent consumer, 'not a horse and buggy and bicycle.' 'You get what you pay for', replies the businessman. 'See to it that I do', replies the consumer.

Exercise:
(1) Draw a diagram similar to Figure 8.8, but show a firm making a profit. Illustrate what will happen to supply and price.
(2) Suppose demand remains the same, but technical progress in this industry reduces overhead costs. What will happen to marginal cost, supply and to equilibrium price? What if technical progress affects variable costs? How would an increase in variable costs, resulting, say, from a shortage of petroleum, affect firms?
(3) Do you think the system of allocation of resources in a perfectly competitive market is similar to the voting procedure in a political democracy? That is to say, are pounds and pence the same as ballots?

A businessman is out to make money. Efficiency in the sense of the term used by the engineers is not really his concern. To the engineer, the measure of efficiency of an engine is the cost ratio of inputs to output; he sees the most efficient point as the minimum of the *ATC* curve. But if high price warrants additional output the rational capitalist couldn't care less about efficiency.

Owners of every engineering works know full well that by running the factory three shifts around the clock they use labour less efficiently on the night shifts. When they put their employees on piecework and pay them by results, they realize that the workers will speed up the machines, overheat the tools, and burn out the bearings on the drills and lathes. Defective work will increase, Everyone knows that this is inefficient in the technological sense of the word. Old-time craftsmen fume and sputter at this way of working. Look at the waste and the shoddy workmanship! Are their employers blind? Of course not! They are out to maximize profit by – let us say it again – producing up to the point where price equals marginal cost.

All is not lost to the craftsman and engineer in the long run. Behind the backs of the profit maximizing managers the market is still at work. Firms making extra profits attract competitors. Price falls from the lucrative levels that permit efficient operation. Firms begin to take losses. Eventually some leave the industry. Slowly – sometimes too slowly – but inexorably the market price is driven toward the point where it equals the *ATC* of a typical, representative firm. Equilibrium in the long run can only occur where price is neither more nor less than average total cost, for profits must be large enough to keep the firm in business, yet small enough not to attract others. Excess profits must be zero in long run equilibrium.

At the same time as the long-run condition is met the short-run condition always also must be met: $P = MC$. The long run, after all, is made up of many short runs. There is only one point where both long- and short-run conditions can be met. It is at the output level, where marginal cost equals average total costs: $P = MC = AC$. This is the minimum of the average costs. In the long run, under perfect competition, firms are driven to produce at their most efficient output level, q^* in Figure 8.9.

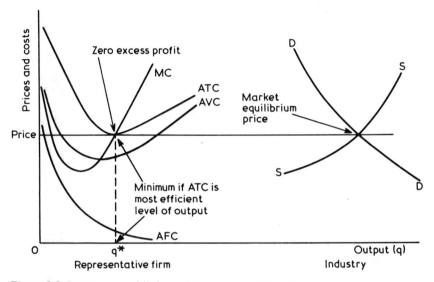

Figure 8.9 Long-run equilibrium of the representative firm

Let us not be too fatuous! In many industries the long run takes a long time. Perhaps Keynes was right: 'In the long run, we are all dead!' While firms are adjusting to supply and demand, the underlying technology and desires are changing as well. Perfect adjustment never comes, even in a completely competitive economy.

How long is the long run? As long as it takes for costs not to be fixed. When is a fixed cost not a fixed cost? When it is variable. Evidently the distinction between fixed and variable costs is a nebulous one. The costs that a firm decides to consider as its overhead expenses depend on the lengthening time horizon of the firm. One by one, fixed inputs will be reviewed in the light of long-term profit prospects. This means that for each

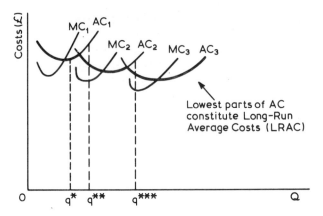

Figure 8.10   Long-run planning curve of firm

production method associated with a set of fixed inputs, there will be a U-shaped average cost curve (*AC*) and an *MC* curve (Figure 8.10). For each set of fixed inputs producers will have to decide how to use the variable inputs in the light of diminishing returns.

Three production methods corresponding to three different sets of fixed inputs are shown. Which will be chosen? The answer depends on the level of output contemplated in the long run. If output q^* is to be produced, method 1 with the lower average cost, *AC*, for that output would be chosen. Why choose the second method when the cost for each unit of output is less in the first? If output q^{**} is desired then the second method is best; if q^{***} is planned, then the third method is used. In general, for each value of q, the lowest of the overlapping *AC* curves will be chosen. We see that the *long-run average cost* (*LRAC*) curve is made up of the lower edge, the envelope, of the family of short-run average cost (*SRAC*) curves. If the number of alternatives of fixed inputs is very large, then the envelope becomes more and more smooth as each *SRAC* contributes only one point to the envelope. There is a long-run marginal cost curve (*LRMC*) associated with the *LRAC* curve. As one would expect, the marginal curve lies below the *LRAC* curve when the latter is falling, and exceeds it when the *LRAC* curve rises (Figure 8.12).

Are these long-run curves U-shaped? If there are no fixed factors in the long run how do we know that the law of diminishing returns is operative? Without diminishing returns what warrant is there for believing that long-run marginal costs rise? They may not! The long-run curves may be horizontal, they may rise, or they may fall. Increasing long-run marginal

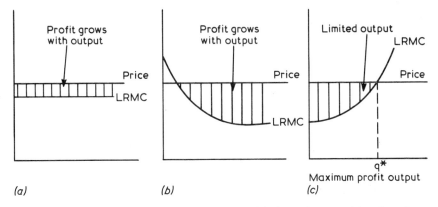

Figure 8.11   Cases of equilibrium and non-equilibrium of competition firms in the long run
(*a*) Constant returns (constant costs)
(*b*) Increasing returns (decreasing costs)
(*c*) Diminishing returns (increasing costs)

costs are associated with diminishing returns. Declining *LRMC* is called either a *decreasing cost* or an *increasing returns* situation. *Constant costs* are, of course, synonymous with *constant returns* (Figure 8.11).

It is important to see that conditions of constant returns or increasing returns to the firm are really incompatible with the maintenance of a competitive industry. Recall that our analysis of competition depended critically on increasing marginal costs to limit the size of the firm's output. Under constant costs (panel (*a*)) production will occur only if *LRMC* lies on or below price. (Why?) The shaded area represents profit. It is obvious that profit will increase indefinitely with increased output. The same is true, with even greater force, with decreasing costs (panel (*b*)). Only when diminishing returns makes the *LRMC* slope upward (panel (*c*)) does it make sense to even speak of a maximum profit, which is attainable at the suitable, limited output q^*.

Without diminishing returns, the output of the firm might tend to increase without bound! What fixed inputs prevent a giant firm from constructing any number of factories each of which might be limited in optimum size due to fixity of local resources? Perhaps nothing. In fact, recent years have witnessed the growth of multinational corporations with worldwide activities. Are there, nonetheless, considerations which can assure us of diminishing returns in the long run? Some authors have suggested that entrepreneurship remains as the ultimate fixed factor of production even to the multi-plant firm. Even though the routine administrative aspect of running a firm can be performed by hired managers, the entrepreneur has to take final responsibility under conditions of uncertainty. Someone must guess at the future of the market. Someone must hire and evaluate these supervisory personnel. Although entrepreneurship is a lot less tangible than other factors of production, it would be hard to overestimate the importance of this innovating, risk-assessing function. Capital can be borrowed, labour can be hired, but somebody has to think up new ideas, decide to reinvest, and shoulder the responsibility for the whole enterprise.

Query: Give examples of the entrepreneurial function in private and public sectors.

The larger the firm, the more thinly the centre of entrepreneurial decision making must be spread. Information of local conditions becomes hard to get. At best it is expensive to find what is really going on down in the ranks, and sometimes it is impossible. Large organizations – public as well as private – tend to develop bureaucratic pyramids to conduct operations. Each executive sees his own particular function, and does not, or cannot, take responsibility for the whole operation. A sales manager is likely to maximize sales oblivious to the fact that the marginal costs of production may be sharply rising and may reduce the firm's profits. Even if he understands production costs he may well say to himself: 'I am chalking up a record as a superior salesman. If I am not rewarded for my efforts at this firm, my reputation will permit me to go elsewhere.' The entrepreneur who sees through this sort of reasoning in the interests of the company cannot be dispensed with.

The 'establishment' – large-scale private or public enterprise – often exhibits diminishing returns in the form of bureaucracy and inability to react to changing circumstances. When it gets too big such a firm cannot keep up with smaller, more aggressive, possibly younger, competitors. If this is the case, then the long-run cost curves of the firm are indeed U-shaped (Figure 8.12). The consequences are extremely important. The long-run equilibrium condition is one in which average total costs equal price, so that only normal profits are earned. The short-run equilibrium condition requires that firms maximize profits, making marginal costs equal to price. Hence equilibrium can only be at the point where marginal and average costs equal each other as well as being equal to price. This is at the minimum of the long-run average cost curve as well as the short. Excess profits are zero and efficiency is maximized.

This reassuring result can only be relied upon to the degree that the law of diminishing returns is operative. Otherwise the outcome of constant or decreasing costs will lead to monopoly as a few firms grow large enough to make competition ineffective. To the extent that firms are likely to exhibit this U-shaped *LRAC*, a strong case may be made for allowing competition

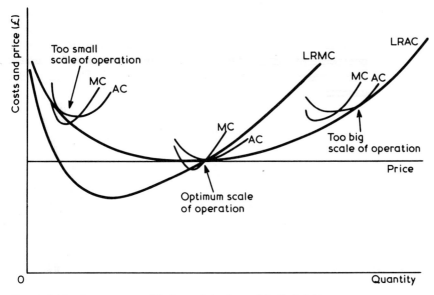

Figure 8.12   Long-run equilibrium of the firm with diminishing returns

to determine the size of the firm. Anti-monopoly laws that might limit firm size to too small a scale of operations would decrease efficiency. The crunch comes when the scale of operations for maximum efficiency is big enough to weaken or postpone effective competition. Then government is in a quandary: should an increase in competition be sought at the expense of smaller scale and inefficient operations?

Joe S. Bain investigated this matter for American firms in his well-known book, *Industrial Organization*. His study of a sample of multi-plant firms showed a typical decreasing long-run average cost up to a critical minimum scale. At larger scales there ensued a range of constant long-run average costs. For many industries, this range of constant returns to scale was sufficient to allow only a few large firms to saturate the market. Increasing costs – where they were observed – often came only at very large scales of production. Clearly there are some – not all – industries where the preservation of competition is not a spontaneous matter and the case for regulation is very strong.

Questions:
(1) Do you think that the corporate form of business organization increases or decreases the efficient use of entrepreneurship? Who is the entrepreneur in the modern corporation? Who is the owner?
(2) How might decentralization of corporations into semi-independent branches affect the efficient use of entrepreneurship?

(3) Are scientific methods of market research, and computerized linear programming methods of making decisions likely to reduce the uncertainties of business? Relate these developments to returns to entrepreneurship and profit. Would there be profit in an economy in which the future could be forecast perfectly? Would there be interest on capital?

The adaptability of production in competitive markets and a look back at the technology matrix

This chapter has traced through the mechanisms whereby businesses adapt to the demands of the consumers. Given the 'state of the technical arts', firms ultimately tend to make the best use of the scarce factors of production available to them. All that takes time. The longer the time period for which a firm can plan, the more flexible and adaptive its production – the fewer of its costs it regards as fixed – and the less important limitations and bottlenecks will be. Hence diminishing returns will be less important and marginal cost curves will rise less sharply than in a shorter time span. Production will have a chance to adapt to limited resources.

Exercise: We measure firm's response to demand by the elasticity of supply. It is the percentage change in quantity produced compared to the percentage change in price. Is the sign of this elasticity positive or negative? What is the elasticity if the same amount of product is offered regardless of price? What if the supply curve is horizontal? Verify that the supply curve representing unit elasticity of supply is any upward sloping straight line through the origin.

One way of analysing the time of adjustment is to divide it into intervals of various lengths and inquire what sort of adjustments can be made in those times. In view of the differences in industries, it would make no sense to define the intervals in actual calendar time – days, weeks, months. Adaptation in agriculture usually involves annual sowing and harvest considerations, while the construction of nuclear power sources involves many years of planning. Instead, economists classify lengths of time by asking what sort of costs and outputs can enterprise change in a given time span. What sort of equilibrium will be struck in a given interval of economic time?

The shortest interval to consider is that required for what is called *market period* or *temporary equilibrium*. Here the amount of product that is available for sale is taken as absolutely fixed, there being not enough time to produce more. Firms must sell the goods they have on hand from day to day at the best price they can get. If there is time to produce more goods by additional production, then we would be dealing with the longer interval called the *short run* (in the short run, some factors of production are variable and others are considered fixed because there is not time to change them. In the *long run*, most, if not all, of the factors of production are adjusted to demand.

   Consider first the market equilibrium for a perishable good like fish. All of it must be sold if we suppose that it is too expensive to store by freezing. Certainly it makes no sense for a fisherman to throw some of his catch away in the hope of raising the price of fish; in a competitive market he is too unimportant. All he would accomplish is to lose out on whatever money his catch might sell for. There is no choice. All of the fish must be sold at the best price it can fetch. Then the supply curve for a 'day' is simply a vertical line indicating that the quantity of fish has nothing at all to do with the price, but is absolutely fixed (Figure 8.13(a)).

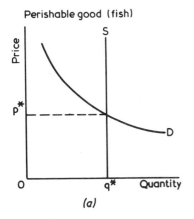
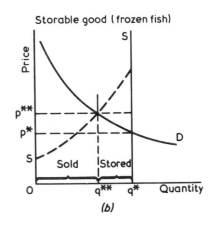

Figure 8.13
(a) Quantity of fish sold is q^* and the equilibrium price is p^*
(b) Quantity of frozen fish sold is q^{**} at price p^{**}. The amount stored is q^* minus q^{**}. If frozen fish were perishable all of it would be sold at the lower price, p^*

   The equilibrium market price must serve to clear the supply. At a higher price fishermen would find themselves with rotting fish. What an incentive to lower the price! At a lower price, customers would queue up at the counters pleading for fish. The price would settle at p^* and the stock of fish, q^*, would be sold.

   If fish could be stored by freezing, an element of flexibility would enter (Figure 8.13(b)). The total supply would be either sold or stored. Fishermen could then decide when to sell – now or later. If the price were too low, fishermen would largely hold their frozen stock until the price rises. If the price were higher, then some would conclude that they ought to sell since it is not likely that prices will go any higher. If the price were still higher, others would sell and fewer would store. At some price, everyone might conclude that prices will not increase further, and they had better sell now before price falls. All of the fish would then be offered for sale. The speculative difference of opinion among these sellers gives rise to the 'supply' curve for a durable good. At some low price all the fish will be held in storage. The market price is p^{**} where the quantity demanded, q^{**}, matches the speculative supply of sellers.

Short-run equilibrium and long-run equilibrium

As a result of the prices which are decreed by the market equilibrium, firms decide upon short-run production plans, changing variable inputs to meet market conditions. As the short run merges into the long run, the marginal cost curve becomes less steeply sloped as more of the inputs fixed in the short run are taken to be variable. Diminishing returns become less effective, and consequently long-run price opportunities bring forth greater output responses when firms have time to adjust themselves until the 'representative firm' has achieved equilibrium.

Exercise: Verify this geometrically by drawing the *LRAC* as the envelope of *SRAC* for increasing, constant and decreasing returns to scale. Show that in each case the *LRMC* is more gently sloped than the *SRMC* curve.

The very long run

There is still more room for adaptation, even after firms have achieved their optimum size. The supply to the industry in the long run could adjust as more (or less) firms of the optimum size enter or leave production depending on demand. Each of these representative firms would have the same long-run average cost curves if the same factors and technology were available to all. The supply curve of the industry would be made up of the straight line forming the lowest point of the *LRAC* curve of each representative firm where $LRAC = LRMC$ (Figure 8.14). If there are no limiting fixed factors facing the industry as a whole, diminishing returns would apply only to firms. The market supply curve would be horizontal. Under these conditions price is entirely set by the infinitely elastic supply. Demand determines the amount of goods by dictating the number of firms, but not price. The demand curves D_1, D_2 and D_3 result in outputs q_1, q_2 and q_3, but the price is always the same at p^*. Price, in the long run, is technically determined by long-run average costs!

Does very long-run equilibrium ever come? It requires that the firms and industry be in long-run equilibrium and that, as the industry expands its

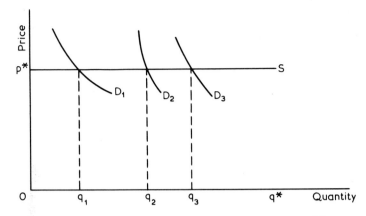

Figure 8.14   Long-run industry supply curve with no fixed factors

outputs, all the inputs to it are available to it at the same factor price. For this to be typical of all firms, there cannot be any fixed supplies of any input to any of the interrelated industries in the economy. Another way of saying this is that all the inputs are produced currently by the economy, and prices are not altered by increasing cost of primary factor inputs such as labour, natural resources, or capital. Labour itself would have to be produced like any other good by inputs of (consumer) goods, and shortages of natural resources could not limit industry output. Then we would be describing a situation where commodities are produced by commodities. Does this all sound familiar? Of course, we saw all this in input-output when we assumed that the inputs were proportional to outputs regardless of the amount of output and the 'wages' of factors of production were constant. This is tantamount to the statement that firms produce at the same average costs in the very long run.

Now we can begin to appreciate the deeper meaning and limitation of the input-output method of fixed technical coefficients of production. It is a rather peculiar situation. At either extreme of complete adaptation to the market or of no adaptation, the input-output analysis is most accurate. Either because there is no other way of doing things, or because we already have reached the ultimate best way, the technical coefficients may be taken as fixed. The real world is somewhere in between. Technical progress changes the technical state of the arts, and shifts cost curves around. When supply curves are never perfectly elastic, changes in demand also cause the technology coefficients to vary with consumer attitudes. The economy is constantly pointing toward very long-term equilibrium, but at the same time changes in knowledge of production and changes in taste point the system in different directions. The real world is in a constant state of flux. It is for this reason that we pointed out that input-output coefficients were always subject to change over time. Now we know why and how.

In actuality it makes a great deal of difference which of the two alternatives is the better explanation for the slowness with which technical coefficients of production change. If there are only a few ways to get goods produced, or if monopoly in its various forms limits the changes that will be considered, then we are dealing with a highly rigid, inflexible economy. Adjustment will not be either easy or automatic. Sharp swings in the trade cycle, unemployment, inflation and instability are likely to be features of our economic future, tempered only by the skill of government in counterbalancing these disturbances.

If, on the other hand, the tendency of a competitive capitalist economy is effectively toward long-run equilibrium, then production, demand and the use of factors would be tolerably close to optimum equilibrium. Despite changes in demand, technical progress and various random shocks, in general the adjustment would take place. The future of capitalism would not be as dim. The role of government would be limited to a mitigator of the painful effects of competition. As the remainder of this book unfolds this vital unresolved question of our times will be renewed with ever increasing urgency.

Exercise:
(1) (*a*) Describe the risks that the fisherman described in the text would face if he could not speculate on future prices by storing his product. How else might he deal with market risk?
   (*b*) How do peasant farmers or herdsmen in a subsistence economy protect themselves against the risk of calamity due to weather or warfare? Explain the persistence of the institutions of extended family and tribal affiliations in less developed countries.
   (*c*) What are risks facing the Soviet factory manager? How does he protect himself?
   (*d*) How does the ordinary person deal with the risk of loss of income to his family if he should die?
(2) Pieces of paper are very durable. Consequently, it is possible to make even a perishable good durable by selling promises to deliver the good at some specified future date. These promises are called futures. Markets such as the commodity markets sell both futures for forward delivery and spot contracts to deliver goods at once. This market now deals in promises. People speculate on the value of these promises.

   People who know a great deal about this market become professional speculators who hope to buy the promises cheap and sell them at a higher price. A farmer who grows grain, or a fisherman who catches fish also is a speculator of sorts, since he is committed to produce a product which will only be available in the future. The market conditions at that date are unknowable. By means of a hedging operation in the market, risk can be shifted to professional full-time speculators. A farmer may sell his promise to deliver wheat at a specified time in the future at a predetermined price, even though the wheat may not yet have been planted. At harvest he gets the price specified. To be sure, if the going spot price at that time is above the contracted arrangement, the farmer has lost income; but he has protected himself against market loss as well. A fisherman might do the same by promising to deliver his catch to the local cannery, freezing plant or wholesale suppliers of fish to restaurants.

How might you protect yourself against market risk under the following circumstances? Work on the reasonable assumption that spot and future prices will move up and down by the same amounts:

(a) You are a manufacturer of soup and are offered a large institutional contract to deliver tomato soup six months hence at a fixed price. If the price of tomatoes rises in the interim you may lose money by having to buy expensive tomatoes to fulfil your contract. What future transactions will permit you to accept the contract?

(b) You are a small potato jobber. Farmers come to you with potatoes for which you must pay cash (spot). By the time you resell the potatoes the price may fall. Your profit comes from handling the potatoes and not speculating. How can you protect yourself against a price fall by a futures operation?

(c) You are a school teacher who lives on a fixed income. Prices may rise, and your income may be worth a lot less in real terms. Should you save your money in cash or should you buy shares of real estate or a house? What would happen to your plan if prices fall? Can you hedge by borrowing money?

(d) You are an exporter of cars to the United States. You are to receive $3000 for each car. Say at that time $1·70 = £1. Suppose you fear the US may devalue to $1·50 per pound, what would you get in sterling for the cars you have shipped? Is there a futures market in money? How can you use it to shift the risk?

(3) Do some library research on the history of the coal mining and auto industry in the UK. Compare their ability or inability to adapt. Come to a conclusion on why Britain has nationalized one industry and not the other. What should be done now in these industries?

(4) (a) Distinguish between MC, AVC, AFC, ATC, LRMC, LRAC.

(b) State the law of diminishing returns and show its importance. Explain why a firm which observes itself to be producing under decreasing MC has not yet advanced the optimum level of output.

(c) Relate MC to opportunity cost.

(d) Relate quasi-rents to profit.

9 Paradise lost: the economics of monopoly

Monopoly and competition

The main trouble with perfect competition is that there is not enough of it. Table 9.1 depicts the concentration of a large share of the market in a few hands and makes for serious doubt that the model of perfect competition among many small firms is a realistic description of the market structure of these two nations.

To spell the matter out, the conditions for perfect competition are:

1 Each industry consists of a very large number of very small firms. No firm is large enough to influence market price by offering more or less goods for sale.
2 Firms in each industry produce identical products. There is perfect substitution between the goods of competing firms. Buyers can choose between sellers entirely on the basis of the price they ask for their wares. Since the goods are identical, no seller can charge more than any other; that is to say, there can be only one price for any good at any one time.
3 Producers and consumers have knowledge of the nature and price of both goods and factors of production.
4 Firms and factors of production may readily enter or leave an industry without legal or other barriers to entry or exit.

Certainly one would not expect that these ideal conditions could be completely met. Nonetheless, when they are approximately true the model of perfect competition is still very useful. But for many industries the

Table 9.1   Per cent of industry output by largest firms in the USA and the UK

Industries	United States* 4 largest firms	United Kingdom† 3 largest firms
Primary aluminium	100	43
Passenger automobiles	98	74
Electric lamps	93	56
Locomotives	91	53
Flat glass	90	51
Cigarettes	82	74
Tyres and tubes	79	73
Trucks	77	86
Matches	74	—
Explosives	72	—
Steel ingots	64	32
Railway cars	64	25
Distilled liquors	64	—
Shortening and cooking oils	55	79
Primary zinc	53	—
Motorcycles	50	87
Aircraft	47	47
Plastic materials	47	51
Shipbuilding and repairing	43	23
Flour and meal	40	46
Farm machinery (excl. tractors)	38	40
Textile machinery	32	36
Petroleum refining	32	93
Cement	31	—
Canned and preserved fruits, vegetables	28	21
Beer and ale	27	11
Paints and varnishes	27	20
Pharmaceutical products	25	24
Hosiery mills	22	12
Wool yarn	20	12
Cotton textiles	18	4
Sawmills and planing mills	7	5

* Per cent of value of shipments, 1954
† Per cent of value added, 1951
Source: J. S. Bain, International Differences in Industrial Structure (1966), p. 78.

divergence is so marked that it is necessary to explain the market conduct of firms in terms of various forms of monopoly.

If utterly perfect competition is an idealized state, so is perfect monopoly. Literally, monopoly means a single seller, a firm with no competitors at all. Its product would have no substitutes. If challenged to produce a monopoly firm one might think of ICI or the frequently nationalized British Steel. In terms of *market structure*, such firms certainly seem to fit the description. Yet British Steel does have competitors, for steel has many substitutes for its various uses. As structural materials, aluminium, plastics, plywood and concrete may be used. For products that range from pots and pans to corrosion-resistant milk tanks it might be worthwhile to use aluminium if the price of stainless steel is too high. In other words, the definition of monopoly in terms of market structure ultimately depends on the definition of the firm's market. Certainly British Steel holds a monopolistic position in the steel market, but not in the market for structural materials, cooking utensils and the like. Ultimately every product is in competition with others for the budget of consumers who are free to spend their money as they see fit. Monopoly is a matter of degree.

What are the dimensions of monopoly? One is the degree of concentration in the market structure of industries. There is a subtlety here since the term industry is essentially arbitrary. It refers to groups of firms producing similar products, so that the degree of concentration depends on how closely goods can be grouped together as similar. The degree to which each firm produces a product which is differentiated from its competitors is the degree to which it possesses concentrated monopoly power. Another way of saying this is that a firm has monopoly power to the extent to which it might reasonably be considered an industry unto itself because of the high degree of product differentiation. Thus at one extreme ICI is virtually identical with the British chemical industry in many lines of output and possesses a high degree of monopoly power. At the other extreme, thousands of news vendors sell identical products.

Exercise:
(1) Go to the library and find the Standard Industrial Classification. Describe the basis for its grouping of firms into industries. Do you agree with its method? What difficulties do you think it encounters?
(2) Evaluate the national and international degree of monopoly in petroleum, cars, grain, coffee.

Matters cannot rest with a description of market structure. The significant issue is, after all, what monopolistic firms do with their power. We have to know the consequences of monopoly in terms of *market conduct*. Are the firms given to 'predatory' forms of competition? Do they conspire to fix prices? Are they conscious of public opinion and public interest? Finally, after all is said and done we must concern ourselves with the *market performance* of firms and industry. Is production efficient? Is the distribution of revenue carried out equitably? Do consumers have the opportunity to be satisfied to the degree they would under perfect competition?

Market structure, conduct, performance

Under perfect competition there is little question about the motives of business firms. They are simply out to maximize their profits. Indeed, competition makes profit maximization the only conduct consistent with long-term survival. Under monopolistic circumstances we cannot be so sure, since competitors are not always breathing hot on the neck of each capitalist. Still the profit motive is very important, so our method will be to first ask how monopolists would act to maximize profits. This will explain a great deal. Then we shall see that they are led to consider other goals as well as profits, once the market structure permits.

The profit maximizing monopoly

The market structure we have in mind is a firm producing a product considerably *differentiated* from its nearest competitors, and protected by formidable *barriers to entry* to potential competing firms. As we have already observed, even the most powerful monopoly cannot force the consumer to buy its product. It must attract customers. If the price is too high, the consumer will buy more of something else. Unlike the small price-taking competitive firm, the monopolist is free to fix his prices as he sees fit. The catch is that if he wants to sell a great deal of merchandise he must lower the price; if he wants to maintain a high price he must face the fact that fewer of his goods will be purchased. Since the monopolist is really an industry unto himself, he faces the downward sloping demand curve associated with any industry. But he faces it alone.

Knowledge about the reaction of the public to different prices is the source of the monopolist's sales problem as well as his profit making power. The monopolist faces opposing tendencies in his marketing policy. For each additional unit that he sells, he must lower the price of all of the merchandise he offers. To maximize profits he must compute the net increase in revenue from an additional sale gained at the expense of lowering price. The increase in revenue is called *marginal revenue (MR)*. We can reproduce this computation from the demand schedule relating price to quantity sold. *Total revenue (TR)* is the schedule of prices times quantities. *Marginal revenue* is the successive increase in *TR* for each unit increase in quantity. Consider a hypothetical monopolistic firm, ABCDE Foundations Ltd (Table 9.2).

The opposing tendencies are at work. The first two columns show that with each increase in quantity of product offered, the price must decrease. Column 3 shows that as sales increase total revenue may increase. But the increase in revenue, marginal revenue, shown in column 4, becomes less and less. There is a fall in the amount by which *TR* grows. Suppose the price were

Table 9.2   ABCDE Foundations Limited

(1) Quantity (Q)	(2) Price (P)	(3) Total revenue (TR = P × Q)	Marginal revenue (MR = ΔTR/ΔQ)
0	£20	£0	£0
1	18	18	18
2	16	32	14
3	14	42	10
4	12	48	6
5	10	50	2
6	8	48	−2
7	6	42	−6
8	4	32	−10
9	2	18	−14
10	0	0	−18

£20. No product would be sold, and total revenue would be zero. If the monopolist cut the price to £18 he would sell one foundation. Hence *TR* is £18. Since £18 is also the increase over his previous revenue, *MR* = £18. Now, to sell two foundations, he will have to sell them both at £16. *TR* will be £32; hence *MR* = £14. Why does his revenue increase by only £14 when he just sold a £16 foundation? Because when a second unit sells for £16, so must the first. If he had been content to sell one article he could have got £18 for it. But if he is ambitious enough to sell two goods, the fall in price of the first must be subtracted from the revenue derived from the second to correctly calculate the gain in revenue.

Exercise:
(1) Compute the marginal revenue (*MR*) for the third unit and explain why the *MR* is less than for the second.
(2) Explain why *MR* is negative for the sixth unit of sales even though the price is £8.
(3) Explain why *MR* is always lower than price after the first unit of sales.
(4) Identify the output that would lead to zero marginal revenue; to zero total revenue.

We know from our study of perfect competition that profit maximization requires the firm to produce up to the point where the additional income it receives for another good just equals the increment in cost. Under perfect competition the additional income was simply the price of the goods; but to a monopolist the increment in income is marginal revenue. Thus a monopolist will maximize his profit if he produces until the marginal revenue (*MR*) just equals the marginal cost (*MC*).

Are we sure there is a point where $MR = MC$? Yes, we have just shown that MR decreases as output increases, whilst MC increases due to the familiar law of diminishing returns. Eventually they meet. If the monopolist miscalculates and produces more than the ouput where $MC = MR$, MC will exceed MR. The firm will lose on the excess items. On the other hand, if a smaller output is manufactured, where MC is lower than MR, additional profit could have been earned had production been extended further.

In its utilization of the marginal principle there are obvious similarities between the monopolist and the firm under perfect competition. But, there is an essential difference: under perfect competition the price was out of the control of the firm and did not change with output. Consequently the perfectly competitive firm increased its revenue by the amount of the price each time it sold another bit of produce. Increased output by a competitive firm did not depress price. Under conditions of perfect competition, the marginal revenue is the same as price. Under monopoly they diverge because price is affected by the output actions of the firm. With this understanding it is possible to use the single rule $MC = MR$ for profit maximization for both perfect competition and monopoly, since under competition price is marginal revenue.

Figure 9.1 contrasts profit maximization for perfect competition and monopoly. In perfect competition (panel (a)), MR is another name for the horizontal price line. Marginal costs rise due to the law of diminishing returns. The firm produces q^*, where $MC = MR$. The difference between total variable costs and total revenues is quasi-rent. In the diagram quasi-rent is the area between the MR curve and the MC curve. In the monopoly

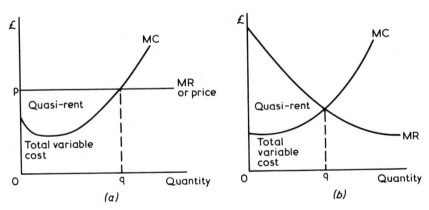

Figure 9.1   Profit maximization under perfect competition and monopoly
(a) Perfect competition
(b) Monopoly

case (panel (b)) MR is downward sloping. To maximize profit, the monopolistic firm produces q^{**}, where $MC = MR$. The area between these two curves represents the quasi-rent to the monopolist.

Query: Suppose a firm under perfect competition acquired monopoly power. What do you think would happen to its output?

More can be learned about the market conduct and performance of the monopolistic firm by considering the average quantities that accompany the marginal ones. The cost curves behave as in competition, since the law of diminishing returns is doing its work under monopoly as well as competition. It is a technical law of production and has nothing to do with market structure or conduct. Matters are different on the demand side. The average revenue (AR) curve is nothing but the downward sloping demand curve facing the monopoly firm. For each quantity of output, total revenue is equal to the corresponding price times quantity: $TR = P \times Q$. But AR is equal to TR/Q, so that average revenue is nothing but the price consumers will pay per unit of product offered for sale.

From what we know about the relationship between all average and marginal quantities, it follows that if the AR demand curve slopes downward, the MR curve must lie below it and slope downward too. As a matter of fact, it can be shown that if the demand curve (alias AR curve) is a straight line, the MR curve is also a straight line and slopes downward twice as fast (Figure 9.2).

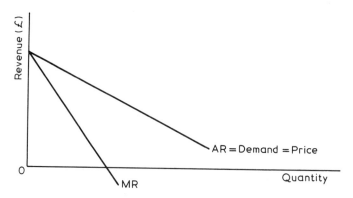

Figure 9.2   Average and marginal revenue

Exercise:
(1) What is the slope of the AR curve under perfect competition? Show that the AR and MR curves coincide under perfect competition.

(2) Show that under monopoly the absolute value of the slope of the MR curve is twice that of a straight line demand curve. (Hint: Choose a point on the AR curve and drop perpendiculars to the axes. Note that the area under the MR curve and the rectangle subtended by the AR curve at that point are equal since they both equal total revenue. Proceed by similar triangles as in school geometry.)

(3) Why is it sensible to draw Figure 9.2 so that AR stays in the positive region while MR may cross the horizontal axis into negative values?

(4) If an increase in output over some intervals of the demand curve results in an increase in revenue, then we may conclude that MR is positive. If the increased quantity results in no increase in total revenue, then MR is zero. And, if an increase in output results in a decrease in revenue (why?) the MR is negative. Relate this result to the concept of elasticity of demand. Show that the linear demand curve can be divided up into regions in which the elasticity of demand takes on values greater than, equal to and less than unity. (Hint: Note that price and quantity vary in opposite directions so that the increase in output is the same as a decrease in price.)

At last we can see the mischief monopoly makes. Superimpose the marginal and average cost curves on the marginal and average revenue curves (Figure 9.3). The firm will maximize its profit if it produces up to the

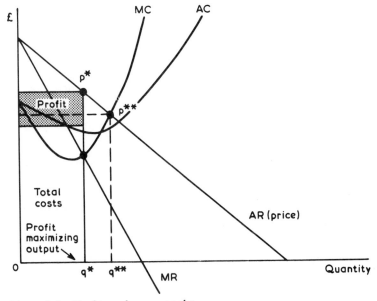

Figure 9.3   Profits under monopoly

point at which marginal cost equals marginal revenue, q^*. What is the associated price? From q^* read up to the demand curve at p^*; this price is how much consumers would be willing to pay for a given quantity of goods. Naturally the monopolist will charge p^*, all that the public will bear.

The firm illustrated is earning a profit greater than the amount necessary to keep it in business. Total revenues can be seen to exceed total costs. Total revenues, as the product of price times quantity, is represented by the rectangle formed by perpendiculars from the AR curve at p^*. Total cost is the product of AC at q^* times quantity. The shaded rectangle is the profit (strictly quasi-rent) to the firm over and above the normal profits included in AC.

In two important respects we can identify this profit with monopoly position of the firm:

1 Since the firm is the sole producer of a differentiated product it has maximized its profit with due regard to the price fall that would have occurred had it attempted to sell more than q^*. By restricting its output to q^* it was able to maintain its price at p^*. If – and one must concede a big 'if' – the demand and cost curves were the same for an industry under perfect competition as the monopoly firms then output would have been q^{**}. This is so because, under perfect competition, the MC curve of the monopoly firm would be the sum of the MC curves of many smaller firms, and would therefore constitute the supply of a competitive industry. AR would be market demand. Price and quantity would be at p^{**} and q^{**}. Under competition prices would be lower and more goods would be produced than under monopoly.
2 Profits in excess of normal can be maintained by the monopolist to the extent that there are barriers to entry into closely related industries. Profits draw competitors like honey draws flies. Competition would reduce the price, and increase the quantity of output. An essential ingredient of profitable monopoly is to keep other firms out.

Exercise:

(1) By completing the following table supplement the information about ABCDE Foundations presented in Table 9.2.

Quantity	Fixed costs	Total variable costs	Marginal costs	Average total costs	Total costs	Profit
0	2	0				
1	2	2				
2	2	5				

Quantity	Fixed costs	Total variable costs	Marginal costs	Average total costs	Total costs	Profit
3	2	10				
4	2	16				
5	2	23				
6	2	33				
7	2	45				
8	2	60				
9	2	77				
10	2	97				

Which output maximizes profit? Show how the monopoly firm earns profit.

(2) Draw diagrams of costs and revenues of monopoly firms under the following circumstances:

(a) Marginal costs cross marginal revenues at a quantity point to the left of the minimum of the AC curve. Draw the AR curve higher than the AC curve at that point.

(b) Marginal costs cross marginal revenues at the minimum of the AC curve.

(c) Marginal costs cross marginal revenues at a point to the right of the minimum of the AC curve.

Discuss the economic situations which correspond to these three diagrams. Show how the public is harmed by the product differentiation and barriers to entry.

Almost every firm possesses some monopolistic power of product differentiation. Product differentiation depends on whether the consumer views the product of one firm as different from its nearest competitor whether or not there is a physical difference. Enlarging and defending a monopoly position is the basis for the strenuous advertising efforts of a firm to convince the public that its product is different.

Query: Explain the impact of the 'star' system of rating the octane level of petrol in the UK. Could this practice be extended to other industries? Would a distressing sort of drab uniformity result? Would monopoly be weakened?

Product differentiation is not always associated with large-scale enterprises. The grocer or local supermarket can make good use of its relationship with customers and location in a city to become a miniature monopolist. This can be inferred from the paradoxical situation that is often observed in the prices of some groceries. Food prices are lower at the weekends and higher during the week. One would think that since the demand for groceries is higher after pay-day, prices would rise before the weekend. Yet Friday is precisely the day that stores run food sales – newspapers are full of advertisements of low prices.

An explanation for this curious pattern of prices lies in the variation in the degree of monopoly as the days of the week change. The grocer differentiates his product by being located close to the customer's home. He accumulates goodwill among his customers. He gives credit. Established customers know that telephone orders will be filled with fresh produce and meats. Children linger over the penny sweets display and neighbourhood gossip is exchanged among adults. For all these reasons the grocer's product, including his services and his smile, is different. These differences are significant during the week for small, convenience, purchases. But what happens to the degree of monopoly on Friday? Prices in competing stores become much more important than convenience because frequently the basic food supply for a whole week is to be purchased. Then it becomes worthwhile to drive to the competing supermarket. As for the grocer's smile – well, money talks! At weekends the monopoly evaporates and the market becomes almost perfectly competitive. Monopolistic firms may be small as well as large. Concentration ratios may be low, as in the grocery business, yet competition may be imperfect. Market conduct must be considered as well as market structure.

Exercise:
(1) Draw graphs of the middle-of-the-week grocery market and the weekend grocery market illustrating the price rise according to the explanation proposed. Is there any way you might test the theory to see if it is correct.
(2) What is the market for used textbooks at the university ? Is it competitive? Should it be?

Monopolistic or imperfect competition

The list of most large national corporations keeps changing from year to year. As time goes on, barriers to entry break down. High profit rates entice new firms to produce competing goods. Patent rights expire and substitute processes are invented. The advantage of large firms is undermined by efficient stock markets which permit the launching of competing business even on a very large scale. New and smaller firms often prove to be more efficient than large and bureaucratic enterprises. Even if barriers to entry withstand these assaults, new products replace the old, so that entrenched positions of monopoly power are bypassed, and foreign competition tends to erode national monopolies. The very expansion of the economy provides room for new large-scale enterprises competing with the older ones that had once saturated the market.

Barriers to entry exist. Most economists would judge them to be harmful. Nevertheless, they are not impregnable fortresses that cannot ultimately be brought down. As a consequence of the constant state of flux in firms' market power monopoly merges into that of imperfect or monopolistic competition. There is a degree of product differentiation shown by the divergence between the *AR* and *MR* curves of the firm. All the same, in the long run barriers to entry are ineffective. Excess profits are wiped out by competing firms. That such a model is typical is the conclusion that one would draw from the study of US firms by Professor George Stigler (Figure 9.4). On the horizontal axis he shows the ranking of manufacturing firms in order of size in their respective industries, and on the vertical axis their

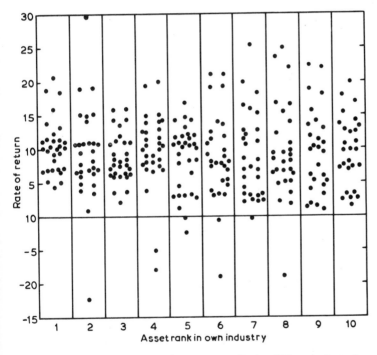

Figure 9.4   Average rates of return, 1959–63, for 290 manufacturing corporations in thirty industries (arrayed by 1963 asset rank in own industry) (George Stigler, *Testimony before Senate Subcommittee on Anti-Trust and Monopoly of the Committee of the Judiciary* (US Senate, 1965), p. 1552)

respective rates of return. Evidently there is little relationship between the relative importance of firms and their profit rate.

Stigler's research was not intended to minimize the monopolistic damage to public welfare. On the contrary, imperfect competition based on product differentiation represents a misallocation of productive resources even when profits are normal. To see this, suppose that the entry of firms into the sale of related products caused excess profits to disappear. That means that at some profit maximizing output where $MC = MR$, it must also be the case that $AR = AC$. (In the previous example, the monopolistic grocer may well maximize his profits. Yet there may be sufficiently many competing grocers that he never can charge higher prices than the amount just necessary to keep him in business with normal profit. The most excess profit he can earn is still zero, even with product differentiation.) That amounts to a situation in which the AR price line is just touching (tangent to) the AC curve at the same quantity as where $MC = MR$ (Figure 9.5). When the monopolist produces at q, he satisfies his own profit maximization conditions ($MC = MR$) *and* the no-profit condition of long-run market equilibrium ($AC = AR$).

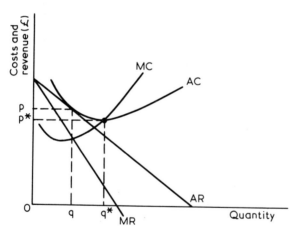

Figure 9.5   Monopolistic competition in long-run equilibrium

How different this is from long-run equilibrium under perfect competition! The firm is not producing at q^* the most efficient level of minimum average cost. The monopolistic firm holds back on output in order not to 'spoil the price'. It produces at less than the most efficient production. Typically the monopolistic firm exhibits underutilized capacity. As a result of restricted production, it sells the limited amount of goods to consumers at a higher price. The monopolistic firm does not earn any extra profit, yet resources have been misallocated nonetheless! No wonder monopoly is regarded as opposed to the public interest.

Monopolistic firms may beat their breasts, and insist that they are not making more than the 'going rate of profit'. Even if this is so, the public is still damaged. Moreover, if monopolistic firms were to be induced to produce at the most efficient output, they would have to earn more than the normal profit (Figure 9.6). Suppose MC were to equal MR where AC is a minimum. Output would be q^* where $AC = MC = MR$. The consumer pays the price P^* found by reading up from q^* to the AR curve. Since the AR curve is always above the MR curve, it is also above the AC curve at that point. Multiplying AC and AR by the output q^* shows the total costs and the excess profit which has to be paid the firm to operate efficiently.

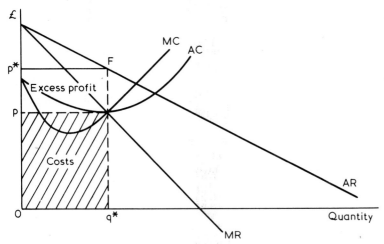

Figure 9.6   Monopolistic firm producing at minimum average cost

Exercise:
(1) Price discrimination:
Suppose a firm produces a single product in one factory, but sells it in two separate imperfect markets.

Step 1
For each market draw AR and MR curves as straight lines. To make the markets really different, be sure that the corresponding curves in each market are not parallel.

Step 2
At each price add up the amount sold in each market by adding the quantities horizontally. This is an aggregate AR curve (if one of the AR

226 Paradise lost: the economics of monopoly

curves starts higher than another, you may find a kink in your aggregate curve).

Step 3

Draw the corresponding aggregate *MR* curve as a straight line with twice the slope of the aggregate *AR*.

Step 4

Draw an *MC* curve for the single factory.

Step 5

Find the total profit maximizing output where the aggregate *MR* curve crosses the *MC*. Divide up the output between the two markets by extending the height of the *MC* = *MR* intersection horizontally over to the vertical axis. For each market the firm will sell where each *MR* equals the aggregate level of *MC*

Step 6

For each quantity sold in each market, read up to each *AR* curve. If you have done the exercise correctly, the prices should be different in each market.

    Repeat the exercise for one perfect market and one monopolistic market. Offer two examples of price discrimination illustrating the analysis.

(2) Might it ever be right for the government to sponsor barriers to entry in the form of patents or licences? Can you think of a practical way of getting firms under monopolistic competition to produce at the most efficient point without letting them earn excess profit?

(3) Choose some of these past and present practices of business and government. Explain their advantages and disadvantages in terms of contributions to productivity on one hand and monopoly on the other. Are any of these illegal?

   (*a*) *Patents* on new inventions. After a period of years the patent expires and the process may be used by anyone. Patents may be sold or licensed.

   (*b*) *Quantity discounts* to retail outlets for large purchases.

   (*c*) *Mergers*: *vertical integration*, the merger of firms producing various stages of the same product; *horizontal integration*, the merger of firms producing the same product at the same level of fabrication; *conglomerate integration*, the merger of unrelated firms.

   (*d*) *Publicly owned* companies in radio and television competing with private broadcasters. *Nationalized* monopolies such as steel, coal and electricity.

   (*e*) *Tying agreements* in which the customer must buy the full line of products produced by a manufacturer to be permitted to buy any.

(f) *Pooling agreements* among firms not to compete in markets assigned to the others

(g) *Franchising of dealers*, which limits wholesale and retail distributors of products to those approved by the manufacturer. The franchised dealer may be required to agree to prices, selling and servicing procedures specified by the manufacturer.

(h) *Agreement* by companies to end a price war.

(i) *Collusion* by engineering companies to fix the price of bids for equipment offered to the government.

(j) *Holding companies* in which the stock of one corporation is owned by another.

(k) *Interlocking directorates* in which the same people may be the boards of directors of several firms.

(l) *Collective marketing organizations* such as trade unions and farm cooperatives.

(m) *Legislation* requiring disclosure of full credit costs on hire purchase agreements.

(n) *Packaging* of groceries in unusual and variable units of weight and volume.

(o) Prepaid private medical insurance, which pays medical bills according to a *fixed schedule of charges*. Drug firms advertising medicines to physicians by brand name as well as chemical content.

(p) *Protective tariffs* on imports of competing goods.

(q) Legislation *illegalizing racial considerations* in employment.

(r) *Minimum wage laws.*

(s) *Resale price maintenance.* Manufacturers determine the price at which retailers may sell their products.

Oligopoly and duopoly

In earlier chapters we were concerned to explain the limits to output of a firm in perfect competition. Whilst the firm could sell all it cared to at the going market price, increasing marginal costs limited the profitable output. Monopolistic firms were seen to consider the reaction of customers as well as costs. These firms did have a sales problem since they had to compare increases in goods sold against their falling prices. This second limitation resulted in a tendency towards further product restriction. Now we turn our attention to market structures composed of few firms: two firms constitute a *duopoly*, and 'a few' are called an *oligopoly*. Oligopolists have still another dimension of concern. They must worry about what the other firms will do as a result of any action they take.

In perfect and imperfect competitive market structures, no identifiable individual was consciously retaliating to the firm's decisions. To be sure, consumers react to the prices of goods, but not with the purpose of causing the firm to change its policies. Under oligopoly, the firm has opponents. The hand of competition is not hidden at all, but is – to overdo the metaphor – sometimes clenched into a fist of price war, or formed in the handshake of a 'live and let live' policy. Thus efforts by a business concern to expand its operations by cutting prices may well be seen by others as the breaking of a truce or as an attempt to take away their market share. Simple profit maximization cannot explain what they may do in response. They may lower their prices. Or, rather than touch off a price war, they may resort to *non-price forms of competition* such as intensified advertising campaigns, improved customer service, better delivery and easier credit terms. The product itself may be changed and more strenuous efforts made to differentiate it from the opposing firm's goods.

I recall an interview my students had with a director of the 'J' Steel Company in a large American city. We asked him if there was a great deal of competition in his business. His affirmative response was accompanied by a grimace at the constant, coercive, exacting, ulcer-generating pressure he had to endure. 'How many firms are there in this industry?' we then asked. 'Eight.' 'And how often do prices change in this highly competitive situation?' The man was visibly agitated at the thought. 'We haven't changed our prices in years. Competition is so terrific that if we changed them by even a little bit, "X" Steel Company would undercut us, and we would lose out in the price war that would result. Oh no, this business is too competitive for that sort of thing!'

'J' Steel Company was fearful of a price war with the more powerful integrated steel firms. These latter firms, in turn, fear government prosecution if they initiated predatory price cutting. They would welcome the excuse 'J' Steel Company's price initiative would provide. Strenuous non-price competition was the only tool available to 'J' market strategists. The firm located supply warehouses and factories at carefully chosen sites so they might be able to deliver steel to their customer's factories within a very short time. They made sure to carry on hand complete inventories of all the various specifications of steel so that the customer would not have to maintain expensive stockpiles. In effect, the 'J' Steel Company was absorbing storage, interest and transport costs which otherwise would have fallen to the company buying the steel.

Image making is another form of non-price competition. The 'J' Steel Company advertised its strict quality control procedures. It polished the steel bars until they shone. One of their advertisements pictured a polished steel bar alongside an elegant sterling silver tea service glittering on a red velvet damask. The picture told the story; 'Buy J Steel, and wealth, respectability and status are yours!'

Query: Are the various forms of non-price competition of the 'J' Steel Company all wasteful?

The complex swirls of conflict between oligopolies are a multidimensional war. It may involve control sources of supply, hiring away of key personnel, and access to financing. Even the control of the enterprise itself may be in dispute. A successful and growing firm may find itself 'raided' by outsiders, who attempt to buy up controlling shares of stock. Yet, despite the obvious explosive potential of oligopoly (perhaps because of it), there often are prolonged periods of rigid unchanging prices, outputs and business practices.

Scientific analysis of oligopoly is very difficult because of its complex, game-like, character. Any well-designed game – chess, bridge, poker – is made interesting by the enormous variety of moves and countermoves open to the players. Only noughts and crosses has a few enumerable outcomes, and that is why it is a game suitable for the limited mentality of either children or computers. Like noughts and crosses, perfect competition and pure monopoly are also reducible to a small set of well-defined moves to maximize profit. In fact the rule is simply $MC = MR$. But each oligopolistic situation is a strategic problem in itself. Every decision is made in the light of the expectation of how others will interpret one's actions, and what their response is likely to be. These decisions are made under conditions of uncertainty. Unforeseen and unexpected outcomes make for a very tricky game!

Some of these ideas of business strategy can be illustrated by a glimpse of the mathematical theory of games, which also has application to conflict situations such as international politics. Consider a very simple two-party game played by Firm A and Firm B. Suppose it is a zero-sum game like dice or poker in which the gains of one player are equal to the losses of others.

Query:
(1) If two firms conspire to fix the price of goods to be sold to the government, are they playing a zero-sum game with each other? Is it a zero-sum game if we consider the two firms and the government as players?
(2) Give some examples of games which you think are not zero-sum games.
(3) Physics students, explain whether or not the law of conservation of energy is a zero-sum game. Who are the players?

To keep matters simple, suppose each player has only two well-defined strategy alternatives, known to both parties. Corresponding to each strategy chosen by player A and the counteracting strategy by player B, we take it that there is a definite resulting payment from one to the other. Therefore, since each player has two alternative strategies, we can make a table called a *payoff matrix* which will have four cells corresponding to the combinations of strategies that are possible. If the entry in a cell is positive, we will take it that B, whose strategies are shown in the columns, makes a payoff to A, whose alternatives are given by the rows. If some of the entries in the payoff matrix are negative, it means that player A has to pay player B. In actual computation, it is easiest to think of B always paying A, but the amount may be negative.

Payoff matrix I

		Firm B		
	Strategy	1	2	Minimum
Firm A	1	−£2	−£1	−£2
	2	£2	£1	£1
	Maximum	£2	£1	

Once again, to keep matters simple, suppose each player 'knows the score', so that there are no secret moves, and the payoff results are understood by each strategist. Then it is easy to deduce what the outcome will be. Imagine that firm B played its strategy 1 in the hopes that firm A would follow with its strategy 1. If A were foolish enough to do so, then B would pay −£2 to A, or, as we have agreed to say, A would have to pay B £2. Would A oblige? Hardly. It would counter B's move with its own strategy 2, which would have a positive £2 payoff from B to A.

If B were clever, it would adopt a more cautious policy, called the *minimax* principle. Firm B should face the inescapable fact that the payoff is going to be a positive amount of money to firm A. It should try to hold that amount down to a minimum if at all possible. B knows that A will choose the maximum value in each column. Therefore, B should choose that strategy for which the *maximum is a minimum*. The maximum values are shown outside the table, so it is easy to see that in this case B will opt for strategy 2, and the minimax is £1.

What will A do? A knows that B will try to have the outcome be the minimum value for each row. Therefore, it should choose the strategy for which the *minimum is maximized*. This is the *maximin* strategy; in our example it is the second alternative facing firm A. The maximin payoff is £1, as is shown by looking at the minimum values recorded outside the table.

Without direct conspiracy, these opponents tacitly agree on policies, so that the payoff from B to A will be £1. Simple prudence leads firm A to strategy 2, and firm B to its strategy 2. Such an agreement on the strategy of minimax-maximin is called a *saddle-point* for technical mathematical reasons. The *value of the game* is the payoff at the saddle-point, in this case £1. Since the payoff is not zero but a certain fixed sum, it has been suggested that these games ought to be called constant-sum games rather than zero-sum games.

Exercise: Repeat the problem with the following payoff matrix.

Payoff matrix I

		Firm B		
	Strategy	1	2	Minimum
Firm A	1	− £2	£2	− £2
	2	− £1	£1	− £1
	Maximum	− £1	£2	

Life is not always so clear cut! Look at this payoff matrix:

Payoff matrix II

		Firm B		
	Strategy	1	2	Minimum
Firm A	1	− £2	£1	− £2
	2	£2	− £1	− £1
	Maximum	£2	£1	

No doubt we are headed for trouble. Since the maximum is − £1, and the minimax is £1, so there is not going to be saddle-point agreement. Suppose firm A plays strategy 2 on the expectation that firm B will play its strategy 1. If B were stupid as well as obliging, it would do so and pay £2 to A. Since B is clever, it disappoints its rival, and replies with strategy 2. That means that the payoff to A is − £1: A must pay B. Since B is playing 2, A replies to his opponent's strategy by playing his first strategy. Now, if B continues to play 2, and A is playing 1, the payoff will be £1 from B to A. But B is not so stupid. He switches back to strategy 1. And, so the game circles on and on without a fixed result. As long as one firm can know the other's strategy, it can employ an effective counter-strategy. If this were the case in the real world, a profit maximizing explanation would not suffice to stop the cycling of strategies.

We would have to explain what firms actually do in terms of habit, ignorance or alternatives, or perhaps sheer fatigue.

Actually, there is a means whereby both firm A and firm B can devise a rational profit maximizing strategy. If they can keep their strategy a secret no reply can be made by opponents before the payoff. The best way of keeping a secret from someone else is to keep it from oneself. A firm might therefore decide its strategy by some sort of chance procedure. The probability of choosing one strategy over another need not be equal as in the case of coin-flipping. The percentages may be weighted 40 and 60 per cent, or some other combination adding up to 100 per cent. In more advanced texts, the reader will learn how probability combinations can be chosen, so both parties agree on the statistically expected final value of the game.

Once we get away from two-person and zero-sum games we frequently run into games that are not strictly determined by any techniques. Heroic attempts have been made to solve some of these games, and some fruitful results have been achieved. Generally, however, the possibility of alliances of some players directed against others brings us back to patterns of shifting allegiances and strategies as the players switch from one solution to another. In the end, the questions that decide oligopoly behaviour have to be descriptions of the behavioural patterns and psychology of the individuals involved. As a matter of fact, psychologists and sociologists have made good use of this feature of games to turn the problem around, and study types of individual reaction by putting people in game situations and watching them choose strategies.

Exercise: Which of the following games are solved by tacit agreement strategies between players and which would cycle unless secret strategies were adopted?

(1)

		Firm B	
	Strategy	1	2
Firm A	1	£2	£6
	2	£3	£5

(2)

		Firm B		
	Strategy	1	2	3
Firm A	1	£5	−£1	£4
	2	−£2	£1	£15
	3	£3	£2	£6

(3) Let the payoff be a percentage of voting stock in a corporation, and play the following game:

		Mr Gould	
	Strategy	1	2
Mr Fisk	1	20%	50%
	2	60%	30%

Before the development of game theory Paul M. Sweezy suggested a way of describing the sort of games oligopolies play as an extension of the theory of monopolistic competition. He argued that the average revenue curve (*AR*) facing an oligopolist curve has a kink or sharp corner at an established 'going' price. To the left of the kink, he suspected the demand curve is elastic, and to the right it is less elastic. If the firm raised its prices, it would fear that the opposing oligopolists might not follow along, and its sales would fall off rapidly and so would its revenues (elastic demand). On the other hand, if the firm lowered its prices, the others would retaliate by lowering theirs, and very little increase in sales would result; the outcome of a price cut might even be a loss of revenue (inelastic demand). An oligopoly would have every incentive to stay at the price indicated by the level of the kink (Figure 9.7).

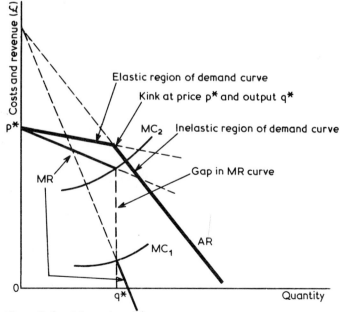

Figure 9.7   Oligopoly pricing

This is a very attractive explanation because it accounts for the frequently observed sticky prices associated with oligopolistic market structures. If we portray the AR curve as composed of two pieces of straight line, segments joined at the kink, we can draw the associated MR curve as a line with twice the slope. The geometry of the diagram shows the MR curve to have a gap, a discontinuity, at the output corresponding to the kink.

One interesting result that Sweezy derived was that technical change would have relatively little to do with prices. Thus the marginal cost curves could shift anywhere within the gap (as high as MC_2 and as low as MC_1) and still MC would equal MR. Only if MC rose very high would a firm cut back on output and raise price; only if MC fell so that it intersected MR beyond the kink might the firm risk a price war.

Alas, like all the other oligopoly models, the kinked demand curve does not explain all the behaviour of firms. First of all, Sweezy's demand curve is a queer sort of game-like creature that reflects a firm's guess about its opponent's actions intermixed with its conceptions as to the tastes of the consumers. Consequently, there is no explanation advanced why the kink is where it is, and not somewhere else.

Secondly, we do find counter-examples to sticky prices in cases of *price leadership*. In some industries price changes by the leading firm are almost automatically accepted by the others. Why is this so in some industries and not others? There seems to be no general answer.

Non profit maximizing oligopoly

A few years ago one of the world's leading economists, Professor William J. Baumol, found himself involved as a consultant to several large oligopolistic corporations. Baumol is a brilliant man, known for his ability to see through complex and apparently paradoxical situations. Yet he confessed himself unable to find the profit maximization process at work in the firms employing him. In a little book, *Business Behavior, Value and Growth*, he developed a model showing how oligopolies might attempt to achieve other goals as well as profit. Baumol's suggestion was that the executive leaders of these firms seemed to be concerned to earn only that profit needed to keep the shareholders satisfied. As executives they were more interested in maximizing their sales and output accomplishments rather than profits as they 'should'. Both pricing policies and advertising were aimed at this goal even though diminishing returns led to profits below the maximum.

Query: What might be meant by maximum sales? Show why it is different from maximum profits.

Another goal is *growth*. It is better for managing directors to report expanding sales rather than irregular profits. Perhaps the organization man anxious to earn the maximum profit this year, lest he not be able to show that he is doing better next year. He expects to be asked: 'What have you done for me lately?' Still other goals of organizational behaviour have been discerned. Increasing market share of sales is important as an indicator of success within a firm. Larger numbers of subordinate employees are a measure of an executive's empire in the organization.

It is not clear which of the possible patterns of oligopoly behaviour will apply in any given situation. We do not seem to be able to derive a general theory of oligopoly behaviour. Maybe it is not that we are inept. Perhaps it is the economy that is disorganized by the lack of perfect competition; for, to the extent that oligopoly is an important feature of our economy, we cannot rely on the efficient coordinating function of competition in the market mechanism. This issue has its ironies. Karl Marx thought that competitive capitalism was disorganized because the absence of planning made for the 'anarchy of production'. We are asking just the reverse: Does the conscious planning by large oligopolistic firms mean that the economy is in an uncoordinated state of anarchy?

It has been suggested that competition and potential competition is far more pervasive than is apparent to casual observation. Stockholders are able to move their capital from low profit to higher profit firms in due course. Moreover, it is too easy to observe bureaucratic rigidity of administered prices and end the inquiry there. Where did the customary prices come from? How do they change? In the long run, as Baumol himself emphasized in his important little book, the hidden hand of competition works. Of course it works more slowly than in competition – that really is the rub. In actual fact, various recent studies have tended to show that the misallocation of resources due to monopoly is surprisingly small. GNP could only be increased by a fraction of one per cent by returning to perfect competition. Part of the reason may be the very inability of the oligopolies to fully utilize their market power. Perhaps equally important is the opposition of oligopoly groups to each other. John Galbraith has called this *countervailing power*.

On the other hand, as one important economist, Harvey Leibenstein, has pointed out, the usual tests for misallocating resources will not always reveal the full tendency of oligopoly to stick to rigid prices and obsolete methods for fear of 'rocking the boat'. He has dubbed the use of all the potential new methods of production x-efficiency. Leibenstein claims that it is this x-efficiency that is lost by oligopoly, more than misallocation or wasted inputs as in monopolistic competition.

Still other economists have stressed the effectiveness of competition despite oligopolistic market structures. Milton Friedman of the University of Chicago has urged that, despite the concentration of market structures, economists make accurate predictions as if a perfectly competitive situation existed. He contends that it is only sensible to ignore monopoly if unified models of perfect competition predict equally well. Perhaps this is an extreme view. Nonetheless, it must be conceded that, despite rigidities in market structure, a blanket case against oligopoly is far from proven.

Controlling monopoly: can paradise be regained?

In one form or another, monopoly poses a basic dilemma for every country in the world. On one hand monopoly entails social evils: output is restricted and prices are higher than the same technology could produce under competitive conditions; oligopoly frequently leads to rigid prices and lagged response to cost changes that may be destabilizing to the economy as a whole (see Chapter 13); monopoly represents a concentration of economic power in private hands that can influence the political machinery in a way that can be worrisome. On the other hand, monopoly may result from economies of large-scale production and so be associated with productive efficiency. Clearly, the larger the efficient plant size, and the smaller the market area, the more difficult it is to condemn monopoly market structures. The more urgent the need to develop modern large-scale technology, the less is the concern with maintaining perfect competition. The more thoroughly an economy is centrally planned, the less will be the dependence on the market mechanisms and the greater will be the tolerable level of monopoly. The more pressing the reed for production to meet a crisis situation, the greater will be the acceptance of monopoly power.

These considerations make for considerable variations in national responses to the problem. In the underdeveloped portion of the world industrialization plans frequently call for the establishment of large-scale enterprises. These are frequently subsidized and licensed by governments. Often they are owned or partly controlled by the state. The issue in Nigeria, for instance, is which international firm should be invited to set up an automobile assembly plant. In addition to its monopoly position, it could receive investment subsidy from the government. Sceptics have argued that what passes for socialism is in fact a system of governmental subsidies and monopolistic powers.

Similar considerations have entered into governmental participation in monopoly power in many of the advanced countries. The *dirigisme* of the French economy, for instance, includes government direction and subsidy and even joint ownership of enterprises with private investors. The European Iron and Steel Community likewise aims at reduction of duplication and small-scale enterprises. The rationale for this is that units large enough to withstand foreign (American) competition must be organized. As long as public funds are going to be used in investment in new capital, it is hard to imagine that the public will set up enterprises of less than the optimal size, leaving it to competition to conduct the weeding out of the inefficient. Here too it is unclear whether these public operations are radical socialist nationalization or conservative support of monopoly power. Operating as it does within a large-scale domestic market, the United States can more easily adopt the official position that monopoly is simply illegal. In addition to criminal prosecution of specific companies, there have been a series of court decisions dismantling some large firms that exhibit a monopolistic market *structure* regardless of their conduct. Yet, at the same time as it takes this anti-monopoly stance (the degree of monopoly has to be shown to be 'unreasonable') the United States promotes less than perfect competition in subsidies to shipping and airline industries. Rates on rail and electric power services are administered by quasi-governmental agencies.

Britain's position is intermediate between the American and the continental approach. A more limited form of anti-monopoly legislation is combined with subsidies, development grants and nationalization which tend to limit competition between private firms. The Restrictive Practices Act of 1956 amended earlier postwar legislation to deal with the two aspects of monopoly control – market conduct and market structure. The Restrictive Practices Court was set up to deal with specific agreements between firms to restrict the supply of goods or to fix prices. That is to say, the court was to be concerned with market conduct. The 1956 act also established the Monopolies Commission, which has been concerned with changes in the market structure through merger of independent firms into more concentrated forms.

Inevitably both these bodies have had to cope with the dilemma of the desire for competition opposed to economies of large scale. Thus the Restrictive Practices Court has not been able to illegalize all restrictive agreements among firms. The 'gateways clause' written into the act permits such agreements if the public is reasonably protected from injury, if consumers benefit, the monopoly power of others is counteracted, local unemployment reduced, or if the Court is satisfied that public interest is fostered. By their very nature, the decisions of the Restrictive Practices Court have raised a furore. In each of the several thousand cases reviewed, it can be taken to task for either failing to deal firmly with monopoly, or for being excessively narrow minded in interpreting the gateways clause. Since there is both benefit and harm associated with most concentrations, the Court has no choice but to use its judgement. Perhaps the most frustrating part of the exercise is the tendency of oligopolies to come to *de facto* price agreements without evidence of collusion.

Even more trying problems face the Monopolies Commission. Defining monopoly as a situation in which one-third of industry output is controlled by a firm or a combination of firms, the act directs the Monopolies Commission to investigate and report whether a monopoly is contrary to the public interest. As one would expect, the criteria the Commission is to use for its guidance include efficient and economic production for home and foreign markets, improvements in technology and the penetration of new markets for British goods. Initially without power to enforce its findings, the Monopolies Commission may now appeal to the enlarged powers of the Board of Trade. Upon referral by the Monopolies Commission, the Board may go as far as limiting or banning mergers and even insisting on the breaking up of existing monopolies. In practice the Board of Trade has not had recourse to these statutory powers. Inquiry by the Commission has led to agreement between the firms and public authorities. As in other countries, legislation to combat monopoly has tended to curb its excesses and lead to 'reasonable' solutions, but the trend toward mergers continues.

Nationalization is, of course, an alternative way in which the public interest can be protected in the face of economies of large-scale production. Once having taken this step, the question becomes: how shall nationalized industries behave? If they are to be efficient, the prices they charge should correspond to shadow prices. This would be possible if the whole economy were centrally planned to perfection. Yet it is not proposed that Britain nationalize all industries. In a mixed economy some are publicly owned and some are private. Should the nationalized industries act as if they were private firms by a programme of marginal cost pricing? If so, they try to produce up to the point where MC equals price. But what price? In the absence of a perfect market that information is missing. If they produce up to the point where $MC = MR$ they will act as monopolists themselves!

Or should they try to define the public interest regardless of efficiency? Should they act to counter monopoly power in the private sector? Should they concern themselves with reducing such external costs as pollution in the public interest, even though it means a loss of profits? Should they price their products so as to redistribute real income by providing services and goods to individual firms that society would like to aid? Should they locate in development regions, even though more profits can be made in more prosperous locations? Should they be instruments of macroeconomic policy by trying to hold the national wage line against inflation while increasing productivity? Should they adjust their product mix and factor use so that directly and indirectly national employment levels will be adjusted in the public interest? Should they adjust themselves to assist in controlling balance of payments problems?

Matters can get more difficult. So long as the preponderance of industry is competitively priced – at home or abroad – the nationalized industry can take the market price of its inputs as reasonably reflective of shadow prices. It can then abandon the marginal pricing principle and maintain a policy of a normal profit mark up over costs and still hope to retain a degree of efficiency. Or, if it chooses, it can deviate from the competitive rule for social reasons which it deems good and sufficient in light of the efficiency sacrificed. But what happens if much of the industrial structure is either nationalized or thoroughly monopolized? What good are the price signals then? Accepting these prices as the basis for a constant per cent mark up is only to pass the distortions through the rest of the economy's interdependent prices. If it is not possible to use prices to determine the contribution of an industry to the economy, how should the government's capital budget be allocated? What reliability can be placed on studies of costs and benefits? Which industries should be encouraged and which cut back?

All this is not to say that nationalization should not be carried on. Only that it is not an instant solution to the problem of bigness. There are not any more neat answers to the questions facing the public sector than there are for the Monopolies Commission in the private sector. In the end, the issue between regulated monopoly and nationalization may be better decided on the practical ground of ease of control and direction in particular cases on one hand, and the loss of efficiency and coordination on the other

There are some glimmers of hope. One is that the economy may be more competitive than it seems. Perhaps, slowly and behind the scenes, the conflicts between opposing monopolistic groups – including the government – ultimately reflect something like supply and demand, even though they give the immediate impression of a chaotic interplay of political and economic power. Another possibility is that mixed methods of planning can be devised for the mixed economy. For instance, by use of input-output tables it is possible to compute shadow prices for the economy given the technology it has. Alternative technology matrices could be compared. Thus, however crudely, the central planners might get an idea of what shadow prices really are and use them in making their decisions. It should be emphasized that only crude first approximations are available this way, but they may provide some guidance to the perplexed.

Exercise:
(1) Read the white paper *Nationalized Industries: A Review of Economic and Financial Objectives*, Cmnd. 3437, and discuss its criteria for government policy.
(2) What is the possible influence of Britain's entry in the Common Market on its market structure, conduct and performance? Explain your views in light of the following data:

Table 1   Shares of the largest EEC firms in the gross domestic product of extractive and manufacturing industries*

Group	1960 %	1965 %	1970 %
Top 4	5·8	6·8	8·1
Top 8	10·4	11·8	14·6
Top 20	20·9	22·6	29·0
Top 50	35·1	35·1	45·7

* Note that gross domestic product is the denominator while sales are the numerator. This biases the ratios upwards.

Table 2   Share of the largest British quoted firms in total net manufacturing assets

Size class	1948 %	1957 %	1968 %
Top 4	10·2	11·4	14·7
Top 12	17·8	20·6	26·2
Top 50	35	39·9	50·8
Top 100	46·5	50·7	63·7

Table 3   Evolution of concentration by industry in Britain

Industry	Percentage of industry net assets held by the 10 largest firms 1954	1965	Number of firms holding 50% or more of the industrial assets 1957	1967
Food	65·7	72·9	7	4
Drinks	41·6	74·9	12	4
Chemicals	81·6	87·7	2	2
Iron and steel	62·8	73·0	6	4
Mechanical engineering	33·8	29·0	—	—
Electrical engineering	61·4	64·6	5	3
Automobiles	50·1	76·4	5	2

Source: A. P. Jacquemin, 'Size, structure and performance of the largest European firms', *Three Banks Review* (June 1974), pp. 62–3. Jacquemin finds no reliable relation between firm size and profit rates, but a lower variability in profits of larger sized firms and conglomerates.

10 The distribution of income

The prices of factors of production

The fundamental theorem of economics stated that the efficient allocation of scarce resources among alternative ends implied a set of prices. Economists did not always regard this as the basic question. The great English economist, David Ricardo, argued that the distribution of income among the various classes of society ought to be the main concern of economic analysis. In this chapter we shall show that these are really two ways of asking the same question. By determining the price of the factors of production and how much of them will be employed, we can determine their owners' share in the national product. It will be seen that the prices of the factors is determined at the same time as the decision is made as to how much of each product to produce.

Suppose that once again we put ourselves in the position of the central planning board of a perfectly planned socialist economy. We would find ourselves making judgements that are strikingly similar to those of directors of a capitalist factory. Just as firms want to maximize their revenue with the scarce factors at their disposal, directors of the nation want to make the most national income with the factors of production available. National planners have a *linear programming* problem to solve (see Chapter 5). National income is their *objective function*, the price of each product times the amount of its final use produced. For two commodities, it is the familiar equation: $Y = p_1 y_1 + p_2 y_2$.

Query: Are society's goals different from individual ones? How? Specify a different objective function.

The *constraints* are the amount of factor inputs available to the economy: land, labour, capital and entrepreneurship available for use directly and indirectly in the production of y_1 and y_2. The linear programme is thus:

Maximize:

$$Y = p_1y_1 + p_2y_2 \qquad \text{National income.}$$

Subject to:

$T_1y_1 + T_2y_2 \leqq B$ T_1 and T_2 are the amount of labour directly and indirectly needed for y_1 and y_2; B is the limiting supply of labour.

$Q_1y_1 + Q_2y_2 \leqq N$ Q_1 and Q_2 are the amount of natural resources (land) directly and indirectly needed for y_1 and y_2; N is the limiting supply of natural resources.

$C_1y_1 + C_2y_2 \leqq K$ C_1 and C_2 are the amount of capital directly and indirectly needed for y_1 and y_2; K is the limiting supply of capital.

$F_1y_1 + F_2y_2 \leqq E$ F_1 and F_2 are the amount of entrepreneurial talent directly and indirectly needed for y_1 and y_2; E is the limiting supply of entrepreneurship.

$y_1 \geqq 0;\ y_2 \geqq 0$ Non-negative amounts of final product.

The feasible set of outputs is represented as the shaded region in Figure 10.1. National income, Y, clearly is a straight line with a negative slope equal

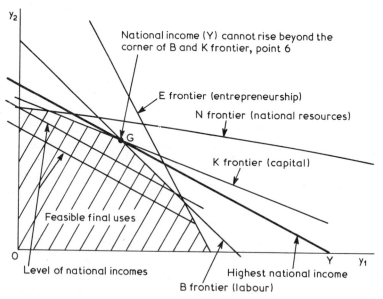

Figure 10.1   Linear programming problem of national planning

to the relative prices of the two final uses. At constant relative prices Y can be maximized by choosing outputs that move it out parallel to itself, until it hits one of the corners or extreme points of the feasible set where two of the constraints cross. G is such a point. At the boundary of the effective constraints, national income can increase no more. The value of final use is limited by the amount of labour and capital left to the nation as the legacy of its history. If the national planners solve the linear programme properly, they will manufacture the amounts of final use indicated by the coordinates of that point. Since the solution is on the frontier of both labour and capital, both of these will be fully used, while land and entrepreneurship will have slack excess capacity.

Exercise: What would be the significance of the point of maximum national income lying within the E and N frontiers? Would the situation change if there were more than two final uses considered? Might it change if the frontiers were non-linear in shape?

For the moment, let us focus our attention on two limiting inputs – labour and capital; they are the bottlenecks, the *effective constraints* at point G. We now ask: What would it be worth to the country if it were possible to ease the labour and capital bottleneck just a bit? The answer is obvious. The gain to the country would be the additional national income that could be produced. Suppose more labour, ΔB, were forthcoming in response to an offer of higher wages. Then the labour frontier would move out parallel to itself, enlarging the feasible set by the dotted region (Figure 10.2). National income can grow until it once more hits the new corner of the labour and capital constraints at G^*. The increase in income is ΔY, proportional to the distance moved outward by the national income line.

Rational socialist planners would compare the additional labour cost with the additional national income it could produce. That is to say, they would continue to hire more and more labour, pushing the labour frontier further and further out as long as the additional cost of labour in wages does not exceed the increase in income. The increase in income, ΔY, is the maximum additional amount that the planners would be willing to pay to get an additional ΔB of labour. This increment in final use which results from an increment in labour employed is called the *marginal product* (*MP*) of labour when measured in physical units (of either good), and the *value of the marginal product* (*VMP*) when measured in money terms. *VMP* is the *shadow price of labour*, equal to the value of the contribution of a further unit of labour to national income.

Query: Locate the marginal product of labour measured in physical units of y_1 or y_2.

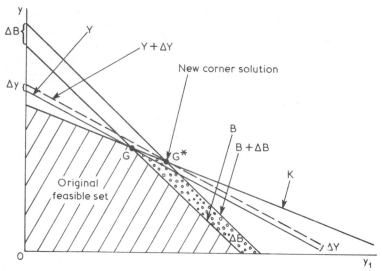

Figure 10.2   Value of an increase in labour

Thus a shadow price is attributed to the factors of production by the efficient allocation of scarce resources among alternative ends. While we have thus far put the issue in terms of the quest of socialist planners for maximum national income, the theorem applied regardless of the sort of society involved. It is the efficient use of resources that imputes the value to factors of production, not the existence or non-existence of planners, capitalists or markets.

To spell this out for capitalist markets, it is necessary to think back to the plywood and lumber mill linear programming problem (Chapter 5). The firm's objective function, total revenue, represents its component of national income; the constraints such as labour, saw-and-machine time, log storage capacity in mill ponds, are recognizable as particular varieties of the factors of production, labour, capital and land. The value of the marginal product of labour (or any other factor) is the additional amount of revenue that would be generated by employing an increased amount of labour. *VMP* is the increase in output of each good (the marginal product) times their respective prices.

The *VMP* is nothing but the firm's *demand price* for the factor; it is the wage that employers would be willing to pay to employ an additional worker. This must be compared with the wage that employees must receive to induce them to supply an additional amount of labour, the *supply price*. At equilibrium the market makes the demand price equal to the supply price; the amount that firms are willing to pay for another unit of labour is equal to the wage necessary to motivate the labour to work. That is to say, supply and demand prices for labour are equal where the quantity of labour supplied equals the quantity of labour demanded. Supply curves and demand curves for the factor of production intersect where the market clears.

Query: Draw supply and demand curves for labour and compare the terms *supply price* and *demand price* with *quantity supplied* and *quantity demanded.*

What makes us so sure that there is actually an intersection point of supply and demand schedules? What forces make for upward sloping supply schedules and downward sloping demand schedules in factor market economies and in planned systems? The *supply* reason is the familiar one that it takes higher wage incentives to get additional labour. Workers have to be induced to leave other occupations. They have to be paid extra to give up more and more of their leisure. Ultimately there are just so many hours of work that people will or can do, and the supply curve relating wages to work becomes simply a vertical line. Similar considerations apply to other factors of production.

Query: Suppose society attempted to force people to work. How much of the preceding analysis would apply? Is forced labour cheap? Can society force people to use their capital? Their land?

The *demand* reason depends on a different version of the law of diminishing returns. Imagine that all the factors of production are fixed except for the labour force. Now trace out what happens to the shadow price of labour as more and more of it becomes available (Figure 10.3). Originally imagine the labour frontier to be B_1. It is situated so close to the origin that it is the sole scarce factor of production, all the others being in slack surplus supply.

We identify firm's revenue (final sales) with national income, shown by the heavy line. It is maximized by choosing the output combination indicated by the point 1 in the diagram (notice, incidentally, that the maximum value of the objective function calls for only one kind of final use to be produced). Now increase the labour force to B_2. Optimum results are obtained at point 2. The distance between the heavy revenue lines through points 1 and 2 shows the increase in revenue that the extra labour has produced.

By again increasing the labour force by the same amount, point 3 appears as the optimal output combination. So far the increase in revenue has been the same. Why should this be so? Because up to now the labour limitation is the only effective one, so the law of diminishing returns is not relevant. (Why?) Equal increases in labour mean equal increases in revenue. But now suppose the labour force is increased to B_4; revenue can be increased by moving to point 4. Labour is not the only scarce factor now, since the natural

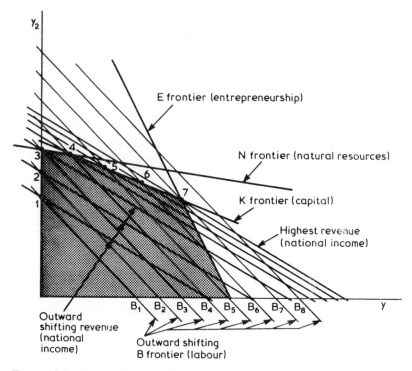

Figure 10.3   The declining shadow price of labour – diminishing returns again

resources constraint has become operative as well. The increase in revenue is plainly smaller due to the smaller slope of the N frontier.

Continue increasing labour, to B_5. Now the capital limitation is relevant as well as the natural resources constraint. Revenue increases by a still smaller amount. As we increase the labour force to B_6 and B_7 the increase in income remains the same since we are still limited effectively by capital. But were we to try to increase the labour force further to B_8, the increase in revenue would fall further. Indeed it would fall to zero since there are no feasible points corresponding to any of the points on B_8. (Why?) So the extra labour would not increase the revenue at all! Indeed, any resource in slack, excess supply will have a price of zero.

Query: Does it follow that a slack resource is unimportant or not used? Give other examples.

Since the amount that would be paid for an additional amount of labour declines as more and more labour is used, the value of the marginal product

demand curve for labour declines. Supply and demand will intersect at a
market price equal to the shadow price which efficiently uses the labour at
the disposal of society (Figure 10.4).

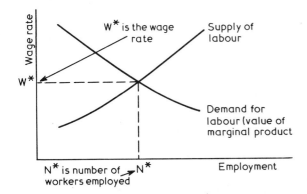

Figure 10.4

We have shown that the optimal solution to the product mix problem
logically implies a set of values to be placed on the factors of production.
This is true of every other factor of production, as well as the labour we are
using as illustration. There is a formal mathematical relationship between
these concepts. The *primal* linear programming problem is one involving the
maximization of the objective function subject to constraints. The solution
to the problem consists in finding final outputs that maximize the revenue
objective. The *dual* problem is one of searching for the values to be placed
on input factors of production that will minimize the costs of the firm. The
constraints are more complicated, but they can be shown to boil down to
producing the final use under competitive conditions which limit a firm to
only normal profits. It can be shown in more advanced study that the
maximum of the objective function in the primal is equal to the minimum of
the objective function in the dual. That is to say, the maximum net national
product that can be produced with given supplies of factors of production is
equal to the minimum amount of national income at factor cost that has to be
paid under competitive conditions to get the output produced.

Certainly this is not the end of the discussion of how income is distributed,
but there are some false notions that can be laid to rest. One such theory is
the 'iron law of wages', which holds that real wages cannot rise above their
'natural' value. In one version of the 'law', it is argued that wages cannot rise
without increasing prices by the same percentage. Real wages are always the
same. The theory might be true enough if, under perfect competition, the
productivity of labour and the supply of the cooperating factors such as

capital were constant. In fact these two considerations actually determine the demands for labour and hence are the means of increasing real wages (look back to Figure 10.3):

1 Suppose labour became more productive, due to increased skill or effort by the labourer or through change in technology. Then moving the labour production frontier one step outward by the distance ΔB actually would require fewer additional man-hours. Each hour of labour by a worker of greater productivity counts for more than one of low productivity. Consequently the increase in income produced by each additional hour is greater, and so is the real wage.
2 Suppose the capital frontier were moved outward. Then, as the amount of labour offered increased, the marginal product of the labourer would increase national income by a larger amount than before. Due to the availability of capital the value of the marginal product of labour rises and so will wages.

Of course it must be conceded that we have only emphasized the demand for labour; it might be that the supply of labour were such that the wage rate would not rise even if demand increased. This would occur if the supply curve for labour were horizontal – infinitely elastic – so that an indefinitely large amount of labour is forthcoming at a constant wage. The demand curve crossing at various points would then determine employment, but not influence wage rate. This condition might occur in a country with a high rate of population growth so that any time wages exceed bare subsistence, more babies are born and the labour force enlarges forcing wages back down to subsistence. A similar situation might occur if there were surplus labour in a backward agricultural sector which would be brought into the cities at the subsistence wage (see Chapter 15). These are hardly the likely circumstances for a modern industrialized nation, but they do shed light on why the notion of an 'iron law of wages' was popular during the Industrial Revolution when supply of labour newly recruited from agriculture was so elastic.

The notion of a fixed 'wages fund' is related to the iron law of wages. This doctrine holds that there is a fixed sum that society has earmarked for subsistence of workers. While the *wage rate* may vary, the total amount of the *wage payments* is fixed. Therefore high wages for some must mean lower wages or unemployment for others. Increased population always means low wages.

There is a certain amount of sense to the concept of a wages fund in a society in which agriculture is the pivotal consumer goods industry. There is then an annual lag between planting and harvest and the amount of foodstuffs cannot be increased in the meantime. Therefore there is a fixed stock of consumer goods available to give the workers as real wages. If the stock were to be enlarged by a bigger harvest, of course, the wages fund would be bigger next year.

As more and more goods are produced by industrial processes, and as international trade makes the goods of the whole world available to any country, the lapse of time entailed in making more consumer goods diminishes. Increased labour productivity can increase the goods available at about the same time as it justifies the competitive demand for higher wages. Even though the justification for a wages fund explanation is now very weak, people often continue to think of income distribution as if there were a fixed fund or pot of money that has to be divided up. The wages fund only makes sense after the fact, as an identity equal to the price of labour times the quantity employed. It is not the fund that determines wage rates and employment, but just the reverse.

Exercise:
(1) Make a graph of supply and demand illustrating the discussion of the 'iron law of wages'.
(2) What is the elasticity of demand for labour assumed in the 'wages fund' doctrine?
(3) The 'lump of labour' theory of employment holds that there is just so much employment available to the workers. If somebody gets a job, it means that somebody else must lose one. Is there any truth to this idea?
(4) Evaluate the following two statements with the aid of the analytic tools you have studied.
(I) Labour increases its wages by the addition of more capital. Even if labour increases its skill it can only use it by operating more complex capital equipment. Most of the high productivity of labour comes from the machinery it operates. Consequently, it is capital that is the cause of high wages. Workers should be grateful to their employers, and realize that it is not the workers who are more productive but the machines. Wage increases should not be granted when more capital is supplied; it is profits that should rise.
(II) Labour is the source of all value. If it were not for the workers the machines would not run. The capitalists do not work, yet they receive income from machines they have not laboured to produce. It is true that machines increase labour productivity, but who made the machines in the first place? The capitalists? No, the workers. Employers might justify their salaries as factory managers or engineers, but they cannot excuse profits made by exploiting the workers.
(5) (*a*) Since there is an unlimited supply of air, what is the price? Why? If there were an unlimited supply of labour what would be the wage rate? Are there places in the world today which fit your description?

(b) Substitute the word land for labour and repeat your answer. Illustrate. What is the relationship between population (labour) and the price of land?

(c) Describe a condition of unlimited supply of capital.

Whilst economic analysis can clear away some misconceptions, it cannot say what income individuals ought to get. It is one thing to point out that a resource is worth so much, it is something else to agree that the situation is 'fair' or equitable. Equity and efficiency are not the same, and frequently conflict. For instance, simply transferring income to the low wage earner by definition means that he must get more than the value of his marginal product. The rest of the labour forces would therefore get less than their VMP.[1] In effect this is a programme of imperfect competition in favour of the poor. While this policy may be judged fair on moral grounds, it could not be considered optimal from an efficiency point of view.

The equity issue can more readily be treated in terms of who shall own the factors of production? One may make a moral decision along this line, and then, after wealth has been transferred, allow it to be put to efficient use. Yet, even when one makes a good equity case for the transfer of wealth, there are difficulties. It is simply hard to transfer the human capital involved in labour skills, since it means shifting people's preferences for work, saving, leisure, and study. One must change a life style. There are other obstacles. When more tangible wealth is transferred, somebody loses. People do not like taxes and death duties. There is the problem of loss of incentive to people who fear that their wealth may be taken away. A person who 'makes it' and accumulates physical and human capital expects to pass it on to his children, in the form of property and education and cultural advantages. Perhaps this accumulation of wealth as a stock is as much a motivation for energetic productive effort as the luxuries that a higher income can bring. Were the possibility of accumulating wealth removed, much of the incentive to work and save might go with it.

The point is that the efficient use of resources is a matter to which we can give fairly clear answers. The sticky question is who ought to own these resources or receive the income they generate. Even stickier is how to bring about the changes in ownership of wealth without at the same time undermining the motivations that make wealth socially useful.

Exercise:

(1) Which of the following methods for redistributing income is best?

(a) Redistribute stocks of wealth to the poor.

(b) Make the labour and capital markets more perfect.

---

[1] Except for 'rent' situations described in the next section.

(c) Give up a degree of productive efficiency and make the labour market imperfect in favour of the poor.
(2) Distinguish between *equity* of income distribution and *equality* of income distribution. What would have to be assumed about utility to make these two ideas synonymous?
(3) Socialists often argue that it is almost as inequitable for capital to be owned privately by capitalists who do not work it as for the slaves to be owned by their employers. Do you agree?
(4) Explain the means whereby wealth in the form of human capital is transmitted from parents to children. To what extent do you think this process is similar to the inheritance of tangible physical property? How is it different? Do you advocate changes in the present arrangements?

Rent

Thus far our attention has been focused on the demand for factors, showing what an enterprise would be willing to pay for another unit of labour, land or capital. Tacitly, this analysis has assumed that if a higher price is offered, more of the factor will be forthcoming. But what if that is not the case? Suppose the factor supply is completely inelastic – or inelastic over a range of offers. Then there is a set of many factor prices at which the same factor supply will be forthcoming, and consequently the output of the product will be the same. The range between the highest price the owner of the factor can receive, and the least he would accept is called *rent*, since this phenomenon was originally associated with returns to land. We shall argue that efficiency considerations require users of the factor to pay the rent so that the scarce factor can be allocated to its most profitable use. Nonetheless, in view of the fact that factor supply is not responsive to factor price over this range, rent constitutes a class of income payments which could be taken away from its present recipients and transferred to others with no loss of output.

What determines the payment for use of land? Demand for use of land depends on marginal productivity. Supply reflects its availability. In this, land is not different from any other factor of production. But there are two special characteristics of land which Ricardo pointed out. First, the supply of land is absolutely fixed. Rent is a payment for what Ricardo called the 'original and indestructible properties of the soil' which he thought were a 'free gift of nature'. Second, the fertility of the land is subject to wide variations and hence its rent should be expected to vary accordingly.

For simplicity, suppose there is only one crop, say wheat, for which land of given fertility was suitable. Then the two alternatives facing the landowner are: (1) let it be used for wheat production by a tenant or himself earning at the best rent it can fetch; (2) let it lie fallow and receive no income. Only the first alternative makes sense. There is no point in forfeiting income by holding land out of production, since no costs are avoided by allowing it to lie fallow. Therefore the supply curve of the piece of land in question is a vertical line indicating that all of this stock of land will be used provided any rent at all is paid for it.

Of course each landowner will want the maximum rent he can get, and so users must bid against one another for it. That is to say, the rent of land is determined by demand (Figure 10.5). When the demand curve for land is D, the rent is r, and all of the land of this type will be used. If the demand curve were to shift downward, the rent would fall, but the amount of land in use would not diminish. At D' rent is zero. If demand fell further to D'' land would be in excess supply, and its rent would be zero.

Query: How much free land would be used? Express this analysis in linear programming terms.

Ricardo was able to extend his analysis to cover lands of different fertility. Suppose that the land shown in Figure 10.5 were the best, grade A land. Suppose further that the demand curve for land of that type were D'. Then rent would be zero on this land of highest fertility. Now suppose that the demand for wheat increased as a result, say, of population expansion. Two things would happen. First of all, the demand curve for land of grade A would shift upward to D, reflecting higher wheat prices, and the rent would

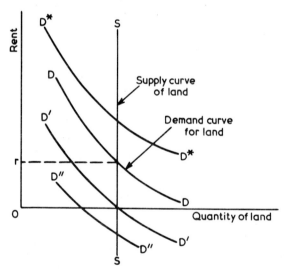

Figure 10.5 Rent of land in wheat production
(grade A land)

increase to r. Secondly, farmers would be on the lookout for more land. Since all of the grade A land is already under cultivation, they will have to use land of poorer quality – say, grade B. Before the rise in demand for wheat, the demand D' for grade B land was so low that to use it, its rent would have to be negative (Figure 10.6). Landlords would have to pay rent to tenants! But now, with the increased demand for wheat, the curve shifts to D. The rent on B rises to zero from a negative value, so landlords would be just willing to have it used and farmers would find it profitable. Figure 10.5 shows that grade A land would earn rent, and Figure 10.6 shows that grade B would earn no rent but it would be cultivated.

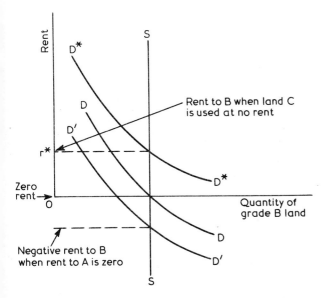

Figure 10.6   Rent of grade B land in wheat production

If the demand for wheat increased the demand for land still further, then grade C land would just be used; the demand for grade B land would shift up further to D^*. Now land of grade C would earn no rent, and grade B would have a greater-than-zero rent. The very best grade A land would have a still higher rent. Land of successively poorer fertility would be drawn into production with increased demand. The poorest land that can be worked without loss is the no rent land. Nothing would be left over above the operating costs to pay anything to the landlords for this worst land, but the better lands would earn higher and higher rents. The different fertility of land gives rise to *differential rent*. Rising demand causes more and more land to be used at the *extensive margin* of farming. The poorest land worth cultivating earns no rent, whilst the more fertile land receives rent due to its differential advantage.

Increased demand for wheat can also be met by using more capital and labour on all types of land. Ricardo called this the *intensive margin* of cultivation. Capital and labour would be used until the law of diminishing returns made the last marginal unit yield just enough to cover marginal costs of production. There will still be a differential rent to owners of more fertile land because they still can earn more revenue from their labour and capital on the better land.

Query: (1) Would there still be zero rent land if the demand for wheat were to increase indefinitely until all the land were occupied?
(2) Is there no-rent land in Britain?
(3) Is there rent to ocean resources? Are ocean natural resources allocated the same way as land resources? Should they be?

Ricardo concluded that rent payments to landlords are not a necessary cost of production to agriculture. The rent is determined by what people will pay for the land, derived from their demand for wheat. Since the supply of land is inelastic, the same amount of land would be forthcoming if the rents were taxed away from landlords. These rents are not a cost of production from a social point of view. Ricardo put the matter in a striking way: the price of wheat determines the rent of land, but the rent of land does not determine the price of wheat.

There is a subtlety here that becomes crucially important in the ecological problems to be discussed in the next chapter where we will be concerned with natural resources use. The fact that rents are not a necessary cost of production does not mean that farmers should not be charged rents in the interest of efficient production. For the rent charge is precisely the market's way of signalling to the farmer whether to till land of given fertility with given intensity of application of labour and capital. If these differential rents were not charged there would be no guidelines to tell the farmers when it is worthwhile to stop trying to use the best grade A land so intensively by employing more and more capital and labour, and to switch over to lower rent, yet more infertile land of grade B. Still, while rent must be paid to serve as a guideline to the efficient use of land resources it could then be taxed away from the landowner without him withdrawing the land from production. The reason for this is the inelasticity of supply of the various lands.

Following Ricardo, some nineteenth century agrarian reformers like Henry George held that landlords should be taxed the full amount of their rental income. Rents, they said, do not constitute a social cost, but supply the income to those who happen to own a scarce and useful means of produc-

tion. There are difficulties with concepts of land rent that make its application to taxation very difficult. Chief among these is that, in practice, it cannot
be ascertained whether anyone owns 'land' or 'capital'. Actually, when one
thinks about it, every piece of property contains an element of natural
resources in its matter; and virtually every natural resource is capital,
touched by the hand of man.

Not only is land virtually impossible to identify, but rent turns out to have
very little to do with land as such. Any factor can earn rent if its supply curve
has some region where the elasticity drops almost to zero. For example,
consider the case of the market for highly skilled and dedicated school
teachers (Figure 10.7). Some people, who love to teach, would be willing to
do so even though the salaries were lower. For these persons the supply
curve is inelastic at Q. At any salary less than P^* some would leave teaching,
and others would spend at least part of their time in other employment. But
at any salary above P^*, say P^{**}, the same teaching effort would be
forthcoming as at P^*. If the demand for these teachers is D', the teachers will
receive P^* as a salary. The income for all the teachers will be P^* times the
number of teachers, Q, equal to the area of the rectangle $OQTP^*$. But if
the demand for these teachers is higher (for instance, if it rises to D)
then the teachers will have P^{**} as their salary. The addition to income
will be the rectangle P^*TFP^{**}, which will be entirely rent. Only P^* is necessary to keep people in the teaching business, but demand enables them to
earn P^{**}.

The concept of *differential rent* can also be applied to this circumstance. It
may be that P^* is the amount necessary to get just any warm body to stand in
front of a class and talk. P^* is the no rent salary of the worst instructor. Gifted

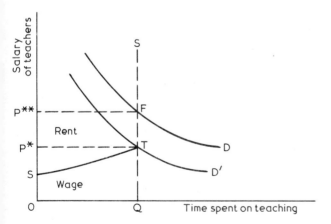

Figure 10.7   Rental income of skilled schoolteachers

teachers come higher; not because they would enter another occupation if they receive only P^*, but because school authorities are anxious to hire such people and so they make competing salary offers to get the superior services.

This example shows that only a portion of the supply curve need be inelastic to produce a rent situation. Under such circumstances only a portion of the price paid for a factor is a rent, the amount paid over and above that necessary to bring the factor into production. On reflection, we see that Ricardo considered a special, extreme case, in which land was either used only as wheat acreage or allowed to be fallow, producing nothing.

If there were an alternative to wheat use of land, say lettuce production, then the cost of putting the land to wheat would be the lettuce crop foregone. The value of the wheat crop over the lettuce is the rent to wheat growers. In other words, rent does not depend on the 'original and indestructible' property of the ground, but on the existence of a difference between one use of a factor and its next best use. This different next best use is the *opportunity cost* of the factor that causes the supply curve to be less than infinitely elastic.

Query: Sketch the supply curve for Ricardo's wheat land if there were some constant cost involved in using it such as fixed use tax which could be avoided if the land were to lie fallow.

How small can this difference between alternatives be and still bear the name rent? Could there be a continuous gradation of alternatives each infinitesimally different from the next one? Why not? If so, then any factor with an upward sloping supply curve will contain an element of rent in its price. This can be seen in Figure 10.8, which illustrates the rent element even in the usual supply curve for, say, labour.

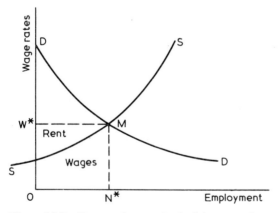

Figure 10.8   Rent and wages in the labour market

In equilibrium, the wage rate, W^*, is required to induce workers to labour for N^* man-hours. The wage rate is determined at the margin by the requirement to get the last of the N^* man-hours. It would cost less than N^* per man-hour if fewer units of labour were hired, yet the wage rate that must be paid to all the labour in a competitive market is N^*. That means that less would have to be paid as pure wages for all the man-hours except the last one. The balance of the income that workers get above this wage is the rent. Only the last unit of labour earns no rent, and the total labour income ON^*MW^* can be divided into wages and rent components as shown in the diagram.

The conclusion to which we have been driven is that almost every factor of production earns some sort of rent; its upward sloping supply curve requires that the factor price determined at the margin of supply and demand exceed the price at which previous, *intramarginal*, units of the factor would be forthcoming. The examples of pure rent income reflect situations of fixity in supply – absolute inelasticity.

Exercise:
(1) Should schools pay teachers according to a 'salary schedule' based on experience and education? Should teachers' salaries be increased by 'merit raises'? Who should get a 'merit raise'? Discuss in terms of equity and efficiency. Explain why the rent of the teacher's salary can appear as wages in national income accounts.

(2) Describe a situation in which land would earn rent from the national point of view, but not from the viewpoint of the individual farmer. Should a socialist country permit the payment of rent? Should it be taxed? How?

(3) Explain what would be the rent of land if holding it idle or in low productivity use as an estate did give satisfaction in the form of prestige?

Profits: innovation, uncertainty, entrepreneurship or exploitation?

There is no real agreement among economists on the nature of profits. It will be seen, however, that the divergent views are not completely incompatible; the differences are largely of emphasis. Many contend that profit is really a form of differential rent to superior forms of fixed factors of production such as new and better machinery, superior location of factory site, skilled and loyal labour and managerial work force and the like. Of course, these advantages are not permanent like the 'original and indestructible powers of the soil'. In the long run competitors can gain similar advantages, so the profit is always at hazard, existing in the short run but fading away as long run profits entice other firms to acquire similar factors of production. Profits to fixed inputs are what we called *quasi-rent* in earlier chapters. Once the fixed factors are in place the output of the firm depends on marginal increases in variable costs. If there is a net return over and above the total variable costs, then this appears to be a short-run quasi-rent to the fixed factors. If quasi-rents exceed fixed costs, the firms earn profits.

If in the long run all the factors of production are variable, quasi-rents tend to disappear as competing firms adopt the superior methods and equipment. One explanation for the persistence of profit consists in the continual dynamic *innovation* of superior methods of production and distribution by *entrepreneurs*. Saying this another way, the entrepreneur constantly upsets the long-run equilibrium, thus earning a quasi-rent for his enterprise. The better the entrepreneur, the greater will be the quasi-rent he can muster. If innovation stopped, profits would disappear too. Society would enter a *static state*.

This is the view of the late Joseph Schumpeter in his famous books, *Capitalism, Socialism, Democracy* and *Business Cycles*. He stressed the difference between the dynamic *innovation* by businessmen as compared to the *invention* of new machinery or processes by engineers or scientists. It is the introduction of new methods into production and distribution that he calls innovation and that generates the profit. The technical *invention* may be known a long time before it is used by the innovator. The invention may be earth-shattering or almost trivial, but someone must show the way to its use. Then others follow suit.

Related theories of profit pay special attention to entrepreneurial talent. Since the ability to take responsibility for a firm and make imaginative and sound decisions is very unevenly distributed among individuals, entrepreneurs particularly earn a differential rent according to their personal abilities. For example, once when preparing to travel abroad, the author was faced with the necessity of shipping clothes and books ahead by sea. It was a small load, not enough to 'build a crate around'. The alternative was air freight, which was very expensive. One enterprising man made a small fortune for himself by assembling small plywood boxes in his garage to meet the need. For a fee, he provided the box for ocean travel and shipped it. His innovation? A wood box!

Exercise:
(1) Can the creation of a monopoly be an innovation?
(2) Who does the innovating in a communist or socialist society? Does the innovator earn a profit? A rent?
(3) If competition were made more perfect so that there were no lapse of time before innovations were adopted and competitors were able to use them, what would happen to the profits? To innovation?

(4) How is Schumpeter's analysis affected by the ability of firms to 'order up' a new good by having research and development scientists to develop products to meet specifications?

Frank Knight of the University of Chicago argues that profits are a normal return to a factor of production provided by entrepreneurs. It is entrepreneurship, Knight says, that permits producers to carry on in a very uncertain and risky world. Some business risks not associated with profits are routinely shifted over to insurance companies: fire, theft, death, marine loss, are known to occur with such regularity that they are statistically predictable for a large number of cases. Insurance firms share the losses among all the policy holders. In effect every person who owns a fire insurance policy pays a small part of the cost of replacing those homes or businesses that will almost certainly burn down in the near future. Other business risks are unpredictable. Knight reserves the word *uncertainty* for them. Uncertainty is inherent in organizing and operating an enterprise. The innovation and organization of the businessman must confront the hazard. This ability and willingness to cope with uncertainty is a scarce factor of production with profit as its shadow price. Profit is not particularly a rent to Knight, but one of the expenses of living in an uncertain world.

Query: (1) If innovation ceased, do you think uncertainty would continue to exist? What would happen to profit?
  (2) Does a person who likes to gamble and enjoys uncertainty also earn a profit?

Radicals often explain profit quite differently. Karl Marx saw it as a form of *exploitation* of workers by capitalists. Marx's explanation is neither a rent theory nor one based on the supply of entrepreneurial services. In *Das Kapital*, he argued that labour is the only primary input. The value of a commodity is the amount of labour directly and indirectly embodied in the production of goods. But the value of the labourer – his wages – is equal to the labour required to produce the subsistence of the workers. Since labour produces more than its own subsistence, it produces a greater value than it receives. This difference is called *surplus value*, which includes not only profits, but interest and land rent. Marx thought that he had shown that in a perfectly competitive capitalist society labour produces surplus value for capitalists who perform no social function.

Exercise:
(1) Evaluate Marx's labour theory of value in the following steps:
  (*a*) Show how it is similar to our input-output analysis of prices with one primary input.

  (b) Devise an alternative input-output model which would treat labour as one of the produced commodities, treating capital or land as the primary input. Is it possible to construct a 'capital' or 'land' theory of value, showing that these factors are exploited by labour, or is labour a cost to society in some more fundamental sense?

(2) Do you think the effect of a tax on profits would be the same as a tax on rent?

The interest rate and the market for capital

Interest is the payment society makes for the use of capital – goods or equipment produced now for use in the future. To study the capital market we must modify the familiar production possibility frontier. Instead of representing two distinct goods such as motor cars or apples, the axes represent the same good at different times. The value of goods available for consumption this year will be called C_1; if it is available next year instead, we shall call it C_2. To keep matters simple we must hold down the number of goods we must manipulate, so let us imagine that the same good can either be used as a consumer good or as capital. As an example, the famous Austrian economist Eugene Bohm-Bawerk suggested wine stored in a cellar. New wine can be consumed this year as a consumer good, or it can be stored until next. If it is consumed now it is simply C_1. If it is stored, the wine is classified as capital, since it represents a stock of goods to be used in the future. The stored wine plus any new wine produced would constitute C_2.

  Storing wine is more than a matter of good taste. Aging wine brings more enjoyment to the palate, and hence a higher price to the wine merchant. Wine as capital is producing more value by being allowed to 'work' during the time that it is stored. Unless the value of C_2 is greater than C_1, it makes no sense to go to the bother and expense of maintaining a capital stock.

  Think now of national income as if it were a single product like wine. By not consuming all the national income, a nation saves some of it in the form of investment in capital equipment – machinery, buildings and so on. Investment in capital equipment also would make no sense unless it were possible to produce a greater amount of product with the equipment than without it. Otherwise it would pay simply to produce mostly consumer goods each year rather than make them in a roundabout way by first producing extra capital equipment and then using the equipment to make consumer goods. Unless it generates a greater consumption possibility in the future, a roundabout producton method will not be employed. To be sure, round-aboutness does not of itself result in greater output. Not every possible new machine is worth using, but some of them are. That is to say, new possibilities are opened up by roundabout methods.

This permits us to describe the frontier relating C_1 to C_2 (Figure 10.9). First, it will always have a slope of greater than unity because the increase in C_2 has to exceed the decrease in C_1. Second, the frontier must be convex due to the law of diminishing returns applied to additional capital. A socialist planning board considering its plan for national income projected over time would face such a frontier just as much as a capitalist businessman considering new equipment, or an individual deciding whether to guzzle his wine or store it. The reasons for the frontier are efficiency and the law of diminishing returns, and these have nothing to do with social system.

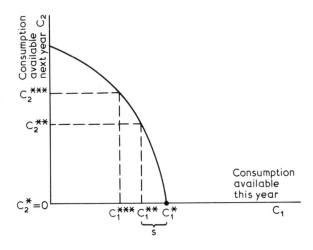

Figure 10.9

It is worthwhile to describe this frontier in some detail. Suppose K_1 was the stock of capital available in year 1. What is the *maximum consumption possible* in year 1? The final use y_1 produced? That is not all. The capital itself could be consumed; in the case of wine it could be drunk. Let the consumption possibility in the year 1 be called $C_1^* = y_1 + K_1$ (Figure 10.9). Decision makers might behave like La Fontaine's cricket who sang all summer and ate up the available food leaving nothing for winter. If cricket minded planners had their way all the available capital would be consumed in the first year as well as the new product. But without capital nothing can be produced or consumed in the second year. Therefore the frontier shows that if consumption in year 1 is C_1^*, then $C_2^* = 0$! This is the point where the production possibility frontier crosses the horizontal axis.

Suppose, like the ant in the fable, society saves. Instead of consuming C_1^*, society consumes only C_1^{**}, saving an amount shown by $C_1^* C_1^{**} = S_1$ on the horizontal axis. Reading from C_1^{**} up to the frontier tells us that C_2^{**} is available for consumption in the second year. In year 2 the decision to consume and save must be made over again.

By saving part of its available goods and investing them, society really acts as if it were lending to itself and paying back with interest. In effect, it is able to obtain an increased return in the year following by using the roundabout method of production. The rate of return on an additional unit of saving and investment is the *marginal efficiency of investment*, m, which is the net increase in year 2, divided by the new savings and investment that is made in year 1. To see this, suppose the saving is the distance $C_1^*C_1^{**} = S_1$. This increase in savings from zero means that there will be less consumption in year 1, and as a result consumption possibilities in year 2 will rise from zero to C_2^{**}. C_2^{**} is equal to the savings carried over from year 1 plus the increased output due to the investment of those savings. The net increase in output in year 2 is the marginal efficiency of investment times the savings, mS_1. C_2^{**} is therefore the sum of these two elements: $C_2^{**} = S_1 + mS_1$. Therefore, $(1 + m)S_1 - C_2^{**}$, and so $(1 + m) = C_2^{**}/S_1$. As the change in C_2 compared to that of C_1, $(1 + m)$ is the slope of the frontier.

From the common sense of borrowing and lending, the rate of return on investment has got to match the interest rate at which people are willing to lend. If the interest rate were higher than m, less investment would occur because it would be too expensive to borrow. Conversely, if the interest rate were lower than m, more investment would take place. It follows therefore, that the slope of the frontier really represents the rate of interest as well as the marginal efficiency of investment. But the slope of the frontier changes according to the law of diminishing returns. Thus, if we were to consider a further act of savings after S_1, we would be reducing consumption this year to C_1^{***} and raising consumption possibilities next year to C_2^{***}. The rate of interest would be less because the frontier has decreased in slope with more capital. The law of diminishing returns serves to diminish the marginal efficiency of investment.

Clearly, the decision to save or consume depends on the rate of interest that people are willing to accept for their savings (supply of savings), as well as the amount of interest that roundabout production method permits firms to pay (demand for savings). If people place a greater emphasis on their present consumption and less on their future satisfactions, they would require a greater rate of interest to convince them to consume less now and save for the future. On the other hand, if they are more future-oriented, it will take a lower rate of interest to induce them to give up present consumption.

The obvious question is why interest must be paid for savings at all. Why don't people simply save their income today simply in order to have income tomorrow? They act as if they were impatient. In fact they are, and for a very good reason: if people have their goods now, they can consume them right away if they so please; or they can store the goods for the future. Neglecting storage expenses, nothing is lost by having the goods now. Even for extremely future-oriented people the lowest rate of interest is zero. It is never negative because nobody will pay for the privilege of getting goods later. On the other hand, there are some impatient people. Many do prefer their goods now, so the only way the interest rate can go from zero is up. For many people, and for different circumstances, future needs are less pressing than present ones. Most of us are not as concerned to provide for consumption in the year 2000 as to see dinner on the table tonight. True, there are misers much concerned about the year 2000; but if they are rational misers, they will never be so concerned as to pay the bank to hold their money for them.

Query: Does money ever have a storage cost? If so, how is it paid?

We can express impatience in technical terms by the time preference indifference map of individuals for C_1 and C_2 (Figure 10.10). Each of the indifference curves has a slope steeper than 45°, because more than the same consumption in year 2 is required to compensate for less consumption in year 1. The slope of each curve is 1 plus the rate of interest that must be paid to induce the consumer to give up a unit of present consumption for the future.

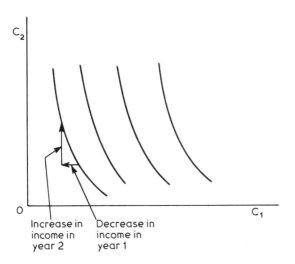

Figure 10.10   The impatient consumer – time preference

Now superimpose the time preference map for two years on the two-year consumption possibilities frontier (Figure 10.11). Individuals are best off by getting to the highest possible indifference curve allowed by the limitation of the consumption possibility frontier. This is done where the frontier is just touching – tangent to – some indifference curve. At this point the rate of interest which expresses the greater consumption the consumer would require tomorrow to induce him to give up an additional unit of satisfaction today just matches the possibility of compensating him by the productivity of roundabout methods accomplished by those savings. Since the indifference curves as well as the consumption possibility frontier all have slopes steeper than 1, the equilibrium of saving and investment occurs at some positive rate of interest equal to the marginal efficiency of investment.

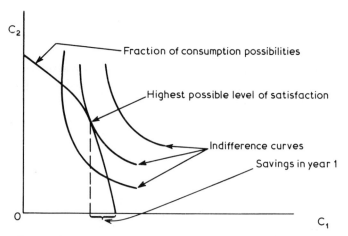

Figure 10.11   Equilibrium of investment and interest

This relationship could be expressed for the market composed of many individuals in terms of the supply and demand. Investment is the demand for savings and depends on the marginal efficiency of investment. At high rates of interest, the marginal efficiency of investment must be high to cover the interest cost. Therefore where the amount of investment is small, individuals are operating on the steepest portion of the consumption possibility frontier. If impatient people dominate the supply of savings it will not pay firms to pay the high interest rates savers require to postpone their satisfaction. Firms will mostly produce consumer goods and little capital equipment. If interest rates are low, the converse is true. By graphing the interest rate against the

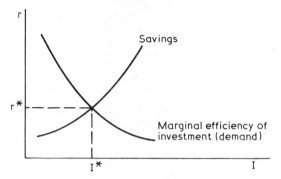

Figure 10.12   Interest and the supply and demand
for investment

amount of investment we have the marginal efficiency of investment demand
curve (Figure 10.12).

The supply of savings involves the release of a portion of income by
impatient people. In a market economy, people are induced to save part of
their income by the offer of interest rates. A supply curve for saving is a
decision by individuals which can be derived from their indifference map.
The capital market tends to clear at the equilibrium rate of interest.

Query: Can a communist economy have a free capital market? Should it?
Describe the capital market for public as well as private expenditures in Britain. Describe the human capital market.

Suppose new investment were to cease – that is to say, suppose the capital
stock were as large as it need be, given the supply of other factors of
production. Would the interest rate go to zero? That would ignore the time
preference of owners of capital; interest must be paid as the (dual) shadow
price to the owners of capital not to convert their assets into consumer
goods. One might smile at this. Only an academic scribbler could seriously
imagine that people can consume engine lathes or harbour cranes; surely the
only possibility of switching assets from capital to consumption is in peculiar
cases like the wine in the cellar. Actually, given the time, it is quite easy to
make the conversion. Simply refuse to replace depreciating machinery as it
wears out, and buy consumer goods instead. Gross investment would then
be zero, but net investment would be negative. The difference would go to
consumption which would eat – or drink – up all the capital.

Obviously someone is going to object to this arrangement. Why should
the capitalists be bribed not to consume? The answer is, of course, that the
capital is their property. If that is granted then there is not much difference
between paying someone not to withhold his capital, sacrificing present

consumption as his labour and giving up leisure. Efficient allocation of resources, we have seen, imputes a shadow factor price to productive property. A person who objects to the distribution of interest income may want to say that he does not think it fair that capital should be privately owned. In saying so he must counter the argument of others that capital is accumulated in private hands through voluntary acts of savings by individuals themselves or by their ancestors, however far removed. The fact remains that, whoever owns the capital, its efficient use entails a shadow price which is interest income. Once having paid the price, perhaps income taxers will try to snatch ill-gotten gains away, but that is an equity question!

Exercise:
(1) Compare rent and interest income with respect to efficiency and equity.
(2) Suppose a socialist society were organized in a decentralized way which gave factory managers wide discretion over the purchase of the inputs into production. What would happen if no interest charges were made for capital? Compare with the case where no rent were charged.
(3) What problems would develop for the accumulation of capital by private individuals if interest were abolished or taxed very heavily? Would the problems be solved by income taxation?
(4) Discuss the wisdom of a government subsidy to farmers to compensate them for interest charges they must pay. Compare this policy with compensating rent payments to farmers who are located on less fertile land than others.
(5) Suppose that Robinson Crusoe finds himself stranded on a desert island with no implements (capital) but with some food that could be gathered for consumption. Explain how he might divide his time between food gathering and constructing implements. Show how the construction of implements can be thought of as a 'roundabout' way of producing food. Explain how much time will be devoted by Crusoe to food gathering and how much to capital accumulation. Does your story have anything to do with money? Would money be involved if a group of people were stranded?

Up until now we have been discussing capital and interest in 'real' terms. We showed why people are unwilling to postpone their consumption unless compensated by getting more goods for future consumption. Money appears to have nothing to do with interest. This could be the case even though goods were measured in money and saving was directed by means of the banking system. Money would serve only as a counting device, as a medium of exchange. Keynes and his followers pointed out that when we consider the element of uncertainty money plays a more important role. We shall discuss this issue in Chapter 12 when we consider the nature of money.

A final amendment. So far we have been merrily talking about *the* rate of interest, when in fact there is a whole range of interest rates. A loan which is more likely not to be repaid at its full value usually carries a higher rate of interest than one that is more secure. In effect, the lender must insure himself against the higher probability of loss by demanding an interest income that will compensate him for the loans that turn out to be bad debts. When we talk of a rise in the rate of interest we mean an increase in the whole pattern of interest rates, the effect of which may vary depending on whether long or short, risky or safer loans are involved.

Wages and labour's share

No distributional issue excites more passion than that of the compensation of labour. Yet, on the face of the matter, the application of our theory is straightforward. The demand for labour depends on its marginal productivity, the value of its marginal product. The supply represents the decision by individuals to divide their time between work and leisure in light of the wages offered them. Under competition wages are determined by the impersonal forces of the market.

Striking statistical support for the theory came from the work of Paul H. Douglas, formerly of the University of Chicago. Douglas asked: is there a law of production which could be written in the form of a *production function* equation relating the inputs of factors of production to the output of national income? From this marginal productivities could be calculated, and the theory tested.

We have seen production functions before. Actually input-output analysis is a very simple sort of production function. It told how much of various final uses could be produced with a given amount of primary input, labour. This simple form would not suit Douglas's purposes since he wanted to investigate conditions where labour and capital could be substituted for each other. He needed an equation relating one output to several inputs. After some experimentation he and a statistician colleague produced what is called the Cobb–Douglas function that seems to fit the facts very well. The output is symbolized by Q, and inputs are labour, L, and capital, K. The function is $Q = AL^{\alpha}K^{1-\alpha}$. Alpha is a constant fraction between zero and unity.

The most important fact to account for in choosing a production function is that wage incomes tend to constitute an amazingly constant portion of national income. Although national income fluctuates, the labour share varies very little. In the USA labour receives about $\frac{2}{3}$ of national income. Before the wars, labour's share in the UK was smaller, but constant nonetheless. Since that time is has approximated the USA distribution. The C–D function explained these results, for it can be shown that if labour is paid its marginal product, the labour share is the constant α, and the remainder, goes to capital, $1-\alpha$ being its marginal product.

The important idea behind using the production function this way is that it is possible to calculate the marginal productivity of labour as the increase in output corresponding to an increase in labour input, holding capital constant. The marginal product of labour will vary with the amount of labour used. Employers will hire workers up to the point where the value of the marginal product equals the wage rates at which labour will be supplied. Multiplying this marginal product by the amount of labour used, L, we get the total labour income. Now if we divide labour's income by the total output, the remarkable fact turns up that the ratio is a constant equal to α regardless of how much labour is employed. (Alas the proof involves some elementary calculus, which is shown in a footnote; non-calculus readers must avert their eyes and take the result on faith.)[2]

Douglas argued that if wage rates rise relative to capital, capital will be substituted for labour. Fewer workers will be employed at higher wages, but labour's share in the national product will be unchanged. Likewise if the income to capital rises, labour will replace capital so as to keep the shares of the parties the same. Within a framework of a perfectly competitive economy, labour's share was determined by the technology of production which permitted the substitution of capital for labour.

One immediate consequence of Douglas's theory is that unions could not increase labour's share in national income simply by holding out for higher wage rates. If wages rose by a given percentage, employment would fall by the same percentage. Those workers who got the higher wage did so at the expense of either their own hours of work or – more likely – the employment and wage rates of other labourers. Wages, labour's real income could rise but only through an increase in productivity. In the Cobb–Douglas function,

---

[2] $Q = AL^{\alpha}K^{1-\alpha}$. Holding K constant, $\delta Q/dL = \alpha AL^{\alpha-1}K^{1-\alpha}$. Since the wage rate equals the marginal productivity of labour, $\delta Q/dL$, labour's total income is $L\,\delta Q/\delta L = \alpha ALK^{1-\alpha}$. Labour's relative share is:

$$\frac{L\,\delta Q/\delta L}{Q} = \frac{\alpha AL^{\alpha}K^{1-\alpha}}{AL^{\alpha}K^{1-\alpha}} = \alpha.$$

Actually there is another way to show this. Take the logarithm of the C–D function to get linear relation between the logs: $\log Q = \log A + \alpha \log L + (1-\alpha)\log K$. Then the slope of this relationship is: $\alpha = \dfrac{\Delta \log Q}{\Delta \log L}$. Since the *change* in a logarithm equals a percentage change in the original variable, we get $(\Delta Q/Q)(\Delta L/L) = \alpha$. But then $[(\Delta Q/\Delta L)L]/Q = \alpha$. Since $\Delta Q/\Delta L$ is the marginal product of labour, which is equal to the real wage rate, w, we have: $wL/Q = \alpha$. The real wage rate times employment is labour's real income. Divide this by Q to get labour's share in national output, which is seen to be α. Perhaps this helps the non-calculus reader.

productivity increase would mean that the constant, A, increased so that the same labour and capital produced more product. But unless the technical progress were biased in favour of capital or labour, i.e. unless the α value changes, the relative shares of national income going to each factor remained unchanged.

Query: Is the constancy of labour's share the same thing as the 'wages fund'? Compare with the 'iron law of wages'.

There have been two lines of criticism of the Cobb–Douglas explanation of the division of the national product between labour and capital. One heard frequently at Cambridge is over the existence and nature of an aggregate production for the country as a whole. Adding up all the various types of product into total output by the device of summing up their money values leaves some economists suspicious that something more than physical production possibilities are involved. Aggregating capital into a single entity carries with it the possibility of circular reasoning; expressing it in money aggregates involves measuring the machinery in terms of its capitalized earning power (see Chapter 1) as much as its physical amount.

A second criticism of this explanation of the constancy of labour's share arises from its dependence on perfect competition in product and factor markets. Recall that *VMP*, the value of the marginal product, is defined as the price of the product times the schedule of marginal product ($P \times MP$). Competitive firms take the product price as a fact they alone cannot alter. But prices, we are forced to realize, are often within the control of the monopolistic firm, and the monopolist may well restrict output below the competitive level (see Chapter 9). Employment will be reduced, as will wage rates. Furthermore, in competitive factor markets, each firm is supposed to take the wage rate as simply given on the labour market. This requires that the employing firm be a small buyer of labour in a market made up of many individual workers. If this condition fails, firms will calculate how much their demand for labour raises the wage rate, and will restrict employment accordingly. Moreover, under competition, workers are supposed to act as individuals who also take the market wage rate as given. Yet in fact labour and management bargain collectively on wages. Large firms, whole industries, and even the government bargain with large unions. Both parties calculate how their demands and supplies for labour will influence the wage rate and employment.

If perfect competition does not hold for individual firms and industries, how can it hold for the country as a whole? Douglas's critics argue that the C–D function is a myth, rationalizing distribution of income bargained by opposing power blocs. His supporters frequently argue that the economy is actually more competitive than the market structure makes it appear;

especially for long-term issues like the distribution of income perfect competition is a tolerably good model of reality. Employees and unions may go through the charade of negotiation, but perhaps they ultimately have to settle for what the workers would have got in any case.

The strongest union rationale for collective bargaining is in industries with concentrated market structures. Very large corporations, they argue, are able to exert downward pressures on wages to individual workers unless they are organized into equally powerful unions. The condition described is called *monopsony* – a market with a single buyer. In this case the employing firm is the single buyer of labour. Monopsony is the mirror image of the monopoly seller. The monopsonist employer knows that if he increases his demand for workers, the wage rate will rise. That is to say, he takes the rising supply curve of labour into account, just as the monopolist takes the falling demand curve into his reckoning. Consequently, he adjusts his demand for labour so that the value of the marginal product is not equal to the wage rate, but to the marginal increase in labour cost. This increase in labour cost depends on the increase in wage rate that results from greater employment. In Figure 10.13 the increase in labour cost is shown by the curve, *M*, marginal to the supply curve of labour, *S*. In general reference to all factors *M* is called the curve of *marginal factor cost*.

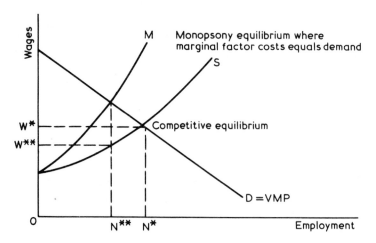

Figure 10.13 Monopsonistic market for labour

Instead of an industry hiring workers up to the point where the supply (*S*) and demand (*D*) for labour cross as in a competitive market, the monopsonistic firm hires where the marginal factor cost curve (*M*) crosses the demand curve. Wages are then at W^{**} instead of at the competitive wage rate W^*. Employment is reduced from N^* to N^{**}. The establishment of a uniform union wage by collective bargaining certainly eliminates monopsony. Nevertheless, it leaves open the question as to what that bargained wage will be.

Exercise:
(1) Describe the working of monopsony in a pre-war mining village in County Durham. Does the same apply now that coal is nationalized? Is there monopsony in Manchester?
(2) Compare monopsony with monopoly. Compare socialism with monopsony and monopoly. Can underdeveloped countries be exploited by the monopsony of the developed?

The big question today is: what determines wages and employment when large firms and large unions confront one another? Although the term monopoly has a stigma which unions are anxious to avoid, in the technical sense of the word large union–employer relations are similar to the oligopoly conflict that we studied earlier. Once again it is very hard to say how different the net result is from what it would have been under perfect competition.

One very ingenious way of avoiding the whole perplexed issue has been suggested by an English economist, Nicholas Kaldor, by an appeal to macroeconomic, Keynesian, thinking (see Chapter 1). He points out that labour's income is very nearly the same thing as consumption by the nation as a whole. But consumption is given by income. In turn income is determined by investment that firms are willing to do. But investment is that portion of national income which is saved and not consumed. Income not consumed by workers must be the profits of capitalists. Amazingly, capitalist 'animal spirits' prompting investment in expectation of profits are suggested as the cause of the profits themselves! By deciding to invest capitalists create profits equal to the investment. Labour gets the balance as consumption. While Kaldor's explanation has some fervent adherents, it is also criticized by those who demand a further explanation of what determines investment apart from animal spirits.

Tutorial exercise

How can change in the degree of inequality in income distribution be measured? One device is to construct a *cumulative frequency curve*, sometimes called a Lorenz curve. For example, suppose we had the following distribution of incomes for the years 1803 and 1804 in East Hypothetica:

Distribution of incomes in East Hypothetica, 1803–4

Income class (£)	Number of income receivers		Amount of incomes in each class (£)	
	1803	1804	1803	1804
0–99	5	10	100	500
100–199	10	35	500	4,000
200–299	20	40	500	1,000
300–399	15	5	400	500
400–499	0	10	500	4,000
Total	50	100	2,000	10,000

Step 1: Cast the data in terms of per cent of total so as to be able to compare them.

Distribution of incomes in East Hypothetica, 1803–4, in per cent of totals

Income class (£)	Per cent of number of income receivers in each class		Per cent of the amount of income in each class	
	1803	1804	1803	1804
0–99	10	10	5	5
100–199	20	35	25	40
200–299	40	40	25	10
300–399	30	5	20	5
400–499	0	10	25	40
Total	100	100	100	100

Step 2: Cumulate the percentages in each column. That is, say for 1803 what per cent of income receivers get less than £100? Obviously 10 per cent. What per cent get less than £200? 10 per cent plus 20 per cent for the next class is 30 per cent. This procedure is carried on for the rest of the table as follows:

Cumulative distribution of incomes in East Hypothetica, 1803–4, in per
cent

	Per cent of number of income receivers		Per cent of amounts of income	
Income class	*1803*	*1804*	*1803*	*1804*
Less than £100	10	10	5	5
Less than £200	30	45	30	45
Less than £300	70	85	55	55
Less than £400	100	90	75	60
Less than £500	100	100	100	100

Step 3: (*a*) Plot these results for each year. On the horizontal axis show
the cumulative per cent of number of income recipients and on the vertical
axis show the cumulative per cent of amounts of income. Both axes will run
from zero to 100 per cent.

(*b*) Draw a diagonal line from the origin to the extreme northeast corner
of your axes where both scales show 100 per cent. This is the line of equality,
because it corresponds to the locus of points where the cumulated per cent of
number of income recipients is equal to the cumulated per cent of the
amounts of income. If income were equally distributed, 10 per cent of the

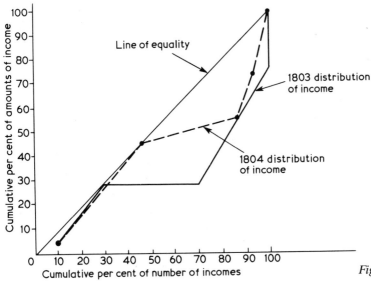

Figure 10.14

number of income recipients would receive 10 per cent of the income, 20 per cent of the number of income recipients would receive 20 per cent of the income, and so on (refer to Figure 10.14).

Because we have examined so few income classes, these Lorenz curves are lumpy, when usually they turn out to be smooth bow-shaped affairs. Nevertheless, the principle is clear. In the metropolis of East Hypothetica income distribution in 1803 was more equal than it was a year later. This is shown by the fact that the Lorenz curve lies closer to the line of equality in 1803 than in 1804 (even though the curves do cross for a small interval). If one wanted to be precise, one could measure the degree of inequality by the area between the Lorenz curves and the line of equality.

Distribution of personal incomes before and after tax in the UK
Years ended 5 April

	1954–5 quinquennial survey					
	Number of incomes	*Income before tax*			*Tax*	*Income after tax*
		Earned	*Invest-ment*	*Total*		
	Thousands	*£million*				
Income £						
180–199	395·0	71	4	75	—	75
200–249	1,048·0	223	13	236	2	234
250–274	1,181·0	307	17	324	6	318
275–299	—	—	—	—	—	—
300–399	2,332·0	776	37	813	32	781
400–499	2,347·0	1,017	41	1,058	53	1,005
500–599	2,657·0	1,423	39	1,462	79	1,383
600–699	2,602·0	1,650	38	1,688	94	1,594
700–799	2,217·0	1,622	36	1,658	103	1,555
800–999	2,931·0	2,541	65	2,606	194	2,412
1000–1499	2,272·0	2,529	134	2,663	300	2,363
1500–1999	448·0	662	102	764	137	627
2000–2999	287·0	543	145	688	162	526
3000–4999	156·6	413	175	588	190	398
5000–9999	64·7	253	177	430	195	235
10,000–19,999	13·7	87	94	181	111	70
20,000 and over	3·0	33	66	99	77	22
Totals	20,955	14,150	1,183	15,333	1,735	13,598

	Number of incomes	Income before tax	Tax	Income after tax
	Thousands		*£ million*	
Income £				
180–199	—	—	—	—
200–249	—	—	—	—
250–274	—	—	—	—
275–299	271	77·7	0·1	77·6
300–399	1,196	418·0	8·4	409·6
400–499	1,407	632·1	29·8	602·3
500–599	1,527	837·1	59·6	777·5
600–699	1,429	927·2	75·4	851·8
700–799	1,477	1,106·9	105·2	1,001·7
800–999	2,865	2,573·3	288·2	2,285·1
1000–1499	6,485	8,005·6	1004·8	7,000·8
1500–1999	3,573	6,108·8	917·2	5,191·6
2000–2999	1,304	3,054·7	605·1	2,449·6
3000–4999	437	1,626·6	435·1	1,191·5
5000–9,999	173	1,144·2	415·3	728·9
10,000–19,999	37	488·2	261·1	227·1
20,000 and over	7	220.6	164·9	55·7
Totals	22,188	27,221·0	4370·2	22,850·8

1968–9 annual survey

Source: Annual Abstract of Statistics 1971, pp. 320–1.

Now for the exercise. In the table above are the distributions of earned and investment income before and after taxes for the UK for 1954–5 and 1968–9. Go through the same three steps and draw Lorenz curves for these years before and after tax.

(1) When was income before taxes more or less equally distributed?
(2) Was income more equally distributed before or after taxes in each period? In which period did taxes most affect the distribution of income?
(3) Is distribution of investment income more or less equal than earned income? Why?
(4) Did the shape of the income distribution change in the two periods as well as its degree of inequality? Did taxes contribute to any change?

(5) Do you think incomes ought to be equally distributed? If not, please describe what you think ought to be the optimum degree of inequality. If you cannot come up with a number, then indicate the principles involved in arriving at an optimum income distribution.

(6) Write an essay in which you explain why the efficient use of resources requires that users pay the full shadow price. If you believe that this shadow price will not result in an equitable distribution of income, devise a system of taxation to take away the income received as the shadow price of factors of production without at the same time reducing efficiency by causing them to provide less of their primary inputs or inducing firms to use the primary inputs in less efficient combinations. Even if this cannot be done perfectly, then offer guidelines to indicate the degree and method by which inequality in income distribution can be reduced. After you have concluded your recipe for taxation and subsidy, consult the *Annual Abstract of Statistics* and compare with taxes and subsidies in the UK.

(7) Construct the Lorenz curves for the distribution of income in other countries. Most of them publish an annual statistical abstract with data suitable for your use.

(8) Compare the changes in inequality between dates in the UK, and between countries with the share of wages in national income. Do these move in the same direction?

11 Is competition really efficient? The environment, pollution, and public goods

The problem stated

Today people are asking whether perfect competition is really efficient. Natural resources are being squandered and despoiled in a way that seems blatantly inefficient, precisely because firms are under competitive pressures to produce at their own minimum cost without regard to the costs to society. Critics of competition point to environmental social costs which are not taken into reckoning by private firms (indeed, looking back to the industrial revolution, one wonders if it ever really was efficient in the social sense to doom generations to unwholesome labour in mines and mills at minimum wages because competition demanded it).

Where is the efficiency, many people wonder, in a situation in which consumers enjoy themselves individually by acquiring more goods and devastate consumers collectively through noise, fumes and carnage on the motorways? How can it be efficient to have so much of the nation's resources devoted to the production of goods for private use ranging from the utilitarian to the inane, while important public services such as health and education are forced to limp along on a restrictive budget?

To provide some answers to these questions, let us first take the time to restate and unify some of the ideas of the efficient working of the market mechanism. Then we will be in a position to see how far this efficiency can go and understand why it breaks down so dramatically.

The efficient economy once more

At the risk of straining the reader's impatience to grapple with immediate world problems of pollution and social conflict, we pursue our theory a bit further. Look at a simple situation in which there is a single will deciding what to produce and what to consume. Let us also take it that the production or consumption of goods does not materially damage (or encourage) the output of others except as they make scarce resources unavailable for alternative uses. There are no pollution problems to speak of, no externalities, no groups with conflicting notions of equity. In a word, we are residents on Robinson Crusoe's desert island. It is not nostalgia or desire to seek a paradise in the sun that brings us here. Rather, we are putting the vexing problems aside so that we can bring them back in the proper place. If the reader yearns for realism – not an unreasonable desire – he might think of the choices of planners in communist countries expressing one will.

First we shall restate how Robinson Crusoe alone, without the possibility of exchange, could maximize his satisfactions by trying to get as much happiness as his production possibilities will allow. Then we shall suppose that Crusoe has developed schizophrenia: he is to regard himself as a profit maximizing competitive capitalist producer on one hand, and as a utility maximizing household on the other. We shall show that trading his labour for products between his two selves leads Crusoe to select the same set of activities and products as if he maximized his utility directly. After this escapist detour through a desert island we will return to the familiar reality of motorways, smog and urban problems.

Consider the production possibility frontier limiting the final uses of Crusoe the producer (Figure 11.1). On the same axes, draw the indifference curves of Crusoe the consumer showing higher levels of satisfaction as he contemplates moving to higher levels of satisfaction. Clearly, Crusoe will choose the highest possible level of satisfaction, C, where he is able to reach happiness level III. This is better than a point within the feasible set such as M, and even better than other points on the boundary such as A, B or D. Of course, E is impossible, since it lies beyond the production possibility frontier.

How might Crusoe find a point like C? Lacking an indifference map or schedule of production possibilities he would have to feel his way by trial and error. He would certainly soon choose a point like A on the boundary of the frontier, because he can have more of both goods on the frontier than at points inside.

A lies on the frontier and also on indifference curve I. The indifference curve slope at A tells us how much of y_2 he would be willing to give up to get more y_1 and still feel as well off. That is to say, he would be just as happy at

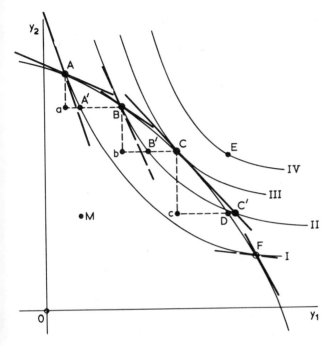

Figure 11.1

A' as at A since they both lie on the same indifference curve. So he would trade aA of y_2 for aA' of y_1. But Crusoe's production possibilities at point A might permit him to do better. If he gives up aA of y_2, he is able to produce aB amount of y_1. Crusoe is willing to give up aA for only aA' of y_1, but in fact he gets more: aB! Would he be willing to trade with himself in this manner? Of course! At point B he would be willing to trade bB for bB', but in fact can get bC. Thus he moves to point C.

This is his best point, as we suspected all along. Were he to make another move, he could get cD by reducing his output of y_2 by cC. But this amount cD is not enough to compensate him for the loss of cC; he requires cC' to stay on the same indifference curve, and that is infeasible! C is best.

Exercise: Start from F and work back to C.

Suppose we say this a slightly different way. The slope of the dashed line, tangent at A to the *indifference curve*, tells what another bit of y_1 is worth to Crusoe in terms of the amount of y_2 he would be willing to give up for it. This amount of y_2 is the shadow price he would be willing to pay for a unit of y_1 at point A. The slope of the *production possibility frontier* at A is given by the solid line tangent to the frontier at that point. It expresses the shadow price that Crusoe has to pay. The slope of the production possibility frontier is less than that of the indifference curves in absolute value. The price he has to pay is less than the price he would be willing to pay. He gets even more of y_1 than he would be willing to accept to give up the unit of y_2 (aB is greater than aA'). Crusoe makes the trade-off with himself, and prefers point B to point A. Repeating the process he moves to point C.

Exercise:
(1) Explain how, at point B, the price Crusoe will pay for more y_1 is less than the price he is required to pay.
(2) Start from F and return to point C in terms of prices that an individual is willing to pay, and that he has to pay.
(3) Express these results in terms of supply curves and demand curves.
(4) Rework this analysis in terms of a flat-faced production possibility frontier and set of indifference curves. Are your results different?

Now suppose poor old Crusoe's case of schizophrenia becomes aggravated. Crusoe the producer confronts Crusoe the consumer as profit maker and market oriented purchaser. Start at point A again. Crusoe the producer attempts to maximize his revenues (see Chapter 5). He observes the prices that his goods can fetch on the market (consisting, of course, of his *alter ego*, Crusoe the consumer). These will be given by the slope of the dashed line tangent to the indifference curve at A; these are the prices that the consumer is willing to pay if he were to have A goods. That makes the dashed line at A the *revenue line* of Crusoe the producer. Is this the maximum revenue he can attain? Certainly not, for he could push the revenue line 'northeast', making more money and still remaining in the feasible set of outputs. He moves towards a point like B in order to raise his revenue. But what is happening? As Crusoe the producer tries to make more money by moving his revenue line towards B, its slope changes reflecting the fact that, having more y_1 and less y_2, his other personality, Crusoe the consumer, will be willing to pay a lower price for y_1 – the slope of the indifference curve at B. Nevertheless, point B represents a greater income than point A. A similar process moves Crusoe to point C. We knew he would end up there all along!

Now look at this problem from the point of view of Crusoe the consumer. His problem is to maximize his happiness by getting to the highest indifference curve permitted by his budget limitation. What is his budget at A? Where does he get his money from? Despite his dual role both Crusoes are really one human being, so that as consumer Crusoe's income is the amount of income that could be generated by selling goods at their shadow prices in the amounts shown at point A. In other words, Crusoe the consumer has as his budget the solid revenue line at A. Clearly the consumer is not maximizing his satisfactions by buying bundle of goods A. His indifference curve and budget lines are not tangent to one another. It would appear to him that, given the money budget shown at A, he would try to move toward indifference curve II from its present position on I. But, as Crusoe the consumer does this, the slope of his budget line increases in steepness; the law of diminishing returns in the slope of the frontier makes it harder to produce the additional y_1 required. The process takes him to B and finally on to C. At C, the budget line and the revenue line coincide. Crusoe's case of split personality is cured by the hidden hand of the market rather than by the consoling couch of Dr Freud!

Exercise:
(1) How much of this analysis of the separating line must be altered when working in terms of a flat-faced curve? Diagram situations in which there is more than one point on the separating line. Draw the possibility where the solution will not be at an extreme point. How much must you modify the discussion in the text to deal with these cases?
(2) Draw a situation in which all the indifference curves lie beyond the production possibility frontier. Describe the economy it implies.

So Robinson Crusoe is as happy as he can be! His schizophrenic and efficient world gets the most happiness for his resources. It would also be possible for the planners of a centrally directed economy to be happy too. They also face a production possibility boundary made up of all the industries in their country. They also have a set of indifference curves representing happiness levels. Why not simply go to a point like C and call that the best of all possible worlds? Indeed, there is no reason why planners could not make themselves as happy as possible, but that is not the problem! The problem is to make society as well off as possible. Society is composed of many individuals. It would be nice if the planners' desires coincided with that of all individuals, but that is not necessarily so. Indeed, the social problem is reconciling individual desires with those of society as a whole. Planning from the centre does not eliminate the problem, but simply puts it in the hands of the planners.

A market economy also has to make the reconciliation of social and individual choices. It is too much to hope that there will be a single best, most efficient choice as in the Crusoe case. Clearly, in a society of many individuals one member could always be made more happy by taking goods away from others. Nonetheless, we can show that the concept of efficient choice still has meaning, but in a much weaker sense. Competition will be seen to lead to a set of alternative efficient points, which shows no clear way to choose among them, but nonetheless excludes inefficient points from consideration. Outputs and resource allocations are inefficient when it is possible to rearrange matters so that at least some people would be better off and nobody would be worse off. A condition where all the possibilities for improving some without hurting others are exhausted is said to be *Pareto optimal* after Vilfredo Pareto, who invented the idea. Thus a point inside the production possibility frontier is not Pareto optimal since it is possible to produce more of everything on the frontier and make at least some people better off without taking goods away from others. But which point on the frontier should be chosen? Crusoe would choose point *C* in Figure 11.1, but his friend Friday with a different set of preferences would choose another point on the frontier. Whose preferences should rule? Crusoe cannot be happier without making Friday less happy, and conversely. Both points are Pareto optimal. Both are efficient. Optimality is a nice weasely word which allows us to avoid saying which is best – Friday's choice, Crusoe's choice or some combination of the two.

The demonstration that the competitive market made up of many persons is Pareto optimal depends on mathematical ideas about sets which will be expressed informally here, but which are treated in a readable and yet elegant way by T. Koopmans in *Three Essays on the State of Economic Science*. When we first discussed the feasible set under the production possibility frontier for a particular firm, we showed that it was convex. It can be shown that the set which is the sum of the elements of all these sets is also convex. Likewise efficient consumers construct convex sets of preferences, which we have called indifference curves. The sum of preference sets for all consumers is also convex. Now, if each individual firm maximizes the value of a linear relationship like the revenue line over all of these feasible production sets the revenue line will be maximized over the set which is the sum of individual firms' sets. Likewise, if consumers individually minimize their expenditure for any given level of happiness, they will minimize their total expenditures as a group.

Now for the demonstrations.

(1) We show that it is self-contradictory to have competitive equilibrium and not have Pareto optimality. Suppose it were the case that we had competitive equilibrium and not Pareto optimality. Then there would be a consumer who would prefer a point that lay on or within the feasible production possibility set which he preferred to his present position. Yet he did not choose such a point. Why not? The only reason is that the other point would cost him more money. That means that consumers would be willing to pay more to producers than they are already getting. But then the producers would not be maximizing their incomes after all, and would be contradicting the meaning of competitive equilibrium. So it is not possible for individuals to be in competitive equilibrium without also being Pareto optimal as well!

(2) It is also possible to prove the converse – that any Pareto optimal resource allocation is attainable as a competitive market equilibrium. What this boils down to is the question of the existence of the line serving both as

maximum revenue and minimum budget that separates the possible production possibility set of firms and the indifference curves of consumers. Such a line can be drawn provided that the consumers' and producers' sets are convex. Then the line fits between them, as in Figure 11.1. In turn, convexity is the case when individual producers and consumers make efficient choices.

While we are quite sure of the conclusions we have proved, we must take pains to be equally sure of what we have not proved. We have not said that allowing the market to work is the only thing to do. The reason for this, even under the assumptions we have made, is that there are many Pareto optimal points. For if we consider the sum of all individual indifference curves, we realize that we would have a different sum if each individual made different choices. Now the choices that people make – to buy certain goods, to work or to retain some more leisure, to part with their wealth for a period of time – all depend on how much wealth each individual has in the first place. So, for each distribution there is no logical way to justify one Pareto optimal point over another; but there is no way to condemn it either. To repeat an old idea, the decision among various efficient points is a normative, ethical question of critical importance, but one that must be asked and answered in normative terms of what ought to be done. The issue can be construed to be a positive, scientific one only to the degree to which individuals in society agree on what is sometimes called a *social welfare function*, which includes value judgements about fairness and equity. Alas, it is precisely the agreement that is so hard to reach!

Nonetheless, the two theorems are frequently cited as the basis for the strongest reliance on the market rather than governmental planning. The argument goes like this: the only choices worth considering are Pareto optimal ones, since, by definition, any other choice of activities can be improved upon. No doubt it is necessary to make moral judgements about distribution, but one should not allow these judgements to render the economy inefficient – less than Pareto optimal. Therefore government should not interfere with the market and competition, but should frankly redistribute to the stocks of wealth initially in the hands of individuals in whatever way one can devise, and then let the market work to achieve the desired Pareto optimum. To interfere with the market is to direct the arrow to the wrong mark, because it is the distribution of stocks of wealth that is at issue, not prices. The outcome of the planning exercise can never be better than Pareto optimal, and may well be worse; if so, some people will be less well off than is really necessary.

In recent years the glories of perfect competition have come under fire. It has been argued that the competitive market does not really lead to Pareto optimal solutions because it fails to reflect collective features of our society which have become increasingly important as population and production grow. It was assumed that the satisfaction achieved by a consumer was determined by the goods he buys and uses; the more he bought, the better off he was. Likewise, firms' production depended only on the factors of production they hired, not on the output of other firms. Yet whilst goods may create happiness for the people that own them, they may be 'bads' because they produce pollutants and damage to others either directly or through the environment which all share. Self-interested owners of the pollutant producing goods do not take this cost into account, and under competition cannot be expected to do so. These considerations are called *externalities* because they are outside individual calculation. Since, by definition, the market reflects individual goals and preferences, prices do not accurately reflect those elements of social cost which are external to private calculation.

Aside from such costs the market cannot cope with collective wants. Public goods are those items from which everyone derives benefit without being able to own them. They range from man-made goods such as public highways to natural resources like the sea or the landscape. Since everyone can use these without paying for them, society cannot rely on the market mechanism to pay for them. Who would pay for that which others (government) will provide free of charge? Nor can the market provide an automatic guide to government as to their value, because the market measures the value of things by *willingness to pay*. Yet government must decide how much of the public goods should be provided. (How many motorways should be built? Which natural resources shall be preserved for public use and which may be used for private benefit?)

Frequently the problems of external social costs and public goods are intertwined in the same situation. For instance, when a firm dumps cyanide or other toxic materials into waste tips, or an oil tanker ruptures and spills oil into the sea, the cost is borne by others than those discharging the noxious materials. If the only damage is to nearby private property, this is an external cost imposed on others. If, however, the damage is to the public's interest in the environmental beauty of the seaside, or the safety of streams to swimming or fishing, then the external cost is in the damage of these public goods. Whilst it will be helpful to think about these two problems in separate categories, the arts of the applied economist and skilful legislator combine. their analysis in a creative way in the solution of current problems.

External bitter with internal sweets: the simple case of bargaining between the polluter and his victim

Consider the case of a negative externality – production by one firm causes damage to another's enterprise. Here competitive markets will not lead to Pareto optimal results because the cost of the damage is not included in the calculation of their producer. Suppose, however, that both the producer and the victim can identify each other and negotiate. The way in which they may come to agreement depends on their bargaining position and the legal framework in which they operate. Thus the courts might award damages to the injured party equal to the amount of the loss; alternatively, it might be that it is not possible to make a legal case for damages and the party suffering the injury might pay (bribe?) the other to limit his production. Either way the external costs become internalized into one or the other enterprise. There are other methods of internalizing these costs so that the pollution or other external damage is an internal cost to the combined operation. The firms might merge or the victim might buy out the polluter.

Ronald Coase of the University of Chicago proved a most remarkable theorem relating to these circumstances. He showed that, provided the parties can identify and negotiate with each other, any solution that they arrive at will be Pareto optimal. That is to say, the same resources and the same outputs will result regardless of the way damages are assessed. There may well be an enormous difference in the distribution of income generated by the enterprises if damages, bribes or mergers are the result of lawsuit and bargaining, but he concluded that this is a question of fairness – equity. Efficiency is not affected. So long as economists insist that they cannot choose on positive grounds between Pareto optima, the issue must be left to the courts or other dispensers of morality for equity judgement. But there is no clear efficiency case for government intervention in abating pollution under the circumstances in the public interest. This is not quite market equilibrium, but it is still *laissez-faire*!

Coase took the example of a corn farm adjacent to a cattle farm, so that the cattle regularly trample some of the corn crop. The Coase result is that the same amount of corn and cattle would be produced regardless of whether the cattle raiser paid damages to the corn farmer, the corn farmer decided to buy out the cattle raiser to reduce the trampling, or the cattle raiser bought out the corn farmer to avoid paying damages awarded by the court!

First consider labour and capital production possibility frontiers for final uses of cattle (y_1) and corn (y_2) producible with the combined resources of the two enterprises. Actually there are two frontiers to be considered for labour and two for capital (Figure 11.2). The frontier shown as a light line represents the outputs of corn and cattle if the two farms were not located next to each other and there were no trampling; the heavy lines show production possibilities with the negative externality.

For simplicity, say that the production possibilities for corn are reduced by a constant percentage of the cattle output. An odd way of saying this is that corn in trampled form is a necessary input into cattle production. Ruined

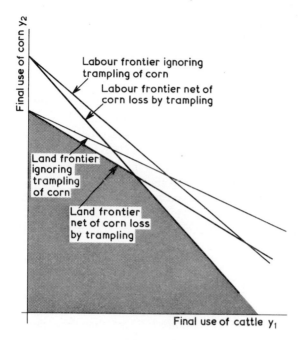

Figure 11.2

corn represents a shipment from the corn operation to cattle production as an intermediate good just as if it were fed to the cattle as fodder.

Suppose, first, that the two firms are merged. Then there is no doubt that the management will have to consider corn trampling as one of the expenses of production. The cost will be internalized and the firm will maximize profit by going to an extreme point on the heavy lined frontier such as A in Figure 11.3. The revenue line Y^* indicates the income achieved by the merged firm.

Now suppose the enterprises are separated, so the labour and capital involved in each phase of the joint operation are parcelled out to separate firms. If he were free from worry about paying for damage to his neighbour's corn crop the cattle farmer would be moved to produce more cattle than at A. What does he care if corn is trampled? He would produce up to his apparent frontier, whilst the corn farmer would continue to suffer and would market the same amount as at A. It would appear that output would be at B. The combined income of both firms would seem to have increased to Y^{**} shown by the revenue line as a result of the extra cattle marketed. Since the increase is due to cattle sales, the distance Y^*Y^{**} represents the gain to the cattle farmer.

But matters cannot rest here because B is beyond the realistic frontier given by the heavy production possibility frontiers. The additional cattle

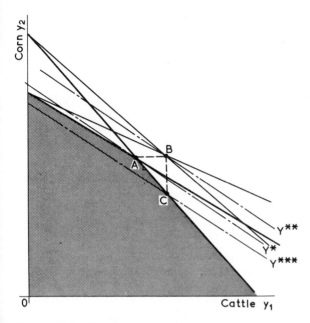

Figure 11.3   The Coase theorem

cause more trampling and consequently corn marketings must be less than before. In fact the combined production would be at C on the effective frontiers, BC of corn being trampled. Thus the joint income of the two firms would be at Y^{***}, which is an income level less than either Y^{**} or Y^{*} due to the convex shape of the frontier.

What happens now? The farmer may take the cattleman to court and collect damages from the cattleman equal in value of the lost corn. Or the farmer might pay a bribe to the cattleman to induce him to curtail production, and compensate the cattleman for the loss of income. In the first case, since the loss to the farmer is BC amount of corn, the damages he could collect is the difference between Y^{**} and Y^{***}. The value of the additional cattle is only the distance between Y^{**} and Y^{*}, because the law of diminishing returns bends the production frontier inward in going from A to C. The cattle raiser would have to pay more in damages to the corn farmer than he gains by selling the additional cattle, so he desists from increasing his herd beyond the amount shown at A.

But now suppose there was no way for the farmer to collect damages. By giving the cattleman a bribe equal to $Y^{*}Y^{**}$ he could induce him to restrict his herd to A again. This would be worthwhile since he would get $Y^{**}Y^{***}$

in additional value of corn sales. Either way, the two parties go back to the same solution. By allowing the two parties to bargain or sue as the law allows, society avoids this loss and has the proper amount of corn and cattle produced to make the most efficient use of productive factors without direct controls, or even knowledge of the amount of the damage.

'Bribe' and 'damages' are loaded words. With equal justice the bribing of the cattleman could be called the 'farmer's payment for the damage caused by the restriction of cattle production'; the damages won at lawsuit could equally be called the 'bribe' which the courts give the farmer to put up with having his corn trampled. Either way efficiency considerations are satisfied. But what of equity? Somehow courts and parliaments are able to make decisions in these cases, as to who should bear the internalized cost. How do they do it? I don't know?

Exercise:
(1) Show how a collective body of city residents might bargain with a smoke producing firm to internalize the cost of smoke damage and reduce it to the proper amount. Would the amount be zero? What difficulties would be involved in this procedure?
(2) Introduce the possibility of building a fence by either party into the previous analysis of the Coase theorem. How much would each be willing to pay? Who should build the fence?
(3) Specify cases of air and water pollution where the considerations for the Coase theorem are met?

Unfortunately, much of the time it is impossible for those causing a negative externality to be individually identified for negotiation. Who is responsible for a particular bit of smoke, street litter or petrol fumes in London? Nor is it possible for the individuals damaged to be precisely identified. It is not easy for those damaged to bargain or sue those responsible. For these reasons, it is frequently impossible to rely on the Coase theorem and leave the problem to those directly concerned. This puts government in the position of dealing with the estimation of and remedy of external costs in the most efficient and equitable manner possible. Nonetheless, one ought not to dismiss Coase's result as irrelevant to many practical situations. All too frequently it is possible for parties to come to agreement and yet insist on government intervention. This places government in the position of making equity rather than efficiency decisions on grounds that are frequently hard to justify. The courts long have accepted this truth and tend to decide as little as possible. Often this is frustrating to the petitioners, but the conservatism has some economic analysis to recommend it.

Pollution and the public interest

Often the Coase theorem does not apply and the public must enter to protect itself from 'bads' as well as enjoying the goods. Every adult knows that it is necessary to take the bad with the good. The only question worth investigating is: How much of each?

The problem has become more urgent. As population and productivity have grown, it becomes increasingly difficult to rely on the natural capacity of the environment to costlessly disperse pollutants into the air, water and soil ecological system where it can be broken down into harmless elements by bacteria, chemical actions, ground water filtering through rocks and the like. Pollutants break down over time, so there is always a certain amount of these 'bads' with us: smoke, noise, animal wastes in the streams, radioactive and heavy metals in the sea, excessive algae growth in lakes and rivers due to run off of fertilizers, and so on. When do these become a problem? How much is it worth to us to reduce the level of pollution by a given amount? How shall we deal with pollution in a Pareto optimal, efficient, way?

To answer these questions let us try to build pollution into our notion of a production possibility frontier. Recall how we computed the amount of labour directly and indirectly required for each final use. Starting from the inverse $X = (I - A)^{-1} Y$, we multiplied each industry output by the amount of labour associated with a unit of output by each industry. That is to say, we multiplied each X_i by the appropriate labour coefficient, l_i. Thus the left hand side of each equation told us the amount of labour involved in that industry, and the right hand side told us the amount of labour per unit final use of each industry. Then, adding the equations, we were led to the production possibility frontier: total labour on the left hand side, and the labour directly and indirectly required for each final use on the right hand side.

Can we not use the same technique to arrive at a *pollutant possibility frontier* relating final uses to tolerable pollution levels? Instead of multiplying by the inverse equation of labour, multiply by the amount of pollutants produced per unit of output in each industry. Let S_1 be the amount of soot produced in industry 1; then the coefficient $s_1 = S_1/X_1$ is the soot per unit of output of the first industry. Similarly, $s_2 = S_2/X_2$. Now, multiplying each of the equations by s_1 and s_2 respectively:

$$s_1 X_1 = S_1 = s_1 J_{11} y_1 + a_1 J_{12} y_2$$
$$s_2 X_2 = S_2 = s_2 J_{21} y_1 + s_2 J_{22} y_2.$$

Adding and collecting terms:

$$S = S_1 + S_2 = (s_1 J_{11} + s_2 J_{21}) y_1 + (s_1 J_{12} + s_2 J_{22}) y_2.$$

The left hand side is the total soot produced. The terms in parentheses on the right hand side tell us the amount of soot pollutant directly and indirectly produced per unit of final use y_1 and y_2. What name shall we apply to these? Let H_1 and H_2 stand for horrible odour 1 and horrible odour 2. For any given amount of S that we can accept, we have a pollutant possibility frontier limiting final uses, $S = H_1 y_1 + H_2 y_2$.

For example, suppose industry 1 is lorry and automobile production, and industry 2 is plastic and synthetic chemical products. Sanitary engineers will be able to tell us s_1 and s_2, the number of particles of soot (particulants) thrown off into the atmosphere per vehicle and per pound of plastic and chemical products. We economists will use the inverse table and compute the direct and indirect amount of soot particulants per unit of final use. These indirect effects may be very important. At first sight, perhaps, the automobile industry seems the cleaner of the two, and the temptation would be to discourage the chemical industry. Yet automobiles use chemicals and plastics in their manufacture (and of course chemical industries use lorries and cars). When the indirect effects are totted up, the more correct policy might be to control the automobile industry.

To locate the frontier we also need to know S, how much pollutant is harmful. The health experts are having a great deal of difficulty in deciding this exactly, but a reasonable number in use is 100 micrograms of a particulant per cubic metre of air.

When we compare the pollutant frontier with the labour and capital production possibility frontiers, we can see at once why pollution has become a problem for an advanced, ostensibly prosperous, economy (Figure 11.4).

The diagram depicts a situation of 'before' and 'after' a country has experienced economic growth. The inner pair of frontiers in the diagram represent the capital and labour constraints before growth. The dashed lines going through A represent the level of national income that can be achieved with the existing supply of capital and labour before growth. Beyond these frontiers is the black, sooty, pollutant possibility frontier representing the 100 micrograms of particulant per cubic metre of air, and the danger to health it represents. Nobody worries about that frontier in a poor country even though it is there as a potential hazard. National income is held in to a feasible set by the limited amount of resources of labour and capital available. There is no question about it, the market is working beautifully in a situation like this.

Now suppose that economic growth occurs, and the capital and labour frontiers move out parallel to themselves because there is more capital and labour. National income would move out parallel to itself to the new extreme point, B. Pollution suddenly becomes an urgent issue. The point

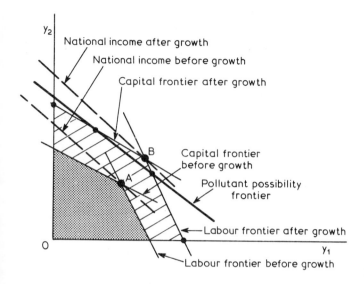

National income after growth

National income before growth

Capital frontier after growth

B

Capital frontier
before growth

A

Pollutant possibility
frontier

←Labour frontier after growth

Labour frontier before growth

Figure 11.4

shown on the diagram where national income is maximized is beyond the pollutant possibility frontier, and hence more than 100 micrograms of noxious matter is thrown off into the air. Breathing has become hazardous to health.

Query: Explain why underdeveloped countries are opposed to banning the use of DDT.

How can production take place beyond the pollution frontier? The answer is simple and important. Labour and capital cost money to the firms using them whilst use of the atmosphere as a sewer for soot is free! Of course the air is not free to society, but it is free to firms and individuals. From a social point of view, they may produce too much, regardless of cost. Yet what is there in the market mechanism to stop them from doing so? Nothing, unless they are somehow compelled or induced to desist. The labour and capital frontiers represent the private property of individuals. To get an individual to sell more labour involves paying him higher wages. But nobody charges for the use of the air, and so it may be over used because there is no automatic check at work.

Clean air is the socially owned common property factor of production that does not appear as a scarce factor of production to any given firm. It has a shadow price given by the same dual linear programming problem as any other factor. But unlike the shadow price of labour and capital it does not have to be paid by a firm; it is external to their calculations. The cost represented by the shadow price of pollution is passed on to others, rather than being borne by those that generate it. Clearly if the producers did have to pay the cost, if the market or some other device coerced them into doing so, they would reduce their output of pollutant accordingly.

Exercise:

(1) Compare the use of land held as private property and the sea as a common property resource. Explain how the use of land is limited by the rent charged for its use. Show why the sea tends to be over used as a source of food and as a dump for wastes. Interpret the current tendency of nations to extend their fishing territorial waters to 200 miles from their coasts in this context. How ought a 'law of the sea' be formulated to apply to undersea resources such as petroleum and manganese nodules? What are the conflicts of interest and how might they be resolved?

(2) Does the abuse of land through soil erosion, urban blight and overgrazing invalidate the argument you have made?

(3) If all property were publicly owned as in a socialist commonwealth, would pollution represent more or less of a problem? How might the USSR deal with pollution? What has its experience been?

One solution, then, to the problem of external costs is to internalize them one way or another. When common property resources are involved, making them over into private property is one way. This is not always easy. For one thing, who shall get the resources? How shall present users be compensated? In mixed economies the public also can influence the use of private property through taxation, by assessing damages to polluters who injure others, subsidy of those who desist, direct regulation and nationalization.

Clearly there are two issues that must be faced: (1) How much pollution to eliminate? (2) What instruments should be used? In order to come to a decision on how much pollution to eliminate, we have to know how much it costs society. The money measure of the damage done is computed as the dual linear programming problem. Glance back to Figure 11.2 where we showed how the pollutant possibility frontier became a limiting constraint on society (although not on individuals) after economic growth had occurred. We now ask how much national income would society lose if it were to restrict output to the set bounded by the external limitation of the pollutant frontier as well as internal considerations such as labour and capital. This is done in Figure 11.5 by drawing a new reduced income line, Y^{**}, limited by the social constraint of keeping the air from exceeding 100 micrograms of particulant per cubic metre. Y^{*} is the level of national income that would be achieved if the pollutant frontier were ignored. The distance $Y^{*}Y^{**}$ is the cost to society of restricting final use within the specified limit.

Once having measured the cost of pollution, it is possible to decide on the degree to which it is worthwhile to attempt to alleviate it. Clearly the

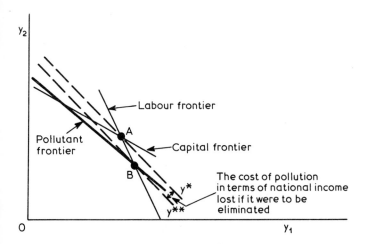

Figure 11.5

distance Y^*Y^{**} is nothing but the shadow price of the amount of pollutant that an unrestricted competitive economy would produce. If a new regulation is to be introduced to restrict pollution from that level, the satisfaction gained by society from that pollution abatement must be compared with the satisfaction lost through the decrease in the level of national income. The more pollution is abated, the greater will be the loss of national income, due to the convex slope of the frontier and hence the law of diminishing returns. The shadow price of pollution thus appears as the supply curve for clean air.

Exercise: Use the previous analysis to show how you would decide whether to install a smoke removal device in factories that eliminated enough smoke to push the pollution frontier out so as to pass through point A. Your answer should be in terms of the costs and benefits of the device. Would you install a more effective but more costly device?

What is the demand for clean air? It is the amount of national income that society is willing to sacrifice to get a bit more of it. Governments may estimate the demand by examining what people will pay in terms of lower incomes to live away from congested cities. Other estimation procedures might be attempted, but however the social desire is translated by the political process into government action, once the demand is determined the level of pollution that ought to be accepted is a straightforward exercise in supply and demand (Figure 11.6).[1] Horizontally we show q, the percentage

---

[1] The problem is complicated by the fact that pure air is largely a public good and so is not ordinarily offered for sale. We will deal with this aspect of the problem in the next section of this chapter.

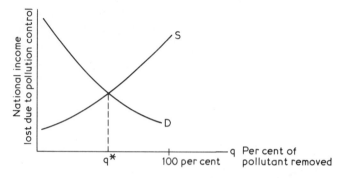

Figure 11.6

of pollutant removed from the air. Vertically we measure the loss in national income. The supply curve slopes upward showing that, as we increase the percentage of pollutant removed closer to 100 per cent, the amount of national income sacrificed gets larger and larger. Society's demand for clean air slopes downward for the same reason as any other demand curve. As people get more and more clean air, they are willing to sacrifice less additional national income as the price of more air purity.

Assuming that society can agree on its demand for clean air, it should remove q^* per cent of pollutant. Environmentalist purists will be displeased with this conclusion, because it implies that $1 - q^*$ per cent of the pollutant should remain; those who believe that 'where there's muck there's money' will also be unhappy. Nevertheless, this equilibrium represents a compromise between costs and benefits.

Exercise: Imagine that Robinson Crusoe faced a pollution-production dilemma on his desert island. Show that a production possibility frontier could be drawn with clean air on the horizontal axis and real income in goods measured on the vertical axis. Draw Crusoe's indifference curves for clean air and goods and show his choice. Explain that the choice is not affected by the existence or non-existence of a market or money measures. Is the choice still Pareto optimal if the desert island includes Friday? Show how placing a proper price on clean air could lead to a market equilibrium that is Pareto optimal.

Having decided how much pollution to endure, how shall the limit be enforced? There are two basic approaches: (1) direct controls on the amount and type of pollutant which may be emitted by firms and consumers; (2) internalization of the social cost into the operating costs, letting the market make the rest of the adjustment.

Of course direct controls are often unavoidable, but they have the serious drawback that they are always too general. Regulations such as 'Reduce effluent sewage by 50 per cent! The use of DDT is forbidden! All automobiles must employ pollution control systems!' tend to deal in averages rather than marginal quantities. Rational economic decisions have to be made at the margin of costs and benefits. One has to decide whether it is worthwhile to produce one more microgram of air particulant in a particular situation in order to get an additional amount of income or other benefit. The issue is not whether the total amount of particulant divided by the total output coincides with regulations. To obey an average is to misallocate resources and have too much pollution in some situations and too little in others. The case of outright prohibition of certain activities is a special case of such regulation. In some remote Scottish town, for instance, there is no need to forbid the odd automobile exhaust or noise. It might make good sense to discharge some pollutant into the atmosphere rather than waste petrol, but blanket regulations may forbid the practice. Moreover, regulations are hard to enforce and interpret. Frequently regulation becomes a legal matter, involving delays as well as fees.

Indirect measures through internalization of social cost are more flexible, since they require firms to calculate social as well as private costs and benefits. They are then led to an optimal solution which takes social costs of pollution into account. The most obvious method is through tax and subsidy programmes which alter the market price of the final uses and thus influence the revenue maximizing choice of firms. This is shown in Figure 11.7, which

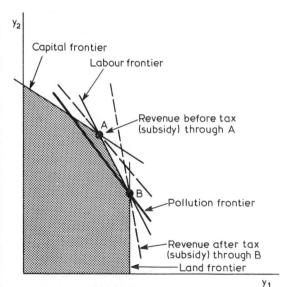

Figure 11.7   (Shaded area shows private view of the feasible set)

is similar to the preceding diagrams except that a land frontier is added to the labour and capital constraints. Suppose one wanted to guide firms to choose point B since it is on the pollution possibility frontier, rather than A which is beyond it. A tax might be imposed on y_2 (or a subsidy on y_1). This would have the effect of making the revenue line after tax (the light dashed line) more steeply sloped than the one before tax (heavy dashed line). Point B would be a revenue maximizing point, and also one which satisfies the pollution possibility frontier.

Exercise: Go back to the isoquant diagrams and show how a tax subsidy programme might be used to direct firms to choose techniques of production that are more in keeping with social cost considerations.

The tax subsidy method of controlling pollution has been criticized on practical grounds. The authorities have to know the social cost of pollution with great precision, as well as its interrelationship with other constraints. When one considers that there are many sorts of pollution and other private constraints it has been suggested that there is not much gain over direct controls.

One ingenious way to internalize the external effects of pollution is to simply sell rights to pollute! Perhaps the idea is not as mad as it sounds. After all, if the difficulty arises because the environment is 'everybody's property and therefore nobody's property', why not make it property? Property is the exclusive right to objects with respect to use, purchase or sale. Normally we think of land, bottles of beer or shares of stock in this connection. Could not the government sell rights to produce pollutant to the highest bidder? By limiting the number of such rights to, say, 100 micrograms per cubic metre of air, the pollution possibility frontier would automatically be respected. Then firms could buy or sell these rights among themselves. Like land, the price of using the air as sewer would equal the value of its marginal product. Firms who make the most marginal contribution to national income by polluting the air would be able and willing to buy away rights from firms for which the marginal product would be less. Government would decide to create these pollution rights by comparing the danger to society of an increase in pollution against the increase in national income. The market would then distribute these rights in an optimal fashion.

While the thought of a pollution licence sounds absurd, perhaps it is only the brazen faced way in which the proposal is made that makes it seem so. Licences are currently sold as rights to use refuse tips and this would be an extension of this practice. However, unless these rights were made restrictive as to area and time of pollution, the solution would not overcome the difficulty of clustering of these licences in limited spaces. At least some of the arbitrariness of direct controls would still remain, since local information on the appropriate amount of pollutant might be hard to obtain. Nonetheless, the market solution remains an interesting idea.

We conclude that whilst there are weaknesses in all the methods of pollution control – regulation, tax subsidy, and selling of licences – they show how the problem is to be dealt with. Limiting pollution involves paying the social cost in order to achieve the social benefit. Whether it be by internalized costs or by establishing regulatory constraints, society can limit pollution if it is willing to pay the price. Determining the price is the really difficult problem. Thus far we have discussed the supply side of the problem; now it is time to ask what determines the demand for social amenities.

The demand for public goods

Many cases involving pollution control and environmental protection entail a certain amount of publicness. That is to say, the benefits accruing from the protection of the environment are available, usually, to a large number of people collectively. This being so, the demand for these goods must originate from society as a whole, through the power of government. No individual would be willing to pay voluntarily for a product which might be paid for by others and which he might then enjoy free of charge. Individuals are collectively compelled to pay in the form of taxes or diversion of resources for that which they would not be willing to buy separately. What then is the collective demand for a public good? How can the authorities' estimate of the benefits of these goods compare with the costs? How does the public demand differ from private demand? More precisely, what governmental demand policies will lead to Pareto optimality?

The market for private goods, it will be recalled, led to Pareto optimality when everybody faced the same market price as required by perfect competition. Then each person arranged his affairs to maximize his private welfare by adjusting the quantity of goods of various types he buys until the rate at which he is willing to give up one good for another (the slope of the indifference curve) equals that market price. His mental state, the marginal rate of substitution, just matched the objective reality of the market price. The price of the good is a measure of how much more each person wants of a certain good; so the sum of the quantities in which everybody wants those goods at each price indicates the demand for a private good in a market economy.

Now, in the case of the pure public good, everybody gets to have the same amount of the good if anybody does. Since price is a measure of the benefits each person gets from the goods, then the demand curve of a public good is the sum of the prices each person would be willing to pay for each quantity of the public goods if he had to do so! Thus, while the demand curve for a private good is the horizontal sum of the quantities each person would buy at any given market price, the demand for a public good is the vertical sum of individual demand curves for each possible quantity. Everybody gets the same quantity of the goods, since it is provided to all.

Not everybody would be willing to pay the same price for the public good. On the contrary, each individual places a different value on a quantity of public goods provided him by the government (if he had to pay for it). The collective satisfaction of society is measured by the vertical sum of the prices people would have paid for any given quantity publicly provided. Figure 11.8 shows a group of individual demand curves for, say, flowers. Lying to the right of these is the market demand curve if the good were a private good in some person's garden; the quantities are added up horizontally for each price. Above these individual demand curves is the public demand for flowers in the park as prices are summed for each quantity the government chose to produce. The Pareto optimal amount of the public good which the government could provide for citizens to use collectively is given by the intersection of the dashed heavy line with the appropriate supply curve. The amount which would be privately produced is given by the intersection of the solid heavy line with a supply curve. At that latter intersection, of course, the goods would be sold to the individuals at the market price given by the intersection of supply and demand.

Consider, as we frequently must, whether goods ought to be publicly or privately owned. To keep issues clear, suppose the conversion of public into private goods and back again were costless. What comparison could we make of the demand for the same good under the two alternative methods of providing it? For concreteness, imagine that the three individuals where demand curves for flowers are illustrated in the diagram, Jones, Smith, and Brown, have gardens separated from each other by high garden walls and they each have a gardener plant similar flowers in their garden. The flowers are then private goods since their use as objects of beauty is blocked to non-owners. Now suppose that at no cost the local authorities were able to remove the walls thereby converting the gardens into a park. The flowers would become public goods available to all three persons and would have to be provided by them collectively through local government. Should the government plant the same sized garden for the collective as the private individuals would separately? The answer depends on the supply curve for flowers. If it crosses above the intersection of the two demand curves in Figure 11.8, then the public good arrangement will result in more flowers being planted than for the private arrangement. The reverse would be the case if the supply curve crossed below the intersection.

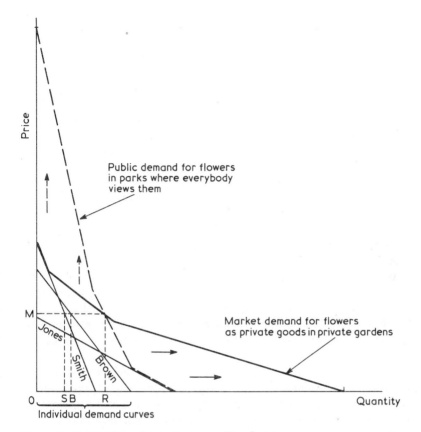

Figure 11.8   Public and private demand for flowers

Query: What can be said about the elasticity of demand for public and
private goods?

A most revealing situation is the point where the public and private
demand curves cross. Now the same amount of flowers will be produced by
both arrangements. Both arrangements will be Pareto optimal, and both
involve the same cost of production. Yet the arrangements are very different
in the way in which the satisfactions from public and private goods are
distributed. In the case of private goods, the price for everybody is *OM*.
Jones does not want any flowers at that price. Smith buys *OS* and Brown
buys *OB*. Together they buy the *OR*. The total satisfaction they get is the
area under their demand curves up to *OS* and *OB* respectively. Now
consider the public good case. *OR* amount of flowers is available for
collective use by everybody. Jones now gets flowers up to *OR* just like

everybody else, even though he would not have paid for them as a private citizen. His satisfaction is the area under his demand curve up to *OR*. Brown also gets *OR* flowers. Look at Smith. He gets *OR* flowers, even though sick of looking at them!

Which of these two situations is preferable? When should a good or service be provided by the public, and when by private business? In some cases the issue is clear because goods cannot be provided by private agencies – national defence is an example. But in the many practical cases facing nations today, the choice does exist. What is to be done? Both alternatives are Pareto optimal. One must choose between the additional happiness of Jones in the public good case and that of Smith in the private good case if Smith has to bear a proportional part of the cost of producing more flowers than he cares to see. And what of Green who has hay fever and is allergic to flowers which the local authorities insist on planting behind his house?

Here is a concrete case in which choice has to be made among Pareto optimal situations in terms of the distribution of benefits. Evidently society must have some criterion for making these decisions. It must decide whether an increment of happiness given to Jones at the expense of Smith represents an increase in social welfare. Society must make some sort of estimate of the satisfactions of its members and then must come to a decision on whether an increase in satisfaction to one member is worth the reduction in welfare of another.

Plainly society does make such decisions through the political process. Hidden away in the minds of decision makers is some sort of social welfare function which includes terms for the happiness of each of the members of society. Notice how vague and question begging is the notion of a social welfare function. It requires that a measurement be made for the happiness of each of the individuals in society based on a common cardinal unit for counting and comparing happiness of different people. In general each person will have a different social welfare function.

A parliamentary democracy must choose decision makers who have in their minds the same social welfare function as the people who elected them. A list of the considerations involved shows how difficult the choice must be:

1 A measure must be found to compare the welfare of individuals. The price which each would be willing to pay is not entirely satisfactory because there is no surety that each person gets the same satisfaction for each unit of expenditure. That is to say, there are no clear ways to make inter-personal comparisons of utility.
2 The social welfare function of each individual depends on more than his own satisfactions derived from goods and services, but includes a judge-ment about the happiness of others. Regard for others, envy, keeping up

with the Joneses, attitudes about the propriety of the social structure are all involved.

3 A way must be found to combine these individual social welfare functions. In the case of both private and public goods discussed above, it was assumed that this would consist in the simple sum of their individual demands. This need not always be the case. One might feel that children should be cared for more than adults. Perhaps artists, shop workers or the elderly should be favoured so that the sum should be weighted in some way. Perhaps the welfares might be combined in some other way such as the sum of their logarithms.

4 A decision must be made whether the welfare of society depends entirely on the welfare of the individuals within it. Does a nation as a corporate entity have values of its own?

5 Political institutions must somehow function to translate the individual welfare functions into the collective action of the state. How is this to be done if the functions are all different?

The questions we are now asking are not to be answered in terms of economics. They involve broader issues of politics and ethics, and one is not at all sure that answers will be forthcoming from those fields.

Exercise:
(1) Suppose our social welfare function were such that we could make a direct comparison of the happiness of Smith, Jones and Brown from their demand curves by simply saying that a penny spent on a good by one person involves the same as the other. That is to say, suppose they were identical in the way their utility were measured by money. Moreover, suppose we were to say that the welfare of society were the simple sum of the welfare of the three individuals who comprise it. Draw a supply curve for flowers through the intersection of the public and market demand curves in Figure 11.8.
   (*a*) Should the good be provided publicly or privately?
   (*b*) Recalling that the cost to society is the area under the supply curve, show the net social benefit of the flowers produced as the difference in area between social welfare and social cost.
   (*c*) Draw a supply curve that would cause you to reverse your judgement about whether the good should be publicly or privately provided.
   (*d*) Criticize the social welfare function you have used and show how a different choice of welfare function would cause you to reverse your judgement on how the good ought to be provided.
(2) Using clippings from the press illustrate how the five concerns involved in social decision making have entered into public controversy.

Should there be limits to growth?

While none of the methods outlined in this chapter have been without difficulty, the principles were laid down for the inclusion of social cost and collective needs in directing economic growth. Suppose these objectives were met, would it satisfy the objections of environmentalists who are opposed to further economic growth? After all, the size of the planet is limited. Is it enough to compel individuals to pay the full social cost of their efforts to maximize their income or welfare, or must we inhibit the maximizing process itself?

The debate is an old one and first emerged as the contradiction between the scarcity of resources and the presumed tendency of the population to indefinite growth. The spectre of eventual starvation was first raised by the Reverend Thomas Malthus in *An Essay on the Principle of Population* (1978) which created a sensation when it first appeared. Almost as great a stir was recently aroused by a recent computer study strikingly similar in assumptions and conclusions.[2] The issue is whether the economy is capable of adapting to the scarcity of resources.

The discussion was advanced by David Ricardo's great work *Political Economy and Taxation* (1817) which included adjustment of population in the adaptation process. He distinguished between fixed constraints such as land, and expandable resources such as labour and capital. Even though population provided labour as well as demand for consumables, the law of diminishing returns meant that the increased use of labour would tend to increase output by smaller amounts for each additional unit of labour.

As the demand for food rose with population, additional land of lesser fertility would be drawn into production. As we have seen, the result would be higher differential rents for lands of greater fertility. This rent was of crucial significance in the optimal adaptation to scarcity of natural resources. One could only afford high rent land if it were used to produce crops which were of high value. Moreover, the high productivity of such natural resources led to greater intensity in the use of labour and capital on such lands where the return would be greater. Ricardo essentially pointed to the market solution to the product mix and factor mix problems which we studied in Chapters 5 and 6. Nonetheless, Ricardo felt that the population could not grow indefinitely because eventually the increment in output of food, obtainable from either using poorer land or more capital and labour, would be less than the subsistence of the labourers. Labour would have reproduced itself to the point of bare subsistence. Since the supplies of all three factors of production would be constant, there would be no further growth in either population or national income. Society would have entered

[2] J. W. Forrester, *World Dynamics* (1971); D. H. Meadows *et al.*, *The Limits to Growth* (1972).

a *static state* of *no growth*. The presumed inevitability of such a prospect was the reason for economics being dubbed 'the dismal science'.

The predictions of Ricardo and Malthus did not prove operative for two basic reasons. First of all, production possibilities are larger than one might think from the fixity of natural resources inputs. Reproducible factors of production – labour and capital – are substitutes for natural resources. At a given state of technique this substitution is subject to diminishing returns, but technical progress serves to push out production possibility frontiers with the same physical inputs.

Secondly, population is not directly proportional to national income. Indeed, the evidence is that population tends to increase more slowly as income rises due to smaller families, later marriages, emancipation of women, and technical progress in contraception. Thus it is the poorer countries that experience high population growth rate, whilst countries such as the US and USSR are virtually on a path of zero population growth.[3]

The reasons for the declining increase in population of high income nations is open to some debate, but at least part of it can be explained in simple economic terms. At low levels of income, especially in agrarian countries, children are an asset as potential labourers. The opportunities for profitable female labour outside the home are small, so that shadow price to the family of having wives tied down with child rearing is very small. High income countries, in contrast, place a higher value on the female labour potential outside the home due to technical progress in labour not demanding of physical strength. Moreover, the home itself is the scene of much mechanization so the shadow price to families of working wives' time away from home and child rearing is much smaller.

The question is not settled by an appeal to the past. There is no guarantee that population growth rates will continue to slow, nor is there assurance that technical progress will continue to accommodate the population growth that does occur. At the same time, mere appeal to the fixity of resources does not itself guarantee that such adaptations as we have outlined will not occur.

Exercise:
(1) Express the analysis in the text in terms of production possibility frontiers for two final uses: food and manufactured goods. Frontiers should be constructed for land of a single type, capital and labour. Show the substitution of reproducible factors for land, as the result of their growth and the search for higher national income. Show the limitation to this process due to the law of diminishing returns. Illustrate the effect of technical progress on the frontiers. Is there a limitation on the

---

[3] The reader might wish to contrast the Forrester and Meadows books cited above with William Nordhaus and James Tobin, *Economic Growth* (1972) and W. D. Nordhaus, 'World dynamics: measurement without data', *Economic Journal* (December 1973), pp. 1156–83.

effectiveness of technical progress in enlarging the feasible set as a result of the fixed supply of natural resources?

(2) Express the production possibility frontiers for land of several different qualities. Show the shadow price (rent) of each of these types of land. Show the intensive margin of land use by increasing labour or capital and relate the shadow price of these factors to the quality of land.

(3) Write an essay on the current 'energy crisis' or the 'petroleum shortage' in terms of the analysis provided. Discuss the role of the prices of these inputs in adaptation of their use, of national income growth and population changes.

(4) Consult the *Annual Abstract of Statistics* and compute the percentage increase in population of the UK. Compare this with the percentage increase in GNP in the same years by graphing population increase on the vertical axis and that of GNP horizontally.

The current discussion goes further than Malthus and involves the danger of depletion of natural resources – not simply its fixity. It is this concern that leads to moves to limit growth in national income rather than simply population. Unlike Ricardo's definition of land as the 'original and indestructible powers of the soil', such resources as petroleum are not only destructible but may be depleted in the foreseeable future. The use of such resources is certainly related to national income, and the danger is that unlimited growth in national income will simply use them up. This would be the case, it is felt, if the increase in national income were either the result of population growth demanding greater output, or simply greater technical capability to use these resources.

Much of what we have said about the old debate still remains relevant. Increased prices of scarce resources will prompt substitution both in products and factor combinations. Technical progress may relax the constraints of the increasingly scarce resources either through enhanced productivity, or the development of new substitutions. The possibility of atomic energy as a substitution for petroleum fuels is certainly familiar to the reader, although its practicality is a matter for further research and development.

The special aspect of using up resources hinges on when it is that they should be consumed. Clearly, if we permit ourselves to use them up more rapidly, national income will be greater now, but less in the future. When one puts the matter in terms of deciding whether to have present versus future income, it is clear that we are dealing with a problem in the rate of interest (see Chapter 10). The issue is whether decisions made in terms of the market rate of interest, dominated by private considerations, should be allowed to determine the use of depletible resources in producing income over time.

How would the market deal with a resource which is used up – say, an oil well? Would a private owner pump his well dry as quickly as possible? He might if he expected the price of petroleum to be the same (or less) in the future than it is today. There would be no incentive to save oil in the ground this year for use in the future if there were no additional income to be earned. The driller would be better advised to sell his oil as quickly as possible and invest his receipts in some other way, earning the market rate of interest. At falling prices petroleum in the ground is unlike wine in the cellar in that its value does not increase through age (present readers may forget that only a few years ago petroleum prices were sagging, and producers were complaining about the oversupply of oil on the world market). Clearly this sort of situation tended to aggravate the tendency to pump out the oil at an accelerated rate. If the prices were expected to fall, then the return to storing oil in the ground would be negative. Petroleum would be like wine spoiling in the cellar!

The problem of conservation, then, becomes one of expressing *society's interest rate* which is different from the signals the market gives to the individual producer. Society may wish to save petroleum for future years and future generations, yet income maximizing firms may well be led to ignore this social interest rate and use up the natural resource too rapidly. The problem of conservation of depletible resources is therefore one of determining and enforcing the social rate of interest when it diverges from the individual ones.

Defenders of the *laissez-faire* solution to the problem will be quick to argue that the market does not ignore the dangers of depletion. On the contrary, as these resources become more scarce, their price rises and the expectation is that their price will rise further. Saving petroleum today for pumping and sale tomorrow at a higher price means that it is like wine in the cellar after all. The higher price, they would argue, is not an accident of Middle East politics, but reflects the way in which the market is estimating the future income that can be obtained by producing the oil at a future date. Income maximization is therefore said to be a conservation measure, rather than a danger to depletion of resources. If government would not attempt to hold down the price the problem of conservation would solve itself!

The conservationist debate then turns on whether the social willingness to postpone income is the same as the individual willingnesses. Let us say that individuals are more impatient than society as a whole. Then the market rate of interest will be higher than the social rate. Since an owner of a natural resource compares the rate of return he can get by saving his property for future sale at a higher price with the rate of interest the market offers on the investment of proceeds of immediate sale, he will be tempted to conserve less and deplete his resource more rapidly than society would wish.

Those arguing for limits to growth are in effect maintaining that the social welfare function dealing with the production over time should consider a lower rate of interest than the consensus of private interest. Basically this is a normative argument in which conservationists express their time preferences and their opponents advocate the social rate of interest they prefer.

Externalities add a further dimension to the debate. Ezra Mishan has recently argued that social costs must be included in the calculation as well as the shadow prices of depleted resources.[4] This brings us back to the issues discussed earlier in this chapter. It may be that when the costs of pollution and crowded living are included in the calculation, increasing national income will move us beyond the pollution possibility frontier that we wish to maintain. That is to say, the fixed resource in our time may be clean air and living space rather than Ricardo's land.

The real issues in this debate are where ought the frontier to be drawn and how may an economy adapt to it. The first question is clearly one of value judgements. Mishan would argue that traditional life styles ought to be weighed heavily in society's values and increasing supplies of consumer and producer goods tend to erode these ill-defined but very important considerations. He would insist that pollution was so damaging that national income ought to be severely restricted rather than allowing it to continue. Of course he is opposed by those who argue for the increase in the material well being of the population based on an increasing flow of goods and services.[5]

The second question of adaptation turns on the ability of society to internalize the costs of pollution. If it is possible to include all the social costs in the decisions of producers and consumers, then the market economy is capable of finding the Pareto optimal solution in the social sense of the word. If this should prove impossible, then Mishan's medicine or restricting the private incentive would have wider appeal.

There is one final aspect to this issue, which must be dealt with in Chapter 15, which discusses economic growth. It will be shown there that macro-economic considerations of employment are involved in no growth policies. Wealthy societies tend to save a high proportion of their national income. For these savings not to represent unsalable goods, there must be a correspondingly high level of investment in new machinery and other capital goods. In turn, investment depends on the belief of firms that the new equipment will really be needed – that is, national income will grow.

[4] See, for instance, E. J. Mishan, *Growth, The Price We Pay* (1969) or his *The Costs of Economic Growth*.
[5] An attempt to estimate whether welfare has increased in recent years taking social costs into account is in W. Nordhaus and J. Tobin, *Economic Growth*. These authors conclude that real welfare has increased by using the income that people forego by living in rural or less polluted areas as a measure of the opportunity cost of the negative externalities.

Consequently, the alternatives that Mishan's analysis presents us are either to find a way to reduce the propensity of the population to save, or to face the danger of severe unemployment resulting from a glut of unsold product. After reading Chapter 15 the reader might well return to Mishan's proposals and reconsider the alternatives facing the industrialized world.

Exercise:
(1) How might monopolistic (oligopolistic) elements in the production and sale of petroleum affect its price and conservation?
(2) Review the argument for Pareto optimality of a market solution in which the two final uses are petroleum today and petroleum tomorrow. What would be the production possibility frontier if the price of petroleum were expected to be constant for each year? What would be the revenue line taking the market rate of interest into account? Draw society's indifference curves and show the solution it would choose. By what measures do you think the social choice ought to be effected?
(3) Look back to Chapter 1 in which the interest rate was used to discount future income in order to compute present value. Explain that the statement that the market rate of interest may be lower than the social rate amounts to the difference between the market rate of discount of interest and the social rate of discount. What would happen to the present value of an asset which produced a given stream of income for a long period of time, but which might be discounted at these different rates? How might this affect the conservation of that asset? How might a lower rate of discount affect the length of time over which one would use that asset, extracting less income each year but for more years?
(4) How might problems of conservation over time work in different social systems?
(5) Show how the interest of unborn generations can be reflected in the present value of a long lived asset sold on the market. Discuss whether the social and market rates of interest (discount) diverge when the time horizon is very long.
(6) How might the uncertainty about market risks affect social and market rates of discount? Do you believe this factor ought to be considered in conservation policy?
(7) Write an essay on the distribution of the benefits of clean air by showing how it might pass from being available to all as a public good when it is not an effective constraint, to being a private good when places with clean air become expensive and remote holiday resorts. Explain how resources in excess supply may have no shadow price, yet are capable of being used and perhaps used up to the point where they do have a price.

Part 3 Macroeconomics:
income, employment
and prices at home and in
the world economy

12 Money

The problem stated

Thus far our analysis has not mentioned money. Perhaps this has seemed odd to the reader, but it is the shadow prices that express the realities lying behind the 'money veil', not the more familiar money prices. The underlying realities are the relationships between technical possibilities of production and consumers' desires for goods. Prices have been expressed in relative terms, the ratio at which goods exchange, even though it has been convenient from time to time to think of one of the goods as money.

In this chapter we have three tasks. First, we must discover what money is, how it is created and how destroyed. Second, we must translate from shadow prices to prices stated in money terms. Finally, we must ask if money is a neutral counting device or if the use of money has opened the Pandora's box of instability, unemployment and inflation.

What is money?

Human beings exhibit a lamentable propensity to construe processes and functions as if they were things. Primitive man needed a rain god fetish to account for the weather. The Greeks invented Venus to prompt what Freud later told us we do naturally. Even Aristotle's great scientific mind sometimes expressed itself in terms of essences which were 'in things' determining their character. The gold fetish dies hardest of all. Even relatively sophisticated persons believe that the value of money is related to its 'gold backing' in some sense, despite the fact that historically almost every good which has a positive exchange value has at some time served as money: lumps of iron, salt, cattle, wives, sea shells, as well as gold and silver.

In our day, the objects of value that serve as money are the debt of governments and banks. That is to say, the money supply consists of currency in the form of pound notes, and accounts held in banks that may be transferred by cheque or withdrawn in the form of currency. People believe that these debts will be paid in a form which will be exchangeable for the real backing of money, the goods and services that money can buy from apricots to zithers. Hence they serve as money. Believing can make it so.

Money, then, is a convenient standard object of value which performs the following four functions:

1 *Money is a medium of exchange.* Money is needed because other goods are inconvenient to exchange. A farmer is not likely to exchange his truckload of pigs directly for two tickets to the cinema, so money enters as an intermediate stage in the exchange process. Goods are exchanged for whatever commodity is called money, and then money is exchanged for the desired goods. A commodity serves better as money if it is easier to exchange. Perhaps it would be better to say that some goods are more money-like than others, rather than to attempt a distinction between money and not-money. Money is an adjective, not a noun. Money-like goods are said to be more *liquid*.

Perfectly liquid money, then, would be a commodity that is universally desired. In fact, once a commodity is believed to be money, society builds it into a fetish, seemingly desired for its own sake and identified with liquidity. It becomes universally desired because it can buy anything. Gold bricks, bits of paper or computer records of bank deposits have been exchangeable for everything because people believe them to be money. Society chooses the money commodity in a convenient form, appropriate to the size and nature of its markets. It must be sufficiently durable, readily recognized, divisible into appropriate amounts, easy to transport. The quantity of money must be adjustable to meet the needs of trade.

Query: Describe circumstances in which the fetishism of money might collapse? Could it happen to gold money? Is it irrational to hold a fetishistic belief that pound notes are money?

2 *Money serves as a means of payment.* Pound notes are a special sort of money. They are *legal tender.* One can offer (tender) such *currency* and compel its acceptance in payment of debt. Creditors may not refuse to accept these pieces of paper as they may decline payment by cheque.

Most of the money supply is not legal tender, but includes *current accounts* in banks as well as other liquid assets. Current accounts are assets which may be transferred from one person to another by simply writing an order to one's bank to do so in the form of a cheque. This money constitutes over three-fourths of the UK money supply and transacts an ever higher per cent of the nation's business. Current account deposits usually serve perfectly well as a means of payment, even though they do not qualify as legal tender.

Query: How can money serve as a means of paying debts, when the most important money is itself a debt of banks and even currency is a debt of the Bank of England?

3 *Money serves as a standard of value.* Money is needed as a standard to make economic decisions. It converts relative prices of the myriad of goods into a single, comparable, standard. Money is the commodity given the value unity – be it a bit of gold, a green piece of paper marked £1 and printed with the Queen's likeness, or a bookkeeping entry. Without a standard, decisions about buying one good would require consideration of the shadow prices of all the others individually. Simple societies can do this, but our world is too complicated.

4 *Money serves as a store of value.* People use money to store their wealth as well as using it as a medium of exchange. These two functions are related, since the money ought not depreciate in value between the time of a sale and subsequent purchase if it is to function as a medium of exchange. Even though the money commodity is physically durable, it might nonetheless depreciate in value. If prices rise then the value of the money commodity falls. Under conditions of *inflation* – rising prices – currency and deposits function less well as a store of value. Under conditions of *deflation* – falling prices – the value of money increases.

The important fact about debt is that it does not have to be paid right away. That makes it possible for an honest man to make out more promises to pay than he presently has the means to pay. This is perfectly legal. Farmers sell promises to deliver wheat or oats in the future, even though the crop is not yet planted. Professors contract to deliver lectures that exist only potentially in their heads. Trading in promises only gets a person in trouble if he cannot deliver when they come due. Since the debt of banks serves as money, is it possible for bankers to write out more promises to pay (deposits) than they have currency? Can they lend out this money at interest? Certainly. Only a prudent reserve need be held against the deposits which make up the debts of banks. Not everyone wants to withdraw his deposits at once. Some people are depositing money as others are claiming it. Only a *fractional reserve* need be maintained to cover situations in which withdrawals may temporarily exceed new deposits.

Since deposits are the core of the modern money supply, we must study the banking system to understand how this deposit money is created, and how the money supply is regulated by the Bank of England through control over reserves. A bank is one of several types of firms that operate as *financial intermediaries*, middlemen who borrow from some individuals and lend to others. A bank borrows by accepting deposits, and lends in the form of overdrafts or loans. Part of the function of a financial intermediary is to collect funds and make them available in convenient amounts and times. More importantly, by dealing with many borrowers, such a firm is able to convert its risk of loss through non-repayment of loans to a fairly predictable business expense. Thus a bank's ability to repay its depositors – those who have loaned it money – is usually not critically injured by a borrower's failure to pay. Individuals who might be asked to lend directly most frequently would not be able to accept the risk of default and would either refuse to lend, or would lend only at high rates of interest. Since the risk of default by a bank on deposits is so small, it is able to borrow (accept deposits) at low rates of interest and lend at somewhat higher rates. The financial intermediaries collect the difference between these two rates of interest as payment for the service of interposing their much better credit standing between the ultimate lender and the borrower. This is not just a paper transaction, for it serves the economic purpose of pooling the risks and thus serves to reduce them to manageable proportions.

There are all sorts of financial intermediaries. Savings banks, small loan companies and pawnbrokers are all engaged in the business of lending other people's money. Commercial banks do even more: They create the current account money in the process of lending. When a bank lends, say, £1000 to its customer it simply says: 'Now the deposit in your account is increased by £1000. Start spending!' Alternatively, the bank may lend by permitting its customer to write overdrafts creating the deposits as it is required to honour cheques. There are limits to the bank's ability to do this which we shall study. The important point to see now is that money has been created at the stroke of the banker's pen. One may object: the commercial bank seems to have made something out of nothing. Yes it has, for it has promised to deliver money in greater quantity than it has on hand. But as long as a prudent reserve is maintained against the possibility that some depositors may wish to withdraw more money than is deposited by others, the bank is safe. There is no reason why an ordinary, privately owned, commercial bank should not create new deposit money, as well as accept deposits of existing funds from the public.

A bank's business is, as we have said, putting its credit standing between borrower and lender. It promises to keep the depositors' wealth at a high level of liquidity. Each time a bank lends, it gives a highly liquid asset, its own promise to pay cheques drawn on current accounts, in exchange for promissary notes, the less liquid promises to pay of borrowers. The promises to pay which the bank accepts come in various forms. Firms sign notes or write overdrafts for short-term private borrowing; they issue gilt-edged stock for long-term loans; banks may also lend to the Treasury by buying government stocks or bills. A bank is *solvent* as long as good sound promises to pay match the deposit debt created. Each time it lends, the bank earns interest, but it becomes a bit less liquid. Liquidity has been traded for earnings.

We said earlier that money-ness is a matter of degree, so that it is difficult to decide what is money and what is not. The notes and high grade stock taken by banks are less liquid than currency or deposits. They are less money-like. Nevertheless they are still much more liquid than, say, real estate, or sacks of potatoes. Should the depositors clamour for their cash in amounts that threaten the prudent reserve, bankers could convert these earning assets into cash with relative ease. They might sell them or they might use them as collateral to borrow the needed cash from other financial institutions. Such highly liquid assets are somewhat shamefacedly called *near money* by economists, who are unwilling to accept them as money because ultimate payment is deferred into the future when these loans become due.

A much more awkward decision about the definition of money concerns *deposit accounts*. These accounts draw interest like near money, and in fact the depositor may legally be asked to wait for a short period before his money may be withdrawn. However, this option is seldom utilized, so such

Table 12.1   The UK money stock as of 16 January 1974
(millions of pounds)

Notes and coins in circulation with the public	£4,238	
Sterling current account deposits with banks	8,781	
Less 60% of transit items	600	
Money stock, M_1		12,419
Sterling deposit accounts with banks	18,100	
Sterling deposit accounts with discount houses	168	
Other currency accounts	1,475	
Public sector deposits	664	
	20,407	
Money stock, M_3		£32,826

Source: Bank of England Quarterly Bulletin (March 1974), Table 12/1.

funds can be used as a means of payment with only the nuisance of making the withdrawal. The function of money as a store of value, on the other hand, is much more closely related to interest earning deposit accounts rather than to current accounts. Deposit accounts have risen very rapidly and now outstrip current accounts. In practice, two definitions of the money stock are used and reported in the *Bank of England Quarterly Bulletin* (Table 12.1): M_1 is the narrower definition – notes and coins in circulation plus current accounts (minus a portion (60 per cent) of the cheques still in the process of collection called *transit items*); M_3 adds to this sterling deposit accounts with banks and discount houses, deposits in foreign currencies, and the deposits of the public sector. In most of the rest of this section we shall analyse M_1, leaving the increasing divergence between M_3 and M_1 for later study (M_2 is not widely used or reported).

The creation and control of the money supply

Current account money is spent when a depositor draws a cheque. Let us assume that he writes a cheque on bank A in favour of someone who deposits it in bank B. Bank A is indebted to bank B, who is now also indebted to the depositor. When bank A pays bank B for the cheque, it is said to be *cleared*. Direct inter-bank payment of many millions of pounds of bank clearings is, of course, ridiculous. The thought of messengers dashing from bank to bank with great fistfulls of cash and cheques boggles the mind. It is much more sensible to pay through a *clearing house association*.

The London commercial banks are sometimes called *clearing banks* because they are members of the London Clearing House. Banks daily collect their cheques, and their representatives meet to exchange claims so that only balancing payments must be made. For instance, suppose the City had only three banks – inevitably named A, B, and C. Each bank comes to the clearing house with cheques payable to the others. Table 12.2 shows the amount each bank named in the rows owes to the others shown in the columns. The amount due each column bank from the others is therefore shown in the columns.

Bank A is seen to owe £250 million to the other banks. It is also owed £375 million. It has a net claim of £125 million. Bank B owes exactly as much as it has due from others. Bank C owes £275 million, and has claims of £150 million, and owes £125 million. The easy way of resolving the balance would be for C to pay the £125 million to A, thereby effectively clearing £875 million in cheques.

The process can be facilitated even further if each member of the clearing house keeps deposits with a bankers' bank, a *central bank*. In the UK the Bank of England is the central bank. Then there need be no actual transfer

Table 12.2 Clearing house
(millions of pounds)

		Money due from other banks			Total owed
		A	B	C	
Money	A	—	150	100	250
owed	B	300	—	50	350
other	C	75	200	—	275
banks					
Total due		375	350	150	Row totals = 875
					Column totals = 875

of funds. All that has to be done is to *shift deposits* in the books of the central bank. Cheque clearing is reduced to a bookkeeping transaction.

In most countries the deposits of commercial banks with the central bank form an important part of their reserves. In turn, as we shall presently see, the size of the reserves in commercial banks determines the amount of deposit money they can create. In the interest of simplicity, we will illustrate the money creation process as if commercial bank reserves consisted entirely of deposits held at the central bank. This is not entirely the case in Britain where some of the near money liquid assets may also be counted, but we shall introduce this complication after the main principle has been established. We shall see how the money supply depends both on the amount of bank reserves, and on the prudent ratio of reserves to deposits maintained by commercial banks.

Again for simplicity imagine first the case of a small country with a single bank firm. Assume that all payments are made by cheque and that no funds flow to neighbouring countries. That is to say, suppose that all payments are simply bookkeeping entries made in the single bank, and there are no *leakages* of funds in the form of withdrawals of deposits in the form of currency, or foreign transfers. How much current account money could the bank create? Obviously an indefinitely large amount, since by the assumptions made nobody would ever draw out any of its reserves. Consequently, its deposit liabilities to depositors would not be limited by a reserve shortage.

Once we admit that leakages are possible then the money supply is limited. People might want to convert their current accounts faster than others were depositing currency in the bank. A reasonable safety margin for the bank would be to maintain a reserve ratio equal to, say, 20 per cent of its deposits. A little bit of algebra tells us how much money could be maintained with a given amount of reserves. Let M be the amount of money in the form of demand deposits. Let R be the amount of reserves either in the form of cash in the bank vault, or, more important, deposits with the central bank. Then $20\% \times M = R$ and $M = R/20\%$ or $M = 5R$. The bank could create five times as much money as it has reserves.

Exercise: Assume the reserve ratio is 20 per cent. If the bank held £1000 in reserve, how much could it hold in current deposits? Repeat with ratios of 10 per cent and 30 per cent. Why would a bank want to have a large amount of demand deposits? If the bank had £500,000 in deposits, how big would its reserves have to be?

Taken together the many banks making up the banking system for a nation act as if they were a single bank. This is so even though the existence of several banks presents different reserve problems to the individual bankers, for whom there is no longer any reason to believe that cheques drawn against deposits a bank creates will be deposited back in the same bank. Each banker must reckon on the likelihood that when the cheques have cleared he will have to transfer reserves to another bank equal to the amount of the new money.

Imagine that bank A has £100 in current account deposits and £100 on deposit in the Bank of England as reserves. Its balance sheet appears as follows:

Balance sheet bank A

Assets	Liabilities
£100 reserves on deposit at Bank of England	£100 deposits

The books balance, of course, but the banker is not earning income. He must lend in order to earn. How much can he lend on the assumption that a loan will result in cheques being drawn on his bank and deposited in another bank? Prudence requires that the banker lend no more than would maintain his reserve ratio after the new deposits were withdrawn. To maintain a reserve ratio of, say, 20 per cent the bank can lend only an additional £80, or 80 per cent of his reserve. It creates a current deposit of £80 in exchange for a loan or overdraft of £80. The bank has added an £80 liability and an £80 asset. The books still balance.

Balance sheet bank A

Assets	Liabilities
£100 reserves	£100 + £80 = £180 deposits
£80 loans (or overdraft)	

Then, after cheques have been drawn against the loan, deposited in another bank and cleared, the books of bank A will be reduced in liabilities by the £80 no longer owing the depositor. A like amount will have been deducted from the reserves that have been transferred to the second bank through the clearing house. The balance sheet continues to balance:

Balance sheet bank A

Assets	Liabilities
£20 reserves	£100 deposits
£80 loans	

But now the bank has only £20 reserves against £100 deposits. It may not lend any further. The net result of the transaction has been to convert £100 of no-interest deposits with the Bank of England into £80 of interest earning loans plus the remaining £20 reserves.

In the process, £80 of new deposits were created, and deposited in bank B. Bank B now has £80 of new reserves, matching £80 current account deposit liability:

Balance sheet bank B

Assets	Liabilities
£80 reserves	£80 deposits

Bank B can lend out 80 per cent of its new reserves. It creates £64 of new deposits. They are deposited in bank C. After the deposits are created, spent and cleared, the balance sheet of bank B is:

Balance sheet bank B

Assets	Liabilities
£16 reserves	£80 deposits
£64 loans	

In the process bank B has created £64 of deposit money which ultimately went to bank C. Bank C repeats the same calculation as the preceding banks. It lends out 80 per cent of its new reserves against its deposits. The new deposits of C go on to bank D, and so on indefinitely. Each bank creates a new amount of money, 80 per cent as big as the preceding bank.

Query: How much money can be created by bank D?

How much money in all has been created, including the original £100 deposit in bank A? We have one of those infinite geometric series, each term is a multiple (80 per cent) of the preceding one. The sum of the series is the created current account deposits.

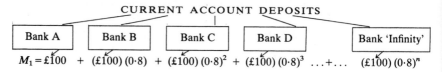

CURRENT ACCOUNT DEPOSITS

| Bank A | Bank B | Bank C | Bank D | Bank 'Infinity' |

$$M_1 = £100 \quad + \quad (£100)(0\cdot8) \quad + \quad (£100)(0\cdot8)^2 \quad + \quad (£100)(0\cdot8)^3 \quad\ldots+\ldots \quad (£100)(0\cdot8)^n$$

The sum of the infinite geometric series $S = a + ar + ar^2 + ar^3 \ldots + \ldots ar^n$ is $[1/(1-r)]a$, provided r is less than 1. In our banking problem, a represents the £100 reserve: r is the 80 per cent of reserves in each bank that go into new loans. The sum is the additional money, M;

$$M = \frac{1}{1-0\cdot8}(100) = \frac{£100}{0\cdot2} = 5 \times £100 = £500.$$

The term $1/(1-r)$ is called the *bank multiplier*. If r is 80 per cent, the multiplier is 5. Algebraically, it behaves like all the multiplier examples we have studied previously. The total of the infinite series of repeated bank deposits is exactly equal to what happened with only one bank in a closed system.

Exercise:
(1) Would the bank multiplier be different if borrowers decided to withdraw cash from the banks that lent them money instead of writing cheques?
(2) Suppose bankers become more cautious and decide to keep a higher reserve ratio. What will happen to the money supply? Give a numerical illustration.
(3) Suppose people decline to borrow all that banks are willing to lend because there is no profitable way of using the money. What would happen to the money supply?

It is clear that a nation's central bank has enormous power to control the money supply by manipulating the amount of reserves in the hands of the banks, and by regulating the ratio of reserves to deposits which commercial banks must keep. A small change in reserves results in a large, multiplied, change in the money supply. Reserves are called *high powered money* for just this reason. When the central bank lends reserves to commercial banks it creates deposits in favour of these banks in the books of the central bank, just as the commercial banker does when he lends to his customers. The central bank creates the high powered money. These created deposits then are the basis for further expansion by the bank multiplier process.

A classic tool of governmental monetary policy is the terms under which central banks lend. The rate which the Bank of England charged was called the *bank rate* for many years, but under new circumstances which we will describe in the next section it is called the *minimum lending rate* (MLR). A low interest rate charge by the central bank served to encourage borrowing by commercial banks and to increase the money supply. High bank rates resulted in net repayment of previous loans back to the central bank and reduction in the money supply.

Central banks have also found a more direct way to alter the reserves in the hands of commercial banks – *open market operations*. Under the circumstances described in this section where bank reserves are deposits with the central bank, the central bank can enter into the market for the near money debt of government, local authorities and commerce held by banks and others. When the central bank buys some of these assets, it pays in the form of a cheque drawn on itself. Thus it creates an additional deposit with the central bank that ultimately is owned by some commercial bank. If the securities had been bought directly from a commercial bank, it would have been credited with a deposit with the central bank at once; if the purchase had been made from a private individual or firm, the cheque would have been deposited with a commercial bank which, upon clearing, would acquire the deposit with the central bank. Thus, without waiting for banks to borrow reserves, the central bank can foist them upon the bankers. These reserves are then lent and re-lent until the multiplier process has worked itself out. When a central bank sells securities, the process is reversed. As cheques made out in favour of the central bank clear, the deposits of commercial banks with it are reduced, and the reserve base of the money supply is contracted.

The banking system in Britain has always departed from this model because the reserves of commercial banks have not been simply deposits with the Bank of England. Moreover, recent changes have tended to enable commercial banks to count various forms of near money as reserves even more than they had been in the past. We shall review this, but the important principle of open market operations remains. When the central bank buys up less liquid assets and at the same time increases the amount of more highly liquid ones that can be counted as reserves, it expands the base of the money supply. This is certainly so when buying securities in exchange for deposits at the central bank, but it is also true in the more complicated present circumstances. The reverse is also true, that the liquidity of the commercial banks can be reduced by selling less liquid assets and reducing the amount of those that can count as reserves.

In addition to altering the amount of the reserve assets, the central bank can adjust the money supply by altering the ratio of reserves to deposits, the *reserve ratio*, r. Thus in the formula $M = [1/(1-r)]a$, an increase in r will reduce the size of the multiplier and effectively reduce the money supply with the same amount of reserves. This principle has also been applied in special ways in Britain.

The way in which banks use their money creating power also is susceptible to the pressure and direction of the central bank by what is politely called *qualitative guidance,* or *moral suasion.* This pressure is effective for a simple reason. Banks are in the fractional reserve business of lending other people's money. No matter how stable and solvent, they never know when they will have to borrow to meet the demands of their depositors. Of course the central banker stands ready as the *lender of last resort* to avert a financial panic by providing reserves through loans and open market operations. Nonetheless, if banks are forced to borrow this can be expensive, especially if the central banker wants to make it so by charging a high bank rate. Moreover, commercial bankers know that the central bank has the power to create a climate of monetary ease or tightness by the instruments discussed. Consequently banks adjust themselves to the climate they expect to face, which very frequently is exactly what the central bank wishes to see come about.

For instance, if the Bank of England were making statement after statement about the danger of inflation, the need to keep interest rates up to attract foreign funds and the desirability of restricting loans of a more risky sort, this would be a clear signal that clearing banks ought to restrict their lending policies and increase their liquid reserve position. Sometimes the Bank of England 'requests' that they do so. These speeches and 'requests' are a clear signal that credit is going to be tightened. Often the central bank need not act further. If the bankers believe credit is going to be tight, they will act to limit loans and thus bring the tight credit result about. The central bankers can manipulate the market in subtle ways through this self-fulfilling prophecy.

In addition to its informal pressures, central banks are frequently charged with a list of *direct controls* over the creation and use of the money supply. Typically these are *selective controls* aimed at particular problem areas. Thus the Bank of England controls hire purchase terms. Perhaps more importantly, it regulates the foreign exchange transactions which involve the flow of funds in and out of Britain.

In summary, central banks are charged with the control over the money supply, largely through the regulation of the use of high powered money. This is accomplished by the exercise of five instruments:

1 The lending of reserves to commercial banks at a rate of interest determined or influenced by the central bank.
2 Open market operations which increase or decrease the supply of reserves which form the base of the money supply.

3 Regulations regarding the ratio of reserves to deposits.
4 Qualitative guidance or moral suasion.
5 Direct controls.

The way in which these instruments are used varies from country to country as a result of the differing history and banking procedures which they have developed. Nonetheless, the principles involved are the same, and with a little patience can be discerned in the monetary institutions of every nation.

Money and banking in Britain

Until recently British central banking more or less followed the pattern of controls described in the previous section; it involved peculiarly British financial institutions, but the main role of the bank rate, open market operations, reserve ratios and so on were plainly at work in the classical manner. This system had been under criticism for many years for two basic reasons which were to be remedied by the 1971 reform called *competition and credit control* (CCC).

One criticism of the traditional system was its tendency to identify the liquidity of commercial banks largely with their deposits with the Bank of England rather than with the general liquidity of their portfolio of assets. Thus the Bank of England required that clearing banks maintain an 8 per cent *cash ratio* reserve against deposits in the form of cash in vault and deposits with the Bank of England. To be sure, the central bank also required that commercial banks maintain a *liquid assets ratio* of approximately 30 per cent against deposits, but the existence of the second standard did not serve to make the cash ratio any less binding. Clearly, if the distinction between money and near money is an arbitrary one, it made little sense to insist on the particular form of cash reserves. A bank with highly liquid assets held in other forms might be perfectly able to sustain a lower cash ratio since the assets could be readily converted to cash at short notice.

A second criticism was that the rate of interest was excessively controlled by the Bank of England through setting the bank rate. As we studied in Chapter 10, the interest rate has a profound significance as a signal to firms. It is the price to which firms react in deciding whether to increase their stock of capital. If the rate is high, firms are discouraged from investing further, and if it is low investment is stimulated. Under competition in the capital market the rate was itself to be determined by the productive opportunities for the use of capital constituting the demand for savings, and the willingness of people to postpone their consumption which underlay the supply. Now if the central bank were to set the rate at which financial institutions borrowed, the effect would be to have the Bank of England set the interest rate rather than supply and demand. To be sure the central bank attempted to consider the market forces at work, but there was always the element of administrative setting of this critical factor price not reflective of the shadow price of capital.

The new system can best be understood by comparison with the old. Prior to CCC, the cash reserves of clearing banks consisted of deposits with the Bank of England, and cash in vault. They did not include such near money as short-term debt of the government, *Treasury bills*, the *commercial bills* of private firms or those of local authorities. Indeed, it was through the influence that the Bank of England had on the interest charged for near money that it influenced the interest rate everywhere else.

When the government borrows it sells either long-term British government stocks or short-term Treasury bills. The form of the interest included in these instruments is different. 'Gilt edged' government stock specifies the principal of the loan (the *par value*) and an interest rate. Supposing that the stock had a par value of £100 and the stated rate of interest were 5 per cent, each year the owner would receive £5 interest. Of course the price at which the stock might be sold on the open market is subject to supply and demand. But no matter what the price on the market, the stock still says £100 and 5 per cent so the owner still receives £5 each year. As we explained in Chapter 1 and in its appendix, the price of the stock reflects what one would be willing to pay for £5 annually for the life of the bond, plus the final payment on maturity when such a date is specified.

Bills are different. They do not have a stated interest rate printed on them at all, although they do show a par value. They are simply promises to pay a fixed lump sum of money to the holder at a specified future date – usually one to three months. The interest payment takes the form of *discount houses* buying these bills from the Treasury at less than the stated nominal par value. They buy at a discount. Since the Treasury pays the par value on maturity, the discount is the interest payment.

Each week the Treasury sells a new batch of bills, either to borrow more funds, or to pay off other bills that have come due. If the price offered the Treasury is high – close to the par value – then the amount of the discount is small and a low rate of interest is being charged the government. Conversely, if the price of bills is low, the discount is high and so is the interest rate. The rate of interest is the amount of the discount divided by the price of the Bill, the amount of money actually loaned to the government by the discount houses.

Exercise:
(1) Calculate the effective interest rate of the £200 discount of a £10,000 three month bill.

Step 1: Compute the amount that the buyer of the bill actually lends the Treasury.

Step 2: Divide the £200 by this amount. This is the interest rate for three months. What is the annual rate of interest?

(2) Suppose the discount house in (1) were to sell the bill to a person after two months. How much would it sell for based on the same annual rate of interest as when it was purchased? What would he sell it for if the interest rate doubled? Halved?

(3) Suppose a gilt edged stock with a par value of £10,000 and 5 per cent interest rate were sold for £100 more than its face value. That is to say, suppose it sold at a *premium*. What would be the *effective rate of interest* (sometimes called the *yield*)? Compare the yield with the stated (*nominal*) interest rate.

(4) In what ways is a Treasury bill different from a pound note?

The Bank of England, the government Treasury and the discount houses are involved in what can best be described as a triangular love-hate relationship. The discount houses make themselves responsible to make a market for all the Treasury bills that the government wishes to sell. Whilst the bills may be sold to others, the discount houses tender a discounted price for the entire issue. They agree to take all the bills that the Treasury cannot sell elsewhere at a higher price, i.e. at a lower rate of interest. This is an important commitment in a country like Britain which has a heavy debt burden that has to be refinanced as the debt becomes due.

How can the discount houses be sure of the money to honour their commitment? Usually the discount houses borrow the money *at call* from commercial banks and other financial intermediaries. A *call loan* is one that must be repaid within twenty-four hours of demand by the lender. These loans are highly liquid investments for commercial banks. Should the discount house find it difficult to borrow from the banks, they can borrow from the Bank of England. The rate of interest they are charged used to be called the bank rate, and under CCC is now called the *minimum lending rate*.

In fact, then, the Bank of England creates funds in the form of deposits on itself, which it lends to discount houses simply by writing them a cheque. The security for the loan to the discount house is the Treasury bills which the discount house has purchased. Thus the Bank of England is printing and lending money which is re-lent to the Treasury. When the money is spent, the effect is to distribute the new deposit money in the Bank of England to commercial banks. As we have seen, these deposits constitute cash reserves which can then be multiplied up through the bank multiplier (new reserves are not created each time the Treasury borrows from the general public, but only when the bills are paid for by Bank of England loans to discount houses).

Thus the Bank of England supports the discount houses which in turn support the Treasury. The Bank of England urges the discount houses to borrow from the commercial banks, and sees itself as the *lender of last resort*. It will always lend to the discount houses, when they are in need, and they will always buy bills. Indirectly the Bank of England also serves as the lender of last resort to the commercial banks, for they are always able to call their loans out of the discount houses, who in turn can seek funds from the central bank.

The bank rate was a crucial instrument of central bank policy under the old system. By charging a higher rate it discouraged the discount houses from borrowing from the Bank of England and pushed them in the direction of seeking more of their call money from the commercial banks. As a result of this additional demand for funds, reserves were diverted from loans to other individuals and businesses. As the discount houses continued to write cheques drawn on commercial banks in favour of the central bank, reserves were thus drawn out of the banking system. The supply of money was contracted. Conversely, a low discount rate increased the money supply. Thus the Bank of England as the lender of last resort supported the other financial institutions, but it also was their disciplinarian. All the same, it could not be too strict a mentor, because it has to provide sufficient liquidity to permit the refinancing of the government debt as portions of it came due.

It is important to note that the Bank of England has been able to control the money supply or the rate of interest but not independently of each other. Raising the bank rate decreased the money supply but by charging more to discount houses and draining reserves from commercial banks the effect was to raise the interest rates. Conversely, decreasing the bank rate lowered interest rates, but only by increasing the base of the money supply. This same sort of relationship applied when the Bank of England engaged in *open market operations*, buying and selling bills rather than lending reserves. When it bought bills on the open market, it wrote cheques on itself which increased the supply of bank reserves, and hence the money supply. But it thereby raised the price of bills, reducing the discount, and thus lowering the interest rate. Selling bills worked in the opposite direction.

The new competition and credit control regulations make basic changes in the nature of commercial bank reserves and the way in which these reserves are provided by the Treasury and Bank of England. CCC provides much greater flexibility in banks' reserves. They may hold a wide variety of near money debt instrument for this purpose. Thus *eligible assets* that may be used as reserves are defined as balances with the Bank of England (other than *special deposits*, to be discussed shortly): Treasury bills, money at call,

British government stocks with less than one year to maturity, local authority and commercial bills, as well as a few smaller items. Money at call makes up over half of these reserves. *Eligible liabilities* are the deposits of the banks with some adjustment for foreign currency transactions and interbank deposits excluding some long-term deposits. The regulations call for banks to maintain no less than a $12\frac{1}{2}$ per cent of eligible reserve assets to eligible liabilities. Banks are under pressure to maintain the ratio close to 16 per cent, although recent experience has found it to be approximately 14 per cent.

The rationale for the new regulations is that the general liquidity of the clearing banks should be the basis for further money creation. Since the distinction between money and near money reserves is a vague one, the regulation looks toward the holding of reserves as a device for restraining the amount of money that banks can create, rather than as a cash reserve held against depositor's withdrawals. If banks are liquid in the overall sense, then they can easily convert their assets into currency without locking themselves into a restrictive form of reserves. Even though call loans and bills represent loans by the banks, they can serve as reserves as well. For assets to function well as reserves, the main requirement is that they must be scarce, yet sufficient to ensure an adequate yet not excessive money supply. There is no reason why reserves cannot be held in a near money form that earns interest.

The interest earning nature of reserves under CCC is the key to its functioning. Commercial banks may now buy reserves for the system by purchasing bills on their own account or lending call money to the discount houses so that they may buy them. A greater part of the burden of controlling the money supply now falls on the Treasury. The sale of new bills by the Treasury is not designed as an 'open market operation' designed to reduce the reserves of the banking system. On the contrary, it has the capacity to increase the amount of high powered money in the hands of banks. This is because the initial exchange between the Treasury selling bills to the banks for cash does not reduce the reserves of the banks. They can count the Treasury bills as reserves under the CCC regulations. However, as a result of the sale of the bills the Treasury has new money to spend which it can inject into the banking system as expenditures are made. Thus the new debt which the Treasury has created by the printing and sale of bills amounts to an increase in the money supply.

There is one great advantage to making money at call and bills for eligible reserve assets. Banks must bid competitively for reserves, and consequently the interest rate that they are willing to pay more nearly reflects the market demand for loans. It responds more automatically to the market determination of the productivity of capital and more flexibly to the needs of commerce. To be sure, the Treasury still maintains control of the supply side of the market for reserves and so it cannot be said that competition determines the rate of interest regardless of government policy. Nonetheless CCC is a step in that direction.

What does all of this make of the bank rate as an instrument of the Bank of England? A lot less. Whilst the Bank of England continues to lend to discount houses in return for their guarantee to make a market for the sale of government debt, the bank rate is supposed to follow the market for credit rather than dominate it. Accordingly the bank rate has had its name changed

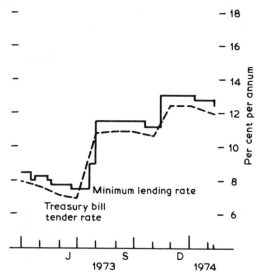

Figure 12.1 Short-term interest rates in London
(*Bank of England Quarterly Bulletin* (March 1974), p. 16)

to the minimum lending rate (MLR), and is to be $\frac{1}{2}$ per cent above the average rate of discount for Treasury bills at their most recent tender (Figure 12.1). The point is that variations in MLR are to be automatic and not to be interpreted as major policy signals by the Bank of England as in the past.

The new procedure also makes open market operations by the Bank of England a lot less important than they were when there was a sharp distinction between cash reserves and short-term debt. Under the new arrangement, if the Bank of England were to sell off some of these instruments from its portfolio it would not be reducing the reserves of the banks. The effect would simply be to trade reserves in the form of deposits with the Bank of England for reserves in the form of Treasury bills. Since both count as reserves, the reserve base of the money supply would not be affected. Of course, if the central bank were to go into the market and sell long-term securities – government stocks – then they would be trading assets that were not eligible as reserves for the deposits with the Bank of England that are eligible. In this way they could affect the money supply. The Bank of England does not like to enter into the long-term capital market. Since long-term rates reflect basic decisions to invest even more than short-term rates, such involvement will tend to distort decisions about capital equipment accumulation. While the Bank of England does intervene in the long-term market to correct disorderly or irregular variations in stock prices, it does not wish to do so as a matter of policy.

Whatever the gains in competitive determination of interest rates, CCC has resulted in a weakening of the traditional tools of control over the money supply. Particularly the wider definition of money, M_3, rose rapidly since its introduction, even though M_1 increased at a more moderate pace (Figure 12.2). While there are other causes for this development aside from the new

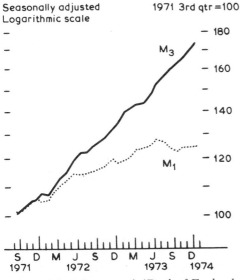

Figure 12.2   Money stock (*Bank of England Quarterly Bulletin* (March 1974), p. 13)

regulations, it is clear that the Bank of England is in some difficulty in controlling money.

In order to attempt to cope, the central bank has had recourse to its remaining instruments. Initially the central bank responded to the situation by altering the reserve ratio in the form of requiring special deposits of up to 2 per cent of commercial bank deposits to be held with the Bank of England. While these deposits earned interest at the Treasury bill rate, they were not available for lending and thus reduced the bank multiplier. In December

1973 the Bank of England attempted to reinforce this policy and direct it specifically at pressuring banks to reduce lending the components of M_3 to the private sector. Non-interest-bearing supplementary deposits are to be held with the central bank by banks (and other deposit taking financial intermediaries) if their interest-bearing eligible liabilities expand at more than an 'allowable rate'. There is a progressive scale for these deposits up to 50 per cent of the amount over the allowable rate.

Generally central banks in most countries have shied away from tinkering with reserve requirements. It has tended to be an inflexible tool. If the amount and frequency of changes is great, banks will tend to keep extra reserves as a precaution. Generally their use is a signal that substantial changes are required. The new scheme of progressive special deposits is an attempt to add flexibility to this tool now that it is difficult to use the others. Before we are in a position to examine this situation further, we must study the theory of money both as a means of expressing shadow prices and as an independent influence on economic events.

Exercise:
(1) Suppose the Bank of England increases special deposits by an average of 5 per cent. What would the change in the money supply be if the ratio of reserves to deposits were 15 per cent, and the volume of reserves were £5000 million?
(2) Suppose the Bank of England were to buy £1 million of long-term British government stocks. What would happen to the money supply if the ratio of reserves were 15 per cent?
(3) Write out the likely course of events if the *Bank of England Quarterly Bulletin* were to contain a leading article expressing concern over high levels of unemployment, excessive interest rates and the urgent need to stimulate the economy.
(4) Consult the *Bank of England Quarterly Bulletin* and find the current MLR. Has it risen or fallen in recent years? Explain the changes by comparing it with changes in prices, GNP and employment.
(5) Compare MLR with interest rates charged on other private and public debt. How closely have they moved together? How will you measure the degree of closeness?
(6) Suppose you were a businessman and the interest rate on long-term bonds you wished to sell was very high, but the money market for short-term obligations showed that small discounts were being charged. What would you do? Explain why long- and short-term debt interest charges tend to increase and decrease together.
(7) Explain why the pound note prominently displays the picture of the Queen next to the words 'I promise to pay the Bearer on Demand the

sum of One Pound'. The promise is signed by the Chief Cashier of the Bank of England. In what does the Cashier propose to pay?

Money prices and the value of money

Earlier in this chapter we commented on the fetishistic character of money. Originally deriving from an identification of a particular commodity such as gold with a universal medium of exchange, we saw how the belief that certain pieces of paper or bank deposits are money suffices to make them perform money's functions. Matters cannot rest at this point, because the really important question is: how much is a unit of money worth? That is to say, the belief that something is money is really a matter of degree. How much can one pound buy? To ask the question is to answer it. Obviously the value of money is nothing but the price of everything else! What is the money price of the commodities that money will buy? Recall that input-output analysis only told us the relative prices of goods, the shadow price ratio linking one to another. Now we need to link these prices to money as a standard.

In Chapter 4 we came to the conclusion that the relative prices of goods in a competitive market economy would be the slope of the 'labour' production possibility frontier. To analyse the nature of money we need not involve ourselves in the complications of several frontiers. Once more lumping all the factor inputs together as 'labour', the production possibility frontier in physical units is:

Theory	*Example*
$B = T_1 y_1 + T_2 y_2$	$50 = 0{\cdot}60 y_1 + 0{\cdot}51 y_2$

where the T_1 and T_2 are the labour directly and indirectly required per unit final use of each type. These physical amounts of labour could be translated into money terms by multiplying both sides of the equation by the wage rate:

$$wB = wT_1 y_1 + wT_2 y_2 \qquad 50w = 0{\cdot}60wy_1 + 0{\cdot}51wy_2$$

The prices of the two final uses could then be expressed as:

$$p_1 = wT_1 \qquad p_1 = 0{\cdot}60w$$

$$p_2 = wT_2 \qquad p_2 = 0{\cdot}51w$$

Is it possible to use these last two equations to solve for prices stated in money terms? Alas, no. We have two equations and three unknown quantities: p_1, p_2 and w, the prices of the two goods and the wage rate. The wage rate is the price of the primary input, labour. Obviously we cannot solve for all three without an additional equation. If we try to solve these equations simultaneously by eliminating one of the prices, we will arrive at one equation relating two prices.

Query: Show that this still involves only pairs of relative prices. List the possible price ratios and interpret them in economic terms.

There has to be an additional money equation to close the system of relative prices and arrive at money prices. This turns out to be a controversial question because money is a human invention and its behaviour has reflected different economic circumstances. It is not always easy to distinguish between the actual working of money under different situations from opinions as to how people feel money ought to work. We shall discuss three explanations of money that can be expressed in money equations, leaving it to the reader to form his own judgement over the controversies.

Commodity money

This is by far the simplest explanation, which only applies when a physical good such as a lump of metal is used as a unit of money. Thus the pound sterling originally was literally a pound of osterling (eastern) silver. By putting his stamp on a coin, the sovereign declares the price of so much metal to be equal to unity – that is, £1. Thus if silver is commodity 1, the money equation is simplicity itself: $p_1 = £1$. The first commodity is said to serve as the *numeraire*, or counting device serving as a standard of value. It is easy to continue the previous algebra to carry out the computation of the other prices:

Theory		*Example*
	Since:	
$p_1 = 1$		$p_1 = £1$
	and since	
$p_1 = wT_1$		$p_1 = 0.60w$
	then:	
$w = p_1/T_1$, so $w = 1/T_1$		$w = £1/0.60$, so $w = £1.67$
	Now solving for p_2:	
$p_2/p_1 = T_2/T_1$, so $p_2 = T_2/T_1$		$p_2/£1 = 0.51/0.60$, so $p_2 = £0.85$

We now have computed the prices of the two commodities and the wage rate of labour.

Labour as the numeraire – money illusion

The commodity money solution only makes sense when money consists of some produced good whose shadow price can then be assigned the value unity. Clearly such an explanation breaks down under modern circumstances when money consists of paper debts created by governments, banks and central banks. One has to find a way to link the paper money to goods.

In his famous book, *The General Theory of Employment, Interest and Money*, John Maynard Keynes suggested that the link was the wage rate. Especially during periods of depression and unemployment Keynes argued that workers accepted the going wage rate as normal, so that money wages tended to be unchanging – sticky – over a period of time. It is important to see in this what Keynes called 'money illusion'. That is to say, the wage rate is not the real income per hour of the worker – it is not his ability to buy food, clothing and shelter with his pay packet. So much money per hour was considered to be normal. The fetishistic character of money was transferred from gold to the labour market.

As a result workers would consider themselves worse off if money wages fell, even if prices also fell. They would bitterly resist a pay cut. Indeed it was this feature of workers' behaviour that made money wage rates sticky downward even during a period of depression. Partly as a result of habit and partly as a result of union wage agreements money illusion was so strong that wages could not be reduced in money terms. Moreover, even if the demand for labour were to increase, Keynes argued that money wage rates would not rise as long as there was a substantial amount of unemployment. He believed that the unemployed would rather take a job at the going wage than hold out for more money. Hence under unemployment conditions, wages would tend neither to rise nor fall. The money wage rate was simply given as a fact of life.

Now if money wage rates are fixed, labour becomes the numeraire. In the problem we have been discussing the money equation becomes $w = w^*$. In our numerical illustration let us take it that $w = £1·67$. The arbitrariness of this figure – designed by the author to make the results come out the same as our other solution – should serve to alert the reader to the fetishistic nature of a 'money illusion' solution to the problem. But so long as the belief in a certain wage rate holds, all the other prices are determined:

Theory	*Example*
$w = w^*$	$w = £1·67$
$p_1 = w^* T_1$	$p_1 = £1·67(0·60) = £1·00$
$p_2 = w^* T_2$	$p_2 = £1·67(0·51) = £0·85$

The price of each good is nothing but the wage rate times the amount of labour directly and indirectly employed in producing it. The amount of labour, in turn, is ultimately derived through the Leontief inverse from the technical coefficients of production. Prices are determined by the belief that wage rates are going to be what they seem always to have been. By determining prices, the element of belief in money wage rates also expresses a belief in the value of paper money.

Exercise:

(1) Suppose the wage rate were £3·00, what would be the prices of commodities 1 and 2?
(2) By real wages we mean the amount of goods that are bought with a given amount of money wages. What is the real wage rate in terms of the amount of commodity 1 that could be bought with £1·67? Commodity 2?
(3) Given fixed technology coefficients, what does sticky wages imply about the rigidity of prices?

Keynes's theory of the value of money was a crucial part of a larger analysis designed to cope with the unemployment of the interwar years. Money illusion was built into his picture of the supply and demand for labour (Figure 12.3). Employment (N) is measured horizontally and the wage rate is measured vertically. Keynes argued that the supply curve for labour, SS', is L-shaped; that is to say, it is horizontal up to the full employment level N_f. Once full employment is reached SS' turns sharply upward. This is a diagrammatic expression of Keynes's belief that more and more workers could be recalled to work without increased wage rates. As greater national income shifted the demand curves for labour to the right from Y_1 to Y_2 and so on, workers would prefer to get a job rather than remain unemployed in the hopes of getting a higher salary.

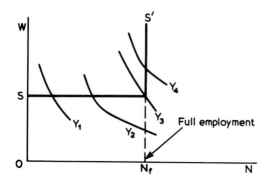

Figure 12.3

Once full employment had been attained at Y_3 the situation would be different. Employment could not be increased further by the very definition of full employment. If the demand for labour increased to Y_4 employers would bid against one another for the scarce labour. Unions would find their bargaining position much strengthened. Wages would rise, and so would prices. Increasing the final demand up to the point of full employment will not result in inflation, Keynes asserted; however, if final demand is so large that more labour is demanded than is available at the conventional wage, money illusion will break down and wages and prices will rise.

The standard 'classical' medicine for unemployment before Keynes was to work along one of the demand curves for labour rather than try to shift them. By allowing wages to fall during a depression as a result of the pressure of unemployment, prices of goods would fall and stimulate people to buy more of them, reducing unemployment. Also, momentarily putting aside our simplification of labour as the only factor of production, lowered wages would induce a substitution of cheaper labour for relatively more expensive capital and natural resources. Moreover, some workers would respond to lower wages by dropping out of the labour force, substituting leisure for wage income. This classic viewpoint relied upon the *substitution effect* rather than the income effect to make the labour market clear. More cheaper goods and factors of production are purchased as prices decline because it is possible to substitute them for dearer ones.

Keynes opposed this view. If his labour market diagram were correct, the downward stickiness of wages would prevent the substitution effect from bringing greater employment. Moreover, wages reductions might turn out to be counterproductive. Lower wage rates would reduce the incomes of workers since it is difficult to change technology quickly and substitute cheap labour intensive methods. Wage cuts would cause substantially the same number of workers to be earning lower wages. The substitution effect might be swamped by the income effect in which the demand curve for labour would be shifted to the left corresponding to the reduced demand for final use. Each gain in employment brought on by wage reductions would be more than matched by a corresponding loss of employment through the income effect. The only sensible way to fight unemployment, Keynes insisted, was to increase demand for final use. Business investment should be encouraged. Government should undertake programmes to spend money. If anything wages ought to be raised! What a startling idea!

Keynes's money illusion theory argument is certainly open to question. Why does money illusion settle at any given wage rate? What makes money wages change? Are workers so near sighted as to ignore prices while businessmen adjust prices sensibly to costs of production? In fairness the important thing to see is that Keynes was not addressing himself to long-run theoretical explanations. His main concern was the immediate problem of escaping from depression. One of the overriding realities with which he grappled was that in the short run wages change slowly. During the rapid downswing of business activity in a depression there is not much chance for wage rates to be renegotiated downward quickly enough to outweigh income effects and do much good. Moreover, whether or not wages are in fact subject to money illusion, a period of major depression was no time to start cracking down on trade unions. Politically that would be suicide. Better accept the going wage rates, he counselled, and find the way out of the collapse of incomes through increasing investment and government expenditures.

The quantity theory of money and its value

The notion that the value of money depends on the quantity of it in circulation is nothing but a restatement of supply and demand applied to money. An increase in the quantity of money supplied tends to reduce its value. Since the value of money is the price of everything else, the increase in the quantity of money would be responsible for inflation in prices. Conversely, a reduction in the quantity of money would increase the value of money and lower the average price level of everything else.

Query: What characteristics of the demand for money might frustrate this tendency?

The quantity theory of money can be summarized in the *equation of exchange, $MV = PT$.* The reader should pay close attention to the units in which the terms are defined:

M is the *quantity of money*, the number of pounds or dollars in existence.

V is the *velocity of money*, the number of times the stock of money is used in a given year. It is the turnover of the money stock, and is simply a pure number.

P is the *price of the average commodity*. Add up all the prices of all the goods sold, and then divide by the number of sales. P is in money units in the equation, although it is usually reported as a percentage of prices in some base year in official statistics. Such percentage figures are usually called *index numbers*.

T is the *number of transactions*, also a pure number.

A mini-example will illustrate the equation. Suppose the money supply is £10. Now suppose this M is used to buy one hat for £3, one hamburger for £1, three theatre tickets for a pound apiece, a book for £2 and two 50 pence bottles of aspirin. Then the whole money supply has been used once. There has been one turnover of the stock of money. We draw a silly picture to show this (Figure 12.4).

Suppose now that there were a second set of transactions. Those who received the cash spend it again. These are also shown in Figure 12.4. The

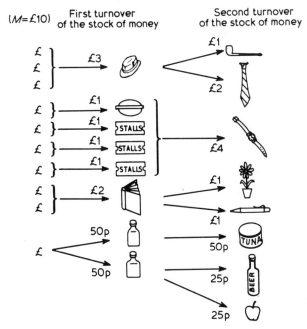

First turnover of the stock of money

Second turnover of the stock of money

(*M*=£10)

Figure 12.4

money stock has now been turned over a second time, so $V = 2$. The value of all the transactions is MV, the amount of money times the number of times which the stock of money has been turned over: £10×2 = £20.

Now we show that PT is also equal to the same value of all the transactions. The number of transactions, T, is 16, as can be seen by counting them in Figure 12.4. To find the average price, P, we add the prices of the goods sold and divide by 16. The sum of the prices is £20, so $P = £20/16 = £1·25$. It is easy to verify that $MV = PT$: £10×2 = £20 = £1·25×16.

The secret of the success of the equation of exchange is no secret. The turnover of the money supply is defined in such a way as to make MV equal to the value of all the transactions; similarly the price of the average commodity is also defined to make PT also equal to the value of all the transactions. After all, what did we really mean by 'using the money stock twice'? We used the money stock once as soon as £10 worth of goods were sold, and we used it again when another £10 were sold. Hence the turnover of the money supply is defined as the value of all the transactions divided by the stock of money. If the value of all the transactions had been £30, the turnover would have been 3 instead of 2. Since V equals the value of all the transactions divided by M, clearly multiplying V by M makes MV equal to the value of all the transactions.

Query: Explain how one would compute the number of times a grocer turned over his stock of merchandise in a year. Compare this definition to the turnover of money.

Similarly, the price of the average commodity is defined as the sum of all the prices of all the transactions divided by the total number of transactions. That is to say P equals the value of all the transactions divided by T. Multiplying P by T makes PT equal to the value of all the transactions. $MV = PT$ because the terms are defined to always be equal.[1]

Exercise:
(1) Let the quantity of money be £100, and let the number of turnovers of the stock of money be 5. What is the average price if there are twenty goods to be sold? What would be the effect if the quantity of money were to increase, but V and T were unchanged?
(2) Does the equation of exchange prove that an increase in the money supply always results in inflation?
(3) Distinguish clearly between the number of turnovers of the money stock and number of transactions.
(4) Using gross social product from the input-output transactions matrix as a measure of the total value of all transactions, and the size of M_1 for the same year, estimate the velocity of money. How would your results change if M_3 were used? What transactions are not included in gross social product that might enter into the value of all the transactions as defined in the equation of exchange?

The equation of exchange provides an explanation of how the economy closes the system of relative prices. If the sizes of M, V and T are given, the price of the average commodity is also determined, since $P = MV/T$. At the same time the average price is the sum of the individual prices of the various goods and services divided by the number of them. If there were only one unit each of the final uses and labour involved then $P = (p_1 + p_2 + w)/3$.[2] This average provides an alternative money equation to the two preceding explanations. It is easy to see how money prices are determined:

Theory	*Example*
Given M, V and T, find $P = MV/T$	Suppose $M = £6$, $V = 3$ and $T = 3$, then $P = £36/3 = £12$.

[1] Later we shall have occasion to relate the velocity of money to national income rather than the value of all the transactions. Then we shall make a distinction between *income velocity of money* and the present *transactions velocity*.
[2] Of course if more than one unit of each commodity were sold then the average price would be computed by weighting the price of each good by the number of goods sold. Thus if two units of the first commodity were sold and one of the others, $P = (p_1 + p_1 + p_2 + w)/4$, or $P = (2p_1 + p_2 + w)/4$.

The money equation needed to close the system is therefore:

$$P = (p_1 + p_2 + w)/3 \qquad\qquad P = £12 = (p_1 + p_2 + w)/3$$

The two *price equations* are:

$$p_1 = wT_1 \qquad\qquad p_1 = 0\cdot60w$$
$$p_2 = wT_2 \qquad\qquad p_2 = 0\cdot51w$$

The easiest way to find the solution is to substitute the price equations in the money equation and solve for w:

$$P = (wT_1 + wT_2 + w)/3 \qquad £12 = (0\cdot60w + 0\cdot51w + w)/3$$
$$P = (w(T_1 + T_2 + 1))/3 \qquad £12 = 2\cdot11w/3$$
$$w = 3P/(T_1 + T_2 + 1) \qquad w = £36/2\cdot11$$
$$\qquad\qquad\qquad\qquad\qquad w = £1\cdot71$$

Now substituting w in the price equations gives us p_1 and p_2:

$$p_1 = 3T_1P/(T_1 + T_2 + 1) \qquad p_1 = 0\cdot60 \times £1\cdot71, \text{ so } p_1 = £1\cdot03$$
$$p_2 = 3T_2P/(T_1 + T_2 + 1) \qquad p_2 = 0\cdot51 \times £1\cdot71, \text{ so } p_2 = £0\cdot87$$

The equation of exchange enables us to compute money prices from the relative prices given by the real sector of the economy. All we really need to know are M, V and T. The rest is arithmetic.

Exercise:
(1) What are p_1, p_2 and w if $M = £10$, $V = 20$, and $T = 3$.
(2) Repeat the derivation of p, p_2 and w if M and V are as given in the text, but T is 4, two units of commodity 1 being sold and one unit each of commodity 2 and labour.
(3) Show how prices would react to a doubling of the money supply, all other things remaining the same. Explain in terms of the equation of exchange and also in terms of supply and demand for goods.
(4) How would your explanation have to be changed if the velocity of money were cut in half?

The actual mechanics of the way in which the equation of exchange regulates average prices turns in a crucial way upon the supply of money as related to the demand for it. If more M is supplied than is needed to carry out transactions, individuals and businesses will find themselves holding more cash than they care to keep, and will attempt to buy more goods than are available. The result will be excess demand for goods and services and an inflationary result. Conversely, if less cash is available than can buy all the goods available at current prices, they will be in excess supply and prices fall. So the issue is: what is the supply. and demand for cash?

The equation of exchange forms the basis for discussing this question, since it can be written $M = PT/V$. The supply of money is given as M by the monetary authorities. The demand for it is PT/V, the value of annual transactions divided by the number of times the money stock can be used in a year. According to the traditional interpretation of the equation of exchange, it is P that adjusts so as to maintain the equality between the supply and demand for money. If that is so, it must be that the velocity of money, V, and the number of transactions, T, are somehow determined independently, largely unaffected by the influences of either the money supply on one hand or the price level on the other. The whole impact of money expansion or contraction is thrust upon changes in prices and not much else. Consequently we shall have to take a closer look at V and T, because it is upon these elements that the meaning and validity of the equaton of exchange will depend.

The debate over the equation of exchange turns out to be crucial in the division between the Keynesian advocacy of a managed economy to maintain full employment and the classical reliance on the market. To see this, note that T is closely related to the total final use. Of course, it is not the same, since the total number of transactions includes interindustry sales as well as transfer payments. One can make the relation precise by redefining the right hand side of the equation of exchange. Instead of T, we can use an average of the physical output going to final use. Symbolize this quantity by Q. The right hand side of $MV = PT$ becomes PQ, the value of final use. This is nothing but national income, which we shall indicate by the letter Y.

Hence, if total final use is determined by 'real' forces, rather than by monetary ones, then under conditions of perfect competition a nation will always tend to its production possibility frontier, and consequently the amount of final use will always be large enough to employ the entire labour force. If this is so, the Keynesian programme for management of the money supply is unnecessary, since only the money measure is affected while shadow prices and employment remain the same.

Since the right hand side of the equation of exchange has been adjusted, we must also fiddle the left to match by changing the meaning of the velocity of money. Earlier we had been discussing what strictly speaking is called the *transactions velocity* of money, the value of all the transactions divided by the money stock ($V = PT/M$). Replacing Q for T makes the measure of the value of money $V' = PQ/M$, or alternatively $V' = Y/M$. V' is called the *income velocity of money*, and $MV' = PQ$.

Query: Which is bigger, V or V'?

Believers in the quantity theory of money, often called *monetarists*, basically argue for the stability of V', which is said to relate to 'real' rather than monetary considerations. Confidence in the stability of V' turns crucially on the belief that people will use money only to transact the purchase of goods and services. V' will depend on the value of final use to be transacted, not on speculation as to future contingencies. Another way of saying this is that the amount of money that people and firms hold in the form of cash balances to do their business does not change capriciously or perversely. These balances depend on the national income to be transacted and the velocity of money embedded in customs of trade in paying bills, taxes and wages, as well as the slowly changing technology of making payment in the form of cheques, bankers orders, electronic accounting devices, credit cards and the like. Here again the value of paper money given by P involves an element of faith in the worth of the paper expressed in the stability of cash balances held.

Query: What would happen to V if the faith broke down?

The monetarist programme for dealing with unemployment can now be seen as the direct opposite of Keynes's call for government to add its demand in the public sector to make up for the flagging expenditure in the private sector. Their reasoning was another way of expressing the idea that if supply and demand are allowed to work the market will clear, and the depression would ultimately cure itself. Suppose, monetarists say, there were a temporary drop in physical output of goods, Q, and hence of employment. Manipulating the equation of exchange, $Q = MV'/P$. If V' is steady, and the monetary authorities maintain a stable money supply, the numerator MV' will remain constant. Denying the persistence of sticky wages in the face of competitive pressure, monetarists expect the price level, P, to fall. Hence Q as the ratio of MV' to P will be restored. The fall in prices is the equivalent of an increase in the real amount of money in the hands of the public.

The crucial question is whether V' in the numerator is stable. Originally, early quantity theorists assumed that it was simply constant. At least at first sight the depression seems not to show this to be the case. The graphs prepared for a recent very careful study using different definitions of money show the years of the Great Depression to have been a period of lowered income velocity (Figure 12.5). National income and employment collapsed during these catastrophic years in the UK, as they did elsewhere.

While such observations led Keynes to reject the constancy of V' and to look for more active participation of the government in maintaining full employment, the monetarists restated their belief in somewhat qualified form to account for the facts. The income velocity of money was subject to other considerations besides the stock of money and current levels of

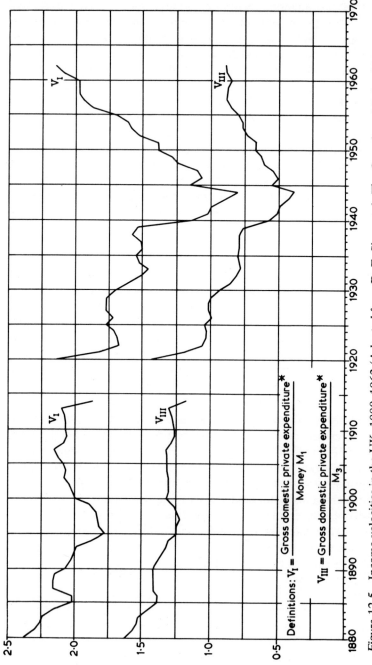

Figure 12.5 Income velocities in the UK, 1880–1962 (Adapted from D. E. Sheppard, *The Growth and Role of UK Financial Institutions 1880–1962* (1972), p. 50)

* Gross domestic private expenditure differs from GNP by the exclusion of government and foreign induced cash balances, and is more meaningful in the estimation of the velocity of money than GNP. In any case Sheppard made the calculations of V_1 and V_{111} using GNP as well and arrived at results similar to those exhibited in the graph.

national income. The influence of the interest rate as the cost associated with holding cash instead of interest bearing assets was conceded, as well as the effect of changes in the price level in determining the value of the money held. Perhaps most important, it was argued that the income velocity of money was related to what Milton Friedman called 'permanent income' rather than 'transitory income'. The former was related to the stock of productive wealth in the public's hands which was capable of producing income over a long period of time, whilst the latter depended on short-term fluctuations.

The main point of the monetarists' view and the statistics they marshal to support it is that the desire to hold cash is not a matter of speculation, but is in a stable relation to such 'real' elements as stock of wealth, the interest rate, and price changes. That is to say, the amount of wealth people wish to hold in the form of money is a limited amount. It can be satisfied by decreasing prices, thus increasing the value of money, or by producing more cash. Either way, 'money matters' as Professor Milton Friedman would put it.

Should governments, therefore, tinker with the money supply? Should central bankers distribute more reserves during a period of recession and contract the money supply during an inflationary period? Monetarists such as Friedman are most emphatic in denouncing such a procedure as leading to greater instability. Rather, they argue, the money supply ought to be allowed to grow as fast as real national income over the long run – say, 3 per cent per annum. Market changes in the price level will re-establish any disequilibrium. By the time the authorities were to act to increase M in a downswing, the recovery process will have already been under way. The net effect would be to increase M unduly, laying the basis for a greater inflation in the next upswing. Moreover, governments should not try to influence employment by expenditures in the public sector. Such programmes, he asserts, only serve to divert factors that would eventually be employed privately, the level of national income being strictly determined by the money supply times the stable velocity of money. Clearly, this issue is not an academic exercise at all. It is a nitty gritty problem of what to do to cure depression on one hand, and avoid inflation on the other.

Keynes and the changing demand for cash: the strength and weakness of monetary policy in dealing with depression and inflation

The Keynesian view of the demand for money was developed in the context of dealing with the inadequate demand for final use and hence for labour. Was it possible, he wondered, to increase demand by lowering the interest rate so that business borrowers will be induced to use bank funds to invest in additional capital equipment? Unfortunately, experience showed that if business prospects were bad interest rates would have to be very low indeed. Could they be driven low enough?

Put the matter in terms of the ability of central banks to flood the banking system with money, by lending reserves, open market operations and the like. We saw that such transactions served to lower the rate of interest. Can the repeated production of money serve to lower the interest rate to almost nothing? Or would the banks decide to hold on to unlimited idle liquid reserves rather than lend on such a basis? Keynes thought the latter possibility was more realistic during the 1930s. Indeed, the decision of the banks to hold their assets in more money-like liquid forms was representative of an even more widespread tendency to hold idle cash balances in virtually unlimited amounts.

Keynes called this phenomenon the *liquidity trap*. Unless significant interest income were sacrificed, he said, nobody gets bored with holding cash. Money does not spoil or decay. At some low interest rate, the demand for money becomes perfectly elastic, and an indefinite amount of it could be held at the minimum rate. If so, the income velocity of money was not stable. Low levels of national income could be associated with very large amounts of money, so that V' could become very low indeed. An increase in M would only cause a corresponding decline in V' so that MV' would not increase. There was no reason to believe that employment could be increased by increases in the money supply.

Before we spell out the Keynesian view of the demand for money, the reader should now see how important the money illusion argument was to the theory Keynes advocated. Clearly, with an unstable velocity of money, it was impossible for him to explain prices by means of the equation of exchange so he had to find another explanation. The convenient stickiness of wages and prices was also central to his disbelief in the monetarist doctrine that price declines would increase the value of the money held by the public to the point where they would start to spend and lend it again. Prices would not decrease sufficiently to guarantee that firms would go out and purchase new capital, or that consumers would buy goods and services.

Query: Why all the fuss about the liquidity trap? Doesn't everyone always want all the money he can get?

To explain his idea, Keynes discussed three motivations for holding cash balances: L_1, L_2, L_3.

L_1 is the *transactions demand* for cash that individuals and businesses need to carry on everyday business. It represents the total of 'cash in till' that people hold as they get ready to spend it for transactions in goods and services. The transactions demand is consistent with quantity theory of money. In fact, we can compute the transactions demand from the equation of exchange. The amount of money needed for transactions purposes is $L_1 = PQ/V'$. The higher the national income, the greater will be the amount of money needed.

L_2 is the *precautionary motive*, holding cash as a store of value against 'a rainy day'. Not much need be said about this component of total cash balances held. In the short run, we may take L_2 as a constant amount.

L_3, the *speculative motive* for holding cash, is more complex and causes the difficulty. Keynes discussed a simplified situation in which an actor on the economic stage is faced with the alternatives of either keeping his cash or buying an *earning asset* symbolized by a bond. The demand for a bond is really an expression of the willingness of a potential investor to give up the safe liquidity afforded by the cash in return for income from the earning asset. By making the alternatives of holding either cash or bonds, Keynes hoped to simplify his analysis. By lumping together all earning assets as bonds, he avoided discussing continuous gradations of liquidity investments ranging from near money to illiquid assets such as machinery or real estate. Bonds were said to earn income, but were not liquid money. By simplifying his analysis in this way, Keynes managed to confuse quite a few economists, most students, and perhaps himself.

Before he buys the bond, Keynes observed, a lender has cash which could be held without risk and used any way he sees fit. But once he buys the bond, the lender has given up his liquid flexibility. If he wants to buy something else, he must first sell the bond. To be sure, buyers are to be had, but the price at which such assets may be sold is uncertain. If the price of the bonds has fallen in the meantime, he will lose money. Of course, if the price of bonds rises he may make money, but to take on the uncertainty about future income a person must be offered the promise of interest payment. It is important to realize that Keynes's demand for cash is really a simplified reflection of a desire to protect oneself against uncertainty. The payment for bearing of uncertainty is the interest paid of bonds.

We saw in Chapter 1 how the price of bonds depends on the interest rate. Consider only the case of a *perpetual* bond, such as the UK War Loan stock, which will not be paid off but sold as a claim on interest income. Long-term bonds of twenty or thirty years or durable assets do not differ a great deal from these perpetual bonds. The bond represents rights to i amount of income each year. If the market rate of interest is r, then we can calculate the market price of the bond. The price, A, will adjust so that it is equal to any other new asset earning the same market rate of interest and yielding the same income. That means $Ar = i$. It follows that $A = i/r$. The bond is equal in price to the income generated, divided by the going market rate of interest. All this means that if a potential investor expects the rate of interest to rise, in effect he expects the price of his bonds to fall. If he expects the interest rate to fall, the price of bonds is expected to rise.

Query: If $i = £10$, and $r = 10$ per cent, compute A. Now suppose r falls to 5 per cent, what is A? Suppose r rises to 20 per cent. What is A?

How do such considerations affect the amount of cash that a person will hold for speculative purposes? If he expects the interest rate to rise, he will be expecting the price of bonds to fall, and therefore will not buy bonds, but will convert his assets into cash. If he expects that interest rates will fall, he will be anticipating an increase in bond prices, and will be willing to transfer his cash into bonds in the hope of making a gain. Conversely, if interest rates are high, people will expect them to fall; therefore, their speculative motive for holding cash will be small. They will speculate on future bond price increases by buying bonds. On the other hand, if interest rates are low, they may be expected to hold a great deal of cash rather than bonds because interest rates are likely to rise. To buy bonds when the price is high means taking a chance that bond prices will fall and loss will be incurred.

Another way of looking at this is the speculative demand curve for liquidity, L_3. Liquidity is the demand for the freedom that one has by not owning a bond. Interest is the price that one has to pay for the freedom money brings because interest is the income foregone by holding cash. At high interest rates very little cash will be held, because the interest tempts individuals into buying bonds. At low interest rates, a great deal of cash money will be held since it is not worthwhile to take the market risk of holding bonds. The demand curve for liquidity is like any other market demand curve. The price of liquidity is the interest rate. The quantity involved is the speculative cash balances, L_3. Sometimes this curve is called the *liquidity preference curve* (Figure 12.6).

Suppose the amount of cash available for speculative holding in liquid form is indicated by L_3^* (the total cash stock minus L_1 and L_2). We draw the supply curve of cash as a vertical line at L_3^*, to indicate that the stock of cash available is created by the authorities at their discretion; their decisions may or may not depend on the market rate of interest. The interest rate at which the supply and demand for cash is available for liquidity purposes is r^*. If the central bank were to increase the quantity of money to provide L_3^{**}, the interest rate would fall to r^{**}. If banks and individuals have more cash on hand, they will be willing to accept a lower interest inducement to part with some of it in exchange for bonds. They will be more willing to lend if their demand for liquidity is more nearly satisfied.

Now come the crunch. Can the liquidity demand for cash be completely satisfied? If so, the interest rate could be forced down close to zero simply by increasing the money supply (Figure 12.7(a)). Then the demand for cash

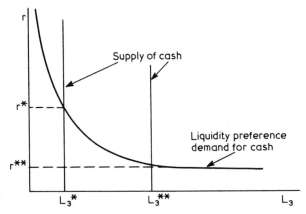

Figure 12.6   Speculative demand and supply for money

would be satiable, and the liquidity preference curve would touch the horizontal axis at some point like L_3^{**} where people are sick of money! On the other hand, if the demand for cash were insatiable (Figure 12.7(b)), it would mean that the liquidity preference demand curve never touches the horizontal axis, but becomes horizontal at some low interest rates. Under these conditions the interest rate could not be reduced to zero by increasing the money available for speculative balances. Below some minimum rate of interest potential lenders will simply hold all the cash they get rather than lend it out. Increasing the supply of money in such a liquidity trap simply increases the idle cash in the hands of firms, businesses and banks.

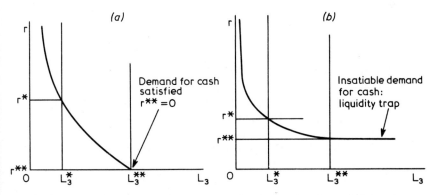

Figure 12.7   Satiable and insatiable speculative demand and supply for cash
(*a*) Satiable speculative demand
(*b*) Insatiable speculative demand

Query: Could the interest rate be negative?

Fundamentally, Keynes believed that there was a floor to the rate of interest because uncertainty is a permanent feature of economic life. In the simplified world of bonds versus money, bondholders can never be sure that the price of their assets will not fall. That is to say, they must always fear a rise in the rate of interest. In order to hedge against this possibility they hold some of their wealth in cash. The higher the price of bonds, the more real this danger becomes, the more people hold cash. Stated differently, the lower the interest rate becomes, the more nearly the bonds approach their maximum price where interest rates would be zero and bond prices have no place to go but down. As long as the uncertainty remained, Keynes felt that the interest rates could not be driven all the way to zero, and that a minimum must exist somewhere where all the additional cash that the authorities generate would be held in idle balances.

Query: Compare this explanation with the speculative demand for fish in the market period (Chapter 8).

Keynes's argument is made more relevant when the simplified picture of only two assets is relaxed. Instead of only bonds and money, we should think of a whole range of assets with varying degrees of liquidity. Some assets are more money-like than others since they can be more readily sold. This coincides with our fundamental understanding of money as the liquidity property of all assets. Because some uncertainty must always exist about the future value of these assets, the more liquid assets will provide an element of security by virtue of the fact that they can be quickly sold.

All of this means that if the liquidity trap exists as Keynes suggested, monetary policy cannot be relied upon to counteract a severe depression. The central bank can increase the money supply all it wishes, yet few will lend or invest in earning assets. Under very bad business conditions, when the risk is great, people clutch their cash rather than invest it at low return. If the authorities act very quickly before the depression gets too severe, a reduction in the interest rate resulting from increased liquidity can act as a stimulant to business. Nevertheless, it is too much to expect that monetary policy alone can do the job once a severe slump is well under way.

Money does not matter as much to Keynesians as to monetarists who focus on transactions demand and hence deny the existence of a liquidity trap. The issue should be tested by appeal to facts. Alas, facts are not very conclusive when exposed to statisticians. The present best evidence is against a liquidity trap. It seems not to be the case under conditions of uncertainty in business affairs that people prefer indefinite amounts of cash to bonds. Of course, this conclusion depends on the rather narrow definition of the alternatives as money or bonds. It still seems plausible to many theorists that people prefer more liquid assets to less liquid ones under unstable conditions, so there are lower limits to interest rates.

If the extreme Keynesian view does not do so well against the facts, neither did the extreme quantity theory of money. On this view, the only demand for cash is the transactions demand which has nothing to do with interest rates. Testing against the facts has led the majority of economists (not all) to conclude that this is not so. If it were so, the velocity of money would be constant and a steady monetary policy would be all that is required to avoid both inflation and unemployment. Interest would be irrelevant.

The balance of present informed opinion is that the velocity of money does respond to the interest rate in a reasonably predictable way. Increasing the money supply does tend to reduce the velocity of money – increases the cash balances held by the public – but not to the point where an indefinitely large amount of cash is held as in a liquidity trap. There is some room for monetary policy to be effective in combating unemployment, but some of the increased money will be held in the form of larger cash balances that might prove difficult to reduce later on during the upswing in business activity.

Exercise:
(1) Show that the formula for the value of a bond can be applied to any earning asset. Show that uncertainty about the earnings can be translated into uncertainty about the market value of the asset. Does your analysis apply to durable consumer goods like refrigerators?
(2) Is it possible that businesses can have large cash balances, and yet be doing very badly? Was this the case during the depression?
(3) If national income falls, what happens to the transactions demand for cash? Will this lower the interest rate? Will it eliminate the liquidity trap?

The fall and rise of monetary policy

We started this chapter with what seemed to be a fairly straightforward trio of questions. What is money? What determines its value? Does the money supply affect the economy in any way other than performing the numeraire function of counting device? Perhaps to the dismay (disgust?) of the reader it first emerged that we were not sure precisely what money was, as distinct from near money. Then we offered three theories of the value of money – commodity money, wage rate – money illusion, and the quantity theory equation of exchange explanation. The last two were competitors for explaining the value of paper money associated with the Keynesians and monetarists respectively. Most disturbing, we discovered that these competing theories were closely linked with the influence of money on employment and prices. Surely experience should provide a clearer basis for passing judgement than we have advanced.

The conclusions drawn from the depression years represented a time of triumph for the Keynesian viewpoint. Belief in the self-regulating capacities of the market had been shattered. The need for government planning and supplementation of private demand to maintain full employment was accepted as a fact of life. Along with the loss of faith in the market regulation of prices came the easier acceptance of the stickiness of money wages as the habitually (or monopolistically) determined price of labour, and through rigid technical coefficients, the determination of the price of everything else. Especially in the short run, it seemed as good an explanation as any, in light of the apparent instability of V'.

A corollary of the Keynesian position was that the main danger facing the postwar economy was incipient depression rather than inflation. The important variable to be maintained in monetary policy was a low interest rate and the general liquidity of the financial system rather than the money supply. Manipulation of the money supply was seen as a means to an end, rather than the key variable to be controlled in its own right. This was the conclusion of the basic Radcliffe Report in 1959. A further commitment to low interest rates arose from the desire of the Bank of England (as well as most other central banks around the world) to refinance the debt of two world wars at modest interest costs. This put the Bank of England in the position of supporting the price of gilt edged securities whenever they tended to fall. This made for a ready market in government debt, but it also meant that the government had chosen not to control the cash reserves of banks. Any time they wished to convert gilt edged securities into cash they could be assured of doing so at no risk. Put bluntly, by concentrating on the interest rate, the Bank of England largely gave up control of the money supply.

Certainly this view was not accepted by the 'classical' economists who relied on the market for full employment. They looked for the underlying faith in the value of money to be expressed in the stable velocity of money. Looking at the same data over a long period of time, they argued that the depression experience was an aberration in the long-term consistency of V'. Indeed, they blamed the apparent variation in the income on the failure of the monetary authorities to realize that the stability of V' depended on permanent income. Consequently they pumped more money into the economy in an effort to rescue it from depression before long-term effects could be effective. The result was a self-fulfilling prophecy in which money was created more rapidly than national income could recoup and so it appeared that the velocity of money was unstable.

Alas both the Keynesian and monetarist views can be defended on factual grounds depending on whether one's focus is only short- or long-run considerations. Keynes liked to dismiss the problem with the quip, 'In the long run we are all dead'. The monetarists reply that the long run always comes and they point to the current worldwide inflation and say that it is here! They charge that the increase in the money supply built up by the short-run reaction to depression, the decision to finance wartime expenditures on a highly liquid low interest basis, and the continuation of increases in the money supply in support of postwar high levels of employment, have all unleashed the forces of inflation that they expected all along.

In attempting to wind down from the monetary stimulus in the past, the authorities have had to move carefully. Interest rates have risen to historically high levels as expectations of inflation have gradually been included in the rates that lenders charge borrowers. The result has been discouragement of investment and employment. At the same time the authorities have been unwilling to drastically reduce the money supply to fight inflation for fear of setting off still higher interest rates. Were the Treasury and the Bank of England to use all their monetary arsenal to stop the inflation, unemployment might well result. The Keynesian expectation that wages and prices are sticky downward has a basis in fact. Workers and businessmen can be expected to fight vigorously to maintain their position, which they view in money terms. 'Let somebody else take the first pay cut! Let the employers first lower prices, then we will lower wages!', say the unions. Businessmen reply, 'Let the unions lower the wages and then we will be able to lower prices!' Chickens and eggs are found everywhere in inflation. Drastically reducing demand might well reduce output and employment before it has an effect on price levels.

To be sure, monetary policy has an important role to play in controlling inflation. If the inflation can be caught early, before the expectations of permanent price rises become part of the national folklore, then monetary restraint has a bit more room to manoeuvre without triggering off a deflationary disaster. Once the cumulative spiral process of increasing wages and prices gets started, the problem becomes very difficult. Workers can argue that they are only trying to catch up with rising prices. Competitive industries raise their prices to reflect the increased costs. Oligopolies use the occasion as a justification to boost prices. The Bank has the ugly choice of providing funds to 'meet the needs of trade' and in effect assenting to inflation, or refusing to do so and accepting unemployment.

To sum up. Under depression conditions the prevailing Keynesian view was that the liquidity trap made manipulation of the money supply unable to cope with unemployment by sufficiently lowering the interest rate. Consequently, while Keynes looked to a minimum rate of interest as a tool for improving the situation he felt that a study had to be made of the structure of demand so that measures could be taken more directly by government to deal with unemployment. Why did consumers buy? Why do businessmen invest? What can be done to influence them in a positive way?

Under the present conditions of inflationary pressures, most nations in the world find that the alternatives seem to be acquiescence to accelerating inflation or unacceptable degrees of unemployment. It is necessary to examine aggregate demand and supply to see why this is so. To what extent is it possible to explain this in terms of the Keynesian apparatus? Should we be looking for a new analysis of the problems facing us? To what extent are the present problems an inheritance from past policies? We turn to these questions in our next chapter.

Exercise:
(1) Do you think inflation is harmful? Why? What do you think the Bank of England ought to do if inflation is accompanied by substantial unemployment – say 4 per cent?
(2) The following table shows instruments of central bank policy as columns and possible goals as rows. In each box indicate the way in which the instrument named in the column would be used to bring about the result shown in the row. If the instrument is inappropriate leave the box empty.

Instruments of central bank policy

Possible goals	Bank rate manipulation	Open market operations	Reserve requirement adjustment	Moral suasion	Selective controls
Increase in money supply					
Decrease in money supply					
Change interest rate					
Tighten credit without altering money supply					
Raise prices					
Lower prices					
Increase employment					

Possible goals	Bank rate manipulation	Open market operations	Reserve requirement adjustment	Moral suasion	Selective controls
Lower the cost of government borrowing					
Discourage spending abroad					
Discourage real estate loans					
Discourage speculation					
Increase the velocity of money					
Encourage economic growth					
Prevent bank runs					
Smooth out seasonal shortages of credit					
Encourage saving					
Encourage the market to make best use of resources in production					

(3) (*a*) Suppose after inverting a Leontief matrix you get the $X = (I-A)^{-1}Y$ to be:

$$X_1 = 1 \cdot 5 y_1 + 3 \cdot 00 y_2$$
$$X_2 = 0 \cdot 5 y_1 + 1 \cdot 75 y_2$$

Suppose the amount of labour directly needed per unit physical output of X_1 were $0 \cdot 1$, and per unit of X_2 were $0 \cdot 5$. Derive:
(i) The production possibility frontier.

      (ii) The relative shadow prices of products 1 and 2.

    (*b*) Suppose we wish to close the input-output system of prices by the quantity theory of money. Let $M = 10$, $V = 5$ and $T = 25$. Compute the money prices of products 1 and 2 and the money wage rate (assume that only one unit each of products 1 and 2 and labour are sold).

(4) Is Andy (Figure 12.8) right?

Figure 12.8   (Daily Mirror Ltd, *Andy Capp* by Reggie Smythe, courtesy of Field Newspaper Syndicate)

(5) Explain to what extent the activities and policies of the Bank of England depend on its organization as a publicly owned central bank. How would it behave if it were privately owned? Make as convincing an argument as you can for a return to pre-war private ownership of the central bank. Explain why most countries have chosen the publicly owned system. Do you think they made the right choice?

13 The structure of aggregate demand: planning for full employment

Aggregate demand

Unadulterated by economics, common sense suggests that the limit to output is productive capacity. Supply considerations, such as production possibility constraints, are the obvious candidates for limits to national income rather than inadequate demand for final use. Indeed, orthodoxy before the 1930s was that 'supply would create its own demand', because the production of final use for sale is precisely equal to the factor incomes needed to purchase it.

The bitter experience of the interwar years was, however, that there was no assurance that the factor incomes would actually be spent, rather than held in the form of idle cash balances. To be sure, the identity of the value of final use and factor incomes holds by definition, but it seemed more reasonable to say that the demand for final use determined the employment of factors of production, rather than that the total availability of factors determined the output of final use. It was more reasonable to say that 'demand created its own supply'; the willingness of people to spend their idle money could easily be matched by the recall of idle factors of production.

J. M. Keynes's *The General Theory of Employment, Interest and Money*, and the tragic decade in which it was written, convinced the world that it was necessary to plan for adequate demand for final use. Such a plan was not particularly concerned with how much of each industry was to go to final use; rather, it was the total, aggregate demand for final use that was at issue. Keynes was concerned with *macroeconomics* to ensure adequate demand for labour and other factor inputs. The structure of demand that Keynes studied was classified not by industry, but by the sources of demand in consumption, investment, government and net export. These categories, when summed, equal the value of final use and hence national income. The analysis was carried on in terms of an essentially linear system, and so will prove familiar to the reader. We proceed by discussing the elements of demand one at a time.

Consumption

Keynes expected that in the long run the most important source of change in aggregate national consumption was the change in national income. He explained aggregate consumption for the whole country in terms of national income by means of the *consumption function*. This function is often written in linear form: $C = cY + A$. C is the consumption expenditure and Y is the income of individuals (for the present we will ignore the distinction between after-tax disposable personal income and national income, and call them both Y). The constant slope of the consumption function, c, is called by the horrendous name the *marginal propensity to consume*. Consumption is thus supposed to have two components, cY and A. The element that is increased by the *income effect* is cY, whilst A refers to the consumption that people do regardless of their income, their *autonomous consumption* (Figure 13.1).

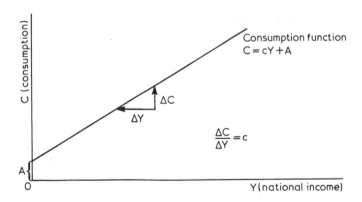

Figure 13.1   The consumption function

The ratio of the change in C compared to the change in Y is the slope of the consumption function, the marginal propensity to consume – that is to say, $C = \Delta C / \Delta Y$. The marginal propensity to consume was assumed to be less than unity because it is unlikely that an increase in income by £1 million would bring on an increase in consumption by more than £1 million, although that is conceivable. (When?) More likely, a portion of that increment in income would be consumed, and a portion not consumed, i.e. saved. The marginal propensity to consume was a positive fraction something like 80 or 90 per cent, depending on precisely which definition of national income was being used.

The element of autonomous consumption arises as a result of habitual and culturally established standards of living. Perhaps it is foolish to take the linear consumption function literally, and say that A is that element of C that would occur even if Y were zero because such a situation has never come about. Rather, the autonomous element should be interpreted as showing that, at sufficiently low levels of national income, total consumption might exceed national income. That is to say, a negative amount of the national income might be saved. That is not impossible. One may consume by drawing down on stocks of previously produced wealth and by receiving transfers from other countries through aid, war reparations, or imperial plunder (university students typically consume more than they earn by drawing on the local authority, using past savings, tapping the wealth of parents, borrowing and miscellaneous panhandling).

Keynes's speculation about the way people consume may be tested for the United Kingdom and United States by a *scatter diagram* (Figure 13.2). It is a plot of points representing consumption and corresponding disposable personal income for each year (points with higher consumption and income will be further from the origin of the graph even though they refer to years that occur earlier than points closer to the origin; thus 1929 was a boom year and showed higher values for C and Y than 1932 which was the depth of the Great Depression).

For both countries a scatter diagram is shown from the depression years.[1] The consumption function can be fitted close to the scatter of points by various statistical methods, although the reader may satisfy himself, by moving a ruler around the page, that the line drawn as the consumption function is as close to the points as any other. For the UK the figures are given *per capita*, so autonomous consumption turns out to be £22·8 per person, and the marginal propensity to consume is 0·65, much as Keynes anticipated.

Keynes used the consumption function to argue that, as national income rose during a period of prosperity, the percentage of final use taken by consumers declined. If other sources of demand were not forthcoming inadequate demand might well result in stagnant depression. At first sight it

---

[1] The depression began earlier in the UK than in the USA and terminated for both countries at the time of their entry into the Second World War.

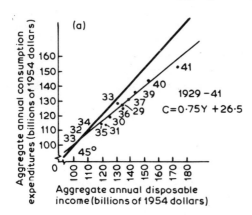

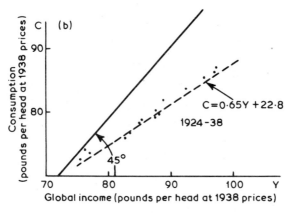

Figure 13.2   The consumption function for
pre-war years
(*a*) United States (G. Ackley, *Macroeconomic
       Theory* (1961), p. 225)
(*b*) United Kingdom (E. Malinvaud, *Statistical
       Methods of Econometrics* (Chicago, Rand
       McNally, 1966), p. 117)

may seem inconsistent to say that the marginal propensity to consume is
constant, and yet the percentage of consumption in national income, the
average propensity to consume, is declining. But the marginal propensity to
consume is the change in consumption compared to the change in income,
$c = \Delta C/\Delta Y$. The average propensity to consume a_c is the ratio of total
consumption to total income: $a_c = C/Y$ (see Chapter 1). The average can
be seen to fall as income rises even though the marginal is constant:

General theory	Example
$$C = cY + a$$	$$C = 0.75Y + 26.5$$

The marginal propensity to consume is constant: $c = 0.75$. The varying average propensity to consume, C/Y, can be found by dividing both sides of the consumption function equation by Y:

$$a_c = \frac{C}{Y} = c + \frac{A}{Y}$$	$$a_c = \frac{C}{Y} = 0.75 + \frac{26.5}{Y}$$

As income rises, the term A/Y gets smaller and smaller since the denominator rises while the numerator is constant. Hence

$$a_c = \frac{C}{Y} = c + \frac{A}{Y} \text{ falls as well.}$$

If $Y = 200$ then $C/Y = 0.75 + 0.13 = 0.88$ but if $Y = 400$, then $C/Y = 0.75 + 0.07 = 0.82$

Query: What is the average propensity to consume if $Y = £1000$?

Look at this important relationship graphically (Figure 13.3) by drawing a ray from the origin to some point (Y^*, C^*) on the consumption function. The slope of the ray is the ratio of the vertical height from the origin divided by the horizontal distance: C^*/Y^*. This is nothing but the average propensity to consume when income is Y^*. The slope of the ray is different from the slope of the consumption function itself. The slope of the ray is the average propensity to consume, while the slope of the consumption function is the *marginal* propensity to consume. Now suppose national income increases to Y^{**}. Consumption also increases. But the ray from the origin to

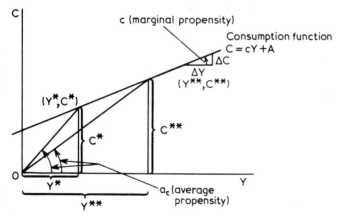

Figure 13.3 The average propensity to consume

(Y^{**}, C^{**}) is less steeply sloped. The average propensity to consume has fallen.

Exercise: Consider the consumption function $C = 0.8\,Y + 50$. Complete the following table:

Y	C	$c = \Delta C/\Delta Y$	$a_c = C/Y$
0			
100			
200			
300			
400			
500			
600			

Draw the graph of the consumption function. Draw the ray representing the average propensity to consume for $Y = 200, 400, 600$. Which changes faster, income or consumption? Why?

It is certainly safe to say that national income received by factors of production may be spent for consumer goods or it may not. Income that is not spent on consumption is called *savings*, S. Since $Y = C + S$, savings is defined as $S = Y - C$. We are not now concerned with the flow of funds that show exactly how the savings, i.e. the not consuming, takes place. People may put their money income in the bank. They may burn it. Firms may save by investing their income directly in capital equipment – a farmer may buy a tractor out of his receipts. Typically, however, saving is done by different people and for different reasons from those that invest. An engineering firm buys a lathe because it is profitable. If it has previously saved for the purchase, well and good; otherwise it borrows other people's savings from the banks, the stock exchange, and the like. An act of saving is not the same as an act of investment. Saving by one person does not amount to investment by another.

Query: (1) Would there be savings in a non-monetary economy? Would savings be automatically invested in such a society?

(2) Describe how the banks function to mobilize the savings of one group of persons to provide funds for the investments of others. Are all the savings invested?

We can relate the average propensity to consume to the *average propensity to save*, $a_s = S/Y$. Divide both sides of the identity $Y = C + S$ by Y. Then $1 = C/Y + S/Y$, or $a_c + a_s = 1$. The average propensity to consume plus the average propensity to save total 1 and $a_s = 1 - a_c$. That is, if the average propensity to consume is 0.8 or 80 per cent, the average propensity to save is 0.2 or 20 per cent. If the average propensity to consume rises, the average propensity to save falls. It follows that, if Keynes was right, the average propensity to save rises as national income grows. Through what means, Keynes asked, can be found a way to keep the growing proportion of savings active in hiring factors of production rather than languishing as unsold goods? Are crises of underconsumption inherent in capitalist money economies?

Exercise:
(1) We define the marginal propensity to save as $s = S/Y$. Continue the previous computational exercise by completing columns for:

$$S \quad s \quad a_s = 1$$

May savings be negative?
(2) A change in income can be written as the sum of the change in consumption plus the change in savings:

$$\Delta Y = \Delta C + \Delta S.$$

Derive the relationship between the marginal propensity to consume and the marginal propensity to save. If the marginal propensity to consume is constant, is the marginal propensity to save constant too? If the marginal propensity to consume were to rise, what would happen to the marginal propensity to save?

Let us present this crucial issue in graphic terms by introducing a convenient device, 'the 45° line', drawn at that angle through the origin (Figure 13.4). If we take any point on the 45° line such as (Y^*, C^*) and drop perpendiculars to each axis, we will have drawn a square with the 45° line as the diagonal. Squares are useful because their sides are equal. This income, Y^*, can be projected vertically by drawing a vertical line from Y^* to the 45° line. Y^* can then be compared with consumption, which is measured on the vertical axis.

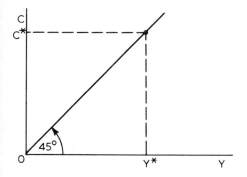

Figure 13.4   The 45° line

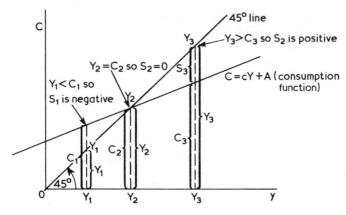

Figure 13.5 Consumption and savings

In Figure 13.5 we superimpose the consumption function on the 45° line. Then we may specify points on the income axis, and measure the same amount of expenditure vertically by reading up to the 45° line. For each level of income we may measure the amount of consumption that will take place by reading up to the consumption function. The difference between the two heights is the income that is not consumed, savings. Suppose that national income is at Y_3. How much of it will be consumed? Read up from Y_3 to the consumption function to see that C_3 will be spent on consumption. So the difference, S_3, is saved. If national income were lower, Y_2, then consumption would exactly equal income and savings would be nil. If income were still less, say Y_1, then consumption would exceed income and S_1 would be negative! It is obvious from the figure that as income rises the *savings gap* between income and consumption widens, even though consumption is rising. Furthermore, as we have shown, the declining average propensity to consume means that the proportion of savings in income is rising as well as its amount.

Exercise: Using a 45° line and the function $C = 0.8Y + 50$, graphically illustrate the result of this section. Compare with your earlier computations.

Determining national income

We are now in a position to understand an *equilibrium level of national income,* a position of rest when there is no tendency for it to move to another level. Solely for purposes of exposition, let us assume that the only demand is for consumption. Of course, investment, exports and government also provide demand, but these are to be brought in later. Then the only possible equilibrium is where consumer demand equals national income (in input-output terms, the only column of final use is consumption, so aggregate of consumption comprises the total demand for final use). All goods produced over and above the amount people will buy for consumption are not salable. In such a condition of disequilibrium, either output or prices will fall until consumer expenditure demand equals national product (if fewer goods are produced than are demanded, higher price and more output will result). The equilibrium level is where the value of consumption equals income: $C = Y$.

What sort of graph would represent all the possible equilibrium situations? That is to say, what is the graph of $C = Y$? The 45° line, of course. However, only one point of the 45° line is also consistent with the consumption function, their intersection (point $(Y_2 C_2)$ in Figure 13.5). To the right of this point, where income is higher, such as Y_3, more final use is produced than people are willing to buy. Unsold goods pile up and income falls. Consumption falls too, but since the marginal propensity to consume is less than 1, consumption declines less rapidly than income. Consequently, consumption demand catches up with national income at Y_2. Thus, if income were originally at Y_3, it would tend to return to equilibrium.

Conversely, income at Y_1 would tend to rise. People would be willing to buy C_1, but only Y_1 would be produced. More workers would be hired and final use increased. Since consumption increases more slowly than income, eventually income would catch up with consumption at Y_2.

Macroeconomic equilibrium can be stated usefully in terms of savings. If the only demand for final use is consumption, then savings represent new value produced but not sold. The equilibrium condition is where $S = 0$. But S is positive when national income exceeds Y_2 and is negative when it is less. Hence the equilibrium at income level is Y_2 where savings are nil.

Our pedagogical device of limiting demand to consumption is not completely far-fetched. There are very poor underdeveloped regions where virtually the entire final use must be devoted to consumption to avoid starvation and thus nothing can be saved. But actually we have a quite different circumstance in mind. A wealthy country does a great deal of saving, but the difficulty which may lead to depression lies in finding demand for those goods produced but not consumed. Aside from government and export demand, which are treated later, investment is the main sink for savings.

An act of investment in additional capital clearly involves an estimate on what the future is likely to bring. If capitalists expect greater sales they will need more equipment; if the expectations are for a slump in capital purchase will be postponed or dropped. Firms may even disinvest, by allowing the equipment to depreciate without replacement or repair.

What will be the equilibrium level of national income when investment demand is added to consumer demand? The equilibrium level of national income must be equal to the total demand for final use, $Y = C + I$. In Figure 13.6 we continue to show income Y on the horizontal axis, but now measure consumption plus investment vertically, so that the 45° line becomes $Y = C + I$, the locus of all possible points of equilibrium. The consistent point of equilibrium will be at Y^* where consumption plus investment demands

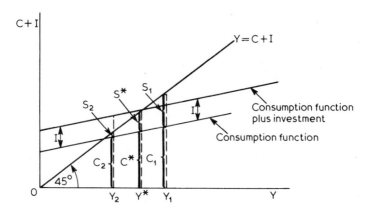

Figure 13.6   Equilibrium with investment demand

cross the 45° line. At Y^* the savings, S^*, is just matched by the investment: $S^* = I$. The banking system, the money market and the securities market are able to act as intermediaries and bring together the savings of some and put them to work as the investment of others.

Equilibrium is achieved much as before. If income were at Y_1, consumption would be C_1 and savings S_1. But income would fall because $C_1 + I$ would be less than Y, so goods would be unsalable. Investment would be insufficient to absorb S_1 savings. Income would fall towards the equilibrium value, Y^*, where $S^* = I$. Conversely, if income were at Y_2, savings would be S_2 and less than investment. Income would rise because there would be an excess demand for goods; $C_2 + I$ would be greater than Y_2 because firms intended to invest more than would be left over as savings after consumption were taken out of national income. Therefore:

Planned savings and investment[2]	National income
$S > I$	Falls
$S < I$	Rises
$S = I$	Equilibrium

One of Keynes's most striking conclusions was that an equilibrium level of income need not be at full employment. Much of the labour force might be unemployed, indefinitely! The days of reliance on self-regulation were over. To be sure, before *The General Theory* governments had reacted to the Depression by stimulating private investment and substituting public works projects for private spending. Nonetheless, *The General Theory* revolutionized the fundamental relationships between government and business by rationalizing government direction of a mixed market economy. Government no longer simply enforced the rules governing the pursuit of livelihood, but was committed to ensure that the pursuit would be successful.

Exercise: In the numerical example used in the exercises find the equilibrium level of income with no investment. Determine equilibrium income when investment is 30. What is the income when investment is 70? Which is bigger, the increase in investment or the increase in income? Can you tell why before it is explained in the next section?

The multipliers: direct and indirect demand

Demand for final use can be summarized in the form of two linear equations:

$C + I = Y$ is the equation for the 45° line.
$cY + A = C$ is the consumption function.

---

[2] There is a minor accounting bug here. The savings and investment we have been discussing are those planned by individuals and business. Yet planned investment decisions may not match the actual savings at all. If $S > I$, goods are unsold. However involuntary or undesired, such goods constitute an addition to stock and therefore must be counted as part of investment. The effect of unwanted goods is to curtail future output and income. Nevertheless, including as investment in stocks anything that is not sold makes the statistical tabulations of investment always equal to savings by identity. Since $Y \equiv C + I$ and $Y \equiv C + S$, $I \equiv S$ by the way the terms are defined. The identity does not mean that the economy is always in equilibrium.

Planned decisions are called *ex ante* savings or investment, and the actual events are called *ex post*. At equilibrium, of course, there is a matching of *ex ante* and *ex post* values effectuated by the process described in the test.

Exercise: In a firm's balance sheet are assets always equal to liabilities plus net worth *ex ante* or *ex post*?

This description of aggregate demand is strikingly similar to the structure of supply given by the balancing equations in the input-output analysis of production. It will be recalled that the goal of input-output was to determine equilibrium total outputs that were consistent with the final use. What determined the final use? We didn't concern ourself with that question, but simply took the information as a fact determined outside our analysis; desired final use was *exogenous* to our model of production. The required outputs of each industry were to be determined by the working out of the model; they were determined within the system, and are called *endogenous* variables. In the model of aggregate demand we take investment and autonomous consumption as brute facts given to us outside the system; I and A are exogenous. Consumption and income are determined within the system and so C and Y are endogenous. We shall now see that the analysis of national income equilibrium is nothing more than the simultaneous solution of the two linear equations, to find the endogenous consumption and national income generated directly and indirectly by the exogenous demand for investment and autonomous consumption.

Recall that at the penultimate step of input-output analysis we wrote the equations in Leontief form with the exogenously given quantities on the right hand side. Similarly, in the analysis of demand we rewrite the previous equations with I and A on the right hand side to get:

$$Y - C = I$$
$$-cY + C = A.$$

Detaching coefficients we can write these as a matrix equation:

$$\begin{bmatrix} 1 & -1 \\ -c & 1 \end{bmatrix} \begin{bmatrix} Y \\ C \end{bmatrix} = \begin{bmatrix} I \\ A \end{bmatrix}.$$

The next step is to invert the equations, solving for the endogenous variables, Y and C.

Theory	*Example* (assume $c = 0\cdot8$)
$Y - C = I$	$Y - C = I$
$-cY + C = A$	$-0\cdot8Y + C = A$

Add to eliminate C:

$Y - cY = I + A$	$Y - 0\cdot8Y = I + A$

Factor Y out on the left hand side and divide by $1 - c$:

$Y = \dfrac{A}{1-c} + \dfrac{A}{1-c}$	$Y = \dfrac{I}{0\cdot2} + \dfrac{A}{0\cdot2}$
	$Y = 5I + 5A$

To eliminate Y, multiply the first equation by c:

$$cY - cC = cI \quad \bigg| \quad 0.8Y - 0.8C = 0.8I$$

Add to the second equation to get:

$$C - cC = CI + A \quad \bigg| \quad C - 0.8C = 0.8I + A$$

Factoring C and dividing by $1-c$:

$$C = \frac{c}{1-c}I + \frac{1}{1-c}A. \quad \bigg| \quad C = \frac{0.8}{0.2}I + \frac{1}{0.2}A$$
$$\quad\quad\quad\quad\quad\quad\quad\quad\quad\quad\quad C = 4I + 5A$$

Collected together the solutions are:

$$Y = \frac{1}{1-c}I + \frac{1}{1-c}A \quad \bigg| \quad Y = 5I + 5A$$

$$C = \frac{c}{1-c}I + \frac{1}{1-c}A \quad \bigg| \quad C = 4I + 5A$$

The inverse matrix of demand is:

$$\begin{bmatrix} \dfrac{1}{1-c} & \dfrac{1}{1-c} \\[2ex] \dfrac{c}{1-c} & \dfrac{1}{1-c} \end{bmatrix} \begin{bmatrix} I \\ A \end{bmatrix} = \begin{bmatrix} Y \\ C \end{bmatrix} \quad \bigg| \quad \begin{bmatrix} 5 & 5 \\ 4 & 5 \end{bmatrix} \begin{bmatrix} I \\ A \end{bmatrix} = \begin{bmatrix} Y \\ C \end{bmatrix}$$

The inverse matrix of demand is a *table of multipliers* which tells what the level of Y and C will be when a programme of investment and autonomous consumption is carried on. The first row of the matrix shows how national income is determined by multiplying investment by $1/1-c$, and adding to autonomous consumption which also is multiplied by $1/1-c$. The first row is therefore made up of *income multipliers*. The second row permits us to compute consumption by multiplying investment by $c/1-c$ and adding to autonomous consumption multiplied by $1/1-c$. These are the *consumption multipliers* – notice that they are different for I and A.

It is possible to make much more elaborate tables of this sort by breaking the endogenous and exogenous variables down into smaller categories, including complicated monetary and tax variables, price changes, allowing for foreign trade and the like. The principle, however, remains as we have explained it. These are frequently called tables of *impact multipliers*, for they show how a change in one of the exogenous variables will be multiplied in its effect on the endogenous ones. Such studies are the basic instrument for planners attempting to regulate the economy.

Like the inverse Leontief table of production, the table of impact multi-pliers tells the ultimate direct and indirect result of an ongoing programme of investment and autonomous consumption. They shed considerable light on the way the economy works. In order to satisfy the exogenous original demand, factors of production are put to work. The income they bring home is purchasing power that they will use to buy consumer goods. But the consumer goods they buy constitute an additional demand for goods and services over and above the initial I and A. To satisfy this demand further national product is needed, adding further to national income. Thus direct demand for national product results in further indirect increases in con-sumption as incomes rise. The new indirect demand causes still more demand. The process goes on indefinitely. Where will it all end? The answer is that it converges to the matrix of multipliers just as it did in the input-output analysis of production. The step by step working out of this process is carried out in the appendix to this chapter, where it will be seen to be the result of a converging geometric series much like the series of adjustments in production (see Chapter 3). The working out of the multi-pliers takes some time. Obviously, there are lags involved between receiv-ing extra income and adjusting consumption. It appears to take a year for the bulk of the multiplier effect to be felt.

Exercise:
(1) In the matrix of multipliers derived in the text, let $I = 30$, and $A = 50$. Compute Y and C. Now increase I to 50, and repeat. Repeat with $I = 80$ and $A = 80$. By how much has income increased each time? Compare with the previous numerical results you have worked out.
(2) How are the multipliers going to be affected by a change in the marginal propensity to consume? Are the multipliers affected by a change in autonomous consumption?

Private investment and public spending

Since Keynes wrote, governments have accepted the necessity to plan aggregate demand at a high enough level to maintain full employment, and yet not so high as to cause inflation. The first step in such a procedure is to determine the desired level of national income, and then compute the level of exogenous expenditures required to produce it. Since autonomous con-sumption is usually considered beyond the reach of short-run manipulation, attention tends to focus on investment. If the investment level falls short of the required amount, there is said to be a *deflationary gap*; if there is an excess of investment planners speak of the *inflationary gap*.

Suppose, for instance, that the actual level of national income in the UK were £5 million less than is required for full employment. By how much would investment have to increase, i.e. what is the deflationary gap in investment? Since our table of impact multipliers shows that for a marginal propensity to consume of 0·8 the investment income multiplier is 5, the gap in investment is £1. A similar calculation could be made if it were desired to 'cool off' the economy, reducing national income by inhibiting investment.

Exercise:
(1) Suppose that the marginal propensity to consume is 0·9, and that investment is £20 million. What is national income? Suppose a national income of £80 million were required to maintain full employment; would the situation constitute a deflationary gap or inflationary gap? How big is the gap, and how much must investment be altered to eliminate it? Illustrate graphically.
(2) What is wrong with the crude underconsumption theory which explains depressions on the grounds that workers do not get back the full value they produce because employers receive profit incomes? Would raising wages avoid a depression?

Since investment is the engine that drives national income, what determines the level of investment? In Chapter 12 we said that it was supply and demand, along with the classical economists. In this view the supply of savings available was expected to react positively to the rate of interest; the investment demand for savings was inhibited by high interest rates. Thus the interest rate was the price of saving, on the one hand which induced people to postpone consumption, and the cost of investment on the other. At some equilibrium rate of interest saving and investment were equilibrated. The market for savings and investment cleared just like the market for peas.

We have already seen part of the reason for Keynes's distaste in this mechanism. Savings, he argued, were the result of income shifts, rather than of interest incentives. Keynes was only slightly less sceptical of the ability of interest rates to affect investment, especially in the short run. To be sure, at low rates of interest firms will find it less expensive to borrow and investment will be encouraged; high rates of interest will discourage investment. Firms will indeed invest until the interest rate is equal to the expected rate of return on investment – the *marginal efficiency of investment.* Nonetheless, Keynes remained unconvinced. The keyword to Keynes was one we left out of our analysis: '*expected*'. That is to say, it was not so much the abstract shadow price of installing an increment of capital in one's factory that mattered to a capitalist, but his belief that such an increment would earn a return commensurate with the interest cost in a world fraught with uncertainty and sometimes fear. By its very nature, investment is a venture into the future, an action in the present dependent on what might happen in the future. More than simple linear programming is involved in investment decisions. Keynes argued that the state of mind of potential investors is more likely to be the key to their spending on additional capital.

The shorter the time period for which planning takes place, the more the marginal efficiency of investment is dominated by the psychology of the investor. In the short run in which Keynes lived, if businessmen feel optimistic about the future, they will invest. As a result business may very well be booming; the investment will be multiplied up into increased national income demand for final use. The prophecy will be self-fulfilling. On the other hand, if businessmen feel that the uncertain future will not be so profitable, they will usually turn out to be right. Pessimism makes it so. When firms postpone investments, the level of income will fall through the multiplier. As we have explained, the reduction in investment will cause a further reduction in income. Businessmen will congratulate themselves on how astute they were to have foreseen all this before anybody else. Investment depends, some modern Keynesians say, on capitalist 'animal spirits'. Shifts in short-run psychology governing decisions to invest frequently swamp the modest effect of interest rate changes.

This *interest-inelasticity of investment* depends on the possibility of postponing or accelerating a planned programme of capital accumulation. Critics of Keynes's theory argue that the longer time goes on, the less the investment decision can be said to be one of mood and attitude. Keynes's point was that when a depression is precipitated it will bring about conditions that make pessimism self-justifying. The long run may never come.

During the Depression the Keynesian view was hard to fault. Governments were unable either to shift in the marginal efficiency of investment by reassurance, or to reduce the rate of interest below the liquidity trap level by increasing the money supply. Money did not much matter. It was necessary to try to escape from the depression by direct government expenditure to supplement private spending. Fiscal policy, the power of government to spend and tax, now must be included in our model as a third exogenous variable, G. In its simplest form we can discuss G in a situation in which there are no taxes to counteract the spending of government. Where would the money come from? Simple. Government may print it or, if the public is squeamish, do what amounts to the same thing, borrow it from the banks (an insight into tax-financed government expenditure will be found in an exercise in the end of this section).

Now we have a simple three sector model of demand to consider:

$$Y = C + I + G$$
$$C = cY + A$$

$G = G_0$, a constant amount of government spending.

It is very easy to manipulate this little model. Simply substitute G_0 in the last equation for G in the first one to indicate that government will spend G_0 amount of money. Government spending is then an exogenous input just like investment, and may be lumped together with it. Repeating the inversion we have gone through, it is easy to see that we have:

$$\begin{bmatrix} Y \\ C \end{bmatrix} = \begin{bmatrix} \dfrac{1}{1-c} & \dfrac{1}{1-c} \\ \dfrac{c}{1-c} & \dfrac{1}{1-c} \end{bmatrix} \begin{bmatrix} I+G_0 \\ A \end{bmatrix}.$$

The first row of this matrix equation is:

$$Y = \frac{1}{1-c}I + \frac{1}{1-c}G_0 + \frac{1}{1-c}A.$$

Government expenditures would act just like investment or autonomous consumption in raising income.

During the Depression governments attempted a programme of 'pump priming'. By pouring some government expenditure into the economic pump they hoped to increase national income by a multiple of the initial expenditures. Hopes went a bit further. By bringing about better business conditions in the form of greater national income, they expected that the programme would restore business confidence and trigger off more private investment as well. Orthodox as 'pump priming' is today, this Keynesian programme triggered off a storm of protest in the 1930s. It seemed absurd on the very face of the matter to attempt to 'spend ourselves rich'. Businesses were failing everywhere, government tax revenues declined, millions were unemployed. Yet Keynes advocated spending money!

Nonetheless, the Keynesian medicine was swallowed. It was learned that the fiscal problem of a nation was not the same as that of an individual or business. The whole is not the same as the sum of its parts. Government money spent within the country is not lost, but employs factors of production that otherwise would be idle. The problem in the Depression years was not that the nation was poor in the sense that it could not produce, but rather it did not have enough demand generated from its private sector. Individuals and businesses were not doing enough consumption and investment to employ all the factors of production. It was necessary for the government to spend, at least until private demand picked up.

At the time, many orthodox economists criticized the programme of government expenditures. Increasing the money supply would simply cause inflation. But that possibility seemed remote in 1936. Growing government debt to pay for the spending also aroused fears that the country was heading for bankruptcy. Would not an individual or business go bankrupt if it owed too much money? Surely the same held true for a nation. But, Keynes was able to argue, debt itself is nothing more than a means of channelling savings to a useful purpose. As a matter of course, business firms borrow as long as expectation of profit exceeds interest cost. Likewise government can borrow so long as it is willing to tax enough to pay the interest cost. Government could go further and create the money to pay the interest. In fact, in 1944 Evsey D. Domar showed that, as a result of the working of the multiplier, the tax rate would not have to be raised in per cent to pay the interest on most programmes of government spending. The increase in income would bring in more income taxes to pay for the interest that the borrowing cost.

With more than a little show of patronage, Keynes conceded that the inflation fears of the conventional wisdom would apply under full employment circumstances. Additional demand is no magic wand that permits output beyond the production possibility frontier of fully utilized resources. Increasing the money supply during a such a period does indeed result in inflation, with disastrous results. It may turn out to be very difficult to finance the government debt at anything but high interest rates. It is not impossible that there might be a loss of confidence in the ability of a government to pay the interest. Other nations might not want to hold the currency of a country with steadily rising prices and might try to convert their assets into the money of more stable nations. All this is true, Keynes agreed. Conventional economists were not simply stupid, but they were applying the wisdom of a full employment situation to a depression economy. Keynes's *General Theory* claimed to be general because it dealt with the Depression situation rather than restricting economic analyses to full employment.

Around the world Keynes's thinking became the new orthodoxy. Governments were committed to the maintenance of full employment levels of national income by instruments that they felt were adequate to do the job. In the next section we shall see some of the problems they have encountered.

Exercise:
(1) The world of Keynes may seem inside out because of the identification of limited demand as the source of poverty rather than insufficient productive resources. Indeed the *paradox of thrift* he advanced was that excessive savings can cause poverty because it might exceed investment plans and cause national income to fall.
   (*a*) Use the paradox of thrift to show how excessive *ex ante* plans to save can result in lower actual, *ex post*, savings.
   (*b*) Does the paradox of thrift apply to underdeveloped countries?
(2) How was the Second World War related to the recovery from the Depression? Can there be prosperity without war?

A tutorial exercise

Prove the *balanced budget multiplier theorem*, which states that even if government should take in taxes as much as it spends, national income will nonetheless increase by the amount of the tax.

Step 1: Enlarge the structure of demand by considering a new variable, T for taxation. Then the model becomes:
(a) $Y = C + I + G$. As before the demand for final use is C, I, G.
(b) $C = c(Y - T) + A$. Consumption depends on income earned by individuals less taxes (disposable personal income), plus A.
(c) $G = T$. Government spending equals taxes – the budget balances.

Step 2: Substitute T for G in the first equation to get $Y = C + I + T$ and rewrite the system of equations with exogenous I, A, G on the right hand side.

$$Y - C - T = I$$
$$-cY + C + cT = A$$
$$T = G$$

Express these in matrix terms.

Step 3: Invert by solving for the endogenous variables Y, C, T. Derive a matrix of multipliers. Show that the first equation of the inverse reads:

$$\frac{1}{1-c}I + \frac{1}{1-c}A + T = Y$$

Step 4: Show that Step 3 proves that if Y increases so does T by an equal amount. Write a short essay in which you explain why there may be inflation even though the budget is balanced at full employment. Illustrate by supposing that the marginal propensity to consume were 0.8, tax revenues were £100 million, investment £50 million, and autonomous consumption £50 million. What would happen if taxes and government spending both increased by 10 per cent? By how much would investment and autonomous consumption have to change to avoid inflation if the 10 per cent increase occurred at full employment?

Full employment and inflation

In the famous 1944 White Paper Britain's plans were laid for the management of aggregate demand to ensure postwar full employment and price stability. The programme operates on the basis of Treasury forecasts of economic trends made three times a year. The spring forecast is the immediate background for the annual budget proposed by the Chancellor of the Exchequer. It prescribes the government fiscal and monetary policy:

expenditures and taxes, subsidies and investment grants, and the line to be taken by the nationalized Bank of England.

Keynesian policy won a great victory by the very existence of such plans. Moreover it has avoided repetitions of the pre-war depressions due to inadequate demand. Yet there has also been a history of menacing inflation combined with sluggish growth. In an open economy this has also represented itself by recurrent international balance of payments problems which we shall study in a later chapter. Even more disturbing is the appearance of both unemployment and inflation. What would Keynes say to that?

After thirty-five years, Keynes's critics have had romp. The warnings of inflation by the 'classical economists', which seemed so ridiculous in 1936, may have come to pass. Monetarists point out that concern with maintaining the interest rate at low levels in order to eliminate unemployment amounts to an abandonment of control over the money supply. As they expected, the velocity of money returned to its normal levels, so MV spells inflation. Keynes's explanation of wages and prices by money illusion never made sense, they argue. In fact, as inflation continues money illusion is replaced with *money disillusion* as workers and employers expect prices to rise and make their contracts accordingly. Over the long run the velocity of money has been more stable than wage rates.

The critique goes further. The reason that the labour market does not clear even in the face of an inflationary gap is the result of the new Keynesian economics. By effectively promising that aggregate demand would be increased any time depression threatened, the way has been opened for more highly organized and powerful unions to win greater wage claims than they would if unemployment threatened them. Wages are sticky downward, but are flexible upward. Similarly, oligopolistic firms are able to raise their prices secure in the knowledge that they will not price themselves out of the market. 'Lame duck' firms in trouble may apply for government subsidy and investment grant assistance. Government, the argument goes, has simply underwritten the monopolistic and non-competitive elements in the economy. They cause the emergence of *cost-push* inflationary effects which supplement the *demand-pull* cause of inflation caused by excess demand. Government must increase the money supply to be sure that products are sold in order to prevent further unemployment. But, at the same time, for fear of uncontrolled inflation, the government does not dare to increase demand enough to bring the jobs to those workers and firms that are not already organized and politically powerful in the club. Too bad for those elements of society not in the club!

Classical economists go all the way with the argument. The guarantee of full employment to the highly organized, and minimum welfare to the rest, reduces the competitive pressures. As a result Britain faces inefficiency and sluggish growth. Productivity lags and real wages fail to increase as fast as expectations or comparison with other countries. There is little incentive to reorganize industry so as to take advantage of idle labour and other resources; similarly, there is less motivation for the workers in declining industries to move to new locations and skills. Unions and firms bicker over slices of meagre cake. The game is holding onto one's job or subsidized position, rather than risk a move to a new one. A more competitive economy, it is argued, would increase productivity and allow higher real wages without inflation. But this cannot be achieved as long as the Keynesian programme is the guide to public policy.

To be fair, Keynes was aware of the danger of inflation, but felt that it was remote as long as there was substantial unemployment. His supply curve for labour was horizontal at less than full employment and then turned up sharply. Ideally it was the heavy L-shaped curve drawn in Figure 13.7. Under unemployment conditions, Keynes argued that workers would prefer a job to holding out for higher wages. Thus the demand curve for labour could shift from Y_1 to Y_2 – in fact up to Y_f – without causing an increase in wages or prices over W^*. Y_f was the full employment level of national income that was supposed to be the goal of macroeconomic planning. Employment at N_f would represent full employment. If demand were excessive, say Y_3, then wages and prices would rise in a demand-pull inflationary situation.

In fact Keynes realized that there would be cost-push elements as well. Wages and prices would tend to rise before full employment was reached. Unions and oligopolies are able to take advantage of strengthened bargaining positions before absolutely everyone has found a job. Moreover, the

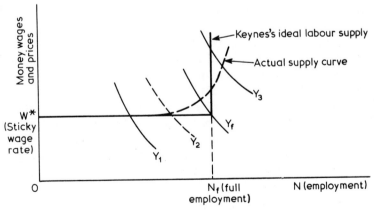

Figure 13.7   Keynes's supply and demand for labour

actual supply of labour (and other factors) is not one homogeneous entity. Consequently there may be shortages or bottlenecks of particular types of labour forcing up prices, while others are still unemployed. These are structural problems in the labour force. Racial discrimination, insistence on remaining in certain occupations or regions, inadequate training of youth, and the like, add to the structural inflexibility of the labour force. In Figure 13.7 the supply curve for labour drawn as a dotted line reflects the emergence of cost-push elements even before full employment is achieved. The curve rises before the corner of the L in Keynes's ideal, so that as full employment is approached, economic planners face an ugly choice between the degree of unemployment they are willing to allow to continue, and the additional inflation of prices they will tolerate. While Keynes realized the necessity of the choice, his critics contend that the commitment he led us to make to full employment weakened the competitive pressures which are needed to break down structural rigidities. Rather than face the crunch, they say, both firms and unions look to government to save them from the force of the market. The question is whether the planning for full employment is simply a realistic recognition of the inability of the market to provide a tolerable level of stability, or whether it has unnecessarily underwritten structural and monopolistic maladjustments, thus making the unemployment–inflation choice progressively more difficult.

Inflation thus seems to be a side effect of the medicine given to achieve full employment. To pursue the medical analogy, the mere existence of side effects does not rule a medicine out of the pharmacopoeia. The question is always how much therapy is achieved at the cost of how much side effect. A. W. Phillips undertook to answer this question in an article entitled 'The relation between unemployment and the rate of change of money wage rates in the United Kingdom 1861–1957'.[3] Over the long period he studied, Phillips fitted a fairly stable relationship between the percentage increase in the wage rate and the percentage of unemployment. The Phillips curve is a downward sloping affair, bending inward toward the origin. It suggests that if unemployment in the United Kingdom were reduced to 1 per cent, wage rates would rise by 8·7 per cent; if an unemployment rate of 3 per cent were tolerated the wage rate increase would be only 1·2 per cent.

Actually, an increase in wage rates does not in itself mean price inflation. If through greater productivity the labour directly and indirectly used in final use fell at the same rate as the wage rate rose, prices would remain the same. A very rough measure of labour productivity is gross domestic product per man which has increased at a rate of approximately 2·3 per cent since 1957.

---

[3] A. W. Phillips, 'The relation between unemployment and the rate of change of money wage rates in the United Kingdom 1861–1957', *Economica* (November 1958), pp. 283–99.

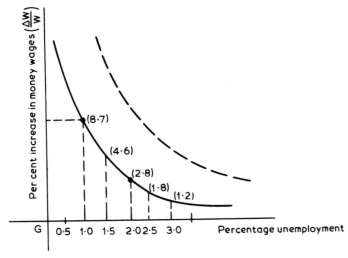

Figure 13.8   The Phillips curve

That means that an unemployment rate between 2 and 2·5 per cent should be attainable without inflation according to the Phillips curve. The actual unemployment rate from 1965 to 1969 is given in Table 13.1, so Britain should not be experiencing any inflation at all!

Table 13.1   Unemployment rate in the United Kingdom

Year	Rate
1965	1·5
1966	1·6
1967	2·3
1968	2·5
1969	2·5
1970	2·6
1971	3·4
1972	3·8
1973	2·7

Source: *Annual Abstract of Statistics*; *Economic Trends*.

In the mournful words of one eminent economist, 'What hath gone wrong?' Evidently the Phillips curve is not a stable relationship. It does not stand still for extended periods of time like some sort of production possibility frontier. Rather it seems to be drifting outward in a northeasterly direction. Perhaps we are now on a Phillips curve represented by the dashed curve in Figure 13.8. If so, then the choice we now have is between higher rates of both unemployment and wage-price inflation. What will tomorrow bring? Matters could be worse. It is possible although not likely that there is no Phillips curve at all, and that wages and unemployment simply go up together.

The reason that we are so distressed by the fact that the Phillips curve is behaving like the Flying Dutchman goes much deeper than the pique of statisticians who turn out to be wrong. It cuts at the very basis of a macroeconomic policy which has been willing to accept a controlled amount of inflation in order to achieve reasonably full employment. If the Phillips curve were stable, then we could swallow our medicine and endure the side effect. Most people would say that a 2·8 percentage increase is not too high a price to pay for holding unemployment down to 2 per cent; if labour productivity continues to grow at 2·3 per cent, prices would rise by only 0·5 per cent.

The administration of controlled inflation requires a controlled wage – price spiral. In turn this depends on the retention of at least a vestige of money illusion on the part of workers and other factors of production. To be sure an increase of wages beyond productivity will cause an increase in prices which will prompt an increase in wages, and so on indefinitely in a geometric series. Previously each round in the series tended to be less than the previous ones; that is to say, the series converged. This was consistent with Phillip's observations and the Keynesian analysis of money wages. Evidently what we have seen in recent years is breakdown of money illusion as price increases of a sufficient magnitude led to massive money disillusion. Wage claims tend to be fully adjusted for price increases so as to raise the real income of labour. Frequently cost of living adjustments are written into labour agreements. Even when they are not formalized, price rises are an accepted justification for wage raises. Matters can deteriorate further as the claims are made in terms of the expected price rise, and may exceed the previous rise. Perhaps inflation is not a mild chronic disease which one endures. It may be more like a pregnancy, a condition which always becomes acute no matter how small the beginning.

Wages are not the only factor price that responds to expectations of inflation. Interest rates are peculiarly sensitive to anticipated changes in the price level, because loans are to be paid back in the future when money is worth less. Thus rates of interest must exceed the anticipated rate of inflation, if there is to be any real interest income received by lenders. The rate of interest stated in money terms – sometimes called the *nominal rate of interest* – actually consists of two components: the *real rate of interest* and the *rate of anticipated inflation*. Like wage claims, the nominal rate of interest may be out of control since price increases keep pushing up expectations. These interest costs, in turn, enter into the price of goods and raise them further. Moreover, because increases in the money supply tend to aggravate inflation they also tend to increase the expected interest rate rather than decrease it. Thus, as we saw in the previous chapter, the money supply is increasing rapidly even while interest rates climb well into the two-digit range!

If the monetary authorities increase the money supply inflation will fuel price expectations and the interest rates may continue to soar. Yet if the monetary authorities restrict the money supply, as they may be forced to do, they may raise the real element of the rate of interest and precipitate the unemployment by discouraging investment. It is a fearful dilemma!

The situation is highly dangerous for several reasons. Inflation itself may go completely out of control. The psychology of panic can drive prices wildly upward, leaving the monetary authorities in the position of issuing fantastic amounts of cash simply to meet the needs of trade. The pre-Hitler experience in Germany was such a situation, where common postage stamps were denominated in thousands of millions of marks! The savings of the thrifty were demolished, as money ceased to perform its function as a store of value. Even when the quantity of money is restricted, expectations of inflation serve to drive people to spend it quickly before its value diminishes, and so the velocity of money also goes out of control. The ultimate breakdown possible in such a runaway inflation destroys even the medium of exchange function of money as people get rid of it as quickly as possible and resort to barter. It is not unusual for such a situation to culminate in demands for political stability, law and order, and authoritarian control.

There is one other grim possibility that should not be ignored. Since increases in the money supply merely increase the rate of inflation and the nominal rate of interest in equal steps, it may prove to be impossible to lower the real rate of interest. Ironically, it might be the case that in real terms the interest rate may have a floor not dissimilar to the Keynesian liquidity trap even while nominal rates of interest soar. It is not inconceivable, therefore, that there will be insufficient real investment demand. Unemployment of the type Keynes analysed might accompany rising prices! Weakening of the stock markets in the major capitals of the world in response to high interest rates is symptomatic of tendencies to put one's assets in near money forms of debt such as Treasury bills currently earning phenomenal rates of return.

Query: What would happen to real rates of interest if expectations of inflation drove the nominal rate up faster than inflation?

One can meet an inflationary psychology by the imposition of wage and price controls to attempt to break the self-fulfilling prophecy of price rises.

Such programmes are called 'prices and incomes policy' in the UK, 'wage–price freeze' in the United States, and similar titles elsewhere. The first effect of controls is almost always success in halting the self-fulfilling psychology of inflation that predicts that price increases will be followed by greater price increases in the future.

Then what happens? The controls have to be retained in whole or in part; or they have to be dismantled once the wave of inflation expectation is over for the moment. Suppose an incomes policy is maintained. What happens to the pressure for higher wages and prices? Does it disappear? Not very likely. The bargain becomes one to be fought out in the political arena between representatives of government, the trade unions, and industry organizations. Indeed, this is likely to be the case even in the absence of an official incomes policy. Clearly part of the reason for the major strikes in the British public sector and nationalized industry is the feeling that issues of overall wage levels were to be decided between labour and the government on a national basis.

The next question is whether wage and price controls can be enforced over extended periods of time even in the presence of an overall agreement. It is certainly very difficult to simply freeze them. Clearly workers in many industries will claim that the inequities are simply being perpetuated. Low profit firms will argue likewise. Moreover, as time goes on, shadow prices change due to alterations in technology and tastes. These also will change with time. Now what should be done? First of all, the existence of wage distortion has to be registered in the incomes regulating agency. That can be very difficult since what is involved is a policy made for the whole economy, not in all its parts and places. Second, even if the authorities convince themselves of the need for wage and price adjustments, they must then carry them out. Some workers must be told that they get less money whilst others are to get more. Clearly those suggestions will fly like a lead balloon!

The really dangerous part of the problem is that administrators of controls will neither have the knowledge nor the power to enforce an efficient allocation of resources. Yet if efficiency and productivity do not increase, wage and price demands will be even more inflationary than ever and the need to maintain controls will be all the more pressing.

Hopefully there is a middle ground between controls and efficient resource allocation. Perhaps there is a bargained, loosely defined agreement that can be arranged which responds to market signals in a reasonable way. Whether such a formula can be developed is yet to be seen. In the absence of such an arrangement, the authorities have little choice but to use macro-economic controls to face the most immediate danger. Hence the development of what have been called 'stop and go' policies. As the economy approaches full employment inflation threatens and the monetary and fiscal brakes are put on, frequently accompanied by price and wage freeze. The result is depressed conditions, restricted investment and considerable unemployment. Instead of 'stop', the signal is 'go' and public policy swings toward inflation again.

What should be done about it? The Keynesian approach is to impose more refined control measures designed to avoid the swings of stop and go. Perhaps a formal or informal sort of arrangement can be made to limit pay and price claims to give more room for maneuvre to macroeconomic fiscal and monetary measures. The monetarist-classical approach agrees that controls might be used as a stop gap to break the inflation expectation syndrome. But then the market mechanism should be allowed to play a decisive role in allocating labour, fixing wages, pricing goods. Full employment should be attained over the long run by a steady increase in the money supply to match the real growth in national income, but day to day surveillance over unemployment is doomed to be self-defeating.

It is now up to the reader to choose his medicine!

Exercise:
(1) What would happen to the multiplier if people increased consumption by more than the increase in income under inflationary conditions? What would happen to the velocity of money?
(2) Distinguish between cost-push and demand-pull inflation. Which is operative in the UK today?
(3) Review the budget statement by the Chancellor of the Exchequer and analyse his proposals in the light of this chapter.
(4) Is inflation anybody's fault? Whose?
(5) Distinguish between short-term measures to halt inflationary spirals and long-term solutions. Are these consistent with each other?

Appendix: multipliers as a series of adjustments

The working out of the convergence of the multipliers is worth the bit of arithmetic involved. Suppose we take the numerical example that has been the subject of various exercises in this chapter: the marginal propensity to consume is 0.8, $I = 30$ and $A = 50$. Then, as the reader has already found out for himself, it is easy to compute Y and C:

Theory	Example
$\dfrac{1}{1-c}I + \dfrac{1}{1-c}A = Y$	$5(30) + 5(50) = 400 = Y$
$\dfrac{c}{1-c}I + \dfrac{1}{1-c}A = C$	$4(30) + 5(50) = 370 = C$

Now suppose that the amount of investment that firms are willing to do increases by 20. The change in I can be written $\Delta I = 20$ and $I + \Delta I = 50$, whilst A is unchanged. What will be the new levels of income and consumption? The ultimate result is known in advance by simply applying the matrix of multipliers:

$$5(50) + 5(50) = 500 = Y$$

$$4(50) + 5(50) = 450 = C.$$

Income will have increased by 100 and consumption by 80.

Let us work out this result as a series of successive adjustments towards the new equilibrium, going through periods 0, 1, 2, 3, and so on. The time periods are shown as subscripts.

Theory   Example

Period 0: The original values of $I = 30$ and $A = 50$. At initial equilibrium:

$$Y_0 = C_0 + I_0 \qquad\qquad 400 = 370 + 30$$

$$C_0 = cY_0 + A \qquad\qquad 370 = (0 \cdot 8)(400) + 50$$

Period 1: Increase I by $\Delta I = 20$; so the immediate direct effect is that income increases by 20 in period 1:

$$Y_1 = C_0 + I + \Delta I \qquad\qquad Y_1 = 370 + 30 + 20 = 420$$

or

$$Y_1 = Y_0 + \Delta I.$$

If income increases consumption follows:

$$C_1 = cY_1 + A \qquad\qquad C_1 = (0 \cdot 8)(420) + 50 = 386$$

or

$$C_1 = cY_0 + A + c\Delta I$$

so

$$C_1 = C_0 + c\Delta I.$$

Period 2: Consumption has increased in period 1, so income must be higher in period 2:

$$Y_2 = C_1 + I + \Delta I \qquad\qquad Y_2 = 386 + 30 + 20 = 436$$

or

$$Y_2 = C_0 + c\Delta I + I + \Delta I$$

or

$$Y_2 = Y_0 + \Delta I + c\Delta I.$$

Since income is higher, so consumption must be higher:

$$C_2 = cY_2 + A \qquad\qquad C_2 = 0.8(436) + 50 = 398.8$$

or

$$C_2 = cY_0 + A + c\Delta I + c^2\Delta I$$

or

$$C_2 = C_0 + c\Delta I + c^2\Delta I.$$

Period 3: Consumption has increased in period 2, so income must be higher in 3:

$$Y_3 = C_2 + I + \Delta I \qquad\qquad Y_3 = 398.8 + 30 + 20 = 448.8$$

or

$$Y_3 = C_0 + c\Delta I + c^2\Delta I + I + \Delta I$$

or

$$Y_3 = Y_0 + \Delta I + c\Delta I + c^2\Delta I.$$

Income has increased in period 3, so consumption must be higher:

$$C_3 = cY_3 + A \qquad\qquad C_3 = 0.8(448.8) + 50 = 409.0$$

or

$$C_3 = cY_0 + A + c\Delta I + c^2\Delta I + c^3\Delta I.$$

or

$$C_3 = C_0 + c\Delta I + c^2\Delta I + c^3\Delta I$$

Exercise: Continue the analysis for period 4 and period 5.

   Income in period 3 is 448.8. Ultimately it will approach 500, as we expect. To see this we compute the increase in income since Y_0. Since $Y_3 = Y_0 + \Delta I + cI + c^2\Delta I$, the increase is $Y_3 - Y_0$. But $Y_3 - Y_0 = \Delta I + c\Delta I + c^2\Delta I$. As we go on to further periods, the string of terms would continue:

$$Y_n - Y_0 = \Delta I + c\Delta I + c^2\Delta I + c^3\Delta I + \ldots + c^{n-1}\Delta I.$$

This is nothing but our old friend, the infinite geometric series. The first term is ΔI, and each term is multiplied by c. Since c is less than unity, the sum of the series is:

$$Y_n - Y_0 = \frac{1}{1-c}\Delta I.$$

Writing $Y_n - Y_0$, the increase in Y, as ΔY, we get

$$\Delta Y = \frac{1}{1-c}\Delta I.$$

That is to say, the increase in investment is multiplied by the same multiplier we predicted from our simultaneous solution. Its numerical value is 5 and so the increase in investment by 20 will ultimately increase income by 100 after the series of adjustments converges.

Query: How do we know c is less than 1? What would happen if it were not?

How do we know that consumption will converge to the value predicted? The increase in consumption is:

$$C_3 - C_0 = c\Delta I + c^2\Delta I + c^3\Delta I$$

for three periods and for n periods is:

$$\Delta C = C_n - C_0 = c\Delta I + c^2\Delta I + c^3\Delta I + \ldots + c^n\Delta I.$$

This is interesting because the geometric series for the increase in consumption is exactly c times as big as the series for the increase in income.

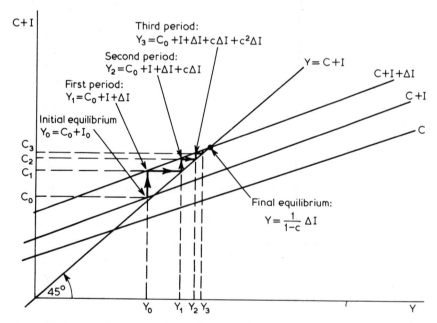

Figure 13.9   Step-by-step working of the multiplier (heavy line shows the path of adjustment to new equilibrium)

(Surprised?) Therefore the investment consumption multiplier will converge to

$$\Delta C = C_n - C_0 = \frac{c}{1-c}\Delta I$$

just as the computation of the inverse predicted. The process is illustrated in Figure 13.9. At time zero start from equilibrium values Y_0 and C_0. Increase I_0 by ΔI. Then in the first period income is increased by the amount of extra investment. The consumption function plus investment is shifted upward. Initially, this results in an increase in income to Y_1. But reading horizontally over to the 45° line shows that Y_1 does not bring us to equilibrium because the increase in income to Y_1 has increased consumption above the 45° line. Income will increase further to Y_2. This is not yet equilibrium, but the difference between consumption and investment and the 45° line is less. The process continues in this step by step fashion until the two lines cross, at which time income and consumption are consistent and equilibrium is achieved.

14 The international economy

National and international economics

The international interaction of national economies amounts to a review of the basic line of micro- and macroeconomic analysis carried out earlier in this book in a wider context. We shall see how the prices implicit in their production possibility frontiers form the basis for efficient international trade promoted by the market mechanism. Then the pathology of the world economy will be studied in terms of the problems of monopoly, unemployment, inflation and monetary considerations. International issues tend to become a bit more complex because of the interactions, but the key to understanding international economies is to observe the basic similarity of most of the issues. As we have done before, we shall make the case for the free market solution and then subject it to criticism, showing how departures from that model have come about.

The gains from trade

In international affairs, the equivalent of the competitive market situation is free trade: no tariffs, licences or quotas on imports or subsidies on exports; no collusive agreements between governments, collecting marketing agencies, monopolies, multinational or otherwise; and no barriers to international payments or transfer of funds.

The message of the market is that economic growth depends on the division of labour which is coordinated and enhanced by the free working of competition. Obstruction of the 'hidden hand of competition' in the form of private monopoly or governmental regulation most often tends to divert the economy from the optimal solutions which it seeks of its own accord. The consensus of economists since the days of Adam Smith was that this idea could be applied to the international commerce of each nation as well. Free trade would serve to maximize the welfare of each nation individually given the resources at their disposal.

To be sure, qualifications have been made to this idea. It is now conceded that tariffs on imports can be made to operate as a sort of monopoly power extracting income from other countries that must export to it. Moreover, restrictions on international trade can be used nationalistically to keep employment within one's own country during periods of depression. Nonetheless the possibility of retaliation tends to make such policies self-defeating to all but the few nations that can ignore the reaction of others. Since the number of such nations may turn out to be nil – it certainly is small – the doctrine of free competition deserves to be taken seriously.

What makes international trade international is that the factors of production normally remain in the home country, and only products are shipped abroad. Whilst we shall retain the convenience of discussing production possibility frontiers in terms of a single 'labour' input, to analyse bilateral trade we need to think of two such frontiers – one for each country. To work out the trade relations between the UK and, say, Mexico, let us tag the various symbols relating to nations with a superscript symbol. Thus the United Kingdom labour force would be B^u, and the Mexican labour force would be written B^m. We continue to identify the commodities by subscripts. Instead of numbering the commodities, let us represent the fanciful trade in gallons of tequila and cars by the subscripts t and c respectively.

With this notation in mind we can write the United Kingdom production possibility frontier as:

$$B^u = T_c^u y_c^u + T_t^u y_t^u$$

and the Mexican frontier as:

$$B^m = T_c^m y_c^m + T_t^m y_t^m.$$

The equations look a bit cumbersome, but all we have done to complicate our familiar equation is to identify the two countries by superscripts.

The impulse to trade derives from the fact that countries have different productivities in these goods, so that national output is differently specialized toward alternative products. This is due to different natural resource endowments and the available inputs of cooperating physical and human capital. True, capital and labour are subject to developmental change as time goes on. But that takes time, so it is fair to say that

Birmingham is better equipped to produce cars than Acapulco. Tequila, a fearful libation fermented from cactus plants, obviously is more readily produced in Mexico.

It follows from the difference in national specializations that the slopes of the two production possibility frontiers, the shadow price of cars compared with that of tequila is different in the two countries. Suppose, for example, $T_c^u = 2$ and $T_t^u = 4$. That means it takes two days of labour directly and indirectly to make a car in the United Kingdom, but it takes four days of labour to make a gallon of tequila in the UK, due to the inferior quality of cactus grown in East Anglia. At the same time suppose that $T_c^m = 10$ and $T_t^m = 1$; it takes ten days of labour in Mexico to make a car, while tequila takes only a day to make with the better Mexican cactus and know-how. The United Kingdom could choose to manufacture domestically any combination of cars and tequila along its own production possibility frontier $B^u = 2y_c^u + 4y_t^u$. Mexico could choose any output along $B^m = 10y_c^m + 1y_t^m$ (see Table 14.1).

Table 14.1   Labour directly and indirectly used by the United Kingdom and Mexico in the production of a unit of cars and tequila (in man-days of labour)

	Cars	Tequila
United Kingdom	2	4
Mexico	10	1

Suppose, further, that the UK has six man-days of labour at its disposal, while Mexico has eleven: $B^u = 6$ and $B^m = 11$. If at first the countries do not trade with each other, they may choose to make one unit of final use of each product to satisfy domestic needs; say the UK uses its labour to produce one car and one gallon of tequila for final use. Similarly, it will take all of Mexico's labour force to produce one car and one gallon of tequila.

Could Britain improve its real income? How might it have more of both cars and tequila? Instead of producing one car and one tequila it could put all six man-days of labour into car production. The UK would then produce three cars. It could keep one car to satisfy its domestic needs[1] and export the other two to Mexico in exchange for tequila. How many gallons of tequila would the UK receive? In Mexico it takes ten times as much labour to manufacture a car as it does a gallon of tequila. Consequently the price of a

---

[1] This simplification could be dropped if we were to examine the influence of expanded trade opportunities on consumers' choice.

car is ten times that of tequila. Cars will be sold for enough pesos to buy twenty gallons of tequila. Instead of one car and one gallon of tequila, the UK has one car and twenty gallons of tequila!

How do Mexicans feel about this? Have they been cheated? Not really. Suppose the Mexicans produce eleven gallons of tequila with their eleven man-days of labour, and prudently continue to consume one gallon themselves. They can trade the remaining tequila to the UK. Remembering that in the United Kingdom shadow prices call for two cars to swap for one gallon of East Anglia grown tequila (!), we conclude that the Mexicans will be able to get twenty cars for their fermented cactus juice! Not bad. Both nations gain from international trade because each produces goods in which it has a comparative advantage and exchanges for those in which it has a relative disadvantage.

A country might decide not to trade as a matter of policy. It would be self-sufficient, but such *autarky* would mean that it would have to donate more of its scarce labour to making goods it could import more cheaply. It takes too much labour to make tequila directly in East Anglia. The UK can make tequila indirectly by building automobiles and trading for tequila with the Mexicans. Why should the Mexicans break their backs making cars? Isn't it easier and cheaper for them to buy from Britain?

Query: (1) The fact of the matter is that the Mexicans actually are breaking their backs to develop industries like auto production. Why?
(2) Compute the products which each country should produce if:

$$T_c^u = 4, \ T_t^u = 2 \quad \text{and} \quad T_c^m = 1, \ T_t^m = 10.$$

In deciding what to produce, each country is concerned only with its own factor cost. It is not in the least concerned with the amount of foreign labour involved in producing the goods it imports. The real issue for the United Kingdom is how much of its own labour would be expended in making tequila directly compared to the amount involved in making autos for export. Britain is not contemplating bringing in Mexicans to East Anglia to make tequila. It only wants to bring the tequila. The UK couldn't care less about how the Mexicans make it; all that matters is the price of cars sold in Mexico compared to that of the tequila it is proposed to buy there. Of course Mexican prices reflect how they allocate their scarce labour resource. That is their problem.

Since it is the ratio of the labour directly and indirectly used that determines the shadow price in two countries, there will be gains from trade to both nations as long as the T_c^u/T_t^u is different from T_c^m/T_t^m. This is the *law of comparative advantage*. It may be the case that labour is more productive in all lines of output in one country compared to another. One might be tempted to say that the more productive country has an absolute advantage. Nonetheless only the comparative advantage counts, since the ratio of the labour inputs into the two products determines their price in each country, not the absolute amount of labour in each good (see exercise 1(a) below). It will always pay to specialize in the product that is valued more highly in foreign markets than it is at home, importing the second product as required.

Exercise:
(1) (*a*) Suppose it took more labour for Mexicans to produce everything. Show that each country should specialize in one commodity nonetheless.

$$T_c^u = 2, \quad T_t^u = 4 \quad \text{and} \quad B^u = 6.$$

$$T_c^m = 50, \quad T_t^m = 5, \quad \text{and} \quad B^m = 55.$$

(*b*) Suppose instead of the United Kingdom and Mexico we were discussing England and Scotland. Would you change any of your conclusions?

(2) Repeat for:

$$T_c^u = 2, \quad T_t^u = 4 \quad \text{and} \quad B^u = 6.$$

$$T_c^m = 5, \quad T_t^m = 10 \quad \text{and} \quad B^m = 15.$$

Why have your conclusions changed drastically? Distinguish again between comparative advantage and absolute advantage.

(3) Can a country have a comparative advantage in everything?

(4) If comparative advantages are not permanent does it affect the conclusion that each country should specialize?

The gains from trade can be seen forcefully in diagrammatic form (Figure 14.1). If the United Kingdom were isolated in the world, it would have to choose to produce at some point on its own production possibility frontier which would limit the nation's welfare. International trade offers the UK an escape from the limitations of its own production possibilities. In Figure 14.1 we draw the UK frontier $B^u = 2y_c^u + 4y_t^u$ where $B^u = 6$; in slope-intercept form it is $y_c^u = -2y_t^u + 3$. The intercept 3 shows that if no tequila were produced three cars could be made. The slope shows that two cars must be given up for each gallon of tequila manufactured.

Suppose, in the absence of trade, the UK initially maximized its welfare at A by making one car and one gallon of tequila. Now Mexico comes along and offers to sell at its shadow price. The ratio of Mexican prices of cars and tequila is $\frac{1}{10}$, as shown by the slope of its frontier $B^m = 10y_c^m + y_t^m$. This widens the possibilities for the UK, as can be seen by the series of parallel dotted lines whose slopes represent Mexican shadow prices. At point A the

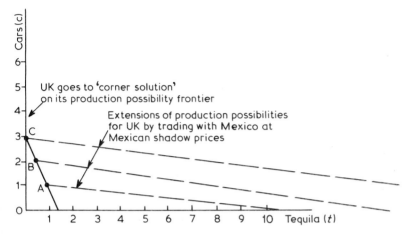

Figure 14.1   The gains from trade

UK has the option of trading one car for ten gallons of tequila. The feasible set includes the set of UK production possibilities and those under the Mexican line passing through point *A*, so the range of choice is widened. The UK can increase its possibilities even further. Moving along its own frontier to point *B*, it produces two cars and half a gallon of tequila; the opportunities for trade with Mexico extend the frontier even further. The maximum set of possibilities is given by going to a corner, *C*, where three cars are made and no tequila. Trade with Mexico extends the frontier to the highest dotted line. If the UK still wants only one car, it can be had, but in addition it can get twenty gallons of tequila. Actually it can choose any point on the enlarged bill of goods available to it to maximize satisfactions.

Query: Draw indifference maps to illustrate the choice.

Reasoning in a similar fashion, Mexico also chooses a corner solution for its production. It finds that, by making eleven gallons of tequila and no cars, it can use the United Kingdom to widen the range of final use from which it can choose.

Exercise:
(1) Graph the Mexican frontier as a solid line and the UK shadow prices as a set of dotted lines for the preceding illustrations. Show how Mexico would choose the corner solution. Repeat for the equations of exercise 2 in the preceding set of exercises. Explain the difference in your answers.
(2) Might it require a great deal of Mexican labour to produce enough tequila to buy the two cars the UK wishes to export? What are the elements of truth and falsity in the assertion 'poor Mexicans have to

work very hard to get goods that the rich British get very easily'? Are the Mexicans being cheated in the exchange? What if there is not enough Mexican labour to make all the tequila Britain can buy?

Now that we know what the two countries ought to do, how is international specialization of production to be brought about? Let the merciless hand of competition do its work! To see this, put a price on labour; assume that in the UK labour gets £6 a day, so that domestic tequila costs £24. (Why?) However, if the UK produces cars and trades these for the tequila, its six days of labour makes three cars, which can bring thirty gallons of tequila in from Mexico. Thus: 1 gallon of imported tequila takes $\frac{6}{30} = \frac{1}{5}$ days of UK labour. Consequently, at £6 per day for UK labour, imported Mexican tequila costs £1·20! A bargain for the UK, but disaster for the home tequila distillers. Britain's tequila makers are being driven out of business, whilst her automobiles are also closing down Mexican automobile manufacturers. East Anglian cactus farmers are being directed by the impersonal working of the market to get a job in the auto factories, like it or not!

Exercise: Suppose the Mexican wage is 100 pesos for a unit of labour. Compute the price in Mexico of Mexican made cars and UK made cars. Repeat for tequila. What will happen to the Mexican car industry? What will happen to its tequila industry?

What should governments do when businessmen demand tariffs, licences (against bad Mexican booze, of course) and import quotas? In all but a few cases the answer is nothing! When workers complain about redundancies in the tequila mills the rational government should turn a deaf ear, except perhaps to assist in relocation elsewhere. To give in to the cries of anguish is to assent to inefficiency and to reduce the wealth of the nation. In effect, it penalizes the public by reducing the goods it can afford to buy in order to keep some working in jobs where they really are not needed.

We exaggerate a bit. Actually the comparative advantage doctrine does not imply that no cars at all should be built in Mexico and no tequila should be produced in the UK. The fixed technology model with one primary input has made our argument too strong by implying that, no matter how much tequila Mexico produced, the shadow price of tequila to cars would not change; likewise, it was presumed that the price of cars in the UK remained unaffected by the number of vehicles produced. Consequently, the two countries were taken as unable to reconcile their internal prices to a common world price for their goods. In fact there can be only one international price for goods (except for transportation costs). The reconciliation process is the result – as the reader has probably guessed – of the working of the law of diminishing returns which becomes operative once we consider that production is carried on by more than one factor of production (see Chapter 5). As

Mexico produces more and more tequila (using land that is better suited to corn growing and oil wells than cactus, and enticing city folk to work in the cactus fields and distilleries), the shadow price of tequila rises. Relative to tequila, the price of cars falls in Mexico in the remaining more efficient auto firms. Similarly in the UK the price of cars rises and that of tequila falls. Eventually, the prices are reconciled (it can also be shown that at that price the amount of cars Mexico is willing to take matches the output Britain is willing to export, and conversely for tequila).

The reconciliation of prices through the working of the international market does not negate the doctrine of comparative advantage. It merely has to be interpreted to mean that each nation is driven to produce more of the product for which it is best suited, and less of the goods for which it does not have a comparative advantage.[2]

A tutorial exercise

(A) If one understands that the case for free trade is fundamentally an extension of a belief in the market mechanism, it is possible to gain insight into the objections to it along lines set forth in earlier chapters: external effects, the existence of monopoly power, considerations of equity in the distribution of income and wealth, and the problem of maintaining full employment while avoiding inflation. Classify the following amendments that have been made to the free trade doctrine in terms of these considerations. Explore the real economic costs associated with each departure from free trade, and explain the benefits that are anticipated. Choose a particular illustration of each and come to a judgement whether the benefits justify the costs (the macroeconomic employment and inflation issues will be explored more thoroughly in the remainder of this chapter).

(1) *National defence and security.* Certain industries have military and diplomatic potential and must be protected by tariffs and subsidies. A nation should assure itself of strategic materials either by making itself as self-sufficient as possible or by stockpiling these items against an emergency.

(2) *Economic development, infant industries and import substitution.* Particularly underdeveloped countries argue for barriers to the import of manufactures from the already industrialized nations. Identifying progress with industrialization, they feel that they cannot permit young local industries to be swamped by the cheaper products of Japan, America and Europe

---

[2] Actually, if it is impossible for the shadow prices to be matched in the two countries due to markedly different production possibilities, then the previous analysis holds and certain goods will not be produced at all. In all likelihood this is the condition for tequila production in the UK, since there is probably no way that even small crops of cactus can be grown which could compete with the foreign imports. The tequila industry is – to the author's knowledge – non-existent in the UK.

until such time as they become equally efficient and can compete in the world market. Moreover, the effect of tariffs or import quotas will serve to raise the price of certain imports – say automobiles – and will force the citizens to spend their money on *import substitutes* such as bicycles. These can be produced locally with available labour. Funds available for imports can then be directed to more socially useful goods ranging from heavy machinery to armaments for national defence.

(3) *Preservation of industries that contribute employment to important groups in the population and which are identified with a national life style.* For example, the price of agricultural products is frequently maintained at a high level by tariff barriers against their importation and governmental purchases of surplus output. Their export is subsidized, government making up the difference between the high domestic price and lower world market prices. Similar arrangements are made with respect to coal mining and shipbuilding in the UK.

(4) *Countering monopolistic power in world markets.* The Argentine economist, Raoul Prebisch, argues that manufactured goods exported by industrial nations are dominated by a few large monopolistic firms and international conglomerate firms. The result is that prices paid by the poorer nations for manufactures are excessively high compared to the prices they get for their primary raw and agricultural produce. The ratio of import to export prices is called the *terms of trade.* In order to improve the terms of trade, and to wield diplomatic and military influence, the primary producing countries have combined to jointly raise their prices for such items as crude petroleum.

(5) *Stabilization of prices of primary products.* The prices of agricultural goods and raw materials are subject to wide swings in price due to the short-run inelasticity of both their supply and demand. (Why is this so?) In order to counter this tendency governmentally sponsored *marketing boards* sell these items on behalf of local producers, offering them prices intermediate between the swings on the world market. Not infrequently, marketing boards will offer low prices to local producers and use their profits to sponsor public projects or industrial development.

(6) *Conservation of natural resources.* Countries often act to limit the export of their natural resources for fear of rapid depletion of such items as oil, timber, mineral deposits and the like. Private interest, it is argued, would produce and sell them abroad in a manner contrary to the long-run welfare of the country. This is especially true if the private firms are foreign owned or controlled.

(B) Having come to some judgements about the case for freer trade and the counteracting considerations, use them to judge the wisdom or folly of the British entry into the European Common Market. Review the debates in Parliament and in the press and interpret them in terms of what you have learned.

Money, employment and prices in the international economy

Just as in domestic matters, the issues surrounding the impact of international commerce on macroeconomic considerations of employment and price levels turn on the meaning of the equation of exchange. The extension of the $MV = PT$ formula to international affairs is actually quite old, having been understood originally in terms of the old *gold standard* system of money which expired with the First World War. In those simpler days, paper money was freely convertible into either gold coin or bullion which could then be disposed of anywhere in the world. Under such circumstances the value of currency was nothing but the price of the lump of gold for which it could be redeemed.

What would happen, free traders were asked, if a nation paid out more in gold for its imports than it received for its exports? Would not such an unfavourable *balance of trade* result in a draining off of its money supply? Applying this idea to the tequila and cars illustration, suppose police warnings not to drink and drive resulted in an international tendency to give up driving. Then Britain would continue to import tequila, paying for it in gold, but Mexico would not buy many cars in return, so the gold would only flow out from the UK.

The equation of exchange shows that changes in the price level set up counteracting changes that stop such an unbalanced gold flow. The self-limiting process is called the *price level specie-flow mechanism*. If the money supply in Britain were to fall, so would its prices compared with those of Mexico. Mexicans would be more strongly attracted to British cars, once more increasing UK exports. Moreover, the relative price of Mexican tequila would rise as the result of the inflow of money to Mexico. This would cause British consumers to drink beer and whisky rather than tequila, thus reducing imports. The unbalanced gold movement would stop itself.

Actually the tendency towards a balance in payments does not depend on the continuation of the gold standard. If British firms are writing more cheques to make payments to Mexican enterprises than the reverse, the reserves of the British banks will be reduced, and those of Mexico will increase. Unless counteracting measures are taken by the monetary authorities, money will flow out of Britain and the consequent reduction in its money supply will lower the price level just as effectively as a gold flow.

The conversion of paper pounds into foreign currencies introduces an element into the adjustment process that operates much more quickly than changes in price levels. It involves equilibration of the world market in money and near money instruments. Take a slightly different example. To pay for the import of a British shirt, an American importer might buy a cheque in sterling from a bank or individual who owns sterling. Alternatively, if the shirt is to be paid for in the future, he might buy an interest-bearing promise to pay pounds such as a *bill of exchange*. Collectively such foreign monies are called *foreign exchange*.[3]

How much would the pound cost the American importer of British shirts under modern conditions where national currencies are not convertible into gold? Provided the government does not intervene, the price of pounds is determined by supply and demand, just like the price of tomatoes or anything else. Suppose the price of the pound were permitted to *float* in the world money markets? Then if more Americans wanted pounds than were made available by those desirous of dollars, the price of pounds would rise. One pound would be worth more dollars – the pound would be *revalued*. By definition the dollar would be worth fewer pounds, so that if the pound were revalued with respect to the dollar, the dollar would be *devalued* with respect to the pound. Instead of £1 = $1·70, the pound might be worth $1·90.

Just as in the market for any other product, the supply and demand mechanism for foreign exchange would tend towards equilibrium. A rise in the price of pounds would make it more expensive for Americans to buy British goods. In terms of dollars, the shirt would rise in price in America, even though it may still sell for £1 in the UK. At the same time US goods are cheaper in England, since each pound fetches more dollars. As a result, British exports are discouraged, and imports from America are encouraged. The excess demand for pounds tends to disappear and equilibrium reasserts itself.

The price level adjustment does not become irrelevant under such circumstances. In due course the devaluation which causes the price of imports to rise and that of exports to fall will bring changes in domestic prices. Imported goods will be more expensive, and greater exports will drain away production to be sold abroad. An increase in domestic prices will occur due to higher costs and fewer goods. Conversely, if the value of foreign exchange of a country rises in the money markets, the price of imported goods will fall,

---

[3] A market in foreign exchange existed even under the gold standard due to the greater convenience in making payments in the form of claims on gold and currency rather than by shipping gold. But so long as the currency was convertible into gold, the price of foreign exchange could not vary from the gold content by more than the cost of shipping the gold itself.

and the volume of its exports will decrease. The net result, in the long run, should be the same as the price level specie-flow mechanism.[4]

In Figure 14.2 we represent the market for sterling foreign exchange by the familiar supply and demand diagram. On the vertical axis we show the price of pounds, i.e. the number of pounds per dollar. On the horizontal axis we represent the number of pounds to be bought and sold. The supply of pounds results from imports into the UK and other UK payments to foreigners. The demand for pounds results from exports from the UK to foreigners for which they must pay, as well as other payments by foreigners to Britons.

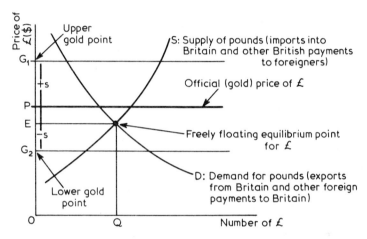

Figure 14.2   The market for sterling in terms of dollars

[4] We have overstated the case for treating the price of foreign exchange like that of tomatoes just a bit. The amount of foreign exchange that a country earns by its exports depends on the nature of the demand for those goods. Some goods are such that the quantity of them that is demanded does not respond very much to changes in price. If the price of goods in such inelastic demand should rise, then the expenditure on those goods rises as well, because the increase in price more than counteracts the slightly smaller number of physical items sold. Consequently, if the world's demand for a nation's exports is inelastic, an imbalance of trade will not be automatically self-adjusting. The increased price of the exports will bring more – not less – foreign exchange into the country. Neither the specie-flow nor the foreign exchange market adjustment mechanisms will bring them back to equilibrium. It is hard to imagine that this is a realistic possibility for very large changes in the price of foreign exchange, since that would require that buyers are almost impervious to changes in the price of things they buy, nor is it likely to be the case for the exports of a nation that produces a wide variety of goods with many competing nations for similar reasons. It can happen, however, that the exports of underdeveloped nations – tropical produce and mineral raw materials – do face an inelastic world market demand. Typically these nations prefer to have their currencies overvalued in the world market because they would end up with a more serious disequilibrium if they devalued their currency.

In a free market for sterling, the rate of exchange will fluctuate until it finds equilibrium at E. At that equilibrium price, the market clears at quantity of pounds, Q. The number of pounds that are demanded for remittance to the United Kingdom to pay for its exports is just equal to the supply of pounds offered by the UK money market for payments abroad.

Under the gold standard matters are complicated by the definition of the value of currencies in terms of specific amounts of gold. There was an official ratio of pounds to dollars based on their respective gold content: price P. As long as the equilibrium exchange rate, E, on the free foreign exchange market is close to P, sterling still will be bought and sold by using paper and credit instruments rather than expressive gold shipments. However, if the price of foreign exchange exceeded P by the cost of shipping and insurance, it would become worthwhile to ship the gold physically. Consequently, E could fluctuate only a little from P. If we designate the gold shipping costs by s, the price of foreign exchange was restricted to the range between $P + s = G_1$ and $P - s = G_2$. G_1 and G_2 were known as the *gold points*. Foreign exchange rates never varied beyond these points.

The gold standard, then, was not a freely fluctuating market at all. In fact, except for the leeway between the gold points, the prices of various currencies were rigidly locked together regardless of the working of supply and demand. If the supply and demand for sterling were such that their intersection at E would lie above the upper gold point, then the quantity of pounds sterling demanded would exceed the quantity supplied at the rigidly fixed price. Sterling would be said to be *undervalued* in such a *disequilibrium*, and gold would flow into England to be converted into more pounds. Conversely, if the crossing of supply and demand were below the lower gold point, the quantity of sterling supplied would be greater than the amount demanded and gold would flow out of Britain to pay for its excessive imports. Sterling would have been *overvalued*.

Exercise: Draw graphs of supply and demand' displaying the situations described in the preceding paragraph. If the shipment of gold were costless would the system be more flexible?

Under the gold standard of rigid exchange rates the only adjustment available was through the price level specie-flow mechanism. That is to say, the money supply was really out of the control of the monetary authorities. Indeed, this was considered a virtue; allowing money to flow in and out of the country in response to price changes was considered 'playing the game' of free trade.

The gold standard collapsed as a result of the stresses of the First World War and the ensuing Depression. The war entailed enormous transactions that were not controlled by changes in relative international prices. Military exigency dictated the purchases of food and munitions. The Depression demolished the system altogether because reduction in demand for a nation's imports reduced the demand for its final use in real terms rather than adjusting its price level. The relative stickiness of prices and wages meant that an unfavourable balance of trade led to further unemployment. Nobody could, or would, 'play the game' according to the old rules.

To understand these developments we must pause to make a more detailed study of the categories involved in the international flow of funds in what is called the *balance of payments*.

The balance of trade and the balance of payments

The import and export of goods and services are recorded in what is called the *balance of trade*, or the *current balance* (Table 14.2). In addition to payments for tangible goods, the current balance includes payments for intangible items. These *invisible items* of export and import include shipping, insurance, and financial services, the earnings from tourism, and the payments for foreign use of British factors of production in foreign countries such as profits, interest and dividends.

Besides the balance of trade a great part of the international flow of funds has very little to do with currently produced goods and services. When transactions arising from capital and other *transfers* of wealth are consistent the balance of trade is expanded to become the *balance of payments* (or total currency flow). The relationship between the two balances is given in Table 14.2.

Exercise:
(1) An excess of exports over imports is called a favourable balance of trade. Did Britain show a favourable or unfavourable balance of trade in Table 14.2? Is it possible to have a favourable balance of trade and an unfavourable balance of payments? Is a favourable balance good?
(2) Is the balance of payments about the *stock* or *flow* of wealth? Which is more like a profit and loss statement – the balance of payments or the balance of trade?

In the balance of payments one may distinguish three basic sources for the transfer of funds:

(1) *Long-term investments* largely represent the working of the international capital market as funds are transferred for the purchase of factories, real estate, railroads and the like. Not infrequently such long-term transfers will take the form of the purchase of shares or long-term loan stock in foreign enterprises. These transfers may originate in intergovernmental loans as well as private investment.

(2) *Short-term investment for commercial purposes* reflects the international money market in Treasury bills, bills of exchange and other

Table 14.2   UK balance of payments 1972 (£ million)

Exports (fob)	9135	
Imports (fob)	9827	
Visible balance	−692	
Invisibles (services, profits, dividends, interest and transfers, public and private sector)		
Credits	5864	
Debits	5135	Balance of trade
Invisible balance	+729	
CURRENT BALANCE	+37	
Investment and other capital flows*		Long-term
Official long-term capital	−249	investment
Overseas investment in UK	+756	
UK private investment overseas	−1350	
Foreign currency borrowing (net) by UK banks to finance UK investment overseas	+715	
Other foreign currency borrowing or lending (net) by UK banks	−232	
Exchange reserves in sterling, British government stocks	+104	Short-term investment for
Banking and money market liabilities	+220	commercial trade,
Other external banking and money liabilities in sterling	−92	financing and
Import credit	+168	speculative
Export credit	−249	reasons
Other short-term flows	−481	
Total investment and other capital flows	−690	
Balancing item	−612	Large 'balancing item' suggests
TOTAL CURRENCY FLOW	−1265	'hot money' flow into UK from US before dollar devaluation
Allocation of SDR	+124	Balance of
Gold subscription to IMF	—	payments
Total official financing	−1141	

Source: Adapted from *Economic Trends* (June 1973).
* Assets: increase −/decrease +. Liabilities: increase +/decrease −.

short-term business and public debt. Like the internal money market, these transactions permit borrowers to finance merchandise shipments, the carrying of inventories and the payment of wage and tax expenses. At the same time it permits banks and business lenders to earn income by holding their liquid assets in near money form rather than in unproductive cash.

(3) *Speculative and 'hot money' flows.* Clearly the short-term money market is highly sensitive to international differences in rates of interest. Some governments may be trying to restrain inflation by high interest rates and others might be trying to stimulate investments by lowering them. The result is a tendency of funds to move from the low interest country to the high. Speculation on the future course of interest rates (and hence on the value of securities) is an additional cause of massive flows of short-term investments. Fears, rumours, expectations and inside information make for rapid and destabilizing flows of funds between countries.

Still other sorts of expectations and anxieties may cause money movements. It may be expected that a nation is going to devalue its currency with respect to others, prompting many to shift their liquid, short-term, near money assets into other *hard currencies* or even into gold. Fears that *exchange controls* are about to be established forbidding the conversion of currency into other money prompts people to 'get their money out' while they still can. Fear of war or of government confiscation of wealth makes for a move to get the money to a safe place. Collectively these speculative flows are called *hot money*. Hot money may constitute a very large part of private short-term capital flows, yet it is often impossible to distinguish hot money from short-term transfers for commercial purposes. An indication of the existence of sizable hot money transfers is the large size of the *balancing item* in the balance of payments. People taking their money to foreign countries – both legally and illegally – appears as a flow of funds not recorded as related to merchandise or capital movements.

Hot money flows are often a disruptive element in the international money market. Justified or not, in the face of a speculative outflow a country may be forced to devalue its own currency in order to make the conversion into foreign currencies less attractive. But if devaluation under speculative pressure prompts the fear of further devaluations, the hot money flows may be even greater. Then the self-fulfilling prophecy of devaluation requires further devaluations and the breakdown in the orderly market for funds.

To sum up, the balance of payments consists of the balance of trade (visibles and invisibles) plus transfers of funds on capital account for investment and speculation. The table is completed by *allocations of special drawing rights* (SDR) and *gold subscriptions to the International Monetary Fund* (IMF) which will be discussed later in this chapter.

Who killed Cock Robin? The breakdown of international payments

War is not only hazardous to the health, but incredibly expensive. Britain entered into the First World War as a *mature creditor nation*. That is to say, its world holdings of earning assets brought back more than was annually invested. The pound and the gold standard seemed indestructible. Convertible into gold on demand, the pound was literally 'as good as gold'. England was the mercantile centre of the world and most nations did their international business in terms of pounds. Indeed, it was probably more truthful to say 'gold was as good as sterling', and that the world was on a sterling standard. Sterling balances were held as bank reserves. Much of the financing of world trade passed through the 'city' of London.

By 1917 Britain was forced to share this role with the United States. Massive military expenditures required huge import purchases that were not checked by the automatic specie-flow mechanism. Accentuated by hot money transfers, funds continued to flow out of Britain which drained the gold reserve and forced the selling off of much of its overseas earning asset holdings. Ultimately, Britain had to suspend the convertibility of sterling into gold. The cord had been cut. Thenceforth the value of the pound depended on the world demand for sterling as a paper currency.[5] Yet it was not the abandonment of the gold standard that deprived the pound of its role as the unique reserve currency, but the lessened demand for sterling. The world slipped off dependence on the sterling standard, and the termination of convertibility was but a symptom of that development.

Despite the end of gold convertibility the pound continued as an *international standard* and *store of value*. Traders continued to clear their accounts by exchanging payments in sterling through London. Central banks and commercial banks all over the world held pounds as a *reserve* or *key currency*. To be sure, much of the pound had to share its role with the dollar; nonetheless the supply and demand for sterling was sufficiently stable to establish its value without recourse to gold convertibility. Until the middle of the depression the United States retained a policy of unlimited convertibility of dollars into gold, but eventually joined the rest of the world in severing the link between its domestic money supply and the gold reserve.[6]

Although the departure of nations from the gold standard was certainly a dramatic development, its real significance during the Depression was as a symptom of the breakdown of the old system whereby nations were content to allow the base of their domestic money supply to be influenced by events occurring abroad. It had formerly been believed that the price level specie-flow mechanism assured that an unfavourable balance of trade was both innocuous and self-correcting. To be sure, the resulting outflow of gold money reduced the demand for domestic goods and services. This reduction of MV in the equation of exchange was expected to induce a fall in the price level only, leaving the level of employment of factors of production at full

---

[5] Over Keynes's objections an attempt was made in 1925 to restore convertibility but it proved abortive.

[6] Dollars were exchangeable for gold in international transactions at the fixed rate of $35 an ounce until 1969.

employment. Nations were expected to simply 'play the game' and allow the imbalances to continue for as long as it took for equilibrium to restore itself.

Alas, as Keynes pointed out, during the depression prices were sticky. Reductions in final demand caused output and employment to fall more than prices. It is the old criticism of the quantity theory of money all over again. A reduction in the money demand reduces $MV = Y = PQ$, except that it reduces Q more than P.

Keynes showed that there is an automatic mechanism at work that prevents permanent imbalance of trade, but it works by keeping incomes of all nations moving together rather than their price level. What made the whole situation so devastating was that the gold standard international payments mechanism worked in such a way as to prevent one nation from increasing its national income faster than others. Keynes showed that the income effect – the demand for imports – increases roughly in proportion to national income. If one nation increases its income faster than others its imports will increase faster than its exports. The resulting imbalance of trade will divert employment away from domestic to foreign labour and other factors. The increase in national income generated by a rise in the trade balance will disappear as soon as imports overtake exports. If, through monetary and fiscal policy, a country insists on continuing to raise income and employment faster than other nations, then imports will continue to rise in excess of exports. Unless some means were found to insulate the national economy from the effects of this imbalance of payments, either gold and foreign exchange would drain out of the nation experiencing the more rapid improvement in employment until its reserves were exhausted, or it would have to curtail its monetary and fiscal policies to recover from depression.

One way of coping with the dilemma was to detach the internal money supply from gold. Then monetary policy could be expansionary within the country regardless of the outflow of gold and foreign exchange as long as reserves lasted. Gold reserves could be economized and used only for foreign transactions. Another method was to attract more exports and discourage imports by lowering the value of the national currency – *devalu-ation*. Finally, export markets could be captured by direct recourse to the power of governments in a wide variety of forms ranging from such 'conventional measures' as restrictive quotas and licences on imports, tariffs on imports and subsidies to exports, to Hitler's use of political and military power to control and conquer markets.

Planning aggregate demand to maintain full employment levels of national income has, since those days, taken on an international as well as domestic aspect. In the expression for national income $Y = C + I + G + E$, the last term equals the difference between exports and imports so that E is nothing but the *balance of trade*. For E to make a net contribution to employment, exports must exceed imports in a 'favourable balance of trade'.

Query: Why is E not the balance of *payments*?

When we confined ourselves to the domestic sector of the economy we wrote $Y = C + I + G$ and the consumption function $C = cY + A$ as a pair of simultaneous equations. Lumping private investment (I) and government spending (G) together in matrix form we had:

$$\begin{bmatrix} I+G \\ A \end{bmatrix} = \begin{bmatrix} 1 & -1 \\ -c & 1 \end{bmatrix} \begin{bmatrix} Y \\ C \end{bmatrix}$$

Inverting we got a table of multipliers:

$$\begin{bmatrix} Y \\ C \end{bmatrix} \begin{bmatrix} \dfrac{1}{1-c} & \dfrac{1}{1-c} \\ \dfrac{c}{1-c} & \dfrac{1}{1-c} \end{bmatrix} \begin{bmatrix} I+G \\ A \end{bmatrix}.$$

Now we add the foreign trade sector of demand to this structure. Let X stand for gross exports, and M for gross imports, so that net exports, $E = X - M$. Following Keynes suppose that imports are approximately proportional to national income; m is the *marginal propensity* to import, $m = M/Y$. Then $M = mY$ and $E = X - mY$. The equations for structure of demand of the economy including foreign trade are:

$$Y = C + I + G + E$$

$$C = cY + A$$

$$E = X - mY.$$

The exogenous terms are I, G, A and X, since exports are determined by what is happening to demand in other nations. Grouping these together and rewriting the equations in matrix form:

$$\begin{bmatrix} 1 & -1 & -1 \\ -c & 1 & 0 \\ m & 0 & 1 \end{bmatrix} \begin{bmatrix} Y \\ C \\ E \end{bmatrix} = \begin{bmatrix} I+G \\ A \\ X \end{bmatrix}.$$

To find the table of impact multipliers we invert. The result is:

$$\begin{bmatrix} Y \\ C \\ E \end{bmatrix} = \begin{bmatrix} \dfrac{1}{1-c+m} & \dfrac{1}{1-c+m} & \dfrac{1}{1-c+m} \\ \dfrac{c}{1-c+m} & \dfrac{1+m}{1-c+m} & \dfrac{c}{1-c+m} \\ \dfrac{-m}{1-c+m} & \dfrac{-m}{1-c+m} & \dfrac{1-c}{1-c+m} \end{bmatrix} \begin{bmatrix} I+G \\ A \\ X \end{bmatrix}$$

Exercise:
(1) Check on the inverse by solving the original equations for Y, C, E.
(2) Suppose that $c = 0\cdot8$ and $m = 0$. $I = 7, G = 3, A = 5, X = 5$. What would the economy be like? What would its trade balance be? Compare the values of the multipliers with those given in the two-sector model of demand.

Now suppose $m = 0\cdot1$. What has happened to the multipliers? What has happened to the export balance? What has happened to national income?

Repeat for $m = 0\cdot2$ and compare the incomes and export balances when $m = 0, m = 0\cdot1$ and $m = 0\cdot2$. How do these illustrate the general argument in the text?
(3) Suppose $c = 0\cdot8$ and $m = 0\cdot1$. Increase I from 7 to 15, and increase A from 5 to 10. What has happened to Y? What has happened to E?

The inverse matrix of impact multipliers illustrates the dilemma which nations face when trying to increase national income by manipulating investment and government expenditures, whilst living within their means with respect to the balance of payments. In the first row of the matrix which relates to national income as the endogenous variable, the multiplier of $I + G$ is the *positive* quantity $1/(1-c+m)$; in the third row, which treats the balance of trade as the endogenous variable, the multiplier of $I + G$ is a *negative* number, $-m/(1-c+m)$. Therefore, attempting to *raise* the level of national income by increasing $I + G$ would, at the same time, *reduce* the trade balance and contribute to a more serious problem in the balance of payments!

The balance of payments constitutes the constraint within which a country must conduct its international relations if it is not to see its foreign exchange reserves disappear abroad. Since the balance of trade forms the largest component of the payments balance, the latter constrains domestic policies to manage national income and employment. Suppose the balance of trade had to be a certain fixed value to live within the balance of payments, then the third equation limits I, G and A. In the particularly simple case where trade must balance, then imports must equal exports, so $E = 0$. The third row simplifies to

$$0 = \left(\frac{-m}{1-c+m}\right)(I+G) + \left(\frac{-m}{1-c+m}\right)A + \left(\frac{1-c}{1-c+m}\right)X.$$

Multiplying through by $(1-c+m)$ and simplifying leads to the striking result: $(I+G+A)m = (1-c)X$. The amount of stimulation which can be given through investment and government is strictly limited by the amount of exports, given the marginal propensity to consume and export. If $I+G+A$ are limited then so must Y.

Exercise:

(1) Suppose $c = 0.8$ and $m = 0.1$, and $X = 10$. What is the highest possible level of national income achievable consistent with a balance of trade? What is the highest level of consumption?

(2) Suppose there were a surplus on capital accounts due, say, to petroleum producing countries depositing funds in the London money market. This would permit a negative balance of trade consistent with balance in total payments. Taking $E = -20$, express the resulting limitation on the size of $I + A + G$ given by X. Using the values for c, m and X in exercise 1, compute the maximum possible level of national income and consumption. Compare the results.

There are several ways in which a country can raise national income:

(1) It can export more. Observe that the multipliers of X are positive in both the first and third rows. By exporting more, income rises, and the balance of trade improves as well. The difficulty is that, by definition, a nation can only export if others import! The nicest way exports and income can increase is for other nations to increase their income as well. They will then increase their purchases, and incomes will increase in step without creating balance of payments problems for anyone. If a nation cannot, or will not, keep income growth in step with the others, it must export more by means fair or foul.

(2) By tariffs, quotas and payments restrictions it can reduce the marginal propensity to import, the portion of the increased national income that is spent abroad. This possibility is obvious from the fact that all the multipliers in the first row relating to national income are $1/(1 - c + m)$. The larger m becomes, the smaller will be the multipliers of investment, government, autonomous consumption and exports, and the less effective these exogenous stimulants to national income will be. With a high marginal propensity to import, most of the stimulus given by these demands leaks off to buy imported goods rather than domestically produced goods and services.

(3) A nation with a substantial store of gold or other foreign exchange may simply let matters slide, and accept an unfavourable balance of payments resulting from high level of Y. Since the internal paper money supply can be managed in spite of the outflow of reserves, this policy can continue until reserves are exhausted or some good fortune reverses the imbalance.

(4) It can allow the excess supply of its currency on world money markets due to the excess of imports over exports to be resolved by a fall in the value of the currency. This can be accomplished by allowing the currency to 'float', finding its own equilibrium level, or by deliberately devaluing it in terms of other money or gold. In part this is an instrument to accomplish (1) and (2) and in part it aims to stem capital transfers by making the foreign exchange

more expensive. Whether this is a market clearing stabilizing device, or the prelude to further destabilizing shifting of the supply and demand for the currency depends on whether the nation plans to further increase its national income more than 'in step' as well as speculative responses to the actions taken.

In the nationalist climate of the interwar years, keeping in step was out of the question. The councils of state were concerned with how to export more and import less; how to penetrate the markets of others and protect domestic producers from foreign competition; how to prevent the hard won domestic investment from stimulating other economies rather than one's own; how to insulate oneself; how to escape from the balance of payments constraint. One very important device was *devaluation*. A government would declare its currency to be worth less in terms of gold or key currencies. It would offer to exchange more of its money for other foreign money. Business was attracted away from other countries. At the same time imported goods were made expensive for its own citizens and were discouraged. Instant prosperity! Under full employment conditions, as aggregate demand rose, domestic prices would increase too. But during the Depression this was not likely. The greater danger was that, with increased incomes, imports would increase and some of the benefits of devaluation would be siphoned off to others. As a result controls were placed on imports in various forms. *Exchange controls* were introduced to limit payments abroad. Licences on imported goods were required and issued in small amounts. Imports of certain goods were subject to *quotas*. *Tariffs* were increased to further discourage imports.

Of course this system could not work! What nation would sit idly by and see itself thrown deeper into depression by devaluation of others? Retaliation in the form of *competitive devaluation* broke out. There was an international price war in cheap money. What a spectacle! Travellers who had some hard currency to spend scratched their heads in wonderment at the enormous sheaf of bills thrust at them in exchange. Thousands and even millions of francs or lire were not unusually large amounts of money to carry around!

Another consequence of devaluation was the writing down of the value of money claims in devalued currencies. Suddenly a thousand franc note was worth half as many pounds, dollars, gold or imported goods. Consequently at the mere rumour of devaluation hot money fled the country and made devaluation even more likely. Indeed any time a nation's balance of payments worsened hot money flows anticipated devaluation and all but made it necessary. Legally or illegally speculators traded money far below the government stated price, and eventually governments had to follow suit.

Nobody could win in the 'beggar my neighbour' game. International money processes and the peace-making function of the international gains from trade all collapsed. Disaster had befallen the wealthy nations. A world carnage followed.

A brave new world?

By the end of the Second World War it was perfectly obvious to the hard headed as well as to the idealistic that the world game of beggar my neighbour could have no winners. Keynes had shown a way out. Nations could maintain full employment by monetary and fiscal policy. It was not necessary to steal an export surplus away from some other country, as long as nations maintained their incomes more or less in step with one another. Freer trade seemed a real possibility.

The keystone to the series of treaties directed to this purpose was the International Monetary Fund (IMF) designed to maintain the free convertibility of currencies at fixed rates of exchange. The price of each nation's currency was to be maintained within 1 per cent of the stated par value by appropriate open market purchase and sales by the financial authorities. The United States was to peg the system to gold by standing ready to buy and sell gold or dollars at the fixed price of $35 per ounce of gold. Since the US was the only nation committed to gold convertibility, in effect the IMF agreement made every nation able to state its currency relative to the dollar. Devaluation of any currency beyond the 1 per cent margin required approval by the other members of the IMF. It was to be justified to them on the grounds that there is a 'structural disequilibrium' in exchange rates so that the price of a currency does not reflect the relative productivity of that nation.

In order to provide a source of short-term credit for nations with temporary or hot money balance of payments problems, the IMF was to stand ready to lend gold and foreign exchange of 'scarce' currencies for short periods of time. The funds are obtained from quotas subscribed in the currency of each nation. These loans were solely to ease temporary strains in order to lessen pressures to devalue – not to provide long-term funds for economic development. The IMF was not intended to cover up structural disequilibrium or grant loans to countries that are not attempting to control increases in national income that keep them out of step.

This system survived from the end of the Second World War until it collapsed in 1971. It finally gave way when the United States announced that it could no longer make its dollars convertible into gold. In the resulting floating market it would not peg the dollar in fixed ratio to other currencies.

What was wrong with the IMF system? In a nutshell, it was a fixed exchange rate system that required that nations keep in step in their national incomes. It broke down when they were no longer willing or able to do so. Unlike the Depression era, the increase in national incomes was associated more with inflation than with increased employment and output.

Under the IMF arrangement, the postwar world really was on a *dollar standard* in much the same way as it had been on a sterling standard. The United States, undamaged by the war, emerged as the major source of goods for reconstruction and development. The US also emerged as the world's unofficial banker. Dollars were used as international means of payment, and nations held dollars as reserves against their own currency. By spending and lending dollars the US was responsible for creating international reserve money.

Could a situation arise in which nations would not be anxious to hold dollars? The possibility seemed far fatched, and yet that is precisely what happened! The postwar era opened with an American balance of trade surplus, which was only brought near balance by capital outflows from the United States: private investments, official loans and grants such as the Marshall Plan, and military spending. The end of the era found the United States with an unfavourable balance of trade and the rest of the world flooded with dollars. Holders of dollars seriously questioned how long the US would be able to continue to convert them into gold and other currencies. Inevitably, this speculation resulted in a further speculative hot money demand to convert dollars. Its position having become untenable, America abandoned its pledge to redeem dollars by gold and allowed the dollar to float. The dollar declined in value, effectively devaluing it.

How did this turnabout in the American fortunes come to pass? Part of the answer is the increased level of national income in the United States, due to inflation as well as increased real output. The increase in imports that implies placed a strain on the US payments balance. There was much more involved, however. The fixed values of European and Japanese currencies had been determined in the immediate postwar era when the productivity of these areas was low. As the years went on, this changed and at least the developed areas of the world came closer to American productivity. Yet their currency was valued at ratios to the dollar reflecting bygone circumstances. Europe and Asia had caught up, and yet the old exchange rates still prevailed. Particularly the Japanese yen and the German mark were undervalued below the equilibrium level. Finally, the massive military and aid programmes undertaken by the US had drained reserves in a way not responsive to market collection.

The outflow of dollars constituted a threat to the stability of other economies as it entered into their monetary system. Under the IMF, nations were obliged to receive all the dollars offered them at the fixed rates of exchange. Their central banks had to buy dollars by writing cheques in their own currency which functioned as high powered money. Also, European banks loaned deposits in dollars, *Eurodollars*, employing the same multiplying fractional reserve system. The effect was to create a multiplied increase in the money stock of all nations. Under the depression conditions which were the background for the Keynesian thinking behind the IMF, this would have been a positive development for the recipient nations. Foreign demand would be added to domestic demand to raise total national income and employment. But under the circumstances of full employment, the addition of further demand and the increase in the money stock only served to aggravate the epidemic tendencies toward inflation.

Keynes succeeded only too well. Full employment became the commitment of all nations, and the rigid international payments machinery designed to complement the commitment served to inflame its inherent inflationary tendency. The IMF system made it impossible for a country to restrict its money supply in the face of massive flows of funds from abroad. It turned out that a favourable balance of payments is not always so favourable. The inflationary pressures were compounded by political considerations. Nations such as France strongly disapproved of the US military and political actions and felt that they were accepting the burden of financing these expenditures by taking all the dollars the US cared to create.

When the Americans eventually allowed the dollar to float, they cut ties represented by the balance of payments constraint. Unless income and speculative destabilization effects recur, allowing the dollar to find the value given by supply and demand means that the market will always clear at some value – for dollars as surely as tomatoes. Once having stopped worrying about the value that dollars will ultimately find on the market, the Americans were able to stop worrying about the loss of foreign exchange.

After several months of very difficult negotiations it was decided that at least a provisional return to the IMF system of fixed exchange rates was in order. This stopgap measure advocated by Europe also broke down as inflationary pressures in Britain forced it to allow its currency to float. At the moment continental countries are jointly floating their currencies versus the dollar whilst holding their own monies in relatively fixed values.

Everyone agrees on the need for a new international monetary system. There is general agreement that the dollar should give up its role as a key currency. The special status of the dollar is objectionable to nations other than the US because it had tended to spread US inflationary pressures to the rest of the world. The Americans are anxious to give up the role of a world central banker, since maintaining a stable dollar convertible to other currencies and gold prevents it from looking after its own self-interest. Here agreement ends. What should replace the dollar as international reserve money? What should be done about the huge 'overhang' of dollars currently held by the rest of the world?

A British suggestion is that the dollar be replaced by the SDR (special drawing rights) which had been created earlier during a period of inadequate international liquidity. Special drawing rights are often called 'paper gold', since they are a reserve asset created by the IMF which can be loaned as any other scarce currency or gold. The proposal is to 'fund' (i.e. exchange) the dollar overcharge into SDR which would then be subject to regulation by the International Monetary Fund which would act like a central bank does in any country. The Americans are much in favour of such an arrangement. France is opposed to the idea since it fears it would permit further money creation. It is much concerned that excess new money should not be created to dispose of the old dollar system.

Even more important than the reserve asset question is what sort of understanding can be achieved on the vexed issue of flexible versus rigid exchange rates. *Fixed exchange rates* arising either from the old gold standard or international treaty mean that nations must keep in step or face balance of payments crises. Nations learnt to keep in step to maintain full employment, but they have not been able to keep in step in controlling inflation. *Flexible exchange rates* arising either from fully floating foreign exchange markets or periodic decisions to devalue remove the necessity for keeping in step and allow each country to pursue its own national economic plan for better or worse, but at the same time remove the discipline of the balance of payments constraint.

Britain and international markets

Britain entered this century as an exporter of manufactured goods and services, and an importer of food and raw materials. The market for manufactures was concentrated in western Europe and the sterling area (roughly the Empire excluding Canada); food and raw material supplies came from all the world's regions (Table 14.3). The unfavourable balance of trade in merchandise was more than made up by the large volume of invisible exports of financial and shipping services, and income from investments abroad.

The Depression era witnessed a dramatic decline in the volume of international trade. In 1936 exports from the UK dropped below the level achieved in 1913! Like the rest of the world, Britain's trade became more concentrated in its own trading area, the sterling bloc. Nonetheless, the structure of imported raw materials and exported manufactures remained constant.

Table 14.3 The structure of Britain's trade: merchandise imports and exports

			Imports			
				Origin (*per cent*)		
Year	Value (£ million)	% of finished mfg.	West Europe	Stlg. area	North Amer.	Rest of world
1913	769	6·4	35·5	20·8	22·8	20·9
1936	848	6·8	25·8	29·6	20·3	24·3
1955	3860	5·3	25·9	39·2	19·8	15·1
1970	9048	22·9	37·8	27·2	20·6	14·5

			Exports			
				Destination (*per cent*)		
Year	Value (£ million)	% of non-mfg.	West Europe	Stlg. area	North Amer.	Rest of world
1913	525	19·8	31·4	32·6	10·5	25·5
1936	441	20·9	25·6	43·5	12·1	18·8
1955	2877	14·8	27·4	48·0	11·3	13·3
1970	7741	11·6	40·5	28·0	15·3	16·1

Source: The British Economy: Key Statistics 1900–1970, pp. 14–15.

After the Second World War Britain's competitors in world markets – Germany, France, Italy, Japan and the United States – made rapid progress in reconstruction of damage and in modernizing their industrial plants, forcing Britain to rely even more heavily on its traditional market. The continental powers organized themselves into the European Economic Community, achieving free trade among themselves, as well as free movement of capital and labour. The law of comparative advantage worked. EEC countries eventually abandoned empire and grew rapidly on the basis of larger European markets and consolidation and coordination of industries such as iron and steel. Applying the infant industry argument for protection from foreign (mostly American) competition during the postwar era of reconstruction, the EEC developed a common tariff barrier against outside competition, while reaping the advantages of free trade among themselves.

Britain elected not to join the EEC, and found itself facing stiff competition in exports from all quarters of the world. Its inability to adequately cope with the competition resulted in chronic balance of payments crises. Successive devaluations did not save the situation as increased domestic prices consumed the temporary commercial advantage. What was needed was higher productivity, lower costs and improved export performance. Yet it proved increasingly difficult to achieve this economy in the absence of an adequate market area to reap the benefits of economies of large-scale production.

In the course of the past two decades it has proved increasingly difficult to rely on the traditional sterling area as the large-scale market. Part of the reason is the development of political independence of the region. While independence certainly does not contradict trade, the degree of exclusiveness of trading and commercial ties to Britain have been weakened. More important is the remarkable shift towards manufactured goods as the main item in world trade. Look at Table 14.3. Who would have thought that by 1970 Britain would devote almost 23 per cent of its imports to finished manufactures after having gone through the first three-quarters of the century with only 5 to 6 per cent of manufactured imports? World trade patterns are shifting away from the exchange of raw materials from underdeveloped primary producing countries for the manufactured goods produced by developing nations. The emphasis on trade is moving toward trade in manufactured and otherwise highly fabricated goods between the developed nations. It is cheaper to create synthetic materials in modern industrial plants than to buy natural raw materials; evidently people prefer to consume more sophisticated goods produced by technologically advanced industries rather than the exotic natural products so popular in the past. The world trend towards trade in manufactures certainly represents a threat to the development plans of the newly independent underdeveloped nations. It also means that Britain no longer can concentrate its trading efforts within the less developed sectors of the commonwealth.

Increased imports of manufactures does not of itself imply balance of payments difficulties. The example of EEC countries shows that it is perfectly possible to balance imports of manufactured goods with exports of other manufactured goods. Nevertheless, Britain has to be able to compete and penetrate markets in a difficult new world market situation. Should it fail to do this, then the analysis of the preceding parts of this chapter can be used to foresee the results. The decline in net exports would multiply up to tend to reduce national income and employment. Should Britain decide to maintain full employment anyway by expansive fiscal policy, essentially substituting G for the lagging E, imports will increase and a balance of payments crisis will result. Were this to happen then the alternatives would be: (a) maintain the value of the pound and meet the imbalance by restricting imports through a system of tariffs, licences, import quotas, more rigorous exchange controls – the effect would be to maintain employment, but to restrict the goods available for final use; (b) allow the pound to fall in value either through periodic devaluations or by floating it, thus making imports more expensive and exports cheaper. This also would have the effect of restricting imports, as well as diverting resources toward goods to be shipped abroad.

Should Britain decide not to attempt to maintain full employment by fiscal policy – an almost unimaginable alternative in the current political framework – then wages and incomes would have to decline until full employment and the balance of payments were both restored at a much lower standard of living. None of these prospects – or any combination of them – is very inviting.

Competition in world markets today involves more than productivity. In a manner alarmingly reminiscent of the interwar years, the world has divided up into multinational trading areas protected from foreign competition by tariffs, exchange controls, devalued (floating) currencies and the like. The EEC, the US market, the Soviet bloc, and the growing Japanese market are examples. After much soul searching and debate, Britain negotiated its entry into the Common Market. The many issues involved all boil down to whether Britain is willing to keep in step with its new partners. That means unemployment or balance of payments problems may only be met by either increasing exports through efficiency or cutting imports resulting in lower levels of income, wages, standard of living.

Originally entry into the EEC implied the acceptance of the doctrine of 'compete or else', with no leeway for devaluation or floating of the pound with respect to European currencies. The pound was to be held as a 'snake in a tunnel' linked to the high and low values of other currencies. The argument for British acceptance of these terms was that there was no longer a choice whether to be competitive, but only where to be competitive. The argument against entry turned on a desire to pursue an independent prices and incomes policy at variance with European countries. In 1972, shortly after the entry into the EEC was voted, inflationary pressures in Britain and hot money flows forced the abandonment of the policy and the floating of the pound. Sterling slipped out of the tunnel. At this writing the question is open once again whether Britain can, or ought, to link itself strictly to the Continent. If so, then Britain will have to restrict its domestic inflation by monetary and other means even at the price of less employment so that it keeps in step with Europe without further devaluations. If not, then Britain will have to find large-scale markets elsewhere, or penetrate European markets by heightened productivity as well as economic diplomacy. It is a critical question involving painful choices either way.

Exercise:
(1) The 1972 decision to float the pound was made inevitable by the hot money flows. What could have been done to prevent the flight from

sterling, and what ought to be done in future? Do you think the problem would be solved if all EEC members had a common currency?

(2) What special contributions can Britain bring to the EEC? What contributions can the EEC make to solving some of the UK regional and employment problems? Will Britain's entry make any of these problems more severe?

(3) Would Britain be better off to align itself more closely with the United States market than with the EEC? Should Britain try to go it alone?

(4) What are the issues raised by the different ways in which EEC countries and Britain support agriculture? How will the entry into the market affect the welfare of farmers and that of consumers?

(5) In what way was Britain's tie to the Commonwealth involved in working out the conditions for entry? How does entry affect New Zealanders? Nigerians?

(6) Compare the arguments of the left wing of the Labour Party and the right wing of the Conservative Party opposing entry into the EEC.

(7) Is the expectation of gains from trade within the EEC compatible with the high degree of government sponsorship, semi-official cartels in many industries and overall *dirigisme* exhibited on the continent? Can there be gains from trade without competition, i.e. under total planning?

(8) Apply the theory of international payments to two regions of the same country – say Wales and England. Treat them as if they were two countries with a fixed relation between their currencies: one Welsh pound equals one English pound. Describe the mechanism by which their economies are kept in step. Explain the causes of higher unemployment and lower levels of personal income in Wales. Would Wales benefit from a more flexible arrangement whereby it could alter the value of its currency relative to England? Would the United Kingdom as a whole benefit? Apart from the legal and political considerations, how does the two-country explanation differ from the regional picture within the UK? What are the consequences for regional and overall development of the difference? Can an analogy be drawn between the position of Wales within the UK and the position of the UK within the Common Market?

(9) A large volume of European trade and finance is carried on in *Eurodollars*. These are claims on dollars which are held by European banks and loaned to both European and American firms. Eurodollars are convenient, because they avoid the regulations of trade, lending and the like that each country has set up with regard to its own currencies.

It has been argued that much of the overhang of dollars has arisen out of a bank multiplier in Eurodollar deposits. Show how this might happen so that the supply of dollars available in Europe is a multiple of the actual US balance of payments deficit.

Do you think there ought to be some sort of regulation of the Eurodollar market? If so, what do you think the goals of such regulations ought to be? How do you think the goals could be implemented?

(10) Review the effect of the increase in the price of petroleum by the OPEC countries on the international position of:

(a) non-oil producing less developed countries

(b) large energy importers among the developed countries such as the US, Japan and some EEC countries

(c) Great Britain and other nations sharing in the North Sea oil discoveries.

(11) To what extent do you feel the current inflation-combined-with-unemployment syndrome is the product of the oil crisis? What policies should oil importers take toward the OPEC group?

15 Economic growth in nations rich and poor

The problem stated

The concern that growth in national income might be excessive in view of scarce and irreplaceable resources is relatively new (see Chapter 11). Most of the time, and in most places, economic growth has been considered desirable. In the wealthy developed nations, high levels of national income were relied upon not only to increase the material well-being of the population but as the means of mitigating the conflicts of interest between classes and groups. If each got a larger income, then the struggles over sharing the pie were that much easier to contain. Moreover, as will be shown in this chapter, it turns out that growth in national income is a virtual necessity to maintain high levels of employment – a decline in growth tending to induce a further decline which might well end in depression. In the less developed countries, growth was taken as an essential to escape from poverty. Specifically industrial development was seen as the means of obtaining some of the means to a better life. Economic development was a prerequisite to genuine national independence from the richer industrial powers.

   In this final chapter we study how developed nations have attempted to maintain a steady growth. This will permit us to gain some insight into the problems of development of the poorer countries, as well as the wealthy.

Consumption and savings revisited

During the terrible years of the 1930s it appeared that capitalism was doomed. This forecast, known as the *stagnation thesis*, was based on the expectation of the tendency of the average propensity to consume to fall as income rose. As the autonomous component of the consumption function becomes relatively less important, a greater proportion of the income of society is not consumed. If this saving were not funnelled back into expenditures by growing investment, a deflationary gap would develop. Keynes seemed to be spelling out what Marx has predicted in the *Communist Manifesto*: the very wealth of society had become a fetter upon itself.

Would there be sufficient investment to close a growing gap? It didn't seem very likely. After all, net investment involves the acquisition of new plant and equipment. Businessmen buy new capital goods when they expect business to get better. But Depression business was in a chronic state of despair. Unused equipment was everywhere. Monetary policy had brought on the very lowest interest rates, and yet investment stagnated. Nor did there seem to be a new upsurge of technical changes which would require the scrapping of old machinery.

There seemed no way out but massive deficit expenditures by the government. To be sure, attempts were made to increase consumption by raising the autonomous element of consumption – shifting the consumption function forward. These included redistribution of income to low income families through wage increases and social security transfer payments. Yet a foregone conclusion was that the consumption function would not really budge. Government expenditure would have to increase indefinitely to achieve full employment. Like it or not, the public sector appeared to be on the way to dominating the economy.

Many did not like it. A famous book by F. A. Hayek argued that increased public expenditure was the *Road to Serfdom*. He cited Adam Smith to the effect that each individual was the best judge of his own self-interest. Free choice by individuals in economic life was identified with political and social freedom. Milton Friedman has enlarged on this theme in forceful and readable terms in the more current *Capitalism and Freedom*.

Others did like it. John Galbraith in *The Affluent Society* argued that there was an urgent need for enlarged expenditure for public goods such as schools, hospitals and roads. The Marxist, Paul M. Sweezy, contended in *The Theory of Capitalist Development* that whilst it might be in their enlightened self-interest, capitalists were not capable of allowing 'their' government to spend money on public welfare for peaceful purposes. There was a consensus, however, that in the absence of massive government spending the same depressed situation would be resumed after the war.

Economists measured the unemployment that could be expected. The world braced itself.

The anticipated postwar depression never materialized, due largely to an amazing increase in consumer demand. To the astonishment of those who took the consumption function as a law of human nature, the relation between consumption and income changed dramatically. The consumption function shifted. Economists scurried back to their statistics, and discovered that as they reviewed longer and longer time spans, consumption seemed to become more nearly proportional to income. In terms of the language we have been using, the average propensity to consume seemed more nearly constant, rather than tending to decline.

Something of this long-run behaviour in consumption can be seen in Figure 15.1, which charts the US long-run consumption function from the depression through the 1950s. If a consumption function line is fitted only for the years 1929–40, the consumption function has a slope of 0·79 and an intercept of $171·6 billion. However, if the scatter for the whole period 1929–58 is used (not considering the war years) the consumption function has a greater slope equal to 0·86 and a lower intercept of $104·9 billion.

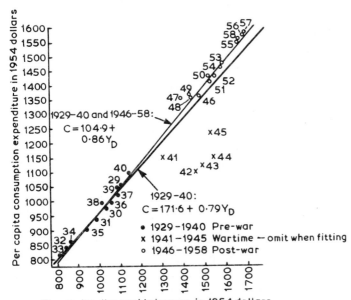

Figure 15.1   Long-run consumption functions (G. Ackley, *Macroeconomic Theory* (1961), p. 247)

Much the same situation occurred in the United Kingdom (Figure 15.2). Based on prewar information, the equation for the consumption function was $C = 0·65Y + 22·8$. All the statistical tests showed this line to be a good

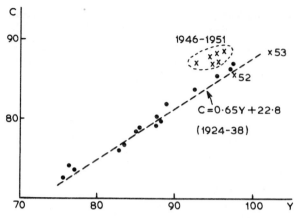

Figure 15.2   Consumption and per capita disposable income in the UK (E. Malinvaud, *Statistical Methods of Econometrics* (Chicago, Rand McNally, 1966), p. 117)

estimate; yet, as Malinvaud, one of the world's leading economic statisticians, writes, 'In fact predictions made in this way turn out to be very poor. Thus in 1948 disposable income per head in the United Kingdom was £92·6 at 1938 prices. The regression [i.e. the equation *mw*] gives a consumption of £83·0 as against an observed £87·0. Saving should have been £9·6 according to the regression, but in fact came to £5·6' (E. Malinvaud, *Statistical Methods of Econometrics*, p. 118). The little crosses in Malinvaud's figure show the actual postwar consumption pattern. Obviously they do not belong to the same consumption function as the years 1924–38.

At first it was thought that the heightened consumption was merely a temporary phenomenon resulting from pent-up demand after the war. However, when longer periods were tested, the average propensity to consume seemed more stable than ever. The average propensity to consume for the UK seemed stable at about 0·95 of disposable income. Back to the drawing boards!

Two main explanations emerged for the unexpected result. Milton Friedman's view amounts to an attack on the whole Keynesian apparatus. He denies the existence of an autonomous element in consumption, and argues that it is only a statistical 'fluke' that makes it appear otherwise. The error, he says, derives from the preposterous belief that people adjust their consumption to their current income. Factory workers are paid fortnightly. Does that mean that they only eat on alternate Fridays and consume nothing the rest of the time? In fact, Friedman says, people sensibly adjust their life styles to their long-run earnings. They do this not just for a fortnight, but for their likely earnings for longer periods of time – up to a lifetime. He calls this their *permanent income*. On theoretical and statistical grounds, he says, human behaviour is such that a constant portion of the permanent income is devoted to consumption and the rest is saved. The average propensity to consume permanent income is constant.

The actual income of individuals, Friedman observes, is composed of a *transitory income element* as well as permanent income. In any particular year people earn more or less than their permanent income. Transitory income is a random matter, by definition. It may be positive or negative. Therefore, if consumption is related only to permanent income it is unrelated to the transitory income.

The crucial point is that if the random transitory income is not related at all to consumption, it will appear as if consumption contains the autonomous element. This is easy to see graphically (Figure 15.3). C is proportional to permanent income, Y_p, so the constant average propensity to consume is $a_c = C/Y_p$. Then $C = a_c Y_p$ is a straight line through the origin.

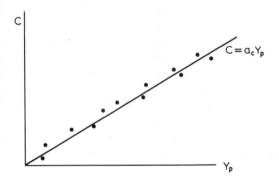

Figure 15.3   Consumption and permanent income

In Figure 15.4 we display total income on the horizontal axis, and continue to show consumption vertically. Friedman's thesis is that consumption is unaffected by the addition of transitory to permanent income to make up total income. If this were the case, then for each of the dots making up the scatter diagram in Figure 15.3 the vertical consumption coordinate would not be changed. But the horizontal income measure would change by the amount of the randomly distributed, positive or negative, transitory income. This is illustrated in Figure 15.4. If transitory income is randomly distributed, it is just as likely that each of the dots will move to the left representing negative transitory income, as to the right for positive transitory income.

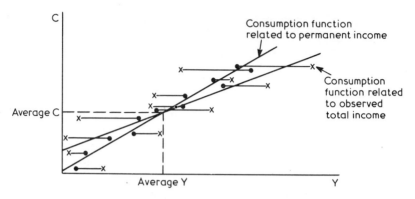

Figure 15.4   Consumption and permanent plus transitory income

It is also true that the average income and average consumption should not be affected by random changes in income – the sum of the transitory components should be zero. To illustrate this (Figure 15.5), one half of the dots of Figure 15.3 are moved to the left and the other to the right. The new locations of the dots are indicated with little x's. Then, by inspecting the diagram, it is clear that a line fitted to the x's passing through the same average consumption and average income point would have a smaller slope than one fitted to the dots. The line through the x's is what the Keynesians actually observed – consumption and total income. It appears, says Professor Friedman, that there is a constant element of autonomous consumption since the line goes through the consumption axis at some vertical point. In reality; consumption is determined by permanent income, and the transitory element of short-run income has nothing to do with consumption. The Keynesian prediction of increasing average propensity to consume is therefore a misleading bogey. Long-run consumption will cluster around the line of consumption and permanent income.

The alternative explanation is associated with James Duesenbery of Harvard. In his view, the consumption function does contain components of autonomous consumption that reflect basic standards of living. However, this element is not engraved in stone, but is historically and culturally conditioned largely by one's neighbours and associates. If the standard of living that people regard as normal should change, the consumption function will shift. A rise in A shifts up consumption function equation, $C = cY + A$, parallel to itself. The shifting of *short-run consumption functions* in this fashion can be seen to give rise to a *long-run consumption function* which appears to be more nearly a line drawn through the origin. In the long run,

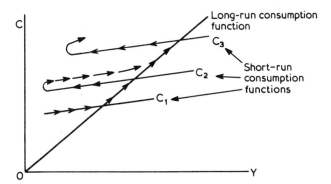

Figure 15.5   The ratchet effect of long- and short-run consumption functions

then, the marginal and average propensities to consume would be identical since they would be the slope of the long-run relationship (Figure 15.5).

Consumption, Duesenbery tells us, acts like the ratchet device fitted to a mechanic's spanner. The tool locks as pressure is applied, but the ratchet releases when the tool is drawn back. Hence the bolt advances as the spanner is moved up and back. In the same way, with each swing of the trade cycle, consumption is driven to higher levels by the rise of national income, but does not fall back to its previous level when the rise of income is reversed. In Figure 15.5 suppose the consumption function relevant to the Depression years was C_1. Consumers emerged from the war with both cash and pent-up desire for consumer goods. Having achieved a higher consumption level, they moved up to a higher short-run consumption function, C_2. Even though income fell with the next cycle, the consumer retreated along the function C_2, as shown by the arrows. Once business picked up again, he moved to a still higher function, C_3. In the long run consumption is seen to be related to the line drawn through the origin, which shows the trend of the shifting of the short-run relationships.

Whether one accepts the Duesenbery ratchet or the permanent income hypothesis of Milton Friedman, the evidence is that in the long run consumption is more or less proportional to income. That puts a different light on the stagnation thesis, because if the long-run average propensity to consume is constant, so is the average propensity to save! The amount of savings that has to be invested increases, but the proportion to national income stays about the same. The question still is: where is this investment going to come from? This may be a difficult problem, but it is not the impasse that the stagnationists anticipated.

Induced investment: the Harrod–Domar treadmill

The important thing to see about investment is that it is a link between the present and the future. Investment, the accumulation of capital, is undertaken because capitalists expect that more equipment will be needed. Keynes was certainly right to point out that over short periods of time expectations may be influenced by the mood of businessmen and the temper of the times. Capitalists may decide to postpone investment because they feel business is going to be bad whether or not they have substantial evidence for their judgement. If businessmen think things are going to be rosy, they may invest before their competitors think of it!

Yet the very success of Keynes's programme in dealing with short-term factors requires that we ask: what are the underlying causes that make businessmen believe that investment is called for? Why do firms invest in new machinery? The answer still depends on the entrepreneur's time perspective. Over the long run the motivation might reflect a change in technical coefficients of production: thus labour saving machinery might be introduced if wages rise, new inventions might render the old processes and equipment obsolete. Consider, however, the very important situation which is intermediate between the short-run situation dominated by business psychology, and the long-run where technology is subject to substantial change and adaptation. This is the fixed technology situation such as is envisioned in input-output analysis. In this time frame, we shall show how investment depends on the amount of growth in national income.

Recall that the technology matrix described ratios of the *flow of materials* and semi-finished goods to the *flow of outputs*. The constancy of these ratios over reasonable time spans justified their use in further analysis. Now we must consider slightly different coefficients which relate the *stock of capital* used in each industry to the flow of output – how much machinery, equipment and building must be on hand to permit a unit of output to flow from each industry. Unlike the earlier technology matrix we are not looking at the intermediate inputs used up per unit of output, but at the plant that must be there for the work to get done.

In order to carry on the analysis, let us not deal with the whole matrix of such capital coefficients, since that will involve us in more mathematics than is necessary to get at the basic issues. Instead we simply will speak to the stock of capital in general, K, as if it were a single type of machine. Then the coefficient we need is the ratio of capital stock to the flow of national income, $v = K/Y$. This ratio is called the *capital-output* ratio,[1] or the *accelerator*. It follows from this statement that the needed capital stock is proportional to

---

[1] Strictly the ratio relates capital to the value of final use (net output) rather than total output. Nevertheless, we shall use the customary name for v.

national income, that $K = vY$, and that the increase in capital that firms will demand is proportional to the increase in income: $\Delta K = y\Delta Y$. But the change in capital stock is investment, I, so investment is proportional to the change in income, $I = v\Delta Y$. For investment to be carried on at all income must grow!

This puts the problem of investment in a rather peculiar light. If there is to be any investment at all, income must grow. The issue is not whether income is high or low, but how much it increases. If the income level were to increase faster, it would call forth additional investment, causing income to grow further. But if income fails to increase – or increases too slowly – then investment will fall and the multiplier process will reduce income further still! We ask: how much must income increase to permit sustained growth in investment? Clearly enough to absorb the additional savings that are also generated as national income gets higher and higher. The delicacy of the balance suggested by this view of economic growth requires that we state it very carefully in symbolic terms. Savings is equal to income times the average propensity to save, $S = a_s Y$. Since we require that $S = I$, to prevent a recession, it follows that we must have $a_s Y = v\Delta Y$. The necessary condition to prevent a fall in income is therefore: $\Delta Y/Y = a_s/v$. This analysis, called the Harrod-Domar model after Sir Ray Harrod and Evsey Domar who independently discovered it, shows the per cent increase in national income $\Delta Y/Y$ is required to equal a_s/v. Harrod called this the *warranted rate of growth*, the average propensity to save divided by the capital-output ratio.

Warranted growth must take place if a cumulative decline in income is to be avoided. Notice that we are not saying that it will be so, only that, if it does not, a depression will occur. Make a very crude calculation: If a_s is roughly 0·2, and v is approximately 3, it follows that the economy must grow very roughly at a bit less than 7 per cent for there to be adequate investment demand. Undoubtedly this is too large when other factors are considered, but the figure gives some idea of the magnitudes involved. The consequence of a 7 per cent annual increase in national income is that in each year national income must be 107 per cent of the year preceding. But since the base of the percentage grows each year, the amount of annual growth gets bigger and bigger. As the table accompanying Figure 15.6 shows, in eleven years national income would have had to more than double, from, say, £100 in year zero to £210·50 in year eleven! If income can grow at the warranted rate, growth creates its own demand by generating enough investment to absorb savings. Can it be done?

Exercise:
(1) Explain how a rate of growth in national income less than the warranted rate will result in inadequate demand because output has not increased enough.

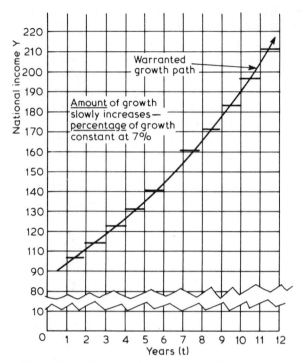

t	Y
0	100
1	107
2	114·49
3	122·50
4	131·08
5	140·26
6	150·08
7	160·59
8	171·83
9	183·86
10	196·73
11	210·50

Figure 15.6   Warranted growth path after eleven years of expansion at 7 per cent

(2) UK national income in 1969 was £35·4 million and in 1970 was £38·7 million. Using the values for the average propensity to save and for the accelerator suggested in the text calculate:
  1. Required investment in 1970.
  2. Savings in 1970.
  3. Actual investment in 1970 was £9330 million. Would 1971 show a business depression due to inadequate demand? Did it?
  4. What would 1970 income have to be to avoid a depression at the start of 1971?
  5. How might changes in v and a_s affect your forecast? Explain in terms of the components of aggregate demand for final use $Y = C + I$.

(3) Let income in year zero be called Y_0 and income in year 1 be called Y_1. In the example each year is 107 per cent of the preceding year. Clearly $Y_1 = 1·07 Y_0$. Income in year 2 is obviously $Y_2 = 1·07 Y_1$. Now express Y_2 in terms of Y_0. Show that for any year, t, income in that year is $Y_t = (1·07)^t Y_0$.

In general if each year is a multiple, M, of the preceding year, $Y_t = MY_0$. Show what will happen if M is a positive number greater than, equal to or less than 1. Give examples with particular values of M. What will happen if M is equal to -2 or $-\frac{1}{2}$?

(4) What must the average propensity to save be to avoid depressions if the capital-output ratio is 3 and the annual growth rate is 3 per cent? How does excess idle capital equipment on hand during a depression affect new investment when income rises?

(5) Consult the Blue Book and compute the average propensity to consume for the past five years. Using the average of these figures, and taking the capital-output ratio to be 3, compute the percentage by which this year's national income would have to exceed last year's to stay on the warranted growth path. Did Britain stay on the growth path? Describe the economic events of the past year in terms of your findings.

Warranted and natural rates of growth

Can an economy continue to grow indefinitely by the same per cent each year? Is it feasible indefinitely to increase national income by increasing amounts? The answer lies in the nature of the production possibility frontiers that limit the final use that constitutes national income. We have seen that as time passes these frontiers are subject to shifts. Thus the labour and capital frontiers shift outward as the labour force grows and capital is accumulated through investment. Moreover, as technical progress reduces the labour (and capital) directly and indirectly required for each unit of final use, the effect also is to shift the frontiers outward. To be sure most – not all – natural resource frontiers represent inputs that are not renewable. Here continued growth depends on technical progress in the use of these resources, using those in plentiful supply as substitutes for scarce items, and substituting capital and labour for natural resources (see Chapter 11).

A convenient way for us to express the possibilities of growth is to identify it with the rate of growth of the labour force, plus the rate of growth of labour productivity due to the increase in the other cooperating factors and technical progress in their use. The rate of growth in potential national income is called the *natural rate of growth*. The central issue that concerns us is the relation between the natural and the warranted rates of growth. The warranted rate can exceed the natural rate, which, as we shall see, is the most likely eventuality for industrially developed countries; the warranted rate can be less than the natural rate, corresponding to the situation in many less developed countries; and the two rates can coincide in a situation in which adjustment has been made between the maintenance of full employment

levels of investment and savings on one hand, and the technical possibilities
of production on the other.

In *A Contribution to the Theory of the Trade Cycle*, Sir John Hicks
examined the high rate of savings in wealthy countries, and the relatively low
rate of increase in population and labour productivity and concluded that
the warranted growth rate would exceed the natural. Graphing the corresponding *growth paths* (Figure 15.7), he concluded that the warranted growth
path would overtake the natural. Once having reached the limits of potential
output, growth along the warranted path would be impossible. Due to the
failure of national income to increase further, investment would fall to zero
(or to a greatly diminished amount) whilst savings were still at a high level.
The inevitable result would be a contraction in national income and employment through the multiplier process. The resulting business recession would
continue until investment were renewed through the physical depreciation
of the old capital equipment, obsolescence as a result of technical progress,
or government monetary and fiscal policy designed to restimulate the
accumulation of capital. The expansion would operate until the next recession.

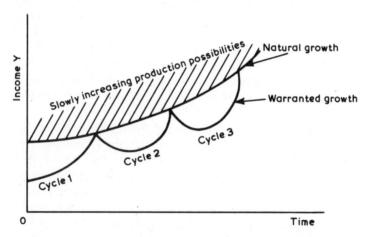

Figure 15.7   The warranted growth rate exceeds the natural

The trade cycle can be seen as a form of forced adjustment of production
possibilities. The rate of growth required to absorb savings requires that
national income grow more rapidly than it physically can. The trade cycle
represents the adaptation to that reality through repeated approaches to the
limits on output, and swings away from it as the warranted growth path
'bounces off the ceiling' of potential national income. The symptoms of

recession are inadequate demand for investment and hence for consumption. The cause of the cycle, however, is the limitation in supply possibilities. Paradoxical as it may seem, the burden of the analysis is that inadequate demand exists because it is impossible to produce enough!

If Hicks is right, then governmental intervention in the system to maintain full employment by suppressing the recessions must be seen in a new light. A firm commitment to continue along a warranted growth path by monetary expansion and government demand amounts to a decision to a continued state of excess demand. It is simply a recipe for continuing inflation. Moreover, it is questionable whether it is possible to continue to do so if money illusion breaks down and the public learns to anticipate empty price rises and make their decisions to consume and invest in terms of real national income.

The urgent question is whether other forms of adaptation are possible, or whether accelerating inflation will ultimately compel the abandonment of the full employment commitment. What sort of adaptation? Obviously one in which the warranted rate of growth is reduced, whilst the natural rate is raised so as to make them more nearly equal. Since the warranted rate is the average propensity to save divided by the capital–output ratio, a decline in the numerator or a rise in the denominator will be helpful; the natural rate of growth is the growth of the labour force plus the growth in the productivity of labour, so a rise in either of these will also help reduce the discrepancy.

Certainly it is an open question whether a competitive market economy is capable of making these adjustments fast enough, but it should be clear to readers of Part 2 of this book that the law of variable proportion tends toward such adaptation. As full employment of the labour force is achieved, it becomes relatively scarce compared to capital. Rising wages stimulate the introduction of labour saving machinery thus raising the capital–output ratio on one hand and increasing labour productivity on the other. Increased wages have the further effect of enlarging the labour force, since additional workers respond to the incentives offered. Housewives take factory jobs, partially unemployed workers in depressed regions migrate to high employment areas, workers accept overtime hours and so on.[2] Moreover, the increased supply of capital relative to labour reduces interest rates by lowering the marginal productivity of capital. The result is a reduced tendency to save, which can be seen as a response to the interest incentive as the 'classical economists' maintained, rather than as a response to income as the Keynesians would have it. In any case, since savings originate more in the

---

[2] It should be pointed out that higher wages sometimes have a negative effect on labour force participation if there is an 'income effect' in which workers prefer more leisure to money income after having achieved a certain level of wage improvement.

profits and interest incomes of capitalists than in the wage incomes of workers, the relative decline in the income of capital relative to that of labour tends to lower the average propensity to save.

All in all, the market mechanism points in the direction of equalizing the natural and warranted rates of growth. In this dynamic growth situation the economy adapts to scarcity through substitution of plentiful for scarce resources for exactly the same reasons that it did in the situations analysed in Part 2 where production possibility frontiers were taken as static rather than growing. Can one rely on the market mechanism to carry out the adaptation? Here agreement among economists ends. Unlike the static situations in which, in effect, we allowed as much time as necessary to carry out adjustments, everything in this dynamic growth situation depends on how fast adaptation takes place.

The view descended from Keynes is one of a fairly rigid economic system in which responses are more to income rather than price incentives; technical coefficients of production tend to be sticky relative to the speed with which national income can rise or fall. Investigations into long-run adaptations are purely an academic exercise having little to do with the real world, not only because people are short sighted and concerned only with immediate problems, but because income effects, monopolistic elements of rigidity and the limited number of technical alternatives actually available inhibit the substitution effect from being adequate to the situations actually facing society. Probably the best known exponent of this view is Joan Robinson of Cambridge University. She has dubbed the congruence of the natural and warranted growth paths the 'golden age of economic growth' to 'emphasize its mythical character.'

The alternative view which relies on the adaptive mechanism argues that by government adopting the policy of attempting to direct and adjust the level of national income toward full employment, such rigidities are compounded and reinforced. While this view accepts the possibilities of dynamic systems going off the rails due to income effects and price rigidities as they did during the Depression, it is argued that massive governmental intervention ought to be largely reserved for such circumstances. This view was advanced by Paul Samuelson and Robert Solow of the Massachusetts Institute of Technology located in Cambridge, Massachusetts, in the United States. It would be incorrect to dub one view the 'English' view and the other the 'American', since proponents of each school of thought are to be found on both sides of the Atlantic. Nonetheless, a highly sophisticated debate between these scholars took place and the opposition has come to be known as the 'Cambridge versus Cambridge' controversy. This is no academic exercise, since the fate of the economic system depends on who turns out to be right.

Exercise:
(1) In the light of what we have discovered about the warranted and natural growth, reconsider the arguments for no growth made on environmentalist or ecological grounds. What would the value of the average propensity to save have to be for the warranted rate of growth to be zero? What would happen if the propensity were larger? What are the implications for the amount of consumption society would have to do to maintain full employment? What are the implications for the distribution of income between capitalists and workers and between rich and poor? Do you think that no growth in national income is compatible with the present social order? Should it be changed? Is no population growth compatible with these other goals? Come to a judgement about the amount and type of growth that is compatible with preservation of the environment and irreplaceable resources on one hand, and reasonable levels of employment and price stability on the other.
(2) Where is Britain now in the Hicks model of the trade cycle? What ought to be the policy of the government?

Growth in the less developed countries

If the problem of wealthy nations is that staying on the warranted growth path tends to outstrip production possibilities, in many ways the situation of less developed countries (LDCs for short) is just the reverse. As if to mock the high hopes that attended the independence of many new nations, growth has been painfully slow. India and Pakistan, for instance, have per capita incomes of $100 compared to roughly $4000 for the USA. Operating at very low levels of per capita national income, most of the final use must go to consumption if the population is to survive. Consequently the average propensity to save is very small. At the same time, the capital–output ratio is not markedly lower than the developed nations, especially when it is stated in incremental terms; additional capital is needed for an additional unit of final use. In the absence of modern roads, power facilities, rail and harbour facilities, communications and the like, it is necessary to make a large capital outlay to initiate industrial and agricultural growth. As a result, the warranted rate of growth has frequently been inadequate to make significant progress either absolutely or in comparison with the already wealthy, developed nations.

The problem is compounded when the warranted rate is compared with the natural rate. Population growth rates in LDCs are approximately 2–3 per cent, compared to fractions of 1 per cent in such wealthy countries as the USA or the USSR. As a result, the natural growth path remains above the warranted, and a widening gap of unemployment opens between them

(Figure 15.8). The population increase is the result of improved sanitation and medicine which tends to lower the death rate, whilst the sluggish growth in national income does not unleash the tendencies towards lower fertility observed in wealthy countries.

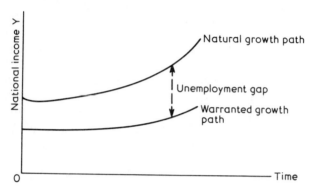

Figure 15.8   Natural and warranted growth – sluggish growth

A little arithmetic makes the point unmistakable. If a country attempts to maintain a warranted growth rate of 5 per cent, and if the capital–output ratio is about 3, then it must save 15 per cent of its national income. If the population growth is 2 per cent, then to increase per capita income by 5 per cent requires a 7 per cent growth in national income, and the nation must save 21 per cent of its final use! In fact, typical growth rate in national income is at 2 to 3 per cent, roughly keeping up with the growth of population.[3]

The key in this application of macroeconomic reasoning to LDCs is the constancy of the capital–output ratio. So long as this is taken as a fixed datum, the underdevelopment syndrome is reduced to a problem of capital shortage. Limited capital means limited output. And the low level of national income means that capital cannot be accumulated out of normal savings. The LDCs are caught in a 'circular trap' of poverty and frustrated hopes for a better life.

Other circular traps are derivative of capital shortage. Education and good health which might lead to increased productivity can be seen as a sort of accumulation in *human capital*. Yet, like physical capital accumulation, it is expensive and cannot be provided by a low income country. High rates of *population growth* are also derived from poverty situations. In developed countries, as income rises the birth rate falls for a number of reasons.

[3] These calculations are lucidly discussed in Walter Elkan, *An Introduction to Development Economics* (1973).

Effective and acceptable means of contraception are provided as a feature of adequate education and health services. Even more important, perhaps, is the change in the status of the female labour force which takes place at higher income levels. The enhanced labour productivity of women working outside the home makes for later marriage and fewer children. It pays to limit family size. Moreover, the traditional views that family prestige depends on the number of children tends to give way to economic advancement. With inadequate rates of economic growth none of these takes place. The population trap tends to reinforce and perpetuate the inability of poor countries to escape from sluggish growth. It appears necessary to find a way to break out by some dramatic burst of capital accumulation.

The classic example of this growth strategy is to be found in the industrialization of the USSR (see Chapter 4). Using their powers of direct capital planning the Soviets broke the capital bottleneck by sharply restricting consumption, even when their GNP was very low. The first products of manufacturing were items of 'heavy industry' – machines that could be used to build other machines. Peasants on collective farms worked harder for less compensation in order to support the industrialization process. Even in the face of famine and near famine conditions, grain exports were maintained to earn the foreign exchange to import capital equipment. It was not a pretty picture. Central planning may be inefficient, but even with the waste, self-sustained growth was achieved.

Exercise:
(1) By what means was the capital accumulation carried on during England's industrial revolution? Was consumption restricted? If so, how?
(2) Will cartels such as the oil cartel break the capital bottleneck for LDCs?

Western economists have also drawn up strategies for development based on a programme of rapid capital accumulation. One of the most influential has been W. W. Rostow, who expressed his ideas in a little book called *The Stages of Economic Growth*. In this book Rostow divided the history of nations into a series of stages of economic maturity. In the course of these stages income rose and technical skills accumulated in the labour force. The decisive moment was what he called the *take off into self-sustained growth*. When income levels became high enough, high levels of savings and investment accumulated capital and in turn increased income further. The process continued until very high levels of income were reached – the United States being the prime example – at which point there was a transition to a high consumption, low savings economy. Having achieved the desired level of income, the growth rate tapered off as people consumed most of the national product.

Despite his anti-communist politics, Rostow's ideas are similar to Karl Marx's stages of history account of economic development. In fact Rostow subtitled his book 'a non-communist manifesto'. Much theoretical and historical debate has arisen over whether it is possible to identify stages of history, and whether the course of history progresses in such a similar way from one nation to another. Aside from questions of historical theory, the practical question is Rostow's assertion that the take off must be a departure from past stages in a more or less abrupt way, and that it is associated with the rapid growth of capital.

If one accepts the idea of breaking through the bottleneck of capital shortage, the question becomes: how to do it? Not a few people in under-developed countries accept Stalin's method as the only way. They are willing to do whatever is necessary to save the required 20 per cent of their national income (as the USSR actually still does).

Another alternative is to rely on the developed countries to supply the needed savings in the form of gifts and long-term loans. There are a large number of agencies and resolutions directed toward this end. Thus alongside the IMF, the International Bank for Reconstruction and Development (the 'World Bank') was established after the Second World War to guarantee long-term loans to LDCs. Resolutions have been passed – but not carried through – to the effect that the developed countries should provide 1 per cent of their GNP for assistance to LDCs.

A third strategy has developed in Latin America where so much wealth is tied up in the hands of landed families. It is proposed that the wealth be seized by revolutionary means and converted into capital for economic development. A related tactic is deliberately using inflation as a device to transfer real wealth into investments. If prices were made to rise rapidly, the landowners living on fixed rental incomes would lose part of their real incomes. Likewise workers whose money incomes are 'sticky' would also have to forego a portion of their claim to final use. Private investors and government sponsored investments would be able to utilize this *forced saving* to accumulate capital.

Whatever the method employed, these strategies identify capital as the bottleneck. In linear programming terms it is the only effective constraint. Since the labour production possibility frontier lies beyond the capital frontier, the shadow price of labour is zero, prompting W. A. Lewis to write a famous article entitled 'Economic development with unlimited supplies of labour'. Specifically, Lewis argued that there would be no loss in agricultural output if the surplus labour were diverted to the industrial sector to build the necessary capital equipment. Labour only appeared to be employed in the countryside, when in fact agriculture was in a condition of *hidden employment*. Farmers were busy doing things, but they could not work to their capacities with limited capital equipment. Rather, such social devices as the extended family kept large numbers of extra workers in agriculture, sharing the income of their families. The same agricultural output could be achieved with less labour. Why not put this free resource to work?

Query: Review the discussion of the dual shadow price of factors of production in Chapter 10, and apply it to this case.

The Lewis analysis, then, amounts to a statement that the factors of production in LDCs have been somehow misallocated. Excess labour has been devoted to agriculture, and the breakout can be accomplished by reallocated labour to industry. If he is right, the changeover would increase total national income, most of which would be saved and invested in machinery and equipment.

Lewis's critics such as Hyla Myint of the London School of Economics have been quick to take him up on this point. How have the resources come to be misallocated? Is misallocation a proper description of the shortage of capital which keeps the natural growth path above the warranted (or, alternatively, keeps the capital production possibility frontier inside the labour limitation). It is hard to see how a reallocation of labour from agriculture would solve the problem. Where is the capital going to come from to operate the projected urban enterprises if it is not now available to cooperate with rural labour? It takes capital to make capital.

If Lewis is right, then capital formation can be accomplished without sacrifice of food and consumables. But if he is wrong, then either workers will be unemployed in the cities because the capital is not available to cooperate with the labour, or the capital really will be accumulated in the Stalin model of requiring the remaining farmers to work harder for the same or less compensation. That is to say, the forced-draft model of economic growth through rapid accumulation of capital requires a milking of the agricultural sector of the population if it is to work at all.

This general line of criticism is taken further by Professor Theodore Schultz of the University of Chicago, who denies the premise that there is a shortage of a single capital bottleneck. Given the technical knowledge at their disposal, he says, the labour force is in fact not actually underutilized even though it may appear so to Western observers. This is especially true in agriculture where the marginal product of labour is small, but not zero as it seems to persons coming from industrial cultures. In addition to more formal anthropological studies, Schultz found that even though he is an authority in agricultural economics, there were no significant ways in which he could suggest that traditional agricultural methods reallocate their resources.

While not opposed to foreign aid in the form of capital equipment, Schultz's investigations convinced him that the highest return was to increasing the human capital in the form of scientific and technological skills. The peasant farmer would then save his income of his own accord in order to obtain such capital equipment that could be shown to pay off. Schultz talked about 'penny capitalists' in the farm village who would save for machinery and fertilizer. The traveller from an industrialized country watching a Nigerian farmer chopping at the dry, rock-hard laterite soil with a mattock inevitably conjures up a vision of how much more ground could be turned over with a gang of ploughs drawn by a powerful tractor. Only later does he learn that such technology is ill suited to the tropical soils, which require intensive agronomic research before such methods are usable. He finds that the labour force is not trained to maintain the complicated equipment, supply the needed parts, or transport and market the produce.

No sooner does the traveller step off the plane than he is struck by the fact that somebody is always willing to carry his bag, clean his house, or work in his factory, all for a pittance. In the terrible slums surrounding many cities in the underdeveloped world, unemployed or casually employed labour is already in plentiful supply. What would be simpler, it seems, than to put them to work with additional capital equipment? Yet not only are the requisite labour skills missing due to inadequate education and health, but capital equipment embodying new technology frequently is associated with *less* use of labour and greater unemployment. If the low wage and unskilled labour is to be utilized in industry, then, just as in agriculture, a new technology has to be developed. The simple importation of foreign equipment may turn out to be self-defeating. It leads to the development of a *dual economy* with a small modern sector maintained by an elite labour force, and a stagnant and poverty stricken existence for the rest. Yet development engineering to find suitable techniques is expensive, and in many industries is it not clear that there exist technologies that can utilize the present labour force and still be cost-competitive with production methods of the advanced countries.

The conclusion drawn by Schultz, Myint and others is that the economies of LDCs will be furthered best by a programme of *balanced growth*. Developed countries can help most by providing the scientific and technical information, to a large degree leaving it to the LDCs to accumulate or borrow the capital, train the labour force and allocate their resources. The incentive for self-gain is sufficient to ensure that through individual response to market opportunities the most efficient allocation of resources will be found. They argue that the pace of growth will probably not be as rapid as the hopes of the LDCs. It may well be that they must give up the idea of overtaking the developed nations in a short time and content themselves with raising their absolute standard of living without regard to the relative position they hold in world economies.

The opposing conclusion is drawn by the circular trap capital shortage theorists who point to apparent misallocation of resources caused by the shortage of capital. Some argue that social rigidities of traditional society are such as to interfere with adequate response to market incentives. Poor societies are neither able nor willing to accumulate the capital that is required and a massive breakthrough has to occur for the situation to change at all.

The reader will doubtless realize that this debate is another manifestation of the opposing views that we have explained at many other points in this book. On one hand the classical economists have pointed to the adaptive microeconomic forces of adjustment at work in the economy through the principle of substitution. Efficient factor combinations are chosen in production in response to interest rates. On the other hand the Keynesian tradition stresses the disruptive income effects which frustrate the substitution process. Savings depend on income rather than interest. Individuals cannot be relied upon to work towards the social goals because the rigidities in the economy prevent such adaptation. These rigidities are expressed in fixed capital–output ratios, propensities to save, and the like. In part they arise from monopolistic forces, partly they reflect the stickiness of human behaviour.

In the end, in LDCs as in the developed world, the difference between these views boils down to a matter of time perspective. In the long run the classical view is that adaptation will occur and that the adopting of short-run policies that run counter to the long-run solutions is the height of short sightedness. The Keynesian view is that 'in the long run we are all dead', and, if this is not to be a grim joke for LDCs, drastic policies must be adopted with lesser regard for balance and efficiency.

The last word on these issues must remain with the reader and the future!

A final tutorial exercise

In 1964 the United Nations published condensed Transactions and Inverse Input-Output Matrices for several Asian countries in its *Economic Survey of Asia and the Far East*. Consider the tables presented below for two developed and two less developed countries.

(1) Describe the structure of production of these economies. Are they complete or incomplete; open or closed; triangular or decomposed? Determine which are the most important industries, referring to the footnotes for more detailed descriptions. How is the importance of agriculture related to

the structure? How is it related to whether the country is developed or less developed? Repeat for mining as the other main extractive industry. Where are these raw materials processed? What is their final use? How important is manufacturing?

(2) Describe the structure of demand of these economies. Compare their average propensities to consume. Compare the components of their consumption vector. How are these related to degree of development? How large is their investment compared to national income? In what industries is investment carried out? How does this relate to their output in these industries? What are the main export industries? In all but the Japanese table, imports are reported by the industry they serve. Which industries are the most important recipients of imported goods?

(3) Describe the problems that these countries are likely to face in terms of natural and warranted growth. To what extent would they benefit from a government sponsored programme of stimulating exports? Evaluate the wisdom of the policy of stimulating domestic industries to replace imported goods called *import substitution*. Compare the likely result with similar programmes in Britain. What are the consequences of a shortage of foreign exchange on the LDCs resulting from an increased price of crude petroleum?

Australia: abridged input-output table, 1958–9
(million Australian pounds, purchasers' prices; imports allocated indirectly

To From	Agriculture	Manufacturing				Mining
		Important input of agriculture	*Textiles*	*Food, beverages and tobacco*	*Other manufacturing*	
Agriculture	69·8	5·6	54·4	284·3	43·6	1·7
Manufacturing						
Important input of agriculture	145·3	45·6	23·7	45·6	37·9	37·6
Textiles	0·2	3·9	116·0	3·1	15·3	0·2
Food, beverages and tobacco	30·7	4·7	—	56·9	1·0	—
Other manufacturing	8·6	43·9	27·0	36·4	83·2	3·0
Mining	0·5	100·8	1·3	13·3	3·2	29·7
Construction utilities and services	415·1	698·9	189·4	317·6	192·5	128·5
Subtotal	670·2	903·4	411·8	757·2	376·7	200·7
Wages and profit	805·3	810·5	182·1	204·7	320·3	197·7
Imports	34·2	536·5	102·0	20·2	113·6	33·3
Indirect tax and subsidies	51·7	98·2	14·7	181·0	15·2	5·2
Total inputs	1,561·3	2,348·5	710·6	1,163·0	825·8	437·0

From \ To	Construction, utilities and services	Subtotal	Consumption	Capital formation	Exports	Total output
Agriculture	12·5	471·9	505·9	102·7	470·4	1,561·3
Manufacturing						
Important input of agriculture	641·5	977·2	767·7	510·0	126·7	2,348·5
Textiles	28·0	166·7	489·6	11·7	40·5	710·6
Food, beverages and tobacco	12·4	105·7	907·1	12·3	137·2	1,163·0
Other manufacturing	319·5	521·6	265·7	38·9	10·4	825·8
Mining	224·0	372·8	24·1	3·4	49·6	437·0
Construction utilities and services	799·7	2,741·7	2,163·5	446·9	90·5	5,431·5
Subtotal	2,037·6	5,357·6	5,123·6	1,125·9	925·3	12,477·7
Wages and profit	3,010·0	5,530·6	—	—	—	5,530·6
Imports	76·5	916·3	65·0	—	—	981·3
Indirect tax and subsidies	307·5	673·5	19·7	—	—	693·2
Total inputs	5,431·5	12,477·7	5,211·1	1,117·8	930·6	19,737·2

Source: *Input-Output Tables, 1958–9* (Commonwealth Bureau of Census and Statistics, Canberra, Australia).

Note: Distributed figures in row 'Unallocated' according to weights of each industry regrouped.

Agriculture: Agriculture, dairying, other pastoral and forestry and fishing.

Important input of agriculture: Chemicals, mineral oil, and metals, engineering and vehicles.

Textiles: Textiles and clothing.

Food, beverages and tobacco: Grain products, confectionery, jam and fruit canning, dairy products, other food, alcoholic drink and tobacco.

Other manufacturing: Wood products, rubber, leather, paper products and printing, paper making and other manufacturing.

Mining; Coal mining, other mining and non-metal mine products.

Construction, utilities and services: Building and construction, gas, water, electricity, trade and transport, dwelling rent, finance, personal and government services and business services.

(4) Which industries are likeliest to contribute to greater employment? Evaluate the wisdom of stimulating some of these industries in order to combat unemployment. To what extent would such an employment generating programme coincide with other dimensions of economic advance? What would be the consequence of programmes to control pollution in Japan by limiting the manufacturing sector? What would be the consequences of a programme to eliminate the use of polluting insecticides such as DDT in the agriculture of these countries? How would they adjust themselves to these environmental programmes?

(5) In what ways could the developed countries most effectively aid the LDCs? What would be the consequences for their own economies?

Australia: input-output data: demand generated per unit of final demand, 1958–9

Induces demands in	Each unit of final demand from Agriculture	Manufacturing Important input of agriculture	Textiles	Food, beverages and tobacco	Other manu- facturing	Mining	Construction, utilities and services
Agriculture	1·053	0·008	0·103	0·277	0·068	0·009	0·010
Manufacturing							
Important input of agriculture	0·146	1·080	0·115	0·136	0·110	0·154	0·166
Textiles	0·004	0·006	1·200	0·009	0·028	0·005	0·010
Food, beverages and tobacco	0·022	0·004	0·004	1·058	0·004	0·002	0·004
Other manufacturing	0·036	0·051	0·085	0·075	1·142	0·041	0·089
Mining	0·025	0·069	0·029	0·042	0·027	1.100	0·065
Construction, utilities and services	0·388	0·420	0·480	0·505	0·390	0·449	1·285
TOTAL	1·674	1·638	2·016	2·102	1·769	1·760	1·629

India: abridged input-output table, 1960–1
(ten million rupees, 1950–60 producers' prices)

From \ To	Agriculture	Food industry	Textiles	Chemical fertilizer	Transport amd electricity	Manufacturing and mining
Agriculture	604·7	795·0	371·0	—	11·0	143·1
Food industry	55·0	48·4	5·6	—	—	12·9
Textiles	3·9	6·6	25·3	0·9	0·4	18·8
Chemical fertilizer	30·3	—	—	—	—	—
Transport and electricity	8·0	5·8	25·5	0·3	13·4	37·0
Manufacturing and mining	49·4	22·2	62·2	5·5	264·1	555·4
Construction	—	—	—	—	—	—
Subtotal	751·3	878·0	489·6	6·7	288·9	767·2
Value added	6,752·0	271·2	325·6	9·2	750·1	905·5
Margin	44·4	67·4	36·8	1·7	31·6	201·2
Value of output	7,577·0	1,323·0	930·0	20·7	1,164·0	2,164·1

From \ To	Construction	Subtotal	Consumption	Gross fixed capital formation	Net exports	Output
Agriculture	68·9	1,993·7	5,412·6	83·6	−113·0	7,577·0
Food industry	—	121·9	1,072·2	102·3	26·6	1,323·0
Textiles	—	55·9	713·9	10·8	144·8	930·0
Chemical fertilizer	—	30·3	—	1·3	−10·7	20·7
Transport and electricity	—	90·0	302·9	175·5	−68·7	1,164·0
Manufacturing and mining	630·4	1,589·2	687·2	499·6	−631·2	2,164·1
Construction	—	—	104·0	1,360·0	—	1,617·0
Subtotal	699·3	3,881·0	8,292·8	2,233·1	−652·2	14,795·8
Value added	636·6	9,650·2	860·0	—	—	13,734·2*
Margin	281·1	664·2	4,646·8	276·0	164·8	—
Value of output	1,677·0	14,795·8	13,984·9	2,509·1	−457·6	—

Source: Interindustry Transactions (*India*), *1960–1* (Planning Commission, India).
Note: Agriculture: Plantations, animal husbandry, food grains, other agriculture, forestry products and rubber.
 Food industry: Food industries.
 Textiles: Cotton and other textiles, and jute textiles.
 Chemical fertilizer: Chemical fertilizers.
 Transport and electricity: Transport equipment, motor transport, railways and electricity.
 Manufacturing and mining: Electrical equipment, non-electrical equipment, iron and steel, iron ore, cement, other metals, other minerals, leather and leather products, glass, wooden and non-metallic mineral products, petroleum products, crude oil, rubber products, chemical and coal.
 Construction: Construction, urban and industrial, and construction, rural.
* Gross value added.

India: input-output data: demand generated per unit of final demand, 1960–1

induces demands in	Each unit of final demand from Agriculture	Food industry	Textiles	Chemical fertilizer	Transport and electricity	Manu-facturing and mining	Construction
Agriculture	1·093	0·686	0·461	0·050	0·036	0·109	0·089
Food industry	0·008	1·043	0·011	0·003	0·002	0·009	0·004
Textiles	0·001	0·006	1·029	0·048	0·003	0·012	0·005
Chemical fertilizer	0·004	0·003	0·002	1·000	—	—	—
Transport and electricity	0·002	0·006	0·031	0·022	1·017	1·024	0·009
Manufacturing and mining	0·012	0·033	0·107	0·369	0·311	1·355	0·529
Construction	—	—	—	—	—	—	1·000
TOTAL	1·120	1·777	1·641	1·492	1·369	1·509	1·636

Japan: abridged input-output table, 1960
(billion yen, producers' prices)

From \ To	Agriculture	Food processing industry	Textiles	Manu-facturing	Transport and electricity	Construc-tion and service industries
Agriculture	500	1,609	341	543	—	33
Food processing industry	127	550	6	42	—	2
Textiles	35	2	728	269	6	54
Manufacturing	261	287	297	710	393	2,302
Transport and electricity	32	76	44	523	107	338
Construction and service industries	80	222	101	786	131	1,176
Mining	1	13	6	608	83	94
Subtotal	1,036	2,760	1,524	9,875	720	4,000
Wages and profits	1,839	358	360	3,205	817	5,613
Capital consumption allowance	210	47	44	408	350	700
Indirect tax and subsidies	47	481	11	173	92	259
Others	7	33	18	182	51	436
Total output	3,138	3,629	1,957	13,951	2,030	11,008

To From	Mining	Subtotal	Consump- tion expenditure	Gross domestic fixed capital formation and increase in stock	Less exports of goods and services	Subtotal	Total output
Agriculture	14	3,039	586	114	61	761	3,138
Food processing industry	—	728	2,928	86	61	3,075	3,629
Textiles	2	1,096	472	52	302	827	1,957
Manufacturing	43	10,688	1,123	2,106	907	4,136	13,951
Transport and electricity	33	1,152	624	20	144	789	2,030
Construction and service industries	33	2,530	5,251	3,058	153	8,462	11,008
Mining	7	812	14	−1	1	14	393
Subtotal	132	20,045	11,000	5,436	1,628	18,064	36,105
Wages and profits	205	12,396	—	—	—	—	—
Capital consumption allowance	34	1,793	—	—	—	—	—
Indirect tax and subsidies	10	1,072	—	—	—	—	—
Others	12	739	—	—	—	—	—
Total output	393	36,105	—	—	—	—	—

Source: 1960 Interindustry Economic Tables (Government of Japan, Tokyo, Japan, 1964).

Note: Distributed figures in row 'Unallocated' according to weight of each industry regrouped.

Agriculture: General crops, industrial crops, livestock for textile industry, other livestock, forestry, fisheries.

Food processing industry: Slaughter, meat and dairy, rice and flour milling, marine food products, other food products, beverages, tobacco.

Textiles: Natural fibre spinning, chemical fibre spinning, other spinning.

Manufacturing: Belongings, lumber and wood products, furniture, paper, pulp and paper products, printing and publishing, leather, rubber, basic and intermediate chemicals, oils, fats and final chemicals, petroleum products, coal products, ceramic, stone and clay products, iron and steel primary products, steel casting, forging and hot-rolled products, non-ferrous primary products, metal products, general machineries, electric machineries, automobiles, other transport equipments, precision machineries, other manufacturing.

Transport and electricity: Electricity, railroad, road transport, other transport.

Construction and service industries: Housing, non-housing, public works, other works, gas, water and sanitary works, commerce, real estate, communication, banking and insurance, official business, public services, other services.

Mining: Coal, iron ore, non ferrous metal ore, crude oil and natural gas, other mining.

Japan: input-output data: demand generated per unit of final demand, 1960

Each unit of final demand from / induces demands in	Agriculture	Food processing industry	Textiles	Manu-facturing	Transport and electricity	Construction and service industries	Mining
Agriculture	1·241	0·665	0·384	0·131	0·033	0·039	0·067
Food processing industry	0·060	1·212	0·027	0·014	0·004	0·004	0·005
Textiles	0·031	0·027	1·623	0·073	0·023	0·027	0·020
Manufacturing	0·271	0·402	0·680	2·221	0·509	0·546	0·350
Transport and electricity	0·029	0·057	0·079	0·106	1·087	0·064	0·112
Construction and service industries	0·062	0·136	0·159	0·167	0·120	1·165	0·132
Mining	0·015	0·026	0·040	0·105	0·069	0·037	1·040
TOTAL	1·709	2·525	2·992	2·817	1·845	1·882	1·726

Malaysia (Malaya): abridged input-output table, 1960
(million Malayan dollars, producers' prices)

From / To	Agriculture	Food processing	Textiles, clothing and footwear	Manu-facturing	Rubber industry	Electricity, water, transportation and communications and services
Agriculture	12·8	321·3	—	198·4	1,199·0	38·3
Food processing	57·0	36·4	0·1	0·1	—	8·6
Textiles, clothing and footwear	—	—	5·2	0·4	3·5	—
Manufacturing	85·1	11·0	2·7	65·9	4·7	313·4
Rubber industry	—	—	—	0·1	66·9	—
Electricity, water, transportation and communications and services	53·7	24·4	1·4	45·4	7·5	309·4
Mining	6·6	—	—	567·2	—	2·2
Subtotal	215·2	393·1	9·4	877·5	1281·6	673·0
Wages and profits	1986·3	72·9	3·4	172·4	196·9	2444·6
Indirect tax and subsidies	58·9	0·4	—	4·6	—	767·0
Imports	90·2	107·7	6·6	212·1	62·9	195·8
Others	60·7	54·6	1·3	88·3	33·1	135·2
Grand total	2,260·4	466·3	12·7	1,054·5	1,478·5	3,920·1

From	Mining	Subtotal	Consumption	Capital formation	Exports	Others	Grand total
Agriculture	—	1,769·8	480·1	144·2	71·7	3·3	2,260·4
Food processing	—	102·2	374·6	24·6	40·3	1·3	466·3
Textiles, clothing and footwear	—	10·2	8·0	0·6	3·7	0·4	12·7
Manufacturing	30·9	513·7	158·2	43·2	650·0	58·2	1,054·5
Rubber industry	—	67·0	22·4	19·8	1,418·7	5·6	1,478·5
Electricity, water, transportation and communications and services	75·8	517·6	2,225·4	387·1	418·1	520·8	3,920·1
Mining	—	576·0	—	− 31·4	154·2	0·2	495·1
Subtotal	106·7	3,556·5	3,268·7	588·1	2,756·7	589·8	9,687·6
Wages and profits	305·6	5,182·1	—	—	—	—	5,182·1
Indirect tax and subsidies	82·8	913·7	—	—	—	—	913·7
Imports	30·9	706·2	1,252·5	196·7	187·7	2,405·8	4,748·9
Others	28·1	401·3	−94·0	90·0	131·7	—	529·0
Grand total	495·1	9,687·6	4,427·2	874·8	3,076·1	2,995·6	21,061·3

Source: National Accounts of the State of Malaya 1955–61 (Department of Statistics, State of Malaya, Kuala Lumpur, Malaysia).

Note: Distributed figures in row 'Unallocated' according to weights of each industry regrouped.

Agriculture: Agriculture and livestock, rubber planting, forestry, fishing.

Food processing: Food industries, beverages, tobacco.

Textiles, clothing and footwear: Textiles, clothing and footwear.

Manufacturing: Wood and cork, furniture and fixtures, paper and paper products, printing and publishing, leather and leather products, chemical products, non-metallic mineral products, basic metal industries, metal products, machinery, etc., miscellaneous manufacturing industries.

Rubber industry: Rubber processing, rubber products.

Electricity, water, transportation and communications and services: Construction, electricity, water, transportation and communications, wholesale and retail trade, banking, insurance, etc., dwellings, other service industries.

Mining: Mining.

Malaysia (Malaya): input-output data: demand generated per unit of final demand, 1960

Each unit of final demand from induces demands in	Agriculture	Food processing industry	Textiles, clothing and footwear	Manu-facturing	Rubber industry	Electricity, water, transportation and communications and services	Mining
Agriculture	1·035	0·781	0·096	0·220	0·147	0·032	0·019
Food processing	0·028	1·106	0·018	0·007	0·004	0·004	0·001
Textiles, clothing and footwear	—	(^{a})	1·694	0·001	0·004	0·001	(^{a})
Manufacturing	0·047	0·070	0·426	1·130	0·012	0·099	0·086
Rubber industry	—	—	—	(^{a})	1·047	—	—
Electricity, water, transportation and communications and services	0·035	0·093	0·264	0·160	0·012	1·100	0·179
Mining	0·028	0·040	0·230	0·609	0·007	0·054	1·046
TOTAL	1·173	2·090	2·728	2·127	1·233	1·290	1·331

[a] Less than 0·0005.

Bibliography

For the convenience of the reader, the symbol * indicates supplementary material which may be read concurrently with the text to provide background and additional information. The symbol ** indicates somewhat more advanced material supplementing the text and advancing somewhat further, while *** indicates advanced material which may be studied after achieving a thorough grasp of the content of the text. To avoid duplication, the references are grouped according to the parts into which the text is organized. Basic sources of statistics are presented separately.

Sources of statistical information

Annual Abstract of Statistics. London, Central Statistical Office (annual).
Balance of Payments Yearbook. Geneva, International Monetary Fund (annual).
Bank of England Quarterly Bulletin. London, Bank of England Economic Intelligence Department.
Direction of Trade. Geneva, International Monetary Fund and the International Bank for Reconstruction and Development (monthly).
Economic Trends. London, Central Statistical Office (monthly).
Input-Output Tables for the United Kingdom, 1968. London, Central Statistical Office, 1973.
National Income and Expenditure (Blue Book). London, Central Statistical Office (annual).
Statistical Abstract of the United States. Washington, DC, US Government Printing Office (annual).
The British Economy: Statistics 1900–1970. London, Times Newspapers Ltd.
Yearbook of National Accounts Statistics. New York, United Nations (annual).

Preface and Chapter 1

** ALLEN, R. G. D. *Mathematical Analysis for Economists*. London, Macmillan, 1938.

* DINWIDDY, CAROLINE. *Elementary Mathematics for Economists*. London, Oxford University Press, 1967.

** HADLEY, G. *Linear Algebra*. Reading, Mass., Addison-Wesley, 1961.

*** HICKS, JOHN R. *Value and Capital*. London, Oxford University Press, 1939, 2nd ed. 1946.

** KEMENY, J. G., SCHLEIFER, A. Jun., SNELL, J. L. and THOMPSON, G. L. *Finite Mathematics with Business Applications*. Englewood Cliffs, New Jersey, Prentice-Hall, 1962.

** KEYNES, JOHN MAYNARD. *The General Theory of Employment, Interest and Money*. London, Macmillan, 1936.

** KUHN, THOMAS S. *The Structure of Scientific Revolutions*. Chicago, Illinois, University of Chicago Press, 1962.

** MARSHALL, ALFRED. *Principles of Economics*. London, Macmillan, 1927 (8th ed.).

** POPPER, KARL R. *The Logic of Scientific Discovery*. New York, Science Editions New York, 1961 (translated from the German).

* PUCKETT, R. H. *Introduction to Mathematical Economics, Matrix Algebra and Linear Economic Models*. Lexington, Mass., D. C. Heath, 1971.

*** SAMUELSON, PAUL A. *Foundations of Economic Analysis*. Cambridge, Mass., Harvard University Press, 1947.

Part 1

* BAIN, J. S. *Industrial Organization*. New York, Wiley, 1968 (2nd ed.).

* BERGSON, ABRAM. 'Toward a new growth model', *Problems of Communism*, March–April 1973.

** CHENERY, H. B. AND CLARK, P. G. *Interindustry Economics*. New York, Wiley, 1959.

* DENISON, E. F. *Why Growth Rates Differ, Postwar Experience in Nine Western Countries*. Washington, DC, The Brookings Institution, 1967.

* DOBB, M. H. *Soviet Economic Development Since 1917*. New York, International Publishers, 1948.

** DORFMAN, R., SAMUELSON, P. A. AND SOLOW, R. M. *Linear Programming and Economic Analysis*. New York, McGraw-Hill, 1958.

* GALBRAITH, J. K. *The Affluent Society*. Boston, Mass., Houghton Mifflin, 1958.

* HAYEK, F. A. *Collectivist Economic Planning*. London, Routledge, 1935.

** HICKS, J. R. *Capital and Growth*. London, Oxford University Press, 1965.

* LANGE, O. R. AND TAYLOR, F. M. *On the Economic Theory of Socialism* (ed. B. E. Lippincott). New York, McGraw-Hill, 1938.

* LEONTIEF, W. *Input-Output Economics*. London, Oxford University Press, 1966.

** LEONTIEF, W. *The Structure of the American Economy, 1919–1939*. London, Oxford University Press, 1951.

** LEONTIEF, W. *et al. Studies in the Structure of the American Economy*. London, Oxford University Press, 1953.

* MIERNYK, W. H. *The Elements of Input-Output Analysis*. New York, Random House, 1965.
* MONTIAS, J. M. 'Planning with material balances in Soviet type economies', *American Economic Review*, December 1959.
* NOVE, A. *The Soviet Economy, An Introduction*. New York, Praeger, 1969 (2nd ed).
* POWELL, R. P. 'Economic growth in the USSR', *Scientific American*, December 1968.
** SAMUELSON, P. A. 'Parable and realism in capital theory', *Review of Economic Studies*, June 1962.
* SMITH, A. *An Inquiry into the Nature and Causes of the Wealth of Nations*. New York, Random House, 1937.
* UTTON, M. A. *Industrial Concentration*. Harmondsworth, Penguin Books, 1970.
** WILES, P. J. D. *The Political Economy of Communism*. Cambridge, Mass., Harvard University Press, 1964.
* YAN, C. *Introduction to Input-Output Economics*. New York, Holt, Rinehart & Winston, 1969.

Part 2

* BAIN, J. S. *International Differences in Industrial Structure*. New Haven, Conn., Yale University Press, 1966.
* BATOR, F. M. 'The simple analytics of welfare maximization', *American Economic Review*, March 1957.
** BAUMOL, W. J. *Business Behavior, Value and Growth*. New York, Macmillan, 1959.
* BAUMOL, W. J. *Economic Theory and Operations Analysis*. Englewood Cliffs, New Jersey, Prentice-Hall, 1965 (2nd ed.).
* BRONFENBRENNER, M. *Income Distribution Theory*. Chicago, Aldine-Atherton, 1971.
** BROWN, M. *On the Theory and Measurement of Technological Change*. Cambridge, Cambridge University Press, 1966.
* CHASE, S. B. (ed.). *Problems in Public Expenditure Analysis*. Washington, DC, The Brookings Institution, 1968.
** COASE, R. H. 'The problem of social cost', *Journal of Law and Economics*, October 1960.
* COBB, C. W. and DOUGLAS, P. H. 'A theory of production', *American Economic Review*, March 1928.
* Command 3437. *Nationalized Industries: A Review of Economic and Financial Objectives*. London, HMSO.
* DORFMAN, R. (ed.). *Measuring Benefits of Government Investment*. Washington, DC, The Brookings Institution, 1965.
* DORFMAN, R. '"Mathematical" or "linear" programming: a non-mathematical exposition', *American Economic Review*, December 1953.
*** FERGUSON, C. E. *The Neoclassical Theory of Production and Distribution*. Cambridge, Cambridge University Press, 1969.
** FORRESTER, J. W. *World Dynamics*. Cambridge, Mass., Wright-Allen Press, 1971.

* GEORGE, H. 'A single tax on land values'. Reprinted in Gherity, J. A., *Economic Thought, A Historical Anthology*. New York, Random House, 1965.

* HARBERGER, A. C. 'Monopoly and resource allocation', *American Economic Review*, May 1954.

** ISARD, W. *et al. Ecologic-Economic Analysis for Regional Development*. Glencoe, Ill., The Free Press, 1972.

* JACQUEMIN, A. P. 'Size, structure and performance of the largest European firms', *Three Banks Review*, June 1974.

** KALDOR, N. 'Alternative theories of distribution', *Review of Economic Studies*, 1955-6.

** KNIGHT, F. H. *Risk, Uncertainty and Profit*. New York, Harper & Row, 1921.

** KOOPMANS, T. *Three Essays on the State of Economic Science*. New York, McGraw-Hill, 1957.

* LEIBENSTEIN, H. 'Allocative efficiency vs. "X-efficiency"', *American Economic Review*, June 1966.

* LEONTIEF, W. 'Environmental repercussions and the economic structure: an input-output approach', *Review of Economics and Statistics*, August 1970.

* MALTHUS, T. R. *An Essay on the Principle of Population* (reprinted). Harmondsworth, Penguin Books, 1970.

** MARX, K. *Capital* (Volume I) (reprinted). London, Everyman Library, Dent, 1972.

* MEADOWS, D. H. *et al. The Limits to Growth*. New York, Universe Books, 1972.

** MILL, J. S. *Principles of Political Economy* (reprinted). Toronto, University of Toronto Press, 1965.

* MISHAN, E. J. *Growth: The Price We Pay*. London, Staples Press, 1969.

* MUNDELL, R. A. *Man and Economics*. New York, McGraw-Hill, 1968.

*** NORDHAUS, W. 'World dynamics: measurement without data', *Economic Journal*, December 1973.

* NORDHAUS, W. AND TOBIN, J. *Economic Growth*. New York, National Bureau of Economic Research, 1972.

* OLSON, M. *The Logic of Collective Action*. Cambridge, Mass., Harvard University Press, 1965.

** PEACOCK, A. T. AND WISEMAN, J. *The Growth of Public Expenditures in the United Kingdom*. Princeton, New Jersey, National Bureau of Economic Research and Princeton University Press, 1961.

* PREST, A. R. *The UK Economy, A Manual of Applied Economics*. London, Weidenfeld & Nicolson, 1970.

** PREST, A. R. AND TURVEY, R. 'Cost-benefit analysis: a survey', *Economic Journal*, December 1965.

** RICARDO, D. *The Principles of Political Economy and Taxation* (reprinted). London, Everyman Library, Dent, 1911.

** ROBINSON, J. *The Economics of Imperfect Competition*. London, Macmillan, 1933.

*** SAMUELSON, P. A. 'The pure theory of public expenditures', *Review of Economics and Statistics*, November 1954.

** SCHUMPETER, J. A. *Business Cycles*. New York, McGraw-Hill, 1939.

* SCHUMPETER, J. A. *Capitalism, Socialism and Democracy*. New York, Harper & Row, 1950 (3rd ed.).

* STIGLER, G. *Testimony before the Subcommittee on Antitrust and Monopoly.* Committee on the Judiciary, United States Senate, 1965.
* STONIER, A. W. AND HAGUE, D. C. *A Textbook of Economic Theory.* London, New York, Longmans Green, 1964 (3rd ed.).
* SWEEZY, P. M. 'Demand under conditions of oligopoly', *Journal of Political Economy*, August 1939.
** TURVEY, R. 'On divergence between private and social costs', *American Economic Review*, August 1963.
** VAJDA, S. *An Introduction to Linear Programming and the Theory of Games.* London, Methuen, 1960.
* WILLIAMS, J. D. *The Compleat Strategyst.* New York, McGraw-Hill, 1954.
** WOLFSON, M. *A Reappraisal of Marxian Economics.* New York, Columbia University Press, 1966.
* WOLFSON, M. 'Was Marx right?', *The Australian Quarterly*, December 1972.

Part 3

* ACKLEY, G. *Macroeconomic Theory.* New York, Macmillan, 1961.
*** ALLEN, R. G. D. *Macro-Economic Theory, A Mathematical Treatment.* New York, Macmillan, 1967.
* AMES, E. *Introduction to Macroeconomic Theory.* New York, Holt, Rinehart & Winston, 1968.
* BARAN, P. *The Political Economy of Growth.* New York, Monthly Review Press, 1957.
** BAUMOL, W. J. *Economic Dynamics, An Introduction.* New York, Macmillan, 1959 (2nd ed.).
** DOMAR, E. D. 'Expansion and employment', *American Economic Review*, March 1947.
** DUESENBERRY, J. *Income, Saving and the Theory of Consumer Behavior.* Cambridge, Mass., Harvard University Press, 1949.
* ELKAN, W. *An Introduction to Development Economics.* Harmondsworth, Penguin Books, 1973.
*** FRIEDMAN, M. *A Theory of the Consumption Function.* Princeton, New Jersey, Princeton University Press, 1957.
* FRIEDMAN, M. *Capitalism and Freedom.* Chicago, University of Chicago Press, 1962.
** FRIEDMAN, M. (ed.). *Studies in the Quantity Theory of Money.* Chicago, University of Chicago Press, 1956.
** FRIEDMAN, M. 'The case for flexible exchange rates', in Caves, R. E. and Johnson, H. (eds.) *Readings in International Economics.* Homewood, Ill., Irwin, 1968.
** GLAHE, F. R. *Macroeconomics: Theory and Policy.* New York, Harcourt Brace, 1973.
** HACCHE, G. 'The demand for money in the United Kingdom: experience since 1971, *Bank of England Quarterly Bulletin*, September 1974.
** HARROD, R. 'An essay in dynamic theory', *Economic Journal*, March 1939.
* HAYEK, F. A. *The Road to Serfdom.* London, Routledge, 1944.
** HICKS, J. R. *A Contribution to the Theory of the Trade Cycle.* London, Oxford University Press, 1950.

**   HICKS, J. R. 'Mr Keynes and the "classics": a suggested interpretation', *Econometrica*, April 1937.

*   HIGGINS, B. *Economic Development, Principles, Problems and Policies.* New York, W. W. Norton, 1968 (rev. ed.).

***   KEMP, M. C. *The Pure Theory of International Trade and Investment.* Englewood Cliffs, New Jersey, Prentice-Hall, 1969.

**   KINDLEBERGER, C. *International Economics.* Homewood, Ill., Irwin, 1968.

**   KINDLEBERGER, C. 'The case for fixed exchange rates', *The International Adjustment Mechanism.* Federal Reserve Bank of Boston, 1970.

*   LAIDLER, D. E. W. *The Demand for Money: Theories and Evidence.* Scranton, Pa., International Textbook Company, 1969.

**   LEIJONHUFVUD, A. *On Keynesian Economics and the Economics of Keynes.* London, Oxford University Press, 1968.

*   LEONTIEF, W. 'Domestic production and foreign trade: the American capital position re-examined' (reprinted), *Input-Output Economics.* London, Oxford University Press, 1966.

*   LEWIS, W. A. 'Economic development with unlimited supplies of labour', *The Manchester School*, May 1954.

*   MCGRAE, H. AND CAIRNCROSS, F. *Capital City, London as a Financial Centre.* London, Methuen, 1973.

*   MARX, K., *The Communist Manifesto* (reprinted). Feuer, L. S. *Marx and Engels, Basic Writings on Politics and Philosophy.* New York, Doubleday, 1959.

*   MYINT, H. *The Economics of the Developing Countries*, New York, Praeger, 1964.

*   PARKIN, M. 'United Kingdom inflation: the policy alternatives', *National Westminster Bank Quarterly Review*, May 1974.

**   PATINKIN, D. 'Price flexibility and full employment', *American Economic Review*, September 1948.

**   PHILLIPS, A. W. 'The relation between unemployment and the rate of change of money wage rates in the United Kingdom, 1861–1957', *Economica*, XXVI, November 1958.

**   ROBINSON, J. *The Accumulation of Capital.* London, Macmillan, 1966.

*   ROSTOW, W. W. *The Stages of Economic Growth, A Non-Communist Manifesto.* Cambridge, Cambridge University Press, 1964.

*   SAYERS, R. S. *Modern Banking.* London, Oxford University Press, 1969 (7th ed.).

*   SCHULTZ, T. W. *Transforming Traditional Agriculture.* New Haven, Conn., Yale University Press, 1964.

**   SEN, A. (ed.). *Growth Economics.* Harmondsworth, Penguin, 1970.

**   SHEPPARD, D. K. *The Growth and Role of UK Financial Institutions 1880–1962.* London, Methuen, 1972.

***   SOLOW, R. M. 'Technical change and the aggregate production function', *Review of Economics and Statistics*, August 1957.

*   SWEEZY, P. M. *The Theory of Capitalist Development.* London, Oxford University Press, 1942.

***   TOBIN, J. 'Liquidity preference as behavior toward risk', *Review of Economic Studies*, February 1958.

*   United Nations, *Economic Survey for Asia and the Far East.* New York, United Nations, 1964.

(i) Summary input-output transactions matrix, United Kingdom, 1968

Sales by ＼ Purchases by	1 Agriculture	2 Forestry and fishing	3 Coal Mining	4 Other mining and quarrying	5 Food	6 Drink and tobacco	7 Mineral oil refining	8 Coke ovens	9 Chemicals, etc.	10 Iron and steel	11 Non-ferrous metals	12 Mechanical engineering	13 Instrument engineering	14 Electrical engineering	15 Shipbuilding, etc.	16 Motor vehicles, etc.	17 Aerospace equipment	18 Other vehicles	19 Other metal goods	20 Textiles	21 Leather, etc.	22 Clothing and footwear
1 Agriculture	—	—	—	—	881·7	41·5	0·3	—	4·0	—	—	—	—	—	—	—	—	—	—	8·0	15·3	—
2 Forestry and fishing	—	—	—	—	28·0	—	—	—	0·4	—	—	—	—	—	—	—	—	—	—	—	—	—
3 Coal mining	1·6	—	—	0·8	5·4	2·5	0·5	138·1	16·6	15·6	—	0·7	0·2	1·5	0·2	2·9	0·7	0·3	0·8	7·9	0·3	0·5
4 Other mining and quarrying	7·6	—	0·1	—	2·1	—	—	—	22·6	0·1	21·5	—	—	—	—	—	—	—	—	—	—	—
5 Food	413·3	0·5	—	—	7·7	32·8	1·7	—	87·6	—	—	—	—	—	—	—	0·3	0·6	63·4	8·1	—	—
6 Drink and tobacco	3·9	—	—	—	—	—	0·3	—	—	—	—	—	—	—	—	—	0·2	—	31·7	—	—	—
7 Mineral oil refining	26·1	5·3	2·6	2·6	16·1	6·3	38·4	—	4·9	—	—	12·5	—	6·7	—	10·1	—	—	8·9	8·2	0·5	—
8 Coke ovens	0·9	—	0·1	2·6	1·4	0·4	—	—	60·2	30·2	1·1	2·5	—	—	—	0·5	—	—	1·1	—	—	1·1
9 Chemicals, etc.	119·1	0·1	4·5	11·7	41·6	19·3	1·6	0·6	28·1	102·2	5·2	31·5	0·9	6·0	1·4	23·0	4·8	1·0	36·9	136·6	11·7	1·3
10 Iron and steel	0·6	—	32·6	0·3	6·2	0·6	0·4	7·9	4·7	40·1	2·3	363·5	5·0	0·8	39·3	221·1	0·2	0·2	306·1	0·6	1·0	0·1
11 Non-ferrous metals	1·3	—	0·3	14·7	11·1	8·8	—	1·1	42·2	63·6	13·6	112·0	8·8	75·0	0·3	68·8	2·7	3·1	156·8	11·5	0·1	9·3
12 Mechanical engineering	7·6	0·6	38·5	0·9	14·7	15·2	12·4	1·6	28·5	74·3	7·7	19·0	4·6	77·1	12·3	53·1	21·6	16·6	26·7	1·0	0·1	1·6
13 Instrument engineering	0·3	—	0·6	0·1	0·4	0·4	0·3	0·1	11·7	1·6	1·4	—	32·4	119·6	5·2	5·5	24·1	3·3	1·7	0·7	0·1	0·3
14 Electrical engineering	1·4	—	12·0	14·7	6·1	5·1	0·8	3·9	20·0	21·2	16·4	81·3	14·9	106·7	19·0	118·2	16·8	14·5	17·3	3·2	1·9	8·3
15 Shipbuilding, etc.	—	6·7	0·4	0·4	0·3	0·2	0·1	—	0·1	2·2	1·8	10·3	—	68·6	1·7	1·6	—	0·1	0·6	0·6	—	0·3
16 Motor vehicles, etc.	5·1	0·4	1·6	3·6	3·0	1·6	0·5	1·2	5·7	19·4	33·7	25·7	0·1	3·4	13·2	—	17·9	6·8	7·0	0·9	0·6	2·1
17 Aerospace equipment	—	—	—	—	0·3	0·2	—	—	0·7	—	—	2·9	—	7·6	—	1·7	39·4	1·1	—	2·6	—	0·7
18 Other vehicles	20·0	—	0·2	0·2	0·6	0·4	0·1	—	0·6	1·4	0·8	3·0	0·7	3·5	1·8	2·5	0·3	4·7	1·8	2·1	0·1	0·2
19 Other metal goods	5·0	—	1·2	2·2	63·4	31·7	10·7	0·3	68·4	6·5	36·6	181·9	6·9	113·0	64·9	165·9	48·8	5·0	—	9·4	0·1	15·5
20 Textiles	0·3	0·5	7·6	0·2	8·1	0·5	—	0·1	27·6	31·0	5·3	6·5	0·2	1·2	0·5	23·9	—	0·3	0·9	23·6	5·3	268·4
21 Leather, etc.	15·3	—	8·6	0·1	—	0·3	—	—	1·8	1·3	2·0	2·0	0·1	12·9	—	3·3	0·5	0·4	6·8	7·9	4·7	64·0
22 Clothing and footwear	—	—	3·1	5·3	—	—	—	1·1	0·4	0·1	2·4	0·1	3·4	8·3	1·8	1·0	2·0	0·2	0·8	0·9	—	—
23 Bricks, etc.	18·6	5·6	6·2	0·9	11·9	27·1	0·1	0·2	24·8	33·0	1·4	18·5	2·2	33·9	2·6	14·1	0·7	0·5	3·3	2·7	0·4	0·4

24 Timber and furniture	3·9	0·4	9·8	0·9	4·1	15·5	0·7	—	8·5	4·0	1·0	17·3	4·9	35·0	8·2	51·4	1·1	1·5	5·0	1·8	0·4	1·1
25 Paper and printing	4·2	0·2	1·8	6·0	118·9	72·4	3·0	0·4	82·9	6·4	8·3	26·9	11·7	37·7	1·3	15·7	4·1	0·9	20·7	27·6	2·3	15·4
26 Other manufacturing	9·0	—	5·5	2·6	14·2	5·5	0·8	0·2	43·6	13·0	2·9	59·7	6·3	52·0	3·3	115·3	6·0	4·5	13·2	22·1	6·2	16·4
27 Construction	41·1	2·2	19·4	5·6	6·0	14·6	0·4	0·3	24·9	5·9	1·5	10·8	0·5	6·2	2·7	5·1	2·3	0·6	4·2	4·7	0·6	1·3
28 Gas	0·6	—	0·1	0·1	6·0	0·4	0·2	7·7	4·6	39·4	6·6	10·2	1·0	5·8	1·0	5·4	1·1	0·8	11·3	2·3	0·1	1·1
29 Electricity	23·6	0·5	31·8	7·2	26·5	6·5	8·8	2·5	68·6	63·9	14·4	29·7	3·3	18·4	5·3	21·5	6·0	0·9	24·1	33·7	1·3	4·9
30 Water	7·0	0·2	2·7	0·4	3·3	1·7	1·3	0·3	8·0	0·4	0·8	2·5	0·1	1·3	0·2	1·1	0·3	0·1	1·1	2·4	0·2	0·3
31 Transport	22·2	6·6	16·6	55·7	133·9	27·5	182·8	14·6	87·9	73·4	25·7	43·8	12·7	24·9	3·6	31·9	2·5	1·5	36·0	58·9	4·0	13·3
32 Communication	6·4	0·5	1·3	1·5	9·3	4·5	0·3	0·2	13·8	4·0	2·1	21·9	2·7	11·4	1·2	6·1	3·3	0·5	9·6	7·4	1·0	4·2
33 Distributive trades	146·8	2·9	11·5	6·9	77·1	19·9	5·3	0·9	50·8	50·6	33·4	83·1	5·3	49·7	13·0	56·4	13·6	4·1	63·7	52·3	5·5	17·0
34 Miscellaneous services	44·3	7·4	1·4	28·5	144·1	100·3	36·5	1·0	220·6	17·1	25·8	129·7	11·5	130·5	23·0	60·6	8·2	1·2	80·5	84·4	7·3	32·9
35 Public administration, etc.(1)	—	—	—	—	—	—	—	—	—	—	—	—	—	—	—	—	—	—	—	—	—	—
36 Imports of goods and services	108·0	1·4	6·6	4·6	722·0	155·6	492·5	0·6	377·6	143·4	399·9	134·9	19·5	231·2	20·7	119·1	31·6	9·0	180·1	367·0	51·4	88·6
37 Sales by final buyers(2)	1·5	—	—	0·7	-1·6	2·3	0·5	0·2	6·4	48·9	51·8	10·8	1·3	7·3	1·6	6·3	12·3	5·3	9·6	4·9	0·3	2·4
38 Total goods and services (1 to 37)	1051·3	42·0	228·7	182·2	2372·3	621·7	802·0	184·0	1460·0	920·0	726·3	1457·3	161·2	1249·1	249·2	1213·2	275·6	89·2	1036·7	895·3	122·9	572·2
39 Taxes on expenditure less subsidies	-198·2	-4·6	-0·5	13·1	55·6	21·6	6·7	2·1	47·2	26·6	7·5	23·7	6·0	24·0	-3·9	30·6	6·2	0·9	24·0	22·2	2·0	16·0
40 Income from employment	329·0	40·0	511·0	66·0	596·9	203·2	38·2	22·7	545·4	509·3	157·1	1176·9	185·4	794·2	216·9	639·0	307·5	75·6	565·5	601·1	44·2	328·6
41 Gross profits and other trading income(3)	710·0	46·0	74·0	45·0	322·6	263·7	45·2	22·1	410·8	179·5	70·9	358·7	50·9	234·2	18·3	177·7	50·6	0·2	200·9	243·4	7·9	70·4
42 Total input(4)(38 to 41)	1892	123	813	306	3347	1110	892	231	2463	1635	962	3017	404	2302	481	2061	640	166	1827	1762	177	987

(1) Public administration and defence, public health and educational services, ownership of dwellings; domestic services to households and services to private non-profit-making bodies serving persons.

(2) The sales by final buyers consists of scrap materials and fees and charges for government services. These inputs are not the output of any industry in 1968 and are therefore treated as primary inputs.

Final buyers

Sales by	23 Bricks, etc.	24 Timber and furniture	25 Paper and printing	26 Other manufacturing	27 Construction	28 Gas	29 Electricity	30 Water	31 Transport	32 Communication	33 Distributive trades	34 Miscellaneous services	35 Public administration, etc.[1]	36 Total intermediate output (1–35)	37 Consumers	38 Public authorities	39 Fixed	40 Stocks	41 Exports	42 Total final output (37–41)	43 Total output[4] (36+42)
1 Agriculture	—	1·3	0·4	—	—	—	—	—	3·8	—	—	16·5	—	972·8	791·1	42·6	18·1	-5·9	73·4	919·3	1892
2 Forestry and fishing	—	13·3	—	—	—	—	0·4	—	0·8	—	—	—	—	42·1	42·0	1·6	—	31·9	5·8	81·3	123
3 Coal mining	16·8	0·4	9·6	2·8	1·6	57·2	313·5	0·6	0·8	0·4	1·0	0·9	—	595·3	177·4	34·1	10·0	-15·7	12·1	217·9	813
4 Other mining and quarrying	49·9	0·7	6·7	0·2	106·7	13·9	—	0·6	0·1	1·1	—	—	—	250·7	7·7	10·3	2·7	1·9	33·0	55·6	306
5 Food	1·8	—	—	8·2	—	—	—	—	10·9	—	—	15·6	—	590·5	2475·6	87·4	—	47·3	146·6	2756·9	3347
6 Drink and tobacco	27·8	—	11·3	5·0	—	—	—	1·1	—	2·0	33·1	15·5	—	32·0	811·6	4·9	—	15·4	246·3	1078·2	1110
7 Mineral oil refining	3·5	3·6	1·5	0·7	31·6	60·0	42·1	0·2	98·1	—	0·5	30·6	—	570·0	100·9	38·6	—	7·5	175·1	322·1	892
8 Coke ovens	37·8	0·3	—	—	0·5	2·1	0·6	—	—	—	—	2·2	—	155·1	57·7	12·9	0·2	-1·8	6·8	75·8	231
9 Chemicals, etc.	6·6	30·2	88·1	161·2	67·0	1·9	3·2	2·0	19·8	0·3	14·3	111·8	—	1186·7	364·5	206·3	19·6	41·1	645·2	1276·7	2463
10 Iron and steel	6·1	7·8	2·8	7·6	162·5	22·3	1·3	7·9	13·2	0·1	1·2	2·5	—	1344·7	11·6	5·1	8·9	11·5	253·6	290·7	1635
11 Non-ferrous metals	18·0	8·1	16·2	5·4	61·1	1·4	0·1	1·0	0·5	—	0·6	12·7	—	747·9	10·0	2·4	2·3	11·7	187·5	213·9	962
12 Mechanical engineering	0·7	5·9	27·4	10·3	100·4	12·8	15·6	4·0	11·0	0·2	15·4	8·6	—	732·3	41·4	92·9	1237·5	-10·7	923·2	2284·3	3017
13 Instrument engineering	7·9	0·2	1·9	0·9	2·4	0·4	0·5	0·2	—	0·4	4·5	5·7	—	154·6	22·4	53·3	45·6	1·3	126·3	248·9	404
14 Electrical engineering	0·3	6·9	7·1	4·9	127·4	2·8	60·1	1·1	3·8	41·7	17·6	119·7	—	851·8	245·4	202·1	584·3	-20·2	438·1	1449·7	2302
15 Shipbuilding, etc.	4·5	0·2	0·5	0·2	0·9	0·2	0·4	—	30·1	—	0·2	0·2	—	81·2	0·3	160·0	133·6	-2·4	107·8	399·3	481
16 Motor vehicles, etc.	0·5	1·7	1·5	2·0	11·6	1·1	1·7	0·3	49·5	0·9	7·5	55·0	—	220·0	350·3	65·0	602·2	-7·6	830·6	1840·5	2061
17 Aerospace equipment	0·7	0·2	0·8	0·3	1·4	0·9	—	—	32·7	0·2	0·2	0·8	—	47·8	0·9	386·7	72·9	-60·6	192·2	592·1	640
18 Other vehicles	25·1	0·2	7·3	0·4	1·5	—	0·2	—	28·2	—	—	0·8	—	92·7	9·0	2·4	25·7	-2·6	38·7	73·2	166
19 Other metal goods	7·2	37·3	25·7	26·9	128·8	5·0	1·4	0·3	64·2	0·5	41·3	79·9	—	1265·7	170·1	17·0	69·2	11·2	293·9	561·4	1827
20 Textiles	—	29·7	1·5	61·6	12·7	0·2	5·1	0·8	14·5	—	92·8	13·8	—	633·6	667·7	20·8	0·6	7·3	432·0	1128·4	1762
21 Leather, etc.	0·2	—	0·6	2·5	0·1	—	—	1·5	0·2	—	—	1·8	—	80·6	43·1	0·3	—	2·6	50·4	96·4	177
22 Clothing and footwear	—	0·5	1·2	0·4	0·3	0·2	—	0·4	6·1	3·0	8·0	9·6	—	35·8	787·2	30·2	0·1	13·8	120·1	951·4	987
23 Bricks, etc.	—	12·2	—	1·6	573·9	6·1	4·7	1·0	2·7	—	0·3	4·8	—	813·3	54·1	8·3	16·6	6·4	99·1	184·5	998

Columns 37–38: Current expenditure. Columns 39–40: Gross domestic capital formation (Fixed; Stocks).

24 Timber and furniture	7·8	—	6·9	10·8	329·3	0·2	4·1	—	4·0	—	18·3	0·7	—	558·6	266·4	33·6	40·1	15·2	19·6	374·9	934
25 Paper and printing	31·9	23·3	—	39·3	9·0	7·3	2·6	0·3	31·3	11·8	125·6	480·0	—	1231·2	343·5	118·9	1·7	12·9	179·9	656·9	1888
26 Other manufacturing	10·1	20·3	20·5	—	90·0	0·9	1·1	1·0	36·1	1·9	36·7	50·7	—	671·6	158·5	42·0	19·9	11·9	181·4	413·7	1085
27 Construction	2·2	3·2	4·8	1·7	—	20·5	3·3	0·6	21·5	4·7	54·1	34·3	—	310·3	594·9	399·0	3753·6	10·8	37·7	4796·0	5106
28 Gas	9·4	0·7	2·5	1·7	1·6	—	0·9	0·2	—	—	9·2	34·8	—	166·8	339·5	19·4	31·6	−3·8	4·7	391·4	558
29 Electricity	32·5	6·7	22·0	17·9	12·0	6·9	—	9·9	30·0	9·9	113·8	90·2	—	755·2	620·0	98·4	124·9	0·6	2·2	846·1	1601
30 Water	0·9	0·8	1·7	0·7	0·5	1·6	—	—	2·0	0·1	4·4	8·2	—	56·7	74·7	10·2	30·2	—	0·3	115·4	172
31 Transport	79·3	36·2	77·2	28·4	56·3	18·8	57·0	0·1	—	42·2	378·8	30·6	—	1685·0	807·9	100·0	34·6	1·0	1273·2	2216·7	3902
32 Communication	6·7	5·8	26·6	5·3	18·5	3·5	5·2	1·2	9·6	—	172·5	206·4	—	574·5	261·0	84·0	48·0	—	38·5	431·5	1006
33 Distributive trades	29·1	15·2	66·6	18·8	76·9	10·0	9·9	1·6	37·3	4·2	—	28·2	—	1067·5	4026·3	149·2	288·9	—	426·0	4890·4	5958
34 Miscellaneous services	21·9	55·3	154·9	66·8	176·2	18·5	44·1	0·5	63·4	8·6	363·9	—	—	2170·9	3675·7	928·4	241·9	—	633·5	5479·5	7650
35 Public administration, etc.(1)	—	—	—	—	—	—	—	—	—	—	—	—	—	—	2308·0	4084·0	—	—	—	6392·0	6392
36 Imports of goods and services	49·2	211·6	297·4	91·1	177·8	36·7	17·6	0·5	889·7	39·9	40·4	77·6	—	5594·8	2012·7	445·5	583·3	79·0	465·7	3586·2	9181
37 Sales by final buyers(2)	2·9	2·2	5·8	2·6	17·9	—	—	—	—	—	34·7	38·0	—	276·9	529·0	−597·3	−335·5	—	126·9	−276·9	—
38 Total goods and services (*1* to *37*)	499·3	542·0	899·0	588·4	2358·4	313·2	596·7	39·0	1515·0	174·1	1591·0	1588·7	—	26617·2	23260·1	7400·5	7713·3	211·0	8827·4	47412·3	74029
39 Taxes on expenditure *less* subsidies	27.6	20·2	28·5	17·4	216·9	15·0	64·6	16·1	99·7	28·9	464·9	468·7	—	1597·3	3957·9	338·5	170·7	—	−36·4	4448·7	6046
40 Income from employment	336·8	277·8	723·2	349·5	1873·0	149·0	310·0	54·0	1578·0	575·0	2487·0	4054·0 (5)	4584·0	25305·0	—	—	—	—	—	—	25305
41 Gross profits and other trading income (3)	134·1	93·5	237·4	130·0	658·0	81·0	630·0	63·0	709·0	228·0	1415·0	1539·0	1808·0	11329·0	—	—	—	—	—	—	11329
42 Total input(4) (*38* to *41*)	998	934	1888	1085	5106	558	1601	172	3902	1006	5958	7650	6392	64848	27236	7739	7884	211	8791	51861	116709

(3) Before providing for depreciation, but after deducting stock appreciation.
(4) Measured free from duplication.
(5) Including the Residual error shown in Table 1.

(ii) Technology matrix: direct requirements per £1 of industrial output

Purchases by (columns 1–18):
1 Agriculture · 2 Forestry and fishing · 3 Coal Mining · 4 Other mining and quarrying · 5 Food · 6 Drink and tobacco · 7 Mineral oil refining · 8 Coke ovens · 9 Chemicals, etc. · 10 Iron and steel · 11 Non-ferrous metals · 12 Mechanical engineering · 13 Instrument engineering · 14 Electrical engineering · 15 Shipbuilding, etc. · 16 Motor vehicles, etc. · 17 Aerospace equipment · 18 Other vehicles

Sales by	1	2	3	4	5	6	7	8	9	10	11	12	13	14	15	16	17	18
1 Agriculture	0	0	0	0	·263	·037	·000	0	·002	0	0	0	0	0	0	0	0	0
2 Forestry and fishing	0	0	0	0	·008	0	0	0	·000	0	0	0	0	0	0	0	0	0
3 Coal Mining	·001	0	0	·003	·002	·002	·001	·598	·007	·003	·001	·001	·000	·001	·000	·001	·001	·002
4 Other mining and quarrying	·004	0	·000	0	·001	0	·001	0	·009	·010	·022	·000	0	0	0	0	0	0
5 Food	·218	·004	0	·008	0	·030	·002	0	·036	·000	0	0	0	·003	0	0	0	0
6 Drink and Tobacco	·002	0	·000	0	·002	0	0	0	·002	0	0	0	0	0	·003	·005	·007	·006
7 Mineral oil refining	·014	·043	·003	·038	·005	·006	0	0	·024	·018	·005	·004	·002	·002	·011	·000	·000	·001
8 Coke ovens	·000	0	·000	·001	·000	·000	0	0	·011	·063	·002	·001	·000	·004	·082	·011	·004	·019
9 Chemicals, etc.	·063	·001	·006	·048	·012	·017	·043	·003	0	·025	·014	·010	·037	·033	·026	·107	·034	·100
10 Iron and steel	·000	0	·040	·003	·002	·001	·018	·034	·018	0	·008	·120	·011	·033	·040	·033	·038	·020
11 Non-ferrous metals	·001	0	·000	·000	·003	·008	·005	·007	·017	·039	0	·037	·022	·052	·004	·026	·026	·087
12 Mechanical engineering	·004	·005	·047	·048	·004	·003	·004	·017	·012	·045	·017	0	·012	·046	·027	·003	·028	·001
13 Instrument engineering	·000	0	·001	·001	·000	·004	·002	0	·005	·001	·002	·006	0	·030	0	·057	·062	·041
14 Electrical Engineering	·001	0	·015	·012	·002	·000	·002	·005	·008	·013	·035	·027	·080	0	·004	·001	·000	·007
15 Shipbuilding etc.	0	·054	·000	·001	·000	·000	0	0	·000	·001	·001	·003	·000	·001	·001	0	·000	·028
16 Motor vehicles, etc.	·003	·003	·002	·007	·001	·001	·001	·001	·002	·012	·006	·009	·002	·003	·004	·001	·004	·002
17 Aerospace equipment	0	0	·000	·001	·001	·001	·001	·001	·000	·001	·002	·001	·003	·002	·001	·001	0	0
18 Other vehicles	0	0	·001	·000	·000	·000	·000	0	·000	·004	·002	·001	·000	·001	·000	·001	·001	·002
19 Other metal goods	·011	·004	·009	·017	·019	·029	·012	·000	·028	·019	·038	·060	·017	·049	·027	·080	·076	·030
20 Textiles	·003	·046	·011	·003	·002	·000	·000	·005	·011	·001	0	·002	·008	·006	·004	·012	·003	·002
21 Leather, etc.	0	0	0	0	0	0	0	0	·001	·001	0	·001	0	0	0	·002	·002	·001
22 Clothing and footwear	·000	0	·004	·008	·004	·024	·001	·001	·010	·020	·001	·006	·005	·015	·005	·007	·003	·003
23 Bricks, etc.	·010	·003	·008	·003	·001	·014	·003	·000	·003	·002	·001	·006	·012	·015	·017	·025	·002	·009
24 Timber and furniture	·002	·002	·012	·008	·036	·065	·001	·002	·034	·004	·009	·029	·009	·016	·003	·008	·006	·005
25 Paper and printing	·002	0	·002	·004	·005	·005	·000	·001	·018	·008	·003	·020	·016	·023	·007	·056	·009	·027
26 Other manufacturing	·005	·018	·007	·018	·001	·001	·000	·001	·010	·004	·002	·004	·001	·003	·002	·002	·004	·004
27 Construction	·022	0	·024	·000	·002	·013	·000	·033	·002	·024	·007	·003	·002	·003	·011	·003	·002	·005
28 Gas	·000	·004	·000	·000	·008	·006	·010	·011	·028	·039	·015	·010	·008	·008	·002	·010	·009	·005
29 Electricity	·012	·002	·039	·024	·001	·002	·001	·063	·003	·000	·001	·010	·000	·001	·011	·003	·002	·001
30 Water	·004	·054	·003	·003	·002	·001	·001	·001	·000	·045	·001	·000	·000	·000	·000	·010	·009	·009
31 Transport	·012	·004	·020	·005	·040	·025	·205	·063	·036	·002	·027	·015	·031	·007	·007	·015	·004	·003
32 Communication	·003	·024	·002	·002	·003	·004	·000	·001	·006	·031	·002	·007	·007	·005	·002	·003	·005	·003
33 Distributive trades	·078	·014	·023	·014	·023	·018	·004	·004	·021	·010	·035	·028	·013	·022	·027	·027	·021	·025
34 Miscellaneous services	·023	·060	·002	·093	·043	·090	·006	·004	·090	·027	·027	·043	·028	·057	·048	·029	·013	·007
35 Public administration, etc.	0	0	0	0	0	0	0	0	0	0	0	0	0	0	0	0	0	0

Sales by \ Purchases by	19 Other metal goods	20 Textiles	21 Leather, etc.	22 Clothing and footwear	23 Bricks, etc.	24 Timber and furniture	25 Paper and printing	26 Other manufacturing	27 Construction	28 Gas	29 Electricity	30 Water	31 Transport	32 Communication	33 Distributive trades	34 Miscellaneous services	35 Public administration, etc.[1]
1 Agriculture	0	·005	·086	0	0	·001	·000	0	0	0	0	0	·001	0	0	·002	0
2 Forestry and fishing	0	0	0	0	0	·014	0	0	0	0	·000	0	0	0	0	0	0
3 Coal mining	·000	·004	·002	·001	·017	·000	·005	·003	·000	·103	·196	·003	·000	·000	·000	·000	0
4 Other mining and quarrying	0	0	0	0	·050	·001	·004	·000	·021	·025	0	·003	·003	·001	0	·002	0
5 Food	0	·005	·003	0	·002	0	0	·008	0	0	0	0	·003	0	0	·001	0
6 Drink and tobacco	·005	·007	·006	·001	·028	·004	·006	·005	·006	·108	·026	·006	·025	·002	·006	·003	0
7 Mineral oil refining	·001	·001	·001	·000	·004	·000	·001	·001	·000	·004	·000	·001	0	0	·000	·003	0
8 Coke ovens	·020	·078	·066	·009	·038	·032	·047	·149	·013	·003	·002	·012	·005	·000	·002	·015	0
9 Chemicals, etc.	·168	·000	·001	·002	·007	·008	·001	·007	·032	·040	·001	·046	·003	0	·000	·000	0
10 Iron and steel	·086	·000	·001	·008	·005	·009	·009	·005	·012	·003	·000	·006	·003	0	·000	·002	0
11 Non-ferrous metals	·015	·013	·011	·008	·018	·006	·015	·009	·020	·023	·010	·023	·003	·000	·003	·001	0
12 Mechanical engineering	·001	·000	0	·000	·001	·000	·001	·001	·000	·001	·000	·001	·001	·000	·001	·001	0
13 Instrument engineering	·009	·004	·003	·002	·008	·007	·004	·005	·025	·005	·038	·006	·008	·041	·003	·016	0
14 Electrical engineering	·000	0	0	0	·000	·000	0	·000	·000	·000	·001	0	·013	·001	·000	·000	0
15 Shipbuilding, etc.	·004	·002	·001	0	·005	·002	·001	·002	·002	·002	·001	·002	·008	·001	·001	·007	0
16 Motor vehicles, etc.	·001	0	·001	0	·000	·000	0	·000	·000	·002	·001	0	·007	·000	·001	·000	0
17 Aerospace equipment	·000	·001	0	·000	·001	·000	0	·000	·000	·002	·001	·002	·016	0	0	·000	0
18 Other vehicles	0	·005	·030	·016	·025	·040	·004	·025	·025	·009	·003	·005	·004	·000	·007	·010	0
19 Other metal products	·003	0	·027	·272	·007	·032	·014	·057	·002	0	0	·009	·000	0	·016	·002	0
20 Textiles	·000	·001	0	·065	0	·001	·001	·002	·000	·000	0	0	0	·003	·001	·000	0
21 Leather, etc.	0	0	·002	0	·000	·013	·000	·001	·000	·011	·003	·002	·002	0	·001	·001	0
22 Clothing and footwear	·002	·001	·002	·000	·008	0	·000	·010	·000	·000	·003	·006	·001	0	·000	·001	0
23 Bricks, etc.	·003	·001	·013	·008	·032	·025	·002	·026	·112	·013	·003	·007	·001	0	·003	·004	0
24 Timber and furniture	·011	·001	·035	0	·010	·022	·011	·005	·064	·002	·001	·006	·008	·012	·006	·007	0
25 Paper and printing	·007	·016	·003	·000	·002	·003	·003	·017	·020	·037	·001	·003	·009	·002	·009	·004	0
26 Other manufacturing	·002	·013	·001	·000	·009	·001	·001	·062	·018	0	·002	·001	·006	·005	·002	·005	0
27 Construction	·006	·003	·007	·001	·033	·007	·012	·002	0	·012	·001	·001	0	0	·002	·012	0
28 Gas	·013	·001	·001	·005	·001	·007	·012	·016	·002	·003	·012	·058	·008	·010	·019	·005	0
29 Electricity	·001	·001	·007	·000	·079	·001	·001	·001	·000	·034	0	0	·001	·000	·001	·012	0
30 Water	·020	·019	·001	·013	·001	·039	·041	·026	·011	·006	·036	·001	0	·042	·064	·004	0
31 Transport	·005	·001	·023	·004	·079	·006	·014	·005	·004	·018	·003	·007	·002	0	·029	·027	0
32 Communication	·035	·033	·006	·017	·029	·016	·035	·017	·015	·033	·006	·009	·010	·004	·004	·004	0
33 Distributive trades	·044	·004	·031	·033	·022	·059	·082	·062	·035	·018	·028	·003	·016	·009	·061	0	0
34 Miscellaneous services	0	·030	·041	0	0	0	0	0	0	·033	0	0	0	0	0	0	0
35 Public administration, etc.	0	0	0	0	0	0	0	0	0	0	0	0	0	0	0	0	0

(iii) Inverse Leontief matrix: total requirements, direct and indirect, per £1 of final industrial output

	1	*2*	*3*	*4*	*5*	*6*	*7*	*8*	*9*	*10*	*11*	*12*	*13*	*14*	*15*	*16*	*17*	*18*
1 Agriculture	1·0625	·0020	·0005	·0040	·2806	·0489	·0021	·0010	·0127	·0009	·0006	·0008	·0011	·0019	·0008	·0013	·0005	·0010
2 Forestry and fishing	·0021	1·0001	·0002	·0002	·0090	·0006	·0001	·0002	·0006	·0001	·0001	·0002	·0002	·0003	·0003	·0004	·0001	·0002
3 Coal mining	·0086	·0034	1·0123	·0128	·0080	·0080	·0053	·6131	·0231	·0561	·0095	·0135	·0067	·0092	·0123	·0145	·0087	·0139
4 Other mining and quarrying	·0069	·0011	·0023	1·0024	·0034	·0032	·0017	·0031	·0114	·0134	·0236	·0041	·0022	·0038	·0035	·0040	·0025	·0034
5 Food	·2355	·0057	·0010	·0128	1·0634	·0420	·0049	·0025	·0399	·0023	·0016	·0018	·0028	·0057	·0017	·0027	·0013	·0022
6 Drink and tobacco	·0030	·0002	·0001	·0004	·0032	1·0005	·0002	·0002	·0024	·0002	·0001	·0002	·0002	·0003	·0002	·0002	·0001	·0001
7 Mineral oil refining	·0222	·0474	·0085	·0490	·0147	·0122	1·0082	·0154	·0311	·0291	·0113	·0123	·0079	·0097	·0108	·0140	·0127	·0142
8 Coke ovens	·0023	·0010	·0039	·0033	·0019	·0019	·0016	1·0038	·0129	·0648	·0043	·0103	·0026	·0048	·0087	·0096	·0045	·0101
9 Chemicals, etc.	·0784	·0119	·0148	·0627	·0398	·0334	·0487	·0469	1·0163	·0383	·0231	·0268	·0505	·0489	·0267	·0366	·0179	·0367
10 Iron and steel	·0093	·0113	·0537	·0207	·0108	·0126	·0098	·0465	·0149	1·0212	·0231	·1402	·0241	·0550	·1178	·1349	·0586	·1293
11 Non-ferrous metals	·0072	·0052	·0086	·0100	·0092	·0155	·0050	·0093	·0245	·0481	1·0093	·0533	·0231	·0651	·0487	·0543	·0545	·0387
12 Mechanical engineering	·0111	·0114	·0548	·0566	·0109	·0203	·0179	·0538	·0198	·0577	·0249	1·0142	·0218	·0558	·0532	·0422	·0375	·1019
13 Instrument engineering	·0012	·0008	·0021	·0033	·0010	·0014	·0013	·0020	·0059	·0028	·0037	·0082	1·0033	·0313	·0058	·0058	·0308	·0036
14 Electrical engineering	·0073	·0065	·0219	·0227	·0076	·0116	·0065	·0220	·0168	·0241	·0411	·0374	·0866	1·0124	·0386	·0684	·0717	·0530
15 Shipbuilding, etc.	·0008	·0555	·0013	·0037	·0015	·0010	·0030	·0019	·0011	·0027	·0017	·0043	·0012	·0023	1·0010	·0019	·0012	·0078
16 Motor vehicles, etc.	·0049	·0053	·0041	·0115	·0036	·0039	·0035	·0052	·0050	·0149	·0076	·0123	·0040	·0065	·0078	1·0043	·0068	·0324
17 Aerospace equipment	·0005	·0007	·0007	·0024	·0007	·0007	·0018	·0010	·0009	·0017	·0026	·0017	·0012	·0021	·0018	·0017	1·0006	·0025
18 Other vehicles	·0010	·0014	·0025	·0041	·0014	·0014	·0037	·0033	·0016	·0058	·0035	·0025	·0011	·0016	·0016	·0029	·0017	1·0015
19 Other metal goods	·0238	·0172	·0192	·0314	·0294	·0384	·0183	·0214	·0376	·0332	·0466	·0737	·0294	·0636	·1494	·0982	·0891	·0512
20 Textiles	·0078	·0476	·0143	·0072	·0071	·0049	·0020	·0099	·0155	·0048	·0028	·0065	·0127	·0107	·0080	·0194	·0066	·0079
21 Leather, etc.	·0002	·0002	·0004	·0007	·0002	·0002	·0001	·0003	·0010	·0003	·0001	·0009	·0002	·0003	·0002	·0020	·0002	·0015
22 Clothing and footwear	·0006	·0003	·0040	·0007	·0004	·0007	·0005	·0026	·0006	·0006	·0005	·0004	·0003	·0003	·0003	·0009	·0002	·0003
23 Bricks, etc.	·0160	·0035	·0131	·0137	·0091	·0285	·0017	·0108	·0137	·0242	·0042	·0116	·0090	·0186	·0111	·0132	·0052	·0093
24 Timber and furniture	·0058	·0064	·0154	·0069	·0039	·0168	·0021	·0104	·0064	·0060	·0033	·0089	·0150	·0181	·0204	·0290	·0051	·0134
25 Paper and printing	·0219	·0105	·0078	·0357	·0480	·0794	·0118	·0110	·0477	·0137	·0166	·0203	·0393	·0302	·0153	·0222	·0156	·0162
26 Other manufacturing	·0111	·0043	·0116	·0169	·0101	·0107	·0057	·0107	·0230	·0146	·0077	·0262	·0218	·0293	·0142	·0641	·0156	·0363
27 Construction	·0265	·0200	·0258	·0223	·0101	·0167	·0031	·0194	·0134	·0086	·0042	·0068	·0037	·0057	·0089	·0062	·0059	·0071
28 Gas	·0021	·0012	·0024	·0025	·0033	·0023	·0012	·0356	·0042	·0283	·0086	·0088	·0045	·0060	·0074	·0083	·0050	·0100
29 Electricity	·0236	·0103	·0458	·0342	·0187	·0147	·0157	·0426	·0369	·0503	·0216	·0229	·0160	·0190	·0241	·0254	·0183	·0187
30 Water	·0048	·0021	·0037	·0021	·0026	·0023	·0019	·0039	·0039	·0011	·0012	·0014	·0008	·0012	·0010	·0012	·0009	·0012
31 Transport	·0433	·0721	·0344	·2073	·0617	·0443	·2133	·0925	·0597	·0737	·0437	·0377	·0465	·0321	·0308	·0428	·0219	·0329
32 Communication	·0103	·0083	·0044	·0120	·0092	·0108	·0037	·0053	·0119	·0071	·0063	·0125	·0111	·0109	·0086	·0091	·0094	·0081
33 Distributive trades	·0951	·0312	·0224	·0351	·0536	·0325	·0126	·0223	·0322	·0432	·0427	·0422	·0237	·0356	·0440	·0457	·0340	·0412
34 Miscellaneous services	·0583	·0764	·0168	·1204	·0712	·1141	·0550	·0252	·1119	·0341	·0448	·0650	·0516	·0817	·0737	·0608	·0345	·0343
35 Public administration, etc.	0	0	0	0	0	0	0	0	0	0	0	0	0	0	0	0	0	0

	19	20	21	22	23	24	25	26	27	28	29	30	31	32	33	34	35
1 Agriculture	·0009	·0076	·0942	·0086	·0018	·0028	·0015	·0051	·0010	·0008	·0005	·0004	·0021	·0003	·0006	·0034	0
2 Forestry and fishing	·0001	·0001	·0003	·0001	·0002	·0143	·0001	·0003	·0010	·0001	·0004	·0001	·0001	·0001	·0000	·0001	-0001
3 Coal mining	·0161	·0121	·0081	·0070	·0309	·0063	·0110	·0128	·0088	·1136	·1998	·0199	·0034	·0032	·0058	·0051	0
4 Other mining and quarrying	·0052	·0015	·0020	·0011	·0518	·0029	·0048	·0029	·0283	·0280	·0010	·0051	·0007	·0015	·0007	·0011	0
5 Food	·0020	·0099	·0273	·0054	·0052	·0031	·0030	·0153	·0024	·0018	·0010	·0011	·0040	·0006	·0010	·0039	0
6 Drink and tobacco	·0002	·0003	·0006	·0002	·0002	·0003	·0003	·0006	·0002	·0002	·0001	·0001	·0001	·0000	·0002	·0021	0
7 Mineral oil refining	·0145	·0123	·0129	·0078	·3084	·0103	·0112	·0136	·0157	·1153	·0303	·0114	·0272	·0043	·0096	·0071	0
8 Coke ovens	·0126	·0021	·0025	·0016	·0057	·0024	·0021	·0039	·0041	·0078	·0017	·0049	·0010	·0004	·0006	·0011	0
9 Chemicals, etc.	·0346	·0859	·0866	·0445	·0526	·0465	·0553	·1632	·0324	·0192	·0102	·0188	·0116	·0046	·0097	·0223	0
10 Iron and steel	·1785	·0072	·0118	·0099	·0212	·0206	·0080	·0184	·0471	·0570	·0168	·0541	·0114	·0038	·0048	·0062	0
11 Non-ferrous metals	·0980	·0053	·0081	·0056	·0142	·0166	·0128	·0142	·0228	·0106	·0059	·0115	·0043	·0035	·0029	·0059	0
12 Mechanical engineering	·0298	·0181	·0169	·0168	·0288	·0127	·0190	·0177	·0308	·0384	·0243	·0301	·0081	·0038	·0059	·0054	0
13 Instrument engineering	·0026	·0014	·0011	·0012	·0022	·0013	·0020	·0025	·0023	·0020	·0022	·0020	·0019	·0019	·0013	·0017	0
14 Electrical engineering	·0213	·0100	·0094	·0083	·0167	·0136	·0100	·0126	·0330	·0148	·0445	·0130	·0122	·0436	·0084	·0199	0
15 Shipbuilding, etc.	·0014	·0008	·0007	·0006	·0020	·0019	·0011	·0010	·0011	·0017	·0012	·0005	·0130	·0007	·0010	·0003	0
16 Motor vehicles, etc.	·0082	·0036	·0028	·0028	·0075	·0041	·0028	·0044	·0054	·0052	·0031	·0034	·0097	·0018	·0028	·0080	0
17 Aerospace equipment	·0018	·0005	·0005	·0004	·0013	·0008	·0005	·0008	·0009	·0008	·0007	·0003	·0074	·0006	·0006	·0003	0
18 Other vehicles	·0024	·0015	·0009	·0011	·0029	·0014	·0015	·0015	·0015	·0035	·0022	·0024	·0168	·0009	·0013	·0005	0
19 Other metal goods	1·0150	·0129	·0397	·0252	·0358	·0477	·0112	·0364	·0405	·0212	·0121	·0113	·0108	·0046	·0110	·0150	0
20 Textiles	·0072	1·0038	·0327	·2773	·0116	·0363	·0169	·0617	·0089	·0040	·0040	·0111	·0023	·0019	·0177	·0046	0
21 Leather, etc.	·0006	·0014	1·0004	·0654	·0002	·0008	·0010	·0027	·0003	·0002	·0001	·0003	·0002	·0002	·0002	·0005	0
22 Clothing and footwear	·0004	·0008	·0026	1·0006	·0007	·0003	·0007	·0008	·0004	·0011	·0009	·0025	·0017	·0031	·0017	·0015	0
23 Bricks, etc.	·0078	·0040	·0039	·0027	1·0036	·0155	·0028	·0053	·1163	·0190	·0069	·0087	·0024	·0016	·0020	·0024	0
24 Timber and furniture	·0054	·0029	·0047	·0031	·0106	1·0021	·0053	·0123	·0676	·0061	·0069	·0018	·0028	·0014	·0046	·0017	0
25 Paper and printing	·0221	·0261	·0262	·0297	·0429	·0363	1·0117	·0525	·0168	·0224	·0079	·0061	·0122	·0148	·0284	·0668	0
26 Other manufacturing	·0134	·0170	·0406	·0258	·0165	·0265	·0151	1·0077	·0250	·0080	·0056	·0089	·0121	·0043	·0092	·0097	0
27 Construction	·0059	·0054	·0082	·0044	·0069	·0061	·0052	·0056	1·0032	·0420	·0081	·0053	·0066	·0055	·0107	·0059	0
28 Gas	·0125	·0024	·0022	·0027	·0112	·0026	·0026	·0036	·0038	1·0027	·0017	·0032	·0009	·0004	·0023	·0052	0
29 Electricity	·0278	·0261	·0172	·0164	·0428	·0152	·0184	·0283	·0147	·0259	1·0119	·0636	·0010	·0120	·0231	·0157	0
30 Water	·0012	·0020	·0021	·0012	·0017	·0014	·0014	·0017	·0007	·0038	·0009	1·0003	·0007	·0002	·0010	·0014	0
31 Transport	·0456	·0476	·0416	·0355	·1113	·0549	·0545	·0484	·0423	·0772	·0521	·0145	1·0109	·0465	·0724	·0142	0
32 Communication	·0107	·0087	·0112	·0100	·0119	·0112	·0192	·0113	·0090	·0295	·0061	·0091	·0044	1·0015	·0322	·0293	0
33 Distributive trades	·0501	·0369	·0477	·0340	·0406	·0263	·0416	·0306	·0289	·0559	·0142	·0158	·0141	·0074	1·0049	·0098	0
34 Miscellaneous services	·0653	·0671	·0679	·0646	·0502	·0797	·0981	·0944	·0604		·0391	·0146	·0254	·0160	·0710	1·0138	0
35 Public administration, etc.	0	0	0	0	0	0	0	0	0	0	0	0	0	0	0	0	1·0000

Index